CAMBRIDGE
EDUCATIONAL SERVICES®

AMERICA'S PREMIERE TESTING READINESS PROGRAM

Victory
for the
ACT® Test

S T U D E N T   T E X T

Our Mission: Progress Through Partnership
Cambridge Educational Services partners with educators who share the significant mission of educational advancement for all students. By partnering together, we can best achieve our common goals: to build skills, raise test scores, enhance curriculum, and support instruction. A leading innovator in education for over twenty years, Cambridge is the nation's premiere provider of school-based test preparation and supplemental curriculum services.

Cambridge Publishing, Inc.
www.CambridgeEd.com

© 1994, 1995, 1996, 1997, 2000, 2003, 2004, 2005, 2009, 2010, 2011, 2014, 2015 by Cambridge Publishing, Inc.
All rights reserved. First edition 1994
Thirteenth edition 2015

Printed in the United States of America
18 17 16 15   1 2 3 4 5

ISBN-13: 978-1-58894-239-5

MIX
From responsible sources
FSC® C099992

TABLE OF CONTENTS

How to Use This Book..vii

PRE-ASSESSMENT/COURSE PLANNING   1

Pre-Assessment Administration 3
How to Use the Pre-Assessment Reports...4
Setting a Test Score Target 7
Planning a Schedule for the Course 9

TEST MECHANICS, CONCEPTS, AND STRATEGIES   11

English   13

Course Concept Outline...13
Test Mechanics..17
Lesson 25
Quizzes 47
Review 69
Strategy Summary 79

Reading   83

Course Concept Outline...83
Test Mechanics..85
Lesson 97
Quizzes 131
Review 153
Strategy Summary 165

Writing   169

Course Concept Outline...169
Test Mechanics..171
Lesson 177
Quizzes 179
Strategy Summary 183

Mathematics   185

Course Concept Outline...185
Test Mechanics..189
Lesson 201
Quizzes 251
Review 269
Strategy Summary 277

Science   281

Course Concept Outline..281
Test Mechanics..285
Lesson...295
Quizzes..325
Review...341
Strategy Summary...355

CAMBRIDGE PRACTICE TEST REINFORCEMENT   357

Directed Study Practice Test   359

Section 1: English...361
Section 2: Mathematics...394
Section 3: Reading..419
Section 4: Science...435
Section 5: Writing (Optional)..456

Practice Test I   461

Section 1: English...464
Section 2: Mathematics...478
Section 3: Reading..498
Section 4: Science...509
Section 5: Writing (Optional)..523

Practice Test II   525

Section 1: English...528
Section 2: Mathematics...542
Section 3: Reading..560
Section 4: Science...568
Section 5: Writing (Optional)..582

Practice Test III   583

Section 1: English...586
Section 2: Mathematics...602
Section 3: Reading..622
Section 4: Science...633
Section 5: Writing (Optional)..646

POST-ASSESSMENT

Post-Assessment Administration 649
How to Use the Post-Assessment Reports 650
Planning for Further Study 652

APPENDIX A: ANSWERS AND EXPLANATIONS

Item Index 767

Error Correction and Suggestion Form 783

HOW TO USE THIS BOOK

Cambridge's *Victory* Program

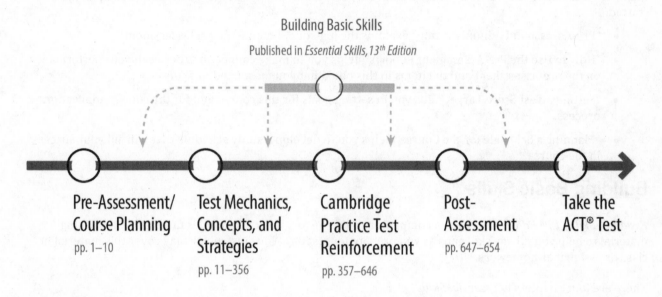

Building Basic Skills
Published in *Essential Skills, 13th Edition*

Pre-Assessment/
Course Planning
pp. 1–10

Test Mechanics,
Concepts, and
Strategies
pp. 11–356

Cambridge
Practice Test
Reinforcement
pp. 357–646

Post-
Assessment
pp. 647–654

Take the
ACT® Test

This course is organized into six parts, which are outlined in the chart above:

- **Pre-Assessment/Course Planning.** A diagnostic pre-assessment and score reports help you identify your starting point and prepare for the course.

- **Building Basic Skills.** This review material, found in *Essential Skills, 13th Edition,* serves as a refresher on topics you may not have studied in a while.

- **Test Mechanics, Concepts, and Strategies.** Most items resemble those on the real tests, which your instructor will use to teach tested concepts and applicable strategies.

- **Cambridge Practice Test Reinforcement.** Four full-length practice tests allow you to practice your skills in a testing format.

- **Post-Assessment.** A diagnostic post-assessment helps you to see how far you've come, and recommended courses of action help you to continue your study after the course.

- **Take the ACT® Test.** After you complete the course you will take the test, using everything you will learn throughout this course to succeed on test day.

The following introduction will briefly explain how to use each part of this program.

Pre-Assessment/Course Planning

In order to know where to begin preparing for the real test, you have to find out what you already do well and what you could learn to do better. The pre-assessment serves this purpose. First, you will take an ACT, Inc. ACT practice exam as the pre-assessment. Then, with the help of your instructor, you will examine your Student Summary and Student Item Analysis reports and determine exactly which topics to review, for how long, and in what order.

There are four sections in the Pre-Assessment/Course Planning chapter of this book that will help get you started:

- "Pre-Assessment Administration" explains the logistics of taking the pre-assessment.
- "How to Use the Pre-Assessment Reports" helps you to make connections between your performance on the pre-assessment and the items in this book that you most need to study.
- "Setting a Test Score Target" aids you in setting goals for this course and for the college application process.
- "Planning a Schedule for the Course" helps you to develop a study schedule that will aid your success in the course.

Building Basic Skills

Essential Skills, 13th Edition serves as a companion to this *Victory* book. It provides targeted skill building material to help you fill any skill gaps as you prepare for test day. Your instructor may cover this material in class or assign it as homework.

There are four chapters in *Essential Skills*:

- English and Writing
- Reading
- Mathematics
- Science

The English and Writing (except the Writing an Essay section), Reading, Mathematics, and Science chapters are organized into three sections: basic, intermediate, and advanced. Each section addresses a group of skills essential for college and career success.

Test Mechanics, Concepts, and Strategies

Test Mechanics, Concepts, and Strategies make up the heart of this course. This part of the book contains items that look like those found on the real test. When compared with items on the real test, the items in this part of the book have similar content, represent the same difficulty levels, and can be solved by using the same problem-solving skills and alternative test-taking strategies.

There are five chapters in Test Mechanics, Concepts, and Strategies, each chapter representing a core component of the exam:

- English
- Reading
- Writing

- Mathematics
- Science

Each of the above chapters begins with a Course Concept Outline, which acts as a syllabus, listing the concepts that are tested for each item type. The items in each chapter are organized to correspond with the respective outline. For each concept in the outline, there is a group of items. The group contains a greater number of items if the item type appears with great frequency on the real test, and it contains a lesser number of items if the item type appears with less frequency. Although the concepts are not grouped in this way on the real test, we organize the lessons in this manner so that the concepts are emphasized and reinforced. After you learn the concepts, you will be able to practice applying this conceptual knowledge on the practice tests.

Cambridge Practice Test Reinforcement

In the Cambridge Practice Test Reinforcement portion of this book, there are four full-length practice tests. In these tests, the items not only mimic the real test in content and difficulty level, but they are also arranged in an order and with a frequency that simulates the real test.

The first test is arranged as a Directed Study Practice Test. You will see the test problems alongside the correct answers and explanations. This format allows you to work through a test with some guidance before tackling a practice test that functions like the real exam. After you complete the Directed Study Practice Test, you will complete three additional practice tests with time restrictions. You may complete these tests in class or your instructor may assign them as homework. Either way, adhering to the time restrictions forces you to pace yourself as you would on the real test. If you complete all four of the practice tests, any test anxiety you may have will be greatly reduced. Answers and explanations to Practice Tests I–III are located in Appendix A of this book.

Post-Assessment

In order to know how far you've come since the pre-assessment, you will take a second ACT, Inc. ACT practice exam. You will take this post-assessment under actual testing conditions. You will then receive a second set of Student Summary and Student Item Analysis reports to help you determine final areas for review.

The Post-Assessment contains three sections to help you see how far you've come:

- "Post-Assessment Administration" explains the logistics of taking the post-assessment.

- "How to Use the Post-Assessment Reports" shows you how to use the Student Summary and Student Item Analysis reports you will receive to identify areas of study, as well as particular items in your textbook, upon which to focus as you continue to prepare for the real test.

- "Planning for Further Study" includes advice on how to make the most of an effective and concrete action plan. You will learn how to maximize your remaining course time and prioritize material to be reviewed before you take the actual test.

Pre-Assessment/ Course Planning

Building Basic Skills

Published in *Essential Skills, 13th Edition*

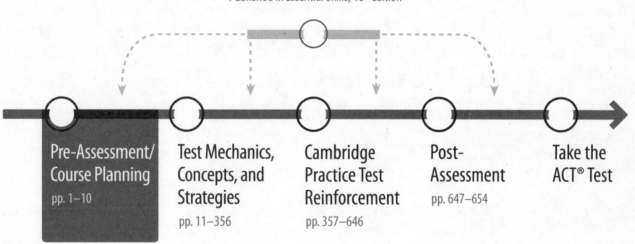

Pre-Assessment/
Course Planning
pp. 1–10

Test Mechanics,
Concepts, and
Strategies

pp. 11–356

Cambridge
Practice Test
Reinforcement

pp. 357–646

Post-
Assessment
pp. 647–654

Take the
ACT® Test

CAMBRIDGE
VICTORY FOR THE
ACT® TEST

PRE-ASSESSMENT
ADMINISTRATION

At the beginning of the course, you will take a pre-assessment. This pre-assessment is an ACT, Inc. ACT practice exam. When you take the pre-assessment, you should bring the following items to the classroom, in addition to anything else your teacher instructs you to bring:

1. Sharpened, soft-lead No. 2 pencils

2. A calculator that is approved for use on the test. This includes any four-function, scientific, or graphing calculator, except for the following:

    *   Devices with built-in computer algebra systems

    *   Pocket organizers or PDAs

    *   Handheld, laptop, or tablet computers

    *   Electronic writing pad or pen-input devices

    *   Calculators built into any electronic communication device, such as a cell phone

    *   Models with a QWERTY (typewriter) keypad (Calculators with letters on the keys are permitted as long as the keys are not arranged in a QWERTY keypad.)

    You may use the following types of calculators if you make appropriate modifications:

    *   Calculators that can hold programs or documents: remove all documents and remove all programs that have computer algebra system functionality.

    *   Models with paper tape: the paper must be removed.

    *   Models that make noise: the sound feature must be turned off.

    *   Models that have an infrared data port: the port must be covered with duct tape, electrician's tape, or another heavy, opaque material.

    *   Models that have a power cord: the power cord must be removed.

        (For more detailed information on calculator usage, go to www.actstudent.org/faq/calculator.html.)

3. A watch (to pace yourself as you work through each test section)

If your program has ordered pre-assessment Student Summary reports, you will receive one of these reports with your pre-assessment results. This report will help you determine the areas in which you need the most study and enable you to target the skills that are necessary to lay a foundation for success in the course. You can then utilize the course time to prepare in those areas so that when you take the real test, you are ready to do your best. You will learn more about how to read and use the Student Summary report in the "How to Use the Pre-Assessment Reports" section on page 4.

HOW TO USE THE PRE-ASSESSMENT REPORTS

In the transition from Pre-Assessment/Course Planning to Test Mechanics, Concepts, and Strategies, you and your teacher will use the results of your pre-assessment to recognize your individual strengths and weaknesses. Having this valuable information will allow you to create a realistic study plan for the course so that you can effectively manage your time.

You will receive the results of your pre-assessment in the form of a Student Summary and a Student Item Analysis. These reports provide details about your performance and will help you to determine where to focus your efforts during the course by strategically targeting those skills that will help you to improve in your areas of weakness. Review the details of the sample Student Summary and Student Item Analysis reports on the next two pages so that you are familiar with their contents.

Sample Student Reports

On the following pages are a sample Student Summary report and Student Item Analysis report.

Student Summary

The Student Summary report summarizes all your scaled scores based on your test performance. In addition, you are able to see how you performed within specific categories for each of the four subject tests (English, Mathematics, Reading, and Science). For example, English includes the categories Rhetorical Skills (RH) and Usage/Mechanics (UM).

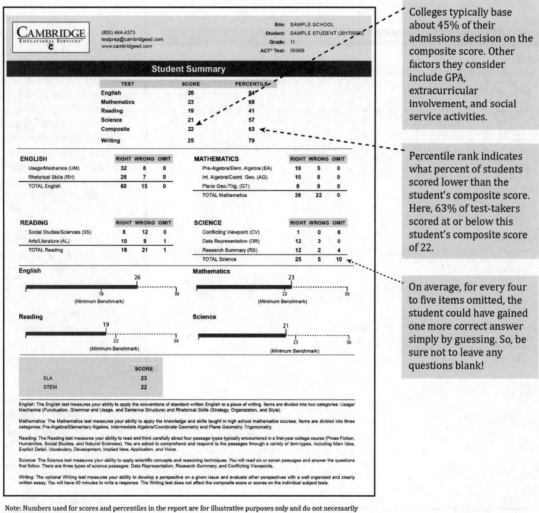

Colleges typically base about 45% of their admissions decision on the composite score. Other factors they consider include GPA, extracurricular involvement, and social service activities.

Percentile rank indicates what percent of students scored lower than the student's composite score. Here, 63% of test-takers scored at or below this student's composite score of 22.

On average, for every four to five items omitted, the student could have gained one more correct answer simply by guessing. So, be sure not to leave any questions blank!

Note: Numbers used for scores and percentiles in the report are for illustrative purposes only and do not necessarily represent a valid correlation.

Student Item Analysis

The Student Item Analysis provides a comprehensive breakdown of each item: its category (corresponding to the categories listed on the Student Summary), the correct answer, and how you answered each item.

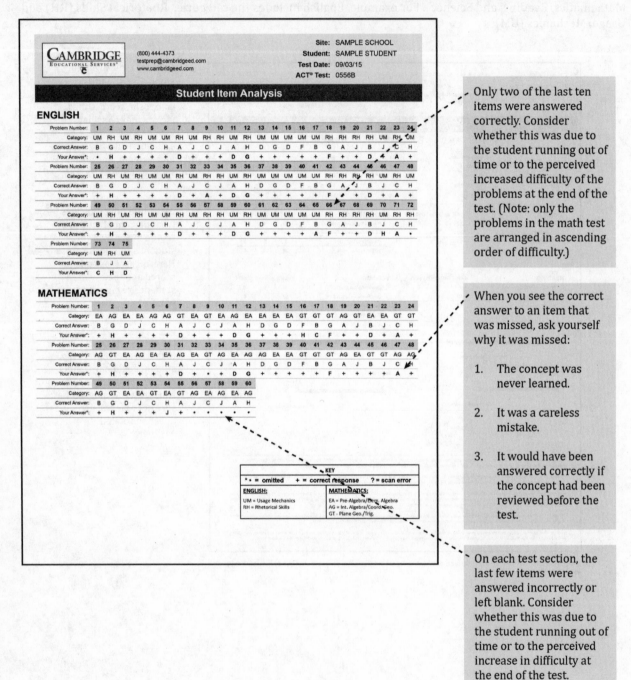

Only two of the last ten items were answered correctly. Consider whether this was due to the student running out of time or to the perceived increased difficulty of the problems at the end of the test. (Note: only the problems in the math test are arranged in ascending order of difficulty.)

When you see the correct answer to an item that was missed, ask yourself why it was missed:

1. The concept was never learned.

2. It was a careless mistake.

3. It would have been answered correctly if the concept had been reviewed before the test.

On each test section, the last few items were answered incorrectly or left blank. Consider whether this was due to the student running out of time or to the perceived increase in difficulty at the end of the test.

SETTING A TEST SCORE TARGET

Your test score target is unique to you and depends on your future educational and career goals. Setting your test score target also involves several steps, outlined below: test, research, and action.

Test

Your first step is to take the pre-assessment that is part of your Cambridge course. After you take this test, you will receive a score report that gives you a very accurate measure of where you stand. To begin the process of setting a test score goal, fill in your pre-test scores below:

TEST SECTION	SCORE
English	
Mathematics	
Reading	
Science	
Writing	
Composite	

As you use these scores to make a plan for improvement throughout this course, remember that if you had a bad test day (for example, if you were ill or distracted by personal problems), your scores may not be reflective of your true abilities. Be sure to take this into account as you set a goal for your post-test and your real ACT test.

Research

Now, make a list of schools that you are interested in attending and research the average scores and GPAs of admitted students so that you can get an idea of how you stack up. Fill in the score that you estimate you need for each school. If you are interested in applying for scholarships, make sure you also research the scores each school requires for scholarship eligibility.

School: _____	Average ACT Test Score of Admitted Students: _____ Average GPA of Admitted Students: _____ Scholarship Score Requirement: _____ Estimated ACT Test Score Needed: _____ Additional Points Needed: _____
School: _____	Average ACT Test Score of Admitted Students: _____ Average GPA of Admitted Students: _____ Scholarship Score Requirement: _____ Estimated ACT Test Score Needed: _____ Additional Points Needed: _____
School: _____	Average ACT Test Score of Admitted Students: _____ Average GPA of Admitted Students: _____ Scholarship Score Requirement: _____ Estimated ACT Test Score Needed: _____ Additional Points Needed: _____
School: _____	Average ACT Test Score of Admitted Students: _____ Average GPA of Admitted Students: _____ Scholarship Score Requirement: _____ Estimated ACT Test Score Needed: _____ Additional Points Needed: _____

Once you have this chart filled in for several schools, you should have a good idea of the difference between your pre-test score and the score you will need to get into your schools of interest. Fill in this information below:

Pre-Test Date: _____	**Score:** _____

Action

How do you translate these numbers into an action plan? See your Student Item Analysis report. This report gives you valuable information for every question on the pre-test. You'll see your answer, the correct answer, and the type of question that was asked. With a little analysis, you can see exactly where your weaknesses are and make a plan to address them. Also, make sure to review the "Planning a Schedule for the Course" section on the next page.

PLANNING A SCHEDULE FOR THE COURSE

The most significant aspect of an effective study plan is that it is a written plan. A written study plan is more concrete than one that you simply draw on from memory. So, when creating your plan, write out a day-by-day schedule for reviewing all of the materials that are necessary for success in the course. This written format will provide a clear and dependable guide for study. The schedule should be prioritized according to the time that you need to devote to each of the different subjects, based on the amount of time that you have.

Consider how you can plan your study time so that it corresponds with the course topics. In addition to assignments given in class, you may wish to devote extra study time to your particular areas of weakness. The "to do" list you created based on your Student Summary report is a good place to start. Use the calendar template that follows to develop a plan of action with your teacher, determining what topics you will study each day and allotting time to study those sections of the book and complete the relevant exercises. Remember that it is not necessary for you to do everything all at once. Instead, picking a few things to focus on each week will help you to better manage your time.

Use the following empty calendar as a template, filling in your assignments and study plan for each day. Your teacher can help you set goals for each subject.

MONTH: _____						
Sunday	**Monday**	**Tuesday**	**Wednesday**	**Thursday**	**Friday**	**Saturday**

Test Mechanics, Concepts, and Strategies

Building Basic Skills

Published in *Essential Skills, 13th Edition*

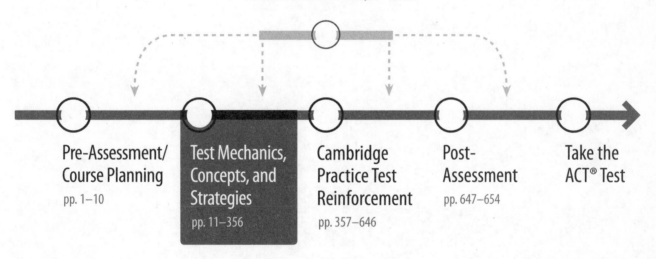

Pre-Assessment/
Course Planning
pp. 1–10

Test Mechanics,
Concepts, and
Strategies
pp. 11–356

Cambridge
Practice Test
Reinforcement
pp. 357–646

Post-
Assessment
pp. 647–654

Take the
ACT® Test

CAMBRIDGE
VICTORY FOR THE
ACT® TEST

English

Course Concept Outline

I. Test Mechanics (p. 17)

A. Overview (p. 17)

B. Anatomy (Items #1–4, pp. 18–19)

C. Pacing (p. 20)

D. Time Trial (Items #1–8, pp. 21–22)

E. Game Plan (p. 23)

1. Don't Read the Directions
2. Do the Passages in Order
3. Start Each Set of Items by Reading the Passage
4. Read Any Items with Underlined Parts, Looking for Errors
5. Work Backwards from the Answer Choices
6. Don't Look for Spelling or Capitalization Errors
7. Make Educated Guesses
8. Don't Be Afraid to Pick "No Change"
9. Remember to Review
10. Don't Be Distracted by the Clock

II. Lesson (p. 25)

A. Preliminaries[1]

1. What Is Tested
2. Directions
3. Item Profiles

---

[1] Some concepts in this Course Concept Outline are not illustrated through examples in your student text but may be covered by your instructor in class. They are included here to provide a complete outline of your course.

4. Notational Information
   a) Underlined Words or Phrases
   b) Boxed Numbers
   c) Bracketed Numbers
   d) Boxed Information

B. Item-Types

1. Grammar and Usage
2. Sentence Structure
3. Punctuation
4. Strategy
5. Organization
6. Style

C. Usage and Mechanics Review (p. 25)

1. Grammar and Usage (p. 25)
   a) Subject-Verb Agreement (Item #1, p. 25)
      (1) Material Inserted Between Subject and Verb (Items #2–7, pp. 25–26)
      (2) Inverted Sentence Structure (Items #8–9, p. 26)
      (3) Compound Subjects (Items #10–12, p. 26)
   b) Pronoun Usage (p. 26)
      (1) Pronouns Must Have Antecedents (Items #13–14, p. 26)
      (2) Antecedents Must Be Clear (Item #15, p. 26)
      (3) Pronoun-Antecedent Agreement (Items #16–19, pp. 26–27)
      (4) Pronouns Must Have Proper Case (Items #20–21, p. 27)
   c) Adjectives versus Adverbs (p. 27)
      (1) Adjectives Modify Nouns; Adverbs Modify Verbs, Adjectives, and Other Adverbs (Items #22–23, p. 27)
      (2) Linking Verbs (Items #24–25, p. 27)
      (3) Watch for Adjectives Posing as Adverbs (Items #26–28, p. 28)
   d) Double Negatives (Items #29–30, p. 28)
   e) Nouns and Noun Clauses (Items #31–33, p. 28)
   f) Faulty or Illogical Comparisons (Items #34–38, pp. 28–29)
   g) Verb Tense (p. 29)
      (1) Principal Parts of Verbs (Items #39–41, p. 29)
      (2) When to Use the Perfect Tenses (Items #42–44, p. 29)
      (3) The Subjunctive Mood (Items #45–46, p. 30)
   h) Sequence and Verb Tense (Items #47–50, p. 30)
   i) Diction (p. 30)
      (1) Wrong Preposition (Items #51–52, p. 30)
      (2) Wrong Word Choice (Items #53–54, p. 30)
      (3) Gerund versus Infinitive (Items #55–56, pp. 30–31)
2. Sentence Structure (p. 31)
   a) Run-On Sentences (Items #57–58, p. 31)
   b) Comma Splices (Items #59–60, p. 31)
   c) Fragments (Items #61–62, p. 31)
   d) Problems of Coordination and Subordination (Items #63–70, p. 32)
   e) Faulty Parallelism (Items #71–73, p. 33)
   f) Incomplete Split Constructions (Items #74–75, p. 33)
   g) Misplaced Modifiers (Items #76–78, pp. 33–34)
   h) Unintended Meanings (Items #79–80, p. 34)
3. Punctuation (p. 34)
   a) Commas (Items #81–100, pp. 34–36)
   b) Semicolons (Items #101–105, p. 37)
   c) Colons (Items #106–107, p. 37)
   d) End-Stop Punctuation (Item #108, p. 37)

e) Dashes (Items #109–110, p. 38)
     f) Quotation Marks (Item #111, p. 38)
     g) Apostrophes (Items #112–114, p. 38)
     h) Punctuating for Clarity Exercise (Item #115, pp. 38–39)

D. Rhetorical Skills Review (p. 39)

  1. Strategy
     a) Appropriate Supporting Material (Item #116, p. 39; #125, p. 42)
     b) Effective Opening, Transitional, and Concluding Sentences (Item #117, p. 40; #122, p. 41; #126, p. 42)
     c) Main Idea (Item #118, p. 40; #127, p. 42)
     d) Audience (Item #119, p. 40)
  2. Organization
     a) Sentence-Level Structure (Item #124, p. 42)
     b) Paragraph-Level Structure (Item #120, p. 40)
     c) Passage-Level Structure (Item #121, p. 41; #123, p. 41)
  3. Style
     a) Conciseness (Items #128–133, pp. 42–43)
     b) Clarity of Meaning (Item #134, p. 43)
     c) Idiomatic Expression (Item #135, p. 43)

E. General Strategies (Items #136–145, pp. 44–46)

III. Quizzes (p. 47)

A. Quiz I (Items #1–32, pp. 47–52)

B. Quiz II (Items #1–29, pp. 53–58)

C. Quiz III (Items #1–31, pp. 59–64)

D. Quiz IV Brain Buster (Items #1–20, pp. 65–68)

IV. Review (Items #1–48, pp. 69–77)

V. Strategy Summary (p. 79)

TEST MECHANICS

Overview

The English Test consists of 75 questions. You'll have 45 minutes to read the passages and answer the questions. It doesn't seem like a lot of time, but you are being tested on what you should already know so you won't have to spend a lot of time on each question. You are not being tested on spelling or vocabulary or even the exact rules of grammar. Rather, you are being tested on your understanding of the rules of grammar and your ability to apply those rules.

For example, you might be asked to correct an error.

Example:

The recently created wildlife refuge, which includes nearly 30 small ponds for migrating geese and ducks, <u>were</u> made possible by substantial gifts from an anonymous donor to the Wildlife Protection Fund.

A.   NO CHANGE
B.   was
C.   have been
D.   being

The correct answer is (B) because the sentence should read "refuge . . . was," not "refuge . . . were." *A verb must agree in both number and person with its subject.* You must be aware of this grammatical rule in order to answer the question correctly, but you would not be asked to state the rule that explains why your choice is correct.

The items used by the English Test fall into one of two categories: Usage and Mechanics or Rhetorical Skills. The Usage and Mechanics category (UM) includes all of the items that you would normally associate with a writing test, such as choosing proper verb tense and pronoun usage, while the Rhetorical Skills category (RH) includes items that ask about the development of a selection, such as crafting topic sentences and selecting effective transitions. You'll see specific examples of both types in the "Anatomy" section that follows.

Anatomy

> **DIRECTIONS:** In the passage below, certain parts of the sentences have been underlined and numbered. In the right-hand column, you will find different ways of writing each underlined part; the original version is indicated by the "NO CHANGE" option. For each item, select the choice that best expresses the intended idea, is most acceptable in standard written English, or is most consistent with the overall tone and style of the passage.
>
> There are also items that ask about a section of the passage or the passage as a whole. These items do not refer to an underlined portion of the passage; these items are preceded by statements that are enclosed in boxes.
>
> Read the passage through once before you begin to answer the accompanying items. Finding the answers to certain items may depend on looking at material that appears several sentences beyond the item. So, be sure that you have read far enough ahead before you select your answer choice.

The directions for the English Test are fairly long, and it would take you a while to read them during the test. You'd be wasting valuable time that could be used to answer questions. By the time you get to the test, you'll know what to do in the English Test, so skip the directions altogether.

Coastal Polynyas in Antarctica

Although you might not think it, the Antarctic

waters are rich in nutrients. The lack of <u>ice, combined</u>
1

with shallow coastal waters, provides the top layers of

1. A. NO CHANGE
B. ice combined
C. ice combined,
D. ice—combined

1. **(A)** *This item tests punctuation. When you insert an aside or clarifying remark, you need to set off that material from the main part of the sentence, usually with commas—one at the start and one at the end of the material. The original sentence is correctly punctuated.*

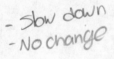
- Slow down
- No change

the ocean with added sunlight, so polynyas <u>(large open</u>

<u>areas of waters surrounded by sea ice)</u> offer ideal
  2

conditions for phytoplankton blooms. Because the ice

around polynyas is thin in the early spring when the

long days begin, they are the first areas to get strong

sunlight. The open waters retain more heat, further

thinning ice cover and leading to early, intense, and

short-lived plankton blooms. These blooms feed krill, <u>a</u>
                                                        3
<u>tiny, shrimp-like animal</u>, which in turn are eaten by
  3
Adelie penguins, seals, whales, and other seabirds and

animals.

   <u>Because</u> relatively small in area, coastal polynyas
    4
play an important role. In eastern Antarctica, more than

90 percent of all Adelie penguin colonies live next to

coastal polynyas. Polynya productivity explains, to a

great extent, the increase and decrease in penguin

population.

2. The writer is considering deleting the information in parentheses. If the writer removed this material, the essay would primarily lose:

  F. a transition from the first paragraph to the second paragraph.
  G. further examples of the animals that depend upon krill for food.
  H. a definition of a term that might be unfamiliar to the reader.
  J. additional information about the climate of Antarctica.

2. **(H)** *Why does the writer include the parenthetical material? The writer includes the parenthetical material to define a key term that might otherwise be unfamiliar to the reader.*

3. A. NO CHANGE
  B. tiny, shrimp-like animals
  C. a tiny animal like a shrimp
  D. an animal like a tiny shrimp

3. **(B)** *The original sentence lacks parallelism. In the main part of the sentence, the writer is talking about krill in the plural: "krill . . . which in turn are eaten." But in the appositive phrase, the writer uses the singular "animal." In order to be parallel to the plural noun "krill," "animal" must be changed to "animals."*

4. F. NO CHANGE
  G. Although
  H. Therefore
  J. Furthermore

4. **(G)** *"Because" is a word used to introduce an explanation, so the reader expects the information in the independent clause to be the outcome of the information provided in the dependent ("because") clause. The writer, instead, intends to contrast the two ideas in the sentence: even though polynyas are small in area, they are very important to Adelie penguins.*

Pacing

The English Test consists of five passages, each approximately 300 words in length and with 15 corresponding items, for a total of 75 items. The time limit is 45 minutes. So, a fairly simple and easy-to-follow plan is to allocate nine minutes to each of the five passages:

TASK	ALLOTTED TIME	REMAINING TIME
Read first passage	1.5 minutes	43.5 minutes
Answer accompanying items	7.5 minutes*	36 minutes
Read second passage	1.5 minutes	34.5 minutes
Answer accompanying items	7.5 minutes*	27 minutes
Read third passage	1.5 minutes	25.5 minutes
Answer accompanying items	7.5 minutes*	18 minutes
Read fourth passage	1.5 minutes	16.5 minutes
Answer accompanying items	7.5 minutes*	9 minutes
Read fifth passage	1.5 minutes	7.5 minutes
Answer accompanying items	7.5 minutes*	0 minutes

*Approximately 30 seconds per question

This schedule describes what would happen in a perfect world; but, of course, the ACT test does not take place in a perfect world. Some items are going to take longer than others, particularly those that ask about the overall development of the passage. This means that you'll need to spend less time on the simple grammar items, building up a time reserve for those more difficult items that are coming. And the more difficult items are usually placed at the end of a passage because that's where it makes sense to ask, "What is the main idea?" and "How could the passage be improved?" The schedule actually gives you a feedback loop that lets you know whether you need to skip some items. For example, if you are nearing the "36 minutes left in the section" mark and still have two or three items to do on the first passage, then skip any Rhetorical Skills items and go straight away to the next passage. The Rhetorical Skills items take longer, and there will be some simple grammar items waiting to be cherry-picked in the next passage.

Time Trial

(8 items; 5 minutes)

DIRECTIONS: In the passage below, certain parts of the sentences have been underlined and numbered. In the right-hand column, you will find different ways of writing each underlined part; the original version is indicated by the "NO CHANGE" option. For each item, select the choice that best expresses the intended idea, is most acceptable in standard written English, or is most consistent with the overall tone and style of the passage.

There are also items that ask about a section of the passage or the passage as a whole. These items do not refer to an underlined portion of the passage; these items are preceded by statements that are enclosed in boxes.

Read the passage through once before you begin to answer the accompanying items. Finding the answers to certain items may depend on looking at material that appears several sentences beyond the item. So, be sure that you have read far enough ahead before you select your answer choice.

Passage I

The Orchid Family

The orchids are the most diverse plant family with 20,000 to 30,000 species in over 800 genera. This represents about 10 percent of all flowering plant species. DNA research <u>suggesting</u> that the orchids are
₁
among the most ancient flowering plant families, as old as 90,000,000 years. They are still evolving rapidly into new species. For example, many endemic species in the genus *Telipogon* are found in the Andes Mountains in areas that were buried under glaciers

1. A. NO CHANGE
   B. suggest
   C. suggests
   D. to suggest

as recent as 10,000 years ago. Orchids are found on
      2

all continents except Antarctica.

2. F. NO CHANGE
    G. as recently as
    H. so recently as
    J. recently

Like all monocots, including lilies orchids are
                                3

flowering plants that have only one seed leaf and

determines verb ← *which or who*
↓ *lack*

typically lacks woody tissue.) All orchids have a single
          4

3. A. NO CHANGE
    B. lilies orchids,
    C. lilies, orchids,
    D. lilies, orchids

4. F. NO CHANGE
    G. lacking
    H. lack
    J. lacked

reproductive structure, called the column, which is
                                                   5

forming by the fusion of the male stamens and
   5

female style. These structures are separate in the

flowers of most other families. Orchids also have a

If both sentence before + after, need comma.

sentance ↓ *not sentance*

modified third petal called a lip, and produce enormous
                                          6

G

numbers of very tiny seeds.

5. A. NO CHANGE
    B. forming
    C. are formed
    D. is formed

6. F. NO CHANGE
    G. lip and produce
    H. lip and produce,
    J. lip, and produces

The vast majority of orchid species are native to

the tropics, and its numbers increase with proximity to
                 7

B

7. A. NO CHANGE
    B. their
    C. one's
    D. your

the equator. The most richest diversity of orchid
                8

species is found in the lush tropical forests of

equatorial South America, Southeast Asia, and New

Guinea. New species are constantly being discovered in

these areas.

8. F. NO CHANGE
    G. more richer
    H. richest
    J. richly

Game Plan

Don't Read the Directions

By the time you get to the test, you'll know what to do when you see the English Test just by the way it looks. Let the appearance of the items on the page be all the direction you need, and get started on reading the first passage immediately.

Do the Passages in Order

Unlike the Reading Test with passages that fall into categories such as Humanities and Natural Science, the passages on the English Test are not really about any particular subject area. Of course, the passages do have a topic and some items do ask Reading-type questions, but the English items mainly test usage, not reading comprehension. In Reading, there is an advantage to predetermining an order for the passages; in English, however, you should just do them in the order presented.

Start Each Set of Items by Reading the Passage

You really need to read the passage before you start answering questions because some items will not make sense without the proper context. Since the passages are about 300 words in length, you can finish a read-through in a little more than a minute. Read primarily for overall development so that you'll understand the logic in the author's presentation, and don't worry overly much about the details. Later, you can study the specific parts of the passage in which the various items appear.

Read Any Items with Underlined Parts, Looking for Errors

When an item asks about rewriting an underlined part, begin by reading the sentence, looking for an error. If you can spot an error, then you're more than halfway home. Later in the English Lesson, you'll cover the important principles of writing and grammar that are tested, and there is a list of these principles provided in the English "Course Concept Outline" (p. 13). You can treat this outline as a checklist of important things to look for in English items.

Work Backwards from the Answer Choices

If you are having difficulty locating the right answer, use the answer choices to help you. Compare each answer choice with the original, and explain to yourself what the important difference is between the two of them. This can help you see an error that you may have overlooked. Additionally, you can compare choices to each other, asking yourself in what way one choice is better or worse than another one. Again, this technique can help you uncover a hidden error and make the right choice.

Don't Look for Spelling or Capitalization Errors

These topics are not tested, so don't waste your time looking for errors of this sort. Even if you think you've found a spelling mistake (and you're almost certain to be wrong anyway), there is nothing you can do with the information. The correct response is correct because it "follows the requirements of standard written English."

Make Educated Guesses

You should be able to eliminate some answer choices on most items because they introduce new errors that are not found in the original. Or, a choice may fail to correct an error that you know to be in the underlined part of the sentence. You should always guess, even if you are unable to eliminate any answer choices, because there is no penalty for guessing on the ACT test. However, your chances improve if you are able to eliminate even one answer choice.

Don't Be Afraid to Pick "No Change"

Choose "NO CHANGE" if you think that the original is correct as written. Many students automatically refuse to pick "NO CHANGE" because they figure that there must be something wrong with the original—even if they are unable to say what. But this reasoning is faulty. "NO CHANGE," when it is an option, is statistically as likely to be correct as is one of the other three choices.

Remember to Review

If you are taking the test on a computer, you will be able to flag questions you may want to review. Use the flag to your advantage, but watch out for three potential pitfalls. First, make sure to at least guess before moving on to the next question in case time runs out and you aren't able to review as you had planned. Second, don't flag too many items, or you won't have time to review all the items you flagged. Save the flags for items on which you guess or about which you are very unsure. And use the answer eliminator tool to eliminate answers you are sure are wrong, to save you time when you review. Third, time your review just right. Wait until you have answered every item before clicking the review button to return to the items you flagged.

Don't Be Distracted by the Clock

If you are taking the test on a computer, you will see a clock onscreen while you are testing. Don't let it distract or worry you. Look at it periodically to make sure you are staying on track, but don't try to time your responses to every item. Try to check the clock every 15 minutes, and in the last 15 minutes of the exam try to check the clock every 5 minutes to help you prioritize any review time.

LESSON

The items in this section accompany the in-class review of the skills and concepts tested by the ACT English Test. You will work through the items with your instructor in class. Answers are on page 657.

DIRECTIONS: Items #1–114 consist of two types of items: (1) When four separate parts of a sentence are underlined, identify the underlined part that contains an error. Some of these sentences may not contain any errors; in such a case, choose "No change." No sentence contains more than one error, and no sentence contains an error that is not underlined. (2) When a single part of a sentence is underlined or the entire sentence is underlined, identify the re-phrasing that best expresses the meaning of the underlined material. The answer choice "NO CHANGE" indicates that the underlined material is correct as written.

Usage and Mechanics Review

Grammar and Usage

Subject-Verb Agreement

1. The professor <u>were traveling</u> in Europe <u>when</u> she
       A   B
   <u>received</u> notice of <u>her</u> promotion. <u>No change</u>
    C   D   E

Material Inserted Between Subject and Verb

2. The professor <u>voted Teacher of the Year</u> by the
           F
   students <u>were traveling</u> in Europe <u>when</u> she
        G   H
   received notice of <u>her</u> promotion. <u>No change</u>
         J   K

3. Most teachers, unless <u>they have</u> an appointment
           A
   to a prestigious university, <u>earns</u> relatively <u>less as</u>
            B   C
   a teacher <u>than they might</u> in business. <u>No change</u>
       D   E

4. Many nutritionists now <u>believe</u> <u>that</u> a balanced
           F G
   diet and not large doses of vitamins <u>are</u> the <u>best</u>
               H   J
   guarantee of health. <u>No change</u>
            K

5. Television <u>comedies</u> <u>in which</u> <u>there is</u> at least one
           A   B
   <u>really detestable</u> character <u>captures</u> the interest of
     C   D
   viewers. <u>No change</u>
        E

6. The opposition to smoking in public places <u>are prompting many state legislatures to consider</u> banning smoking in such locations.

   F. NO CHANGE
   G. is prompting many state legislatures to consider
   H. are prompting many state legislatures considering
   J. is prompting many state legislatures considering
   K. is prompting many state legislatures' consider

7. Diplomats sent to an unstable region or a genuinely hostile territory usually <u>is assigned an aide or chauffeur who function</u> also as a bodyguard.

   A. NO CHANGE
   B. are assigned an aide or chauffeur who function
   C. are assigned an aide or chauffeur who functions
   D. is assigned an aide or chauffeur that function
   E. are assigned an aide or chauffeur which functions

Inverted Sentence Structure

8. <u>Though</u> this is the wealthiest country in the
   F
   world, within a <u>few</u> blocks of the White House,
   G
   <u>there is</u> scores of homeless people <u>who live</u> on
   H   J
   the streets. <u>No change</u>
                    K

9. <u>Just</u> a few miles from the factories and
   A
   skyscrapers <u>stand</u> a medieval <u>castle</u> <u>that looks</u>
               B   C
   <u>exactly as</u> it did in the twelfth century. <u>No change</u>
   D   E

Compound Subjects

10. John, his wife, and the rest of his family <u>plans</u>
                                                 F
    <u>to attend</u> the award dinner <u>to be given</u> by the
    G   H
    company for the employees with the <u>most</u>
                                          J
    seniority. <u>No change</u>
                   K

11. Either the governor or one of his close aides
    <u>prefer</u> <u>not to have</u> the senator <u>seated at</u> the head
    A   B   C
    table where he <u>would be</u> conspicuous. <u>No change</u>
                     D   E

12. <u>Surrounded by</u> layers of excelsior, none of the
    F
    crystal goblets <u>were broken</u> <u>when</u> the workers
                     G   H
    <u>dropped</u> the crate. <u>No change</u>
    J   K

Pronoun Usage

Pronouns Must Have Antecedents

13. During her rise to fame, she betrayed many of her friends, <u>and because of it</u>, very few people trust her.

    A. NO CHANGE
    B. and in spite of it
    C. and because of her friends
    D. and even though
    E. and because of her behavior

14. In New York City, <u>they</u> are brusque and even
    F
    rude <u>but</u> quick <u>to come to</u> one another's
    G   H
    assistance <u>in a time of</u> crisis. <u>No change</u>
    J   K

Antecedents Must Be Clear

15. Ten years ago, the United States <u>imported</u> ten
    A
    times <u>as much</u> French wine as Italian wine, but
    B
    today Americans <u>are drinking</u> more of <u>it</u>.
    C   D
    <u>No change</u>
    E

Pronoun-Antecedent Agreement

16. Although a police officer <u>used to be</u> a symbol of
    F
    authority, today <u>they receive</u> <u>little</u> respect
    G   H
    <u>from most</u> people. <u>No change</u>
    J   K

17. The abbot <u>was</u> an effective administrator
A

<u>who attempted to</u> assign each monk a task
B

<u>particularly suited</u> to <u>their</u> talents and training.
C   D

<u>No change</u>
E

18. After three years of college education, a person

<u>should be allowed to</u> apply to graduate school,
F

<u>because</u> by that time <u>you are</u> ready <u>to choose</u> a
G   H   J

profession. <u>No change</u>
K

19. <u>If one wishes</u> <u>to apply for</u> a scholarship, <u>you</u>
A   B   C

must submit a <u>completed</u> application by March 1.
D

<u>No change</u>
E

Pronouns Must Have Proper Case

20. The judges <u>were</u> unable to make a final decision
F

on a single winner, so <u>they</u> divided the first prize
G

<u>between</u> John and <u>he</u>. <u>No change</u>
H   J   K

21. Although Peter <u>had been looking</u> <u>forward to</u> the
A   B

debate for weeks, a sore throat <u>prevented him</u>
C

taking <u>part</u>. <u>No change</u>
D   E

Adjectives versus Adverbs

Adjectives Modify Nouns; Adverbs Modify Verbs, Adjectives, and Other Adverbs

22. The company's mission statement took into consideration the <u>significant changes</u> that were made in the field of technology.

F. NO CHANGE
G. significantly changes
H. significant changed
J. significantly changed
K. significantly to change

23. When asked about the chance that the defenders might concentrate their forces at the beachhead, the general responded <u>tart that he was fully</u> aware of all the possibilities.

A. NO CHANGE
B. tartly that he was full
C. tart that he was full
D. tart that he fully was
E. tartly that he was fully

Linking Verbs

24. When the door burst open, Kevin <u>looked up angry</u> from his desk.

F. NO CHANGE
G. was looking up angry
H. looked up angrily
J. looks up angrily
K. looked angry up

25. The director explained that the scene required Edmund <u>to look distraughtly</u> on hearing the news of his sister's death.

A. NO CHANGE
B. looking distraughtly
C. to have looked distraughtly
D. to have looked distraught
E. to look distraught

✷ short

Watch for Adjectives Posing as Adverbs

26. Some psychologists maintain that a child <u>who</u>
....F

<u>has seen</u> violence on television <u>is</u> more likely to
.....G..H

react <u>violent</u> in situations of stress. <u>No change</u>
............(J) ly...K

27. The <u>recent created</u> commission <u>has done</u> nothing
.............(A)..ly....................................B

to address the problem <u>except to approve</u> the
....C

color of <u>its</u> stationery. <u>No change</u>
.................D.........................E

28. The track meet begins at 10:00 a.m., so the
G.....team needs to depart from the school <u>at a
.......reasonable early hour</u>.

    F. NO CHANGE
    (G.) at a reasonably early hour
    H. during a reasonable early hour
    J. while a reasonably early hour
    K. at a reasonably hour that is early

Double Negatives

29. <u>Not hardly</u> a sound <u>could be heard</u> in the
.............(A)......................B

auditorium <u>when</u> the speaker <u>approached</u> the dais
...................C...............................D

to announce the result of the contest. <u>No change</u>
....E

30. Although she <u>had been hired</u> by the magazine
............................F

<u>to write</u> book reviews, <u>she knew</u> <u>scarcely nothing</u>
....G...........................H.............(J)

about current fiction. <u>No change</u>
...................................K

Nouns and Noun Clauses

31. The reason Harriet <u>fired</u> her secretary is <u>because</u>
B....................A...........................B

he <u>was</u> <u>frequently</u> late and spent too much time
......C........D

on personal phone calls. <u>No change</u>
..................................(E)

Cannot use reason + b/c in the same sentence

32. The reason the manager changed catchers was
short...because he hoped that the opposing side
would put in a left-handed pitcher.

    F. NO CHANGE
    G. The reason that catchers were changed by
        the manager was because
    H. The reason the manager changed catchers
        which
    (J.) The manager changed catchers because
    K. The manager changed catchers, the reason
        being

only location

33. I read in a magazine <u>where</u> scientists <u>believe</u>
....(A)..............B

<u>they</u> <u>have discovered</u> a new subatomic particle.
...C.........D

<u>No change</u>
......E

Faulty or Illogical Comparisons

34. The company <u>offers</u> a plastic key card
J.........................F

so that <u>employees</u> <u>can carry</u> it in <u>their</u> <u>wallet</u>.
...............G..................H...............(J)

<u>No change</u>
...(K̶)

35. The great pianist Vladimir Horowitz <u>played</u> the
D...A

music <u>of</u> the Romantic Era <u>better than</u> <u>any pianist</u>
...........B...........................(C)...........D

in history. <u>No change</u>
........................E   *other*

36. <u>Like Neil Simon, many of Tennessee Williams'
G...plays</u> reflect a culture familiar to the
playwright.

    F. NO CHANGE
    (G.) Many of Tennessee Williams' plays, like
        Neil Simon's,
    (H.) Many of Tennessee Williams' plays, like
        Neil Simon,
    J. Many of Neil Simon and Tennessee
        Williams' plays
    K. As with the plays of Neil Simon, many of
        Tennessee Williams' plays

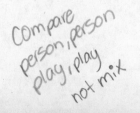
compare person, person play, play not mix

37. Educators <u>are</u> now expressing <u>their</u> concern that
         A   B

American school children <u>prefer</u> watching
                              C

television <u>to books</u>. <u>No change</u>
            Ⓓ ↖   E

Don't watch books

38. The novels of Nathaniel Hawthorne <u>contain</u>
                                             F

characters who <u>are</u> every bit <u>as</u> sinister and
                 G   H

frightening <u>as the master</u> of cinematic suspense,
            Ⓙ

Alfred Hitchcock. <u>No change</u>
                     K

Verb Tense

Principal Parts of Verbs

39. After the broken glass and other debris were
cleaned up, we realized that the thief <u>had took</u>
not only the necklace but a valuable ring as
well.

A. NO CHANGE
B. had taken
C. was took
D. was taken
E. were took

40. Everyone was very surprised <u>when Sylvia</u>
<u>brought</u> her grandfather to music class and
asked him to perform several Spanish songs on
the guitar.

F. NO CHANGE
G. because Sylvia bringing
H. while Sylvia brought
J. that Sylvia brang
K. for Sylvia to bring

41. The sheriff called off the search for the escaped
convict because he doubted that <u>the convict</u>
<u>can successfully cross the river because the</u>
<u>current was so swift</u>.

A. NO CHANGE
B. the convict successfully crossed the river
because the current was so swift
C. the convict successfully crossed the river
being that the current was so swift
D. the convict would have been successful in
crossing the river, the current being so
swift
E. a successful attempt to cross the river was
made by the convict because the current
was so swift

When to Use the Perfect Tenses

42. Elaine is the favorite to win the final event
because she <u>had always run</u> well at the 100-
meter distance.

F. NO CHANGE
G. has always run
H. have always run
J. always ran
K. will always run

43. My computer crashed several times before I
<u>finally figured out that I had loaded</u> a
corrupted copy of the program.

A. NO CHANGE
B. had finally figured out that I loaded
C. had finally figured out that I had loaded
D. finally had figured out that I loaded
E. figured out finally that I would load

44. At the current rate of consumption, we <u>have</u>
<u>exhausted</u> our supply of firewood before the
weather turns warm.

F. NO CHANGE
G. had exhausted
H. exhausted
J. will exhaust
K. will have exhausted

The Subjunctive Mood

45. The will is going to be read at 3:00 p.m., so the lawyer has asked that all family members <u>are present</u> in the office at that time.

   A. NO CHANGE
   B. are presently
   C. are going to be present
   D. be present
   E. being present

46. A dangerous situation could arise if the override switch were left open and the water <u>drops</u> below 50 percent of capacity.

   F. NO CHANGE
   G. dropped
   H. allowed to drop
   J. allowed dropping
   K. allows to drop

Sequence and Verb Tense

47. The teacher began <u>to discuss</u> the homework
                      A
assignment <u>when</u> he <u>will be</u> interrupted <u>by</u> the
          B   C   D
sound of the fire alarm. <u>No change</u>
                       E

48. The conductor <u>announced</u> that the concert would
                F
resume <u>as soon as</u> the soloist <u>replaces</u> the broken
       G   H
string on <u>her</u> violin. <u>No change</u>
       J   K

49. <u>Many</u> patients begin <u>to show</u> symptoms again
    A   B
after <u>they</u> <u>stopped</u> taking the drug. <u>No change</u>
     C   D   E

50. The winter was so severe <u>that</u> <u>several</u> of Hillary's
                   F   G
prize rose bushes <u>had sustained</u> <u>serious</u> damage
            H   J
from the frost. <u>No change</u>
            K

Diction

Wrong Preposition

51. <u>In contrast of</u> the prevailing opinion, the
     A
editorial <u>lays</u> the blame <u>for</u> the strike on the
      B   C
workers and <u>their</u> representatives. <u>No change</u>
         D   E

52. Although ballet and modern dance are both

<u>concerned in</u> movement in space to musical
   F
accompaniment, the training for ballet <u>is</u> <u>more</u>
                          G H
rigorous <u>than that</u> for modern dance. <u>No change</u>
       J   K

Wrong Word Choice

53. By midnight the guests still <u>had not been served</u>
                        A
anything <u>to eat</u>, so <u>they</u> were <u>ravishing</u>.
       B   C   D
<u>No change</u>
  E

54. The <u>raise</u> in the number of accidents <u>attributable</u>
     F   G
to drunk drivers <u>has prompted</u> a call for <u>stiffer</u>
          H   J
penalties for driving while intoxicated.

<u>No change</u>
  K

Gerund versus Infinitive

55. The idea of trying <u>completing</u> the term paper <u>by</u>
             A   B
Friday <u>caused</u> Ken <u>to cancel</u> his plans for the
      C   D
weekend. <u>No change</u>
        E

56. Psychologists <u>think</u> that many people eat
            F

<u>satisfying</u> <u>a need</u> for affection that is not
G   H

otherwise <u>fulfilled</u>. <u>No change</u>
        J   K

Sentence Structure

Run-On Sentences *before + after complete thoughts*

57. The armor plating on the new tank protects more vulnerable <u>areas than the armor on the old tank, it costs</u> about three times as much to manufacture and install. *, and*

  A. NO CHANGE
  B. areas than the armor on the old tank, because it costs
  (C.) areas than the armor on the old tank, and it costs
  D. areas than the armor on the old tank which costs
  E. areas than the armor on the old tank, it costs

58. <u>The filibuster continued late into the night some</u> senators slept sitting upright in the chairs while others slumped over their desks.

  F. NO CHANGE
  G. As the filibuster continued late into the night, some
  H. Because of the filibuster continuing late into the night, some
  J. The filibuster continued late into the night with
  K. The filibuster, which continued late into the night, some

Comma Splices

59. The weather forecast predicted heavy <u>rain, the</u> baseball game was postponed until the following day.

  A. NO CHANGE
  B. rain while the
  (C.) rain, so the
  D. rain the
  E. rain or the

both complete thought , plus fanboy or . or ;

60. The devastation caused by the flood was <u>so complete, it</u> was impossible to tell that the pile of debris had once been a house.

  F. NO CHANGE
  G. so complete, and it
  H. so complete that it
  J. so completely, it
  K. so that it

Fragments

61. <u>The audience, dazzled by the sequined costumes and brilliant lights and applauded wildly.</u>

  A. NO CHANGE
  B. The audience, dazzled by the sequined costumes and brilliant lights, applauded wildly.
  C. The audience was dazzled by the sequined costumes and brilliant lights applauding wildly.
  D. The audience, applauding wildly and dazzled by the sequined costumes and brilliant lights.
  E. Dazzled by the sequined costumes and brilliant lights, the applauding audience.

62. <u>Most of the delegates, who were from smaller villages and rural areas and so opposed any plans to improve conditions in the large cities.</u>

  F. NO CHANGE
  G. Most of the delegates from smaller villages and rural areas and so opposed any plans to improve conditions in the large cities.
  H. The delegates, most of whom were from smaller villages and rural areas and so opposed any plans to improve conditions in the large cities.
  J. The delegates who opposed any plans to improve conditions in the large cities and were from smaller villages and rural areas.
  K. Most of the delegates, who were from smaller villages and rural areas, opposed any plans to improve conditions in the large cities.

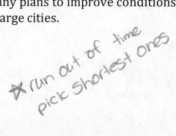

★ run out of time pick shortest ones

*Problems of Coordination and
Subordination*

63. Carlos telephoned to say that weather had
delayed his <u>plane, but he will</u> not be able to
attend the meeting.

   A. NO CHANGE
   B. plane, so he will
   C. plane, but he was
   D. plane when he will
   E. plane because he could

64. By the fifth inning, Cindy was showing signs of
fatigue and walked three consecutive <u>batters,
so</u> the coach refused to take her out of the
game.

   F. NO CHANGE
   G. batters, when
   H. batters, moreover
   J. batters during
   K. batters, but

65. <u>Because</u> the wetlands were protected by
federal law, the owners were not able to build
the shopping center that they had planned.

   A. NO CHANGE
   B. In fact
   C. However
   D. Moreover
   E. So that

66. Victoria was nominated to the office of club
<u>president, or</u> it is doubtful that she would
serve even if elected.

   F. NO CHANGE
   G. president so
   H. president, though
   J. president, in that
   K. president, even

67. The driving snow made the roadway slippery
and reduced visibility to no more than a few
feet, <u>and fortunately there were no</u> accidents
despite the heavy volume of traffic.

   A. NO CHANGE
   B. but fortunately there were no
   C. and fortunately there were some
   D. while fortunately there were no
   E. so fortunately there were no

68. The land surrounding Las Vegas is
characterized by parched red dunes and flats
with dry ravines, <u>but it is</u> almost entirely
lacking in vegetation.

   F. NO CHANGE
   G. and they are
   H. and it is
   J. but they are
   K. but are

69. Kari was just about to mail in her deposit for
her second-choice school <u>and that was when
the letter arrived notifying her</u> of her
acceptance at her first choice.

   A. NO CHANGE
   B. and then the letter that arrived notified
       her
   C. when she received notification by letter
   D. and then they told her
   E. when she learned

70. <u>Although the American relay team did not
qualify for the finals, the</u> anchor runner
dropped the baton shortly after the hand-off.

   F. NO CHANGE
   G. When the American relay team did not
       qualify for the finals, the
   H. The American relay team did not qualify
       for the finals, and the
   J. The American relay team did not qualify
       for the finals because the
   K. Not qualifying for the finals, the American
       relay team's

Faulty Parallelism

71. To abandon <u>their</u> homes, leave behind their
                  A

families, and <u>traveling</u> across the ocean <u>required</u>
              B   C

great courage on the part of the immigrants

<u>who moved</u> to America. <u>No change</u>
    D   E

72. The review <u>praised</u> the wit, charm, and
                F

<u>interpreting</u> of the recitalist <u>but never once</u>
    G   H

<u>mentioned</u> her voice. <u>No change</u>
    J   K

73. To acknowledge that <u>one has</u> something to learn
                     A B

to take

<u>is</u> <u>taking</u> the first step on the road to true
 C   (D)

wisdom. <u>No change</u>
          E

Incomplete Split Constructions

74. The students are <u>critical of</u> the dean because he ~~is~~
                  F   G

is   w/

either <u>unfamiliar or</u> doesn't care about the urgent
        H

<u>need for</u> new student housing on campus.
   J

<u>No change</u>   *unfamilar w/ <u>not about</u>*
  K

75. Baseball <u>has</u> and probably always will be the
            (A)

sport <u>that</u> <u>symbolizes</u> for people <u>in</u> other
      B   C   D

countries the American way of life. <u>No change</u>
                                  E

Misplaced Modifiers

76. <u>Letters were received by the editor of the
newspaper that complained of its editorial
policy.</u>

  F. NO CHANGE
  G. Letters were received by the editor of the
       newspaper having complained of its
       editorial policy.
  H. The editor of the newspaper received
       letters complaining of the newspaper's
       editorial policy.
  J. Letters were received by the editor in
       which there were complaints to the editor
       of the newspaper about its editorial policy.
  K. Letters were received by the editor
       complaining of the newspaper's editorial
       policy by the editor.

77. Riding in a coach and wearing the crown
     jewels, <u>the crowd cheered the royal couple</u>.

  A. NO CHANGE
  B. cheering for the royal couple was done by
       the crowd
  C. the royal couple was cheered by the crowd
  D. the royal couple's cheering was done by
       the crowd
  E. the royal couple, who was being cheered
       by crowd

78. <u>Wrapped in several thicknesses of newspaper, packed carefully in a strong cardboard carton, and bound securely with tape, the worker made sure that the fragile figurines would not be broken.</u>

   F. NO CHANGE
   G. Wrapped in several thicknesses of newspaper, packed carefully in a strong cardboard carton, and then binding the carton securely with tape, the worker made sure that the fragile figurines would not be broken.
   H. The figurines, having been securely wrapped in several thicknesses of newspaper, packed carefully in a strong cardboard carton which was then securely bound with tape, the worker made sure would not be broken.
   J. The worker, wrapping the figurines in several thicknesses of newspaper, packing them carefully in a strong cardboard carton, and securely binding the carton with tape, made sure that they would not be broken.
   K. To make sure that the figurines would not be broken, the worker wrapped them in several thicknesses of newspaper, packed them carefully in a strong cardboard carton, and securely bound the carton with tape.

Unintended Meanings

79. Mary Lou was awarded the gold medal because she scored <u>more points than any child participating</u> in the field day.

   A. NO CHANGE
   B. more points than any other child participating
   C. most points than any child participating
   D. more points than any child who had participated
   E. more points as any child participating

80. <u>(Appearing in his first American tour)</u> the British singer's album rose to the top of the charts.

   F. NO CHANGE
   G. While appearing
   H. While he was appearing
   J. When appearing
   K. Upon appearing

Punctuation

Commas

81. I think that Doré's illustrations of Dante's *Divine Comedy* <u>are excellent; but my favorite drawing is "Don Quixote in His Library."</u>

   A. NO CHANGE
   B. are excellent, but my favorite drawing is "Don Quixote in His Library."
   C. are excellent and my favorite drawing is "Don Quixote in His Library."
   D. are excellent in that my favorite drawing is "Don Quixote in His Library."
   E. are excellent even though "Don Quixote in His Library" is my favorite drawing.

82. <u>Practically</u> all nitrates are crystalline and <u>readily</u>
       F   G
   <u>soluble, and</u> they are characterized by marked
       H
   decrepitation <u>when</u> heated on charcoals by a
                    J
   blowpipe. <u>No change</u>
                    K

83. The door <u>was</u> <u>ajar,</u> and the house <u>had been</u>
             A   B   C
   <u>ransacked.</u> <u>No change</u>
       D   E

84. Since many diseases and insects cause serious

damage to <u>crops,</u> special national legislation has
            F

been passed to provide for the quarantine of

imported <u>plants;</u> and under provisions of various
         G

<u>acts,</u> inspectors are placed at ports of entry to
H

prevent smugglers from bringing in plants

<u>that might be</u> dangerous. <u>No change</u>
   J   K

85. <u>A full train crew consists of a motorman, a</u>
<u>brakeman, a conductor, and two ticket takers.</u>

  A. NO CHANGE
  B. A full train crew consists of a motorman, a
      brakeman, a conductor and two, ticket
      takers.
  C. A full train crew consists of a motorman,
      brakeman, conductor, and two ticket
      takers.
  D. A full train crew consists of, a motorman, a
      brakeman, a conductor, and two ticket
      takers.
  E. A full train crew consists of a motorman a
      brakeman a conductor and two ticket
      takers.

86. The procedure requires that you open the outer

cover <u>plate,</u> remove the <u>thermostat,</u> replace
       F   G

the broken <u>switch, and then</u> replace the
          H   J

thermostat. <u>No change</u>
            K

87. <u>After</u> Peter finished painting the bird <u>feeder</u> he
  A   B

<u>and</u> Jack <u>hung it</u> from a limb of the oak tree.
C   D

<u>No change</u>
 E

88. <u>When</u> Pat explained to his mother that ten was
  F

the highest mark <u>given</u> on the entrance <u>test</u> she
             G   H

<u>breathed</u> a sigh of relief. <u>No change</u>
  J   K

89. <u>Tim hopes to score well on the exam because</u>
<u>he plans to go to an Ivy League school.</u>

  A. NO CHANGE
  B. Tim hopes to score well on the exam and
      he plans to go to an Ivy League school.
  C. Tim hopes to score well on the exam,
      because he plans to go to an Ivy League
      school.
  D. Tim hopes to score well on the exam, and
      he plans to go to an Ivy League school.
  E. Tim hopes to score well on the exam he
      plans to go to an Ivy League school.

90. <u>In this impoverished region with its arid soil a</u>
<u>typical diet may contain only 800 calories per</u>
<u>day.</u>

  F. NO CHANGE
  G. In this impoverished region with its arid
      soil; a typical diet may contain only 800
      calories per day.
  H. In this impoverished region, with its arid
      soil, a typical diet may contain only 800
      calories per day.
  J. In this impoverished region with its arid
      soil, a typical diet may contain only 800
      calories per day.
  K. In this impoverished region with its arid
      soil: a typical diet may contain only 800
      calories per day.

91. <u>Begun</u> in 1981 and completed in <u>1985</u> the bridge
  A   B

<u>provided</u> the first link <u>between</u> the island and the
  C   D

mainland. <u>No change</u>
                  E

92. <u>To slow the bleeding Van tied a pressure
bandage around the lower portion of the leg.</u>

  F. NO CHANGE
  G. To slow the bleeding—Van tied a pressure
      bandage around the lower portion of the
      leg.
  H. To slow the bleeding, Van tied a pressure
      bandage around the lower portion of the
      leg.
  J. To slow the bleeding, Van tied a pressure
      bandage, around the lower portion of the
      leg.
  K. Van tied a pressure bandage, to slow the
      bleeding, around the lower portion of the
      leg.

93. <u>Niagara Falls,</u> <u>which</u> forms part of the border
  A   B

between the United States and <u>Canada,</u> was the
                                  C

site of a saw mill <u>built by the French in 1725.</u>
                          D

<u>No change</u>
  E

94. Secretary of State <u>Acheson,</u> <u>however,</u> made a
                        F   G

<u>reasoned</u> defense <u>of</u> the treaty. <u>No change</u>
  H   J   K

95. Until the end of the eighteenth <u>century,</u> the only
                                        A

musicians in <u>Norway,</u> were simple,
                B

unsophisticated peasants <u>who</u> traveled <u>about</u> the
                            C   D

countryside. <u>No change</u>
                    E

96. Prizes <u>will be</u> awarded in each <u>event,</u> and the
            F   G

<u>participant, who compiles the greatest overall</u>
                        H

<u>total,</u> <u>will receive</u> a special prize. <u>No change</u>
  H   J   K

97. Since learning of the dangers of <u>caffeine,</u> <u>neither</u>
                                        A   B

my wife <u>nor</u> I have consumed any <u>beverage,</u>
          C   D

containing caffeine. <u>No change</u>
                          E

98. After months of separation, Gauguin finally
joined Van Gogh <u>in Arles in October of 1888,
Gauguin left a few weeks later.</u>

  F. NO CHANGE
  G. in Arles in October of 1888; Gauguin,
      however, leaving a few weeks later
  H. in Arles in October of 1888, while Gauguin
      left a few weeks later
  J. in Arles in October of 1888, it was three
      weeks later when Gauguin was gone
  K. in Arles, in October of 1888, but left a few
      weeks later

99. <u>By the middle of June,</u> the foliage on the trees
        A

and the underbrush <u>was</u> lush and green and so
                      B

thick <u>that</u> it was impossible to see <u>very far, into</u>
        C   D

the woods. <u>No change</u>
                  E

100. Students who plan to graduate with joint
majors <u>must, declare</u> their intention and
identify the two areas of study by the end of
their junior years.

  F. NO CHANGE
  G. must declare
  H. must, declaring
  J. must declaring
  K. must declared

Semicolons

101. <u>He grew up on a farm in Nebraska; he is now the captain of a Navy ship.</u>

A. NO CHANGE
B. He grew up on a farm in Nebraska, he is now the captain of a Navy ship.
C. He grew up on a farm in Nebraska he is now the captain of a Navy ship.
D. He grew up on a farm; in Nebraska he is now the captain of a Navy ship.
E. He grew up on a farm in Nebraska but he is now the captain of a Navy ship.

102. <u>The Smithtown players cheered the referee's decision; the Stonybrook players booed it.</u>

F. NO CHANGE
G. The Smithtown players cheered the referee's decision the Stonybrook players booed it.
H. The Smithtown players cheered the referee's decision, the Stonybrook players booed it.
J. The Smithtown players cheered the referee's decision: the Stonybrook players booed it.
K. The Smithtown players cheered the referee's decision; but the Stonybrook players booed it.

103. <u>When</u> John entered the <u>room; everyone</u> stood <u>up.</u>
   A   B   C   D

<u>No change</u>
E

104. Clem <u>announced</u> <u>that</u> the prize <u>would be</u> donated to
            F   G   H

Harbus <u>House;</u> a well-known charity. <u>No change</u>
       J   K

105. The nineteenth-century composers Wagner and Mahler did more than just write <u>music, they conducted</u> their own works.

A. NO CHANGE
B. music, in that they conducted
C. music; they conducted
D. music, with their conducting of
E. music; as conductors, they did

Colons

106. The <u>seemingly</u> tranquil lane has been the scene of
           F

many crimes <u>including: two</u> <u>assaults,</u> three
                 G   H

<u>robberies,</u> and one murder. <u>No change</u>
J   K

107. In addition to test <u>scores, college</u> admissions
                         A

officers take into consideration many other

factors such <u>as: grades,</u> extracurricular <u>activities,</u>
           B   C   D

<u>and</u> letters of recommendation. <u>No change</u>
D   E

End-Stop Punctuation

108. <u>Peter notified Elaine. The guidance counselor, that he had been accepted.</u>

F. NO CHANGE
G. Peter notified Elaine the guidance counselor, that he had been accepted.
H. Peter notified Elaine, the guidance counselor that he had been accepted.
J. Peter notified Elaine, the guidance counselor, that he had been accepted.
K. Peter notified Elaine that the guidance counselor had been accepted.

Dashes

109. <u>Peanuts—blanched or lightly roasted, add an interesting texture and taste to garden salads.</u>

    A. NO CHANGE
    B. Peanuts—blanched or lightly roasted— add an interesting texture and taste to garden salads.
    C. Peanuts: blanched or lightly roasted, add an interesting texture and taste to garden salads.
    D. Peanuts, blanched or lightly roasted—add an interesting texture and taste to garden salads.
    E. Peanuts blanched or lightly roasted; add an interesting texture and taste to garden salads.

110. The rug gets its striking colors from the weaver's skilled use of <u>dyes—both natural and synthetic to create</u> shades in subtle variations.

    F. NO CHANGE
    G. dyes—both natural and synthetic, to create
    H. dyes, both natural and synthetic—to create
    J. dyes—both natural and synthetic—to create
    K. dyes—both natural and—synthetic to create

Quotation Marks

111. <u>The first chapter of *The Scarlet Letter* is "The Custom House."</u>

    A. NO CHANGE
    B. The first chapter of *The Scarlet Letter* is "The Custom House".
    C. The first chapter of *The Scarlet Letter* is The Custom House.
    D. The first chapter of *The Scarlet Letter* is *The Custom House.*
    E. The first chapter of "*The Scarlet Letter*" is "The Custom House."

Apostrophes

112. According to legend, <u>King Arthurs court</u> consisted of twenty-four knights, each of whom was chosen by Arthur for a special talent or virtue.

    F. NO CHANGE
    G. King Arthurs' court
    H. King Arthur's court
    J. King's Arthur court
    K. Kings' Arthur court

113. In the turmoil of our <u>modern times</u>, it is important to try to keep in mind the fundamental moral values that structure our society.

    A. NO CHANGE
    B. modern times'
    C. modern time's
    D. modern-like times'
    E. modern and time

114. While he addresses the barbell, <u>a weightlifters face</u> has an expression of deep concentration which immediately gives way to one of complete exertion during the lift and to total exhaustion as the bar is allowed to fall to the ground.

    F. NO CHANGE
    G. the weightlifters face
    H. the weightlifters faces
    J. the weightlifters' face
    K. a weightlifter's face

Punctuating for Clarity Exercise

> **DIRECTIONS:** Item #115 requires punctuation of the paragraph.

115. On Monday Mark received a letter of acceptance from State College He immediately called his mother herself a graduate of State College to tell her about his acceptance When he told her he had also been awarded a scholarship she was very excited After hanging up Mark's mother decided to throw a surprise party for Mark

She telephoned his brother his sister and several of his friends Because the party was supposed to be a surprise she made them all promise not to say anything to Mark Mark however had a similar idea a party for his mother to celebrate his acceptance at her alma mater He telephoned his brother his sister and several of his parents' friends to invite them to a party at his house on Saturday night and he made them all promise to say nothing to his mother On Saturday night both Mark and his mother were surprised

Rhetorical Skills Review

Items #116–120 are based on the following essay, which is a response to an assignment to write about an issue that is facing America and what might be done to resolve it.

[1] In my mind, one of the most pressing issues facing America today is healthcare. [2] One aspect of the problem is lack of access to a doctor. [3] Many people just cannot afford to pay for a visit to a doctor. [4] They avoid going to the doctor until they are really sick. [5] If they were treated in the first place, they wouldn't get so sick. [6] This practice not only causes human suffering but is wasteful. [7] Health insurance for surgery is also an issue. [8] Many people do not get adequate health insurance with their jobs and cannot afford to pay for it. [9] The inability to pay for health insurance also creates an unfair distribution of healthcare in America.

[10] An even more important aspect of the healthcare problem in America is the choices that people make for themselves. [11] Take smoking for example. [12] Scientific evidence proves that smoking causes lung cancer and other diseases. [13] Yet, many people continue to smoke, and young people continue to start smoking. [14] There are other health problems such as being overweight and using drugs that may also come from private choices.

[15] Some government assistance is needed for those who cannot afford medical care or health insurance. [16] The most important thing is for people to be concerned with their own health. [17] If we take care of ourselves by eating better, exercising more, and avoiding destructive choices, we will all live longer, healthier, and happier lives.

116. The author considers inserting the following factual statement between sentences 13 and 14:

> Nicotine, which is found in tobacco, is one of the most addictive chemicals known to science.

Would this statement add to the development of the paragraph?

A. Yes, because the paragraph identifies smoking as a serious problem.
B. Yes, because the sentence explains why young people start to smoke.
C. No, because scientific evidence is irrelevant to the author's point.
D. No, because the addictive mechanism behind smoking is not relevant.
E. No, because essays should emphasize positive points, not negative ones.

117. Which of the following revisions to Sentences 15 and 16 best clarifies the author's position?

    F. NO CHANGE
    G. Some government assistance is needed for those who cannot afford medical care or health insurance and people need to be concerned with their own health.
    H. The most important thing is for people to be concerned with their own health and for them to ask for government assistance.
    J. Even though some government assistance is needed for those who cannot afford medical care or health insurance, the most important thing is for people to be concerned with their own health.
    K. OMIT Sentence 15

118. In context, which of the following best describes the main purpose of the essay?

    A. To expose faulty reasoning
    B. To evaluate a theory set forth earlier
    C. To provide specific illustrations
    D. To propose a solution to a problem
    E. To persuade the reader to change an opinion

119. In writing this passage, the author was most probably addressing:

    F. a convention of surgeons.
    G. a group of concerned citizens.
    H. a meeting of insurance executives.
    J. a conference of tobacco executives.
    K. an assembly of noted scientists.

120. What should be done to Sentence 7 to strengthen the organization of the essay?

    A. NO CHANGE
    B. Begin a new paragraph
    C. Switch Sentence 6 with Sentence 7
    D. Switch Sentence 7 with Sentence 8
    E. OMIT Sentence 7

Item #121 is based on the following essay, which is a response to an assignment to write about a chore for which you have a responsibility and why you like or dislike doing the chore.

[1]

Each year, my family plants a vegetable garden. Both my parents work, and with this, it is the job of the children to tend the garden.

[2]

Work starts several weeks before the growing season actually begins. We put little pots of soil containing seeds that must sprout before they are planted outdoors on the sun porch. Then, my father prepares the ground with a rototiller. When the danger of frost is past, it is time to plant.

[3]

For the first few weeks, we water the seed beds regularly and pull weeds by hand. Once the plants are established, the leaves of the good plants block the sunlight so weeds can't grow. However, there are other jobs such as staking tomatoes and tending to running vines.

[4]

Then the blossoms appear and are pollinated by bees and other insects. As small vegetables appear, the blossoms drop off. They continue to grow and later in the summer begin to ripen. Up to this point, tending the garden has been a chore, but now it becomes a pleasure. Each afternoon, we pick the ripe ones and wash them so that they are ready for cooking. I suppose that I feel proud that I have helped to feed my family. I have to admit that my greatest enjoyment is the taste of the freshly picked vegetables.

121. The overall organization of the passage can best be described as:

F. chronological development.
G. explanation of two sides of an issue.
H. generalization of a statement with illustrations.
J. posing a question and then answering it.
K. citing an authority and then drawing a conclusion.

> Items #122–127 are based on the following essay, which is a response to an assignment to write about a significant activity or experience from the summer vacation.

[1]

On my vacation to Alaska, I took a trip to Porcupine. In 1905, Porcupine was a thriving town of 2,000 people, retail stores, and a post office. Hardly any of the town remains today, but there is still gold there, and our guide showed us how to pan for gold. It's easy to learn how, and anyone can do it. 122

[2]

The technique of panning depends on the weight of gold. It's about 20 times heavier than water, so the gold stays at the bottom of a stream and gets caught in the sand in slow-flowing water around bends and along the edge of the stream. It can also get stuck in small crevices of rock and even wedged into pieces of wood. 124

[3]

You need to find where the gold is. There's no sense in panning for gold in a stream where there isn't any, so go to a stream where people have found gold before. Then concentrate on those areas that are most likely to trap the little bits of gold.

[4]

Keep moving the pan until about half the original material has been carried away. Lift the pan out of the water, tilt it toward the side with the riffles (the small ridges), 125 and swirl until the water is gone. Repeat this process until nearly all the material is gone.

[5]

To start panning, put a few handfuls of material into your gold pan. Then submerge the pan in the water of the stream. Hold the pan under the surface and move it in a circular motion so that the lighter material sloshes over the edge. You have to be careful not to be too aggressive or you'll send your gold downstream along with the silt and other debris.

[6]

Use a small stream of water suction pipette (or even a spray bottle with a concentrated setting on the nozzle) to sort the gold from the remaining debris. Pick up the flecks with a tweezers or your fingers and place them in a small glass container such as a test tube or a medicine bottle.

[7]

Panning takes practice, patience, and luck, but even a little bit of gold is a big thrill. 126 You're probably not going to find a lot of gold.

122. Which of the following sentences inserted at 122 would best introduce the remaining paragraphs of the essay?

A. Gold is one of the most valuable substances on earth.
B. Just follow these simple instructions.
C. I try to do a lot of different things on my vacations.
D. Did you even know that there was a gold rush in Alaska?
E. Porcupine, the town, was named for the small quilled animal.

123. Which of the following sequence of paragraphs is most logical?

F. NO CHANGE
G. 6, 4, 5
H. 4, 6, 5
J. 5, 4, 6
K. 5, 6, 4

124. The best placement for the final sentence in Paragraph 2 would be:

A. where it is now.
B. as the first sentence of Paragraph 2.
C. in Paragraph 2, following the sentence ending ". . . weight of gold."
D. as the first sentence of Paragraph 3.
E. as the last sentence of Paragraph 4.

125. Is the parenthetical note following the word "riffles" in Paragraph 4 appropriate?

F. Yes, because it clarifies a technical term for the reader.
G. Yes, because it presents an idea that is essential to the passage.
H. No, because it distracts the reader from the directions for panning.
J. No, because the author does not cite a source for the definition.
K. No, because technical jargon is out of place in this essay.

126. The best placement for the sentence: "Panning takes practice, patience, and luck, but even a little bit of gold is a big thrill" would be:

A. where it is now.
B. at the end of the passage.
C. at the beginning of Paragraph 2.
D. at the beginning of Paragraph 6.
E. at the beginning of the essay.

127. Suppose the author had been assigned to write a brief essay on an interesting travel destination. Assuming that all of the following statements are true, would this essay successfully fulfill the assignment?

F. Yes, because many gold-seekers came to Porcupine during the nineteenth century.
G. Yes, because panning for gold would be a fun activity on a trip.
H. No, because very little remains today of the town of Porcupine.
J. No, because most people have never before heard of Porcupine.
K. No, because many people prefer silver jewelry to gold jewelry.

DIRECTIONS: Items #128–135 consist of two types of items: (1) When four separate parts of a sentence are underlined, identify the underlined part that contains an error. Some of these sentences may not contain any errors; in such a case, choose "No change." No sentence contains more than one error, and no sentence contains an error that is not underlined. (2) When a single part of a sentence is underlined or the entire sentence is underlined, identify the re-phrasing that best expresses the meaning of the underlined material. The answer choice "NO CHANGE" indicates that the underlined material is correct as written.

128. Angela is hoping to save enough for a trip to Europe, during which the small village where her grandparents were born will be visited.

A. NO CHANGE
B. the small village where her grandparents had been born will be visited
C. she will visit the small village where her grandparents were born
D. there will be a visit to the small village where her grandparents were born
E. a visit to the small village where her grandparents were born will be included

129. Finally and at long last the old dog opened his eyes and noticed the intruder.

F. NO CHANGE
G. Finally
H. So finally
J. Yet at long last
K. Finally and long lastingly

130. The speaker declared that alternative ways of utilizing waterfront land ought to be explored.

A. NO CHANGE
B. alternatives of use for
C. alternative utilizations of
D. alternative ways of utilization of
E. alternate uses of

131. <u>Since only</u> the ruling party <u>is allowed to</u> vote, <u>its</u>
     F   G   H

members are able to maintain the <u>existing</u> status
                                    J

quo. <u>No change</u>
      K

132. Each year, the geese <u>make</u> their <u>annual</u> <u>migration</u>
                            A   B   C

from Northern Canada to <u>their winter habitats</u> in
                                 D

the United States. <u>No change</u>
                    E

133. <u>Although</u> the committee met for over two weeks
     F

and issued a 50-page report, <u>its findings</u> were
                             G

<u>of little</u> <u>importance or</u> consequence. <u>No change</u>
  H   J   K

134. <u>Along with an end to featherbedding and no-show jobs</u>, the new head of the Transit Authority has eliminated many other inefficient employment practices.

  A. NO CHANGE
  B. In addition to eliminating featherbedding and no-show jobs
  C. Not only did he end featherbedding and no-show jobs
  D. Besides featherbedding and no-show jobs coming to an end
  E. Together with the ending of featherbedding and no-show jobs

135. <u>Being that</u> the hour <u>was</u> late, we <u>agreed</u> to
     F   G   H

adjourn the meeting and <u>reconvene</u> at nine
                              J

o'clock the following morning. <u>No change</u>
                                K

General Strategies

DIRECTIONS: Items #136–145 are based on the passage below. In the passage, certain parts of the sentences have been underlined and numbered. In the right-hand column, you will find different ways of writing each underlined part; the original version is indicated by the "NO CHANGE" option. For each item, select the choice that best expresses the intended idea, is most acceptable in standard written English, or is most consistent with the overall tone and style of the passage.

There are also items that ask about a section of the passage or the passage as a whole. These items do not refer to an underlined portion of the passage; these items are preceded by statements that are enclosed in boxes.

Read the passage through once before you begin to answer the accompanying items. Finding the answers to certain items may depend on looking at material that appears several sentences beyond the item. So, be sure that you have read far enough ahead before you select your answer choice.

Appalachia's European Settlers

The first Europeans who adopted Appalachia as

<u>home, followed</u> the trails pounded out by those earliest
136

mountain <u>engineers: the</u> buffalo, elk, deer, and other
137

136. A. NO CHANGE
B. home followed
C. home: followed
D. home; followed

137. F. NO CHANGE
G. engineers, the
H. engineers the
J. engineers. The

wild game. (Later, they found the great traces forged
138
by the Indian tribes on their trading and fighting
138
forays.) Gradually, these first Europeans hewed out
138

passages that become part of America's history, and
139
portions of which may still be discovered along today's

interstates and back roads. Their very names connect us
140
to the past in the region: The Great Warrior's Trail,
140
Boone's Trace (which became the Wilderness Road),

and the Cumberland Gap.

Geographic isolation greatly influenced the
141
region's culture. From the beginning, numerous ethnic

groups contributed to Appalachian settlement. During

the late 1600s and into the next century, Germans from

the Rhineland settled in the Great Appalachian Valley.
142
Building fat barns and tight houses on the fertile fields
142
of Pennsylvania, Maryland, Virginia, and North

Carolina. They were the "Pennsylvania Dutch."

The German settlers made important
143
contributions. One of the important contributions made
143
by German settlers to frontier life was the Pennsylvania

rifle—also called the Kentucky rifle or the Long rifle.

A weapon born of necessity and economy, its extended

---

138. A. NO CHANGE
   B. Great traces forged by the Indian tribes, however, were later found on their trading and fighting forays.
   C. (Finding later, great traces forged by the Indian tribes, on their trading and fighting forays.)
   D. Later, they found the great traces forged by the Indian tribes on their trading and fighting forays.

139. F. NO CHANGE
   G. will become a part of
   H. became part of
   J. became part

140. A. NO CHANGE
   B. connecting us to
   C. connected us to
   D. connect us

141. F. NO CHANGE
   G. Geographically isolated
   H. Isolated geographically
   J. Isolated geography

142. A. NO CHANGE
   B. Valley, building
   C. Valley: building
   D. Valley,

143. F. NO CHANGE
   G. (The German settlers made important contributions.)
   H. "The German settlers made important contributions."
   J. OMIT the underlined portion.

barrel assured greater <u>accuracy and precision</u> than
                                          144
could be achieved with the old muskets, and its smaller

bore required less powder and lead for each shot

<u>(precious commodities)</u>. Such rifles were highly prized
     145
possessions, and their manufacture was one of the

central industries of pioneer Appalachia.

144. A. NO CHANGE
B. accuracy as well as precision
C. accuracy plus precision
D. accuracy

145. The most appropriate placement of the underlined phrase in this sentence would be:

F. where it is now.
G. after the word *powder*.
H. after the word *lead*.
J. after the word *each*.

QUIZZES

This section contains four English quizzes. Complete each quiz under timed conditions. Answers are on page 658.

Quiz I
(32 items; 20 minutes)

Passage I

Shakespeare's Mirror of Life

No writer can please many readers and please them for a long time <u>excepting by</u> the accurate
1

1. A. NO CHANGE
   B. except by
   C. except for
   D. excepting

representation of human nature. Shakespeare, <u>however,</u>
                                                    2
is above all writers, the poet of human nature, the

writer who holds up to his readers a <u>faithful and true</u>
                                                3
mirror of manners and life.

    Shakespeare's characters are not modified by

the customs of particular places unknown to the rest

of the world, by peculiarities of study or professions

known <u>to just a few, or</u> by the latest fashions or
           4

popular opinions. Shakespeare's characters are <u>each</u>
                                                      5
genuine representations of common humanity. Hamlet

and Othello <u>act and speak</u> according to the general
                  6
passions and principles that affect all of us. In the

writings of other poets, <u>whoever they may be,</u> a
                                   7

character is too often an individual; in <u>that of</u>
                                               8
<u>Shakespeare,</u> it is commonly a species.
      8
    Other dramatists can gain attention only by using

exaggerated characters. Shakespeare <u>has no heroes; his</u>
                                              9

2. F. NO CHANGE
    G. moreover
    H. therefore
    J. furthermore

3. A. NO CHANGE
    B. faithful
    C. faithfully true
    D. true and real

4. F. NO CHANGE
    G. about by only a few, and
    H. to just a few, but
    J. to only a few, since

5. A. NO CHANGE
    B. every
    C. all
    D. each one a

6. F. NO CHANGE
    G. acting and speaking
    H. acted and spoke
    J. acted and spoken

7. A. NO CHANGE
    B. whoever they may be
    C. whomever they may be,
    D. OMIT the underlined portion.

8. F. NO CHANGE
    G. the one of Shakespeare,
    H. those of Shakespeare's,
    J. those of Shakespeare,

9. A. NO CHANGE
    B. has no heroes: his
    C. has no heroes his
    D. has no heroes, his

scenes <u>only</u> are occupied by persons who act and
10

speak as the reader thinks he or she <u>would of spoken</u>
11
or acted on the same occasion. This, therefore, is the

praise of <u>Shakespeare that</u> his drama is the mirror of
12
life. ☐ 13

10. The most appropriate placement of the underlined phrase in this sentence would be:

F.   where it is now.
G.   after the word *act*.
H.   before the word *act*.
J.   after the word *occupied*.

11. A.   NO CHANGE
B.   would have speaked
C.   would have spoken
D.   would speak

12. F.   NO CHANGE
G.   Shakespeare,
H.   Shakespeare. That
J.   Shakespeare: that

13. Is the final sentence an appropriate ending?

A.   Yes, because it makes a final point about Shakespeare that was not previously mentioned and will leave the reader with something to think about.
B.   Yes, because it is a summary of what was said in the introductory paragraph and will give the reader a sense of closure.
C.   No, because it is irrelevant to the essay and will leave the reader confused.
D.   No, because it is so repetitious that it will make the reader impatient.

Items #14–17 ask about the preceding passage as a whole.

14. What assumption is the essay's author making?

F.   Everyone believes Shakespeare is a good writer.
G.   No one has ever heard of Shakespeare.
H.   An accurate representation of human nature is important for great art.
J.   We could not understand Shakespeare's characters in the twentieth century.

15. Where might you find this essay published?

    A. In a book of literary criticism
    B. In a journal for Renaissance scholars
    C. In a Shakespeare biography
    D. In a sociology textbook

16. Which of the following is NOT a strategy the author uses to make his/her point?

    F. Comparison
    G. Argument
    H. Examples
    J. Personal anecdote

17. Which of the following would most strengthen the author's argument that Shakespeare is the poet of human nature?

    A. A discussion of Shakespeare's poetry
    B. An analysis of the characters Hamlet and Othello
    C. Biographical background on Shakespeare
    D. A description of Shakespeare's Globe Theater

Passage II

Diary of a Black Hole

[1]

In the course of billions of years, millions of stars may <u>sometimes occasionally</u> be concentrated
₁₈
into a region, or regions, only a few light years across,

18. F. NO CHANGE
    G. sometimes, occasionally
    H. occasionally
    J. off and on

<u>and in these crowded conditions colliding</u> with one
₁₉

19. A. NO CHANGE
    B. colliding
    C. and in these crowded conditions, they collide
    D. which causes them to collide

another. Some of these collisions <u>would occur</u> at
20
high speeds, in which case the stars are partially or

completely torn apart. Other collisions are gentle

<u>bumps, but the stars coalesce</u>. The bigger the star
21

<u>becomes, the more likely</u> it is to be hit again and the
22
faster it grows until it reaches instability, collapses on

itself, <u>and forms a black hole</u>.
23

[2]

When most of the stars and gas in the core of a

galaxy <u>has been</u> swallowed up by the black hole, the
24

nucleus of the galaxy settles down <u>to a relative</u> quiet
25
existence. This is probably the state of the nucleus

of our own galaxy, but every hundred million years or

so it may flare <u>for</u> a brightness 100 times its present
26
level when a globular cluster or especially large gas

cloud <u>of enormous size</u> spirals into the nucleus.
27
[3]

Once formed, a central "seed" black hole grows

mainly through the accretion of gas accumulated in

20. F. NO CHANGE
G. will occur
H. to occur
J. occur

21. A. NO CHANGE
B. bumps, since the stars
C. bumps, and the stars coalesce
D. bumps, with the stars coalescing

22. F. NO CHANGE
G. becomes the more
H. becomes the more,
J. becomes; the more

23. A. NO CHANGE
B. and a black hole is formed
C. and when this happens a black hole is formed
D. and thus a black hole is formed at this very moment

24. F. NO CHANGE
G. have been
H. will have been
J. would have been

25. A. NO CHANGE
B. to a relatively
C. for a relative and
D. relatively

26. F. NO CHANGE
G. by
H. up to
J. OMIT the underlined portion.

27. A. NO CHANGE
B. of great enormity
C. which is huge
D. OMIT the underlined portion.

the <u>nucleus; gas</u> obtained from disrupted stars, from
      28

supernova explosions, or from stars torn apart by the

gravitational field of the black hole. Perhaps an entire

galaxy can collide with another <u>galaxy, and the result</u>
                                            29

<u>would be</u> the transfer of large amounts of gas from one
   29

galaxy <u>to each other</u>.
            30

28. F. NO CHANGE
    G. nucleus and gas
    H. nucleus. Gas
    J. nucleus gas

29. A. NO CHANGE
    B. galaxy to result in
    C. galaxy. Such a collision could result in
    D. galaxy with the results that

30. F. NO CHANGE
    G. to the other
    H. an other
    J. and another

Items #31–32 ask about the preceding passage as a whole.

---

31. Which of the following represents the most logical sequence for the paragraphs?

    A. 1, 2, 3
    B. 1, 3, 2
    C. 2, 3, 1
    D. 3, 1, 2

32. The author's intended audience is most likely:

    F. astronomers.
    G. young children.
    H. high school students.
    J. physicists.

Quiz II
(29 items; 20 minutes)

Passage I

The Influence of the Southwest on Artists

Georgia O'Keeffe, <u>who's</u> death <u>at age ninety-</u>
₁   ₂

<u>eight</u> closed one of the most fertile chapters of
₂

1. A. NO CHANGE
   B. which
   C. that
   D. whose

2. F. NO CHANGE
   G. at the old age of ninety-eight
   H. at the age of ninety-eight years
   J. when she was ninety-eight years old

American <u>creativity and flourished</u> as a maverick in her
₃

3. A. NO CHANGE
   B. creativity, and flourished
   C. creativity—flourished
   D. creativity, flourished

life and work. <u>Since other</u> painters spent a season or
4

two in the country trying to come to terms with the

scenes and settings of the Southwest—O'Keeffe stayed

a lifetime. When the canvases of other <u>artists, working</u>
5

<u>in the region</u> faded from view and <u>then were neglected</u>
5   6

<u>in the chronicle of American visual history</u>, her stylized
6

images made an <u>indelible and permanent</u> impression
7

on countless eyes.

Between 1900 and 1945, the region now called

New Mexico both fascinated <u>and also it perplexed</u> two
8

generations of American artists. <u>Despite their successes,</u>
9

many of those artists wearied of the industrial world of

the east. <u>The vast expanse of the West offered a</u>
10

<u>promise for inspiration.</u> For these artists, life and art, so
10

separate in New York and Paris, seemed <u>inextricably</u>
11

<u>bounded</u> in Southwestern cultures. Painters of every
11

---

4. F. NO CHANGE
G. Because other
H. In that other
J. Other

5. A. NO CHANGE
B. artists working in the region,
C. artists working in the region
D. artists, who worked in the region

6. F. NO CHANGE
G. got neglected then in the chronicle of American visual history
H. were also then neglected in the American visual history chronicle
J. then they were also totally neglected in the chronicle of American visual history

7. A. NO CHANGE
B. indelible
C. indelible—and permanent—
D. indelible but permanent

8. F. NO CHANGE
G. and perplexed
H. while perplexing
J. but perplexed

9. A. NO CHANGE
B. Despite their having many successes
C. In spite of their having their successes
D. Ensuring successes,

10. F. NO CHANGE
G. America's West, with its vast expanse, offered an inspiring promise.
H. America's vast expanse of the West offered a promise for inspiration.
J. Offering a promise of inspiration to the artists was the vast expanse of the American West.

11. A. NO CHANGE
B. inextricably bound
C. inextricable bounding
D. inextricably bounding

persuasion <u>were convinced</u> that sampling this
₁₂

mysterious phenomenon <u>will strengthen</u> and enrich
₁₃

their own work. Most were touched by what D. H.

Lawrence called the "spirit of the place." Besides the

scenic beauty bathed in clear golden <u>light. The</u> rich
₁₄

traditions of New Mexico's Indian and Hispanic people

<u>who were living there</u> became frequent subjects of the
₁₅

artists who traveled to Taos and Santa Fe.

12. F. NO CHANGE
    G. could be convinced
    H. will be convinced
    J. are convincing

13. A. NO CHANGE
    B. would strengthen
    C. strengthens
    D. strengthening

14. F. NO CHANGE
    G. light, the
    H. light the
    J. light: the

15. A. NO CHANGE
    B. who lived there
    C. living there
    D. OMIT the underlined portion.

Items #16–17 ask about the preceding passage as a whole.

---

16. Is the author's quote of D. H. Lawrence in the last paragraph appropriate?

    F. Yes, because the author is talking about how this spirit inspired artists, and the quote strengthens his argument.
    G. No, because the author has already made his point about the spirit, and the quote is redundant.
    H. No, because the author does not make it clear that Lawrence is an authority on the subject.
    J. Yes, because it is always a good idea to end an article with a quotation.

17. How might the author have developed the essay so that it was more interesting?

A. The author could have told an anecdote about D. H. Lawrence.
B. The author could have eliminated all mention of Georgia O'Keeffe.
C. The author could have discussed the settling of New Mexico.
D. The author could have been more specific about the other artists who went to the Southwest.

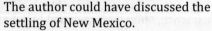

Passage II

Chippewa Chief Demands Timber Payment

Early in November 1850, the work of a logging detail from Fort Gaines in the Minnesota Territory was interrupted by a party of Chippewa warriors who demanded payment for the timber. The loggers refused,
                                                          18
so the Indians, acting at the direction of Chief
18   **19**

Hole-in-the-Day confiscated the government's oxen.
19

The loggers had established their camp on Chippewa

lands without his authorizing it. Therefore, in a move
       20   **21**
designed to force reimbursements for the timber, Hole-

18. F. NO CHANGE
G. The loggers refused—
H. The loggers refused:
J. The loggers refused so

19. A. NO CHANGE
B. that acted at the direction of Chief Hole-in-the-Day,
C. acting at the direction of Chief Hole-in-the-Day,
D. (acting at the direction of Chief Hole-in-the-Day),

20. F. NO CHANGE
G. without his authorization
H. without their authorizing it
J. without his authorization of it

21. A. NO CHANGE
B. Henceforth
C. Since
D. On the contrary

in-the-Day <u>was ordering</u> his braves to seize the oxen.
22

Captain John Todd, the commanding officer at

Fort Gaines, demanded <u>that the cattle had to be</u>
23

<u>returned to them</u>. The chief's reply was firm, <u>and at the</u>
23   24

<u>same time, it was friendly</u>. In his message to Captain
24

Todd, Hole-in-the-Day explained that he had <u>delayed</u>
25

<u>to seize</u> the cattle until he could meet Todd in council
25

and had sent a messenger to the officer requesting a

conference at Crow Wing. When Todd did not come,

he <u>acted, additionally</u> he later decided that since the
26

army had not paid for timber cut the previous winter,

he intended to keep the oxen until the tribe <u>was</u>
27

<u>reimbursed by</u> all the timber taken for the fort. Hole-in-
27

the-Day concluded by saying, "Do not think hard of

me, but I do as others would—the timber is mine." 28

22. F. NO CHANGE
G. gave orders that
H. orders
J. ordered

23. A. NO CHANGE
B. the return of the cattle
C. the cattle's returning
D. that they return the cattle

24. F. NO CHANGE
G. but, at the same time, it was friendly
H. yet friendly
J. at the same time—friendly

25. A. NO CHANGE
B. delayed to have seized
C. delayed to seized
D. delayed seizing

26. F. NO CHANGE
G. acted but additionally
H. acted. Additionally,
J. acted additionally,

27. A. NO CHANGE
B. reimbursed for
C. reimbursed
D. was reimbursed for

28. Is the author's use of the quote in the final paragraph appropriate?

F. Yes, because it neatly summarizes the main point of the essay.
G. No, because the chief's thoughts were irrelevant to the events.
H. Yes, but the author should have included a quotation from Captain Todd.
J. No, because quotations have no place in expository writing.

Item #29 asks about the preceding passage as a whole.

29. Which of the following best describes the overall character of the essay?

   A. Description of a scene
   B. Narration of events
   C. Comparison of two theories
   D. Argument for a change

Quiz III

(31 items; 20 minutes)

DIRECTIONS: In the passages below, certain parts of the sentences have been underlined and numbered. In the right-hand column, you will find different ways of writing each underlined part; the original version is indicated by the "NO CHANGE" option. For each item, select the choice that best expresses the intended idea, is most acceptable in standard written English, or is most consistent with the overall tone and style of the passage.

There are also items that ask about a section of the passage or the passage as a whole. These items do not refer to an underlined portion of the passage; these items are preceded by statements that are enclosed in boxes.

Read the passage through once before you begin to answer the accompanying items. Finding the answers to certain items may depend on looking at material that appears several sentences beyond the item. So, be sure that you have read far enough ahead before you select your answer choice.

Passage I

The Con Game Is No Game

Most people have a certain crime <u>that one</u>
₁

<u>believes</u> should be ranked as the worst of all crimes.
₁

For some, <u>its'</u> murder; for others, it may be selling
₂

drugs to children. I believe, <u>moreover</u>, that the worst of
₃

all crimes may be the confidence scheme.

1. A. NO CHANGE
B. that they believe
C. which one believes
D. that you believe

2. F. NO CHANGE
G. they are
H. it's
J. its

3. A. NO CHANGE
B. however
C. further
D. therefore

The confidence scheme may seem an <u>odd</u> choice
                                          4
for the worst crime since con games are usually

<u>nonviolent. Although,</u> it is a crime that ranks in
         5
heartlessness. Con artists are the most devious, the

most harmful, and the most disruptive members of

society because <u>they break</u> down <u>honesty, and trust, the</u>
                       6   7

most important bonds of social order.

The con games themselves are <u>simplistic almost</u>
                                              8
<u>infantile</u>. They work <u>on account of a con artist can</u> win
    8   9
complete confidence, talk fast enough to keep the

victim slightly confused, <u>and dangling</u> enough
                                 10
temptation to suppress any suspicion or skepticism.

The primary targets of these criminals <u>will be</u> the
                                            11

4. F. NO CHANGE
G. obvious
H. irrelevant
J. apt

5. A. NO CHANGE
B. nonviolent, though
C. nonviolent, but
D. nonviolent, and

6. F. NO CHANGE
G. it breaks
H. of its breaking
J. of them breaking

7. A. NO CHANGE
B. honesty, and trust the
C. honesty and trust, the
D. honesty and trust the

8. F. NO CHANGE
G. simplistic; almost infantile
H. simplistic, almost infantile
J. simplistic, yet almost infantile

9. A. NO CHANGE
B. on account of a con artist's ability to
C. owing to a con artist's ability to
D. because a con artist can

10. F. NO CHANGE
G. and dangles
H. and has dangled
J. and dangle

11. A. NO CHANGE
B. to be
C. are
D. is

elderly and <u>women. (And they prefer to work in large</u>
<u>12</u>

<u>crowds.)</u>
12

12. F. NO CHANGE
G. women, and the con artists prefer to work in large crowds.
H. women, preferring, of course, to work in large crowds.
J. women (who prefer to work in large crowds).

Items #13–15 ask about the preceding passage as a whole.

---

13. Which of the following is most probably the author's opinion rather than a fact?

A. The most disruptive members of society are con artists.
B. The majority of con games are nonviolent.
C. The targets of con games are mostly the elderly and women.
D. The con artists succeed when they win the complete confidence of their targets.

14. What would be the most logical continuation of the essay?

F. A description of some confidence games
G. An account of the elderly as crime victims in society
H. An account of the author's experience with con artists
J. An explanation of crowd psychology

15. What would strengthen the author's contention that con games rank first in heartlessness?

A. Statistics to show the number of people who were taken in by the con artist
B. A discussion of the way the police handle the problem
C. An example that shows how the con artist breaks down honesty and trust
D. An example to illustrate that con games are nonviolent and simple

Passage II

Elizabeth I's Intellect Ruled Supreme

Elizabeth I had a sensuous and indulgent nature

that she inherited from her mother, Anne Boleyn <u>(who</u>
                                                   16

<u>was beheaded by Henry VIII)</u>. Splendor and pleasure <u>is</u>
     16   17

the very air she breathed. She loved gaiety, laughter,

and wit. Her vanity <u>remained even, to old age. The</u>
                         18

vanity of a coquette.

The statesmen <u>who she outwitted</u> believed,
                    19

almost to the end, that Elizabeth I was little more than

a frivolous woman <u>who was very vain</u>. However, the
                       20

Elizabeth whom they saw was far from <u>being</u> all of
                                           21

Elizabeth, the queen. The willfulness of her father,

Henry VIII, and the triviality of Anne played over

the surface of a nature <u>so hard like</u> steel—a purely
                             22

intellectual temperament. Her vanity and caprice

16. F. NO CHANGE
    G. (having been beheaded by Henry VIII)
    H. beheaded by Henry VIII
    J. OMIT the underlined portion.

17. A. NO CHANGE
    B. is,
    C. were
    D. were,

18. F. NO CHANGE
    G. remains, even to old age, the
    H. remains, even to old age the
    J. remained, even to old age, the

19. A. NO CHANGE
    B. that she outwitted
    C. whom she outwitted
    D. who she was outwitting

20. F. NO CHANGE
    G. and she was also very vain
    H. known for her great vanity
    J. OMIT the underlined portion.

21. A. NO CHANGE
    B. to be
    C. having been
    D. OMIT the underlined portion.

22. F. NO CHANGE
    G. as hard as
    H. so hard as
    J. as hard like

carried no weight <u>whatsoever</u> in state affairs.
23

The coquette of the presence chamber

<u>had became</u> the coolest and hardest of politicians at
24

the council board.

It was this part that gave her marked <u>superiority</u>
25

<u>over</u> the statesmen of her time. No <u>more nobler a group</u>
25   26

of ministers ever gathered round the council board than

those of Elizabeth, but she was the instrument of none.

She listened and she weighed, but her policy, as a

whole, was her own. It was the policy of good sense,

<u>not genius, she</u> endeavored to keep her throne, to keep
27

England out of war, <u>and she wanted</u> to restore civil and
28

religious order.

23. A. NO CHANGE
    B. no matter what
    C. whatever, at all
    D. whatever, despite everything

24. F. NO CHANGE
    G. became
    H. used to become
    J. becomes

25. A. NO CHANGE
    B. superiority in regard to
    C. superiority about
    D. superior quality to

26. F. NO CHANGE
    G. nobler a group,
    H. nobler a group
    J. more nobler of a group,

27. A. NO CHANGE
    B. not genius she
    C. not genius. She
    D. —not genius, she

28. F. NO CHANGE
    G. wanting
    H. and wanting
    J. and

Items #29–31 ask about the preceding passage as a whole.

29. What might logically have preceded this essay?

    A. Some biographical background on Elizabeth I
    B. A discussion of the wives of Henry VIII
    C. A discussion of the politics of Tudor England
    D. A discussion of the policies of Elizabeth's ministers

30. This essay is most probably taken from a:

   F.   scholarly work on Renaissance England.
   G.   biography of Elizabeth I.
   H.   diary kept by one of Elizabeth's ministers.
   J.   political science textbook.

31. Which of the following would most strengthen the essay?

   A.   Knowing who the ministers were and what their policies were
   B.   Examples of Elizabeth's dual nature
   C.   A discussion of Henry VIII's policies
   D.   A discussion of the role of the woman in Tudor England

Quiz IV Brain Buster
(20 items; 10 minutes)

DIRECTIONS: The following sentences test correct, effective expression. Each sentence contains an underlined portion, or the entire sentence may be underlined. Following each sentence are five ways of phrasing the underlined portion. The first choice repeats the original; the other four choices are different. If you think the original is better than any of the other choices, choose "NO CHANGE," otherwise, choose one of the other choices.

In choosing answers, follow the conventions of standard written English. Make sure to consider issues of grammar, word choice, sentence construction, and punctuation. Your choice should produce the most effective sentence. It should be clear, precise, and free of ambiguity or awkwardness.

1. More than just a movie star, Audrey Hepburn was celebrated for her luminous beauty, for her acclaimed acting ability, <u>and everyone knew of her humanitarian work with organizations</u> such as UNICEF.

    A. NO CHANGE
    B. and everyone knew of her humanitarian organizations work
    C. and for her humanitarian work with organizations
    D. and her humanitarian work with organizations
    E. along with her humanitarian work with organizations

2. Many geologists believe that the likelihood of a devastating earthquake of magnitude 8 or higher <u>is as great or greater in the eastern part of the United States than</u> in California.

    F. NO CHANGE
    G. may be at least as great or greater in the eastern part of the United States than
    H. is so great or greater in the eastern part of the United States than
    J. is at least as great in the eastern part of the United States as
    K. can be at least so great in the eastern part of the United States as

3. The industry has seen a dramatic <u>increase in the churn of cell phone accounts caused by customer willingness to act on new promotional offers to switch</u> providers.

    A. NO CHANGE
    B. increase in the churn of cell phone accounts caused by willingness of customers to act on new promotional offers switching
    C. increasing churn of cell phone accounts caused by willingness of customers to act on new promotional offers by switching
    D. churn of cell phone accounts increase because of customer willingness to act on new promotional offers to switch
    E. increase in the churn of cell phone accounts because of customer willingness to act on new promotional offers to switch

4. <u>The Bichon Frisé is a breed of non-sporting dog, descending from the water spaniel and originating</u> in ancient times in the Mediterranean area.

    F. NO CHANGE
    G. The Bichon Frisé, which is a breed of non-sporting dog descending from the water spaniel, originated
    H. The Bichon Frisé, a breed of non-sporting dog descended from the water spaniel, originated
    J. The Bichon Frisé, a breed of non-sporting dog, descended from the water spaniel which originated
    K. A Bichon Frisé is a breed of non-sporting dog, descended from the water spaniel, and has its origin

5. Although the defense found the only lead that was likely to defeat the contract, the declarer <u>ruffed in, sloughed her losing club on dummy's ace of diamonds,</u> after drawing trumps, was able to score six spade tricks to make the grand slam.

    A. NO CHANGE
    B. ruffed in and sloughed her losing club on dummy's ace of diamonds
    C. ruffing in, sloughed her losing club on dummy's ace of diamonds
    D. ruffed in, sloughed her losing club on dummy's ace of diamonds, and
    E. ruffed in, sloughing her losing club on dummy's ace of diamonds,

6. <u>Lincoln, discovering in young manhood the secret that the Yankee peddler has learned before him, knew</u> how to use a good story to generate good will.

    F. NO CHANGE
    G. Discovering in young manhood the secret that the Yankee peddler has learned before him, Lincoln knew
    H. Lincoln, discovering the secret that the Yankee peddler had learned in young manhood before him, knew
    J. In young manhood Lincoln discovered the secret that the Yankee peddler had learned before him:
    K. Lincoln, discovered in young manhood the secret that the Yankee peddler had learned before him, knew

7. The portfolio, which was apparently <u>left inadvertent on the bus, contained three completed watercolors, including several uncompleted sketches.</u>

    A. NO CHANGE
    B. left inadvertently on the bus, contained three completed watercolors, including several uncompleted sketches
    C. inadvertently left on the bus containing three completed watercolors, including several uncompleted sketches
    D. inadvertently left on the bus, contained three completed watercolors and several uncompleted sketches
    E. left inadvertently on the bus with three completed watercolors and several uncompleted sketches

8. Recent tests on a variety of herbal supplements designed to reduce cholesterol found that half did not contain the listed <u>ingredients, were so poorly manufactured that the active ingredients, when present,</u> could not be absorbed.

    F. NO CHANGE
    G. ingredients, which were so poorly manufactured that the active ingredients, when present,
    H. ingredients or were so poorly manufactured that the active ingredients, when present,
    J. ingredients were so poorly manufactured that the present active ingredients,
    K. ingredients, were so poorly manufactured, and that the active ingredients, when present,

9. Both Samuel Beckett and Joseph Conrad were brought up speaking one language <u>and they wrote in another language when they wrote novels.</u>

    A. NO CHANGE
    B. having written novels in another language altogether
    C. but wrote their novels in another language
    D. yet when they wrote novels, they wrote them in another language
    E. with their novels being written in a different language

10. <u>The relationship of smoking and lung cancer have been firmly established, yet people continue to ignore warnings, jeopardizing their health and that of others.</u>

    F.   NO CHANGE
    G.   The relationship of smoking to lung cancer has been firmly established, yet people continue to ignore the warnings, jeopardizing their health and that of others.
    H.   The relationship of smoking to lung cancer has been firmly established, yet people continually ignore the warnings that jeopardize their own health and that of others.
    J.   The relationship between smoking and lung cancer has been firmly established, yet people continue to ignore warnings, jeopardizing their own health and that of others.
    K.   The relationship of smoking with lung cancer has been firmly established, with people continuing to ignore the warnings and jeopardizing their own health and others.

11. <u>Thrown onto the stage by adoring fans, the prima ballerina knelt gracefully and gathered up the bouquets of red roses.</u>

    A.   NO CHANGE
    B.   Throwing onto the stage by adoring fans, the prima ballerina knelt gracefully and gathered up the bouquets of red roses.
    C.   Thrown onto the stage by adoring fans, the prima ballerina had knelt gracefully before gathering up the bouquets of red roses.
    D.   Thrown onto the stage by adoring fans, the bouquets of red roses were gathered up by the prima ballerina after she had knelt gracefully.
    E.   The prima ballerina knelt gracefully and gathered up the bouquets of red roses that had been thrown onto the stage by adoring fans.

12. Although the Battle of Fort Ann is rarely mentioned in history texts, it <u>may have been the most significant engagement of the Revolutionary War because it led</u> ultimately to General Burgoyne's defeat at Saratoga.

    F.   NO CHANGE
    G.   could have been the most significant engagement of the Revolutionary War because it led
    H.   could have been the most significant engagement of the Revolutionary War if it led
    J.   might have been the most significant engagement of the Revolutionary War leading
    K.   might have been the more significant engagement of the Revolutionary War that led

13. The driving snow made the roadway slippery and reduced visibility to no more than a few feet, <u>and fortunately there were no</u> accidents despite the heavy volume of traffic.

    A.   NO CHANGE
    B.   but fortunately there were no
    C.   and fortunately there were some
    D.   while fortunately there were no
    E.   so fortunately there were no

14. India's movie industry <u>may not be as well known as the United States, but it is much bigger because</u> film is the principal storytelling vehicle in a country where more than 40 percent of the population is illiterate and the cheapest ticket costs no more than a quarter.

    F.   NO CHANGE
    G.   may not be as well known as that of the United States, but it is much bigger because
    H.   might not be as well known as that of the United States, but it is much bigger on account of
    J.   could not be as well known as the United States, but they are much bigger because
    K.   may not be as well known as that of the United States and bigger because

15. <u>Although the American relay team did not qualify for the finals, the</u> anchor runner dropped the baton shortly after the hand-off.

A. NO CHANGE
B. When the American relay team did not qualify for the finals, the
C. The American relay team did not qualify for the finals, and the
D. The American relay team did not qualify for the finals because the
E. Not qualifying for the finals, the American relay team's

16. The <u>newly released worm is especially dangerous because</u> it directs infected computers to launch a distributed denial of service attack on the very web sites that offer instructions for combating the worm.

F. NO CHANGE
G. released new worm is especially dangerous because
H. released new worm is dangerous especially because
J. newly released worm is especially dangerous on account of
K. new released worm is dangerous especially as it

17. <u>To protest their being underpaid in comparison to other city agencies, a strike was called by the sanitation workers.</u>

A. NO CHANGE
B. To protest them being underpaid in comparison with other city agencies, the sanitation workers called a strike.
C. To protest their being comparatively underpaid with other city agencies, a strike was called by the sanitation workers.
D. To protest their being underpaid in comparison with workers of other city agencies, the sanitation workers called a strike.
E. The sanitation workers called a strike to protest them being underpaid in comparison with other city workers.

18. Learning of the fall of Constantinople to the Turks in 1453, <u>the failure of the crusading movement became apparent to Christian Europe which had ignored earlier major defeats.</u>

F. NO CHANGE
G. Christian Europe realized that the crusading movement had failed, which had ignored earlier major defeats
H. Christian Europe, which had ignored earlier major defeats, realized that the crusading movement had failed
J. Christian Europe, ignoring earlier major defeats, realized that the crusading movement had failed
K. Christian Europe ignored earlier major defeats and realized that the crusading movement had failed

19. <u>Insofar as poultry is a good bargain and often less than a dollar a pound</u>, the per-person consumption of chicken and turkey has increased in the last ten years, while that of the more expensive meats such as beef and lamb has declined.

A. NO CHANGE
B. Because poultry is a good bargain and often less than a dollar a pound
C. For the reason that poultry is a good bargain at less than a dollar a pound
D. Because poultry is a good bargain at less than a dollar a pound
E. Insofar as poultry is a good bargain, selling for under a dollar a pound

20. Because of the number of colleges and universities in and around the city, <u>the population of Boston has more percentage of students than any other</u> city in the United States of comparable size.

F. NO CHANGE
G. the population of Boston has more percentage of students than any
H. Boston's population has a greater percentage of students as any other
J. Boston has a higher percentage of students as any
K. Boston has a higher percentage of students than any other

REVIEW

This section contains additional English items for further practice. Answers are on page 658.

DIRECTIONS: In the passages below, certain parts of the sentences have been underlined and numbered. In the right-hand column, you will find different ways of writing each underlined part; the original version is indicated by the "NO CHANGE" option. For each item, select the choice that best expresses the intended idea, is most acceptable in standard written English, or is most consistent with the overall tone and style of the passage.

There are also items that ask about a section of the passage or the passage as a whole. These items do not refer to an underlined portion of the passage; these items are preceded by statements that are enclosed in boxes.

Read the passage through once before you begin to answer the accompanying items. Finding the answers to certain items may depend on looking at material that appears several sentences beyond the item. So, be sure that you have read far enough ahead before you select your answer choice.

Passage I

Significance of Symbolism in Medieval Art

Art of the Middle Ages is first and foremost a sacred script, the symbols and meanings of which <u>are well settled</u>. A circular halo placed vertically behind
1

the head of a figure signifies <u>sainthood, meanwhile</u> the
2

halo impressed with a cross signifies divinity.

1. A. NO CHANGE
   B. is well settled
   C. are settled well
   D. would be settled

2. F. NO CHANGE
   G. sainthood, because
   H. sainthood because
   J. sainthood, while

A tower with a window indicates a village, and
3
should an angel be watching from the battlements, that
city is thereby identified as Jerusalem.

Mathematics is also an important element of this
iconography. "The Divine Wisdom," wrote Saint
Augustine, "reveals itself everywhere in numbers." A
4
doctrine derived from the Neoplatonists who revived
4   5
the teachings of Pythagoras. Furthermore, numbers
require symmetry. At Chartres, a stained-glass
window shows the four prophets Isaac, Ezekiel, Daniel,
and Jeremiah carrying on their shoulders the four
evangelists Matthew, Mark, Luke, and John.

Every painting is also an allegory, showing us
6

one thing and inviting us to see another. In this respect,
7
the artist was asked to imitate God, who had hidden a
7

profound meaning behind the literal and who wished
8
nature to be a moral lesson to man. In a painting of the

final judgment, the foolish virgins can be seen by us at
9
the left hand of Jesus and the wise on the right, and we
understand that this symbolizes those who are lost and

3. A. NO CHANGE
B. (Do NOT begin a new paragraph) A tower
C. Towers
D. Having a tower

4. F. NO CHANGE
G. numbers," which
H. numbers." This doctrine was
J. numbers" which

5. A. NO CHANGE
B. Neoplatonists that
C. Neoplatonist's that
D. Neoplatonist's who

6. F. NO CHANGE
G. (Do NOT begin a new paragraph) Every painting
H. However, every painting
J. (Do NOT begin a new paragraph) However, every painting

7. A. NO CHANGE
B. Furthermore, the artist was
C. The artist, however, was
D. Generally, artists are

8. F. NO CHANGE
G. meaning which was behind
H. meaning being behind
J. meaning behind and in back of

9. A. NO CHANGE
B. by all of us
C. by each of us
D. OMIT the underlined portion.

those that have been saved.
10

Within such a system, even the most mediocre
11

talent was elevated by the genius of centuries, and the
12
first artist of the Renaissance broke with the tradition
at great risk. Even when they are great, medieval
artists are no more than the equals of the old masters
who passively followed the sacred rules. When they
are not outstanding, they scarcely avoid banality and
13
insignificance in their religious works.

10. F. NO CHANGE
  G. those who have been saved
  H. those who are saved
  J. the saved

11. A. NO CHANGE
  B. (Do NOT begin a new paragraph) Within such a system,
  C. (Do NOT begin a new paragraph) Inside of such a system,
  D. (Do NOT begin a new paragraph) To be inside such a system,

12. F. NO CHANGE
  G. with
  H. however
  J. since

13. A. NO CHANGE
  B. always
  C. ever
  D. OMIT the underlined portion.

Items #14–16 ask about the preceding passage as a whole.

14. The author most likely wrote this essay for which of the following?

  F. A scholarly art journal
  G. A book tracing the history of mathematics
  H. A history of the Catholic Church
  J. A book surveying the history of Western art

15. The author relies on which of the following to develop the passage?

    A. Examples
    B. Extensive quotations from other authorities
    C. Statistics
    D. Personal experience

16. The author probably quotes Saint Augustine in order to:

    F. ridicule his position.
    G. emphasize the importance of numbers and symmetry.
    H. prove the importance of Church teaching.
    J. illustrate Augustine's knowledge of art.

Passage II

Pursuit of the Bottomless Pit

A persistent and universal symbol in the mythology of virtually every <u>culture, is</u> that of a
₁₇
bottomless pit or an engulfing whirlpool. It was the

maw of the <u>abyss: and those</u> venturing too close were
₁₈
dragged inward toward chaos by an irresistible force.

Socrates <u>(a Greek philosopher who committed
₁₉
suicide)</u> talked of a chasm that pierced the world
₁₉
straight through from side to side. Ulysses <u>also
₂₀
encountering it,</u> as did a mythical Cherokee who
₂₀
escaped, but not before he was drawn down to the

narrowest circle of the maelstrom where he could peer

17. A. NO CHANGE
    B. culture is
    C. culture are
    D. cultures are

18. F. NO CHANGE
    G. abyss, and those
    H. abyss meanwhile those
    J. abyss due to the fact that

19. A. NO CHANGE
    B. (a philosopher from Greece who committed suicide)
    C. (a Greek philosopher who had committed suicide)
    D. OMIT the underlined portion.

20. F. NO CHANGE
    G. also encountered it,
    H. also encountered them,
    J. encountered them also,

into the netherworld of the dead. <u>Many primitive</u>
<u>21</u>
<u>cultures bury their dead with tools in the belief that</u>
<u>21</u>
<u>the tools will be useful to them in the afterlife.</u>
<u>21</u>

     <u>On the other hand, the search</u> for a solution to
       22

one of <u>astronomys'</u> most persistent and perplexing
   23

riddles, black holes, could be viewed <u>by one</u> as a
         24

<u>continuation of the search for</u> the whirlpool that is the
   25

maw of the abyss, a depth our telescopes cannot reach

and from which nothing <u>will have returned</u>. What is
        26

incredible to contemplate, <u>and what sets us</u> apart from
        27

the ancients, is that we think we have a fair idea <u>not</u>
       28

<u>only as to</u> how they are formed, but also how large they
  28

are and so forth. A combination of theory and

21. For the sake of the logic and coherence of this paragraph, the underlined sentence should be:

   A. left as it is now.
   B. placed before the word *Ulysses*.
   C. placed at the end of the passage.
   D. omitted.

22. F. NO CHANGE
   G. The search
   H. (Do NOT begin a new paragraph) The search
   J. Also, the search

23. A. NO CHANGE
   B. astronomy's
   C. astronomy
   D. astronomys

24. F. NO CHANGE
   G. by one astronomer
   H. by those
   J. OMIT the underlined portion.

25. A. NO CHANGE
   B. continuing the search of
   C. continuation to the search for
   D. continuation for the search for

26. F. NO CHANGE
   G. will return
   H. returns
   J. returning

27. A. NO CHANGE
   B. setting us
   C. and that sets us
   D. and we are set

28. F. NO CHANGE
   G. about
   H. not about
   J. OMIT the underlined portion.

observation <u>have led to</u> the growing suspicion among
₂₉

astrophysicists that the nucleus of virtually every

galaxy harbors a massive black hole.

29. A. NO CHANGE
    B. has led to
    C. has led
    D. led

Passage III

Tradition Preservation During Meiji Restoration

Instead of casting aside traditional values during

the Meiji Restoration of 1888, those who strove to

dismantle feudalism and to modernize the country

chose to preserve three traditions as the foundations <u>on</u>
₃₀

<u>which they could build a modern Japan upon</u>.
₃₀

30. F. NO CHANGE
    G. on which they could be building a modern
       Japan upon
    H. upon which they could build a modern
       Japan
    J. upon which they someday could probably
       build a modern Japan

The <u>older</u> tradition and basis of the entire
₃₁

31. A. NO CHANGE
    B. oldest
    C. old
    D. OMIT the underlined portion.

Japanese value system was <u>respect for and even</u>
₃₂

<u>worshipping</u> the Emperor. During the early centuries
₃₂

32. F. NO CHANGE
    G. respecting and even worshipping
    H. respect for and even worship of
    J. respect and even worship

of Japanese history, the Shinto cult, in which <u>the</u>
₃₃

<u>Imperial family traced its ancestry to the Sun Goddess</u>,
₃₃

33. A. NO CHANGE
    B. the Imperial family got its ancestry traced
       back to the Sun Goddess
    C. the Imperial family's ancestry was traced
       back to the Sun Goddess
    D. the Sun Goddess was considered to be the
       ancestor of the Imperial family

became the people's sustaining faith. <u>Being later</u>
₃₄

<u>subordinated</u> to imported Buddhism and Confucianism,
₃₄

Shintoism was perpetuated in Ise and Izumo, the great

shrines of the Imperial family, until the Meiji

modernizers established it as a quasi state religion to

unify the people and restore the Emperor as the

symbol of national unity and the object of loyalty <u>to</u>
₃₅

<u>the Japanese</u>.
₃₅

     <u>Another tradition that was enduring</u> was the
₃₆

hierarchical system of social relations based on

feudalism. Confucianism prescribed

<u>a pattern by</u> ethical conduct between groups
₃₇

of people within a fixed hierarchy. Four of the five

34. F. NO CHANGE
    G. Later subordinated
    H. Later subordinated,
    J. Subordinated later,

35. A. NO CHANGE
    B. the Japanese had
    C. by the Japanese
    D. for the Japanese

36. F. NO CHANGE
    G. Another tradition
    H. (Do NOT begin a new paragraph) Another tradition
    J. The other tradition

37. A. NO CHANGE
    B. patterns by
    C. a pattern for
    D. patterns with

Confucian relationships <u>(those between ruler and</u>
₃₈

<u>subject, husband and wife, father and son,</u>
₃₈

<u>and elder brother and younger brother)</u> <u>were</u> <u>vertical</u>
₃₈   ₃₉   ₄₀

<u>since they</u> required loyalty and obedience from the
₄₀

inferior toward the superior <u>and benevolence and</u>
₄₁

<u>protection from the superior to the inferior.</u> Only the
₄₁

fifth <u>relationship, that</u> between friend and friend—was
₄₂

horizontal. <u>A</u> third tradition was respect for learning,
₄₃

another basic <u>idea of Confucius.</u> In traditional Japan,
₄₄

study was the absolute duty of man. It was a religious

38. Is the author's use of parentheses appropriate?

   F.   Yes, because the examples are irrelevant to the passage.
   G.   Yes, because although the information is relevant, the material is not part of the main development of the passage.
   H.   No, because the examples are relevant to the meaning of the sentence.
   J.   No, because the material is essential to the reader's understanding of the passage.

39. A.   NO CHANGE
       B.   was
       C.   are
       D.   could be

40. F.   NO CHANGE
       G.   vertical, they
       H.   vertical, since it
       J.   vertical, being they

41. A.   NO CHANGE
       B.   and also benevolence and protection from the superior to the inferior
       C.   with the benevolence and protection being from the superior to the inferior
       D.   and from the superior to the inferior, the benevolence and protection

42. F.   NO CHANGE
       G.   relationship that
       H.   relationship—that
       J.   relationship

43. A.   NO CHANGE
       B.   Furthermore, a
       C.   (Begin a new paragraph) A
       D.   (Begin a new paragraph) Also a

44. F.   NO CHANGE
       G.   Confucius idea
       H.   idea of Confucianism
       J.   Confucianism idea

mandate as well as a social duty and was a means of
45

promoting a harmonious and stable society. The
46
individual's behavior was strictly prescribed by
46
law and custom. Only the Samurai had the right to

retaliate with force if they were displeased. But his
47
primary duty was to the lord.

45. A. NO CHANGE
B. mandate as well as being
C. mandate as well,
D. mandate,

46. F. NO CHANGE
G. An individual behavior
H. Behavior by individual's
J. The individuals behavior

47. A. NO CHANGE
B. But their
C. Being that their
D. Because their

> Item #48 asks about the preceding passage as a whole.

48. The best description of the development of this essay would be:

F. argument and rebuttal.
G. a personal narrative.
H. a three-part exposition.
J. question and answer.

STRATEGY SUMMARY

General Strategies

1. After you have memorized the directions, they can be safely ignored; therefore, do not waste valuable test time by re-reading instructions.

2. Read the entire selection for comprehension of the overall meaning. Look for possible errors. Mentally note how to correct possible errors.

3. Study the answer choices, looking for one that matches your anticipated answer.

4. Compare the answer choices. What makes them different from one another?

5. Do not choose answer choices that introduce new errors or change the meaning of the selection.

6. Use the additional strategies presented below when searching for errors.

Strategies for Usage and Mechanics Content Area

Check for Grammatical Errors

a) Look for obvious subject-verb agreement problems. The test-writers may try to obscure agreement by inserting material between the subject and the verb, inverting the sentence structure so that the verb precedes the subject, or introducing compound subjects.

b) Check for proper pronoun usage. Remember that all pronouns must have antecedents. The pronoun must clearly refer to the antecedent and must agree in case, number, and person.

c) Be alert to the proper usage of adjectives and adverbs. Note that adjectives modify nouns, while adverbs modify verbs. Also, adjectives, not adverbs, follow linking verbs. Lastly, watch out for adjectives posing as adverbs. Sometimes, adjectives can be transformed into adverbs by adding "-ly," so it is important to identify whether the modifier is an adjective or an adverb.

d) Watch for double negatives. Even though double negatives are sometimes used colloquially, they are not grammatically correct.

e) Check for proper noun clause introductions. A noun clause is a group of words that functions as the subject of a sentence and must be introduced with "that." Note that "because" and "why" should not be used to introduce noun clauses.

f) Watch for illogical comparisons. Comparisons can only be made between similar objects. Be alert to the use of the comparative form of an adjective (for comparing two objects) and the superlative form of an adjective (for comparing three or more objects). Remember that some adjectives and adverbs express the highest degree of quality; therefore, they cannot be improved upon.

g) Check for improper verb and mood shifts. The same verb tense and mood should be used within a sentence or paragraph unless there is a valid reason for a change. Also, be alert to the improper usage of verb tenses in general. Make sure that the verb tense within a sentence or a paragraph is logical.

h) Make sure that the choice of verb tense in a sentence reflects the sequence and the duration of the events described.

i) Check for diction errors such as wrong prepositions, improper word choice, and gerund-infinitive switching.

Check for Sentence Structure Errors

a) Check to see if the sentence is a run-on.

b) Be aware of comma splice errors in sentences.

c) Check to see if the sentence is a fragment.

d) Make sure the sentence contains logical coordinating conjunctions.

e) Watch for faulty parallelism in a sentence. Note that whenever elements of a sentence perform similar or equal functions, they should have the same form.

f) Be alert for sentence structures in which a thought that is interrupted by intervening material is completed later in the sentence. Check that the interrupted thought is correctly completed. A simple way to check for this type of error is to read the sentence without the intervening material—the sentence should make sense, be grammatically correct, and represent a complete thought.

g) Look for misplaced modifiers. Modifiers should be placed as close as possible to what they modify. Errors in placement of modifiers create ambiguous and illogical constructions.

h) Be alert to misplacements or omissions of certain elements of a sentence. These errors lead to unintended meanings. Make sure the intended meaning of the sentence follows from its logical structure.

Check for Punctuation Errors

a) Check to see if commas are used correctly in the sentence. The following list summarizes the most important uses and misuses of commas:

(1) Use a comma before a coordinating conjunction joining two clauses.

(2) Use commas for clarity.

(3) Use commas to separate words in a series.

(4) Use commas to mark the end of an introductory phrase.

(5) Use pairs of commas to set off appositive, parenthetical, and nonrestrictive elements.

(6) A comma should not be used to separate a subject from its verb.

(7) Commas should not be used to set off restrictive or necessary clauses or phrases.

(8) A comma should not be used in place of a conjunction.

b) Check for correct semicolon usage. The following list summarizes the appropriate uses of semicolons:

(1) Use a semicolon to separate two complete ideas.

    (2) Use a semicolon to separate a series of phrases with commas.

    (3) Use a semicolon to separate independent clauses.

    (4) Do not use semicolons to separate dependent clauses.

c) Check for correct end-stop punctuation. Make sure that any material that has a period is a complete sentence.

d) Check for correct usage of dashes. The following are the rules for situations requiring the use of a dash:

    (1) Use a dash for emphasis or to set off an explanatory group of words.

    (2) Use a dash before a word or group of words that indicates a summation or reversal of what preceded it.

    (3) Use a dash to mark a sudden break in thought that leaves a sentence unfinished.

e) Check for correct apostrophe usage. Apostrophes are most commonly used to show possession. They are also used when a noun is used to modify another noun or a gerund.

f) Check to see if a punctuation mark is needed to clarify the selection.

Strategies for Rhetorical Skills Content Area

Check to See if the Strategy Used by the Writer Is Appropriate

a) Make sure that all supporting material is appropriate to the selection.

b) Be alert to opening, transitional, and concluding sentences. Check to see if they are effective or if they need improvement.

c) Read the selection for the main ideas and identify the main purpose of the entire passage.

d) Look for diction, purpose, and tone clues that identify the writer's audience.

Check for Organization Errors

a) Check the sentence-level structure. Sentences should be in logical and appropriate order within the paragraph.

b) Check the paragraph-level structure. Paragraphs should be divided logically and unified around a central theme.

c) Check the passage-level structure. Passages should follow an identifiable pattern of development, with paragraphs appearing in a logical order.

Check for Stylistic Problems

a) Make sure that the sentences are concise and to the point.

    (1) Look for awkward sentences or weak passive verbs.

    (2) Look for needlessly wordy sentences.

b) Check for ambiguous sentences. Such sentences run two or more ideas together and require further clarification to separate and connect the disparate ideas.

c) Check for idiomatic usage.

Reading

Course Concept Outline

I. Test Mechanics (p. 85)

A. Overview (p. 85)

B. Anatomy (Items #1-4, pp. 86-87)

C. Pacing (p. 88)

D. Time Trial (Items #1-3, pp. 89-90)

E. Game Plan (p. 91)

1. Quickly Preview the Test Section, but Skip the Directions
2. Personalize the Passage Order
3. Read Any Introductory Notes
4. Preview the Passage
5. Preview the Item Stems
6. Read the Passage
7. Answer the Items
8. Remember to Review
9. Don't Be Distracted by the Clock

II. Lesson (p. 97)

A. Preliminaries[1]

1. What Is Tested
2. Directions
3. Passage Profiles
4. Item Profiles

B. Facts about Passages

1. Four Passage Topics, Unfamiliar Subjects
2. Passages Test Comprehension, Not "Speed-Reading"

---

[1] Some concepts in this Course Concept Outline are not illustrated through examples in your student text but may be covered by your instructor in class. They are included here to provide a complete outline of your course.

C. Item-Types

1. Main Idea (Items #1–2, p. 98)
2. Explicit Detail (Items #3–5, p. 98)
3. Vocabulary (Item #6, p. 98)
4. Development (Items #7–8, pp. 98–99)
5. Implied Idea (Items #9–11, p. 99)
6. Application (Items #12–13, p. 99)
7. Voice (Items #14–15, p. 99)

D. Strategies

1. Three Reading Comprehension Levels
   a) General Theme
   b) Specific Points
   c) Evaluation
2. Using the Three Comprehension Levels
3. Five Steps to Approaching Passages
   a) Label Passages as "Easy" or "Hard"
   b) Preview First and Last Sentences of Selection
   c) Preview Item Stems
   d) Read the Passage
   e) Answer the Items (Items #16–24, pp. 100–102)
4. Item-Type Strategies
   a) Main Idea Clues (Items #25–27, pp. 103–104)
   b) Explicit Detail Clues (Item #28, p. 104)
   c) Vocabulary Clues (Items #29–33, p. 104)
   d) Development Clues (Items #34–35, p. 104)
   e) Implied Idea Clues (Items #36–37, pp. 104–105)
   f) Application Clues (Item #38, p. 105)
   g) Voice Clues (Item #39, p. 105)

E. Paired Passages (Items #40–57, pp. 106–109)

F. Further Use of Reading Strategies

1. Prose Fiction (Items #58–82, pp. 110–114)
2. Social Science (Items #83–94, pp. 115–117)
3. Humanities (Items #95–125, pp. 118–124)
4. Natural Science (Items #126–148, pp. 124–130)

G. Pre-Assessment Examples

II. Quizzes (p. 131)

A. Quiz I (Items #1–18, pp. 131–134)

B. Quiz II (Items #1–17, pp. 135–138)

C. Quiz III (Items #1–18, pp. 139–143)

D. Quiz IV Brain Buster (Items #1–29, pp. 144–152)

IV. Review (Items #1–46, pp. 153–164)

V. Strategy Summary (p. 165)

TEST MECHANICS

Overview

The Reading Test consists of four sections, with either one passage or two shorter paired passages (approximately 700-words total), each followed by 10 items. You will read a passage and answer the items based upon what is stated or implied in the reading selection.

You will be given one passage or paired passage from each of the following four categories: Prose Fiction, Social Science, Humanities, and Natural Science. In most cases, the passage will be about a topic with which you are not familiar. The test-writers choose unusual topics so that the Reading Test will assess your reading skill and not your prior knowledge.

The time limit for the 40 items on the Reading Test is 35 minutes. Given the time limit, you obviously need to work quickly. The exam, however, is not a test of "speed-reading." Instead, the exam is a test of reading *comprehension*.

Anatomy

DIRECTIONS: The passage below is followed by a set of items. Read the passage and choose the best answer for each item. You may refer to the passage as often as necessary to answer the items.

The directions make Reading items sound easy: read this and answer the items. As a result, the directions aren't very helpful, and you can ignore them from now on. (NOTE: Given space restrictions, this passage is much shorter than those used on the ACT test.)

Passage I

Read

Social Science: This passage is adapted from a government report about the history of alcohol abuse.

The movement to prohibit alcohol began in the early years of the nineteenth century. Local societies formed in New York and Massachusetts to promote temperance in the use of alcohol. Many of
5 these societies were affiliated with Protestant evangelical denominations and met in local churches. As time passed, most temperance societies changed their goal to call for complete abstinence from all alcohol.

10 In 1919, largely in response to these efforts, the Eighteenth Amendment to the Constitution was passed. This Amendment banned the production, transportation, and sale of all alcoholic beverages. The Amendment, also known as the Prohibition
15 Amendment, provided for concurrent enforcement by both federal and state law. By 1920, in addition to the federal Volstead Act, the nation had laws in thirty-three states prohibiting alcohol entirely.

Prohibition, however, proved unworkable.
20 Bootleggers and speakeasies quickly organized to satisfy the public's thirst for alcohol. Thirteen years later, the "Noble Experiment," doomed by the difficulty of enforcement, ended with the repeal of the Prohibition Amendment.

Most of the passages include an introductory note telling you where the passage comes from. A note may provide some useful information, so you should read it.

Typically, reading passages discuss an unfamiliar topic. Even if you know something about Prohibition, that information may or may not be helpful since you'll only be asked about this particular passage.

This passage is organized chronologically. The first paragraph talks about the "early years of the nineteenth century," in other words, the early 1800s.

The second paragraph starts with 1919. Then, the passage briefly traces the events leading up to Prohibition.

The third paragraph explains why Prohibition failed: people wanted to drink, so bootleggers and illegal clubs satisfied that demand. Eventually, Prohibition was repealed.

1. The passage is primarily concerned with the:

   A. social problems caused by alcohol abuse.
   B. founding of anti-alcohol temperance socie-ties.
   C. origins of Prohibition and its subsequent failure.
   D. efforts to enforce Prohibition legislation.

2. According to the passage, in the early nineteenth century, temperance societies originally:

   F. encouraged moderation in alcohol use.
   G. demanded the repeal of the Eighteenth Amendment.
   H. supported efforts to enforce the Volstead Act.
   J. refused to align with religious groups.

3. The passage implies that Prohibition failed because:

   A. religious organizations withdrew their support for the program.
   B. the repeal of the Eighteenth Amendment was only experimental.
   C. too many states passed laws prohibiting the sale of alcohol.
   D. widespread demand for alcohol made enforcement impossible.

4. In line 15, the word *concurrent* means:

   F. unsuccessful.
   G. shared.
   H. practicable.
   J. intermittent.

1. **(C)** *This is a common type of Reading item: the item asks you to identify the main idea of the passage. The passage discusses the origins and failure of Prohibition.*

2. **(F)** *This item asks about something that is specifically stated in the passage. The author clearly states that the temperance societies were originally founded to "promote temperance" (line 4) as opposed to complete prohibition.*

3. **(D)** *This item requires that you "read between the lines" of the passage. In the third paragraph, the author does not specifically say why Prohibition failed, but you can figure it out from what's said: people simply refused to quit consuming alcohol, even if it was illegal.*

4. **(G)** *This item asks you for the definition of a term in the context of the passage. The passage states that the federal government and the states were given "concurrent" authority and that the states, as well as the federal government, passed laws against alcohol. So, "concurrent" must mean something like "joint" or "shared."*

Pacing

The Reading Test has 40 items and a 35-minute time limit. The fact that there are four sections (with either one passage or two shorter paired passages in each section) of approximately equal length, each with the same number of items, and a 35-minute time limit leads naturally to the conclusion that you should spend eight minutes and 45 seconds on each passage—and that's a pretty good plan. The following table summarizes the timing for this approach.

TASK	ALLOTTED TIME	REMAINING TIME
Read the first selected passage	2.5 minutes	32.5 minutes
Answer the accompanying items	6.25 minutes*	26.25 minutes
Read the second selected passage	2.5 minutes	23.75 minutes
Answer the accompanying items	6.25 minutes*	17.5 minutes
Read the third selected passage	2.5 minutes	15 minutes
Answer the accompanying items	6.25 minutes*	8.75 minutes
Read the fourth selected passage	2.5 minutes	6.25 minutes
Answer the accompanying items	6.25 minutes*	0 minutes

*Approximately 37 seconds per item

Note that the table refers to "first selected passage," "second selected passage," and so on. These references are to the order in which you decide to do the passages, not to the order in which they are presented in your test booklet. For reasons discussed in the "Game Plan" feature, you might choose to start with the passage that appears last. It's up to you.

Time Trial

(3 items; 3 minutes)

> **DIRECTIONS:** The passage below is followed by a set of items. Read the passage and choose the best answer for each item. You may refer to the passage as often as necessary to answer the items.

Passage I

Natural Science: This passage is excerpted from an essay about the possible reasons for the extinction of salmon runs in New England rivers.

Folklore holds that Atlantic salmon were once so abundant in New England rivers that early colonists walked across the backs of the fish as they ran up the rivers in spring. Then, according to the
5 received wisdom, at the turn of the nineteenth century, increasing pollution in the rivers and the construction of large dams across rivers caused salmon to become severely depleted. If this theory were accurate, then there should be ample
10 archaeological evidence that salmon played a major role in the diets of the aboriginal peoples of New England. But in site after site, although bones of many other fish species have been recovered, no salmon bones have been found. It's more likely that
15 the accounts of salmon were embellished by early writers.

In fact, salmon did not begin to colonize New England streams until a period of climatic cooling known as the Little Ice Age (C.E. 1550–1800). At the
20 end of this period, the climatic warming created less favorable environmental conditions for salmon. Thus, their range retracted. The idea that initial colonization did not occur until this time, and then only as a temporary range expansion, explains the
25 lack of salmon in prehistoric sites and the depletion of the fish at the end of the eighteenth century.

While authorities such as D. W. Lufkin have stated that "the circumstances leading to the demise of *Salmo salar* are relatively simple to identify" and
30 have cited dams, pollution, logging practices, and over-fishing, causes behind its demise are more complex, with ecological and climatological bases. If pollution and dams were the major cause of the extinctions, then why were the runs not made
35 extinct on the Penobscot, a heavily dammed and

polluted river in Maine? Why did salmon runs become extinct downstream of the dams on the Connecticut River? The general lack of success in salmon restoration programs over the last two
40 centuries suggests a fundamental ecological cause for impoverished salmon runs in New England rather than an anthropogenic one.

1. The primary purpose of the passage is to:

  A. propose a long term plan for restoring salmon runs to the rivers of New England.
  B. undermine the theory that human activity caused the extinction of salmon runs in New England rivers.
  C. demonstrate that anthropogenic factors are often more powerful than natural ones in shaping the environment.
  D. provide evidence that the disappearance of *Salmo salar* was caused by the damming and pollution of the rivers.

2. The author cites the lack of salmon bones in archaeological digs as evidence that:

  F. the salmon population in New England rivers declined sharply after the end of the Little Ice Age.
  G. aboriginal Americans, who consumed other fish species, refused to eat the abundant salmon.
  H. salmon were not available to aboriginal Americans before the time of the arrival of the first colonists.
  J. anthropogenic factors were largely responsible for the extinction of the salmon runs.

3. It can be inferred that D. W. Lufkin would most likely:

   A. agree with the author that the primary causes of the depletion of salmon stocks are climatological.

   B. accept the author's contention that early reports about the abundance of salmon were greatly exaggerated.

   C. reject the author's thesis and insist that the causes of salmon extinction are anthropogenic.

   D. disagree with the author that salmon stocks have declined precipitously since the end of the eighteenth century.

Game Plan

Quickly Preview the Test Section, but Skip the Directions

Last-minute adjustments to the test format are theoretically possible (though not common), so check the test section before you start to work, especially the number of passages, the number of items, and the time limit. And yes, the test-writers always tell you to "read the directions carefully." But they don't tell you that you have to read them during the test. Instead, become familiar with them *before* test day. That way, you won't waste 30 seconds or more (enough time to answer an item) re-reading directions with which you are already familiar.

Personalize the Passage Order

Remember that you don't have to do the items in the order in which they are presented in the booklet. For some sections, like the math section, doing problems in order (more or less) makes good sense because the difficulty of the questions increases as you move through the test. However, in a Critical Reading section with Passages items, it is a sound strategy to make a choice about the order in which you're going to work through the section. You may decide to do the reading passages in the order presented, or you may want to change the order.

What factors should you consider? First, you may find a topic that seems familiar to you. Of course, you can't expect that you'll already know the answers to the items, but familiarity is a definite advantage. Second, you'll feel more comfortable with some topics than with others. Do you like biology but hate literature or like social science but hate art? Then do the passages about topics that you like first.

This sets up the following personalized order for completion of the passages:

1. Choose familiar topics to do first
2. Otherwise, choose your favorite topic to do first.
3. Choose your second favorite topic to do second, and so on.

When you choose your passages, you should number them in the margin of your test booklet. Put a big "1" by the passage you'll do first, and so on.

Read Any Introductory Notes

Many passages, particularly longer ones, will include an introductory note telling you where the passage comes from and maybe some other information. Sometimes, this information is useful for getting a better understanding of the passage. Therefore, before starting on a passage and items, always read any introductory notes.

Preview the Passage

Before you begin reading a particular passage, take 15 to 30 seconds to preview key sentences. Key sentences are the first and last sentences of the passage and the first sentence of each paragraph. Why preview? First sentences are often topic sentences, so reading a series of topic sentences will tell you what the author is trying to say, and it can give you an outline of the development of the passage. Sometimes, though not always, the last sentence is a conclusion.

To see how this can work, preview the following passage about solar energy, in which only the key sentences are visible.

At the present time, 98 percent of world energy consumption comes from sources such as fossil fuels.

5

10

Our energy consumption amounts to about one-ten thousandth of the energy we receive from the sun.

15

20

It is often stated that the growth rate will decline or that energy conservation measures will preclude any long-range problem.

25

30   The only practical means of avoiding the problem of thermal pollution is the use of solar energy.

35

To see what you can learn from just a few sentences, think about these questions:

What's the passage about?

- Gas mileage.
- Space exploration.
- ⊙ Solar energy.

What is a common attitude about energy conservation?

- That it doesn't work.
- That it might work.
- ⊙ That it will probably work.

What's the author's view on solar energy?

- It doesn't work.
- It's unnecessary.
- ⊙ It's absolutely essential.

The answers can be determined from the few sentences you have previewed: the passage is about solar energy. A lot of people think conservation will probably solve all our problems. The author believes solar energy is necessary.

Preview the Item Stems

Additionally, before reading a particular passage, you may find it helpful to preview the item stems, which are presented either as questions or incomplete statements. If a stem mentions a key word or phrase, make a mental note and look for it as you read the selection. See what you would learn from the following items, in which only the item stems are visible.

1. According to the passage, the most important disadvantage of nuclear energy is:

    A.
    B.
    C.
    D.

Previewing would tell you to look for certain information in your reading. The first stem uses the phrase "most important disadvantage of nuclear energy." So, you know that the passage will discuss disadvantages of nuclear energy. When you find the "most important" one, mark that reference so that you can answer this item.

2. According to the author, shifting climate patterns will have all of the following effects EXCEPT:

    F.
    G.
    H.
    J.

The second stem tells you that the author discusses "shifting climate patterns," probably in some detail since the passage mentions multiple effects. Each time you find one of the effects, mark it so that when you answer this item you can eliminate those choices that mention such effects. ("EXCEPT" means to look for the one NOT mentioned in the passage.)

3. The author's attitude toward scientists who deny that average temperatures are rising can best be described as:

    A.
    B.
    C.
    D.

The third stem lets you know that the passage discusses average temperatures and a theory advanced by some scientists. If you find that reference in your reading, you'll be able to figure out the author's attitude and then you'll have the answer to this item.

4. Which of the following best describes the main point of the passage?

    F.
    G.
    H.
    J.

Finally, the last stem tells you to look for the main idea. That, in and of itself, is not particularly helpful because you're always reading for the main idea—even if you don't get a question that asks about it. So, some stems are general while others are more specific.

Note that some students may not find this technique useful. Try it, and use it if you like it.

Read the Passage

Keep the following points in mind when reading a passage:

- Read the passage(s) quickly but carefully. You'll probably need about two to three minutes to read a passage or set of paired passages. This is about 300 to 350 words a minute.

- Read the passage(s) for important themes. Many of the items will ask about important themes of the passage, such as the main point, the purpose of a particular paragraph, or the author's intention.

- Do not try to memorize details. If you need detailed information, you can always go back to the passage(s) to find it. This is an "open-book" test.

- Pause at the end to summarize your reading. One of the most helpful reading techniques is to summarize in your own words what you have just read. What is the main point? What did the author do in the first paragraph? In the second paragraph? What did the author prove?

Answer the Items

Keep the following points in mind when answering the accompanying items:

- Identify the question being asked. Reading items fall into one of seven categories (such as "Main Idea," "Explicit Detail," and "Vocabulary"). Specific item-types have characteristic kinds of answers. If you identify the category first, it will be easier to find the right answer. You'll learn more about the seven item-types later in the Reading Lesson.

- Answer the question being asked. One of the most common mistakes made by examinees is to read the item stem carelessly and then answer the "wrong" question. That is, they *respond* to what they think they read rather than what is actually on the page. Since wrong answers often sound plausible, if you make this mistake, you're probably going to find a pretty good answer—to the wrong question.

- Read the answer choices carefully. You'll learn how to recognize the seven Reading item-types and what the correct answer to each should look like. Do this experiment: estimate how many words are in the passage and then how many are in the answer choices. The answer choices are just about as long as the passage itself. That means reading comprehension doesn't stop at the end of the last sentence of the passage. It continues all the way through to the last word of the last answer choice to the last item.

- Pay attention to thought-reversers. Thought-reversers are words in the item stem like "NOT," "BUT," and "EXCEPT." These words turn the question upside down. What is normally the right answer is now a wrong answer, and what is normally a wrong answer is the right answer.

- Do not spend too much time on any one item. Remember that you get +1 for the hardest question and +1 for the easiest. With Reading items, the easiest ones can theoretically be the last in the group and the hardest ones can be the first. So, if you sense that you're spinning your wheels, make a guess and then move along. You should always guess, even if you are unable to eliminate any answer choices, because there is no penalty for guessing on the ACT test. However, your chances improve if you are able to eliminate even one answer choice.

Remember to Review

If you are taking the test on a computer, you will be able to flag questions you may want to review. Use the flag to your advantage, but watch out for three potential pitfalls. First, make sure to at least guess before moving on to the next question in case time runs out and you aren't able to review as you had planned. Second, don't flag too many items, or you won't have time to review all the items you flagged. Save the flags for items on which you guess or about which you are very unsure. And use the answer eliminator tool to eliminate answers you are sure are wrong, to save you time when you review. Third, time your review just right. Wait until you have answered every item before clicking the review button to return to the items you flagged.

Don't Be Distracted by the Clock

If you are taking the test on a computer, you will see a clock onscreen while you are testing. Don't let it distract or worry you. Look at it periodically to make sure you are staying on track, but don't try to time your responses to every item. Try to check the clock every 15 minutes, and in the last 15 minutes of the exam try to check the clock every 5 minutes to help you prioritize any review time.

LESSON

The passages and items in this section accompany the in-class review of the skills and concepts tested by the ACT Reading Test. You will work through the items with your instructor in class. Answers are on page 659.

DIRECTIONS: Each passage below is followed by a set of items. Read the passage and choose the best answer for each item. You may refer to the passage as often as necessary to answer the items.

Passage I

Social Science: This passage is excerpted from an essay in a history book about the presidential election of 1796.

To broaden their appeal in the presidential election of 1796, the Federalists selected Thomas Pinckney, a South Carolinian, as running mate for the New Englander John Adams. But Pinckney's
5 Southern friends chose to ignore their party's intentions and regarded Pinckney as a presidential candidate, creating a political situation that Alexander Hamilton was determined to exploit. Hamilton had long been wary of Adams' stubbornly
10 independent brand of politics. He preferred to see Pinckney, who was more pliant and over whom Hamilton could exert more control, in the president's chair.

The election was held under the system
15 originally established by the Constitution. At that time, there was but a single tally, with the candidate receiving the largest number of electoral votes declared president. The candidate with the second largest number was declared vice president.
20 Hamilton anticipated that all the Federalists in the North would vote for Adams and Pinckney equally in an attempt to ensure that Jefferson would not be either first or second in the voting. Pinckney would be solidly supported in the South while Adams
25 would not. Hamilton concluded if it were possible to divert a few electoral votes from Adams to Pinckney, Pinckney would receive more than Adams, yet both Federalists would outpoll Jefferson.

Various methods were used to persuade the
30 electors to vote as Hamilton wished. In the press, anonymous articles were published attacking Adams for his monarchical tendencies and Jefferson for being overly democratic, while pushing Pinckney as the only suitable candidate. In private
35 correspondence with state party leaders, the Hamiltonians encouraged the idea that Adams' popularity was slipping, that he could not win the election, and that the Federalists could defeat Jefferson only by supporting Pinckney.

40 Had sectional pride and loyalty not run as high in New England as in the deep South, Pinckney might well have become Washington's successor. New Englanders, however, realized that equal votes for Adams and Pinckney in their states would defeat
45 Adams; therefore, eighteen electors scratched Pinckney's name from their ballots and deliberately threw away their second votes to men who were not even running. It was fortunate for Adams that they did, for the electors from South Carolina
50 completely abandoned him, giving eight votes to Pinckney and eight to Jefferson.

In the end, Hamilton's interference in Pinckney's candidacy lost him even the Vice Presidency. Without New England's support,
55 Pinckney received only 59 electoral votes, finishing third to Adams and Jefferson. He might have been President in 1797, or as Vice President a serious contender for the Presidency in 1800; instead, stigmatized by a plot he had not devised, he served
60 a brief term in the United States Senate and then dropped from sight as a national influence.

Item-Types

Main Idea

1. The main purpose of the passage is to:

  A. propose reforms to the procedures for electing the President and Vice President.
  B. condemn Alexander Hamilton for interfering in the election of 1796.
  C. describe the political events that led to John Adams' victory in the 1796 Presidential election.
  D. contrast the political philosophy of the Federalists to that of Thomas Jefferson.

2. Which of the following titles best describes the content of the passage?

  F. The Failure of Alexander Hamilton's Plan for Thomas Pinckney to Win the 1796 Presidential Election
  G. The Roots of Alexander Hamilton's Distrust of John Adams and New England's Politics
  H. Important Issues in the 1796 Presidential Campaign as Presented by the Federalist Candidates
  J. The Political Careers of Alexander Hamilton, John Adams, and Thomas Pinckney

Explicit Detail

3. According to the passage, which of the following was true of the Presidential election of 1796?

  A. Thomas Jefferson received more electoral votes than did Thomas Pinckney.
  B. John Adams received strong support from the electors of South Carolina.
  C. Alexander Hamilton received most of New England's electoral votes.
  D. Thomas Pinckney was selected by Federalist party leaders to be the party's presidential candidate.

4. According to the passage, Hamilton's plan included all of the following EXCEPT:

  F. articles published in newspapers to create opposition to John Adams.
  G. South Carolina's loyalty to Thomas Pinckney.
  H. private contact with state officials urging them to support Thomas Pinckney.
  J. John Adams' reputation as a stubborn and independent New Englander.

5. The passage supplies information that answers which of the following questions:

  A. How many electoral votes were cast for John Adams in the 1796 Presidential election?
  B. Under the voting system originally set up by the Constitution, how many votes did each elector cast?
  C. Who was Jefferson's running mate in the 1796 Presidential election?
  D. What became of Alexander Hamilton after his plan to have Thomas Pinckney elected President failed?

Vocabulary

6. In line 11, the word *pliant* most nearly means:

  F. assertive.
  G. public.
  H. national.
  J. yielding.

Development

7. Why does the author refer to the election procedure established by the original Constitution?

  A. To prove to the reader that New England as a whole had more electoral votes than the state of South Carolina.
  B. To persuade the reader that Thomas Pinckney's defeat could have been avoided.
  C. To alert the reader that the procedure used in 1796 was unlike the procedure in use today.
  D. To encourage the reader to study Constitutional history.

8. The overall development of the passage can best be described as:

F. refuting possible explanations for certain phenomena.
G. documenting a thesis with specific examples.
H. offering an explanation of a series of events.
J. making particular proposals to solve a problem.

Implied Idea

9. The passage implies that some electors voted for John Adams because they were:

A. in favor of a monarchy.
B. persuaded to do so by Hamilton.
C. afraid South Carolina would not vote for Pinckney.
D. eager to have a President from their geographical region.

10. Which of the following can be inferred from the passage?

F. Thomas Pinckney had a personal dislike for Jefferson's politics.
G. The Federalists regarded themselves as more democratic than Jefferson.
H. The Hamiltonians contacted key Southern leaders to persuade them to vote for Adams.
J. Electors were likely to vote for candidates from their own geographical region.

11. It can be inferred that had South Carolina not cast any electoral votes for Jefferson, the outcome of the 1796 election would have been a:

A. larger margin of victory for John Adams.
B. victory for Thomas Jefferson.
C. Federalist defeat in the Senate.
D. victory for Thomas Pinckney.

Application

12. The electors who scratched Pinckney's name from their ballots behaved most like which of the following people?

F. A newspaper publisher who adds a special section to the Sunday edition to review the week's political events.
G. A member of the clergy who encourages members of other faiths to meet to discuss solutions to the community's problems.
H. An artist who saves preliminary sketches of an important work even after the work is finally completed.
J. A general who orders his retreating troops to destroy supplies they must leave behind so the enemy cannot use the supplies.

13. Hamilton's strategy can best be summarized as:

A. divide and conquer.
B. retreat and regroup.
C. feint and counterattack.
D. hit and run.

Voice

14. The tone of the passage can best be described as:

F. witty.
G. comical.
H. scholarly.
J. frivolous.

15. The author's attitude toward Hamilton's plan can best be described as:

A. angry.
B. approving.
C. analytical.
D. regretful.

Passage II   100%

Humanities: This passage is adapted from an essay in a philosophy textbook about citizenship.

The liberal view of democratic citizenship that developed in the seventeenth and eighteenth centuries was different from that of the classical Greeks. The pursuit of private interests with little
5 interference from government was seen as the road to happiness and progress rather than the public obligations and involvement that were emphasized by the Greeks. Freedom was to be found by limiting governmental activity, not through immersion in
10 the life of the *polis*. The role of the citizen was to select leaders and keep public authority in check. The rights of citizens against the state were the focus.

Over time, the liberal notion of citizenship
15 developed in two directions. First, there was a movement to increase the proportion of people who were eligible to participate as citizens. Second, there was a broadening of legitimate governmental activities and a use of governmental power to
20 redress economic and social imbalances. Political citizenship became an instrument through which groups with sufficient numbers of votes could use the state's power to enhance their social and economic well-being.

25 Within the liberal view of democratic citizenship, tensions have developed over the degree to which the government can and should be used to promote happiness and well-being. Political philosopher Martin Diamond has categorized two
30 views of democracy. On the one hand, there is the "libertarian" perspective that stresses the private pursuit of happiness. It emphasizes restraint on government and protection of individual liberties. On the other hand, there is the "majoritarian" view
35 that emphasizes the "task of the government to uplift and aid the common man." The tensions between these two views are evident today. Taxpayer revolts and calls for smaller government clash with demands for greater government
40 involvement in the economy and social sphere.

Strategies

Five Steps to Approaching Passages

Answer the Items

16. The author's primary purpose is to:

    F. study ancient concepts of citizenship.
    G. contrast different notions of citizenship.
    H. criticize modern libertarian democracy.
    J. describe the importance of universal suffrage.

17. It can be inferred from the passage that the Greek word *polis* (line 10) means:

    A. family life.
    B. military service.
    C. marriage.
    D. political community.

18. The author cites Martin Diamond in the last paragraph because the author:

    F. regards Martin Diamond as an authority on political philosophy.
    G. wishes to refute Martin Diamond's views on citizenship.
    H. needs a definition of the term "citizenship."
    J. is unfamiliar with the distinction between libertarian and majoritarian concepts of democracy.

19. According to the passage, all of the following are characteristics that would distinguish the liberal idea of government from the Greek idea of government EXCEPT:

    A. the emphasis on the rights of private citizens.
    B. the activities that government may legitimately pursue.
    C. the obligation of citizens to participate in government.
    D. the size of the geographical area controlled by a government.

20. A majoritarian would be most likely to favor legislation that would:

    F.   eliminate all restrictions on individual liberty.

    G.   cut spending for social welfare programs.

    (H.) provide greater protection for consumers.

    J.   lower taxes on the wealthy and raise taxes on the average worker.

Passage III

Humanities: This passage is adapted from an article about John Dewey.

The place of public education within a democratic society has been widely discussed and debated. Perhaps no one has written more widely on the subject in the United States than John Dewey.
5 Sometimes called "the father of public education," his theories of education have a large social component; that is, he places an emphasis on education as a social act and the classroom as a replica of society.

10 Dewey defined various aspects of education. First, it was a necessity of life. Just as humans needed sleep, food, water, and shelter for physiological renewal, they also needed education to renew their minds.

15 A second aspect of education was its social component. It provided the young with a nurturing environment that encouraged the growth of their social customs.

A third aspect of public education was the
20 provision of direction to youngsters who needed the steadying influences of school. Direction was not overt, but rather indirect through the school situations in which the youngster participated.

Finally, Dewey saw public education as a
25 catalyst for growth. Since the young came to school capable of growth, it was the role of education to provide opportunities for that growth to occur. The successful school environment is one in which a desire for continued growth is created. In Dewey's
30 model, the role of education is not seen as a preparation for some later stage in life. Rather, education is seen as a process of growth that never ends, with human beings continuously expanding their capacity for growth. Neither did Dewey's
35 model see education as a means by which the past was repeated. Instead, education was a continuous reconstruction of experiences, grounded very much in the present environment.

21. Which of the following best states the main idea of this passage?

   A. The role of education is extremely complex.
   (B.) Dewey's notion of education contains a significant social component.
   C. Dewey's model of education is not relevant today.
   D. Direction provided in education must not be overt.

22. The phrase "a continuous reconstruction of experiences" (lines 36–37) used in reference to education means that education is:

   F. based in life experiences.
   (G.) a never-ending process.
   H. a meaning-based endeavor.
   J. an individual pursuit.

23. The passage implies that:

   (A.) true education fosters the desire for lifelong learning.
   B. a truly educated person understands physics.
   C. Dewey was a radical philosopher.
   D. education must cease at some point.

24. The tone of this passage can best be described as:

   F. humorous.
   (G.) serious.
   H. dramatic.
   J. informal.

Passage IV

Social Science: This passage is adapted from an article on Aleut language and culture.

The Aleuts reside on several islands of the Aleutian Chain, the Pribilof Islands, and the Alaskan Peninsula. They have possessed a written language since 1825, when the Russian missionary Ivan
5 Veniaminov selected characters of the Cyrillic alphabet to represent Aleut speech sounds, recorded the main body of Aleut vocabulary, and formulated grammatical rules. The Czarist Russian conquest of the proud, independent sea hunters was
10 so devastatingly thorough that tribal traditions, even tribal memories, were almost obliterated. The slaughter of most adults was enough to destroy the continuity of tribal knowledge, which was dependent upon oral transmission. Consequently,
15 the Aleuts developed a fanatical devotion to their language as their only cultural heritage.

The Russian occupation placed a heavy linguistic burden on the Aleuts. They were compelled to learn Russian to converse with their
20 overseers and governors. They also had to learn Old Slavonic in order to take an active part in church services as well as to master the skill of reading and writing in their own tongue. In 1867, when the United States purchased Alaska, the Aleuts were
25 unable to break sharply with their immediate past and substitute English for any one of their three languages.

To members of the Russian Orthodox Church, knowledge of Slavonic remained vital, as did
30 Russian, the language in which one conversed with the clergy. The Aleuts came to regard English education as a device to wean them from their religious faith. The introduction of compulsory English schooling caused a minor renaissance of
35 Russian culture as the Aleut parents sought to counteract the influence of the schoolroom. The harsh life of the Russian colonial rule began to appear more happy and beautiful in retrospect.

Regulations forbidding instruction in any
40 language other than English increased its unpopularity. The superficial alphabetical resemblance of Russian and Aleut linked the two tongues so closely that every restriction against teaching Russian was interpreted as an attempt to
45 eradicate the Aleut tongue. From the wording of many regulations, it appears that American

administrators often had not the slightest idea that the Aleuts were clandestinely reading and writing in their own tongue or that they even had a written
50 language of their own. To many officials, anything in Cyrillic letters was Russian and something to be stamped out. Bitterness bred by abuses and the exploitations that the Aleuts suffered from predatory American traders and adventurers kept
55 alive the Aleut resentment against the English language.

Gradually, despite the failure to emancipate the Aleuts from a sterile past by relating the Aleut and English languages more closely, the passage of
60 years has assuaged the bitter misunderstandings and caused an orientation away from Russian toward English as their second language. However, Aleut continues to be the language that molds their thought and expression.

Item-Type Strategies

Main Idea Clues

25. The author is primarily concerned with describing:

   A. the Aleuts' loyalty to their language and American failure to understand the language.

   B. Russian and American treatment of Alaskan inhabitants both before and after 1867.

   C. how the Czarist Russian occupation of Alaska created a written language for the Aleuts.

   D. American government attempts to persuade the Aleuts to use English as a second language.

26. The author is primarily concerned with:

   F. describing the Aleuts' loyalty to their language and American failure to understand the language.

   G. criticizing Russia and the United States for their mistreatment of the Aleuts.

   H. praising the Russians for creating a written language for the Aleuts.

   J. condemning Russia for its mistreatment of the Aleuts during the Czarist Russian occupation.

27. Which of the following titles best fits the passage?

   A. Aleut Loyalty to Their Language: An American Misunderstanding
   B. Failure of Russian and American Policies in Alaska
   C. Russia's Gift to the Aleuts: A Written Language
   D. Mistreatment of Aleuts During Russian Occupation

Explicit Detail Clues

28. According to the passage, the most important reason for the Aleuts' devotion to their language was:

   F. the invention of a written version of their language.
   G. the introduction of Old Slavonic for worship.
   H. the disruption of oral transmission of tribal knowledge.
   J. the institution of compulsory English education.

Vocabulary Clues

29. In line 18, the word *linguistic* relates to:

   A. orthodoxy.
   B. commerce.
   C. language.
   D. laws.

30. In line 34, the word *renaissance* most nearly means:

   F. resurgence.
   G. rejection.
   H. repeal.
   J. reassessment.

31. In line 48, the word *clandestinely* most nearly means:

   A. secretly.
   B. reliably.
   C. openly.
   D. casually.

32. In line 58, the word *sterile* most nearly means:

   F. germ-free.
   G. unproductive.
   H. fortunate.
   J. ill-timed.

33. In line 60, the word *assuaged* most nearly means:

   A. failed.
   B. created.
   C. intensified.
   D. eased.

Development Clues

34. The passage is developed primarily by:

   F. testing the evidence supporting a theory.
   G. describing causes and effects of events.
   H. weighing the pros and cons of a plan.
   J. projecting the future consequences of a decision.

35. The author mentions that the Russians killed the majority of adult Aleuts to:

   A. call attention to the immorality of foreign conquest.
   B. urge Russia to make restitution to the children of those killed.
   C. stir up outrage against the Russians for committing such atrocities.
   D. explain the extreme loyalty that Aleuts feel to their language.

Implied Idea Clues

36. Which of the following statements about the religious beliefs of the Aleuts can be inferred from the passage?

   F. Prior to the Russian occupation, they had no religious beliefs.
   G. American traders and adventurers forced them to abandon all religious beliefs.
   H. At no time in their history have the Aleuts had an organized religion.
   J. The Russians forced Aleuts to become members of the Russian Orthodox Church.

37. The passage implies that:

   A. the Cyrillic alphabet was invented for the Aleut language.
   B. all of the Cyrillic characters were used in writing the Aleut language.
   C. Russian and the Aleut language have some similar speech sounds.
   D. English is also written using the Cyrillic alphabet.

Application Clues

38. Distributing which of the following publications would be most likely to encourage Aleuts to make more use of English?

   F. Russian translations of English novels
   G. English translations of Russian novels
   H. An English-Russian bilingual text devoted to important aspects of Aleutian culture
   J. An Aleut-English bilingual text devoted to important aspects of Aleutian culture

Voice Clues

39. The author's attitude toward the Aleuts can best be described as one of:

   A. understanding and sympathy.
   B. callousness and indifference.
   C. condemnation and reproof.
   D. ridicule and disparagement.

Paired Passages

Passage V

Humanities: These passages are adapted from essays on the nature of comedy.

Passage A

    Comedy appeals only to the intelligence, for laughter is incompatible with emotion. Depict some fault, however trifling, in such a way as to arouse sympathy, fear, or pity, and it is impossible to laugh.
5 On the other hand, a vice—even one that is, generally speaking, of an odious nature—can be made ludicrous by a suitable contrivance. So long as it leaves our emotions unaffected, it is funny. This is not to say that the vice itself is ludicrous but only
10 that the vice, as embodied in a particular character, is ludicrous. The only requirement is that it must not engage our feelings.

Passage B

    Absentmindedness is always comical. Indeed, the deeper the absentmindedness the higher the
15 comedy. Systematic absentmindedness, like that of Don Quixote, is the most comical thing imaginable; it is the comic itself, drawn as nearly as possible from its very source. Take any other comic character, however unconscious he may be of what
20 he says or does: he cannot be comical unless there is some aspect of his person of which he is unaware, one side of his nature which he overlooks. On that account alone does he make us laugh.

40. The author of Passage A implies that laughter:

    F. is not an emotional reaction.
    G. counteracts feelings of dread.
    H. can correct a vice.
    J. is triggered only by a vice.

41. The author of Passage A discusses vice primarily in order to:

    A. advise the reader on how to avoid certain behavior.
    B. make it clear that comedy does not engage the emotions.
    C. provide an example that the reader will find amusing.
    D. demonstrate that emotions are more powerful than intelligence.

42. In context, "deeper" (line 14) means:

    F. complete.
    G. complex.
    H. courageous.
    J. futile.

43. Which of the following best describes the logical connection between the views expressed in the two passages?

    A. Passage B provides examples that show that the views of Passage A are incorrect.
    B. Passage B redefines a key term that is used by the author of Passage A.
    C. The two passages reach the same conclusion based on different evidence.
    D. The two passages discuss different aspects of the topic.

Passage VI

Prose Fiction: Passage A is an excerpt from the article "The New Sequoia Forests of California" in *Harper's New Monthly Magazine*. Passage B is an excerpt from *Old Indian Days* by Charles Eastman.

Passage A

Shortly after sunrise, just as the light was beginning to come streaming through the trees, I caught the big bright eyes of a deer gazing at me through the garden hedge. The expressive eyes, the
5 slim black-tipped muzzle, and the large ears were perfectly visible, as if placed there at just the right distance to be seen. She continued to gaze while I gazed back with equal steadiness, motionless as a rock. In a few minutes she ventured forward a step,
10 exposing her fine arching neck and forelegs, then snorted and withdrew.

Trembling sprays indicated her return, and her head came into view; several steps later, she stood wholly exposed inside the garden hedge, gazed
15 eagerly around, and again withdrew, but returned a moment afterward, this time advancing into the middle of the garden. Behind her I noticed other pairs of eyes.

It then occurred to me that I might possibly
20 steal up to one of them and catch it, not with any intention of killing it, but only to run my hand along its beautiful curving limbs. They seemed, however, to penetrate my conceit and bounded off with loud, shrill snorts, vanishing into the forest.

25 I have often tried to understand how so many deer, wild sheep, bears, and grouse—nature's cattle and poultry—could be allowed to run at large through the mountain gardens without in any way marring the beauty of their surroundings. I was,
30 therefore, all the more watchful of this feeding flock, and carefully examined the garden after they left, to see what flowers had suffered; I could not, however, detect the slightest disorder, much less destruction. It seemed rather that, like gardeners, they had been
35 keeping it in order. I could not see one crushed flower, nor a single blade of grass that was bent or broken down. Nor among the daisy, gentian, or bryanthus gardens of the Alps, where the wild sheep roam at will, have I ever noticed the effects of
40 destructive feeding or trampling. Even the burly, shuffling bears beautify the ground on which they walk, decorating it with their awe-inspiring tracks, and writing poetry on the soft sequoia bark in boldly

drawn hieroglyphics. But, strange to say, man, the
45 crown, the sequoia of nature, brings confusion with all his best gifts and with the overabundant, misbegotten animals that he breeds, sweeps away the beauty of the wilderness like a fire.

Passage B

The night was intolerable for Antoine. The
50 buffalo were about him in countless numbers, regarding him with vicious glances. It was only due to the natural offensiveness of man that they gave him any space. The bellowing of the bulls became louder, and there was a marked uneasiness on the
55 part of the herd. This was a sign of an approaching storm.

Upon the western horizon were seen flashes of lightning. The cloud that had been a mere speck had now become an ominous thunderhead. Suddenly the
60 wind came, and lightning flashes became more frequent, showing the ungainly forms of the animals like strange monsters in the white light. The colossal herd was again in violent motion. It was a blind rush for shelter, and no heed was paid to buffalo wallows
65 or even deep gulches. All was in the deepest of darkness. There seemed to be groaning in heaven and earth—millions of hoofs and throats roaring in unison.

As a shipwrecked sailor clings to a mere
70 fragment of wood, so Antoine, although almost exhausted with fatigue, stuck to the saddle of his pony. As the mad rush continued, every flash displayed heaps of bison in death's struggle under the hoofs of their companions.

75 When he awoke and looked around him again, it was morning. The herd had entered the strip of timber which lay on both sides of the river, and it was here that Antoine conceived his first distinct hope of saving himself.

80 "Waw, waw, waw!" was the hoarse cry that came to his ears, apparently from a human being in distress. Antoine strained his eyes and craned his neck to see who it could be. Through an opening in the branches ahead he perceived a large grizzly bear
85 lying along an inclined limb and hugging it desperately to maintain his position. The herd had now thoroughly pervaded the timber, and the bear was likewise hemmed in. He had taken his unaccustomed refuge after making a brave stand

90 against several bulls, one of which lay dead nearby, while he himself was bleeding from several wounds.

Antoine had been assiduously looking for a friendly tree, by means of which he hoped to escape from captivity. His horse, by chance, made his way
95 directly under the very box-elder that was sustaining the bear and there was a convenient branch just within his reach. He saw at a glance that the occupant of the tree would not interfere with him. They were, in fact, companions in distress. Antoine
100 sprang desperately from the pony's back and seized the cross-limb with both his hands.

By the middle of the afternoon the main body of the herd had passed, and Antoine was sure that his captivity had at last come to an end. Then he
105 swung himself from his limb to the ground, and walked stiffly to the carcass of the nearest cow, which he dressed, and prepared himself a meal. But first he took a piece of liver on a long pole to the bear!

44. The word "sprays" (line 12) refers to:

F.   minute droplets.
G.   light mist.
H.   thin legs.
J.   small branches.

45. In context, "steal up" (line 20) means:

A.   acquire unlawfully.
B.   prepare for action.
C.   promise faithfully.
D.   approach undetected.

46. In the first two paragraphs, the author of Passage 1 is primarily concerned with:

F.   recounting an experience.
G.   exploring a theory.
H.   teaching a lesson.
J.   offering an opinion.

47. In context, "conceit" (line 23) means:

A.   arrogance.
B.   selfishness.
C.   fanciful notion.
D.   dissatisfaction.

48. According to the passage, the deer and the sheep are alike in that they both:

F.   are wary of human beings.
G.   inhabit remote Alpine gardens.
H.   feed without causing destruction.
J.   live untamed in wilderness regions.

49. The "boldly drawn hieroglyphics" (lines 43–44) are probably:

A.   claw marks.
B.   park signs.
C.   rare flowers.
D.   hoof prints.

50. The author compares the deer to gardeners (lines 34–37) in order to:

F.   encourage the reader to learn more about deer.
G.   refute the idea that deer are aggressive.
H.   illustrate the similarity between deer and humans.
J.   emphasize that deer are not destructive.

51. In context, "wallows" (line 64) means:

A.   deep cave.
B.   shallow depression.
C.   rugged cliff.
D.   low hill.

52. By "the natural offensiveness of man" (line 52), the author of Passage B probably refers to man's:

F.   frequent rudeness.
G.   disagreeable odor.
H.   uncontrolled aggression.
J.   distasteful behavior.

53. All of the following are true of the comparison drawn in the third paragraph of Passage B EXCEPT:

   A. Antoine, like a shipwrecked sailor, is in a desperate situation.

   B. The herd of buffalo are like the storm driven sea.

   C. The environment is filled with dangerous creatures that threaten a sailor the way Antoine fears the buffalo.

   D. Antoine's pony supports him the way that debris might support a shipwrecked sailor.

54. The tone of the first two paragraphs of Passage B is:

   F. frivolous.

   G. suspenseful.

   H. animated.

   J. reserved.

55. The phrase "unaccustomed refuge" (line 89) suggests that the bear:

   A. preferred open areas to confined spaces.

   B. rarely climbed a tree for safety.

   C. did not often encounter buffalo.

   D. was fearful of the presence of a human.

56. In context, "dressed" (line 107) means:

   F. adorned.

   G. clothed.

   H. prepared.

   J. bound.

57. The mood of Passage B moves from:

   A. joy to despair.

   B. hopelessness to hope.

   C. happiness to gloom.

   D. apprehension to courageousness.

Passage VII

Prose Fiction: This passage is adapted from the short story "Mrs. Gay's Prescription" by Louisa May Alcott.

The poor little woman looked as if she needed rest but was not likely to get it; for the room was in a chaotic state. The breakfast table presented the appearance of having been devastated by a swarm
5 of locusts, the baby began to fret, little Polly set up her usual whine of "I want sumpin to do," and a pile of work loomed in the corner waiting to be done.

"I don't see how I ever shall get through it all," sighed the despondent matron as she hastily drank
10 a last cup of tea. Two great tears rolled down her cheeks as she looked from one puny child to the other, and felt the weariness of her own tired soul and body more oppressive than ever.

"A good cry" was impending, when there came
15 a brisk ring at the door and a step in the hall. A large, rosy woman came bustling in, saying in a cheery voice as she set a flower-pot down upon the table, "Good morning! Nice day, isn't it? Came in early on business and brought you one of my Lady
20 Washingtons. You are so fond of flowers."

"Oh, it's lovely! How kind you are. Do sit down if you can find a chair; we are all behind hand today, for I was up half the night with poor baby, and haven't energy enough to go to work yet," answered
25 Mrs. Bennet, with a sudden smile that changed her whole face. Baby stopped fretting to stare at the rosy clusters, and Polly found employment in exploring the pocket of the newcomer, as if she knew her way there.

30 "Let me put the pot on your stand first. Girls are so careless, and I'm proud of this. It will be an ornament to your parlor for a week." Opening a door, Mrs. Gay carried the plant to a sunny bay window where many others were blooming
35 beautifully.

Mrs. Bennet and the children followed to talk and admire, while the servant leisurely cleared the table.

"Now give me that baby, put yourself in the
40 easy chair, and tell me all about your worries," said Mrs. Gay, in the brisk, commanding way which few people could resist.

"I'm sure I don't know where to begin," sighed Mrs. Bennet, dropping into the comfortable seat
45 while baby changed bearers with great composure.

"I met your husband and he said the doctor had ordered you and these chicks off to Florida for the winter. John said he didn't know how he should manage it, but he meant to try."

50 "Isn't it dreadful? He can't leave his business to go with me, and we shall have to get Aunt Miranda to come and see to him and the boys while I'm gone, and the boys can't bear her strict, old-fashioned ways, and I've got to go that long journey all alone
55 and stay among strangers, and these heaps of fall work to do first, and it will cost an immense sum to send us, and I don't know what is to become of me."

Here Mrs. Bennet stopped for breath. Mrs. Gay asked briskly, "What is the matter with you and the
60 children?"

"Well, baby is having a hard time with his teeth and is croupy. Polly doesn't get over scarlet fever well, and I'm used up; no strength or appetite, pain in my side and low spirits. Entire change of scene,
65 milder climate, and less work for me, is what we want, the doctor says. John is very anxious about us, and I feel regularly discouraged."

"I'll spend the day and cheer you up a bit. You just rest and get ready for a new start tomorrow; it
70 is a saving of time to stop short now and then and see where to begin next. Bring me the most pressing job of work. I can sew and see to this little rascal at the same time."

Further Use of Reading Strategies

Prose Fiction

58. The phrase "little woman" (line 1) refers to:

F. Lady Washington.
G. a servant.
H. Mrs. Bennet.
J. Mrs. Gay.

59. When Alcott compares the breakfast table to something "devastated by a swarm of locusts" (lines 4–5), she means:

A. that it is a mess left by an uncaring mob.
B. that children are no more meaningful than insects to Mrs. Bennet.
C. to illustrate the chaos of Mrs. Bennet's life.
D. that the Bennets are pests.

60. Had Mrs. Gay not arrived when she did, the author leads us to suspect that:

F. Mrs. Bennet would have gone back to bed.
G. the children would have continued to cry.
H. Mrs. Bennet would have accomplished little all day.
J. sickness would have overtaken the entire family.

61. The phrase "rosy clusters" (line 27) refers to:

A. Mrs. Gay's cheeks.
B. Mrs. Bennet's cheeks.
C. candies from Mrs. Gay's pockets.
D. flowers.

62. In lines 30–35, the author:

F. reveals Mrs. Bennet's only talent.
G. uses the sunny parlor as a symbol of hope.
H. contrasts Mrs. Gay's sunniness with Mrs. Bennet's dullness.
J. contrasts Mrs. Bennet's plants with her children.

63. When Mrs. Bennet says that she's "used up" (line 63), she means that she:

A. has no energy.
B. is abused.
C. is exploited.
D. has spent all her money.

64. The word *pressing* (line 71) means:

F. heavy.
G. ardent.
H. forceful.
J. important.

65. The disposition of Mrs. Bennet's friend is indicated by:

   I. her name.
  II. her speech.
 III. her clothing.

A. I only
B. III only
C. I and II only
D. I and III only

66. The author implies that Mrs. Bennet's real problem is:

F. her inability to cope.
G. a touch of fever.
H. the cold winter weather.
J. a lack of common sense.

67. Mrs. Gay's primary quality seems to be her:

A. lethargy.
B. anxiety.
C. dignity.
D. practical nature.

Passage VIII

Prose Fiction: This passage is adapted from the memoir series "Old Times on the Mississippi" by Mark Twain that appeared in *Atlantic Monthly*.

At the end of what seemed a tedious while, I had managed to pack my head full of islands, towns, bars, "points," and bends; and a curiously inanimate mass of lumber it was, too. However, inasmuch as I
5 could shut my eyes and reel off a good long string of these names without leaving out more than ten miles of river in every fifty, I began to feel that I could make her skip those little gaps. But of course my complacency could hardly get started enough to
10 lift my nose a trifle into the air, before Mr. Bixby would think of something to fetch it down again. One day he turned on me suddenly with this settler:

"What is the shape of Walnut Bend?"

He might as well have asked me my
15 grandmother's opinion of protoplasm. I reflected respectfully, and then said I didn't know it had any particular shape. My gunpowdery chief went off with a bang, of course, and then went on loading and firing until he was out of adjectives.

20 I had learned long ago that he only carried just so many rounds of ammunition, and was sure to subside into a very placable and even remorseful old smoothbore as soon as they were all gone. That word "old" is merely affectionate; he was not more
25 than thirty-four. I waited. By and by he said:

"My boy, you've got to know the *shape* of the river perfectly. It is all there is left to steer by on a very dark night. Everything else is blotted out and gone. But mind you, it hasn't the same shape in the
30 night that it has in the daytime."

"How on earth am I ever going to learn it, then?"

"How do you follow a hall at home in the dark? Because you know the shape of it. You can't see it."

35 "Do you mean to say that I've got to know all the million trifling variations of shape in the banks of this interminable river as well as I know the shape of the front hall at home?"

"On my honor, you've got to know them *better*
40 than any man ever did know the shapes of the halls in his own house."

"I wish I was dead!"

"Now I don't want to discourage you, but..."

"Well, pile it on me; I might as well have it now
45 as another time."

"You see, this has got to be learned; there isn't any getting around it. A clear starlight night throws such heavy shadows that, if you didn't know the shape of a shore perfectly, you would claw away
50 from every bunch of timber, because you would take the black shadow of it for a solid cape; and you see you would be getting scared to death every fifteen minutes by the watch. You would be fifty yards from shore all the time when you ought to be
55 within fifty feet of it. You can't see a snag in one of those shadows, but you know exactly where it is, and the shape of the river tells you when you are coming to it. Then there's your pitch-dark night; the river is a very different shape on a pitch-dark night
60 from what it is on a starlit night. All shores seem to be straight lines, then, and mighty dim ones, too; and you'd *run* them for straight lines, only you know better. You boldly drive your boat right into what seems to be a solid straight wall (you knowing very
65 well that in reality there is a curve there), and that wall falls back and makes way for you. Then there's your gray mist. You take a night when there's one of these grisly, drizzly, gray mists, and then there isn't any particular shape to a shore. A gray mist would
70 tangle the head of the oldest man that ever lived. Well, then different kinds of *moonlight* change the shape of the river in different ways."

68. In line 12, the word *settler* is used to mean:

    F.   a pioneer.
    G.   a perch on the railing.
    H.   a remark that decides the issue.
    J.   a humbling problem.

69. When the narrator compares Bixby's question to asking his "grandmother's opinion of protoplasm" (line 15), he means that:

   A.   the question is inane.
   B.   the speaker is very old.
   C.   he does not know the answer.
   D.   his grandmother would be able to respond.

70. Comparing the chief to a gun (lines 17–19) points out the chief's:

   F.   accuracy.
   G.   peppery temper.
   H.   love of hunting.
   J.   violent past.

71. When Twain writes that Mr. Bixby "carried just so many rounds of ammunition," he means that:

   A.   Bixby used a pistol to settle arguments.
   B.   Bixby loaded and fired his gun at random.
   C.   Bixby was an impossible employer.
   D.   Bixby's hot temper would soon subside.

72. The narrator's reaction to Mr. Bixby's insistence on the need to know the river at night is:

   F.   despair.
   G.   elation.
   H.   puzzlement.
   J.   anger.

73. In the phrase "pile it on me" (line 44), "it" refers to:

   A.   clothing.
   B.   information.
   C.   the river.
   D.   the shoreline.

74. The word *cape* (line 51) means:

   F.   cloak.
   G.   robe.
   H.   peninsula.
   J.   waterway.

75. Mr. Bixby is shown to be extremely:

   A.   knowledgeable.
   B.   rude.
   C.   condescending.
   D.   fearful.

76. What is the purpose of including the lengthy explanation provided in the last paragraph of the selection?

   I.   To show how well Bixby speaks
   II. To show how much a riverboat captain must know
   III. To show the many modes of the river

   F.   I only
   G.   II only
   H.   I and III only
   J.   II and III only

77. According to the passage, which of the following is true?

   A.   A riverboat should always be within 100 feet of the shore.
   B.   On a clear, starlit night, the shoreline is easy to see.
   C.   On a pitch-dark night, the pilot cannot discern the curve of the shoreline.
   D.   The river's shape gives no hint of underwater snags.

Passage IX

Prose Fiction: This passage is adapted from Nathaniel Hawthorne's *The House of the Seven Gables.*

It still lacked a half hour of sunrise when Miss Hepzibah—we will say awoke, it being doubtful whether the poor old lady had so much as closed her eyes during the brief night of midsummer—but,
5 at all events, arose from her solitary pillow, and began the adornment of her person. She was alone in the old house—quite a house by itself, indeed— with locks, bolts, and oaken bars on all the intervening doors. Inaudible, consequently, were
10 poor Miss Hepzibah's gusty sighs. Inaudible were the creaking joints of her stiffened knees, as she knelt down by the bedside. And inaudible too, by mortal ear, that almost agony of prayer—now whispered, now a groan, now a struggling silence—
15 wherewith she sought the Divine assistance through the day! Evidently this is to be the day of more than ordinary trial to Miss Hepzibah. For above a quarter of a century gone by, she has dwelt in strict seclusion, taking no part in the business of life, and
20 just as little in its intercourse and pleasures.

Here comes Miss Hepzibah. Forth she steps into the dusky, time-darkened passage. A tall figure, clad in black silk, with a long and shrunken waist, she feels her way towards the stair like a
25 nearsighted person, which in truth she is.

Her scowl—as the world persisted in calling it—had done Miss Hepzibah every ill office, in establishing her character as an ill-tempered old maid; nor does it appear improbable that, by often
30 gazing at herself in a dim looking glass, and perpetually encountering her own frown within its ghostly sphere, she had been led to interpret the expression almost as unjustly as the world did. But her heart never frowned.

78. According to the passage, Miss Hepzibah is all of the following EXCEPT:

F. elderly.
G. reclusive.
H. religious.
J. vain.

79. The author's portrait of Miss Hepzibah is:

A. critical and disparaging.
B. loving and intimate.
C. sarcastic and mocking.
D. interested and sympathetic.

80. It can be inferred that Miss Hepzibah views the day's coming events with:

F. apprehension.
G. confidence.
H. eagerness.
J. boredom.

81. Which of the following correctly describes the scene as set by the passage?

I.   The season is summer.
II. The weather is threatening.
III. The time is morning.

A. I only
B. III only
C. I and II only
D. I and III only

82. In the last paragraph, the author implies that Miss Hepzibah is:

F. old and wicked.
G. affable and outgoing.
H. good-hearted but misunderstood.
J. sincere but blasphemous.

Passage X

Social Science: This passage discusses the contest over the vice presidency in the 1792 election.

In 1792, there was no contest for the presidency. George Washington received the unanimous vote of the electors, Federalist and Republican alike. But the struggle over the vice
5   presidency hinted at the rekindling of old divisions sparked by Alexander Hamilton's system. Southern planters who in 1789 had been ready, in fact eager, to cooperate with the monied men of the North, parted with them when they realized that the
10 policies designed to benefit Northern merchants and bankers brought no profit to them. Even more, they saw themselves paying for a system that contributed to another section's prosperity. Although in 1792 they were willing to continue with
15 Washington, they were not as willing to go along with Vice President John Adams, who represented the commerce, shipbuilding, fisheries, and banking institutions of New England and the North. If the Federalists were to have the first office, then the
20 followers of Jefferson—who had already come to call themselves Republicans instead of the unpopular term anti-Federalist—insisted that they were to command the second office.

Appealing to the shopkeepers, artisans,
25 laboring men, and farmers of the North based on their sympathy with the French Revolution, and to the Southern planters with their agrarian bias, the Republicans waged a gallant but losing campaign for the second office. However, the campaign served
30 notice to the overconfident Federalists that when the Republicans became better organized nationally, they would have to be more seriously considered. This did not take long. In 1793, England declared war with republican France over the
35 murder of Louis XVI. And in 1794, John Jay's treaty ending the United States' difficulties with Britain seemed to suggest a sympathetic policy toward monarchical and conservative England, instead of republican, liberty-loving France. The treaty
40 intensified party spirit and gave the Republicans a sense of mission that legitimized their existence. The contest was now between the Republican "lovers of liberty" and the Monocrats.

Social Science

83. Which of the following titles best describes the content of the passage?

A. The Origins of Jefferson's Republican Party
B. Jefferson's Defeat in the 1792 Election
C. The Legacy of Hamilton's Political System
D. Political Differences Between the Rich and the Poor

84. According to the passage, all of the following are true of the Republicans EXCEPT:

F. they opposed the monied interests of the North.
G. they were led by Thomas Jefferson.
H. they disapproved of the French Revolution.
J. they and the Federalists supported the same candidate for president in 1792.

85. It can be inferred from the passage that the term *Monocrats* (line 43) was:

A. used by John Jay in his treaty to refer to France's King Louis XVI.
B. invented by the Federalists to refer to the aristocratic landowners of the South.
C. coined by the Republicans to disparage the Federalists' support of England.
D. employed by Republicans to describe their leader, Thomas Jefferson.

86. The passage implies that Thomas Jefferson was unsuccessful in his 1792 bid for the vice presidency because the Republican Party:

F. did not have a presidential candidate.
G. was not as well organized as the Federalists.
H. refused to support John Adams.
J. appealed to workers in the North.

87. The tone of the passage can best be described as:

A. enthusiastic and impassioned.
B. scholarly and neutral.
C. opinionated and dogmatic.
D. argumentative and categorical.

Passage XI

Social Science: This passage is adapted from an article about attempts to change the healthcare system.

Considerable advances have been made in healthcare services since World War II. These include better access to healthcare (particularly for the poor and minorities), improvements in physical
5   plants and facilities, and increased numbers of physicians and other health personnel. All have played a part in the recent improvement in life expectancy. But there is mounting criticism of the large remaining gaps in access, unbridled cost
10 inflation, the further fragmentation of service, excessive indulgence in wasteful high-technology "gadgeteering," and breakdowns in doctor-patient relationships. In recent years, proposed panaceas and new programs, small and large, have
15 proliferated at a feverish pace, and disappointments have multiplied at almost the same rate. This has led to an increased pessimism—"everything has been tried and nothing works"—that sometimes borders on cynicism or even nihilism.

20   It is true that the automatic "pass through" of rapidly spiraling costs to government and insurance carriers produced for a time a sense of unlimited resources. It allowed a mood to develop whereby every practitioner and institution could "do his own
25 thing" without undue concern for the "Medical Commons." The practice of full-cost reimbursement encouraged capital investment, and now the industry is overcapitalized. Many cities have hundreds of excess hospital beds; hospitals have
30 proliferated a superabundance of high-technology equipment; and structural ostentation and luxury were the order of the day. In any given day, one-fourth of all community beds are vacant; expensive equipment is underused or, worse, used
35 unnecessarily. Capital investment brings rapidly rising operating costs.

Yet, in part, this pessimism derives from expecting too much of healthcare. Care is often a painful experience accompanied by fear and
40 unwelcome results; although there is room for improvement, it will always retain some unpleasantness and frustration. Moreover, the capacities of medical science are limited. Humpty Dumpty cannot always be put back together again.
45 Too many physicians are reluctant to admit their limitations to patients; too many patients and

families are unwilling to accept such realities. Nor is it true that everything has been tried and nothing works, as shown by the prepaid group practice
50 plans at the Kaiser Foundation and Puget Sound. However, typically such undertakings have been drowned by a veritable flood of public and private funds that have supported the continuation of conventional practices and subsidized their
55 shortcomings on a massive, almost unrestricted scale. Except for the most idealistic and dedicated, there were no incentives to seek change or to practice self-restraint or frugality. In this atmosphere, it is not fair to condemn as failures all
60 attempted experiments; it may be more accurate to say that many never had a fair trial.

88. In line 15, the word *feverish* most nearly means:

F. diseased.
G. rapid.
H. controlled.
J. timed.

89. According to the author, the pessimism mentioned in line 37 is partly attributable to the fact that:

A. there has been little real improvement in healthcare services.
B. expectations about healthcare services are sometimes unrealistic.
C. large segments of the population find it impossible to get access to healthcare services.
D. advances in technology have made healthcare service unaffordable.

90. The author cites the prepaid plans (lines 47–50) as:

F. counterexamples to the claim that nothing has worked.
G. examples of healthcare plans that were overfunded.
H. evidence that healthcare services are fragmented.
J. proof of the theory that no plan has been successful.

91. It can be inferred that the sentence "Humpty Dumpty cannot always be put back together again" (lines 43–44) means that:

   A. the cost of healthcare services will not decline.
   B. some people should not become doctors.
   C. medical care is not really essential to good health.
   D. medical science cannot cure every ill.

92. With which of the following descriptions of the system for the delivery of healthcare services would the author most likely agree?

   F. It is biased in favor of doctors and against patients.
   G. It is highly fragmented and completely ineffective.
   H. It has not embraced new technology rapidly enough.
   J. It is generally effective but can be improved.

93. Which of the following best describes the logical structure of the selection?

   A. The third paragraph is intended as a refutation of the first and second paragraphs.
   B. The second and third paragraphs are intended as a refutation of the first paragraph.
   C. The second and third paragraphs explain and put into perspective the points made in the first paragraph.
   D. The first paragraph describes a problem, and the second and third paragraphs present two sides of the dilemma.

94. The author's primary concern is to:

   F. criticize physicians and healthcare administrators for investing in technologically advanced equipment.
   G. examine some problems affecting the delivery of healthcare services and assess the severity of those problems.
   H. defend the medical community from charges that healthcare has not improved since World War II.
   J. analyze the reasons for the healthcare industry's inability to provide quality care to all segments of the population.

Passage XII

Humanities: This passage is adapted from an article about literary genres.

When we speak casually, we call *Nineteen Eighty-Four* a novel, but to be more exact we should call it a political fable. This requirement is not refuted by the fact that the book is about a man,
5 Winston Smith, who suffers from a varicose ulcer, or by the fact that it takes account of other individuals, including Julia, Mrs. Parsons, Syme, and O'Brien. The figures claim our attention, but they exist mainly in their relation to the political system that determines
10 them. It would indeed be possible to think of them as figures in a novel, though in that case they would have to be imagined in a far more diverse set of relations. They would no longer sustain a fable, because a fable is a story relieved of much
15 contingent detail so that it may stand forth in an unusual degree of clarity and simplicity. A fable is a structure of types, each of them deliberately simplified lest a sense of difference reduce the force of the typical. Let us say, then, that *Nineteen Eighty-*
20 *Four* is a political fable, projected into a near future and including historical references.

Since a fable requires a typology, it must be written from a certain distance. The author cannot afford the sense of familiarity that is induced by
25 detail. A fable, in this respect, asks to be compared to a caricature, not to a photograph. It follows that in a political fable there is bound to be some tension between a political sense dealing with the diversity of social and personal life, and a fable sense
30 committed to simplicity of form and feature. If the political sense were to prevail, the narrative would be drawn away from fable into the novel. If the sense of fable were to prevail, the narrative would appear unmediated, free or bereft of conditions. The
35 risk would be considerable: a reader might feel that the fabulist has lost interest in the variety of human life. The risk is greater still if the fabulist projects his narrative into the future: the reader cannot question by appealing to life conditions already
40 known. He is asked to believe that the future is another country and that "they just do things differently there."

In a powerful fable, the reader's feeling is likely to be mostly fear: he is afraid that the
45 fabulist's vision of life may be true. The fabulist's feeling may be more various. A fable such as *Nineteen Eighty-Four* might arise from disgust, despair, or world-weariness caused by evidence that nothing, despite one's best efforts, has changed;
50 it is too late now to hope for the change one wants.

Humanities

95. In line 15, the word *contingent* most nearly means:

    A. dependent.
    B. essential.
    C. boring.
    D. unnecessary.

96. In drawing an analogy between a fable and a caricature (lines 25–26), the author would most likely regard which of the following pairs of ideas as also analogous?

    F. The subject of a caricature and the topic of a fable
    G. The subject of a caricature and the main character in *Nineteen Eighty-Four*
    H. The subject of a fable and the artist who draws the caricature
    J. The artist who draws the caricature and a novelist

97. Which of the following would be the most appropriate title for the passage?

    A. A Critical Study of the Use of Characters in *Nineteen Eighty-Four*
    B. *Nineteen Eighty-Four*: Political Fable Rather Than Novel
    C. *Nineteen Eighty-Four*: Reflections on the Relationship of the Individual to Society
    D. The Use of Typology in the Literature of Political Fables

98. According to the passage, which of the following are characteristics of a political fable?

    F. It is widely popular at its time of development.

    G. The reader is unlikely to experience fear as his reaction to the political situation described.

    H. Its time frame must treat events that occur at some point in the future.

    J. Its characters are defined primarily by their relationship to the social order.

99. The author mentions that Winston Smith suffers from a varicose ulcer to:

    A. demonstrate that a political fable must emphasize type over detail.

    B. show that Winston Smith has some characteristics that distinguish him as an individual.

    C. argue that Winston Smith is no more important than any other character in *Nineteen Eighty-Four*.

    D. illustrate one of the features of the political situation described in *Nineteen Eighty-Four*.

100. The tension that the author mentions in line 27 refers to the:

    F. necessity of striking a balance between the need to describe a political situation in simple terms and the need to make the description realistic.

    G. reaction the reader feels because he is drawn to the characters of the fable as individuals but repulsed by the political situation.

    H. delicate task faced by a literary critic who must interpret the text of a work while attempting to accurately describe the intentions of the author.

    J. danger that too realistic a description of a key character will make the reader feel that the fable is actually a description of his own situation.

101. The author's attitude toward *Nineteen Eighty-Four* can best be described as:

    A. condescending.
    B. laudatory.
    C. disparaging.
    D. scholarly.

102. The author uses the phrase "another country" (line 41) to describe a political fable in which:

    F. political events described in a fable occur in a place other than the author's country of origin.

    G. a lack of detail makes it difficult for a reader to see the connection between his own situation and the one described in the book.

    H. too many minor characters create the impression of complete disorganization, leading the reader to believe he is in a foreign country.

    J. the author has allowed his personal political convictions to infect his description of the political situation.

103. The author's primary concern is to:

    A. define and clarify a concept.
    B. point out a logical inconsistency.
    C. trace the connection between a cause and an effect.
    D. illustrate a general statement with examples.

Passage XIII

Humanities: This passage is adapted from the speech "Is it a Crime for a Citizen of the United States to Vote?" by Susan B. Anthony.

Friends and fellow citizens: I stand before you tonight under indictment for the alleged crime of having voted at the last presidential election without having a lawful right to vote. It shall be my
5   work this evening to prove to you that in thus voting, I not only committed no crime, but, instead, simply exercised *my citizen's rights*, guaranteed to me and all United States citizens by the National Constitution, beyond the power of any State to deny.
10 The preamble of the Federal Constitution says: "We, the people of the United States, in order to form a more perfect union, establish justice, insure *domestic* tranquility, provide for the common defense, promote the general welfare, and secure
15 the blessings of liberty to ourselves and our posterity."

It was we, the people, not we, the white male citizens; but we, the whole people, who formed the Union. And we formed it, not to give the blessings of
20 liberty, but to secure them; not to the half of ourselves and the half of our posterity but to the whole people—women as well as men. And it is a downright mockery to talk to women of their enjoyment of the blessings of liberty while they are
25 denied the use of the only means of securing them provided by this government—the ballot.

For any State to make sex a qualification that results in the disfranchisement of one entire half of the people is a violation of the supreme law of the
30 land. By it the blessings of liberty are forever withheld from women and their female posterity. To them this government has no just powers derived from the consent of the governed. To them this government is not a democracy. It is not a
35 republic. It is a hateful oligarchy of sex. An oligarchy of learning, where the educated govern the ignorant, might be endured; but this oligarchy of sex, which makes father, brothers, husband, sons, the oligarchs or rulers over the mother and sisters,
40 the wife and daughters of every household—which ordains all men sovereigns, all women subjects, carries dissension, discord and rebellion into every home of the nation.

Webster's Dictionary defines a citizen as a
45 person in the United States, entitled to vote and hold office.

The only question left to be settled now is: Are women persons? And I hardly believe any of our opponents will have the hardihood to say we are
50 not. Being persons, then, women are citizens; and no State has a right to make any law, or to enforce any old law, that shall abridge their privileges or immunities. Hence, every discrimination against women in the laws of the States is today null and
55 void.

104. The nineteenth-century feminist leader Susan B. Anthony fought long and hard to guarantee women the right to vote. In this speech, based on her situation at the time, she talks as if she were a:

F.   defendant on trial.
G.   chairperson of a committee.
H.   legislator arguing for a new law.
J.   judge ruling at a trial.

105. Anthony broadens her appeal to her audience by showing how her case could affect all:

A.   existing laws.
B.   United States citizens.
C.   women.
D.   uneducated persons.

106. Anthony quotes the preamble to the Constitution (lines 10–16) in order to:

F.   impress the audience with her intelligence.
G.   utilize a common legalistic trick.
H.   point out which part of the preamble needs to be changed.
J.   add force to her argument.

107. According to Anthony, who formed the Union?

A.   Only one-half of the people
B.   The whole people
C.   White male citizens only
D.   White female citizens

108. When Anthony says that the blessings of liberty are forever withheld from women and their female posterity, she means that:

    F. all classes of women are discriminated against.

    G. women of the past have been victimized.

    H. female children of the poor will be the only ones affected.

    J. women of the present and the future will suffer.

109. Anthony argues that a government that denies women the right to vote is not a democracy because its powers do not come from:

    A. the Constitution of the United States.

    B. the rights of the states.

    C. the consent of the governed.

    D. the vote of the majority.

110. According to this speech, an "oligarchy of sex" would cause:

    F. women to rebel against the government.

    G. men to desert their families.

    H. problems to develop in every home.

    J. the educated to rule the ignorant.

111. In this speech, a citizen is defined as a person who has the right to vote and also the right to:

    A. acquire wealth.

    B. speak publicly.

    C. hold office.

    D. pay taxes.

112. Anthony argues that state laws that discriminate against women are:

    F. being changed.

    G. null and void.

    H. helpful to the rich.

    J. supported by the Constitution.

Passage XIV

Humanities: This passage is adapted from an essay by Oliver Goldsmith that appeared in *The Citizen of the World.*

Were we to estimate the learning of the English by the number of books that are every day published among them, perhaps no country, not even China itself, could equal them in this
5 particular. I have reckoned not less than twenty-three new books published in one day, which makes eight thousand three hundred and ninety-five in one year. Most of these are not confined to one single science, but embrace the whole circle. History,
10 politics, poetry, mathematics, metaphysics, and the philosophy of nature are all comprised in a manual not larger than that in which our children are taught the letters. If then, we suppose the learned of England to read but an eighth part of the works
15 which daily come from the press (and surely none can pretend to learning upon less easy terms), at this rate every scholar will read a thousand books in one year. From such a calculation, you may conjecture what an amazing fund of literature a man
20 must be possessed of, who thus reads three new books every day, not one of which but contains all the good things that ever were said or written.

And yet I know not how it happens, but the English are not, in reality, so learned as would seem
25 from this calculation. We meet but few who know all arts and sciences to perfection; whether it is that the generality are incapable of such extensive knowledge, or that the authors of those books are not adequate instructors. In China, the Emperor
30 himself takes cognizance of all the doctors in the kingdom who profess authorship. In England, every man may be an author that can write; for they have by law a liberty, not only of saying what they please, but also of being as dull as they please.

35 Yesterday, I testified my surprise to the man in black, where writers could be found in sufficient number to throw off the books I daily saw crowding from the press. I at first imagined that their learned seminaries might take this method of instructing
40 the world. But, to obviate this objection, my companion assured me that the doctors of colleges never wrote, and that some of them had actually forgotten their reading. "But if you desire," continued he, "to see a collection of authors, I can
45 introduce you to a club, which assembles every Saturday at seven...." I accepted his invitation; we walked together, and entered the house some time before the usual hour for the company assembling.

My friend took this opportunity of letting me
50 into the characters of the principal members of the club....

"The first person," said he, "of our society is Doctor Nonentity, a metaphysician. Most people think him a profound scholar, but, as he seldom
55 speaks, I cannot be positive in that; he generally spreads himself before the fire, sucks his pipe, talks little, drinks much, and is reckoned very good company. I'm told he writes indexes to perfection: he makes essays on the origin of evil, philosophical
60 inquiries upon any subject, and draws up an answer to any book upon 24 hours' warning...."

113. Goldsmith's disdainful attitude toward English authors is best explicated in:

    A. lines 1–5.
    B. lines 13–18.
    C. lines 31–34.
    D. lines 43–48.

114. Goldsmith believes that:

    F. we can tell how knowledgeable English authors are by counting the number of books they publish.
    G. the number of books published in England is not up to standards set in China.
    H. the number of books published in England says nothing about English scholarship.
    J. every English scholar reads a thousand books a year.

115. Goldsmith calculates the number of books published in England to:

    A. impress his readers with English erudition.
    B. make the point that anyone can be an author.
    C. make a defense for his argument that England is better than China.
    D. make a comparison with publication quotas in other lands.

116. The tone of the second paragraph may best be described as:

    F. self-satisfied.
    G. awestruck.
    H. affectionate.
    J. sardonic.

117. Goldsmith first assumes that English writers come from:

    A. foreign lands.
    B. seminaries.
    C. China.
    D. clubs.

118. The word *obviate* (line 40) means:

    F. clarify.
    G. obscure.
    H. turn.
    J. negate.

119. Goldsmith's opinion of the first member of the club is illuminated by which of the following?

    I. His conversation with the character
    II. The given name for the character
    III. His friend's description of the character

    A. I only
    B. II only
    C. I and III only
    D. II and III only

120. One of Goldsmith's major objections to English authors is their:

    F. deficiency in language skills.
    G. inclination to drink.
    H. tendency to write about everything at once.
    J. inability to retain information.

Passage XV

Humanities: This passage discusses the impact of the Southwest's environment and culture on twentieth-century artists.

Georgia O'Keeffe, whose death at age 98 closed one of the most fertile chapters of American artistic creativity, flourished as a maverick in her life and work. While other painters spent a season or two in
5　the country trying to come to terms with the scenes and settings of the Southwest, O'Keeffe stayed a lifetime. When the canvases of other artists working in the region faded from view, her stylized images and motifs made an indelible impression on
10　countless eyes.

Between 1900 and 1945, the region now called New Mexico both fascinated and perplexed two generations of American artists. Luminaries such as Stuart Davis, Marsden Hartley, and John Sloan, built
15　their reputations on depictions of modern life in Eastern cities. Despite successes, these artists wearied of the industrial world of the East. The vast expanse of the American West offered a promise for inspiration. It was a new world to their eyes—an
20　enchanted land far removed from urban conventions.

For these artists, life and art, so separate in New York and Paris, seemed inextricably bound in Southwestern cultures. Painters were convinced
25　that sampling this phenomenon would strengthen and enrich their own work. Most were touched by what D.H. Lawrence called the "spirit of the place." Besides the scenic possibilities bathed in clear golden light, the rich traditions of New Mexico's
30　Native American and Latino people—their dress, crafts, pueblos, plaza life, rituals, and simple dignity—became frequent subjects of the artists who came to Taos and Santa Fe.

Some of the artists were traditionalists—local
35　color realists; some were modernists—like O'Keeffe, painters of the abstract. Their talents coupled with the appeal of the land gave New Mexico's art centers a status unrivaled among other summer colonies.

121. This passage deals primarily with:

A.　the life of Georgia O'Keeffe.
B.　the major trends of American modern art.
C.　the mystery and spirit of the Southwest.
D.　artists in the American Southwest.

122. The author implies that the Southwest attracted artists for all of the following reasons EXCEPT:

F.　the quality of life was different from that of large urban centers.
G.　the inhabitants and culture provided interesting subject matter.
H.　New Mexico was the only state to support young, avant-garde painters.
J.　the region offered unusual geological features and landscapes.

123. The author implies that most of the artists who painted in the Southwest:

A.　originally studied in Paris.
B.　lived there only temporarily.
C.　painted only landscapes.
D.　received considerable recognition.

124. The author mentions which of the following facts about Georgia O'Keeffe?

　I.　She resided permanently in the Southwest.
　II.　She enjoyed considerable and lasting fame.
　III.　She created modern, abstract paintings.

F.　I only
G.　II only
H.　I and III only
J.　I, II, and III

125. Stuart Davis, Marsden Hartley, and John Sloan were painters who painted mainly in:

A.　Paris.
B.　New Mexico.
C.　cities in the Eastern United States.
D.　Rome.

Passage XVI

Natural Science: This passage discusses the development of basic inheritance theories and the role of DNA in genetic mutation processes.

In 1866, Gregor Mendel published the results of his studies on the breeding of different races of pea plants. Through his experiments, Mendel discovered a pattern of inheritance and
5 subsequently developed the concept of a "unit of inheritance."

Mendel started with a pure stock of pea plants that had recognizably different characteristics. He artificially cross-pollinated the different races of
10 plants and noted the characteristics of the different offspring over several generations. Mendel concluded that a pair of discrete "factors" governed each trait and that they segregated upon the formation of the gametes. This pair of factors is now
15 known as the maternally and paternally derived alleles on homologous chromosomes that first come together at fertilization and later segregate during meiosis.

Subsequent studies have shown that new
20 genes could appear as mutations of existing genes and that crossing over and recombination could redistribute maternal and paternal characteristics. Genes can occur in a linear sequence, and groups of genes that segregate together are called "linkage
25 groups." The chromosome is the carrier of the linear array of genes and the physical basis of the linkage groups.

It was originally thought that proteins were the genetic carrier. In contrast to nucleic acids,
30 proteins were known to mediate complex reactions and to be composed of a variety of different building blocks. There are approximately 20 different amino acids in a protein, but only 4 different nucleotides in a nucleic acid molecule. It was not until 1944 that
35 Avery et al. noted that deoxyribonucleic acid (DNA) was the genetic carrier, not protein. Avery and his co-workers conducted experiments on the transformation in pneumococcus. Two strains of the bacteria had been isolated: one produced colonies
40 having a smooth (S) appearance and was able to cause pneumonia in a suitable host; the other grew into rough (R) colonies because of a defect in its capsule and was non-virulent. When a cell-free extract of the S bacteria was added to the medium
45 in which the R strain was growing, a few of the R

bacteria grew into smooth colonies and were virulent. They had become transformed. From the time of transformation, the progeny of that cell continued to have the properties of the S strain. The
50 transformation was a stable genetic change. Avery and his co-workers purified the contents of cells in detergent after their disruption and found that among the contents of the cells, only the purified DNA was capable of causing the transformation. As
55 a result of these and future experiments, it was determined that in order for transformation to occur, DNA fragments entered the recipient cell intact and substituted in the bacterial chromosome for the original DNA, which was eliminated. This
60 process resulted in the creation of a genetically different microorganism.

DNA is a very long, fibrous molecule with a backbone composed of alternate sugar and phosphate groups joined by 3'-5'-phosphodiester
65 linkages. Attached to each sugar is one of four possible nitrogenous bases. There are two types of bases: the pyrimidines, cytosine (C) and thymine (T); and the purines, adenine (A) and guanine (G). The amount of purine equals the amount of
70 pyrimidine, and, more specifically, the amount of adenine equals the amount of thymine, and the amount of guanine equals the amount of cytosine.

In 1953, Watson and Crick proposed that DNA was made of two chains of nucleotides coiled
75 around a common axis, with the sugar-phosphate backbone on the outside and the bases pointing in toward the axis, and that the two chains were held together by hydrogen bonds. The hydrogen bonds occur between each base of one chain and an
80 associated base on the other chain. Based on the 20-angstrom width of the fiber, a pyrimidine from one chain is always paired with a purine from the other chain. Adenine is the only purine capable of bonding to thymine and guanine is the only purine capable
85 of bonding to cytosine.

Watson and Crick proposed that the information in DNA was coded for by the linear sequence of the base pairs. They theorized that a mutation could be accounted for by a chance
90 mistake in the formation of the sequence during duplication. Another major aspect of the Watson and Crick model was the proposed complementarity between hydrogen-bonded nucleotides. For example, adenine is complementary to thymine,
95 AGC is complementary to TCG, and one chain is complementary to the other. If the base sequence of

one chain is known, then the base sequence of the complementary chain can be derived. The concept of complementarity of nucleic acids in DNA and
100 RNA chains is the basis of most research in which these classes of molecules are involved.

Natural Science

126. Mendel conducted his studies using the method known as:

F. cloning.
G. genetic mapping.
H. cross-pollination.
J. transformation.

127. Mendel's findings were important because they indicated which of the following?

I. DNA fragments can replace original DNA.
II. Specific units, handed down from one generation to the next, govern traits in organisms.
III. Proteins are composed of approximately 20 different amino acids.

A. I only
B. II only
C. I and III only
D. I, II, and III

128. Contrary to earlier beliefs, Avery et al. discovered that:

F. there are only four nucleotides in DNA.
G. pneumonia can be passed from host to host.
H. genes can mutate.
J. DNA, not protein, carries genetic information.

129. If you infected R strain pneumococcus with S extract and saw a few R strain pneumococcus transformed to S strain, you would expect:

A. the remaining R strain pneumococcus to transform later.
B. only the new S strain cells to survive.
C. offspring of those transformed cells to be S strain as well.
D. a few S strain pneumococcus to transform to R strain.

130. The author uses the word *non-virulent* (line 43) to mean:

F. harmless.
G. toxic.
H. bacterial.
J. sweet.

131. In contrast to the paragraphs before, the fifth paragraph is intended primarily to:

A. give historical genetic research information .
B. describe the results of Mendel's experiments.
C. speculate on the future of genetic research.
D. provide a definition for an essential element in genetic research.

132. A chain of DNA with the pattern CAG would bond with a chain with the pattern:

F. GAC.
G. TGA.
H. GTC.
J. Cannot be determined from the given information

133. Which of the following is (are) classified as a purine?

    I.   Cytosine
   II.   Guanine
  III.   Thymine

  A. I only
  B. II only
  C. III only
  D. I and II only

134. Which of the following was Watson and Crick's contribution to the study of genetics?

    I.   Information about the transfer of genes across membranes
   II.   The notion that pairs of genes could work together
  III.   A suggestion about the structure of DNA

  F. I only
  G. II only
  H. III only
  J. I, II, and III

135. The concept of complementarity in DNA is apparently important because:

  A. it contradicts the notion that proteins are the basis for genetic transformation.
  B. hydrogen bonds connect the nucleotides.
  C. if maternally and paternally derived alleles were not complementary, life could not exist.
  D. if you know one chain's sequence, you can determine that of the other.

Passage XVII

Natural Science: This passage is adapted from a science magazine article about galaxies.

Galaxies come in a variety of sizes and shapes: majestic spirals, ruddy disks, elliptically shaped dwarfs and giants, and a menagerie of other, more bizarre forms. Most currently, popular theories
5   suggest that conditions prior to birth—mass of the protogalactic cloud, its size, its rotation—determine whether a galaxy will be large or small, spiral or elliptical; but about 10 percent of all galaxies are members of rich clusters of thousands of galaxies.
10 The gravitational forces of fields of nearby galaxies constantly distort galaxies in the crowded central region of rich clusters. In addition, rich clusters of galaxies are pervaded by a tenuous gas with a temperature of up to 100 million degrees. Galaxies
15 are blasted and scoured by a hot wind created by their motion through the gas. In crowded conditions such as these, environment becomes a more important determinant of the size and shape of a galaxy than heredity. In fact, if our galaxy had
20 happened to form well within the core of a cluster such as Virgo, the Sun would probably never have formed, because the Sun, a second- or third-generation star located in the disk of the galaxy, was formed from leftover gas five billion years or so
25 after the initial period of star formation. By that time, in a rich cluster, the galaxy may well have already been stripped of its gas.

As a galaxy moves through the core of a rich cluster, it is not only scoured by hot gas; it
30 encounters other galaxies as well. If the collision is one-on-one at moderate to high speeds of galaxies of approximately the same size, both galaxies will emerge relatively intact, if a little distorted and ragged about the edges. If, however, a galaxy coasts
35 by a much larger one in a slow, grazing collision, the smaller one can be completely disrupted and assimilated by the larger.

Under the right conditions, these cosmic cannibals can consume 50 to 100 galaxies. The
40 accumulative effect of these collisions is to produce a dynamic friction on the large galaxy, slowing it down. As a result, it gradually spirals in toward the center of the cluster. Eventually, the gravitational forces that bind the stars to the infalling galaxy are
45 overwhelmed by the combined gravity of the galaxies in the core of the cluster—just as the ocean is pulled away from the shore at ebb tide by the

Moon, the stars are pulled away from their infalling parent galaxy. If there is a large galaxy at the center
50 of the cluster, it may ultimately capture these stars. With the passage of time, many galaxies will be torn asunder in the depths of this gravitational maelstrom and be swallowed up in the ever-expanding envelope of the central cannibal galaxy.

55 Galactic cannibalism also explains why there are few if any bright galaxies in these clusters other than the central supergiant galaxy. That is because the bright galaxies, which are the most massive, experience the greatest dynamical friction. They are
60 the first to go down to the gravitational well and be swallowed up by the central galaxies.

Over the course of several billion years, 50 or so galaxies may be swallowed up, leaving only the central supergiant and the 51st, the 52nd, etc.,
65 brightest galaxies. Given time, all the massive galaxies in the cluster will be absorbed, leaving a sparse cluster of a supergiant galaxy surrounded by clouds of small, dim galaxies.

136. In line 3, the word *menagerie* most nearly means:

    F. odd mixture.
    G. open environment.
    H. uniform collection.
    J. flat area.

137. It can be inferred from the passage that the physical features of a galaxy that does not belong to a rich cluster are determined primarily by the:

    A. size and rotation of the protogalactic cloud.
    B. intensity of light emanating from the galaxy.
    C. temperature of the interstellar gas.
    D. age of the protogalactic cloud.

138. The author implies that the currently accepted theories on galaxy formation are:

    F. completely incorrect and misguided.
    G. naive and out-of-date.
    H. speculative and unsupported by observation.
    J. substantially correct but in need of modification.

139. According to the passage, a cluster with a central, supergiant galaxy will:

    A. contain no intermediately bright galaxies.
    B. have 50–100 galaxies of all sizes and intensities.
    C. consist solely of third- and fourth-generation stars.
    D. produce only spiral and disk-shaped galaxies.

140. According to the passage, the outcome of a collision between galaxies depends on:

    F. the relative velocities of the galaxies.
    G. the relative ages of the galaxies.
    H. the relative sizes of the galaxies.
    J. the relative velocities and sizes of the galaxies.

141. According to the passage, as a galaxy falls inward toward the center of a cluster, it:

    A. collides with the central core and emerges relatively intact.
    B. absorbs superheated gases from the interstellar medium.
    C. is broken apart by the gravitational forces of the core.
    D. is transformed by collisions into a large, spiral galaxy.

142. The passage provides information that will answer which of the following questions?

    F. What is the age of our sun?
    G. What proportion of all galaxies are found in clusters?
    H. Approximately how many galaxies would be found in a rich cluster?
    J. What type of galaxy is ours?

143. The tone of the passage can best be described as:

    A. light-hearted and amused.
    B. objective but engaged.
    C. detached and unconcerned.
    D. cautious but sincere.

Passage XVIII

Natural Science: This passage reviews the basic physical chemistry of atoms and radioactive decay.

An atom consists of a nucleus (containing protons and neutrons) surrounded by electrons. Each proton has a positive charge of +1, and each electron has a negative charge of −1. A neutron has
5 no charge. The number of protons in their nuclei determines the identities of the different elements. For example, hydrogen atoms have only one proton, while oxygen atoms have eight protons. The total number of protons in the nucleus is the "atomic
10 number" of that element. The total number of protons and neutrons in the nucleus is the "atomic mass" of the atom. Different atoms of the same element may contain a different number of neutrons, and so have different atomic masses. (But
15 they will have the same number of protons and the same atomic number.) Atoms of the same element with different atomic masses are called isotopes of that element.

Certain elements are radioactive—they emit
20 various types of radiation from their atomic nuclei. Two common types of radiation are alpha particles and beta particles. An alpha particle, which is the equivalent of a helium nucleus, consists of two protons and two neutrons. It is written $_2^4\text{He}$ (the
25 superscript 4 is the mass number of the particle, and the subscript 2 is its atomic number). A beta particle is an electron traveling at high speed. It is written $_{-1}^{0}\text{e}$. Both types of radiation are emitted at a very high speed and can easily penetrate other
30 substances.

When atoms of a substance emit radiation, they are said to undergo radioactive decay. The result is a different element with a different atomic number and a different mass number. For example,
35 when a radium atom emits an alpha particle, it decays into an atom of radon. This reaction is shown in the following equation:

$$_{88}^{226}\text{Ra} \rightarrow _2^4\text{He} + _{86}^{222}\text{Rn}$$

Note that the equation is balanced. That is, the
40 atomic number of the original atom on the left side of the equation equals the sum of the atomic numbers of the products on the right side of the equation. Similarly, the mass number of the original atom equals the sum of the mass numbers of the

45 products. Every nuclear reaction balances in this same manner.

Some types of nuclear radiation take place very slowly; other types are very rapid. The rate of radiation is measured in half-lives. A half-life is the
50 time required for one-half the amount of a given radioactive substance to decay.

144. As radium emits alpha particles, the mass of radium will:

   F. increase.
   G. decrease.
   H. stay the same.
   J. either increase or decrease, depending on the conditions.

145. In nuclear chemistry notation, two isotopes, or forms, of cobalt are written $_{27}^{59}\text{Co}$ and $_{27}^{60}\text{Co}$. The difference between the two isotopes is:

   A. an alpha particle.
   B. a beta particle.
   C. a proton.
   D. a neutron.

146. An alpha particle has:

   F. no electric charge.
   G. a positive electric charge.
   H. a negative electric charge.
   J. a variable electric charge.

147. A beta particle has:

   A. no electric charge.
   B. a positive electric charge.
   C. a negative electric charge.
   D. a variable electric charge.

148. When an atom emits a beta particle, the atomic mass number will:

   F. increase.
   G. decrease.
   H. stay the same.
   J. either increase or decrease, depending on the conditions.

QUIZZES

This section contains four Reading quizzes. Complete each quiz under timed conditions. Answers are on page 660.

Quiz I
(18 items; 15 minutes)

> **DIRECTIONS:** Each passage below is followed by a set of items. Read the passage and choose the best answer for each item. You may refer to the passage as often as necessary to answer the items.

Passage I

Social Science: This passage discusses the economic structure of current healthcare policy.

The healthcare economy is replete with unusual and even unique economic relationships. One of the least understood involves the peculiar roles of producer or "provider" and purchaser or
5 "consumer" in the typical doctor-patient relationship. In most sectors of the economy, the seller attempts to attract a potential buyer with various incentives of price, quality, and utility, and the buyer makes the decision. When the buyer has
10 no choice because there is effectively only one seller and the product is essential, the government usually asserts a monopoly and places the industry under price and other regulations. Neither of these conditions prevails in most of the healthcare
15 industry.

In the healthcare industry, the doctor-patient relationship is the mirror image of the ordinary relationship between producer and consumer. Once an individual has chosen to see a physician—and
20 even then there may be no real choice—it is the physician who usually makes all significant purchasing decisions: whether the patient should return "next Wednesday," whether X-rays are needed, whether drugs should be prescribed, etc. It
25 is a rare and sophisticated patient who will challenge such professional decisions or raise in advance questions about price, especially when the ailment is regarded as serious.

This is particularly significant in relation to
30 hospital care. The physician must certify the need for hospitalization, determine what procedures will be performed, and announce when the patient may be discharged. The patient may be consulted about some of these decisions, but ultimately it is the
35 doctor's judgments that are final. Little wonder, then, that in the eyes of the hospital, the physician is the real "consumer." Consequently, the medical staff represents the "power center" in hospital policy and decision-making, not the administration.

40 Although usually there are in this situation four identifiable participants—the physician, the hospital, the patient, and the payer (generally an insurance carrier or government)—the physician makes the key decisions for all of them. The hospital
45 becomes an extension of the physician; the payer generally meets most of the bona fide bills generated by the doctor/hospital; and for the most part the patient plays a passive role. In routine or minor illnesses, or just plain worries, the patient's
50 options are, of course, much greater with respect to use and price. In illnesses that are more serious, however, such choices tend to evaporate, and it is for these illnesses that the bulk of the healthcare dollar is spent. We estimate that 75 to 80 percent of
55 healthcare expenditures are determined by physicians, not patients. For this reason, economy measures directed at patients or the public are relatively ineffective.

1. In line 1, the phrase "replete with" most nearly means:

   A. filled with.
   B. restricted by.
   C. enriched by.
   D. damaged by.

2. The author's primary purpose is to:

   F. speculate about the relationship between a patient's ability to pay and the treatment received.

   G. criticize doctors for exercising too much control over patients.

   H. analyze some important economic factors in healthcare.

   J. urge hospitals to reclaim their decision-making authority.

3. It can be inferred that doctors are able to determine hospital policies because:

   A. it is doctors who generate income for the hospital.

   B. most of a patient's bills are paid by health insurance.

   C. hospital administrators lack the expertise to question medical decisions.

   D. a doctor is ultimately responsible for a patient's health.

4. According to the author, when a doctor tells a patient to "return next Wednesday," the doctor is in effect:

   F. taking advantage of the patient's concern for his health.

   G. instructing the patient to buy more medical services.

   H. warning the patient that a hospital stay might be necessary.

   J. advising the patient to seek a second opinion.

5. The author is most probably leading up to:

   A. a proposal to control medical costs.

   B. a discussion of a new medical treatment.

   C. an analysis of the causes of inflation in the United States.

   D. a study of lawsuits against doctors for malpractice.

6. The tone of the passage can best be described as:

   F. whimsical.

   G. cautious.

   H. analytical.

   J. inquisitive.

7. With which of the following statements would the author be most likely to agree?

   A. Few patients are reluctant to object to the course of treatment prescribed by a doctor or to question the cost of the services.

   B. The payer, whether an insurance carrier or the government, is less likely to acquiesce to demands for payment when the illness of the patient is regarded as serious.

   C. Today's patients are more informed as to what services and procedures they will need from their healthcare providers.

   D. The more serious the illness of a patient, the less likely it is that the patient will object to the course of treatment prescribed or question the cost of services.

8. The author's primary concern is to:

   F. define a term.

   G. clarify a misunderstanding.

   H. refute a theory.

   J. discuss a problem.

Passage II

Humanities: This passage discusses Leif Ericsson's and Biarni's voyages to North America.

In the summer of 999, Leif Ericsson voyaged to Norway and spent the following winter with King Olaf Tryggvason. Substantially the same account is given by both the Saga of Eric the Red and the Flat
5 Island Book. Of Leif's return voyage to Greenland, the latter says nothing. But according to the former, it was during this return voyage that Leif discovered America. The Flat Island Book, however, tells of another and earlier landfall by Biarni, the son of a
10 prominent man named Heriulf. It makes this trip Leif's inspiration for the voyage to the new land. In short, like Leif, Biarni and his companions discovered three countries in succession before reaching Greenland. To come upon each new land
15 takes one "doegr" more than the last until Biarni comes to land directly in front of his father's house in the last-mentioned country.

Most later writers have rejected this narrative, and they may be justified. Possibly, Biarni was a
20 companion of Leif when he voyaged from Norway to Greenland via America. Or it may be that the entire tale is but a garbled account of that voyage and Biarni is another name for Leif. It should be noted, however, that the stories of Leif's visit to King Olaf
25 and Biarni's to that king's predecessor are in the same narrative in the Flat Island Book. So there is less likelihood of duplication than if they were from different sources. Also, Biarni landed on none of the lands he passed, but Leif apparently landed on one,
30 for he brought back specimens of wheat, vines, and timber. Nor is there any good reason to believe that the first land visited by Biarni was Wineland. The first land was "level and covered with woods," and "there were small hillocks upon it." Later writers do
35 not emphasize forests particularly in connection with Wineland, though they are often noted incidentally; and of hills, the Saga says of Wineland only "wherever there was hilly ground, there were vines."

40 Additionally, if the two narratives were from the same source, we should expect a closer resemblance of Helluland. The Saga says of it: "They found there hellus" (large flat stones). According to the Biarni narrative, however, "this land was high
45 and mountainous." The intervals of one, two, three, and four "doegr" in both narratives are suggestive. But mythic formulas of this kind may be introduced into narratives without altogether destroying their validity. It is also held against the Biarni narrative
50 that its hero is made to come upon the coast of Greenland exactly in front of his father's home. But it should be recalled that Heriulfsness lay below two high mountains that served as landmarks for navigators.

55 I would give up Biarni more readily were it not that the story of Leif's voyage, contained in the supposedly more reliable Saga, is almost as amazing. But Leif's voyage across the entire width of the North Atlantic is said to be "probable"
60 because it is documented in the narrative of a preferred authority. Biarni's is "improbable," or even "impossible," because the document containing it has been condemned.

9. The author's primary concern is to demonstrate that:

A. Leif Ericsson did not visit America.
B. Biarni might have visited America before Leif Ericsson.
C. Biarni did not visit Wineland.
D. Leif Ericsson visited Wineland first.

10. The passage provides information that defines which of the following terms?

I. Doegr
II. Hellus
III. Heriulfsness

F. I only
G. II only
H. I and II only
J. II and III only

11. It can be inferred from the passage that scholars who doubt the authenticity of the Biarni narrative make all of the following objections EXCEPT:

    A. Biarni might have accompanied Leif Ericsson on the voyage to America, and that is why a separate, erroneous narrative was invented.
    B. the similarity of the voyages described in the Saga and in the Flat Island Book indicates that there was but one voyage, not two voyages.
    C. it seems very improbable that a ship, having sailed from America to Greenland, could have found its way to a precise point on the coast of Greenland.
    D. both the Saga of Eric the Red and the Flat Island Book make use of mythic formulas, so it is probable that the same person wrote them both.

12. The author mentions the two high mountains (lines 52–53) in order to show that it is:

    F. reasonable for Biarni to land precisely at his father's home.
    G. possible to sail from Norway to Greenland without modern navigational equipment.
    H. likely that Biarni landed on America at least 100 years before Leif Ericsson.
    J. probable that Leif Ericsson followed the same course as Biarni.

13. All of the following are mentioned as similarities between Leif Ericsson's voyage and Biarni's voyage EXCEPT:

    A. both visited Norway.
    B. on the return voyage, both visited three different lands.
    C. both returned to Greenland.
    D. both sighted Wineland.

14. It can be inferred that the author regards the historicity of the Biarni narrative as:

    F. conclusively proved.
    G. almost conclusively proved.
    H. possibly true.
    J. highly unlikely.

15. In the final paragraph, the author suggests that some authorities who regard the Saga as authentic are guilty of which of the following errors in reasoning?

    A. Oversimplification
    B. Logical contradiction
    C. False analogy
    D. Circular reasoning

16. According to the passage, Heriulf is:

    F. Leif Ericsson's son.
    G. one of Leif Ericsson's sailors.
    H. Biarni's father.
    J. King Olaf Tryggvason's son.

17. According to the author, most authorities regard the Biarni narrative as:

    A. conclusively demonstrated.
    B. probably true.
    C. probably untrue.
    D. an attempted fraud.

18. Biarni's home was in:

    F. Norway.
    G. Greenland.
    H. Wineland.
    J. Flat Island.

Quiz II

(17 items; 15 minutes)

> **DIRECTIONS:** Each passage below is followed by a set of items. Read the passage and choose the best answer for each item. You may refer to the passage as often as necessary to answer the items.

Passage I

Social Science: This passage discusses the 1796 presidential election between Thomas Jefferson and John Adams.

"Heartily tired" from the brutal, almost daily, conflicts that erupted between himself and Alexander Hamilton, Thomas Jefferson resigned his position as Secretary of State in 1793. His Federalist
5 opponents were convinced that this was merely a strategic withdrawal to allow him an opportunity to plan and promote his candidacy for the presidency should Washington step down in 1796. Jefferson, however, insisted that this retirement from public
10 life was to be final.

But even in retirement, the world of politics pursued him. As the election grew nearer and it became apparent that Washington would not seek a third term, rumors of Jefferson's presidential
15 ambitions grew in intensity. He reacted to these continuous insinuations in a letter to James Madison. Jefferson admitted that while his enemies had originated the idea that he coveted the office of chief executive, he had been forced to examine his
20 true feelings on the subject for his own peace of mind. In so doing, he concluded that his reasons for retirement—the desire for privacy and the delight of family life—coupled with his now failing health were insuperable barriers to public service. The
25 "little spice of ambition" he had in his younger days had long since evaporated and the question of his presidency was forever closed.

Jefferson did not actively engage in the campaign on his own behalf. The Republican Party,
30 presaging modern campaign tactics, created a grass roots sentiment for their candidate by directing their efforts toward the general populace. In newspapers, Jefferson was presented as "the uniform advocate of equal rights among the
35 citizens" while Adams was portrayed as the "champion of rank, titles, heredity, and distinctions."

Jefferson was not certain of the outcome of the election until the end of December. Under the original electoral system established by the
40 Constitution, each presidential elector cast his ballot for two men without designating between them as to office. The candidate who received the greater number of votes became the president; the second highest, the vice president. Based on his own
45 calculations, Jefferson foresaw that the electoral vote would be close. He wrote to Madison that in the event of a tie, he wished for the choice to be in favor of Adams. The New Englander had always been his senior in public office, he explained, and
50 the expression of public will being equal, he should be preferred for the higher honor. Jefferson, a shrewd politician, realized that the transition of power from the nearly mythical Washington to a lesser luminary in the midst of the deep and bitter
55 political divisions facing the nation could be perilous. He had no desire to be caught in the storm that had been brewing for four years and was about to break. "This is certainly not a moment to covet the helm," he wrote to Edward Rutledge. When the
60 electoral vote was tallied, Adams emerged as the victor. Rejoicing at his "escape," Jefferson was completely satisfied with the decision. Despite their obvious and basic political differences, Jefferson genuinely respected John Adams as a friend and
65 compatriot. Although he believed that Adams had deviated from the course set in 1776, Jefferson never felt a diminution of confidence in Adams' integrity and was confident he would not steer the nation too far off its Republican tack. Within two
70 years, Jefferson's views would be drastically altered as measures such as the Alien and Sedition Acts of 1798 convinced him of the need to wrest control of the government from the Federalists.

1. The phrase "heartily tired" (line 1) is most probably a quotation from:

   A. Alexander Hamilton.
   B. Thomas Jefferson.
   C. George Washington.
   D. John Adams.

2. The "escape" mentioned in line 61 refers to the fact that Jefferson:

   F.   was no longer Secretary of State.
   G.   would not be burdened with the problems of the presidency.
   H.   fled the country following the election.
   J.   was hoping that the votes would be recounted.

3. According to the passage, the Republican Party appealed primarily to:

   A.   wealthy landowners.
   B.   ordinary people.
   C.   prosperous merchants.
   D.   high society.

4. The author states that all of the following were reasons Jefferson resigned as Secretary of State EXCEPT:

   F.   Jefferson disliked Madison.
   G.   Jefferson wanted to spend time with his family.
   H.   Jefferson was weary of the demands of public service.
   J.   Jefferson wished for greater privacy.

5. The author is primarily concerned with revealing:

   A.   the feud between Alexander Hamilton and Thomas Jefferson.
   B.   the difference between the Federalists and the Republicans.
   C.   the strategies used by early American political parties.
   D.   Thomas Jefferson's character and personality.

6. The author relies on which of the following in developing the selection?

   I.   Personal correspondence
   II.   Newspapers
   III.   Voter registration rolls

   F.   I only
   G.   II only
   H.   I and II only
   J.   I and III only

7. One reason for Jefferson's retirement was his disagreement with:

   A.   Alexander Hamilton.
   B.   George Washington.
   C.   James Madison.
   D.   Edward Rutledge.

8. In the context of the passage, the phrase "covet the helm" (lines 58–59) means:

   F.   to aspire to be President.
   G.   to desire to purchase a boat.
   H.   to wish to be left in peace.
   J.   to hope to become wealthy.

9. The passage suggests that two years after the 1796 election, Jefferson would:

   A.   ally himself with Alexander Hamilton.
   B.   ally himself with John Adams.
   C.   disagree with John Adams.
   D.   disagree with Edward Rutledge.

10. The newspaper depicted Jefferson and Adams as:

   F.   conservative and liberal, respectively.
   G.   liberal and conservative, respectively.
   H.   conservatives.
   J.   liberals.

Passage II

Natural Science: This passage discusses human social evolution and adaptation.

Man, so the truism goes, lives increasingly in a man-made environment. This puts a special burden on human immaturity, for it is plain that adapting to such variable conditions must depend on
5 opportunities for learning, or whatever the processes are that are operative during immaturity. It must also mean that during immaturity, man must master knowledge and skills that are neither stored in the gene pool nor learned by direct
10 encounter. Rather, they are contained in the culture pool—knowledge about values and history, skills as varied as an obligatory natural language or an optional mathematical one, as mute as levers or as articulate as myth telling.

15 Yet, it would be a mistake to leap to the conclusion that because human immaturity makes possible high flexibility, anything is possible for the species. Human traits were selected for their survival value over a four- to five-million-year
20 period with a great acceleration of the selection process during the last half of that period. There were crucial, irreversible changes during that final man-making period: the recession of formidable dentition, a 50-percent increase in brain volume,
25 the obstetrical paradox—bipedalism and strong pelvic girdle, larger brain through a smaller birth canal—an immature brain at birth, and creation of what Washburn has called a "technical-social way of life," involving tool and symbol use.

30 Note, however, that hominidization consisted mainly of adaptations to conditions in the Pleistocene. These preadaptations, shaped in response to earlier habitat demands, are part of man's evolutionary inheritance. This is not to say
35 that close beneath the skin of man is a naked ape, that civilization is only a veneer. The technical-social way of life is a deep feature of the species adaptation. But we would err if we assumed that man's inheritance placed no constraint on his
40 power to adapt. Some of the preadaptations can be shown to be presently maladaptive. Man's inordinate fondness for fats and sweets no longer serves his individual survival well. Furthermore, the human obsession with sexuality is plainly not fitted
45 for survival of the species now, however well it might have served to populate the upper Pliocene and the Pleistocene. Nevertheless, note that the species typically responds to these challenges by technical innovation rather than by morphological
50 or behavioral change. Contraception dissociates sexuality from reproduction. Of course, we do not know what kinds and what range of stresses are produced by successive rounds of such technical innovation. Dissociating sexuality and reproduction,
55 for example, surely produces changes in the structure of the family, which in turn redefines the role of women, which in turn alters the authority pattern affecting the child, etc. Continuing and possibly accelerating change seems inherent in such
60 adaptation. This, of course, places an enormous pressure on man's uses of immaturity, preparing the young for unforeseeable change—more so if there are severe restraints imposed by human preadaptations to earlier conditions of life.

11. The primary purpose of the passage is to:

A. refute some misconceptions about the importance of human immaturity.
B. introduce a new theory of the origins of the human species.
C. describe the evolutionary forces that formed the physical appearance of modern humans.
D. discuss the importance of human immaturity as an adaptive mechanism.

12. It can be inferred that the obstetrical paradox is puzzling because:

F. it occurred very late during the evolution of the species.
G. evolutionary forces seemed to work at cross purposes to each other.
H. technological innovations have made the process of birth easier.
J. an increase in brain size is not an ordinary evolutionary event.

13. Which of the following statements can be inferred from the passage?

    A. Human beings are today less sexually active than were our ancestors during the Pleistocene era.

    B. During the Pleistocene era, a fondness for fats and sweets was a trait that contributed to human survival.

    C. Mathematics was invented by human beings during the latter half of the Pleistocene era.

    D. The use of language and tools is a trait that is genetically transmitted from one generation to the next.

14. As it is used in line 32, the word *preadaptations* refers to traits that:

    F. were useful to earlier human beings but have since lost their utility.

    G. appeared in response to the need to learn a natural language and the use of tools.

    H. humans currently exhibit but that developed in response to conditions of an earlier age.

    J. are disadvantageous to creatures whose way of life is primarily technical and social.

15. The author mentions contraception to demonstrate that:

    A. human beings may adapt to new conditions by technological invention rather than by changing their behavior.

    B. sexual promiscuity is no longer an aid to the survival of the human species.

    C. technological innovation is a more important adaptive mechanism than either heredity or direct encounter.

    D. conditions during the upper Pliocene and Pleistocene eras no longer affect the course of human evolution.

16. With which of the following statements would the author LEAST likely agree?

    F. The technical-social way of human life is an adaptive mechanism that arose in response to environmental pressures.

    G. The possibility of technical innovation makes it unlikely that the physical appearance of humans will change radically in a short time.

    H. Technological innovations can result in changes in the social structures in which humans live.

    J. The fact that humans have a technical-social way of life makes the species immune from evolutionary pressures.

17. The author is most probably addressing which of the following audiences?

    A. Medical students in a course on human anatomy

    B. College students in an introductory course on archaeology

    C. Psychologists investigating the uses of human immaturity

    D. Biologists trying to trace the course of human evolution

Quiz III

(18 items; 15 minutes)

> **DIRECTIONS:** Each passage below is followed by a set of items. Read the passage and choose the best answer for each item. You may refer to the passage as often as necessary to answer the items.

Passage I

Social Science: The following passages are excerpts from two different sources that discuss particular approaches to history.

Passage A

As Carl Hempel demonstrates in his seminal essay "The Function of General Laws in History," a general law plays the same role in both history and the natural sciences. According to Hempel's

5 deductive-nomological model, proper scientific explanation—whether for history or the natural sciences—includes three sorts of statements:

(A) A set of statements about conditions (that can be designated as C1, C2, and so on) that are true

10 at a particular place and time.

(B) A set of universal hypotheses connecting events of type C with events of type E.

(C) A statement asserting that E is logically deducible from the statements of A and B.

15 The "C" events are, of course, causes, while the "E" events are effects. Given a sufficiently precise description of background conditions by Set A and an adequately articulated set of empirical laws in Set B, a conclusion such as "A popular uprising

20 overthrew the government" can be logically deduced with as much certainty as that of a syllogism.*

The notion that a historian cannot study past events in the same way that a chemist studies

25 reactions or a physicist studies falling objects is due to a misunderstanding. Historical explanations intentionally omit from Set A statements about human nature that are well-known to the sciences of psychology and sociology because they are too

30 numerous to mention. Further, many of the general laws used by historians do not seem susceptible to

easy confirmation in the way that laboratory experiments are. It is difficult to find a sufficiently large number of revolutions to assess the validity of

35 the assertion that a drop of a certain magnitude in a population's standard of living will inevitably be followed by revolution.

Thus, we should more accurately speak not of scientific explanations of historical events but of

40 "sketches" of history. This terminology would call attention to the incompleteness and the imprecision in historical explanation, while at the same time reminding us that the form of explanation is the same as that of the natural sciences.

*A syllogism is a form of reasoning in which a conclusion is drawn from two statements:

> Major Premise: All ruminants are quadrupeds.
> Minor Premise: All cows are ruminants.
> Conclusion: Therefore, all cows are quadrupeds.

Passage B

45 The obvious distinction between history and the natural sciences is that history is concerned with human actions. The historian makes a distinction between what may be called the outside and the inside of an event. The outside of the event

50 is everything belonging to it that can be described in terms of bodies and their movements: the passage of Caesar across a river called the Rubicon on a certain date or the spilling of Caesar's blood on the senate-house floor on another. The inside of the

55 event can only be described in terms of thought: Caesar's defiance of Republican law or the clash of constitutional policy between Caesar and Caesar's assassins. The historian is not investigating mere events (a mere event is one that has only an outside

60 and no inside) but actions, and an action is the unity of the outside and inside of an event.

The task of the historian is thus distinguished from that of the natural scientist in two ways. On the one hand, the historian must undertake an

65 additional investigation that is neither needed by nor available to the natural scientist. The historian must inquire after the "why" of an event, that is, the thought behind it. On the other hand, the task of the historian is somewhat simpler than that of the

70 natural scientist because once that question has been answered there is no further question to be raised.

There is no reason to look behind the thought associated with the event for a supervening general law.

75 Since the questions that the historian asks are different from those posed by the natural scientist, the historian will employ a different method. The historian penetrates to the inner aspect of the event by the technique of *Verstehen*.* To be sure, the
80 historian will study whatever documents and other physical evidence are available, but these are important only insofar as they provide an access to the inside of the event.

A purely physical event can only be
85 understood as a particular occurrence governed by a universal or general law, but the inside of an event is a thought—unique, and as such, not subject to a law-like explanation. Nor is this reason for disappointment. It is not the case that there are
90 historical laws but the techniques just do not yet exist to find them. Rather, the laws just do not exist to be found. To expect to find causal explanation in history and to demand of history predictions about the course of future events is an illegitimate
95 expectation conceived and fostered by the false analogy of history to the natural sciences and the incorrect assumption that the natural sciences are the paradigm for all human knowledge.

The positivist will object that this means that
100 history is, in principle, less rigorous than natural science, but this objection ignores the point that there simply are no historical laws to be discovered. In fact, because an historical event has both an inside and an outside, it is the events of natural
105 science that are, in a sense, deficient. As R. G. Collingwood wrote so boldly in the concluding section of *The Idea of History*, "Natural science...depends on historical thought for its existence." In history, there are no general scientific
110 laws to be uncovered, and the search for them is the foolish pursuit of a will-o'-the-wisp that exists only in the fables of positivist literature.

Verstehen is the German word for "understanding."

1. As used in line 5, the word "nomological" most nearly means:

   A. law-like.
   B. historical.
   C. accurate.
   D. logical.

2. In line 18, the phrase "adequately articulated" means:

   F. verbally presented.
   G. only preliminary.
   H. confidently denoted.
   J. sufficiently detailed.

3. In the second paragraph of Passage A, the author suggests that a series of historical events could serve the same scientific function as:

   A. eyewitness accounts.
   B. general laws.
   C. laboratory experiments.
   D. historical sketches.

4. According to the author of Passage A, it is difficult to formulate a general historical law about revolution because:

   F. revolutions, by definition, involve the overthrow of an existing government.
   G. too few revolutions are available for study to yield valid conclusions.
   H. details about a revolution are generally only known to a few key participants.
   J. historical events ordinarily involve a large number of unidentified actors.

5. The attitude of the author of Passage A toward psychology and sociology is one of:

   A. skepticism.
   B. indifference.
   C. confidence.
   D. outrage.

6. Passage A is primarily an argument against the position that:

   F. revolutions are caused by factors that can be identified.

   G. history is not a science like physics or chemistry.

   H. science is an undertaking requiring the use of logic.

   J. history is more important than the physical sciences.

7. Passage B explains that the technique of *Verstehen* is used to enable the historian to study:

   A. the outside of historical events.

   B. motives and intentions of historical actors.

   C. psychology and sociology.

   D. historical laws.

8. The author of Passage A and the author of Passage B would be most likely to agree with which of the following statements?

   F. Psychology and sociology use the same methodology as the natural sciences.

   G. Scientific historians should construct their explanations in the same way that the physicist does.

   H. The inability of historians to conduct laboratory testing shows that history is not a science.

   J. Events that have no element of thought are governed by law-like regularities.

Passage II

Natural Science: This passage reviews the basic physics of electromagnetic waves, specifically radar.

Whether used to control airplane traffic, detect speeding automobiles, or track a hurricane, radar is a very useful tool. Developed during World War II, this technology allows for remote sensing, that is,
5   locating objects that are not seen directly. The word "radar" is a contraction of "radio detection and ranging." It works in much the same way as an echo. When you shout toward a cliff or a large building, part of the sound bounces back. In radar, waves of
10   electromagnetic radiation are sent out. When they strike an object, they bounce back and are picked up by a receiver. The returning signal indicates the direction of the object; the time it takes for the signal to return indicates the distance to the object.
15   Radar waves detect objects by their varying densities. They are not deflected by atmospheric layers and therefore always travel in a straight line—in all weather, both day and night.

Radar waves are electromagnetic waves, as are
20   light waves, electric waves, X-rays, cosmic rays, and radio waves. All electromagnetic waves travel at 300,000 kilometers per second—the speed of light. Waves differ from each other in the number of times they vibrate per second; this variable is
25   known as frequency and is usually expressed as cycles per second. Waves also differ in their size, or wavelength. The speed, frequency, and wavelength of a wave are related by the wave equation in which:

30       $\text{speed} = \text{frequency} \cdot \text{wavelength}$

This shows that the product of the frequency and wavelength of any given wave is always a constant—the speed of light. To find the wavelength of a wave, knowing the frequency, this formula is
35   used:

$$\text{wavelength} = \frac{\text{speed}}{\text{frequency}}$$

For example, if a radio station broadcasts waves at 600,000 cycles per second (cps), the wavelength would be calculated this way:

40   $\text{wavelength} = \dfrac{300{,}000 \text{ km per sec}}{600{,}000 \text{ cps}} = 0.5 \text{ km} = 500 \text{ m}$

If the frequency of the wave is doubled to 1,200,000 cycles per second, its wavelength would be cut in half to 250 meters. Since frequencies are so high, the unit "megahertz" is usually used;
45   1 megahertz $= 1{,}000{,}000$ cycles per second.

Wavelengths within the electromagnetic spectrum vary greatly. Radar has wavelengths that measure from approximately one centimeter (0.01 meters) up to one meter. Each kind of wave has a
50   range of wavelengths. The table compares some sample wavelengths of several kinds of electromagnetic waves.

TYPE OF WAVE (METERS)	SAMPLE WAVELENGTH
cosmic rays	0.0000000000000001
X-rays	0.0000000001
ultraviolet rays	0.00000001
visible light	0.000001
infrared heat	0.0001
microwaves	0.001
radar	0.1
television	1.0
radio	100
long radio waves	10,000
electric power	1,000,000

9. Radio waves and radar waves have the same:

    A. frequency.
    B. wavelength.
    C. cycles per second.
    D. speed.

10. A radar signal having a frequency of 3,000 megahertz would have a wavelength of:

    F. 0.001 km.
    G. 0.01 km.
    H. 10 m.
    J. 0.1 m.

11. A radar set could not locate an airplane if it were flying:

    A. faster than the speed of sound.
    B. above a heavy storm.
    C. above the atmosphere.
    D. below the horizon.

12. It is possible to find the distance to an object from a radar set because the:

    F.   wavelength of radar is known.
    G.   frequency of radar is known.
    H.   speed of radar is 300,000 kilometers per second.
    J.   set operates at 10 megahertz.

13. The relationship between the frequency and wavelength of a wave is:

    A.   constant.
    B.   directly proportional.
    C.   exponential.
    D.   inverse.

14. An antenna picks up a signal that has a wavelength of about one meter. It is likely to be:

    F.   in the visible spectrum.
    G.   an ultraviolet ray.
    H.   a television signal.
    J.   an X-ray.

15. Radio waves will not penetrate the ionosphere, but microwaves will. Would you expect X-rays to penetrate the ionosphere?

    A.   Yes, because they have a shorter wavelength than microwaves and radio waves.
    B.   Yes, because they have a lower frequency than microwaves and radio waves.
    C.   No, because they travel more slowly than microwaves.
    D.   No, because they have fewer cycles per second than microwaves or radio waves.

16. Compared to cosmic rays, the frequency value of visible light waves is:

    F.   higher.
    G.   lower.
    H.   the same.
    J.   Cannot be determined from the given information

17. Which of the following factors would be most important in order for radar to detect and track storms?

    A.   Radar signals travel in straight lines.
    B.   The densities of moist air masses are different from those of dry air masses.
    C.   The atmosphere does not deflect radar signals.
    D.   Radar signals travel much faster than storms.

18. Like a radar reflection, an echo can be used to determine the distance of an object. This must be because:

    F.   sound is a form of radar.
    G.   sound travels at a relatively fixed rate.
    H.   sound waves have different frequencies.
    J.   sound waves are invisible.

Quiz IV Brain Buster
(29 items; 30 minutes)

DIRECTIONS: Each passage below is followed by a set of items. Read the passage and choose the best answer for each item. You may refer to the passage as often as necessary to answer the items.

Passage I

Social Science: This passage discusses agricultural policy during Franklin D. Roosevelt's presidency.

President Roosevelt's administration suffered a devastating defeat when, on January 6, 1936, the Agricultural Adjustment Act of 1933 was declared unconstitutional. New Deal planners quickly pushed
5 through Congress the Soil Conservation and Domestic Allotment Act of 1935, one purpose of which was conservation. It also aimed to control surpluses by retiring land from production. The law was intended as a stopgap measure until the
10 administration could formulate a permanent farm program that would satisfy both the nation's farmers and the Supreme Court. Roosevelt's landslide victory over Landon in 1936 obscured the ambivalent nature of his support in the farm states.
15 Despite extensive government propaganda, many farmers still refused to participate in the Agricultural Adjustment Administration's voluntary production control programs. The burdensome surpluses of 1933 were gone not as the result of the
20 AAA, but as a consequence of great droughts.

In February of 1937, Secretary of Agriculture Wallace convened a meeting of farm leaders to promote the concept of the ever normal granary. This policy would encourage farmers to store crop
25 surpluses (rather than dump them on the market) until grain was needed in years of small harvests. The Commodity Credit Corporation would grant loans to be repaid when the grain was later sold for a reasonable profit. The conference chose the
30 Committee of Eighteen, which drafted a bill. However, the major farm organizations were divided. Since ten of the eighteen members were also members of the American Farm Bureau Federation, the measure was quickly labeled a Farm
35 Bureau bill, and there were protests from the small, but highly vocal, Farmer's Holiday Association. When debate on the bill began, Roosevelt himself was vague and elusive. He didn't move the proposed legislation into the "desirable" category until
40 midsummer. In addition, there were demands that the New Deal's deficit spending be curtailed. Opponents of the bill charged that the AAA was wasteful and primarily benefited corporations and large scale farmers.

45 The Soil Conservation and Domestic Allotment Act had failed to limit agricultural production as the administration had hoped. Farm prices and consumer demand were high, and many farmers, convinced that the drought had ended the need for
50 crop controls, refused to participate in the AAA's soil conservation program. Without direct crop controls, agricultural production skyrocketed in 1937. By late summer there was panic in the farm belt that prices would again be driven down to
55 disastrously low levels. Congressmen began to pressure Roosevelt to place a floor under farm prices by making loans through the CCC. However, Roosevelt made such loans contingent upon the willingness of Congress to support the
60 administration's plan for a new system of crop controls. When the price of cotton began to drop, Roosevelt's adroit political maneuver finally forced congressional representatives from the South to agree to support a bill providing for crop controls
65 and the ever normal granary. The following year Congress passed the Agricultural Adjustment Act of 1938.

1. The primary purpose of the passage is to:

   A. analyze the connection between changes in weather conditions and the movement of agricultural prices.

   B. call attention to the economic hardship suffered by farmers during the 1930s.

   C. pinpoint the weaknesses of the agricultural policies of Roosevelt's New Deal.

   D. describe the events that led to the passage of the Agricultural Adjustment Act of 1938.

2. Which of the following is NOT a statement made by the author about the Soil Conservation and Domestic Allotment Act?

   F. It was intended to be a temporary measure.
   G. It aimed at reducing agricultural production.
   H. It aimed at soil conservation.
   J. It was drafted primarily by the Farm Bureau.

3. According to the passage, the Roosevelt administration wanted agricultural legislation with all of the following characteristics EXCEPT:

   A. it would not be declared unconstitutional by the Supreme Court.
   B. it would provide for direct control of agricultural production.
   C. it would dismantle the Agricultural Adjustment Administration.
   D. it would provide loans to help farmers store surplus grain.

4. According to the passage, all of the following were impediments to the passage of the Agricultural Adjustment Act of 1938 EXCEPT:

   F. initial lack of clear Presidential support.
   G. prosperity enjoyed by the nation's farmers.
   H. opposition to the idea of a Farm Bureau bill.
   J. doubts about the constitutionality of the bill.

5. The author implies which of the following conclusions?

   A. Roosevelt's ability to gain passage of the Agricultural Adjustment Act of 1938 depended on the large harvests of 1937.
   B. Secretary of Agriculture Wallace alienated members of the American Farm Bureau Federation by proposing an ever normal granary.
   C. The Agricultural Adjustment Act of 1933 was declared unconstitutional because it was written by the Farm Bureau.
   D. The Commodity Credit Corporation was created to offer farmers incentives for taking land out of production.

6. It can be inferred from the passage that the Farmer's Holiday Association opposed the bill drafted by the Committee of Eighteen because:

   F. the bill was not strongly supported by President Roosevelt.
   G. the Farmer's Holiday Association opposed the American Farm Bureau Federation.
   H. the Roosevelt administration had incurred excessive debt to finance its New Deal.
   J. its membership consisted primarily of large-scale farmers.

7. It can be inferred that loans granted by the Commodity Credit Corporation would encourage farmers to store surplus grain by:

   A. providing farmers a financial incentive to take arable land out of production.
   B. implementing a comprehensive program of mandatory soil conservation practices.
   C. conditioning financial assistance on a promise to participate in the Agricultural Adjustment Administration's program.
   D. relieving farmers of the need to sell grain in order to obtain immediate cash.

8. The passage provides information that would help answer which of the following questions?

I. Who was Secretary of Agriculture during Roosevelt's second term?
II. Who was Roosevelt's major opponent in the 1936 Presidential election?
III. Who was President of the American Farm Bureau Federation in 1937?

F. I only
G. II only
H. I and II only
J. I and III only

9. Which of the following best describes the author's treatment of Roosevelt's farm policies?

A. Scholarly but appreciative
B. Objective but critical
C. Analytical but abrasive
D. Biased and condemnatory

Passage II

Natural Science: This passage discusses the development of medical views on alcoholism.

The present day view of alcoholism as a physical disease was not a scientific discovery; it is a medical thesis that has developed only slowly over the past 200 years and amidst considerable
5 controversy. Historically, the moral perspective of the Judeo-Christian tradition has been that excessive use of alcohol is a willful act, one that leads to intoxication and other sinful behavior; but in the early nineteenth century, Benjamin Rush, a
10 founder of American psychiatry, proposed that "The habit of drunkenness is a disease of the will." By the late nineteenth century, physicians generally viewed the habitual use of drugs such as opiates, tobacco, and coffee as a generic disorder stemming
15 from biological vulnerability, either inherited or acquired.

Prohibition represented a triumph of the older morality over a modern medical concept. Where physicians who championed the disease concept of
20 alcoholism emphasized the need for treatment, the Temperance Movement stressed that alcohol itself was the cause of drunkenness and advocated its control and later its prohibition. Scientific interest in alcoholism, dampened by Prohibition, revived
25 toward the middle of the twentieth century. This resurgence was not due to any new scientific findings but because of humanitarian efforts to shift the focus from blame and punishment to treatment and concern.

30 The early 1960s witnessed a growing acceptance of the notion that, in certain "vulnerable" people, alcohol use leads to physical addiction—a true disease. Central to this concept of alcoholism as a disease were the twin notions of
35 substance tolerance and physical dependence. Both are physical phenomena. Substance tolerance occurs when increased doses of a drug are required to produce effects previously attained at lower doses; physical dependence refers to the occurrence
40 of withdrawal symptoms, such as seizures, following cessation of a drinking bout. In 1972, the National Council on Alcoholism outlined criteria for diagnosing alcoholism. These criteria emphasized alcohol tolerance and physical dependence. They
45 treated alcoholism as an independent disorder, not merely as part of a more general and underlying personality disorder.

In 1977, a World Health Organization report challenged this disease model by pointing out that not everyone who has alcohol related problems has true alcohol dependence. This distinction between dependence and other drug related problems that do not involve dependence was not immediately accepted by the American Psychiatric Association. The early drafts of the 1980 edition of its *Diagnostic and Statistical Manual of Mental Disorders* described a dependence syndrome for alcohol and other drugs in which tolerance and dependence were important, but not essential, criteria for diagnosis. At the last moment, however, the inertia of history prevailed; tolerance and dependence were both included not as necessary to diagnose dependence but as sufficient indicators in and of themselves.

It was not until 1993 that the American Psychiatric Association changed this position. In the fourth edition of the *Manual*, tolerance and withdrawal symptoms are the first two of seven criteria listed for diagnosing alcohol and other drug dependence. However, the clinician is not required to find whether either is present or to what degree in order to make the diagnosis.

Despite the consensus among professionals, we should not forget that the moral perspective on alcoholism is still very much alive. It perhaps does not surprise us that the Reverend J.E. Todd wrote an essay entitled "Drunkenness a Vice, Not a Disease" in 1882. But we should be concerned that the book *Heavy Drinking: The Myth of Alcoholism as a Disease* was published in 1988. Even as late as the mid-1970s, sociologists were reporting that the term "alcoholic" was commonly used in the United States as a synonym for "drunkard," rather than as a name for someone with an illness or a disorder. Apparently, in the mind of the general public, the contradictory notions of alcoholism as a disease and as a moral weakness can coexist quite comfortably.

10. The author's primary concern is to:

F. refute the notion that drunkenness is a serious social problem.

G. argue that alcoholism is less serious than it was 200 years ago.

H. explain the evolution of the idea that alcoholism is a disease.

J. give an example of the way that medical terminology changes over time.

11. According to the passage, members of the Temperance Movement:

A. agreed with doctors that alcohol abuse was a serious problem.

B. agreed with doctors that the solution to alcohol abuse was treatment.

C. agreed with doctors that drunkenness should be treated as a disease.

D. disagreed with doctors that alcoholism was a serious problem.

12. The author mentions Benjamin Rush in order to:

F. mark the beginning of the concept of alcoholism as a disease.

G. highlight the seriousness of habitual use of certain drugs.

H. discredit a central tenet of the religious view of alcoholism.

J. encourage physicians to treat alcoholism as a physical disease.

13. It can be inferred that the concepts of tolerance and dependence helped to establish the disease model of alcoholism because they:

A. prove that alcoholism is not a manifestation of a fundamental personality disorder.

B. are necessary but not sufficient findings to diagnose alcoholism.

C. demonstrate that alcohol abuse is similar to abuse of opiates and other drugs.

D. are evidence of physical addiction, which is an affliction of the body.

14. The author regards the essay "Drunkenness a Vice, Not a Disease" as:

F. misguided and dangerous.
G. incorrect and harmful.
H. insightful and beneficial.
J. outdated but harmless.

15. The author implies that all of the following are true EXCEPT:

A. the long held view that alcoholism is a moral problem has finally been totally discredited.
B. historically, alcoholism has been regarded as a weakness of the will rather than a disease.
C. in modern times, the medical community has disagreed over the exact definition of alcoholism.
D. the medical profession may make terminological distinctions that are not understood by the general population.

16. According to the fourth paragraph, the draft versions of the 1980 *Diagnostic and Statistical Manual of Mental Disorders* were similar to the final 1993 version in that they:

F. listed tolerance and dependence as both necessary and sufficient conditions for the diagnosis of alcoholism.
G. did not specify tolerance and dependence as essential elements of alcoholism.
H. suggested that alcoholism might be a generic, biological disorder.
J. argued that viewing alcoholism as a disease might actually encourage drunkenness.

17. With which of the following statements would the author most likely agree?

A. Shifting public opinion will force physicians to return to the view that alcoholism is a moral weakness.
B. A physician should not make a finding of alcoholism in a patient in the absence of either tolerance or dependence.
C. The decision to classify a problem as a disease depends in part on whether it is susceptible to medical treatment.
D. New scientific findings on the workings of tolerance and dependence warranted a shift to the disease model of alcoholism.

Passage III

Humanities: This passage discusses the political thought of James Burnham.

Most thinkers have distinguished three political entities: the individual, society, and state. It is normal to begin with the individual and then to consider society as the embodiment of his nature as
5 a social being. Thus, the individual is considered to be both logically and historically prior to society. Furthermore, society is considered both logically and historically prior to the state. But in James Burnham's vision of the future state, the priority of
10 the individual over the state is inverted. Burnham changed his mind on many points of detail between one book and the next, partly because he thought that what was happening in world politics at any given moment was decisive. But his general sense of
15 the form political power would take didn't move far from the version of it he gave in *The Managerial Revolution*. In that book he predicted that the weaknesses of capitalism would eventually prove fatal. However, he thought the downfall of
20 capitalism would not be the victory of the people followed by a Marxist paradise. Instead, capitalism would be replaced by an autocracy even more extreme than that in Stalin's Russia. Under this autocracy, the instruments of production would be
25 controlled by the state. The state, in turn, would be controlled by a ruling elite of managers.

Burnham argued that managers would control the instruments of production in their own corporate favor. The economy of state ownership
30 would provide the basis for domination and exploitation by a ruling class to an extreme never before known. The masses would be curbed or constantly diverted so that they would, as we say, go along with the managerial order. Also in
35 Burnham's future state, history has come to an end. Existence has removed itself from historical process and become pure essence, its attributes those of official meaning. Perfection is defined as the state of being in complete accordance with the terms
40 prescribed for it by the state, much as a proposition in logic or a theorem in mathematics might be faultless.

In *We*, Yevgeny Zamyatin envisaged a one-world state. Burnham allowed for three states.
45 Three superstates would divide the world between them and would enter into shifting alliances with one another. In 1941, Burnham thought the three would be the United States, Europe, and Japan. The superpowers would wage war over territory. The
50 Burnham said, "These wars will be directed from each base for the conquest of the other bases. But it does not seem possible for any one of these to conquer the others. Even two of them in coalition could not win a lasting victory over the third."

55 By 1947, many of Burnham's predictions had already proved false, a result of his tendency to assume that present conditions would persist unchanged; but a more damning indictment of his vision is the hypocrisy concealed behind the attack
60 on power. Burnham was infatuated with the image of totalitarianism; he was fascinated by the power he attacked. He despised the democracy he should have defended. Ultimately, Burnham voiced the secret desire of the English intelligentsia to destroy
65 the old, egalitarian version of Socialism and usher in a new hierarchical society in which the intellectual could at last get his hands on the whip.

18. The author's treatment of James Burnham's writing can best be described as:

F. analytical and condemnatory.
G. insightful and neutral.
(H.) speculative and jaded.
J. cynical and detached.

19. The statement that Burnham inverted the logical priority of the individual over the state means that Burnham believed that:

A. people are seen as aspects of the state and not as individuals.
(B.) history culminated in the existence of an all-powerful government.
C. individuals can reach perfection only as social beings.
D. the existence of individuals can be deduced from the existence of a state.

20. The author criticizes Burnham for:

   F. extrapolating from existing political and social conditions.
   G. failing to show how a totalitarian state could evolve from a democracy.
   H. thinking that democracy is a form of government superior to oligarchy.
   J. reversing the normal relationship between the individual and society.

21. According to Burnham, in the completely autocratic state, history will have come to an end because:

   A. the state will define the social forms to which individuals must conform.
   B. the means of production will be controlled by a managerial elite.
   C. no one superpower will be able to wage war successfully against any other superpower.
   D. individuals will be diverted from a study of past events by the state.

22. The author's primary concern is to:

   F. present his own vision of the future.
   G. prove someone else's predictions were wrong.
   H. critique a political theory.
   J. criticize a literary style.

23. The passage supports which of the following conclusions about the writings of Yevgeny Zamyatin?

   I. They are in large part derivative of the works of James Burnham.
   II. They describe a future society in which the state is all-powerful.
   III. The descriptions they contain are based on conditions that existed at the time they were written.

   A. I only
   B. II only
   C. I and II only
   D. II and III only

Passage IV

Natural Science: This passage describes a meteorite that may have originated on Mars.

Meteorite ALH84001 is a member of a family of meteorites, half of which were found in Antarctica, that are believed to have originated on Mars. Oxygen isotopes, as distinctive as fingerprints,
5 link these meteorites and clearly differentiate them from any Earth rock or other kind of meteorite. Another family member, ETA79001, was discovered to contain gas trapped by the impact that ejected it from Mars. Analysis of the trapped gas shows that it
10 is identical to atmospheric gases analyzed by the spacecraft that landed on Mars in 1976.

The rock of ALH84001 was formed 4.5 billion years ago, but 3.6 billion years ago it was invaded by water containing mineral salts that precipitated
15 out to form small carbonate globules with intricate chemical zoning. These carbonates are between 1 and 2 billion years old. 16 million years ago, an object from space, possibly a small asteroid, impacted Mars and blasted off rocks. One of these
20 rocks traveled in space until it was captured by the Earth's gravity and fell on Antarctica. Carbon-14 dating shows that this rock has been on Earth about 13,000 years.

The carbonate globules contain very small
25 crystals of iron oxide (magnetite) and at least two kinds of iron sulfide (pyrrhotite and another mineral, possibly greigite). Small crystals of these minerals are commonly formed on Earth by bacteria, although inorganic processes can also form
30 them. In addition, manganese is concentrated in the center of each carbonate globule, and most of the larger globules have rims of alternating iron-rich and magnesium-rich carbonates. The compositional variation of these carbonates is not what would be
35 expected from high temperature equilibrium crystallization; in fact, it is more similar to the variation that occurs during low temperature crystallization. Furthermore, it is consistent with formation by non-equilibrium precipitation induced
40 by microorganisms.

There are also unusually high concentrations of PAH-type hydrocarbons. These PAHs are unusually simple compared to most PAHs, including PAHs from the burning of coal, oil, or gasoline or the
45 decay of vegetation. Other meteorites contain PAHs, but the pattern and abundances are different. Of course, PAHs can be formed by strictly inorganic reactions, and abundant PAHs were produced in the early solar system and are preserved on some
50 asteroids and comets. Meteorites from these objects fall to Earth and enable us to analyze the PAHs contained within the parent bodies. While some of these are similar to the PAHs in the Martian meteorite, all show some major differences. One
55 reasonable interpretation of the PAHs is that they are decay products from bacteria.

Also present are unusual, very small forms that could be the remains of microorganisms. These spherical, ovoid, and elongated objects closely
60 resemble the morphology of known bacteria, but many of them are smaller than any known bacteria on Earth. Furthermore, microfossil forms from very old Earth rocks are typically much larger than the forms that we see in the Mars meteorite. The
65 microfossil-like forms may really be minerals and artifacts that superficially resemble small bacteria. Or, perhaps lower gravity and more restricted pore space in rocks promoted the development of smaller forms of microorganisms. Or, maybe such
70 forms exist on Earth in the fossil record but have not yet been found. If the small objects are microfossils, are they from Mars or from Antarctica? So far, studies of the abundant microorganisms found in the rocks, soils, and lakes near the coast of
75 Antarctica do not show PAHs or microorganisms that closely resemble those found in the Martian meteorite.

There is considerable evidence in the Martian meteorite that must be explained by other means if
80 we are to definitely rule out evidence of past Martian life in this meteorite. So far, we have not seen a reasonable explanation by others that can explain all of the data.

24. The main purpose of the passage is to:

F. argue that the available data support the conclusion that life once existed on Mars.

G. examine various facts to determine what thesis about ALH84001 is most strongly supported.

H. answer objections to the contention that Martian meteorites contain evidence of primitive life.

J. pose challenges to scientists who hope to prove that ALH84001 proves that life exists on Mars.

25. According to the passage, what evidence most strongly establishes that meteorite ALH84001 originated on Mars?

A. Comparison of trapped gases and the Martian atmosphere

B. Presence of alternating iron and magnesium carbonates

C. Evidence of shapes that resemble known bacteria

D. Pattern of carbonate globules with unusual zoning

26. The passage mentions all of the following as tending to prove that ALH84001 may once have contained primitive life EXCEPT:

F. distinctive oxygen isotopes trapped in gases.

G. extraordinarily high concentrations of unusual PAHs.

H. presence of iron oxide and iron sulfide crystals.

J. unusual zonings of carbonate globules

27. According to the passage, the compositional variation of the carbonate deposits and the PAH–type hydrocarbons both:

A. result from chemical processes more likely to occur on Mars than on Earth.

B. might be the product of an organic reaction or the product of an inorganic process.

C. tend to occur at relatively cooler temperatures than other, similar reactions.

D. are evidence of chemical processes that occurred during the formation of the solar system.

28. The author mentions lower gravity and restricted pore space (lines 67–68) in order to explain why:

F. bacteria on Mars might be smaller than bacteria found on Earth.

G. no microfossil record of bacteria has yet been found in Antarctica.

H. the spherical, ovoid, and elongated shapes in ALH84001 cannot be bacteria.

J. restricted pore space in Martian rocks would hinder bacterial growth.

29. With which of the following conclusions about the possibility of life on Mars would the author most likely agree?

A. The available evidence strongly suggests that conditions on Mars make it impossible for life to have developed there.

B. The scientific evidence is ambiguous and supports no conclusion about the possibility of life on Mars.

C. Scientific evidence cannot, in principle, ever demonstrate that life existed on Mars.

D. Scientific data derived from ALH84001 is consistent with the proposition that life once existed on Mars.

REVIEW

This section contains additional Reading items for further practice. Answers are on page 660.

> **DIRECTIONS:** Each passage below is followed by a set of items. Read the passage and choose the best answer for each item. You may refer to the passage as often as necessary to answer the items.

Passage I

Natural Science: This passage discusses systems for reporting and investigating adverse drug effects.

A key principle of pharmacology is that all drugs have multiple actions. Actions that are desirable in the treatment of disease are considered therapeutic. Those that are undesirable or pose

5 risks to the patient are called "effects." Adverse drug effects range from the trivial, for example, nausea or dry mouth, to the serious, such as massive gastrointestinal bleeding; some drugs can even be lethal. Therefore, an effective system for the

10 detection of adverse drug effects is an important component of the healthcare system of any nation. Much of the research conducted on new drugs aims to identify the conditions of use that maximize beneficial effects and minimize the risk of adverse

15 effects. The intent of drug labeling is to reflect this body of knowledge accurately so that physicians can properly prescribe the drug or, if it is to be sold without prescription, so that consumers can properly use the drug.

20 The current system of drug investigation in the United States has proven very useful in identifying the side effects associated with new prescription drugs. By the time a new drug is approved by the Food and Drug Administration, its side effects are

25 usually well described in the package insert for physicians. The investigational process, however, cannot be counted on to detect all adverse effects because of the relatively small number of patients involved in pre-marketing studies and the relatively

30 short duration of the studies. Animal studies are, of course, done before marketing in an attempt to

identify any potential for toxicity, but negative results do not guarantee the safety of a drug in humans, as evidenced by such well known examples

35 as the birth deformities due to thalidomide.

In many countries, this recognition prompted the establishment of programs to which physicians report adverse drug effects. The United States and other countries also send reports to an international

40 program operated by the World Health Organization. These programs, however, are voluntary reporting programs and are intended to serve a limited goal: alerting a government or private agency to adverse drug effects detected by

45 physicians in the course of practice. Other approaches must be used to confirm suspected drug reactions and to estimate incidence rates. These other approaches include conducting retrospective control studies, for example, the studies associating

50 endometrial cancer with estrogen use, and monitoring hospitalized patients to determine the incidence of acute common side effects. This approach was typified by the Boston Collaborative Drug Surveillance Program.

55 Thus, the drug surveillance system of the United States is composed of a set of information bases, special studies, and monitoring programs, each contributing in its own way to our knowledge about marketed drugs. The system is decentralized

60 among a number of governmental units and is not administered as a coordinated function. Still, it would be unwise at this time to attempt to unite all of the disparate elements into a comprehensive surveillance program. Instead, the challenge is to

65 improve each part of the system and to take advantage of new online strategies to improve coordination and communication.

1. In line 63, the word *disparate* most nearly means:

    A. useless.
    B. expensive.
    C. temporary.
    D. unconnected.

2. The author's primary concern is to discuss:

    F. methods for testing the effects of new drugs on humans.
    G. the importance of having accurate information about the effects of drugs.
    H. procedures for determining the long-term effects of new drugs.
    J. attempts to curb the abuse of prescription drugs.

3. The author implies that a drug with adverse side effects:

    A. will not be approved for use by consumers without a doctor's prescription.
    B. must wait for approval until lengthy studies prove the effects are not permanent.
    C. should be used only if its therapeutic value outweighs its adverse effects.
    D. should be withdrawn from the marketplace pending a government investigation.

4. Which of the following can be inferred from the passage?

    F. The decentralization of the overall drug surveillance system results in it being completely ineffective in any attempts to provide information about adverse drug effects.
    G. Drugs with serious adverse side effects are never approved for distribution.
    H. Some adverse drug effects are discovered during testing because they are very rare.
    J. Some adverse drug effects cannot be detected prior to approval because they take a long time to develop.

5. The author introduces the example of thalidomide in the last sentence of the second paragraph to show that some:

    A. drugs do not have the same reactions in humans that they do in animals.
    B. drug testing procedures are ignored by careless laboratory workers.
    C. drugs have no therapeutic value for humans.
    D. drugs have adverse side effects as well as beneficial actions.

6. It can be inferred that the estrogen study mentioned in the last sentence of the third paragraph:

    F. uncovered long-term side effects of a drug that had already been approved for sale by the Food and Drug Administration.
    G. discovered potential side effects of a drug that was still awaiting approval for sale by the Food and Drug Administration.
    H. revealed possible new applications of a drug that had previously been approved for a different treatment.
    J. is an example of a study that could be more efficiently conducted by a centralized authority than by volunteer reporting.

7. The author is most probably leading up to a discussion of some suggestions about how to:

    A. centralize authority for drug surveillance in the United States.
    B. centralize authority for drug surveillance among international agencies.
    C. coordinate better sharing of information among the drug surveillance agencies.
    D. eliminate the availability and sale of certain drugs now on the market.

8. The author makes use of which of the following devices in the passage?

    F. Definition of terms
    G. Examples
    H. Analogy
    J. Definition of terms and examples

Passage II

Natural Science: This passage is adapted from a science magazine article that discusses lightning.

Lightning is an electrical discharge of immense proportions. Some 80 percent of lightning occurs within clouds; about 20 percent is cloud-to-ground lightning; and an extremely small percentage is
5 cloud-to-sky lightning.

Cloud-to-ground lightning begins when complex meteorological processes cause a tremendous electrostatic charge to build up within a cloud. Typically, the bottom of the cloud is
10 negatively charged. When the charge reaches 50 to 100 million volts, air is no longer an effective insulator, and lightning occurs within the cloud itself. Ten to 30 minutes after the onset of intracloud lightning, negative charges called
15 stepped leaders emerge from the bottom of the cloud, moving toward the earth in 50-meter intervals at speeds of 100 to 200 kilometers per second and creating an ionized channel. As the leaders near the Earth, their strong electric field
20 causes streamers of positively charged ions to develop at the tips of pointed objects that are connected directly or indirectly to the ground. These positively charged streamers flow upward.

When the distance, known as the striking
25 distance, between a stepped leader and one of the streamers reaches 30 to 100 meters, the intervening air breaks down completely, and the leader is joined to the Earth via the streamer. Now a pulse of current known as a return stroke ranging
30 from thousands to hundreds of thousands of amperes moves at one tenth to one third the speed of light from the Earth through the object from which the streamer emanated and up the ionized channel to the charge center within the cloud. An
35 ionized channel remains in the air and additional negative charges called dart leaders will quickly move down this path resulting in further return strokes. This multiplicity causes the flash to flicker. The entire event typically lasts about one second.

40 The return stroke's extremely high temperature creates the visible lightning and produces thunder by instantly turning moisture into steam. Most direct damage results from the heavy return stroke current because it produces high
45 temperatures in the channel, or from arcing at the point of ground contact. If the lightning current is

carried by an enclosed conductor (e.g., within a jacketed cable, through a concrete wall, or beneath a painted surface), entrapped moisture is turned into
50 high-pressure steam that can cause a cable, wall, or painted object to explode. Arcing frequently ignites combustibles.

Lightning causes hundreds of millions of dollars in property losses annually and the majority
55 of forest fires. Lightning is also the leading weather-related killer in the US, causing from 100 to 200 deaths each year.

9. In line 14, the word *intracloud* most nearly means:

A. between clouds.
B. within a cloud.
C. from cloud to sky.
D. from ground to cloud.

10. The selection defines the striking distance as the distance between:

F. the ground and the cloud.
G. a stepped leader and a dart leader.
H. a dart leader and a return stroke.
J. a streamer and a stepped leader.

11. According to the selection, the flickering appearance of a lightning strike is created by:

A. the stepped movement of leaders.
B. multiple return strokes.
C. water being vaporized.
D. arcing at ground contact.

12. What topic might the author logically address in a continuation of the passage?

F. Precautions to minimize lightning damage
G. Other weather phenomena that cause injury
H. Basic principles governing electricity
J. Identifying different types of clouds

13. According to the passage, which of the following is NOT true of stepped leaders?

    A. They develop 10 to 30 minutes after intracloud lightning.
    B. As they traverse the distance from cloud to ground, they create an ionized channel.
    C. Their powerful positive charge causes streamers to develop in grounded objects.
    D. They emerge from the bottom of the cloud and move downward in intervals of 50 meters.

14. The passage answers which of the following questions?

    F. How does lightning produce the associated thunder?
    G. How far above the ground is the bottom of the typical lightning-producing cloud?
    H. How frequently will lightning strike a given object?
    J. How long does it take a cloud to build up an electrostatic charge?

15. The author's primary concern is to:

    A. warn about the dangers posed by lightning strikes.
    B. describe the sequence of events that make up a lightning strike.
    C. discuss fundamental scientific laws pertaining to electricity.
    D. support the commonly held view that lightning strikes the ground.

Passage III

Social Science: This passage discusses the history of hospitals.

Public general hospitals originated in almshouse infirmaries. Established as early as colonial times, these infirmaries were created by local governments to care for the poor. Later, in the
5 late eighteenth and early nineteenth centuries, the infirmary separated from the almshouse and became an independent institution supported by local tax money. At the same time, private charity hospitals began to develop. Both private and public
10 hospitals mainly provided food and shelter for the impoverished sick. There was little that medicine could actually do to cure illness, and the middle class was treated at home by private physicians.

Late in the nineteenth century, private charity
15 hospitals began trying to attract middle-class patients. Although the depression of 1890 stimulated the growth of charitable institutions and an expanding urban population became dependent on assistance, there was a decline in private
20 contributions to these organizations. This decline forced them to look to local government for financial support. Since private institutions had also lost benefactors, they began to charge patients. In order to attract middle-class patients, private
25 institutions provided services and amenities that distinguished between paying and nonpaying patients, making the hospital a desirable place for private physicians to treat their own patients. As paying patients became more necessary to the
30 survival of the private hospital, the public hospitals slowly became the only place for the poor to get treatment. By the end of the nineteenth century, cities were reimbursing private hospitals for their care of indigent patients. The public hospitals
35 remained dependent on tax dollars.

The advent of private hospital health insurance gave middle-class patients the power to pay for private hospital services and guaranteed the private hospital a regular source of income. Private
40 hospitals could restrict themselves to revenue-generating patients while the public hospitals were left to care for the poor. Although public hospitals continued to provide outpatient services, emergency services, and services for patients with
45 contagious diseases, the Blue Cross plans developed around the needs of the private hospitals and the inpatients they served. Thus, reimbursement for ambulatory care has been minimal under most Blue Cross plans. Provision of outpatient care has not
50 been a major function of the private hospital, in part because private patients can afford to pay for the services of private physicians. Also, since World War II, there has been a huge influx of federal money into private medical schools and their
55 hospitals. Further, large private medical centers with expensive research equipment and programs have attracted the best administrators, physicians, and researchers. Because of the greater resources available to the private medical centers, it is harder
60 for public hospitals to attract highly qualified research and medical personnel. With the mainstream of healthcare firmly established in the private medical sector, the public hospital has become a "dumping ground."

16. In line 34, the word *indigent* most nearly means:

F. without the means to pay.
G. having emergency medical needs.
H. lacking health insurance.
J. reimbursed by the government.

17. According to the passage, the very first private hospitals:

A. developed from almshouse infirmaries.
B. provided better care than public infirmaries.
C. were established mainly to service the poor.
D. were supported by government revenues.

18. It can be inferred that the author believes the differences that currently exist between public and private hospitals are primarily the result of:

F. political considerations.
G. economic factors.
H. ethical concerns.
J. legislative requirements.

19. It can be inferred that the growth of private health insurance:

A. relieved local governments of the need to fund public hospitals.
B. guaranteed that the poor would have access to medical care.
C. forced middle-class patients to use public hospitals.
D. reinforced the distinction between public and private hospitals.

20. Which of the following would be the most logical topic for the author to introduce in the next paragraph?

F. A plan to improve the quality of public hospitals
G. An analysis of the profit structure of health insurance companies
H. A proposal to raise taxes on the middle class
J. A discussion of recent developments in medical technology

21. The author's primary concern is to:

A. describe the financial structure of the healthcare industry.
B. demonstrate the importance of government support for healthcare institutions.
C. criticize wealthy institutions for refusing to provide services to the poor.
D. identify the historical causes of the division between private and public hospitals.

22. The author cites all of the following as factors contributing to the decline of public hospitals EXCEPT:

F. government money was used to subsidize private medical schools and hospitals to the detriment of public hospitals.
G. public hospitals are not able to compete with private institutions for top-flight managers and doctors.
H. large private medical centers have better research facilities and more extensive research programs than public hospitals.
J. Blue Cross insurance coverage does not reimburse subscribers for medical expenses incurred in a public hospital.

23. The author's attitude toward public hospitals can best be described as:

A. contemptuous and prejudiced.
B. apprehensive and distrustful.
C. concerned and understanding.
D. enthusiastic and supportive.

24. The author implies that any outpatient care provided by a hospital is:

F. paid for by private insurance.
G. provided in lieu of treatment by a private physician.
H. supplied primarily by private hospitals.
J. a source of revenue for public hospitals.

Passage IV

Social Science: This passage discusses a conflict that emerged following US military unification.

The National Security Act of 1947 created a national military establishment headed by a single Secretary of Defense. The legislation had been a year-and-a-half in the making. It began when
5 President Truman first recommended that the armed services be reorganized into a single department. During that period, the President's concept of a unified armed service was torn apart and put back together several times; the final
10 measure to emerge from Congress was a compromise. Most of the opposition to the bill came from the Navy and its spokesmen, including Secretary of the Navy James Forrestal. In support of unification (and a separate air force that was part of
15 the plan) were the Army air forces, the Army, and, most importantly, the President of the United States.

Passage of the bill did not end the disputes. Rather than unify, the act served only to federate
20 the military services. It neither halted the rapid demobilization of the armed forces that followed World War II nor brought to the new national military establishment the loyalties of officers steeped in the traditions of the separate services. At
25 a time when the balance of power in Europe and Asia was rapidly shifting, the services lacked any precise statement of United States foreign policy from the National Security Council on which to base future programs. The services bickered over their
30 roles and missions, already complicated by the Soviet nuclear capability that, for the first time, made the United States subject to devastating attack. Not even the appointment of Forrestal as First Secretary of Defense allayed the suspicions of
35 naval officers and their supporters that the role of the US Navy was threatened with permanent eclipse. Before the war of words died down, Forrestal himself was driven to resignation and then suicide.

40 By 1948, the United States military establishment was forced to make do with a budget approximately 10 percent of what it had been at its wartime peak. Meanwhile, the cost of weapons was rising geometrically as the nation came to put more
45 and more reliance on the atomic bomb. These two factors inevitably made adversaries of the Navy and the Air Force as the battle between advocates of the

B-36 and the supercarrier so amply demonstrates. Given severe fiscal restraints on the one hand, and
50 on the other the nation's increasing reliance on nuclear deterrence, the conflict between these two services over roles and missions was essentially a contest over slices of an ever-diminishing pie.

Yet if in the end neither service was the clear
55 victor, the principle of civilian dominance over the military clearly was. If there had ever been any danger that the US military establishment might exploit, to the detriment of civilian control, the goodwill it earned as a result of its victories in
60 World War II, that danger disappeared in the interservice animosities formed by the battle over unification.

25. In line 21, the word *demobilization* most nearly means:

  A. shift to a unified military.
  B. realignment of allies.
  C. change from war to peace.
  D. adoption of new technology.

26. According to the passage, the interservice strife that followed unification occurred primarily between the:

  F. Army and Army air forces.
  G. Army and Navy.
  H. Army air forces and Navy.
  J. Air Force and Navy.

27. It can be inferred from the passage that Forrestal's appointment as Secretary of Defense was expected to:

  A. placate members of the Navy.
  B. result in decreased levels of defense spending.
  C. outrage advocates of the Army air forces.
  D. win Congressional approval of the unification plan.

28. According to the passage, President Truman supported:

    F. elimination of the Navy.
    G. a unified military service.
    H. establishment of a separate air force.
    J. a unified military service and establishment of a separate air force.

29. With which of the following statements about defense unification would the author most likely agree?

    A. Unification ultimately undermined United States military capability by inciting interservice rivalry.
    B. The unification legislation was necessitated by the drastic decline in appropriations for the military services.
    C. Although the unification was not entirely successful, it had the unexpected result of ensuring civilian control of the military.
    D. In spite of the attempted unification, each service was still able to pursue its own objectives without interference from the other branches.

30. According to the selection, the political situation following the passage of the National Security Act of 1947 was characterized by all of the following EXCEPT:

    F. a shifting balance of power in Europe and in Asia.
    G. fierce interservice rivalries.
    H. lack of strong leadership by the National Security Council.
    J. a lame-duck President who was unable to unify the legislature.

31. The author cites the resignation and suicide of Forrestal in order to:

    A. underscore the bitterness of the interservice rivalry surrounding the passage of the National Security Act of 1947.
    B. demonstrate that the Navy eventually emerged as the dominant branch of service after the passage of the National Security Act of 1947.
    C. suggest that the nation would be better served by a unified armed service under a single command.
    D. provide an example of a military leader who preferred to serve his country in war rather than in peace.

32. The author is primarily concerned with:

    F. discussing the influence of personalities on political events.
    G. describing the administration of a powerful leader.
    H. criticizing a piece of legislation.
    J. analyzing a political development.

Passage V

Humanities: This passage is adapted from an article about early American education.

The founders of the American Republic viewed their revolution mostly in political rather than economic or social terms. Furthermore, they talked about education as essential to the public good. This
5 goal took precedence over knowledge as job training or as a means to self-improvement. Over and over again, the Revolutionary generation, both liberal and conservative in outlook, asserted its belief that the welfare of the Republic rested upon
10 an educated citizenry. Schools, especially free public schools, would be the best means of educating the people in civic values and the obligations required of everyone in a democratic society. All agreed that the key ingredients of a civic education were
15 literacy and instruction in patriotic and moral virtues. Some added to these the study of history and of principles of government itself.

The founders, as was the case with almost all their successors, were long on rhetoric regarding
20 the value of civic education. But they left it to the textbook writers to distill the essence of those values for schoolchildren. Texts in American history and government appeared as early as the 1790s. The textbook writers turned out to be largely
25 conservative, more likely Federalist in outlook than Jeffersonian. They almost all agreed that political virtue must rest upon moral and religious precepts. Since most textbook writers were from New England, this meant that the texts were infused with
30 a Protestant, and above all Puritan, view.

In the first half of the Republic, education emphasized civic values. It made little attempt to develop participatory political skills. That was a task left to political parties, town meetings,
35 churches, and the coffee or ale houses where men gathered for conversation. Also, as a reading of certain Federalist papers of the time would show, the press probably did more to provide realistic, partisan knowledge of government than the schools.
40 The goal of education, however, was to achieve a higher form of *unum* for the new Republic. In the middle half of the nineteenth century, the political values taught in the public and private schools did not change much from those of the first fifty years of
45 the Republic. In the textbooks of the day, their rosy hues, if anything, became golden. To the strong values of liberty, equality, and a Christian morality

were now added the middle-class virtues of hard work, honesty, the rewards of individual effort, and
50 obedience to parents and authority. But of all the political values taught in school, patriotism was at the top; and whenever teachers explained to children why they should love their country above all else, the idea of liberty assumed pride of place.

33. In line 5, the phrase "took precedence over" most nearly means:

A. set an example for.
B. formulated a policy of.
C. enlightened someone on.
D. had greater importance than.

34. The passage deals primarily with the:

F. content of textbooks used in early American schools.
G. role of education in late eighteenth- and early to mid-nineteenth-century America.
H. influence of New England Puritanism on early American values.
J. origin and development of the Protestant work ethic in modern America.

35. According to the passage, the founders of the Republic regarded education primarily as:

A. a religious obligation.
B. a private matter.
C. an unnecessary luxury.
D. a political necessity.

36. The author states that textbooks written in the middle part of the nineteenth century:

F. departed radically in tone and style from earlier textbooks.
G. mentioned for the first time the value of liberty.
H. treated traditional civic virtues with even greater reverence.
J. were commissioned by government agencies.

37. Which of the following would LEAST likely have been the subject of an early American textbook?

    A. Basic rules of English grammar
    B. The American Revolution
    C. Patriotism and other civic virtues
    D. Effective farming methods

38. The author's attitude toward the educational system discussed in the passage can best be described as:

    F. cynical and unpatriotic.
    G. realistic and analytical.
    H. pragmatic and frustrated.
    J. disenchanted and bitter.

39. The passage provides information that would be helpful in answering which of the following questions?

    A. Why was a disproportionate share of early American textbooks written by New England authors?
    B. Was the Federalist Party primarily a liberal or conservative force in early American politics?
    C. How many years of education did the founders believe were sufficient to instruct young citizens in civic virtue?
    D. What were the names of some of the Puritan authors who wrote early American textbooks?

40. The author implies that an early American Puritan would likely insist that:

    F. moral and religious values are the foundation of civic virtue.
    G. textbooks should instruct students in political issues of vital concern to the community.
    H. textbooks should give greater emphasis to the value of individual liberty than to the duties of patriotism.
    J. private schools with a particular religious focus are preferable to public schools with no religious instruction.

Passage VI

Social Science: This passage discusses the relationship between the US economy and international commerce.

International commerce is woven thoroughly into the fabric of the American economy. Exports and imports amounted to more than 11 percent of the US gross domestic product (GDP) in 1991. This
5 was up dramatically from 7.5 percent just five years before. More than 7 million American jobs are related to exports. Millions more depend on the overall economic activity generated by export trade. Export-related jobs pay more—almost 17 percent
10 more—than the average American job.

Exports are vital to the economic health of many key sectors of the manufacturing economy. For instance, makers of computers, heavy earthmoving equipment, and farm implements are
15 increasingly dependent on export markets. For these exports, slow growth abroad translates to declining vitality at home. The same picture is true of agriculture. Roughly one in four farm acres is now harvested for the export market. International
20 sales of business-related services—construction, finance, insurance, and engineering, among others—amount to tens of billions of dollars each year.

In the early years of the post-World War II era,
25 the United States stood virtually alone as the industrial and technological leader of the world. At that time, the US produced almost half of the world's GDP. This included much of the world's manufactured goods. The US also had roughly 80
30 percent of the world's hard currency reserves. Today, while the US remains the world's leading economy, its share of world GDP has shrunk to about 24 percent. Its share of world manufacturers is even lower. Experts agree that, relative to the size
35 of the economy and the diversity of its industrial and technological base, the US has lagged far behind its export potential.

Meanwhile, the potential for growth in US exports is enormous. Markets in Europe and Japan
40 are huge and stable. There is growing promise in Asia's $5.7 trillion economy and Latin America's $1 trillion economy. These markets are generating a rapidly growing demand for infrastructure investment, aircraft, and high-technology capital
45 goods—all areas in which the US has real or

potential strengths. In addition, new entrants into the world economy, such as Central and Eastern Europe and the countries of the former Soviet Union, show real promise as potential markets for
50 US exports.

Growing world markets, however, do not automatically translate into US export sales. The fierce competition for international markets comes primarily from the more innovative firms in Europe
55 and Japan. In particular, Japanese companies have set the pace with a mix of aggressive business practices and an economy-wide commitment to quality, rapid time to market, ongoing innovation, and customer satisfaction. American companies are
60 beginning to try to meet the competition abroad, as well as to view their success as a benchmark for improvement, whether that best is in Chicago, Frankfurt, or Osaka.

The new realities of international competition
65 yield lessons for the US government as well. Economic diplomacy and high-level advocacy, competitive and focused export financing, and improved efforts at information-gathering have become necessary components of an export
70 promotion policy. Many foreign governments have been more aggressive and more focused than the US government in working with their firms to secure export sales. Senior government officials, up to and including the President or Prime Minister, often will
75 travel to support the sale of their home country's goods and services. The US government needs to begin to measure its export strategy against the flexibility and effectiveness of the competition. Exports are central to growth, jobs, and a rising
80 standard of living for all Americans. Our role in building a better America at home and acting as an economic leader abroad is dependent on our ability to develop a coherent, aggressive, and effective national export strategy.

41. Which of the following US economic sectors has declined most seriously since World War II?

A. Agriculture
B. Manufacturing
C. High-technology products
D. Business-related services

42. Which of the following best expresses the central point of the passage?

    F. Exports drive the US economy.

    G. US exports have declined since shortly after World War II.

    H. Exports are so important to the US economy that steps should be taken to increase US exports worldwide.

    J. The US government should encourage US corporations to expand into markets in Asia and Latin America.

43. Which of the following areas is NOT mentioned in the passage as a potential market for US goods abroad?

    A. Asia

    B. Latin America

    C. Central Europe

    D. Northern Africa

44. The passage suggests that both US corporations and the US government should:

    F. discourage imports in favor of exports.

    G. focus on improving the quality of American products.

    H. try to meet the competition abroad.

    J. take steps to reduce the economy's dependence on exports.

45. With which of the following explanations for the decline in the United States' share of world GDP would the author be most likely to agree?

    I. Other countries are relatively uninterested in purchasing the goods and services the US has to offer.

    II. Other governments have done more to encourage their countries' exports than has the US government.

    III. Companies in some other countries have been more enterprising in producing high-quality goods and services.

    A. II only

    B. I and II only

    C. I and III only

    D. II and III only

46. According to the passage, an increase in US exports abroad would generate:

    F. more high-paying jobs for American workers.

    G. increased profits for American farmers.

    H. greater diversity in American industry.

    J. resentment among foreign competitors.

STRATEGY SUMMARY

Reading Strategies

Understanding the three levels of reading comprehension and how they relate to the seven Reading item-types will help you to quickly identify the question that is being asked by a particular item.

Level 1—General Theme

The first level of reading, appreciation of the general theme, is the most basic. Main Idea items test whether you understand the passage at the most general level. The first sentence of a paragraph—often the topic sentence—may provide a summary of the content of that paragraph. Also, the last sentence of a paragraph usually provides concluding material that may also be helpful in understanding the general theme of the passage.

Main Idea items ask about the central theme that unifies the passage(s):

- *Which of the following is the main point of the passage?*

- *The primary purpose of the passage is to….*

Level 2—Specific Points

The second level of reading, understanding specific points, takes you deeper into the selection. Explicit Detail, Vocabulary, and Development items all test your ability to read carefully. Since this is an "open-book" test, you can always return to the selection. Therefore, if something is highly technical or difficult to understand, do not dwell on it for too long— you can always come back to it later if necessary.

Explicit Detail items ask about details that are specifically mentioned in the passage. This type of item differs from a Main Idea item in that explicit details are points provided by the author in the passage. Explicit Detail items provide "locator words" that identify the required information in the passage.

- *The author mentions which of the following?*

- *According to the passage,…?*

Vocabulary items test your understanding of a word or phrase in context. The nature of the Vocabulary items indicates two points. First, the correct answer choice will make sense when it is substituted for the referenced word. Second, the correct answer choice may not be the most commonly used meaning of the word; in fact, if it were, then what would be the point of including the item on the test? Thus, the general strategy for this type of item is to favor the less commonly used meaning.

- *The word ------- in line ## means….*

- *In line ##, what is the best definition of the word -------?*

Development items ask about the overall structure of the passage or about the logical role played by a specific part of the passage.

- *The author develops the passage primarily by….*

- *The author mentions…in order to….*

Level 3—Evaluation

The third level of reading, evaluation of the text, takes you even deeper into the selection. Implied Idea, Application, and Voice items ask not just for understanding, but also require a judgment or an evaluation of what you have read. This is why these items are usually the most difficult.

Implied Idea items don't ask about what is specifically stated in the passage; rather, Implied Idea items ask about what can be logically inferred from what is stated in the passage. For example, the passage might explain that a certain organism (X) is found only in the presence of another organism (Y). An accompanying Implied Idea item might ask the following question: "If organism Y is not present, what can be inferred?" Since the passage implies that in the absence of Y, X cannot be present, the answer would be "X is not present." Since this type of item generally builds on a specific detail, "locator words" for identifying information in the passage are often provided in the item stem.

- *The passage implies that….*
- *The author uses the phrase "…" to mean….*

Application items are similar to Implied Idea items, but they go one step further: examinees must apply what they have learned from the passage to a new situation.

- *With which of the following statements would the author most likely agree?*
- *The passage is most probably taken from which of the following sources?*

Voice items ask about the author's attitude toward a specific detail or the overall tone of the passage.

- *The tone of the passage can best be described as….*
- *The author regards…as….*

General Strategies

Reading strategies are not an exact science. Practice is essential to mastering the following techniques:

Preview the Passage

Read the first sentence of each passage in the Reading Test. After reading the first sentence of each passage, label each passage as either "Easy" or "Hard" based on your initial understanding of the material and your level of interest. Analyze the easier passages first.

Preview Each Paragraph

Preview the first and last sentences of each paragraph. There is usually an introductory paragraph for excerpted passages that identifies the author and provides a brief description of the selection. First, read this introductory material to gain clues about the author's point of view. Then, preview the first and last sentences of each paragraph, as they often provide paragraph summaries.

Read the Passage

After previewing each paragraph, ask what the author is attempting to describe, especially in the case of Evaluation items. Bracket difficult material, either mentally or with some sort of a mark, and then simply revisit it if necessary or if time permits. Instead of wasting time re-reading, attempt to understand the context in which the author introduces a particular concept.

Code in Groups

Circle the answers to the items in the test booklet, and transcribe the answers to all the items for a passage to the answer sheet after finishing each passage. This approach helps increase accuracy and makes checking your work easier and more efficient. Only when the time limit approaches should you transcribe each answer individually.

Writing

Course Concept Outline

I. Test Mechanics (p. 171)

A. Overview (p. 171)

B. Anatomy (Essay Prompt, p. 172)

C. Pacing (p. 173)

D. Time Trial (Essay Prompt, p. 174)

E. Game Plan (p. 175)

    1. Use a Pencil
    2. Respond to the Specific Prompt
    3. Write Legibly
    4. Don't Copy the Prompt
    5. Don't Skip Lines
    6. Be Specific

II. Lesson (p. 177)

A. Preliminaries[1]

    1. What Is Tested
    2. Directions
    3. Item Format
    4. Scoring
        a) Essay Scoring Guide
        b) Test Scores

---

[1] Some concepts in this Course Concept Outline are not illustrated through examples in your student text but may be covered by your instructor in class. They are included here to provide a complete outline of your course.

B. Composing the Essay

1. Pre-Writing
2. Beginning the Writing Process
3. The Introduction
4. The Body
5. The Conclusion
6. Revising

C. Essay Writing Strategies

1. Begin with the Prompt
2. Write Only on the Assigned Topic
3. Do Not Try to Do Too Much
4. Outline the Essay (Essay Prompt, p. 177)
5. Organize Ideas into Paragraphs (Essay Prompt, p. 177)
6. Write Using Correct Grammar
7. Punctuate and Spell Correctly
8. Write Clearly, Concisely, and Legibly
9. Proofread the Essay

III. Quizzes (p. 179)

A. Quiz I (Essay Prompt, p. 179)

B. Quiz II (Essay Prompt, p. 180)

C. Quiz III (Essay Prompt, p. 181)

IV. Strategy Summary (p. 183)

TEST MECHANICS

Overview

The Writing Test will assess in broad terms your ability to develop and express your ideas in writing. It is not intended to evaluate whether you'd be a good novelist or how well you'd write if given time to do research and write several drafts. In short, you will produce an on-demand piece of writing that will likely be of rough draft quality.

The Writing Test is also not intended to test your mastery of any body of knowledge. The topic will be sufficiently broad so that arguments and explanations can be drawn from personal experience; for example, the topic might ask you to express your opinions about sports, music, psychology, current events, or even modern technology such as "tweeting" or video games.

The essay topic will be described as a "prompt." The word "prompt" was chosen because it indicates that the topic is really just an *excuse* or *opportunity* for you to write something. The test could just as easily say, "During the next thirty minutes, write an essay on anything of interest to you." However, the readers would then have to deal with essays on an unwieldy number of topics; the prompt keeps everyone more or less on the same page.

Essays are scored *holistically*, which means they are given a grade based on the overall impression created. Bonus points are not awarded for a well-turned phrase, and specific points are not deducted for specific grammatical mistakes. However, consistently poor grammar that interferes with meaning will affect the essay score. You will receive three types of scores for your essay. First, the overall essay score is reported on a scale of 1–36. Second, you will receive additional scores reported within four domains: Ideas and Analysis, Development and Support, Organization, and Language Use and Conventions, on a scale of 2–12 for each domain (the scores of two readers are combined to determine each domain score). Third, the Essay score is combined with your English Test and Reading Test scores to produce an English Language Arts (ELA) score on a scale of 1–36. The Essay score is NOT included in your composite score.

Anatomy

> **DIRECTIONS:** You have 40 minutes to plan and write an essay. Read the prompt carefully and make sure you understand the instructions.

The Electoral College

In light of the results of the 2000 presidential election, our indirect method of selecting our president through the Electoral College (all Electoral College votes are declared to the winning candidate in each of the 50 states) has come into question. Direct popular election is the method most often presented as the fairest way to choose a president. Adoption of this process would mean, simply, that the candidate who received the most votes would become president. Some argue that the Electoral College could be kept and votes in the states could be designated to a candidate in a proportional method, so a person who received 60% of a state's votes would receive 60% of its electoral votes. Those who favor this method argue this is the fairest way to choose who will lead the country, but would changing the constitution to address a situation that was problematic in only one recent election be an extreme and unwise change? No matter which side you may choose, this conversation is an important one for our nation's future.

Perspective 1	Perspective 2	Perspective 3
Direct election of the president by popular vote is the fairest way to choose our chief executive. Such a change in our process of selecting the president would reinforce our view that America is a government of the people, by the people, and for the people.	The Electoral College has served the United States for over 250 years. Radical change is not always the best course. A tweaking of the selection process would provide candidates a percentage of the votes earned in each state.	Changing the constitution is never to be done lightly. The founding fathers thought long and hard about this step. We should think long and hard about such a change to our constitution and the possible consequences of such a decision.

Essay Task

Write a unified, coherent essay in which you evaluate multiple perspectives on the impact of direct popular election of the President of the United States. In your essay be sure to:

- Analyze and evaluate perspectives given
- State and develop your own perspective
- Explain the relationship between your perspective and those given

Your perspective may be in full agreement with any of the others, in partial agreement or wholly different. Whatever the case, support your ideas with logical reasoning and detailed, persuasive examples.

Notice that the prompt does not test a specific body of knowledge. For example, it does not ask, "What were the causes of World War II?" or "What is the best recipe for chocolate cake?" Also, notice that the prompt is constructed so you can provide a very successful response based simply on the perspectives listed and your own personal experience. Finally, notice that the prompt points you in the right direction. It asks you a question, and all you need to do is respond to the question and meet the requirements outlined above. These requirements will be discussed in more detail later in the Writing Lesson.

Pacing

There is one essay prompt with a 40-minute time limit. During the 40 minutes, you must read the prompt, formulate a position, outline your argument or analysis, write your essay, and proofread your essay. Here is a suggested breakdown for those tasks:

TASK	TIME TO EXECUTE	TIME REMAINING
Read the prompt.	1 minute	39 minutes
Evaluate the given perspectives.	2 minutes	37 minutes
Formulate your perspective.	2 minutes	35 minutes
Outline your essay.	2 minutes	33 minutes
Write the introduction.	4 minutes	29 minutes
Write the first paragraph.	7–8 minutes	21–22 minutes
Write the second paragraph.	7–8 minutes	13–15 minutes
Write the third paragraph.	7–8 minutes	5–8 minutes
Write the conclusion.	3 minutes	2–5 minutes
Proofread your essay.	2–5 minutes	0 minutes

If you follow this approximate schedule, it is likely your essay will score at least a 22. After all, your essay will include an introduction that evaluates the given perspectives and states your perspective, three supporting paragraphs (each of which will provide a specific reason in support of your perspective), and a brief conclusion that clearly expresses your point of view. Obviously, if your essay is also expressed in clear and precise language, and if it does not include any major grammatical errors, you will likely receive an even higher score.

Time Trial

(1 prompt; 11 minutes)

DIRECTIONS: Write an outline for your essay. Then write an introductory paragraph.

Planned Obsolescence

Many technology manufacturers follow a policy of planned obsolescence. Obsolescence describes the condition of no longer being used or useful. Planned obsolescence means that manufacturers make products that are designed to wear out and be replaced quickly. New smartphone applications only function on the latest version of a phone. High repair costs encourage consumers to buy a new laptop instead of fixing a broken one. Spare parts for a computer are no longer available after a few years. Planned obsolescence cuts costs for the manufacturer and the consumer, but what are the risks for both parties when the consumer must frequently replace a product? With the prevalent role of technological devices in our society, planned obsolescence has a strong financial impact on our lives.

Perspective 1	Perspective 2	Perspective 3
Planned obsolescence can be unfair to consumers, forcing them to spend more money than necessary on products that do not offer significant improvements to the older ones. Manufacturers should deliver high quality, long-lasting products. From the manufacturer's perspective, flimsy products could also encourage consumers to buy from a company with a more durable product.	Some industries, such as the automotive industry, are focusing on creating new products that are more environmentally friendly than what is currently available. Planned obsolescence could encourage consumers to buy these newer products and ultimately have a positive impact on the environment.	Planned obsolescence cuts manufacturing costs and encourages companies to design better products in a shorter period of time. This allows for greater innovation in products and ultimately gives the consumer a superior product.

Essay Task

Write a unified, coherent essay in which you evaluate multiple perspectives on the impact of planned obsolescence. In your essay be sure to:

- Analyze and evaluate perspectives given
- State and develop your own perspective
- Explain the relationship between your perspective and those given

Your perspective may be in full agreement with any of the others, in partial agreement or wholly different. Whatever the case, support your ideas with logical reasoning and detailed, persuasive examples.

Game Plan

Use a Pencil

Write your essay in pencil. Do not use a pen. Any essay written in pen will automatically receive a "0."

Respond to the Specific Prompt

Write on the topic that is presented. If you write an essay that is off-topic, your essay will automatically receive a "0" because it will be considered "not responsive." Also, remember to evaluate each of the given perspectives, present your own perspective, and describe how your perspective relates to each of the given perspectives. Following all the required steps outlined in the prompt is an easy—and essential—way to earn points.

Write Legibly

Write clearly and legibly. If you write an essay that is illegible, your essay will automatically receive a "0." Readers cannot give a grade to what they cannot read. So, if your handwriting is hard to read, take a little extra time and try printing.

Don't Copy the Prompt

Do not copy the prompt onto the lined paper. The readers know the topic, and it is already written on the page. If you copy the prompt onto the lined paper, it looks like you're simply trying to fill up space.

Don't Skip Lines

Do not skip lines when writing your essay on the lined paper. You should be able to make your essay legible without skipping lines. If you skip lines, it looks like you're trying to "pad" your essay to make it look longer.

Be Specific

When writing your essay, be specific. Avoid vague generalizations. For example, here are a few sentences that are weak because they are too vague:

> *"Perfection in house painting is very time-consuming and requires a lot of hard work. You just can't do it in a short time; you've got to invest a lot of effort."*

If you include specific details, the same point can be made much more persuasively. For example, here is the same argument about house painting but made with specific details:

> *"House painting requires attention to details. You have to prepare the surface by scraping away all old and loose paint and carefully washing it. You have to put down hundreds of strips of masking tape to protect those areas that should not receive paint, like glass panes, trim to be painted a second color, and fixtures. You have to apply a primer, then a base coat, and then the finish coat. Finally, you have to apply the second color and clean up all the mistakes. A perfect paint job would take 6 months or longer, and the cost would be prohibitive. That is why when you look closely you will always see imperfections."*

As you can see, this response is much more compelling because the point of view is supported by specific details. Specific details are frequently the difference between an essay that receives a Development and Support score of 4 or 6 and an essay that receives a Development and Support score of 8 or 10.

LESSON

The following essay topic will be used during the Writing Lesson to illustrate proper essay development and writing skills. Follow along with your instructor to outline and develop sample responses to the prompts. Sample essay responses begin on page 661.

DIRECTIONS: You have 40 minutes to plan and write an essay. Read the prompt carefully and make sure you understand the instructions. A successful essay will have the following features: it will evaluate each of the perspectives given in the prompt; it will state and develop a personal perspective; it will explain the relationship between the given perspectives and your personal perspective; it will present ideas with logical reasoning and clear, persuasive examples; and, finally, it will include clear and effective language in accordance with the conventions of standard written English.

Technological advances have enhanced our capacity to communicate. Email, twitter, Instagram, and social messaging sites have made the sharing of information and networking with others exponentially more efficient. Whether the 'other' is our neighbor next door, or someone or some group halfway around the planet, the ability to connect has been almost infinitely improved. However, critics claim that while we now communicate more quickly, we also interact more superficially, and the ease of interaction has, in many cases, rendered us more isolated. Although technology has made communication easier, are we, in fact, lonelier with more digital and less face-to-face interaction? As more and more communication happens online, it is important to assess the psychological effects of such connections.

Read and consider the perspectives below. Each perspective suggests a particular way of thinking about the impact of technology on human interaction.

Perspective 1	Perspective 2	Perspective 3
Despite the efficiency of moving information, so much of what is shared is facile and empty of real depth. We are now in a "fast food" age of information: quick turnaround with only "empty calories" of communication.	Though we connect more easily with one another, there is a feeling that we are becoming ever more isolated and estranged from each other. We have a need for closer contact with the people we know.	Technological advances have made it far easier to communicate in today's world. We can literally reach out and touch individuals, groups, and societies in an instant and be connected immediately.

Essay Task

Write a unified, coherent essay in which you evaluate multiple perspectives on the impact of technology on human interaction. In your essay be sure to:

- Analyze and evaluate the perspectives given
- State and develop your own perspective
- Explain the relationship between your perspective and those given

Your perspective may be in full agreement with any of the others, in partial agreement, or wholly different. Whatever the case, support your ideas with logical reasoning and detailed, persuasive examples.

QUIZZES

This section contains three Writing quizzes. Complete each quiz under timed conditions. Sample essay responses begin on page 661.

Quiz I
(1 Essay Prompt; 40 minutes)

DIRECTIONS: You have 40 minutes to plan and write an essay. Read the prompt carefully and make sure you understand the instructions.

Fracking

The quest for finding additional sources of energy is almost never-ending, and our demand for fossil fuels has dominated our energy consumption. Fracking (hydraulic fracturing) which "pries" fossil fuel resources from the earth's crust, is one recent development at the forefront of promising innovations making our country energy sufficient. While this process offers great promise in delivering fuel to the world, some critics point to the environmental damage that can be caused by fracking, including pollution and destabilization of the earth's crust. Also, critics say that the success of fracking will bring a halt to the development of renewable energy sources as alternatives to fossil fuel. Although fracking would greatly increase our access to fossil fuel, is it a sustainable solution, given the environmental risks? As other sources of fossil fuels diminish, policymakers must address the benefits and risks of fracking.

Perspective 1	Perspective 2	Perspective 3
Dependence on fossil fuel must stop. We need to find alternative sources that are reliable, renewable, and safe. Human ingenuity and imagination must be put to the test to find such sources as quickly as possible for our survival.	Fracking holds promise for greater energy sufficiency in the US. However, the process also has environmental risks that pose tremendous dangers to human, plant, and animal life.	Fossil fuels are necessary for our societies to function. Methods of extracting fossil fuels from the earth's crust are crucial because there are still great quantities of fossil fuel beneath the earth's surface.

Essay Task

Write a unified, coherent essay in which you evaluate multiple perspectives on the impact of fracking. In your essay be sure to:

- Analyze and evaluate perspectives given
- State and develop your own perspective
- Explain the relationship between your perspective and those given

Your perspective may be in full agreement with any of the others, in partial agreement or wholly different. Whatever the case, support your ideas with logical reasoning and detailed, persuasive examples.

Quiz II

(1 Essay Prompt; 40 minutes)

DIRECTIONS: You have 40 minutes to plan and write an essay. Read the prompt carefully and make sure you understand the instructions.

Introducing Technology in Pre-Kindergarten Programs

Children are often introduced to technology at a young age, sometimes through their preschool programs. Students play educational games on tablets with interactive touch screens. Technology can also help children gain social skills if they play computer games with a partner. Teachers can use digital cameras or videos to document students' progress and share it with their parents. Technology can provide activities that are fun for students and convenient for teachers, but should technology play a central role in preschool classrooms? Since children use technological devices at an increasingly young age, it is important to consider how technology could enhance or inhibit early childhood development.

Perspective 1	Perspective 2	Perspective 3
Technological devices are impractical for pre-K classroom use because they are expensive, are easy for children to break, and quickly become outdated. Furthermore, children should not become too reliant on computers for entertainment.	Games on computers or tablets can make learning basic skills, such as counting or memorizing the alphabet, more entertaining and interactive for children. Children will see the task as a form of play, rather than work.	It is important to make the use of technology a natural and integral part of children's lives. They will be required to use it in the classroom, and eventually in the workforce, and they will adapt to it more quickly if they start using technological devices at a young age.

Essay Task

Write a unified, coherent essay in which you evaluate multiple perspectives on the impact of introducing technology in pre-kindergarten programs. In your essay be sure to:

- Analyze and evaluate perspectives given
- State and develop your own perspective
- Explain the relationship between your perspective and those given

Your perspective may be in full agreement with any of the others, in partial agreement or wholly different. Whatever the case, support your ideas with logical reasoning and detailed, persuasive examples.

Quiz III

(1 Essay Prompt; 40 minutes)

> **DIRECTIONS:** You have 40 minutes to plan and write an essay. Read the prompt carefully and make sure you understand the instructions.

Freedom of Speech Online

Websites can offer open forums for debate and discussion, but sites can monitor users' comments and remove statements considered harmful or obscene. Some sites censor obscene language, such as racial slurs or hate speech. Others try to prevent "trolling," or the use of extreme statements for the purpose of offending readers, rather than contributing to meaningful debate. If a person threatens someone online, his or her comments could have legal consequences. Limiting what is said online might restrict freedom of speech, but should site managers have the power to limit permitted speech on their websites and/or impose legal consequences? With the rise of legal cases about freedom of speech online, it is important to examine what types of speech should be tolerated in certain online settings.

Perspective 1	Perspective 2	Perspective 3
Monitoring comments gives the website too much control over what is said. Although some issues, such as threats, should be monitored, eliminating all "offensive" speech could limit the range of viewpoints that are expressed on a website.	Allowing offensive speech could intimidate writers into silence, especially if they are covering a controversial topic. Some writers receive violent threats from people commenting on their articles. In a real-life setting, this type of speech would have legal consequences, and likewise, it should not be allowed online.	Site administrators argue that the anonymity of posting online can allow people to write offensive comments without ever facing the people they insult. If website users know that offensive speech can be censored, they will conduct themselves more civilly, as if they were talking to people face-to-face.

Essay Task

Write a unified, coherent essay in which you evaluate multiple perspectives on the impact of freedom of speech online. In your essay be sure to:

- Analyze and evaluate perspectives given
- State and develop your own perspective
- Explain the relationship between your perspective and those given

Your perspective may be in full agreement with any of the others, in partial agreement or wholly different. Whatever the case, support your ideas with logical reasoning and detailed, persuasive examples.

STRATEGY SUMMARY

General Strategies

1. Begin with the prompt.

2. Write only on the assigned topic. Writing on any other topic will result in a score of "0."

3. Remember to evaluate the given perspectives, develop your own perspective, and describe how your perspective relates to the given perspectives.

4. Do not try to do too much. Try to limit the scope of your topic to a reasonable effort.

5. Organize your thoughts and write an outline before beginning the essay. Do not spend more than two minutes writing the outline.

   a) Familiarize yourself with the essay prompt and the given perspectives.

   b) Develop your own perspective.

   c) Develop a thesis.

   d) Identify three to four important points.

   e) Decide on the order of presentation of the major points.

6. Organize ideas into paragraphs.

   a) Begin with an introduction.

   b) Create three to four body paragraphs.

   c) End with a conclusion.

7. Write using correct grammar.

8. Write clearly, concisely, and legibly.

9. Punctuate and spell correctly.

10. Spend a few minutes proofreading your essay.

Mathematics

Course Concept Outline

I. Test Mechanics (p. 189)

A. Overview (p. 189)

B. Anatomy (Items #1–4, pp. 190–191)

C. Pacing (p. 192)

D. Time Trial (Items #1–5, pp. 193–194)

E. Game Plan (p. 195)

    1. Quickly Preview the Test Section, but Skip the Directions
    2. Answer the Question That Is Being Asked
       a) Read the Question Carefully
       b) Pay Attention to Units
       c) Pay Attention to Thought-Reversers
    3. Use the Answer Choices
       a) Eliminate Answer Choices That Cannot Be Correct
       b) Use the Answer Choices to Check Your Math
    4. Don't Go Calculator Crazy

E. Calculator Exercise (Items #1–10; pp. 198–199)

II. Lesson (p. 201)

A. Preliminaries[1]

    1. What Is Tested
    2. Directions
    3. Item Profiles

---

[1] Some concepts in this Course Concept Outline are not illustrated through examples in your student text but may be covered by your instructor in class. They are included here to provide a complete outline of your course.

B. Item-Types (p. 201)

1. Arithmetic (Item #1, p. 201)
2. Algebra (Items #2–6, pp. 201–202)
3. Coordinate Geometry (Item #7, p. 202)
4. Geometry (Items #8–9, pp. 202–203)
5. Trigonometry (Item #10, p. 203)
6. Statistics and Probability (Item #11, p. 203)
7. Data Representation (Item #12, p. 204)

C. General Strategies (p. 204)

1. Use the Figures (Items #13–16, pp. 204–205)
2. Use the Answer Choices
   a) Answer Choices Are Arranged in Order
   b) Wrong Choices Correspond to Conceptual Errors (Item #17, p. 205)
3. Pay Special Attention to "Signal" Words (Items #18–21, pp. 205–206)
4. Answer the Question Being Asked (Items #22–30, pp. 206–207)
5. Carefully Consider "Cannot Be Determined" (Item #31, p. 207)
6. Additional Helpful Hints

D. Arithmetic Review and Strategies (p. 207)

1. Simple Manipulations—Just Do It! (Items #32–33, pp. 207–208)
2. Complicated Manipulations—Look for Shortcuts
   a) Simplifying (Item #34, p. 208)
   b) Factoring (Items #35–36, p. 208)
   c) Approximation (Items #37–39, p. 208)
   d) The "Flying-X" Method (Item #40, p. 209)
   e) Decimal-Fraction Equivalents (Item #41–42, p. 209)
3. Complicated Arithmetic Application Items—Bridge the Gap (Items #43–44, p. 209)
4. Common Arithmetic Items
   a) Properties of Numbers (Items #45–53, pp. 210–211)
   b) Scientific Notation (Items #54–57, p. 211)
   c) Sets: Union, Intersection, and Elements (Items #58–62, pp. 211–212)
   d) Absolute Value (Items #63–65, p. 212)
   e) Matrices (Items #66–69, pp. 212–213)
   f) Complex Numbers (Items #70–71, p. 213)
   g) Percents (Items #72–78, p. 214)
   h) Ratios (Items #79–80, p. 215)
   i) Proportions and Direct-Inverse Variation (Items #81–87, pp. 215–216)
5. Arithmetic Strategy: "Test-the-Test" (Items #88–93, p. 216)

E. Algebra Review and Strategies (p. 216)

1. Manipulating Algebraic Expressions
   a) Basic Algebraic Manipulations (Items #94–95, pp. 216–217)
   b) Evaluating Expressions (Items #96–99, p. 217)
   c) Manipulating Expressions Involving Exponents (Items #100–101, p. 217)
   d) Factoring Expressions (Items #102–104, p. 218)
   e) Creating Algebraic Expressions (Items #105–106, p. 218)
   f) Logarithmic Expressions (Items #107–108, pp. 218–219)
2. Evaluating Sequences (Items #109–112, p. 219)
3. Solving Algebraic Equations or Inequalities with One Variable
   a) Simple Equations (Item #113, p. 219)
   b) Simple Inequalities (Item #114, p. 219)
   c) Equations Involving Rational Expressions (Items #115–117, pp. 219–220)
   d) Inequalities Involving Rational Expressions (Item #118, p. 220)

       e) Equations Involving Radical Expressions (Items #119–122, p. 220)
       f) Equations Involving Integer and Rational Exponents (Items #123–126, pp. 220–221)
       g) Equations Involving Logarithms (Items #127–128, p. 221)
       h) Equations Involving Absolute Value (Items #129–130, p. 221)
       i) Inequalities Involving Absolute Value (Items #131–133, pp. 221–222)
   4. Expressing and Evaluating Algebraic Functions
       a) Function Notation (Items #134–141, pp. 222–223)
       b) Concepts of Domain and Range (Items #142–145, p. 223)
       c) Functions as Models (Item #146, p. 223)
   5. Solving Algebraic Equations with Two Variables (Item #147, p. 223)
   6. Solving Simultaneous Equations (Items #148–152, pp. 223–224)
   7. Solving Quadratic Equations and Relations (Items #153–157, pp. 224–225)
   8. Algebra Strategies: "Test-the-Test" and "Plug-and-Chug" (Items #158–169, pp. 225–227)

F. Coordinate Geometry Review and Strategies (p. 227)

   1. The Coordinate System (Items #170–174, pp. 227–228)
   2. Slope of a Line (Items #175–178, pp. 228–229)
   3. Slope-Intercept Form of a Linear Equation (Items #179–183, pp. 229–230)
   4. Distance Formula (Items #184–187, pp. 230–231)
   5. Graphs of Linear Equations (Items #188–189, p. 231)
   6. Graphs of First-Degree Inequalities (Item #190, p. 232)
   7. Graphs of Quadratic Equations and Relations (Items #191–192, pp. 232–233)
   8. Qualitative Behavior of Graphs of Functions (Items #193–194, p. 233)
   9. Transformations and Their Effects on Graphs of Functions and Figures (Items #195–196, p. 234)

G. Geometry Review and Strategies (p. 235)

   1. Geometric Notation
   2. Lines and Angles (Items #197–201, pp. 235–236)
   3. Triangles
       a) Pythagorean Theorem (Item #202, p. 236)
       b) 45°-45°-90° Triangles (Items #203–204, p. 236)
       c) 30°-60°-90° Triangles (Item #205, p. 236)
       d) Properties of Triangles (Items #206–207, p. 237)
   4. Rectangles and Squares (Items #208–210, p. 237)
   5. Circles (Item #211, p. 238)
   6. Properties of Tangent Lines (Items #212–215, p. 238)
   7. Complex Figures (Items #216–221, pp. 238–240)
   8. Solids (Items #222–225, p. 240)
   9. Geometry Strategies
       a) "Guesstimating" (Items #226–228, p. 241)
       b) Measuring (Items #229–230, p. 241)
       c) "Meastimating" (Items #231–232, p. 242)

H. Trigonometry Review and Strategies (p. 242)

   1. Definitions of the Six Trigonometric Functions (Items #233–234, pp. 242–243)
   2. Determining Trigonometric Values
   3. Trigonometric Relationships (Items #235–236, p. 243)
   4. Trigonometry as an Alternative Method of Solution (Items #237–239, pp. 243–244)

I. Statistics and Probability Review and Strategies (p. 244)

   1. Averages (Items #240–244, pp. 244–245)
   2. Median (Item #245, p. 245)
   3. Mode (Item #246, p. 245)
   4. Probability (Items #247–251, pp. 245–246)

5. Data Representation
   a) Bar, Cumulative, and Line Graphs (Items #252–256, pp. 247–249)
   b) Pie Charts (Items #257–258, p. 249)
   c) Tables (Item #259, p. 250)
   d) Scatterplots (Item #260, p. 250)

III. Quizzes (p. 251)

   A. Quiz I (Items #1–20, pp. 251–255)

   B. Quiz II (Items #1–20, pp. 256–259)

   C. Quiz III (Items #1–20, pp. 260–263)

   D. Quiz IV Brain Buster (Items #1–25, pp. 264–267)

IV. Review (Items #1–32, pp. 269–275)

V. Strategy Summary (p. 277)

TEST MECHANICS

Overview

The ACT Mathematics Test, according to the test-writers, presupposes a knowledge of pre-algebra, algebra, intermediate algebra, coordinate geometry, geometry, and trigonometry. The ACT Mathematics Test items are pretty much the same kind of questions you'd see on a regular test—except they are multiple-choice questions.

You do not have to know all of the tested topics to do well on the exam. For example, intermediate algebra, coordinate geometry, and trigonometry combined account for less than 40 percent of the test. Here is the distribution of items by topic on the ACT Mathematics Test:

ACT MATHEMATICS TEST TOPICS (60 items; 60 minutes)		
Content	Approximate Number	Approximate Percent
Pre-Algebra	14	23%
Elementary Algebra	10	17%
Intermediate Algebra	9	15%
Coordinate Geometry	9	15%
Plane Geometry	14	23%
Trigonometry	4	7%

This means that you could choose to skip all of the trigonometry items and the nine most difficult coordinate geometry and intermediate algebra items, miss another nine questions, and still get a 24 on the ACT Mathematics Test, which is a good score. For a very respectable score of 21 (above the national average), you need a raw score of about 33, which you can get if you choose to skip all the trigonometry, intermediate algebra, and coordinate geometry items and keep your wrong answers down to five.

This is not a recommended strategy. You want to make sure that you answer any questions you know how to answer and guess on the rest. But these calculations show that you can do quite well on the math portion of the ACT test even if you're not exactly a math whiz.

Anatomy

> **DIRECTIONS:** Solve each item and choose the correct answer choice. Calculator use is permitted; however, some items are best solved without the use of a calculator.

You really do not need the directions at all. You can use a calculator, and there will be further discussion of this in class.

NOTES: All of the following should be assumed, unless otherwise stated.

1. Illustrative figures are NOT necessarily drawn to scale.
2. The word *average* indicates arithmetic mean.
3. The word *line* indicates a straight line.
4. Geometric figures lie in a plane.

Also, figures are not necessarily drawn to scale. However, in practice, the figures are almost always drawn to scale. Again, this issue will be discussed in detail later during the Mathematics Lesson.

---

1. Paulo bicycled $6\frac{1}{3}$ miles on Wednesday and $8\frac{2}{5}$ miles on Thursday. How many miles did he bicycle during those two days?

A. $14\frac{2}{15}$

B. $14\frac{1}{4}$

C. $14\frac{3}{8}$

D. $14\frac{11}{15}$

E. $14\frac{13}{15}$

1. (D) *This item is solved by addition:*

$$6\frac{1}{3}+8\frac{2}{5}=\frac{19}{3}+\frac{42}{5}$$
$$=\frac{95}{15}+\frac{126}{15}$$
$$=\frac{221}{15}$$
$$=14\frac{11}{15}$$

2. The average weight of 5 packages in a shipment is 8.7 pounds. The weights of 4 of the packages are 6.3 pounds, 7.5 pounds, 8.9 pounds, and 9.6 pounds. What is the weight of the fifth package?

F. 8.5
G. 8.8
H. 9.4
J. 11.2
K. 12.3

2. (J) *This item is a bit more difficult. First, set up an equation for the average:*

$$\frac{6.3+7.5+8.9+9.6+x}{5}=8.7$$

Then, solve for the missing weight:

$$(6.3+7.5+8.9+9.6)+x=(8.7)(5)$$
$$x=43.5-32.3=11.2$$

3. If $3x + 4 = 7x - 2$, $x = ?$

A. $-\dfrac{1}{4}$

B. $\dfrac{1}{2}$

C. $\dfrac{3}{5}$

D. $\dfrac{2}{3}$

E. $1\dfrac{1}{2}$

3. (E) *For this item, you need to solve for x:*

$$3x + 4 = 7x - 2$$
$$3x - 7x = -2 - 4$$
$$-4x = -6$$
$$4x = 6$$
$$x = \frac{6}{4} = \frac{3}{2} = 1\frac{1}{2}$$

4. The ratio of the radii of two circles is $3:4$. What is the ratio of their areas?

F. $7:1$
G. $3:4$
H. $9:16$
J. $3:4\pi$
K. $9:16\pi$

4. (H) *With this item, since the ratio of the radii of the two circles is* $3:4$, *the ratio of their areas is:*

$$\frac{\pi(3)^2}{\pi(4)^2} = \frac{9\pi}{16\pi} = \frac{9}{16} = 9:16.$$

There are three other features of Mathematics items to note:

- ***Answer choices are arranged in order.*** For most Mathematics items, answer choices are arranged from least to greatest or vice versa. However, there are some exceptions. Choices that consist entirely of variables do not follow the rule, and items that ask "which of the following is the largest value?" obviously do not follow the rule. That the answer choices are usually arranged in order makes it easier for you to find your choice in the list. It also sets up an important test-taking strategy of starting with the middle choice when applying the "test-the-test" strategy, which you'll learn about later in the Mathematics Lesson.

- ***Answer choices are carefully constructed.*** The choices are not typically presented so that you have to perform repetitive number crunching to find the correct answer. You are not likely to find a problem with answer choices like the following:

  A. $183.27
  B. $183.28
  C. $183.29
  D. $183.30
  E. $183.31

  The choices on the ACT test usually correspond to errors in thinking—not errors in arithmetic. This feature is important because it is the basis for a couple of time-saving strategies that you'll learn shortly.

- ***Items are arranged on a ladder of difficulty.*** Of course, you can't tell this from the four examples provided here, but the ladder of difficulty is an important feature of the math test. Given that the problems become more difficult as you proceed, you're obviously going to have to make some important decisions about speed and possibly randomly guessing on some items. You'll get more advice on this later in the Mathematics Lesson.

Pacing

The Mathematics Test consists of 60 items. The time limit is 60 minutes. The items are arranged on a ladder of difficulty, so you'll need a pacing plan that helps you move more quickly through the easier items at the beginning of the test and allows you to build up a time reserve for the harder items that are located toward the end. The following table summarizes the timing for this approach:

ITEM NUMBERS	TIME TO SPEND PER ITEM	REMAINING TIME
#1–10	36 seconds	54 minutes
#11–20	42 seconds	47 minutes
#21–30	54 seconds	38 minutes
#31–40	66 seconds	27 minutes
#41–50	72 seconds	15 minutes
#51–60	90 seconds	0 minutes

This table is a schedule for the best of all possible math worlds. It's intended to be a guideline, not a rule. Try to stay on schedule, but be prepared to adjust your timing according to how many items you can realistically complete. Trying to stay on a schedule during the test will help you avoid the two biggest time wasters for timed tests.

First, staying on schedule will ensure that you are not plodding through the easy items at the beginning of the test. At first, with a 60-minute time limit, it will seem like you've got all the time in the world. But you don't. From the moment the test begins, you're behind schedule and playing catch-up. So, keep a sense of urgency.

Second, the schedule will serve as a constant reminder that you cannot afford to spend too much time on any one problem. If you make a mistake and spend three minutes on item #22, you'll find that you're falling behind schedule. Leave that problem, hoping you'll have time at the end of the test to come back and finish it. But spending three minutes to get +1 when three minutes could get you +5 is an inefficient use of time.

Time Trial

(5 items; 5 minutes)

DIRECTIONS: Solve each item and choose the correct answer choice. Calculator use is permitted; however, some items are best solved without the use of a calculator.

NOTES: All of the following should be assumed, unless otherwise stated.

1. Illustrative figures are NOT necessarily drawn to scale.
2. The word *average* indicates arithmetic mean.
3. The word *line* indicates a straight line.
4. Geometric figures lie in a plane.

1. $\dfrac{1}{10^{25}} - \dfrac{1}{10^{26}} = ?$

C

A. $\dfrac{9}{10^{25}}$

B. $\dfrac{1}{10^{25}}$

C. $\dfrac{9}{10^{26}}$

D. $-\dfrac{9}{10^{25}}$

E. $-\dfrac{1}{10}$

$$\frac{10 \cdot \frac{1}{10^{25}}}{10} - \frac{1}{10^{26}}$$

$$\frac{10}{10^{26}} - \frac{1}{10^{26}} = \frac{9}{10^{26}}$$

2. The table below shows readings of water levels for the Red River at various times. If readings of the rise of the water level followed a geometric progression, how many inches above normal was the water level at 3:00 p.m.?

RED RIVER WATER LEVEL READINGS				
Time (p.m.)	1:00	2:00	3:00	4:00
Inches above Normal	0.5	1.5	?	13.5

×3

F. 4
G. 4.5
H. 4.75
J. 5
K. 5.25

3. If s, t, and u are different positive integers and $\dfrac{s}{t}$ and $\dfrac{t}{u}$ are positive integers, which of the following CANNOT be a positive integer?

A. $\dfrac{s}{u}$

B. $s \cdot t$

C. $\dfrac{u}{s}$

D. $(s+t)u$

E. $(s-u)t$

4. In the figure below, $\overline{AD} = \overline{DC}$. What is the
value of $\overline{AD} + \overline{DC}$?

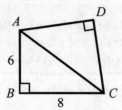

F. $18\sqrt{2}$
G. 18
H. $10\sqrt{2}$
J. 10
K. $6\sqrt{2}$

Pathagorem therom
$a^2 + b^2 = c^2$

5. In the figure below, the length of $\overline{AC}$ is 5 units.
Which of the following is the best
approximation for the number of units in the
length of $\overline{BC}$? ($\tan 22° \approx 0.4$)

A. 2.0
B. 3.0
C. 7.5
D. 12.5
E. 16

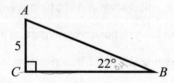

hyp · Sin 40 $\frac{a}{x}$ · hyp
───────────────
Sin 40

hyp = $\frac{a}{Sine\ 40}$

hyp = 14.0

Game Plan

Quickly Preview the Test Section, but Skip the Directions

As you get started on test day, take a few seconds to preview the Mathematics Test. It's 99.99% certain that you're going to find everything in place and just as you expect. But a quick overview will guarantee against any unanticipated changes. Do NOT, however, read the directions. Remind yourself of your pacing plan and then get to work.

Answer the Question That Is Being Asked

Read the Question Carefully

Some problems are fairly simple, but others are more complex, particularly practical word problems and more difficult geometry problems. The more complex the question, the easier it is to misread and set off down the wrong track. If the question is very long, underline key parts of the question.

Example:

If Mark traveled 20 miles in 3 hours and Lester traveled twice as far in half the time, what was Lester's average speed?

A. $3\frac{1}{3}$ miles per hour

B. $6\frac{2}{3}$ miles per hour

C. 12 miles per hour

D. 26 miles per hour

E. $26\frac{2}{3}$ miles per hour

The stem states that Lester traveled twice as far as Mark in half the time, or 40 miles in 1.5 hours.

Therefore, Lester's average speed was $\frac{40 \text{ miles}}{1.5 \text{ hours}} = 26.\overline{666} = 26\frac{2}{3}$ miles per hour, (E).

Pay Attention to Units

Some items require you to convert units (e.g., feet to inches or hours to minutes). The item stem will tell you what units to use. When you see an item stem that includes units, circle the unit and put a star beside it.

Example:

A certain copy machine produces 13 copies every 10 seconds. If the machine operates without interruption, how many copies will it produce in an hour?

F. 780

G. 4,200

H. 4,680

J. 4,800

K. 5,160

Create an expression that, after cancellation of like units, gives the number of copies produced in an hour:

$$\frac{13 \text{ copies}}{10 \cancel{\text{ seconds}}} \cdot \frac{60 \cancel{\text{ seconds}}}{1 \cancel{\text{ minute}}} \cdot \frac{60 \cancel{\text{ minutes}}}{1 \text{ hour}} = 4,680 \text{ copies/hour}.$$ Therefore, the copy machine produces 4,680 copies in an hour, (H).

Pay Attention to Thought-Reversers

A thought-reverser is any word, such as "not," "except," or "but," that turns a question inside out. As shown, below, make sure you mark the thought-reverser so that you do not forget it as you work the problem.

Example:

How many integers in the set of integers from 1 to 144, inclusive, are NOT a square of an integer?

A.   0
B.   2
C.   12
D. 132
E. 144

Since 1 is the square of 1, and 144 is the square of 12, there are a total of 12 integers in the set of integers from 1 to 144, inclusive, that are a square of an integer (1^2 , 2^2 , 3^2 , 4^2 , 5^2 , 6^2 , 7^2 , 8^2 , 9^2 , 10^2 , 11^2 , 12^2). Therefore, there are a total of $144 - 12 = 132$ integers in the set that are NOT a square of an integer, (D).

Use the Answer Choices

In the Mathematics Lesson, you will learn some very powerful test-taking strategies that use the multiple-choice answers to test items to help solve the items. For now, there are two simple suggestions to keep in mind.

Eliminate Answer Choices That Cannot Be Correct

Sometimes, the array of answers will include choices that, taken at face value, seem to be plausible, but when examined more carefully, must be incorrect.

Example:

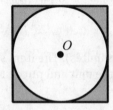

In the figure above, a circle with center O and a radius of 2 is inscribed in a square. What is the area of the shaded portion of the figure?

F. $2 - \pi$
G. $4 - 2\pi$
H. $16 - 2\pi$
J. $16 - 4\pi$
K. $16 - 6\pi$

The shaded area is equal to the area of the square minus the area of the circle. Since the radius of the circle is 2, the side of the square is 4 and its area is $4 \cdot 4 = 16$. The area of the circle is $\pi(2)^2 = 4\pi$. Therefore, the shaded area is $16 - 4\pi$, (J). Notice that without even solving the item, you can eliminate answer choices. Take a closer look at (F), (G), and (K). Since π is approximately 3.14, (F), (G), and (K) are negative. Area, however, cannot be a negative number, so (F), (G), and (K) must be wrong, and you can eliminate them without doing any other work. Now, if you had to, you can make an educated guess from the remaining choices and the odds of guessing correctly are 50 percent. (Note that even if you are unable to eliminate answer choices, you still should guess, since the ACT test does not penalize for wrong answers.)

Use the Answer Choices to Check Your Math

While the ACT test does not test repetitive number crunching, some items do require a calculation or two. One of the fundamental rules of math is to "check your work." On the ACT test, however, this is a real time waster. Let's say you do a calculation (with or without your calculator) and the result is $23.10. If one of the choices is $23.10, pick it, mark your answer sheet, and move on to the next item. Do NOT check your arithmetic. The possibility that you did the arithmetic, made a mistake, and still got a number like 23.10 is just too unlikely to consider. On the other hand, if you do not find a choice that matches your calculation, then you'd better check both your set-up of the problem and your arithmetic to find the error. In this way, the answer choices function as a feedback loop on the accuracy of your calculations.

Don't Go Calculator Crazy

Just because you are allowed to use a calculator on the test does not mean that you should try to solve every problem with your calculator. In fact, for most problems, using the calculator is a less efficient method of arriving at a solution. Assume, for example, that you have to do the following arithmetic to get your answer: $\left(\frac{2}{3}\right)\left(\frac{7}{4}\right)\left(\frac{1}{6}\right)$.

Since this problem involves single digit multiplication, it's going to be easier to do the arithmetic with a pencil than with a calculator: $\left(\frac{2}{3}\right)\left(\frac{7}{4}\right)\left(\frac{1}{6}\right) = \frac{2 \cdot 7 \cdot 1}{3 \cdot 4 \cdot 6} = \frac{14}{72} = \frac{7}{36}$. Use the calculator when it will be a definite advantage, but don't automatically assume that every problem is easier to solve with a calculator.

Calculator Exercise

This exercise is designed to illustrate when and when not to use your calculator. Make sure that the calculator you bring to the ACT test is one with which you are thoroughly familiar. (For more detailed information on calculator usage, including specific models that are prohibited on the test, go to http://www.actstudent.org/faq/calculator.html.) Although no item requires the use of a calculator, a calculator may be helpful at times. It may be useful for any item that involves complex arithmetic computations, but it cannot take the place of understanding how to set up a mathematical item. The degree to which you can use your calculator will depend on its features. Answers are on page 666.

DIRECTIONS: Label each of the items that follow according to one of the following categories. Then solve each item.

Category 1: A calculator would be very useful (it would save valuable test time).

Category 2: A calculator might or might not be useful.

Category 3: A calculator would be counterproductive (it would waste valuable test time).

1. What is the average of 8.5, 7.8, and 7.7?

A. 8.3
B. 8.2
C. 8.1
D. 8.0
E. 7.9

2. If $0 < x < 1$, which of the following has the greatest value?

F. x
G. $2x$
H. x^2
J. x^3
K. $x+1$

3. If 4.5 pounds of chocolate cost \$10, how many pounds of chocolate can be purchased for \$12?

A. $4\frac{3}{4}$

B. $5\frac{2}{5}$

C. $5\frac{1}{2}$

D. $5\frac{3}{4}$

E. 6

4. What is the value of $\frac{8}{9} - \frac{7}{8}$?

F. $\frac{1}{72}$

G. $\frac{1}{8}$

H. $\frac{1}{7}$

J. $\frac{15}{72}$

K. $\frac{15}{7}$

5. Which of the following fractions has the greatest value?

A. $\dfrac{111}{221}$

B. $\dfrac{75}{151}$

C. $\dfrac{333}{998}$

D. $\dfrac{113}{225}$

E. $\dfrac{101}{301}$

6. Dr. Leo's new office is 2.8 yards by 4 yards. She plans to run a decorative border around the perimeter of the office. How many yards of wallpaper border should she purchase?

F.   8
G.   13.2
H.   13.6
J.   14.2
K.   16.7

7. What is the value of $\dfrac{2}{3} - \dfrac{5}{8}$?

A.   1

B. $\dfrac{15}{16}$

C. $\dfrac{3}{24}$

D. $\dfrac{1}{24}$

E. $\dfrac{1}{100}$

8. If $3x + y = 33$ and $x + y = 17$, then what is the value of x?

F.   8
G.   12
H.   16
J.   24
K.   33

9. If the perimeter of the rectangle below is 40, what is its area?

A.   5
B.   15
C.   25
D.   45
E.   75

10. If the price of a book increases from $10.00 to $12.50, what is the percent increase in price?

F.   2.5%
G.   12.5%
H.   25%
J.   33%
K.   50%

LESSON

The items in this section accompany the in-class review of the skills and concepts tested by the ACT Mathematics Test. You will work through the items with your instructor in class. Use any available space in this section for scratch work. Answers begin on page 666.

DIRECTIONS: Solve each item and choose the correct answer choice. Calculator use is permitted; however, some items are best solved without the use of a calculator.

NOTE: All of the following should be assumed, unless otherwise stated.

1. Illustrative figures are NOT necessarily drawn to scale.
2. The word *average* indicates arithmetic mean.
3. The word *line* indicates a straight line.
4. Geometric figures lie in a plane.

Item-Types

Arithmetic

1. If the price of fertilizer has been decreased from 3 pounds for $2 to 5 pounds for $2, how many more pounds of fertilizer can be purchased for $10 than could have been purchased before?

   A.   2
   B.   8
   C.   10
   D.   12
   E.   15

Algebra

2. Five students formed a political club to support a candidate for local office. They project that club membership will double every three weeks. Which of the following can be used to find the number of members that the club projects to have after twelve weeks?

   F. $5\left(2^{\frac{3}{12}}\right)$

   G. $5\left(2^{\frac{2}{3}}\right)$

   H. $5\left(2^{\frac{3}{2}}\right)$

   J. $5\left(2^{\frac{12}{3}}\right)$

   K. $5+5\left(2^4\right)$

3. If $\dfrac{2x-5}{3} = -4x$, then $x = ?$

   A. -1

   B. $-\dfrac{5}{14}$

   C. 0

   D. $\dfrac{5}{14}$

   E. 1

4. The oil-fired boiler in the basement of a school building consumes fuel at a rate of g gallons every h hours. Which of the following expressions can be used to calculate the amount of fuel consumed during m minutes of uninterrupted operation?

F. ghm

G. $\dfrac{g}{hm}$

H. $\dfrac{60g}{hm}$

J. $\dfrac{gm}{60h}$

K. $\dfrac{g}{60hm}$

5. If $f(x) = 2x - 3$ and $g(x) = x^2 - 2$, then what does $f(g(2))$ equal?

A. -1
B. 0
C. 1
D. 4
E. 7

6. If $|x + 3| = 5$, then $x = ?$

F. -8 or 2
G. -2 or 8
H. -8
J. -2
K. 2 or 8

Coordinate Geometry

7. In the figure below, the line has a slope of 1. What is the y-intercept of the line?

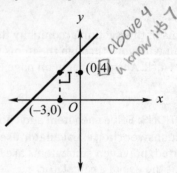

A. -5
B. -3
C. 0
D. 3
E. 7

Geometry

8. In the figure below, $\triangle PQR$ is inscribed in a circle with center O. What is the area of the circle?

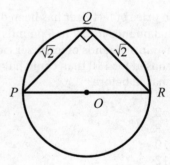

F. $\dfrac{\pi}{2}$

G. $\dfrac{\pi}{\sqrt{2}}$

H. π

J. $\pi\sqrt{2}$

K. 2π

9. In the figure below, $\overline{QP}$ is tangent to circle O at point P, and $\overline{QR}$ is tangent to circle O at point R. What is the degree measure of the minor arc PSR?

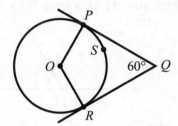

A.   30
B.   60
C.   90
D.   120
E.   180

Trigonometry

10. In the figure below, $\sin A = ?$

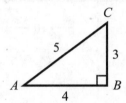

F. $\dfrac{3}{5}$

G. $\dfrac{3}{4}$

H. $\dfrac{4}{5}$

J. $\dfrac{5}{4}$

K. $\dfrac{5}{3}$

Statistics and Probability

11. What is the average of 8.5, 7.8, and 7.7?

A.   8.3
B.   8.2
C.   8.1
D.   8.0
E.   7.9

Data Representation

12. The following graph shows the data for domestic and foreign sales for Company *X* over five years.

Sales of Company *X* (in millions)

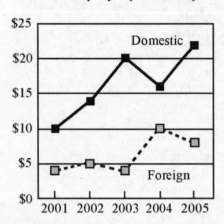

Which of the following pie graphs best represents the division of total sales between foreign and domestic sales for 2004?

F.

J.

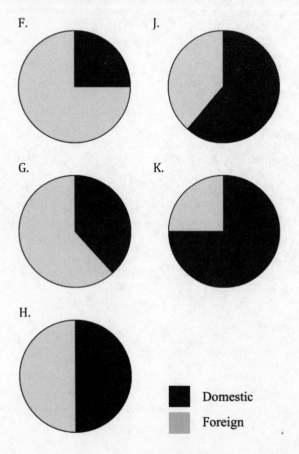

G.

K.

H.

■ Domestic

■ Foreign

General Strategies

Use the Figures

13. In the figure below, *x* = ?

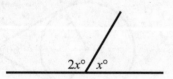

A. 15
B. 30
C. 45
D. 60
E. 120

14. In the figure below, what is the length of $\overline{AB} + \overline{CD}$?

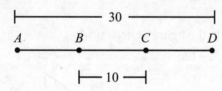

F.   5
G. 10
H. 15
J. 20
K. 40

Items #15–16 refer to the following figure.

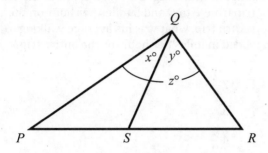

15. Which of the following must be true?

      I. $\overline{PS} < \overline{SR}$
     II. $z = 90$
   III. $x > y$

  A. I only
  B. I and II only
  C. I and III only
  D. I, II, and III
  E. Neither I, II, nor III

16. Which of the following must be true?

      I. $\overline{PR} > \overline{PS}$
     II. $z > x$
   III. $x + y = z$

  F. I only
  G. I and II only
  H. I and III only
  J. I, II, and III
  K. Neither I, II, nor III

Use the Answer Choices

Wrong Choices Correspond to Conceptual Errors

17. In a certain year, the number of girls who graduated from City High School was twice the number of boys who graduated. If $\frac{3}{4}$ of the girls and $\frac{5}{6}$ of the boys went to college immediately after graduation, what fraction of the graduates that year went to college immediately after graduation?

  A. $\dfrac{5}{36}$

  B. $\dfrac{16}{27}$

  C. $\dfrac{7}{9}$

  D. $\dfrac{29}{36}$

  E. $\dfrac{31}{36}$

Pay Special Attention to "Signal" Words

18. A jar contains black and white marbles. If there are ten marbles in the jar, then which of the following could NOT be the ratio of black to white marbles?

  F. $9:1$
  G. $7:3$
  H. $1:1$
  J. $1:4$
  K. $1:10$

19. If n is a negative number, which of the following is the <u>least</u> in value?

  A. $-n$
  B. $n - n$
  C. $n + n$
  D. n^2
  E. n^4

20. If a machine produces 240 thingamabobs per hour, how many <u>minutes</u> are needed for the machine to produce 30 thingamabobs?

F.   6
G.   7.5
H.   8
J.   12
K.   12.5

21. Of the 120 people in a room, $\frac{3}{5}$ are women. If $\frac{2}{3}$ of the people are married, what is the maximum number of women in the room who could be <u>unmarried</u>?

A.   80
B.   72
C.   48
D.   40
E.   32

Answer the Question Being Asked

22. Three friends are playing a game in which each person simultaneously displays one of three hand signs: a clenched fist, an open palm, or two extended fingers. How many unique combinations of the signs are possible?

F.   3
G.   9
H.   10
J.   12
K.   27

23. If $\frac{1}{3}$ of the number of girls in a school equals $\frac{1}{5}$ of the total number of students, what is the ratio of girls to boys in the school?

A. 5:3
B. 3:2
C. 2:5
D. 1:3
E. 1:5

24. Peter walked from point P to point Q and back along the same route, a total distance of 2 miles. If he averaged 4 miles per hour on the trip from P to Q and 5 miles per hour on the return trip, what was his average walking speed in miles per hour for the entire trip?

F. $2\frac{2}{9}$

G.   4

H. $4\frac{4}{9}$

J. $4\frac{1}{2}$

K.   5

25. After a 20% decrease in price, the cost of an item is D dollars. What was the price of the item before the decrease?

A.   0.75D
B.   0.80D
C.   1.20D
D.   1.25D
E.   1.5D

26. On a certain trip, a motorist drove 10 miles at 30 miles per hour, 10 miles at 40 miles per hour, and 10 miles at 50 miles per hour. What portion of her total driving time was spent driving 50 miles per hour?

F. $1\frac{13}{51}$

G. $\frac{5}{7}$

H. $\frac{5}{12}$

J. $\frac{1}{3}$

K. $\frac{12}{47}$

27. What is the <u>maximum</u> number of non-overlapping sections that can be created when a circle is crossed by three straight lines?

    A. 3
    B. 4
    C. 5
    D. 6
    E. 7

28. At Glenridge High School, 20% of the students are seniors. If all of the seniors attended the school play, and 60% of all the students attended the play, what percent of the <u>non-seniors</u> attended the play?

    F. 20%
    G. 40%
    H. 50%
    J. 60%
    K. 100%

29. The water meter at a factory displays the reading below. What is the <u>minimum</u> number of cubic feet of water that the factory must use before four of the five digits on the meter are again the same?

Water Usage in Cubic Feet

    A. 10,000
    B.   1,000
    C.   999
    D.   666
    E.   9

30. A telephone call from City X to City Y costs $1.00 for the first three minutes and $0.25 for each additional minute thereafter. What is the <u>maximum</u> duration of a phone call, in minutes, for $3.00?

    F.   8
    G. 10
    H. 11
    J. 12
    K. 13

Carefully Consider "Cannot Be Determined"

31. In the figure below, $m + n + o + p + q + r = ?$

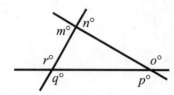

    A. 360
    B. 540
    C. 720
    D. 900
    E. Cannot be determined from the given information

Arithmetic Review and Strategies

Simple Manipulations—Just Do It!

32. $\dfrac{8}{9} - \dfrac{7}{8} = ?$

    F. $\dfrac{1}{72}$

    G. $\dfrac{1}{8}$

    H. $\dfrac{1}{7}$

    J. $\dfrac{15}{72}$

    K. $\dfrac{15}{7}$

33. $\sqrt{1-\left(\dfrac{2}{9}+\dfrac{1}{36}+\dfrac{1}{18}\right)} = ?$

    A. $\dfrac{1}{5}$

    B. $\sqrt{\dfrac{2}{3}}$

    C. $\dfrac{5}{6}$

    D. 1

    E. $\sqrt{3}$

Complicated Manipulations—Look for Shortcuts

Simplifying

34. $\dfrac{1}{2}\cdot\dfrac{2}{3}\cdot\dfrac{3}{4}\cdot\dfrac{4}{5}\cdot\dfrac{5}{6}\cdot\dfrac{6}{7}\cdot\dfrac{7}{8} = ?$ $\dfrac{1}{8}$

Cross of some top+bottom numerator × denominator cancel out

    F. $\dfrac{1}{56}$

    G. $\dfrac{1}{8}$

    H. $\dfrac{28}{37}$

    J. $\dfrac{41}{43}$

    K. $\dfrac{55}{56}$

Factoring

35. $86(37) - 37(85) = ?$

    A. 0
    B. 1 $86(37) - 85(37) = 37$
    C. 37
    D. 85
    E. 86

36. Which of the following is <u>a prime</u> factorization of 120?

    F. $(2)(2)(15)$
    G. $(2)(3)(4)(5)$ *not prime*
    H. $(2)(2)(3)(10)$
    J. $(2)(2)(2)(3)(5) = 120$
    K. $(2)(2)(3)(3)(5)$

Approximation

37. $-4.01(3.2) + 0.2(0.4) = ?$

    A. -12.752
    B. -4.536
    C. 0.432
    D. 1.251
    E. 12.783

38. $\dfrac{0.2521 \cdot 8.012}{1.014}$ is approximately equal to which of the following?

    F. 0.25
    G. 0.5
    H. 1.0
    J. 1.5
    K. 2.0

39. Which of the following fractions is the largest?

    A. $\dfrac{111}{221}$

    B. $\dfrac{75}{151}$

    C. $\dfrac{333}{998}$

    D. $\dfrac{113}{225}$

    E. $\dfrac{101}{301}$

The "Flying-X" Method

40. If $z = \dfrac{x+y}{x}$, $1 - z = ?$

   F. $\dfrac{1-x+y}{x}$

   G. $\dfrac{x+y-1}{x}$

   H. $\dfrac{1-x-y}{x}$

   J. $-\dfrac{y}{x}$

   K. $1-x-y$

Decimal-Fraction Equivalents

41. $0.125 \cdot 0.125 \cdot 64 = ?$

   A.   0.125
   B.   0.5
   C.   0.625
   D.   1
   E.   8

42. $\dfrac{0.111 \cdot 0.666}{0.166 \cdot 0.125}$ is approximately equal to which of the following?

   F.   6.8
   G.   4.3
   H.   3.6
   J.   1.6
   K.   0.9

Complicated Arithmetic Application Items—Bridge the Gap

43. If the senior class has 360 students, of whom $\dfrac{5}{12}$ are women, and the junior class has 350 students, of whom $\dfrac{4}{7}$ are women, how many more women are there in the junior class than in the senior class?

   A. $(360-350)\left(\dfrac{4}{7} - \dfrac{5}{12}\right)$

   B. $\dfrac{(360-350)\left(\dfrac{4}{7} - \dfrac{5}{12}\right)}{2}$

   C. $\left(\dfrac{4}{7} \cdot \dfrac{5}{12}\right)(360-350)$

   D. $\left(\dfrac{4}{7} \cdot 350\right) - \left(\dfrac{5}{12} \cdot 360\right)$

   E. $\left(\dfrac{5}{12} \cdot 360\right) - \left(\dfrac{4}{7} \cdot 350\right)$

44. If the price of candy increases from 5 pounds for $7 to 3 pounds for $7, how much less candy (in pounds) can be purchased for $3.50 at the new price than at the old price?

   F. $\dfrac{2}{7}$

   G.   1

   H. $1\dfrac{17}{35}$

   J.   2

   K. $3\dfrac{34}{35}$

Common Arithmetic Items

Properties of Numbers

45. If n is any integer, which of the following is always an odd integer?

    A. $n-1$
    B. $n+1$
    C. $n+2$
    D. $2n+1$
    E. $2n+2$

46. Which of the following expressions represents the product of two consecutive integers?

    F. $2n+1$
    G. $2n+n$
    H. $2n^2$
    J. n^2+1
    K. n^2+n

47. If n is any integer, which of the following expressions <u>must</u> be even?

    I. $2n$
    II. $2n+n$
    III. $2n \cdot n$

    A.   I only
    B.   II only
    C.   III only
    D.   I and II only
    E.   I and III only

48. If n is the first number in a series of three consecutive even numbers, which of the following expressions represents the sum of the three numbers?

    F. $n+2$
    G. $n+4$
    H. $n+6$
    J. $3n+6$
    K. $6(3n)$

49. If n is an odd number, which of the following expressions represents the third odd number following n?

    A. $n+3$
    B. $n+4$
    C. $n+6$
    D. $3n+3$
    E. $4n+4$

50. If n is any odd integer, which of the following expressions <u>must</u> also be odd?

    I. $n+n$
    II. $n+n+n$
    III. $n \cdot n \cdot n$

    F.   I only
    G.   II only
    H.   III only
    J.   II and III only
    K.   I, II, and III

51. If n is a negative number, which of the following expressions <u>must</u> be positive?

    I. $2n$
    II. n^2
    III. n^5

    A.   I only
    B.   II only
    C.   III only
    D.   I and II only
    E.   II and III only

52. If $0 < x < 1$, which of the following expressions is the largest?

    F. x
    G. $2x$
    H. x^2
    J. x^3
    K. $x+1$

53. If $-1 < x < 0$, which of the following expressions is the largest?

A. -1
B. x
C. $2x$
D. x^3
E. $x-1$

Scientific Notation

54. Which of the following is equivalent to 12,040,000,000,000?

F. 1.204×10^{-14}

G. 1.204×10^{-13}

H. 1.204×10^{12}

J. 1.204×10^{13}

K. 1.204×10^{14}

55. The world's population in 2014 was estimated to be 1,000 times Bulgaria's population of 7.2×10^6. What was the approximate population of the world in 2014?

A. 7.2×10^3

B. 7.2×10^6

C. 7.2×10^7

D. 7.2×10^8

E. 7.2×10^9

56. Which of the following is equivalent to
$$\frac{\left(4 \times 10^7\right)\left(6 \times 10^{12}\right)}{8 \times 10^9}?$$

F. 1.25×10^{10}

G. 2×10^{10}

H. 3×10^{10}

J. 2×10^{28}

K. 3×10^{28}

57. A sound wave travels at approximately 1,125 feet/second. If a person hears a sound two and a half minutes after it happens, how far away, in feet, is the person from the source of the sound?

A. 1.6875×10^1

B. 2.8125×10^3

C. 2.8125×10^4

D. 1.6875×10^5

E. 1.6875×10^6

Sets: Union, Intersection, and Elements

58. If set $S = \{2, 3, 4\}$ and set P is the set of all products of different elements in set S, then set $P = ?$

F. $\{6, 8, 12\}$
G. $\{6, 8, 18\}$
H. $\{6, 8, 12, 24\}$
J. $\{6, 8, 12, 18, 24\}$
K. $\{6, 8, 12, 18, 24, 36\}$

59. If set X is the set of all integers between 1 and 24, inclusive, that are evenly divisible by 3, and set Y is the set of all integers between 1 and 24, inclusive, that are evenly divisible by 4, what is the set of all elements in both sets X and Y?

A. $\{12\}$
B. $\{3, 4\}$
C. $\{12, 24\}$
D. $\{4, 12, 24\}$
E. $\{3, 4, 12, 24\}$

60. If x is an element of set X, in which set X is the set of integers evenly divisible by 3 such that $6 < x < 11$, and y is an element of set Y, where set Y is the set of integers evenly divisible by 4 such that $7 < y < 12$, what is the intersection of sets X and Y?

F. {}
G. {8}
H. {9}
J. {12}
K. {8, 12}

61. If set S is the set of all positive odd integers and set T is the set of all positive even integers, then the union of sets S and T (the set of all elements that are in either set or both sets) is the set of:

A. positive integers.
B. integers.
C. even integers.
D. odd integers.
E. real numbers.

62. In a certain school, each of the 72 music majors must participate in the marching band, the orchestra, or both. If only music majors participate, 48 students total participate in the marching band, and 54 students total participate in the orchestra, how many students participate in both programs?

F. 6
G. 18
H. 24
J. 30
K. 36

Absolute Value

63. $|-2| + 3 - |-4| = ?$

A. −5
B. −4
C. −1
D. 1
E. 9

64. $|5| - |-5| + |-3| = ?$

F. −8
G. −3
H. 3
J. 8
K. 13

65. $|-3| \cdot |-4| \cdot -5 = ?$

A. −60
B. −30
C. −7
D. 20
E. 60

Matrices

66. What is the matrix solution of

$$2\begin{bmatrix} 5 & -1 \\ -3 & 7 \\ 1 & 0 \end{bmatrix} - \begin{bmatrix} -6 & 0 \\ 4 & 2 \\ 11 & -1 \end{bmatrix}?$$

F. $\begin{bmatrix} 4 & -2 \\ -2 & 16 \\ 13 & -1 \end{bmatrix}$

G. $\begin{bmatrix} 16 & -2 \\ -14 & 10 \\ -20 & 2 \end{bmatrix}$

H. $\begin{bmatrix} -2 & -2 \\ 2 & 18 \\ 24 & -2 \end{bmatrix}$

J. $\begin{bmatrix} 16 & -2 \\ -10 & 12 \\ -9 & 1 \end{bmatrix}$

K. $\begin{bmatrix} -60 & 0 \\ -24 & 28 \\ 22 & 0 \end{bmatrix}$

67. Which of the following is the matrix product
$$\begin{bmatrix} -2 & 0 \\ 3 & 5 \end{bmatrix} \cdot \begin{bmatrix} 1 & 2 \\ -1 & 0 \end{bmatrix}?$$

A. $\begin{bmatrix} -2 & -4 \\ -2 & 6 \end{bmatrix}$

B. $\begin{bmatrix} -2 & 0 \\ -3 & 0 \end{bmatrix}$

C. $\begin{bmatrix} -1 & 2 \\ 2 & 5 \end{bmatrix}$

D. $\begin{bmatrix} -1 & -4 \\ -3 & -5 \end{bmatrix}$

E. $\begin{bmatrix} -2 & 2 \\ -3 & 5 \end{bmatrix}$

68. The following matrix shows how many people in a certain company work in each of three departments:

$$\begin{array}{ccc} \text{accounting} & \text{marketing} & \text{human resources} \\ \begin{bmatrix} 35 & 22 & 60 \end{bmatrix} \end{array}$$

The following matrix shows the fractions of each department that take public transportation:

$$\begin{array}{c} \text{accounting} \\ \text{marketing} \\ \text{human resources} \end{array} \begin{bmatrix} 0.2 \\ 0.5 \\ 0.75 \end{bmatrix}$$

Based on the given information, approximately how many people working in the three departments take public transportation to work?

F. 7
G. 11
H. 45
J. 50
K. 63

69. The numbers of male and female students taking each subject at High School X are shown by the following matrix [S]:

$$\begin{array}{cccc} & \text{math} & \text{English} & \text{history} \\ \text{male} & \begin{bmatrix} 120 & 164 & 100 \\ \text{female} & 140 & 180 & 110 \end{bmatrix} \end{array}$$

The estimates of the fractions of female and male students who will receive As are shown in the following matrix [A]:

$$\begin{array}{cc} \text{male} & \text{female} \\ \begin{bmatrix} 0.25 & 0.4 \end{bmatrix} \end{array}$$

Based on the given matrices, how many students are expected to earn an A in English?

A. 41
B. 69
C. 72
D. 86
E. 113

Complex Numbers

70. $(3+i)(4-3i) = ?$

F. $12+3i^2$
G. $12-3i^2$
H. $9-5i^2$
J. $9-5i$
K. $15-5i$

71. $\dfrac{1}{2-i} = ?$

A. -2
B. -1
C. $\dfrac{2+i}{5}$
D. $\dfrac{2-i}{5}$
E. $\dfrac{2+i}{3}$

Percents

72. A jar contains 24 white marbles and 48 black marbles. What percent of the marbles in the jar are black?

F. 10%
G. 25%
H. $33\frac{1}{3}\%$
J. 60%
K. $66\frac{2}{3}\%$

73. A group of three friends shared the cost of a tape recorder. If Andy, Barbara, and Donna each paid \$12, \$30, and \$18, respectively, then Donna paid what percent of the cost of the tape recorder?

A. 10%
B. 30%
C. $33\frac{1}{3}\%$
D. 50%
E. $66\frac{2}{3}\%$

74. Twenty students attended Professor Rodriguez's class on Monday and 25 students attended on Tuesday. The number of students who attended on Tuesday was what percent of the number of students who attended on Monday?

F. 5%
G. 20%
H. 25%
J. 80%
K. 125%

75. If the population of a town was 20,000 in 1997 and 16,000 in 2007, what was the percent decline in the town's population?

A. 50%
B. 25%
C. 20%
D. 10%
E. 5%

Items #76–78 refer to the following table.

CAPITOL CITY FIRES	
Year	Number of Fires
2002	100
2003	125
2004	140
2005	150
2006	135

76. The number of fires in 2002 was what percent of the number of fires in 2003?

F. 25%
G. $66\frac{2}{3}\%$
H. 80%
J. 100%
K. 125%

77. The number of fires in 2006 was what percent of the number of fires in 2005?

A. 90%
B. 82%
C. 50%
D. 25%
E. 10%

Ratios

79. A groom must divide 12 quarts of oats between two horses. If Dobbin is to receive twice as much as Pegasus, how many quarts of oats should the groom give to Dobbin?

A. 4
B. 6
C. 8
D. 9
E. 10

(handwritten: 2x + x = 12; 3x = 12/3; x = 4; 2(4) = 8)

80. If the ratio of John's allowance to Lucy's allowance is $3:2$, and the ratio of Lucy's allowance to Bob's allowance is $3:4$, what is the ratio of John's allowance to Bob's allowance?

F. 1:6
G. 2:5
H. 1:2
J. 3:4
K. 9:8

(handwritten: common denominator; J 3·3/2·3 L 3·2/4·2; 9/6 6/8 9:8)

Proportions and Direct-Inverse Variation

81. If 4.5 pounds of chocolate cost \$10, how many pounds of chocolate can be purchased for \$12?

A. $4\dfrac{3}{4}$

B. $5\dfrac{2}{5}$

C. $5\dfrac{1}{2}$

D. $5\dfrac{3}{4}$

E. 6

82. At Star Lake Middle School, 45% of the students bought a yearbook. If 540 students bought yearbooks, how many students did <u>not</u> buy a yearbook?

F. 243
G. 540
H. 575
J. 660
K. 957

(handwritten: 100/45/55; $\frac{540}{45\%} = \frac{x}{55\%}$; $45\% x = 540 \cdot 55\%$)

83. In the equation $y = kx$, k is the constant of variation. If y is equal to 6 when $x = 2.4$, what is the constant of variation?

A. 0.4
B. 2.5
C. 3.4
D. 3.6
E. 14.4

84. A train traveling at a constant speed, k, takes 90 minutes to go from point P to point Q, a distance of 45 miles. What is the value of k, in miles per hour?

F. 20
G. 30
H. 45
J. 60
K. 75

85. The cost of picture framing depends on the outer perimeter of the frame. If a 15-inch-by-15-inch picture frame costs \$35 more than a 10-inch-by-10-inch picture frame, what is the cost of framing, in dollars per inch?

A. \$3.50
B. \$2.75
C. \$2.25
D. \$1.75
E. \$1.50

86. Walking at a constant speed of 4 miles per hour, it took Jill exactly 1 hour to walk home from school. If she walked at a constant speed of 5 miles per hour, how many <u>minutes</u> would the trip take?

F. 48
G. 54
H. 56
J. 72
K. 112

(handwritten: $\frac{4 mi}{60 min}$ $\frac{5 mi}{x}$; Walking faster, shorter time; $rate_1 \times dist_1 = rate_2 \times dist_2$; $4 mph \times 60 = 5 mph \times 48$; 240 = 240)

87. Ms. Peters drove from her home to the park at an average speed of 30 miles per hour and returned home along the same route at an average speed of 40 miles per hour. If her driving time from home to the park was 20 minutes, how many minutes did it take Ms. Peters to drive from the park to her home?

   A. 7.5
   B. 12
   C. 15
   D. 24
   E. 30

30 mph x 20 = 600

40 mph x ___ = 600

[faster = less time

Arithmetic Strategy: "Test-the-Test"

88. Which of the following is the larger of two numbers the product of which is 600 and the sum of which is five times the difference between the two?

   F. 10
   G. 15
   H. 20
   J. 30
   K. 50

89. If $\frac{1}{3}$ of a number is 3 more than $\frac{1}{4}$ of the number, then what is the number?

   A. 18
   B. 24
   C. 30
   D. 36
   E. 48

90. If $\frac{3}{5}$ of a number is 4 more than $\frac{1}{2}$ of the number, then what is the number?

   F. 20
   G. 28
   H. 35
   J. 40
   K. 56

91. If both 16 and 9 are divided by n, the remainder is 2. What is n?

   A. 3
   B. 4
   C. 5
   D. 6
   E. 7

92. The sum of the digits of a three-digit number is 16. If the tens digit of the number is 3 times the units digit, and the units digit is $\frac{1}{4}$ of the hundreds digit, then what is the number?

   F. 446
   G. 561
   H. 682
   J. 862
   K. 914

93. If the sum of five consecutive integers is 40, what is the smallest of the five integers?

   A. 4
   B. 5
   C. 6
   D. 7
   E. 8

Algebra Review and Strategies

Manipulating Algebraic Expressions

Basic Algebraic Manipulations

94. If $a^3 + b = 3 + a^3$, then $b = ?$

   F. 3^3
   G. $3\sqrt{3}$
   H. 3
   J. $\sqrt[3]{3}$
   K. $-\sqrt{3}$

95. Which of the following expressions is equivalent to $4a+3b-(-2a-3b)$?

A. $2a$
B. $12ab$
C. $2a+6b$
D. $6a+6b$
E. $8a+9b$

Evaluating Expressions

96. If $x = 3$, what is the value of x^2+2x-2?

F. 0
G. 4
H. 6
J. 9
K. 13

97. If $x=2$, then $\dfrac{1}{x^2}+\dfrac{1}{x}-\dfrac{x}{2}=?$

A. $-\dfrac{3}{4}$

B. $-\dfrac{1}{4}$

C. 0

D. $\dfrac{1}{4}$

E. $\dfrac{1}{2}$

98. If $\dfrac{1}{3}x=10$, then $\dfrac{1}{6}x=?$

F. $\dfrac{1}{15}$

G. $\dfrac{2}{3}$

H. 2

J. 5

K. 30

99. If $p=1$, $q=2$, and $r=3$, what is the value of $\dfrac{(q\cdot r)(r-q)}{(q-p)(p\cdot q)}$?

A. -3
B. -1
C. 0
D. 3
E. 6

Manipulating Expressions Involving Exponents

100. $\dfrac{9\left(x^2y^3\right)^6}{\left(3x^6y^9\right)^2}=?$ $\dfrac{9x^{12}y^{18}}{9x^{12}y^{18}}$

F. 1
G. 3
H. x^2y^3
J. $3x^2y^3$
K. $x^{12}y^{12}$

101. $2\left(4^{-\frac{1}{2}}\right)-2^0+2^{\frac{3}{2}}+2^{-2}=?$

A. $-2\sqrt{2}-\dfrac{1}{4}$

B. $2\sqrt{2}-\dfrac{1}{4}$

C. $2\sqrt{2}$

D. $2\sqrt{2}+\dfrac{1}{4}$

E. $2\sqrt{2}+\dfrac{5}{4}$

Factoring Expressions

102. Which of the following expressions is equivalent to $\dfrac{x^2 - y^2}{x + y}$?

F. $x^2 - y^2$
G. $x^2 + y^2$
H. $x^2 + y$
J. $x + y^2$
K. $x - y$

103. Which of the following expressions is equivalent to $\dfrac{x^2 - x - 6}{x + 2}$?

A. $x^2 - \dfrac{x}{2} - 3$
B. $x^2 - 2$
C. $x - 2$
D. $x - 3$
E. x

104. Which of the following is the factorization of $6x^2 + 4x - 2$?

F. $(6x + 1)(x - 3)$
G. $(6x + 3)(x - 1)$
H. $(3x - 1)(2x - 2)$
J. $(2x + 2)(3x - 1)$
K. $(2x + 4)(3x - 2)$

Creating Algebraic Expressions

105. In a certain game, a player picks an integer between 1 and 10, adds 3 to it, multiplies the sum by 2, and subtracts 5. If x is the number picked by a player, which of the following correctly expresses the final result of the game?

A. $x + (3)(2) - 5$
B. $3x + 2 - 5$
C. $2(x + 3 - 5)$
D. $2(x + 3) - 5$
E. $(2)(3)(x) - 5$

106. At 9:00 a.m., when the heat is turned on, the temperature of a room is 55°F. If the room temperature increases by n°F each hour, which of the following can be used to determine the number of hours needed to bring the temperature of the room to 70°F?

F. $(55 + 70)(n)$
G. $(55 - 70)(n)$
H. $\dfrac{(70 - 55)}{n}$
J. $\dfrac{n}{(70 - 55)}$
K. $\dfrac{n}{(55 + 70)}$

Logarithmic Expressions

107. Evaluate $\log_5 125 + \log_2\left(\dfrac{1}{2}\right)$.

$3 + -1 = 2$

A. -1
B. 0
C. 1
D. 2
E. 3

Math
Alpha
Math

108. If $\log_b x = m$ and $\log_b y = n$, then what is $\log_b xy$?

F. $m + n$ (circled)
G. bmn
H. bxy
J. $m - n$
K. mn

$\log_b(xy)$

$\log_b{}^x \cdot \log_b{}^y$

$m + n$

Evaluating Sequences

109. In a geometric sequence of positive numbers, the fourth term is 125 and the sixth term is 3,125. What is the second term of the sequence?

A. 1
B. 5
C. 10
D. 25
E. 50

110. City University projects that a planned expansion will increase the number of enrolled students every year for the next five years by 50%. If 400 students enroll in the first year of the plan, how many students are expected to enroll in the fifth year of the plan?

F. 200
G. 600
H. 675
J. 1,350
K. 2,025 (circled)

$400(1+.5)^4$

$= 2025$

111. Jimmy's uncle deposited $1,000 into a college fund account and promised that at the start of each year, he would deposit an amount equal to 10% of the account balance. If no other deposits or withdrawals were made and no additional interest accrued, what was the account balance after three additional annual deposits were made by Jimmy's uncle?

A. $1,030
B. $1,300
C. $1,331
D. $1,500
E. $1,830

112. A tank with a capacity of 2,400 liters is filled to capacity with water. If a valve is opened that drains 25% of the contents of the tank every minute, what is the volume of water (in liters) that remains in the tank after 3 minutes?

F. 1,800
G. 1,350
H. 1,012.5
J. 600
K. 325.75

Solving Algebraic Equations or Inequalities with One Variable

Simple Equations

113. If $(2 + 3)(1 + x) = 25$, then $x = ?$

A. $\dfrac{1}{5}$
B. $\dfrac{1}{4}$
C. 1
D. 4
E. 5

Simple Inequalities

114. If $2x + 3 > 9$, which of the following can be the value of x?

F. -4
G. -3
H. 0
J. 3
K. 4

Equations Involving Rational Expressions

115. If $\dfrac{12}{x+1} - 1 = 2$, and $x \neq -1$, then $x = ?$

A. 1
B. 2
C. 3
D. 11
E. 12

116. If $\dfrac{x}{x+2}=\dfrac{3}{4}$, and $x \neq -2$, then $x = ?$

    F. 6
    G. 4
    H. 3
    J. 2
    K. 1

117. If $\dfrac{x}{x-2}-\dfrac{x+2}{2(x-2)}=8$, and $x \neq 2$, which of the following is the complete solution set for x?

    A. {}
    B. {−2}
    C. {2}
    D. {4}
    E. {8}

Inequalities Involving Rational Expressions

118. If $\dfrac{3}{x-2}>\dfrac{1}{6}$, which of the following defines the possible values for x?

    F. $x<20$
    G. $x>0$
    H. $x>2$
    J. $0<x<20$
    K. $2<x<20$

Equations Involving Radical Expressions

119. If $\sqrt{2x+1}-1=4$, then $x = ?$

    A. −5
    B. −1
    C. 1
    D. 12
    E. 24

120. Which of the following is the complete solution set for $\sqrt{3x-2}-3=-4$?

    F. {}
    G. {−1}
    H. {1}
    J. {−1, 1}
    K. {1, 2}

121. If $\sqrt{2x-5}=2\sqrt{5-2x}$, then $x = ?$

    A. 1
    B. 2
    C. $\dfrac{5}{2}$
    D. 10
    E. 15

122. Which of the following is the complete solution set for $\sqrt{x^2+9}=5$?

    F. {−4, 4}
    G. {−4}
    H. {0}
    J. {4}
    K. {}

Equations Involving Integer and Rational Exponents

123. If $4^{x+2}=64$, then $x = ?$

    A. 1
    B. 2
    C. 3
    D. 4
    E. 5

124. If $8^x = 2^{x+3}$, then $x = ?$

   F. 0
   G. 1
   H. $\dfrac{2}{3}$
   J. 3
   K. $\dfrac{3}{2}$

125. If $3^{2x} = \dfrac{1}{81}$, then $x = ?$

   A. -2
   B. $-\dfrac{3}{2}$
   C. $-\dfrac{2}{3}$
   D. $\dfrac{2}{3}$
   E. $\dfrac{3}{2}$

126. If $5^3 = \left(\sqrt{5}\right)^{-2x}$, then $5^x = ?$

   F. $\dfrac{1}{125}$
   G. $\dfrac{1}{25}$
   H. $\dfrac{1}{5}$
   J. 5
   K. 25

Equations Involving Logarithms

127. Which of the following is a value of x that satisfies the equation $\log_4 x = 4$?

   A.   4
   B. 16
   C. 160
   D. 256
   E. 512

128. Which of the following is a value of x that satisfies the equation $2\log_x 16 + \log_x 16 = 6$?

   F.   2
   G.   4
   H. 16
   J. 32
   K. 64

Equations Involving Absolute Value

129. Which of the following is the complete solution set for $\left|\dfrac{2x+1}{3}\right| = 5$?

   A. $\{-8, -7\}$
   B. $\{-8, 7\}$
   C. $\{-7, 8\}$
   D. $\{7\}$
   E. $\{8\}$

130. Which of the following is the complete solution set for $|x+6| = 3x$?

   F. $\left\{-3, \dfrac{3}{2}\right\}$
   G. $\left\{-\dfrac{3}{2}, 3\right\}$
   H. $\left\{\dfrac{3}{2}, 3\right\}$
   J. $\{3\}$
   K. $\{\}$

Inequalities Involving Absolute Value

131. Which of the following is the complete solution set for $|2x-1| > 3$?

   A. All real numbers
   B. The null set
   C. All real numbers less than -1 or greater than 2
   D. All real numbers less than -2 or greater than 1
   E. All real numbers less than -3

132. If $|3x - 6| > 9$, then which of the following must be true?

    F. $-3 < x < 2$
    G. $-2 < x < 3$
    H. $x < -3$ or $x > 2$
    J. $x < -1$ or $x > 5$
    K. $x < -1$ or $x > 9$

133. Which of the following identifies exactly those values of x that satisfy $|-2x + 4| < 4$?

    A. $x > -4$
    B. $x < 4$
    C. $x > 0$
    D. $0 < x < 4$
    E. $-4 < x < 0$

Expressing and Evaluating Algebraic Functions

Function Notation

134. If $f(x) = x^2 + x$, what is the value of $f(-2)$?

    F. -8
    G. -2
    H. 2
    J. 8
    K. 12

135. If $y = f(x) = \left(\dfrac{6x^2 - 2^{-x}}{|x|}\right)^{-\frac{1}{2}}$ for all integers and $x = -1$, what is the value of y?

    A. 2
    B. $\dfrac{1}{2}$
    C. $\dfrac{1}{4}$
    D. $-\dfrac{1}{2}$
    E. -2

136. If $f(x) = x + 3$ and $g(x) = 2x - 5$, what is the value of $f(g(2))$?

    F. -2
    G. 0
    H. 2
    J. 4
    K. 10

137. If $f(x) = 3x + 2$ and $g(x) = x^2 + x$, what is the value of $g(f(-2))$?

    A. 15
    B. 12
    C. 6
    D. 3
    E. -2

138. If $f(x) = 2x^2 + x$ and $g(x) = f(f(x))$, what is the value of $g(1)$?

    F. 3
    G. 18
    H. 21
    J. 39
    K. 55

139. If $f(x) = 3x + 4$ and $g(x) = 2x - 1$, for what value of x does $f(x) = g(x)$?

    A. -5
    B. -2
    C. 0
    D. 3
    E. 7

140. If $\boxed{x} = x^2 - x$ for all integers, then $\boxed{-2} = ?$

    F. -6
    G. -2
    H. 0
    J. 4
    K. 6

141. If $\boxed{x} = x^2 - x$ for all integers, then $\boxed{3} = ?$

    A. 27
    B. 30
    C. 58
    D. 72
    E. 121

Concepts of Domain and Range

142. If $f(x) = 3x - 2$ and $-5 < x < 5$, which of the following defines the range of $f(x)$?

    F. $-17 < f(x) < 13$
    G. $-13 < f(x) < 17$
    H. $-5 < f(x) < 12$
    J. $0 < f(x) < 17$
    K. $3 < f(x) < 13$

143. If $f(x) = \dfrac{x+2}{x-1}$, for which of the following values of x is $f(x)$ undefined?

    A. -2
    B. -1
    C. $\dfrac{1}{2}$
    D. 1
    E. 2

144. If $f(x) = \dfrac{2 - 2x}{x}$, which of the following defines the range of $f(x)$?

    F. All real numbers
    G. All real numbers except -2
    H. All real numbers except 0
    J. All real numbers except 2
    K. All real numbers greater than 2

145. If $|4x - 8| < 12$, which of the following defines the possible values of x?

    A. $-8 < x < -4$
    B. $-4 < x < 8$
    C. $-1 < x < 5$
    D. $1 < x < 5$
    E. $4 < x < 8$

Functions as Models

146. The cost of making a call using a phone-card is $0.15 for dialing and $0.04 per minute of connection time. Which of the following equations could be used to find the cost, y, of a call x minutes long?

    F. $y = x(0.04 + 0.15)$
    G. $y = 0.04x + 0.15$
    H. $y = 0.04 + 0.15x$
    J. $y = 0.15 - 0.04x$
    K. $y = 0.04 - 0.15x$

Solving Algebraic Equations with Two Variables

147. If $x + y = 3$, then $2x + 2y = ?$

    A. $-\dfrac{2}{3}$
    B. $\dfrac{1}{2}$
    C. $\dfrac{2}{3}$
    D. 6
    E. Cannot be determined from the given information

Solving Simultaneous Equations

148. If $2x + y = 8$ and $x - y = 1$, then $x = ?$

    F. -2
    G. -1
    H. 0
    J. 1
    K. 3

149. If $7x = 2$ and $3y - 7x = 10$, then $y = ?$

A. 2
B. 3
C. 4
D. 5
E. 6

(handwritten) $-7x = 10 - 3y$ over -7

Solving Quadratic Equations and Relations

153. Which of the following is the solution set for
$2x^2 - 2x = 12$?

(handwritten) B $\dfrac{2x^2 - 2x - 12 = 0}{2 \quad 2 \quad 2}$

A. $\{-2, -3\}$
B. $\{-2, 3\}$
C. $\left\{\dfrac{2}{3}, 3\right\}$
D. $\left\{\dfrac{3}{2}, 2\right\}$
E. $\{2, 3\}$

(handwritten) $x^2 - x - 6 = 0$ $(x-3)(x+2)$ $x = 3$ $x = -2$

150. If $2x + y = 8$ and $x - y = 1$, what is the value of $x + y$?

(handwritten left margin) Substitution

(handwritten) ÷ by coefficient

F. -1
G. 1
H. 2
J. 3
K. 5

(handwritten) $x = 1 + y$
$2(1+y) + y = 8$
$2 + 3y = 8$
$3y = \dfrac{6}{3}$ $y = 2$
$2x + 2 = 8$
$2x = \dfrac{6}{2}$ $x = 3$

151. If $4x + 5y = 12$ and $3x + 4y = 5$, what is the value of $7(x + y)$?

A. 7
B. 14
C. 49
D. 77
E. 91

154. If $x^2 - 3x = 4$, then which of the following shows all possible values of x?

F. $\{4, 1\}$
G. $\{4, -1\}$
H. $\{-4, 1\}$
J. $\{-4, -1\}$
K. $\{-4, 4\}$

152. Which of the equations that follow correctly describes the relationship between the values shown for x and y in the table below?

x	-2	-1	0	1	2
y	$\dfrac{10}{3}$	$\dfrac{8}{3}$	2	$\dfrac{4}{3}$	$\dfrac{2}{3}$

F. $3x + 2y = 6$
G. $3x - 2y = 3$
H. $3x + 3y = -6$
J. $6x + 4y = 7$
K. $2x + 3y = 6$

155. If $x^2 + 30 = 11x$, then which of the following shows all possible values of x?

A. $\{-5, 6\}$
B. $\{5, 6\}$
C. $\{5, -6\}$
D. $\{-3, -10\}$
E. $\{3, 10\}$

156. Which of the following is the solution set for
$3x^2 + 3x = 6$?

F. $\{1, -2\}$
G. $\{1, 2\}$
H. $\left\{\dfrac{1}{2}, 1\right\}$
J. $\left\{\dfrac{1}{2}, \dfrac{1}{3}\right\}$
K. $\{-1, -2\}$

157. Which of the following is the solution set for $2x^2 - 3x = 2$?

A. $\left\{\dfrac{1}{2}, 2\right\}$

B. $\left\{-\dfrac{1}{2}, 2\right\}$

C. $\left\{-\dfrac{1}{2}, -2\right\}$

D. $\{2, -2\}$

E. $\{2, 4\}$

Algebra Strategies: "Test-the-Test" and "Plug-and-Chug"

158. Diana spent $\dfrac{1}{2}$ of her weekly allowance on a new book and another \$3 on lunch. If she still had $\dfrac{1}{6}$ of her original allowance left, how much is Diana's allowance?

F.   \$24

G.   \$18

H.   \$15

J.   \$12

K.   \$9

159. In a certain game, a player had five successful turns in a row, and after each one, the number of points added to his total score was double what was added the preceding turn. If the player scored a total of 465 points, how many points did he score on the first play?

A.   15

B.   30

C.   95

D.   155

E.   270

160. At a certain firm, d gallons of fuel are needed per day for each truck. At this rate, g gallons of fuel will supply t trucks for how many days?

F. $\dfrac{d}{gt}$

G. $\dfrac{gt}{d}$

H. dgt

J. $\dfrac{dg}{t}$

K. $\dfrac{g}{dt}$

161. Y years ago, Paul was twice as old as Bob. If Bob is now 18 years old, how old is Paul today in terms of Y?

A. $36 + Y$

B. $18 + Y$

C. $18 - Y$

D. $36 - Y$

E. $36 - 2Y$

162. After filling the car's fuel tank, a driver drove from point P to point Q and then to point R. She used $\dfrac{2}{5}$ of the fuel driving from P to Q. If she used another 7 gallons to drive from Q to R and still had $\dfrac{1}{4}$ of a tank left, how many gallons does the tank hold?

F.   12

G.   18

H.   20

J.   21

K.   35

163. If pencils cost x cents each, how many pencils can be purchased for y dollars?

   A. $\dfrac{100}{xy}$

   B. $\dfrac{xy}{100}$

   C. $\dfrac{100y}{x}$

   D. $\dfrac{y}{100x}$

   E. $100xy$

164. A merchant increased the original price of an item by 10%. If she then reduces the new price by 10%, the final price, in terms of the original price, is equal to which of the following?

   F.   a decrease of 11%
   G.   a decrease of 1%
   H.   no net change
   J.   an increase of 1%
   K.   an increase of 11%

165. Harold is twice as old as Jack, who is three years older than Dan. If Harold's age is five times Dan's age, how old (in years) is Jack?

   A.   2
   B.   4
   C.   5
   D.   8
   E.   10

166. A tank with capacity T gallons is empty. If water flows into the tank from pipe X at the rate of X gallons per minute, and water is pumped out by pipe Y at the rate of Y gallons per minute, and X is greater than Y, in how many <u>minutes</u> will the tank be filled?

   F. $\dfrac{T}{Y-X}$

   G. $\dfrac{T}{X-Y}$

   H. $\dfrac{T-X}{Y}$

   J. $\dfrac{X-Y}{60T}$

   K. $\dfrac{60T}{XY}$

167. Machine X produces w widgets in five minutes. Machine X and Machine Y, working at the same time, produce w widgets in two minutes. How long will it take Machine Y working alone to produce w widgets?

   A.   2 minutes, 30 seconds
   B.   2 minutes, 40 seconds
   C.   3 minutes, 20 seconds
   D.   3 minutes, 30 seconds
   E.   3 minutes, 40 seconds

168. If a train travels m miles in h hours and 45 minutes, what is its average speed in miles per hour?

   F. $\dfrac{m}{h+\frac{3}{4}}$

   G. $\dfrac{m}{1\frac{3}{4}h}$

   H. $m\left(h+\dfrac{3}{4}\right)$

   J. $\dfrac{m+45}{h}$

   K. $\dfrac{h}{m+45}$

169. On a playground, there are *x* seesaws. If 50 children are all riding on seesaws, two to a seesaw, and five seesaws are <u>not</u> in use, what is the value of *x*?

A. 15
B. 20
C. 25
D. 30
E. 35

Coordinate Geometry Review and Strategies

The Coordinate System

170. In the figure below, what is the length of $\overline{PQ}$?

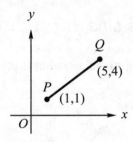

F. $\sqrt{2}$
G. $\sqrt{3}$
H. 3
J. 4
K. 5

171. In the figure below, the line segment joining points (3,3) and (7,3) forms one side of a square. Which of the following CANNOT be the coordinates of another vertex of the square?

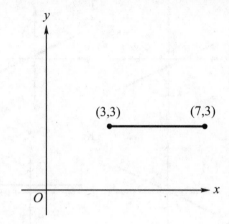

A. (3,−1)
B. (3,7)
C. (7,−3)
D. (7,−1)
E. (7,7)

172. Which of the following is a graph of the line that passes through the points (−5,3), (−1,1), and (3,−1)?

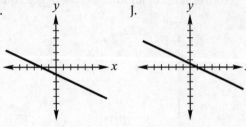

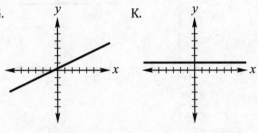

F.

J.

G.

K.

H.

173. If point A is the center of the semicircle in the figure below, what are the coordinates, (x,y), of the point on the semicircle that is farthest from the y-axis?

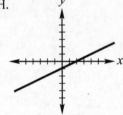

A. (−4,4)
B. (−3,3)
C. (−2,3)
D. (−3,2)
E. (3,2)

174. In the figure below, the area of △ABC is 8. What is the value of k?

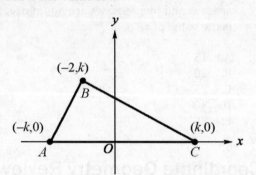

F. 2
G. $2\sqrt{2}$
H. 4
J. $4\sqrt{2}$
K. 8

Slope of a Line

175. In the figure below, what is the slope of the line?

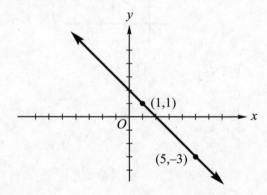

A. −3
B. −2
C. −1
D. 1
E. 2

176. In the figure below, which two sides of polygon *PQRST* have the same slope?

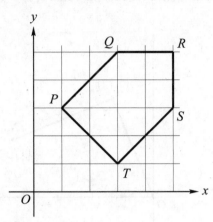

F. $\overline{PQ}$ and $\overline{QR}$

G. $\overline{PQ}$ and $\overline{RS}$

H. $\overline{PQ}$ and $\overline{ST}$

J. $\overline{QR}$ and $\overline{RS}$

K. $\overline{RS}$ and $\overline{ST}$

177. Line *l* is the graph of the equation $y = \dfrac{3x}{2} + 2$.

The graph of which of the following equations is perpendicular to line *l* at $(0,2)$?

A. $y = \dfrac{3x}{2} - 2$

B. $y = \dfrac{2x}{3} - 2$

C. $y = -\dfrac{2x}{3} + 2$

D. $y = -\dfrac{3x}{2} + 3$

E. $y = -3x + 4$

178. If set $A = \{(-2,3),\ (-1,1),\ (-4,-5)\}$, and set $B = \{(3,4),\ (4,3),\ (2,-1)\}$, how many lines can be drawn with a positive slope that include exactly one point from set A and one point from set B?

F. 2

G. 3

H. 4

J. 5

K. 6

Slope-Intercept Form of a Linear Equation

179. A line includes the points $(2,3)$ and $(3,6)$. What is the equation of the line?

A. $y = 2x - 3$

B. $y = 3x - 3$

C. $y = \dfrac{3x - 3}{2}$

D. $y = 3x + 3$

E. $y = x - 3$

180. Which of the following is the equation for the line with slope of 2 that includes point $(0,2)$?

F. $y = x - 1$

G. $y = 2x - 1$

H. $y = 2x - 2$

J. $y = 2x + 2$

K. $y = x + 1$

181. Which of the following is the equation for the line that includes points $(-1,1)$ and $(7,5)$?

   A. $y = \dfrac{x}{2} + 2$

   B. $y = \dfrac{x}{2} + \dfrac{3}{2}$

   C. $y = \dfrac{x}{2} + \dfrac{2}{3}$

   D. $y = 2x + \dfrac{3}{2}$

   E. $y = 2x + 2$

182. If the graph of a line includes the points $(2,4)$ and $(8,7)$, what is the y-intercept of the line?

   F.   6
   G.   4
   H.   3
   J.   −1
   K.   −3

183. If the slope and y-intercept of a line are -2 and 3, respectively, then the line passes through which of the following points?

   A. $(-5,-10)$
   B. $(-5,10)$
   C. $(-2,3)$
   D. $(3,4)$
   E. $(4,-5)$

Distance Formula

184. What is the distance between the points $(-3,-2)$ and $(3,3)$?

   F. $\sqrt{3}$
   G. $2\sqrt{3}$
   H.   5
   J. $\sqrt{29}$
   K. $\sqrt{61}$

185. In the coordinate plane below, $\overline{MO} \cong \overline{MN}$ and $\overline{MO} \perp \overline{MN}$. What is the value of y?

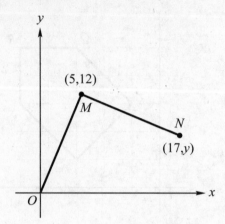

   A.   5
   B.   7
   C.   12
   D.   13
   E.   17

186. In the figure below, what is the area of the square region?

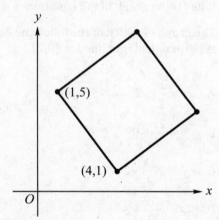

   F.   4
   G.   8
   H. $8\sqrt{2}$
   J.   16
   K.   25

187. In the coordinate plane, what is the midpoint of the line segment with endpoints $(-3,-5)$ and $(5,7)$?

A. $(1,1)$

B. $(1,6)$

C. $\left(3,\dfrac{7}{2}\right)$

D. $(4,6)$

E. $(8,12)$

Graphs of Linear Equations

188. The figure below is the graph of which of the following equations?

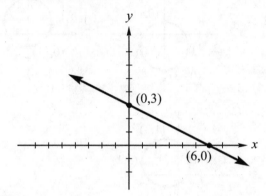

F. $x+2y=6$

G. $2x+y=6$

H. $x+\dfrac{y}{2}=6$

J. $\dfrac{x}{2}+y=2$

K. $x-3y=2$

189. A school rented a hotel ballroom for a dance. The cost of the rental is $1500 plus $5.00 per person who attends. Each person who attends will pay an admission charge of $12.50. If x represents the number of people who attend, which of the graphs can be used to determine how many people must attend for the admission charges to cover exactly the cost of renting the ballroom?

A.
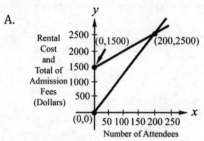

B.
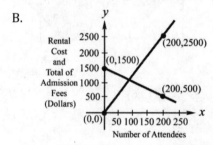

C.
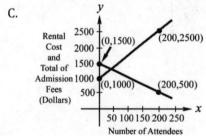

D.
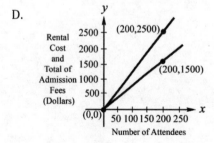

E.
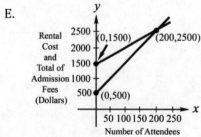

Graphs of First-Degree Inequalities

190. Which of the following is the graph of the inequality $y \geq 2x$?

F.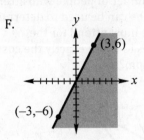

J.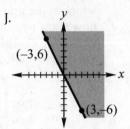

G.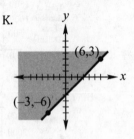

K.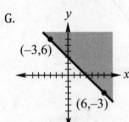

H.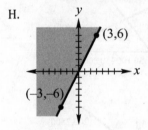

Graphs of Quadratic Equations and Relations

191. Which of the following is the graph of the equation $(x-1)^2 + y^2 = 4$?

A.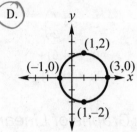

D.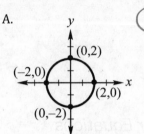

B.

E.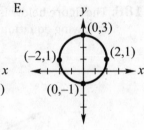

C.

equation of a circle

$r^2 = (x-h)^2 + (y-k)^2$

$r = $ radius

$(h,k) = $ center

$h = 1$ $k = 0$ $(1,0)$ center

192. Which of the following is the graph of the equation $\dfrac{x^2}{9} + \dfrac{y^2}{16} = 1$?

F.

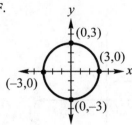

J.

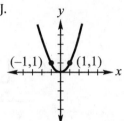

G.

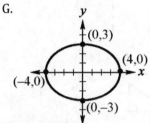

K.

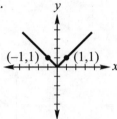

H.

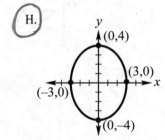

Qualitative Behavior of Graphs of Functions

193. The figure below shows the graph of a function $g(x)$. What is the minimum degree of $g(x)$?

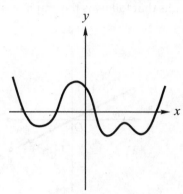

A. 1
B. 2
C. 3
D. 4
E. 5

crosses x-axis
4 times

194. The figure below shows the graph of $f(x)$ in the coordinate plane. For the portion of the graph shown, for how many values of x is $f(x) = 3$?

y = 3

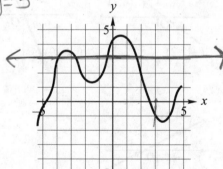

F. 0
G. 1
H. 2
J. 3
K. 4

Transformations and Their Effects on Graphs of Functions and Figures

195. The figure below represents the graph of $y = f(x)$ in the coordinate plane. Which of the graphs that follow is the graph of $y' = f(x-1)$?

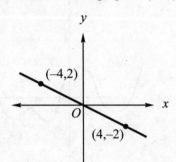

A.
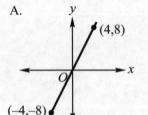

D.
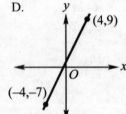

B.
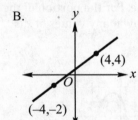

E.
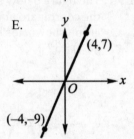

C.
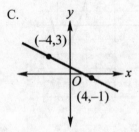

196. If the triangle in the figure below is reflected across the *y*-axis and then reflected across the *x*-axis, which of the graphs that follow shows the resulting position of the triangle?

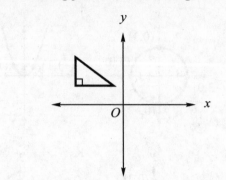

F.   J.
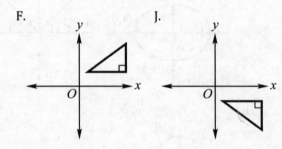

G.   K.
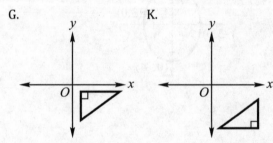

H.
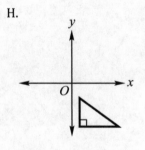

Geometry Review and Strategies

Lines and Angles

197. In the figure below, $x = ?$

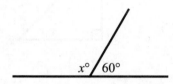

A. 45
B. 60
C. 75
D. 90
E. 120

198. In the figure below, $x = ?$

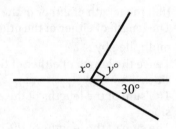

F. 45
G. 60
H. 90
J. 105
K. 120

199. In the figure below, l_1 is parallel to l_2. Which of the following <u>must</u> be true?

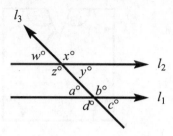

   I. $w = a$
  II. $y + b = 180$
 III. $x + d = 180$

A. I only
B. II only
C. I and II only
D. II and III only
E. I, II, and III

200. In the figure below, $x = ?$

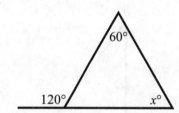

F. 30
G. 45
H. 60
J. 75
K. 90

201. In the figure below, what is the sum of the indicated angles?

A. 540
B. 720
C. 900
D. 1,080
E. 1,260

$180 \cdot 7 - 2 = 900$

Triangles

Pythagorean Theorem

202. In the figure below, what is the length of $\overline{AB}$?

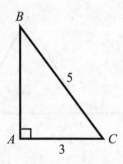

F. $2\sqrt{3}$
G. 2
H. 4
J. $4\sqrt{2}$
K. 8

45°-45°-90° Triangles

203. In the figure below, what is the length of $\overline{PQ}$?

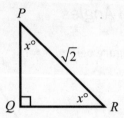

A. 1
B. $\sqrt{2}$
C. $2\sqrt{2}$
D. 4
E. 5

204. In a right isosceles triangle, the hypotenuse is equal to which of the following?

F. Half the length of either of the other sides
G. The length of either of the other sides multiplied by $\sqrt{2}$
H. Twice the length of either of the other sides
J. The sum of the lengths of the other two sides
K. The sum of the lengths of the other two sides multiplied by $\sqrt{2}$

30°-60°-90° Triangles

205. In the triangle below, what is the length of $\overline{AC}$?

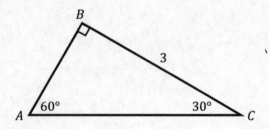

A. 2
B. $\sqrt{3}$
C. $2\sqrt{3}$
D. $3\sqrt{3}$
E. 6

Properties of Triangles

206. In the figure below, the perimeter of $\triangle PQR = $?

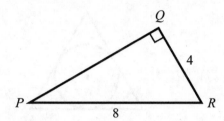

F. $12+\sqrt{3}$
G. $12+2\sqrt{3}$
H. $12+4\sqrt{3}$
J. 28
K. 56

207. In the figure below, what is the area of $\triangle MNO$?

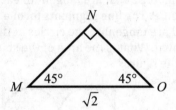

A. $\dfrac{1}{2}$

B. $\dfrac{\sqrt{2}}{2}$

C. 1

D. $\sqrt{2}$

E. 2

Rectangles and Squares

208. If the area of the rectangle below is 18, what is the perimeter?

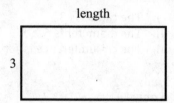

F. 9
G. 12
H. 18
J. 24
K. 30

209. In the figure below, $PQRS$ is a rectangle. If $\overline{PR}$ = 5 centimeters, what is the area, in square centimeters, of the rectangle?

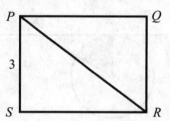

A. 2
B. 3
C. 4
D. 8
E. 12

210. If the width of a rectangle is increased by 10% and the length of the rectangle is increased by 20%, by what percent does the area of the rectangle <u>increase</u>?

F. 2%
G. 10%
H. 15%
J. 32%
K. 36%

Circles

211. If the area of a circle is equal to 9π, which of the following is (are) true?

     I.   The radius is 3.
     II. The diameter is 6.
     III. The circumference is 6π.

    A. I only
    B. II only
    C. III only
    D. I and II only
    E. I, II, and III

Properties of Tangent Lines

212. In the figure below, O is the center of the circle, and $\overline{PQ}$ is tangent to the circle at P. If the radius of circle O has a length of 6, what is the area of the shaded portion of the figure?

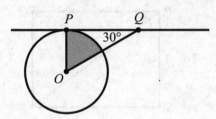

    F. π
    G. 3π
    H. 6π
    J. 9π
    K. 12π

213. The figure below shows two pulleys connected by a belt. If the centers of the pulleys are 8 feet apart and the pulleys each have a radius of 1 foot, what is the length, in feet, of the belt?

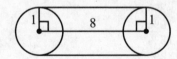

    A. 4π
    B. 8π
    C. $8+\pi$
    D. $16+\pi$
    E. $16+2\pi$

214. In the figure below, a circle is inscribed in an equilateral triangle. If the radius of the circle is 1, what is the perimeter of the triangle?

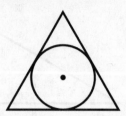

    F. $\sqrt{3}$
    G. $2\sqrt{3}$
    H. $3\sqrt{3}$
    J. 6
    K. $6\sqrt{3}$

215. The figure below shows two circles of diameter 2 that are tangent to each other at point P. The line segments form a rectangle and are tangent to the circles at the points shown. What is the area of the shaded portion of the figure?

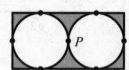

    A. $4-2\pi$
    B. $4-\pi$
    C. $8-2\pi$
    D. $8-\pi$
    E. 2π

Complex Figures

216. If a circle of radius 1 foot is inscribed in a square, what is the area, in square feet, of the square?

    F. $\dfrac{\sqrt{2}}{2}$
    G. 1
    H. $\sqrt{2}$
    J. 2
    K. 4

217. An isosceles right triangle is inscribed in a circle with a radius of 1 inch such that all three vertices of the triangle touch the circumference of the circle. What is the area, in square inches, of the triangle?

A. $\dfrac{\sqrt{2}}{3}$

B. $\dfrac{1}{2}$

C. 1

D. $\sqrt{2}$

E. $2\sqrt{2}$

218. In the figure below, *BCDE* is a square with an area of 4. What is the perimeter of $\triangle ABE$?

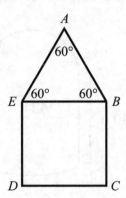

F. 3
G. 4
H. 6
J. 8
K. 12

219. In the figure below, if *QRST* is a square and the length of $\overline{PQ}$ is $\sqrt{2}$, what is the length of $\overline{RU}$?

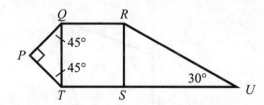

A. $\sqrt{2}$
B. $\sqrt{6}$
C. $2\sqrt{2}$
D. 4
E. $4\sqrt{3}$

220. In the figure below, *PQRS* is a square, and $\overline{PS}$ is the diameter of a semicircle. If the length of $\overline{PQ}$ is 2, what is the area of the shaded portion of the diagram?

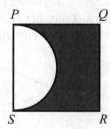

F. $4 - 2\pi$

G. $4 - \pi$

H. $4 - \dfrac{\pi}{2}$

J. $8 - \pi$

K. $8 - \dfrac{\pi}{2}$

221. If the lengths of the sides, in inches, are as marked on the figure below, what is the area, in square inches, of the quadrilateral?

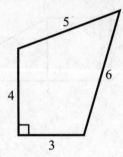

A. 6
B. $6 + \sqrt{3}$
C. 12
D. 18
E. 24

Solids

222. The prism below has bases with sides 12, 16, and 20. The distance between the bases is 30. What is the lateral surface area of the prism?

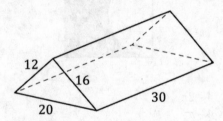

F. 1,632
G. 1,440
H. 600
J. 480
K. 360

223. What is the approximate surface area, in square inches, of a ball of largest circumference 12π inches?

$(SA_{Sphere} = 4\pi r^2)$

A. 12π
B. 36π
C. 144π
D. 576π
E. $2,304\pi$

224. The volume of a cone can be found using the formula $V = \frac{1}{3}\pi r^2 h$. If a cone has a height of 10 cm and a volume of 120π cm^3, what is the diameter of its base, in centimeters?

F. 6
G. 12
H. 36
J. 72
K. 144

225. A construction company is building a silo. The silo is a cylinder with a hemisphere on top. The diameter of the cylinder is 42 feet and the height of the cylinder is 40 feet. How much hay can you store in your silo, in cubic feet?

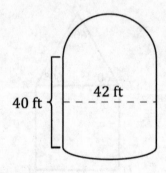

A. $23,814\pi$
B. $29,988\pi$
C. $711,774\pi$
D. $717,948\pi$
E. $70,560 + 6,174\pi$

Geometry Strategies

"Guesstimating"

226. In the figure below, $x = ?$

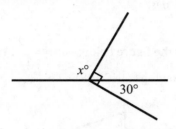

F. 30
G. 65
H. 120
J. 150
K. 170

227. What is the perimeter of the triangle shown below?

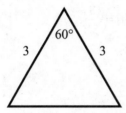

A. $3\sqrt{2}$
B. 6
C. 7.5
D. 9
E. 15

228. In the figure below, $x = ?$

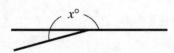

F. 120
G. 150
H. 180
J. 210
K. 240

Measuring

229. In the figure below, $x = ?$

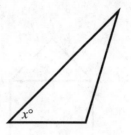

A. 30
B. 45
C. 60
D. 75
E. 90

230. In the figure below, what is the length of $\overline{AC}$?

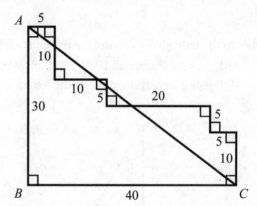

F. $30\sqrt{2}$
G. 50
H. 75
J. $60\sqrt{2}$
K. 100

"Meastimating"

231. In the figure below, what is the area of square *ABCD*?

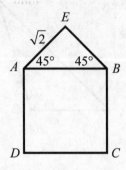

- A.   2
- B. $2\sqrt{2}$
- C.   4
- D. $4\sqrt{2}$
- E.   8

232. In the triangle below, the measure of $\angle BAC$ is 30° and the length of $\overline{AB}$ is 2. Which of the following best approximates the length of $\overline{AC}$?

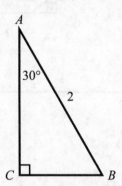

- F.   0.8
- G.   1.0
- H.   1.7
- J.   1.9
- K.   2.3

Trigonometry Review and Strategies

Definitions of the Six Trigonometric Functions

233. For the figure below, $\sin\theta = \dfrac{12}{13}$. Which of the following is INCORRECT?

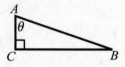

- A. $\cos\theta = \dfrac{5}{13}$
- B. $\tan\theta = \dfrac{12}{5}$
- C. $\cot\theta = \dfrac{5}{12}$
- D. $\sec\theta = \dfrac{13}{5}$
- E. $\csc\theta = \dfrac{12}{13}$

234. In the right triangle below, the length of $\overline{AB}$ is 5 centimeters and $\angle A$ measures 30°. What is the length, in centimeters, of $\overline{BC}$? ($\sin 30° = 0.5$)

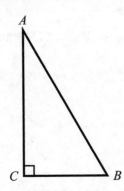

F.   4

G. $3\frac{1}{2}$

H. $2\frac{3}{4}$

J. $2\frac{1}{2}$

K.   2

Trigonometric Relationships

235. If $\sin 60°$ is equal to $\frac{\sqrt{3}}{2}$, what is the value of

$\sin^2 30° + \cos^2 30° = 1$

A. $\frac{\sqrt{3}+1}{2}$

B. $\sqrt{5}$

C. $\frac{\sqrt{5}}{2}$

$\sin^2 x + \cos^2 x = 1$

D. $\frac{3}{4}$

(E.)   1

236. Which of the following is equivalent to $\dfrac{\sin A}{\cos A}$?

(F.) $\tan A$

G. $\cot A$

H. $\sec A$

J. $\csc A$

K. $\dfrac{1}{\tan A}$

Trigonometry as an Alternative Method of Solution

237. In the figure below, $\triangle PQR$ and $\triangle QRS$ are isosceles right triangles. If $\overline{QP} = 3$, what is the length of $\overline{QS}$? ($\sin 45° = \dfrac{\sqrt{2}}{2}$)

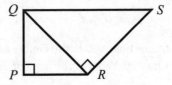

A. $\sqrt{2}$

B. $2\sqrt{2}$

C.   4

D.   6

E.   8

238. If the area of the square *JKLM* in the figure below is 4, what is the sum of the lengths of the diagonals $\overline{JL}$ and $\overline{KM}$? $\left(\sin 45° = \dfrac{\sqrt{2}}{2}\right)$

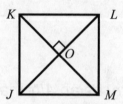

F. $\dfrac{\sqrt{2}}{2}$

G. $2+\dfrac{\sqrt{2}}{2}$

H. $4\sqrt{2}$

J. $4+4\sqrt{2}$

K. $8\sqrt{2}$

239. In the figure below, *O* is the center of the circle with radius 10. What is the area of $\triangle AOB$? $\left(\sin 30° = \dfrac{1}{2}\;;\;\sin 60° = \dfrac{\sqrt{3}}{2}\right)$

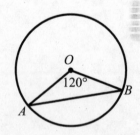

A. $10\sqrt{3}$

B. 10

C. 25

D. $25\sqrt{3}$

E. 50

Statistics and Probability Review and Strategies

Averages

240. If the average of 35, 38, 41, 43, and *x* is 37, what is *x*?

F. 28
G. 30
H. 31
J. 34
K. 36

241. The average weight of 6 packages is 50 pounds per package. Another package is added, making the average weight of the 7 packages 52 pounds per package. What is the weight, in pounds, of the additional package?

A. 2
B. 7
C. 52
D. 62
E. 64

242. The average of 10 test scores is 80. If the high and low scores are dropped, the average is 81. What is the average of the high and low scores?

F. 76
G. 78
H. 80
J. 81
K. 82

243. In Latin 101, the final exam grade is weighted two times as heavily as the mid-term grade. If Leo received a score of 84 on his final exam and 90 on his mid-term, what was his course average?

A. 88
B. 87.5
C. 86.5
D. 86
E. 85

244. In a group of children, three children are 10 years old and two children are 5 years old. What is the average age, in years, of the children in the group?

F.   6
G.   6.5
H.   7
J.   7.5
K.   8

Median

245. The number of employment applications received by All-Star Staffing each month during 2002 was as follows: 8, 4, 5, 3, 4, 3, 1, 0, 3, 4, 0, and 7. What was the median number of applications received per month in 2002?

A.   2.5
B.   3
C.   3.5
D.   4
E.   4.5

Mode

246. William's monthly electric bills for last year were as follows: $40, 38, 36, 38, 34, 34, 30, 32, 34, 37, 39, and 40. What is the mode of the bills?

F. $33
G. $34
H. $35
J. $36
K. $37

Probability

$3 \cdot 2 = 6$

247. If set $A = \{1, 2, 3, 4, 5, 6\}$ and set $B = \{1, 2, 3, 4, 5, 6\}$, what is the probability that the sum of one number from set A and one number from set B will total 7?

$6 \cdot 6 = 36$ $\dfrac{6}{36}$

A. $\dfrac{1}{12}$

B. $\dfrac{5}{36}$ $\dfrac{1}{6}$

C. $\dfrac{1}{6}$

D. $\dfrac{1}{5}$

E. $\dfrac{1}{3}$

248. If a book is selected at random from the collection shown below, which of the following has the greatest probability of being selected?

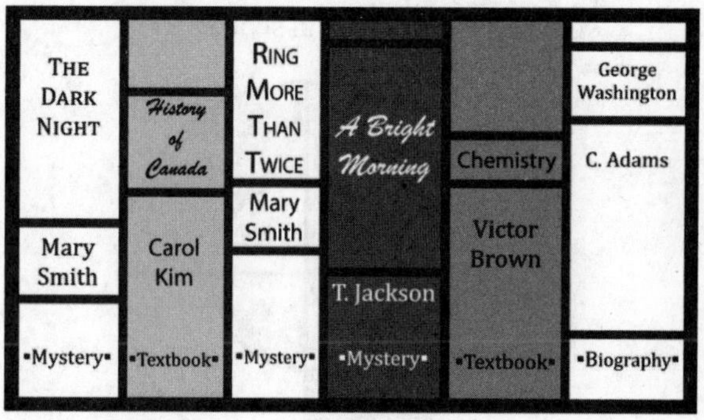

F.   A book by Mary Smith
G.   A textbook
H.   A mystery
J.   A book written by either Carol Kim or Victor Brown
K.   A biography

249. If a jar contains r red marbles, b blue marbles, and g green marbles, which of the following expresses the probability that a marble drawn at random will <u>NOT</u> be red?

A. $\dfrac{-r}{r+b+g}$

B. $\dfrac{r}{r+b+g}$

C. $\dfrac{b+g-r}{b+g+r}$

D. $\dfrac{r}{b+g}$

E. $\dfrac{b+g}{b+g+r}$

250. The figure below shows a dartboard consisting of two concentric circles with center O. The radius of the larger circle is equal to the diameter of the smaller circle. What is the probability that a randomly thrown dart striking the board will score a 3?

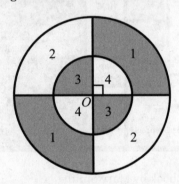

F. $\dfrac{1}{16}$

G. $\dfrac{1}{8}$

H. $\dfrac{1}{4}$

J. $\dfrac{1}{2}$

K. $\dfrac{3}{4}$

251. An underwater salvage team is searching the ocean floor for a lost signal device using a large circular search pattern and a smaller circular search pattern with a radius equal to one-third that of the larger pattern. If the device is known to be inside the boundary of the larger search area, what is the probability that it is NOT located in the shaded portion of the figure?

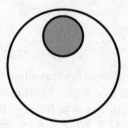

A. $\dfrac{1}{9}$

B. $\dfrac{1}{6}$

C. $\dfrac{1}{3}$

D. $\dfrac{1}{2}$

E. $\dfrac{8}{9}$

Data Representation

Bar, Cumulative, and Line Graphs

252. During the week shown in the graph below, what was the greatest increase in sales from one day to the next?

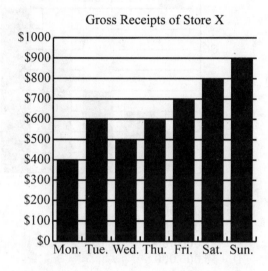

Gross Receipts of Store X

F. $50
G. $100
H. $150
J. $200
K. $250

253. If the graph below represents expenditures by Corporation X in two different years, what was the approximate ratio of expenditures in 2006 to those in 2007?

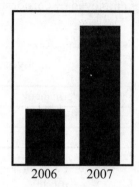

A. $\frac{1}{5}$

B. $\frac{2}{5}$

C. $\frac{1}{2}$

D. $\frac{2}{3}$

E. 2

254. Based on the data presented below, what was the difference, if any, between the number of permanent workers employed by Corporation X on March 1st and the number of permanent workers employed by Corporation X on April 1st?

Number of Corporation X Employees

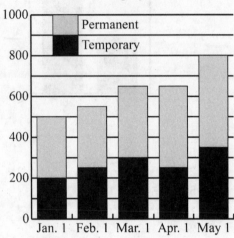

F. 0
G. 50
H. 100
J. 150
K. 200

255. Based on the data presented below, what was the difference in the value of foreign sales by Company T between 2003 and 2005?

Company T Domestic Sales
(in millions of dollars)

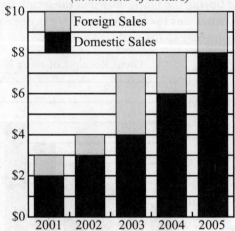

A. $1,000,000
B. $2,000,000
C. $3,000,000
D. $5,000,000
E. $6,000,000

256. Based on the data presented below, what was the approximate total number of packages shipped by PostExpress for the months January, February, and March, inclusive?

Number of Packages Shipped Monthly by PostExpress

F. 40,000
G. 55,000
H. 60,000
J. 70,000
K. 85,000

Pie Charts

257. Based on the data presented below, approximately how much money was spent on the Air Force?

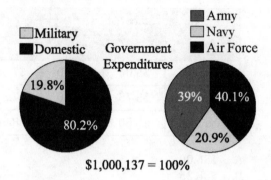

Government Expenditures

$1,000,137 = 100%

A. $39,704
B. $79,409
C. $96,123
D. $198,027
E. $401,054

258. Based on the data presented below, what was the dollar value of foreign sales to Europe by PetProducts in 2002?

PetProducts 2002 Foreign Sales
(Total = $2,000,000)

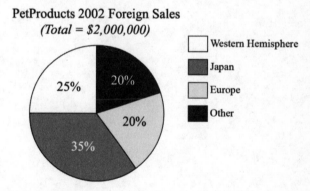

F. $200,000
G. $400,000
H. $1,200,000
J. $1,600,000
K. $2,000,000

Tables

259. Based on the data presented below, what is the total cost of 5 large blue t-shirts, 8 small red t-shirts, and 4 extra large white t-shirts?

T-SHIRT PRICES			
	Blue	Red	White
Small	$5.00	$6.00	$7.00
Large	$5.75	$6.50	$7.25
Extra Large	$6.50	$7.25	$8.00

A. $56.00
B. $88.25
C. $105.50
D. $108.75
E. $135.00

Scatterplots

260. The following scatterplot shows the video-game playing habits of 20 students.

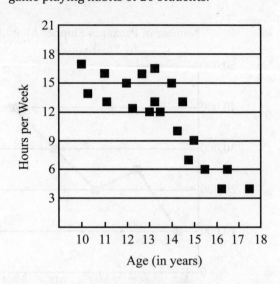

The graph most strongly supports the conclusion that the number of hours per week spent playing video-games:

F. is constant from age 10 to age 18.
G. increases as age increases from 10 to 18.
H. decreases as age increases from 10 to 18.
J. is constant for ages 10 through 14 and then decreases.
K. is constant for ages 10 through 14 and then increases.

QUIZZES

This section contains four Mathematics quizzes. Complete each quiz under timed conditions. Use any available space in the section for scratch work. Answers are on pages 667–668.

Quiz I

(20 items; 20 minutes)

DIRECTIONS: Solve each item and choose the correct answer choice. Calculator use is permitted; however, some items are best solved without the use of a calculator.

NOTES: All of the following should be assumed, unless otherwise stated.

1. Illustrative figures are NOT necessarily drawn to scale.
2. The word *average* indicates arithmetic mean.
3. The word *line* indicates a straight line.
4. Geometric figures lie in a plane.

1. In the triangle below, $x = ?$

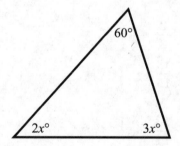

A. 24
B. 20
C. 16
D. 12
E. 10

2. A normal dozen contains 12 items, and a baker's dozen contains 13 items. If x is the number of items that could be measured either in a whole number of normal dozens or in a whole number of baker's dozens, what is the <u>minimum</u> value of x?

F. 1
G. 12
H. 13
J. 25
K. 156

3. In the figure below, what is the degree measure of the <u>smaller</u> of the two angles formed by the hour and minute hands of the clock?

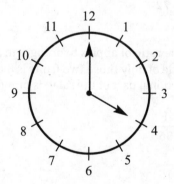

A. 45
B. 60
C. 90
D. 120
E. 240

4. Starting from points that are 200 kilometers apart, two trains travel toward each other along two parallel tracks. If one train travels at 70 kilometers per hour and the other travels at 80 kilometers per hour, how much time, in hours, will elapse before the trains pass each other?

    F. $\dfrac{3}{4}$

    G. 1

    H. $\dfrac{4}{3}$

    J. $\dfrac{3}{2}$

    K. 2

5. A student begins heating a certain substance with a temperature of 50°C over a Bunsen burner. If the temperature of the substance will rise 20°C for every 24 minutes it remains over the burner, what will be the temperature, in degrees Celsius, of the substance after 18 minutes?

    A. 52
    B. 56
    C. 60
    D. 65
    E. 72

6. If the ratio of apples to oranges in a fruit salad made of only those two fruits is 8 to 7, what fractional part of the salad is oranges?

    F. $\dfrac{1}{56}$

    G. $\dfrac{1}{15}$

    H. $\dfrac{1}{7}$

    J. $\dfrac{7}{15}$

    K. $\dfrac{8}{7}$

7. The object of a popular board game is to use clues to identify a suspect and the weapon used to commit a crime. If there are 3 suspects and 6 weapons, how many different solutions to the game are possible?

    A. 2
    B. 3
    C. 9
    D. 12
    E. 18

8. The average weight of three boxes is $25\dfrac{1}{3}$ pounds. If each box weighs at least 24 pounds, what is the greatest possible weight, in pounds, of any one of the boxes?

    F. 25
    G. 26
    H. 27
    J. 28
    K. 29

9. If n subtracted from $\dfrac{13}{2}$ is equal to n divided by $\dfrac{2}{13}$, what is the value of n?

    A. $\dfrac{2}{3}$

    B. $\dfrac{13}{15}$

    C. 1

    D. $\dfrac{13}{11}$

    E. 26

10. In the figure below, what is the area of the quadrilateral?

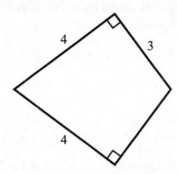

F.   18
G.   15
H.   12
J.   9
K.   8

11. In the figure below, what is the length of $\overline{BC}$? $\left(\sin 30° = \dfrac{1}{2}\right)$

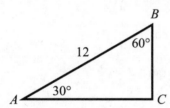

A.   2
B.   3
C. $3\sqrt{3}$
D.   6
E. $6\sqrt{3}$

12. After being dropped from a height of h meters, a ball bounces 3 meters high on the third bounce and $\dfrac{4}{3}$ meters high on the fifth bounce. The height of each bounce is lower by a constant factor. What is the value, in meters, of h?

F. $\dfrac{27}{8}$
G. $\dfrac{9}{2}$
H. $\dfrac{27}{4}$
J. $\dfrac{81}{8}$
K. $\dfrac{27}{2}$

13. Set $A = \{-2,\ -1,\ 0\}$, and set $B = \{-1,\ 0,\ 1\}$. If a is an element of set A and b is an element of set B, for how many pairs (a, b) is the product ab a member of both set A and set B?

A.   0
B.   2
C.   5
D.   6
E.   7

14. Which of the following is the complete solution set for $|2x + 4| = 12$?

F.   {-8, 4}
G.   {-4, 8}
H.   {0, 8}
J.   {4, 8}
K.   {6, 8}

15. If $f(x) = \dfrac{(x-1)^2}{(-2-x)}$, for what value of x is $f(x)$ undefined?

    A. −2
    B. −1
    C. 0
    D. 1
    E. 2

Items #16–17 refer to the following table.

ANNUAL EXPENDITURES FOR THE JONES FAMILY (percent of annual expenditures)		
Category	2006	2007
Rent	23.0%	19.3%
Food	17.6%	18.2%
Clothing	14.2%	15.1%
Automobile	11.3%	12.3%
Utilities	10.9%	10.2%
Savings	6.2%	5.1%
Entertainment	5.2%	5.3%
Medical and Dental Care	4.0%	3.7%
Charitable Contributions	3.2%	3.9%
Household Furnishings	2.9%	3.1%
Other	1.5%	3.8%
Total	100.0%	100.0%
Total Expenditures	$34,987.00	$40,012.00

16. Approximately how much money did the Jones family spend on medical and dental care in 2006?

    F. $1,200
    G. $1,400
    H. $1,520
    J. $2,250
    K. $4,000

17. If the categories in the table are rank ordered from one to eleven in each year, how many categories would have a different rank from 2006 to 2007?

    A. 2
    B. 3
    C. 4
    D. 5
    E. 6

18. For the figure below, which of the following statements is INCORRECT?

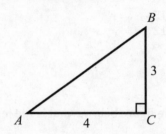

    F. $\sin A = \dfrac{3}{5}$

    G. $\cos A = \dfrac{4}{5}$

    H. $\tan A = \dfrac{3}{4}$

    J. $\cot A = \dfrac{5}{3}$

    K. $\sec A = \dfrac{5}{4}$

19. When the 10-gallon tank of an emergency generator is filled to capacity, the generator operates without interruption for 20 hours, consuming fuel at a constant rate until all the fuel is consumed. Which of the graphs below represents the fuel consumption of the generator over time?

A.

B.

C.

D.

E.

20. In the figure below, $\overline{PQ}$ is tangent to circle O at point S and $\overline{QR}$ is tangent to circle O at point T. If the radius of circle O is 2, what is the area of the shaded portion of the figure?

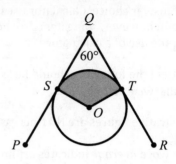

F. $\dfrac{\pi}{3}$

G. $\dfrac{2\pi}{3}$

H. π

J. $\dfrac{4\pi}{3}$

K. 2π

Quiz II

(20 items; 20 minutes)

DIRECTIONS: Solve each item and choose the correct answer choice. Calculator use is permitted; however, some items are best solved without the use of a calculator.

NOTES: All of the following should be assumed, unless otherwise stated.

1. Illustrative figures are NOT necessarily drawn to scale.
2. The word *average* indicates arithmetic mean.
3. The word *line* indicates a straight line.
4. Geometric figures lie in a plane.

1. The figure below is a plan that shows a solid set of steps to be constructed from concrete blocks of equal size. How many blocks are needed to construct the steps?

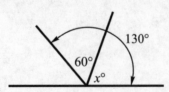

A. 12
B. 15
C. 18
D. 21
E. 24

2. In the figure below, what is the value of x?

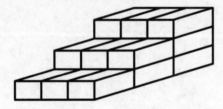

F. 70
G. 60
H. 50
J. 40
K. 30

3. If $2^{x+1} = 4^{x-1}$, what is the value of x?

A. 1
B. 2
C. 3
D. 4
E. 5

4. Of the actors in a certain play, five actors are in Act I, 12 actors are in Act II, and 13 actors are in Act III. If 10 of the actors are in exactly two of the three acts and all of the other actors are in just one act, how many actors are in the play?

F. 17
G. 20
H. 24
J. 30
K. 38

5. In the figure below, $\overline{AB} \cong \overline{BC} \cong \overline{CA}$. What is the value of y?

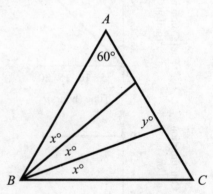

A. 20
B. 60
C. 80
D. 100
E. 120

6. Under certain conditions, a bicycle traveling k meters per second requires $\dfrac{k^2}{20}+k$ meters to stop. If $k=10$, how many <u>meters</u> does the bicycle need to stop?

F.   10
G.   12
H.   15
J.   20
K.   30

7. What is the slope of a line that passes through the origin and $(-3,-2)$?

A. $\dfrac{3}{2}$

B. $\dfrac{2}{3}$

C.   0

D. $-\dfrac{2}{3}$

E. $-\dfrac{3}{2}$

8. An album contains x black-and-white photographs and y color photographs. If the album contains 24 photographs, then which of the following CANNOT be true?

F. $x=y$
G. $x=2y$
H. $x=3y$
J. $x=4y$
K.   Cannot be determined from the given information

9. If $2a=3b=4c$, then what is the average (arithmetic mean) of a, b, and c, in terms of a?

A. $\dfrac{13a}{18}$

B. $\dfrac{4a}{3}$

C. $\dfrac{13a}{9}$

D. $2a$

E. $\dfrac{8a}{3}$

10. If $x=6+y$ and $4x=3-2y$, what is the value of x?

F.   4

G. $\dfrac{11}{3}$

H. $\dfrac{5}{2}$

J. $-\dfrac{2}{3}$

K. $-\dfrac{7}{2}$

11. If $\dfrac{2}{3}$ is written as a decimal to 101 places, what is the sum of the first 100 digits to the right of the decimal point?

A.   66
B.   595
C.   599
D.   600
E.   601

12. In the figure below, O is the center of the circle with radius 1. What is the area of the shaded region?

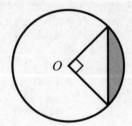

F. $\dfrac{3\pi}{4} + \dfrac{1}{2}$

G. $\dfrac{3\pi}{4} - \dfrac{1}{2}$

H. $\dfrac{\pi}{4} + \dfrac{1}{2}$

J. $\dfrac{\pi}{4} - \dfrac{1}{2}$

K. $\pi - 1$

13. If $f(3) = 5$ and $f(7) = 7$, what is the slope of the graph of $f(x)$ in the coordinate plane?

A. -2

B. $-\dfrac{1}{2}$

C. 1

D. $\dfrac{1}{2}$

E. 2

14. In a list of the first 100 positive integers, the digit 9 appears how many times?

F. 9
G. 10
H. 11
J. 19
K. 20

15. If $\dfrac{x}{x+3} = \dfrac{3}{4}$, and $x \neq -3$, then $x = ?$

A. 3
B. 4
C. 5
D. 7
E. 9

16. Which of the following is the complete solution set for $\sqrt{2x+3} + 2 = 5$?

F. $\{\}$
G. $\{-1\}$
H. $\{3\}$
J. $\{-1, 3\}$
K. $\{1, 2\}$

17. In the figure below, what is the length of $\overline{AC}$?
$\left(\sin \angle ABD = \dfrac{\sqrt{7}}{4} \right)$

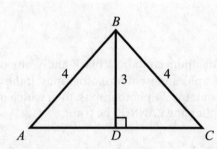

A. 5
B. $2\sqrt{7}$
C. $4\sqrt{3}$
D. 7
E. 10

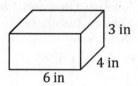

18. A dartboard has four concentric circles with the center as indicated in the figure below. If the diameter of each circle except for the smallest is twice that of the next smaller circle, what is the probability that a randomly thrown dart that strikes the figure will strike the shaded portion of the figure?

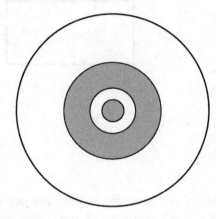

F. $\dfrac{3}{16}$

G. $\dfrac{1}{4}$

H. $\dfrac{13}{64}$

J. $\dfrac{17}{64}$

K. $\dfrac{1}{2}$

19. If $f(3)=4$ and $f(-3)=1$, what is the y-intercept of the graph of $f(x)$ in the coordinate plane?

A. $-\dfrac{5}{2}$

B. $-\dfrac{2}{5}$

C. 0

D. $\dfrac{2}{5}$

E. $\dfrac{5}{2}$

20. A tissue box has dimensions shown below. What is the total surface area of the box, in square inches?

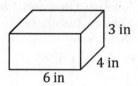

3 in

4 in

6 in

F. 24

G. 36

H. 48

J. 54

K. 108

Quiz III

(20 items; 20 minutes)

> **DIRECTIONS:** Solve each item and choose the correct answer choice. Calculator use is permitted; however, some items are best solved without the use of a calculator.

NOTES: All of the following should be assumed, unless otherwise stated.

1. Illustrative figures are NOT necessarily drawn to scale.
2. The word *average* indicates arithmetic mean.
3. The word *line* indicates a straight line.
4. Geometric figures lie in a plane.

1. What is the average (arithmetic mean) of all integers 6 through 15 (including 6 and 15)?

A. 6
B. 9
C. 10.5
D. 11
E. 21

2. Which of the following is equivalent to $\dfrac{3.2 \times 10^5}{8 \times 10^8}$?

F. 4×10^{-4}
G. 4×10^{-3}
H. 4×10^{-2}
J. 4×10^3
K. 4×10^{13}

3. If the rectangle below has an area of 72, then $x = ?$

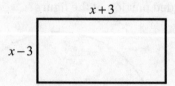

A. 3
B. 4
C. 6
D. 8
E. 9

4. Machine X produces 15 units per minute, and Machine Y produces 12 units per minute. In one hour, Machine X will produce how many more units than Machine Y?

F. 90
G. 180
H. 240
J. 270
K. 360

5. Which of the following pie charts represents the data shown below?

Team Expenses		
Transportation	$240	■
Lodging	$360	▨
Meals	$120	☐

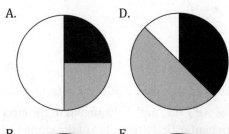

A.   D.

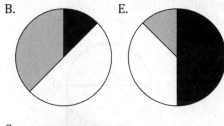

B.   E.

C.

6. On the first day after being given an assignment, a student read $\frac{1}{2}$ the number of pages assigned, and on the second day, the student read 3 more pages. If the student still has 6 additional pages to read, how many pages were assigned?

F. 15
G. 18
H. 24
J. 30
K. 36

7. The average (arithmetic mean) of Pat's scores on three tests was 80. If the average of her scores on the first two tests was 78, what was her score on the third test?

A. 82
B. 84
C. 86
D. 88
E. 90

8. In the figure below, $a + c - b$ is equal to which of the following?

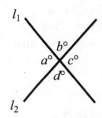

F. $2a - d$
G. $2a + d$
H. $2d - a$
J. $2a$
K. 180

9. If $3a + 6b = 12$, then $a + 2b = ?$

A. 1
B. 2
C. 3
D. 4
E. 6

10. Two circles with radii r and $r + 3$ have areas that differ by 15π. What is the radius of the smaller circle?

F. 4
G. 3
H. 2
J. 1
K. $\frac{1}{2}$

11. If x, y, and z are integers, $x > y > z > 1$, and $xyz = 144$, what is the <u>greatest</u> possible value of x?

    A. 8
    B. 12
    C. 16
    D. 24
    E. 36

12. For all integers, $x \Phi y = 2x + 3y$. Which of the following must be true?

    I. $3 \Phi 2 = 12$
    II. $x \Phi y = y \Phi x$
    III. $0 \Phi (1 \Phi 2) = (0 \Phi 1) \Phi 2$

    F. I only
    G. I and II only
    H. I and III only
    J. II and III only
    K. I, II, and III

13. In the figure below, what is the slope of line l?

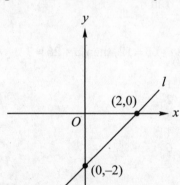

    A. 1
    B. $\dfrac{1}{2}$
    C. 0
    D. $-\dfrac{1}{2}$
    E. -1

14. If Yuriko is now twice as old as Lisa was 10 years ago, how old is Lisa today if Yuriko is now n years old?

    F. $\dfrac{n}{2} + 10$
    G. $\dfrac{n}{2} - 10$
    H. $n - 10$
    J. $2n + 10$
    K. $2n - 10$

15. In the figure below, $ABCD$ is a rectangle with sides $\overline{AB}$, $\overline{BC}$, and $\overline{CD}$ tangent to the circle with center O. If the radius of the circle is 2, what is the area of the shaded region?

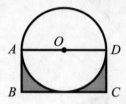

    A. $\dfrac{3\pi}{2}$
    B. $\dfrac{3\pi}{4}$
    C. $8 - 2\pi$
    D. $2 - \pi$
    E. $\pi - 1$

16. The sum of two positive consecutive integers is n. In terms of n, what is the value of the larger of the two integers?

    F. $\dfrac{n-1}{2}$
    G. $\dfrac{n+1}{2}$
    H. $\dfrac{n}{2} + 1$
    J. $\dfrac{n}{2} - 1$
    K. $\dfrac{n}{2}$

17. The table below shows a teacher how to convert scores for a test from the Old Scale to the New Scale. What is the Minimum Passing Score on the New Scale?

	OLD SCALE	NEW SCALE
Minimum Score	0	120
Minimum Passing Score	60	?
Maximum Score	100	180

A. 108
B. 136
C. 156
D. 164
E. 208

18. If a polygon with all equal sides is inscribed in a circle, then the measure in degrees of the minor arc created by adjacent vertices of the polygon could be all of the following EXCEPT:

F. 30
G. 25
H. 24
J. 20
K. 15

19. A jar contains 5 blue marbles, 25 green marbles, and x red marbles. If the probability of drawing a red marble at random from the jar is $\frac{1}{4}$, what is the value of x?

A. 25
B. 20
C. 15
D. 12
E. 10

20. In the figure below, the length of $\overline{AB}$ is 2 units. Which of the following is the best approximation for the number of units in the length of $\overline{BC}$? $(\cos 45° \approx 0.7)$

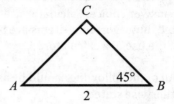

F. 0.7
G. 1.2
H. 1.4
J. 2.9
K. 3.4

Quiz IV Brain Buster
(25 items; 20 minutes)

DIRECTIONS: Solve each item and choose the correct answer choice. Calculator use is permitted; however, some items are best solved without the use of a calculator.

NOTES: All of the following should be assumed, unless otherwise stated.

1. Illustrative figures are NOT necessarily drawn to scale.
2. The word *average* indicates arithmetic mean.
3. The word *line* indicates a straight line.
4. Geometric figures lie in a plane.

1. Maggie has to inventory her employer's collection of books. There are three categories of books. Historical novels account for one-fourth of the books. Classics comprise half of the remaining books and there are 30 travel books. How many books does she have to inventory?

    A.   50
    B.   70
    C.   80
    D. 100
    E. 120

2. The local university's enrollment figures for a six-year period are detailed in the table below. Between which two consecutive years did the university experience the greatest percent increase in student enrollment?

UNIVERSITY ENROLLMENT					
2006	2007	2008	2009	2010	2011
14,000	15,100	15,900	16,500	17,600	17,400

    F. 2006–2007
    G. 2007–2008
    H. 2008–2009
    J.   2009–2010
    K. 2010–2011

3. If $f(x) = \dfrac{x^2 + x}{x - 1}$ and $g(x) = 2x + 3$, then $g(f(-2)) = ?$

    A. $-\dfrac{4}{3}$
    B. $-\dfrac{2}{3}$
    C. 0
    D. $\dfrac{4}{3}$
    E. $\dfrac{5}{3}$

4. Set *A* contains all the positive factors of 24. Set *B* contains all the prime numbers less than 20. How many numbers are elements in both set *A* and set *B*?

    F. Zero
    G. One
    H. Two
    J.   Three
    K. Four

5. The local modeling agency is looking for some new models for a specific job. The job requires that the model's height be within 2 inches of 70 inches. Which of the following absolute value inequalities describe this condition, where *x* is the model's height?

    A. $|x + 2| \le 70$
    B. $|x - 2| < 70$
    C. $|x + 70| < 2$
    D. $|x - 70| < 2$
    E. $|x + 70| \le 2$

6. Tommy has blue, green, and red marbles. The number of blue marbles and green marbles combined total 25. The number of blue and red marbles combined total 30. There are twice as many red marbles as green marbles. How many green marbles does Tommy have?

F.   5
G.   10
H.   15
J.   20
K.   25

7. At a wedding, three entrees are served: chicken, fish, and beef. The total number of people who ordered each entrée are shown in the matrix below:

$$\begin{array}{ccc} \text{chicken} & \text{fish} & \text{beef} \\ \left[\begin{matrix} 85 & 58 & 68 \end{matrix}\right] \end{array}$$

The percentage of each group who ordered potatoes as a side is shown in the matrix below:

$$\begin{matrix} \text{chicken} \\ \text{fish} \\ \text{beef} \end{matrix} \left[\begin{matrix} 20\% \\ 50\% \\ 75\% \end{matrix}\right]$$

Approximately how many servings of potatoes will need to be prepared for this wedding?

A.   17
B.   29
C.   51
D.   97
E.   107

8. In the figure below, line *l* is parallel to line *m*. What is the value of *x*?

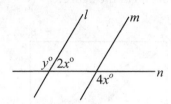

F.   20
G.   30
H.   40
J.   50
K.   Cannot be determined from the given information

9. If $x = a^2 - b^2$, $y = a^2 + 2ab + b^2$, and $a + b \neq 0$, then $\dfrac{x}{y} = ?$

A. $2a^2 + 2ab$

B. $\dfrac{a^2 - b^2}{a^2 + b^2}$

C. $\dfrac{a + b}{a - b}$

D. $\dfrac{-1}{2ab}$

E. $\dfrac{a - b}{a + b}$

10. A 13-foot ladder is leaning against a building and the bottom of the ladder is 5 feet from the wall. The ladder begins to slide down the building. When the bottom of the ladder is 8 feet from the wall, about how far has the top of the ladder slipped down?

F.   less than 1 foot
G.   exactly 1 foot
H.   between 1 foot and 2 feet
J.   exactly 2 feet
K.   more than 2 feet

11. In rectangle *ABCD* below, $\overline{AD} = \overline{DE}$, $\overline{AD} = 2$, and $\angle BAC = 30°$. What is the area of the shaded portion of the figure?

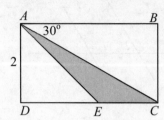

A. $2\sqrt{3} - 2$

B. $4 - 2\sqrt{3}$

C. $2\sqrt{2}$

D. $2\sqrt{2} - 3$

E. $2\sqrt{3}$

12. In the figure below, $\overgroup{DE}$ is the arc of a circle with center *C*. If the length of $\overgroup{DE}$ is 2π, what is the area of sector *CDE*?

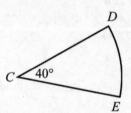

F. 4π

G. 9π

H. 12π

J. 18π

K. 24π

13. If *a* is the greatest prime factor of 24 and *b* is the greatest prime factor of 80, what is *ab*?

A. 4

B. 6

C. 10

D. 15

E. 16

14. If the average (arithmetic mean) of *a*, *b*, and *c* is *z*, which of the following is the average of *a*, *b*, *c* and *d*?

F. $\dfrac{z+d}{3}$

G. $\dfrac{z+d}{4}$

H. $\dfrac{3z+d}{3}$

J. $\dfrac{3z+d}{4}$

K. $\dfrac{3(z+d)}{4}$

15. When 21 is divided by a positive integer *d*, the remainder is 5. For how many different values of *d* is this true?

A. One

B. Two

C. Three

D. Four

E. Five

16. Let the operation ✪ be defined by $x ✪ y = xy + y$ for all numbers *x* and *y*. If $2 ✪ 3 = z ✪ 1$, what is the value of *z*?

F. 6

G. 7

H. 8

J. 9

K. 10

17. In a rectangular coordinate system, the center of a circle has coordinates (3,–10). The circle touches the *y*-axis only once. What is the diameter of the circle?

A. 3

B. 6

C. 9

D. 10

E. 20

18. If $x^2 + 3x - 18 = 0$ and $2m = x$, which of the following could be a value of m?

F. -3
G. 1
H. 3
J. 6
K. 9

19. Which of the following coordinate points lie completely inside the circle whose equation is $x^2 + y^2 = 36$?

A. $(6,0)$
B. $(0,-6)$
C. $(-4,5)$
D. $(2,7)$
E. $(4,4)$

20. If $x - y = 7$ and $x^2 - y^2 = 35$, what is $x + y$?

F. 5
G. 7
H. 10
J. 28
K. 42

21. If m is a positive number such that $\log_m\left(\dfrac{1}{32}\right) = -5$, then $m = ?$

A. $\dfrac{1}{4}$
B. $\dfrac{1}{2}$
C. 2
D. 4
E. 37

22. The expression $\cos^2 x - 7 + \sin^2 x$ is equivalent to:

F. -8
G. -7
H. -6
J. 6
K. 8

23. Which of the following values of x satisfies the equation $\log_x\left(\dfrac{1}{81}\right) = -4$?

A. 3
B. 4
C. 9
D. 18
E. 81

24. Assume an angle with radian measure θ exists such that $\cos\theta = -\dfrac{3}{5}$ and $\dfrac{\pi}{2} < \theta < \pi$. What is the value of $\sin\theta$?

F. $-\dfrac{5}{3}$
G. $-\dfrac{4}{5}$
H. $\dfrac{3}{5}$
J. $\dfrac{4}{5}$
K. $\dfrac{5}{4}$

25. If the polynomial $3x^3 + 12x^2 + 2x + 8 = 0$ has the root -4, which of the following are also roots of the polynomial?

A. $\pm\dfrac{\sqrt{6}}{3}$
B. $\pm\dfrac{\sqrt{6}}{6}$
C. $\pm\dfrac{i\sqrt{6}}{3}$
D. $\pm\dfrac{i\sqrt{6}}{6}$
E. $\pm\dfrac{i\sqrt{3}}{6}$

REVIEW

This section contains additional Mathematics items for further practice. Answers are on page 668.

DIRECTIONS: Solve each item and choose the correct answer choice. Calculator use is permitted; however, some items are best solved without the use of a calculator.

NOTES: All of the following should be assumed, unless otherwise stated.

1. Illustrative figures are NOT necessarily drawn to scale.
2. The word *average* indicates arithmetic mean.
3. The word *line* indicates a straight line.
4. Geometric figures lie in a plane.

1. The approximate distance from earth to the moon is 7,568,352,000 feet. If an astronaut has made three trips to the moon (and back), what is the approximate total distance he has traveled between the earth and the moon?

   A. 1.26×10^6

   B. 7.57×10^6

   C. 1.26×10^9

   D. 7.57×10^9

   E. 7.57×10^{12}

2. If each of the dimensions of a rectangle is increased by 100%, by what percent is the area increased?

   F. 100%
   G. 200%
   H. 300%
   J. 400%
   K. 500%

3. What is 10% of $\dfrac{x}{3}$ if $\dfrac{2x}{3}$ is 10% of 60?

   A. 0.1
   B. 0.2
   C. 0.3
   D. 0.4
   E. 0.5

4. In the figure below, M and N are midpoints of sides $\overline{PR}$ and $\overline{PQ}$, respectively, of $\triangle PQR$. What is the ratio of the area of $\triangle MNS$ to that of $\triangle PQR$?

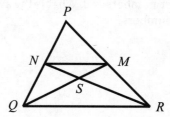

   F. 2:5
   G. 2:9
   H. 1:4
   J. 1:8
   K. 1:12

5. A cube has an edge that is 4 inches long. If the edge is increased by 25%, which of the following is the best approximation of the percent increase in the volume of the cube?

   A. 25%
   B. 48%
   C. 73%
   D. 95%
   E. 122%

6. In the figure below is a portion of the (x,y) coordinate plane. If each small square has an area of 1 and the coordinates of point P are $(3,7)$, what are the (x,y) coordinates of point Q?

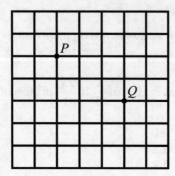

F. (5,6)
G. (1,10)
H. (6,9)
J. (6,5)
K. (5,10)

7. The average of 8 numbers is 6; the average of 6 other numbers is 8. What is the average of all 14 numbers?

A. 6

B. $6\frac{6}{7}$

C. 7

D. $7\frac{2}{7}$

E. $8\frac{1}{7}$

8. Which of the following is the matrix product of
$$\begin{bmatrix} 0.5 & -3 & 0.25 \\ -1 & 2 & 1.5 \end{bmatrix} \text{ and } \begin{bmatrix} 8 & 0 \\ -1 & 2 \\ 12 & 6 \end{bmatrix}?$$

F. $\begin{bmatrix} 10 & -4.5 \\ 8 & 13 \end{bmatrix}$

G. $\begin{bmatrix} 10 & 0 \\ 1 & 4 \end{bmatrix}$

H. $\begin{bmatrix} 10 & -24 & 2 \\ -2.5 & 7 & 2.75 \\ 0 & -24 & 12 \end{bmatrix}$

J. $\begin{bmatrix} 4 & 0 & 0.25 \\ 1 & 4 & 1.5 \\ 12 & 6 & 0 \end{bmatrix}$

K. $\begin{bmatrix} 8.5 & -3 & 0.25 \\ -2 & 4 & 1.5 \\ 12 & 6 & 0 \end{bmatrix}$

9. Doreen can wash her car in 15 minutes, while her younger brother Dave takes twice as long to do the same job. If they work together, how many minutes will the job take them?

A. 5

B. $7\frac{1}{2}$

C. 10

D. $22\frac{1}{2}$

E. 30

10. In the figure below, the sides of the large square are each 14 inches long. Joining the midpoints of each opposite side forms 4 smaller squares. What is the value of y, in inches?

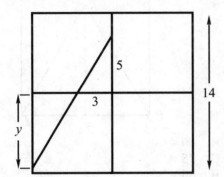

F. 5
G. 6
H. $6\dfrac{5}{8}$
J. $6\dfrac{2}{3}$
K. 6.8

11. In the figure below, $PQRS$ is a parallelogram, and $\overline{ST} = \overline{TV} = \overline{VR}$. If $\angle PTS = 90°$, what is the ratio of the area of $\triangle SPT$ to the area of the parallelogram?

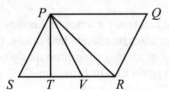

A. $\dfrac{1}{6}$

B. $\dfrac{1}{5}$

C. $\dfrac{2}{7}$

D. $2\dfrac{1}{3}$

E. Cannot be determined from the given information

12. If $p > q$ and $r < 0$, which of the following is (are) true?

I. $pr < qr$
II. $p + r > q + r$
III. $p - r < q - r$

F. I only
G. II only
H. I and III only
J. I and II only
K. I, II, and III

13. A pound of water is evaporated from 6 pounds of seawater that is 4% salt. What is the percentage of salt in the remaining solution?

A. 3.6%
B. 4%
C. 4.8%
D. 5.2%
E. 6%

14. Which of the following expressions correctly describes the mathematical relationship below?

3 less than the product of 4 and x

F. $4x - 3$
G. $3x - 4$
H. $4(x - 3)$
J. $3(4x)$
K. $\dfrac{4x}{3}$

15. In the figure below, what percent of the area of rectangle *PQRS* is shaded?

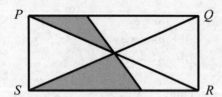

    A. 20%
    B. 25%
    C. 30%
    D. $33\frac{1}{3}$%
    E. 35%

16. A cylindrical container has a diameter of 14 inches and a height of 6 inches. Since one gallon equals 231 cubic inches, what is the approximate capacity, in gallons, of the tank?

    F. $\frac{2}{3}$
    G. $1\frac{1}{7}$
    H. $2\frac{2}{7}$
    J. $2\frac{2}{3}$
    K. 4

17. If $12 + x = 36 - y$, then $x + y = $?

    A. −48
    B. −24
    C.   3
    D. 24
    E. 48

18. In the figure below, *PQRS* is a square and *PTS* is an equilateral triangle. What is the degree measure of ∠*TRS* ?

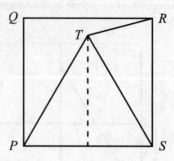

    F. 60
    G. 75
    H. 80
    J. 90
    K. Cannot be determined from the given information

19. Which of the following is equivalent to

$$\log_3 1 + \log_2 16 - \log_7 \frac{1}{49} \text{ ?}$$

    A. 1
    B. 2
    C. 3
    D. 6
    E. 7

20. Paul can paint a fence in 2 hours and Fred can paint the same fence in 3 hours. If Paul and Fred work together, how many hours will it take them to paint the fence?

    F. 5
    G. $2\frac{1}{2}$
    H. $1\frac{1}{5}$
    J. 1
    K. $\frac{5}{6}$

21. A motorist drives 60 miles to her destination at an average speed of 40 miles per hour and makes the return trip at an average speed of 30 miles per hour. What is her average speed, in miles per hour, for the entire trip?

A. 17

B. $34\frac{2}{7}$

C. 35

D. $43\frac{1}{3}$

E. 70

22. If $\log_3 a = x$ and $\log_3 b = y$, what is the value of $\log_3\left(ab^2\right)$?

F. xy^2

G. $x + y^2$

H. $x + 2y$

J. $a + b^2$

K. $a + 2b$

23. A sphere with a diameter of 18 feet sits inside of a cylinder. It is tangent to the top and bottom of the cylinder and has the same diameter as the cylinder. What is the volume of the space outside of the sphere but inside of the cylinder?

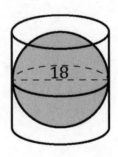

A. 486

B. 486π

C. 972π

D. $1,458\pi$

E. $2,430\pi$

24. Which of the following values of x satisfies the equation $\log_6 x = 3$?

F. 9

G. 18

H. 36

J. 216

K. 729

25. In the figure below, $\overline{AB}$ is three times longer than $\overline{BC}$, and $\overline{CD}$ is two times longer than $\overline{BC}$. If $\overline{BC}$ is removed from the line and the other two segments are joined to form one line, what is the ratio of the original length of $\overline{AD}$ to the new length of $\overline{AD}$?

A. 3:2

B. 6:5

C. 5:4

D. 7:6

E. 11:10

26. If $(x+1)(x-2)$ is positive, then which of the following statements is true?

F. $x < -1$ or $x > 2$

G. $x > -1$ or $x < 2$

H. $-1 < x < 2$

J. $-2 < x < 1$

K. $x = -1$ or $x = 2$

27. In the table below, which yearly period had the smallest percent increase in sales?

ABC SOUND STORES	
Annual Sale of Compact Discs	
Year	Number Sold
2002	7,000
2003	9,000
2004	12,000
2005	16,000
2006	20,000
2007	24,000

A. 2002–2003
B. 2003–2004
C. 2004–2005
D. 2005–2006
E. 2006–2007

28. For the figure below, which one of the following statements is true?

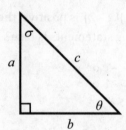

F. $\sin\theta = \dfrac{b}{c}$

G. $\tan\sigma = \dfrac{a}{b}$

H. $\cos\theta = \dfrac{c}{a}$

J. $\sin\theta = \cos\sigma$
K. $\cot\sigma = \tan\sigma$

29. In the figure below, if $\arcsin s = 2(\arcsin d)$, then $x = $?

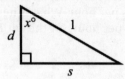

A. 15
B. 30
C. 45
D. 60
E. 75

30. In the figure below, if $\overline{AC}$ is the diameter of the circle, B is a point on the circle, and $\sin\theta = \dfrac{1}{2}$, then $\sin\phi = $?

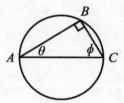

F. $\dfrac{\sqrt{2}}{3}$

G. $\dfrac{\sqrt{3}}{3}$

H. $\dfrac{\sqrt{3}}{2}$

J. $\dfrac{2\sqrt{2}}{3}$

K. $\dfrac{2\sqrt{3}}{2}$

31. The figure below is a possible graph of which of the following equations?

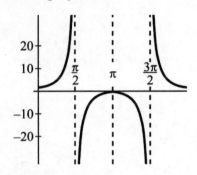

A. $y = 2(\sin x)$
B. $y = \sin x + 2$
C. $y = \csc x + 1$
D. $y = \csc x - 1$
E. $y = \sec x + 1$

32. If θ is an acute angle and $\cos\theta = \dfrac{b}{c}$, $b > 0$ and $c > 0$ and $b \neq c$, then $\sin\theta$ is equal to which of the following?

F. $\dfrac{b}{\sqrt{b^2 - c^2}}$

G. $\dfrac{c}{\sqrt{b^2 - b^2}}$

H. $\dfrac{\sqrt{b^2 - c^2}}{b}$

J. $\dfrac{\sqrt{b^2 - c^2}}{c}$

K. $\dfrac{\sqrt{c^2 - b^2}}{c}$

STRATEGY SUMMARY

General Strategies

When approaching a Mathematics item, there are several things to which you should pay careful attention:

Figures

Figures are usually, but not always, drawn to scale. When all other options for answering the item fail, try the strategy of assuming the figure *is* drawn to scale. Then, use the figure to help you answer the item.

Answer Choices

Most answer choices are arranged in order of ascending or descending value and many incorrect answer choices correspond to conceptual errors.

"Signal" Words

Typically, "signal" words are capitalized (e.g., thought-reversers, such as "NOT," "CANNOT," and "EXCEPT"); however, they may sometimes be underlined or italicized (e.g., specified units). While the specific formatting of these words may vary, they can be critical to correctly understanding the item. Pay careful attention to thought-reversers, as they reverse the apparent meaning of an item.

Ladder of Difficulty

Difficult Mathematics items tend to be clustered near the end of the section. When solving items that are high on the ladder of difficulty, be wary of simplistic answers and the "Cannot be determined..." response. Remember to pace yourself—difficult, time-consuming items have the same value as the easy items.

Item Stems

Read the item stem first. Only then should you read the details of the item, keeping this item stem in mind.

Solutions

Double-check the solution by confirming that it answers the particular question that is being asked. When applicable, this confirmation includes verifying that the solution is given in the units specified by the item stem.

If you are unable to either find an elegant (quick) solution or solve the item directly based on subject knowledge, the following alternative solutions strategies can be extremely helpful:

"Test-the-Test" Strategy

The correct answer to any item is always one of five given choices. Sometimes, the easiest and quickest way to solve an item is to test each of the answer choices. The "test-the-test" strategy can mean plugging answer choices back into the item (starting with the middle answer choice) to test the validity of an expression, or it can mean checking each answer choice against any stated conditions. The "test-the-test" strategy is typically useful for items with numerical solutions or variables and values that meet stated conditions.

"Plug-and-Chug" Strategy

This strategy is similar to the "test-the-test" strategy in that the item stem and answer choices (rather than direct mathematical solution strategies) are used to isolate the correct answer. The difference is that rather than testing the validity of each answer choice against the item stem conditions, the item stem and/or answer choices are evaluated by plugging in chosen numbers: "plug-and-chug." This strategy is especially helpful when solving Algebra items.

"Eliminate-and-Guess" Strategy

If unable to determine the correct answer directly by using mathematical methods or indirectly by using either the "test-the-test" or "plug-and-chug" strategy, eliminate as many answer choices as possible and then guess from the remaining answer choices. For difficult mathematics items, eliminate answer choices that can be reached either by a single step or by copying a number from the item.

Checklist of Skills and Concepts

Arithmetic

___ Simplifying: Fractions, Collecting Terms

___ Factoring

___ Approximation

___ The "Flying-X" Method

___ Decimal/Fraction Equivalents

___ Properties of Numbers (Odd, Even, Negative, Positive, Consecutive)

___ Sets (Union, Intersection, Elements)

___ Absolute Value

___ Percents (Change, Original Amount, Price Increase)

___ Ratios (Two-Part, Three-Part, Weighted)

___ Proportions (Direct, Indirect)

Algebra

___ Evaluation of Expressions (Rational, Radical)

___ Exponents (Integer, Rational, Negative)

___ Factoring

___ Sequence

___ Solving Single Variable Equations and Inequalities

___ Absolute Value

___ Function Math

___ Domain and Range

___ Solving Equations (Multi-Variable, Linear, Simultaneous, Quadratic)

___ Story Problems: Work (Joint Effort), Averages

Coordinate Geometry

___ Coordinate Plane

___ Slope of a Line

___ Slope-Intercept Form of a Linear Equation

___ Distance Formula

___ Graphing Linear Equations

___ Graphing First-Degree Inequalities

___ Graphing Quadratic Equations

___ Permutations of Equations and Graphs

Geometry

___ Lines and Angles (Perpendicular, Parallel, Intersecting, Big Angle/Little Angle Theorem)

___ Triangles (Equilateral, Isosceles, Acute, Obtuse, Perimeter, Area, Altitudes, Angles, Bisectors, Pythagorean Theorem)

___ Quadrilaterals (Squares, Rectangles, Rhombuses, Parallelograms, Trapezoids, Perimeter, Area)

___ Polygons (Sum of Interior Angles)

___ Circles (Chords, Tangents, Radius, Diameter, Circumference, Area)

___ Solids (Cubes, Cylinders, Spheres, Volumes, Surface Areas)

___ Complex Figures

Trigonometry

___ Trigonometric Functions

___ Trigonometric Values

___ Trigonometric Relationships

Statistics and Probability

___ Averages (Simple, Weighted), Median, and Mode

___ Probability

___ Graphs (Bar, Cumulative, Line)

___ Pie Charts

___ Tables

___ Scatterplots

Science

Course Concept Outline

I. Test Mechanics (p. 285)

A. Overview (p. 285)

B. Anatomy (Items #1–4, pp. 286–288)

C. Pacing (p. 289)

D. Time Trial (Items #1–6, pp. 290–291)

E. Game Plan (p. 292)

1. Quickly Preview the Test Section, but Skip the Directions
2. Personalize the Passage Order
3. Read the Passage
4. Answer the Items
5. Use the Answer Choices
6. Eliminate Choices, Guess (If Necessary), and Move On

II. Lesson (p. 295)

A. Preliminaries[1]

1. What Is Tested
2. Directions
3. Item Profiles

B. Facts about the Science Test

1. Three Types of Passages

---

[1] Some concepts in this Course Concept Outline are not illustrated through examples in your student text but may be covered by your instructor in class. They are included here to provide a complete outline of your course.

a) Data Representation
b) Research Summary
c) Conflicting Viewpoints
2. Science Items Test Reasoning, Not Knowledge

C. Item-Types

1. Comprehension
2. Analysis
3. Application

D. General Strategies

1. Plan Your Attack—Easiest Passages First
2. Do Not Preview Item Stems before Reading a Passage
3. Underline Key Words and Phrases
4. Pay Attention to What Is There, Not What Isn't There
5. Pay Attention to Differences
6. Watch for Assumptions
7. Look for Trends
8. Transcribe Answers in Groups
9. Answer the Question That Is Being Asked
10. Work Out the Answer First
11. Make Notes to Clarify Viewpoints

E. Data Representation Review and Strategies (p. 295)

1. Graphs
a) Straight Lines
b) Parabolic Curves
c) Graph Reading Strategy (Items #1–3, p. 295)
2. Tables
a) Understanding the Nature of Data (Items #4–5, p. 296)
b) Recognizing Trends (Items #6–8, p. 296)
c) Drawing Conclusions (Item #9, p. 296)
3. Typical Data Representation Items (Items #10–22, pp. 297–299)
4. Data Representation Strategies (Items #23–40, pp. 299–304)

F. Research Summary Review and Strategies (p. 304)

1. Understanding Design of Experiment
2. Predicting Results
3. Evaluating Data
4. Typical Research Summary Items (Items #41–51, pp. 304–307)
5. Research Summary Strategies (Items #52–74, pp. 307–316)

G. Conflicting Viewpoints Review and Strategies (p. 316)

1. Predicting Results
2. Spotting the Assumptions
3. Picking the Best Argument
4. Typical Conflicting Viewpoints Items (Items #75–85, pp. 316–319)
5. Conflicting Viewpoints Strategies (Items #86–103, pp. 319–323)

III. Quizzes (p. 325)

A. Quiz I (Items #1–16, pp. 325–329)

B. Quiz II (Items #1–16, pp. 330–335)

C. Quiz III (Items #1–16, pp. 336–340)

IV. Review (Items #1–66, pp. 341–353)

V. Strategy Summary (p. 355)

TEST MECHANICS

Overview

The Science Test consists of 40 multiple-choice items divided into six or seven groups. Each group of items is based on a report of data findings, a description of an experiment, or the presentation of a debate on different scientific theories. The time limit for the Science Test is 35 minutes. Calculators are NOT allowed on the ACT Science Test.

We'll call the initial presentation a "passage," whether it is a report of data (Data Representation), a description of an experiment (Research Summary), or a debate of a theory (Conflicting Viewpoints). So, just as the English and Reading Tests have passages with associated items, the Science Test has passages (of the three types) with associated items. We'll use this terminology even though "passage" doesn't quite fit here since the Science Test uses a lot of diagrams, pictures, tables, and graphs.

The Science Test roughly follows the content of science courses taught in grades 7 through 12. Passages use content from the following areas:

- **Biology:** botany, cellular biology, ecology, evolution, genetics, microbiology, zoology

- **Chemistry:** biochemistry, organic chemistry, nuclear chemistry, thermo-chemistry, acids and bases, kinetics and equilibria, properties of matter

- **Earth/Space Sciences:** astronomy, environmental science, geology, meteorology, oceanography

- **Physics:** mechanics, thermodynamics, fluids, solids, electromagnetism, optics

Although these are obviously "science" subjects, you don't really need to know any science—beyond some basic concepts—to do well on this part of the exam. In fact, the ACT Science Test would be more accurately labeled "Science Reasoning" Test because that phrase would emphasize that the items test reasoning ability and not the mastery of some specific body of scientific knowledge.

Anatomy

Now that you've read the directions, you don't need to read them again, especially not during the test. The only thing of real significance is that you CANNOT use your calculator on this part, even though you might think it would be nice. But you should be able to remember that one point without re-reading the directions.

Passage I

A student studied the process by which malodorzane is produced by heating protocrud in a closed system and then releasing it into the surrounding atmosphere.

In this Science passage, there is a single device and a series of tables that report data from the operation of the device. You'll see examples of other types of passages later in the Science Lesson.

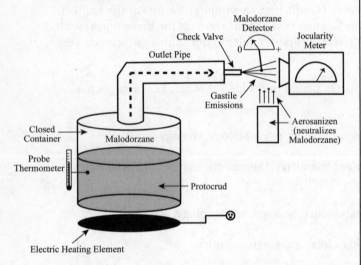

Experiment 1

The concentration of malodorzane produced by the protocrud at various temperatures was measured by determining how much aerosanizen was needed to neutralize the malodorzane (Table 1).

TABLE 1	
Temperature of Protocrud	Aerosanizen (spritz/minute)
20°C	46–198
22.5°C	199–377
25°C	378–612

Experiment 2

The student observed that the release of gastiles, whether or not the malodorzane was counteracted by aerosanizen, produced primary and secondary jocularities. The intensity of the jocularities was measured and recorded for different durations of gastiles (Table 2).

TABLE 2		
	Intensity of Jocularities	
Gastiles (seconds)	Primary Jocularities (decibels)	Secondary Jocularities (decibels)
1.0	30 dB	—*
2.0	35 dB	—*
5.0	40 dB	30 dB
12.0	60 dB	40 dB
19.0	120 dB	60 dB

*Intensity was below measurable levels.

Experiment 3

The student measured and recorded the duration of the jocularities for different durations of gastiles (Table 3).

TABLE 3		
	Duration of Jocularities	
Gastiles (seconds)	Primary Jocularities (seconds)	Secondary Jocularities (seconds)
0.2	3	—*
1.0	7	—*
2.5	13	11
5.0	25	9
12.0	51	4

*Duration was below measurable levels.

1. Data from the passage indicate that duration was greatest for secondary jocularities produced by gastiles of what duration?

   A. 1.0 seconds
   B. 2.5 seconds
   C. 5.0 seconds
   D. 12.0 seconds

2. Gastiles with a duration of 13.0 seconds would probably produce primary jocularities of a duration:

   F. between 3 and 7 seconds.
   G. between 7 and 13 seconds.
   H. between 13 and 25 seconds.
   J. greater than 51 seconds.

3. A primary jocularity of 90 decibels would most likely be produced by a gastile of:

   A. less than 1.0 seconds.
   B. between 1.0 and 2.0 seconds.
   C. between 12.0 and 19.0 seconds.
   D. greater than 19.0 seconds.

4. The data in Table 1 would be most useful in determining whether:

   F. the temperature of aerosanizen affects the chemical's ability to neutralize malodorzane.
   G. the volume of malodorzane varies with the chemical composition of the protocrud.
   H. the closed system produces a greater volume of malodorzane than aerosanizen.
   J. the temperature of the protocrud affects the rate of malodorzane production.

1. **(B)** *Data for the duration of jocularities is given in Table 3, and the greatest entry, 11 seconds, corresponds to gastiles of duration 2.5 seconds.*

2. **(J)** *Again, the answer is in Table 3, but this time there is no entry for 13 seconds. The largest entry is 12.0 seconds. Because primary jocularity duration increases as gastile duration increases, the corresponding entry in the "Primary Jocularities" column, if one existed, would likely be greater than 51 seconds.*

3. **(C)** *The relevant information is located in Table 2, but there is no entry in the table for 90 dB. However, 90 dB is between 60 dB and 120 dB. The most likely conclusion, then, is that the corresponding entry in the first column, if one existed, would be between 12.0 and 19.0 seconds.*

4. **(J)** *Table 1 shows the amount of aerosanizen needed to neutralize the quantity of malodorzane at various temperatures. So, the data in that table would provide information about how the temperature of the protocrud affects the rate of malodorzane production.*

Pacing

The Science Test presents six or seven passages, with a total of 40 items, to be completed in 35 minutes. The table below establishes the time that you can afford to spend on various parts of the Science Test if your goal is to complete the entire test. For many people, completing the entire test may be an unrealistic goal, and a better goal for a test with seven passages is to complete six of the seven passages. Or perhaps even only five passages. If you choose to define your goal differently than completing the entire test, then you can adjust the timing for the remaining passages so that you'll have more time (e.g., four minutes for five items equals 48 seconds per item).

TESTS WITH SIX PASSAGES		
PASSAGE	TIME TO SPEND	REMAINING TIME
I	5 minutes	30 minutes
II	6 minutes	24 minutes
III	6 minutes	18 minutes
IV	6 minutes	12 minutes
V	6 minutes	6 minutes
VI	6 minutes	0 minutes

TESTS WITH SEVEN PASSAGES		
PASSAGE	TIME TO SPEND	REMAINING TIME
I	5 minutes	30 minutes
II	5 minutes	25 minutes
III	5 minutes	20 minutes
IV	5 minutes	15 minutes
V	5 minutes	10 minutes
VI	5 minutes	5 minutes
VII	5 minutes	0 minutes

You should begin work on each passage by reading the passage itself and familiarizing yourself with the main purpose of the data reports or experiments or the focus of the debate. This should be an overview of the information, not a detailed study. You are reading primarily to learn where information is located so that you can retrieve it—if an item asks about it.

Preview the number of questions associated with each passage. Allow yourself one minute to learn about the passage, then spend between 40 and 50 seconds answering each item. Thus, the time you spend on each passage will vary depending on the number of items associated with that passage. So, on the Science Test (perhaps more so than on any other test), time is of the essence.

Time Trial

(6 items; 5 minutes)

> **DIRECTIONS:** The passage below is followed by several items. After reading the passage, choose the best answer to each item. You may refer to the passage as often as necessary. You are NOT permitted the use of a calculator.

Passage I

How old is the earth? Two opposing views are presented.

Scientist 1

The earth is approximately five billion years old. We know this to be true because of radioactive dating. Some chemical elements are unstable and will fall apart into smaller pieces over time. This disintegration occurs over a period of time that is very regular for the particular element. In general, we talk about the half-life of the element, which is the time necessary for one-half of the material to disintegrate. This time is constant whether we have an ounce or a ton of the material. So, by measuring the relative amounts of the material left and the disintegration products, we can form an accurate idea of how old the earth is by determining how many half-lives have occurred.

Scientist 2

The argument that supports the hypothesis that the earth is only five billion years old is seriously flawed. What the argument fails to take into account is that the earth is the constant recipient of a shower of cosmic debris in the form of meteorites. These meteorites replenish the stock of radioactive material on the surface of the earth, making it seem as though the earth has gone through fewer half-lives than it really has. Therefore, all estimates of the age of the earth based on radioactive dating are too low.

1. Which of the following is a major assumption of Scientist 1?

   A. The earth has life that recycles carbon-14.
   B. The half-life of all radioactive elements is five billion years.
   C. The radioactive material was formed at the same time as the earth.
   D. There is no longer any radioactivity on the earth.

2. Which of the following is a major assumption of Scientist 2?

   F. The meteorites that land on the earth are radioactive.
   G. Few meteorites have landed on the earth.
   H. The earth is more than five billion years old.
   J. The earth is highly radioactive.

3. Which of the following, if true, would best refute Scientist 2's argument?

   A. Recent meteorites have been found to be radioactive.
   B. The earth has a greater amount of radioactive material on the surface than in the mantle.
   C. The earth's orbit intersects the orbits of a number of meteorites.
   D. Few meteorites have been found to contain radioactive material.

4. Which of the following would be most likely if Scientist 2's hypothesis were correct?

    F. The amount of radioactive material and its disintegration products on the earth has decreased over time.

    G. The amount of radioactive material and its disintegration products has increased over time.

    H. The amount of radioactive material and its disintegration products has stayed essentially the same over time.

    J. The earth will reach a critical mass and explode.

5. Which of the following would be most likely if Scientist 1's hypothesis were correct?

    A. The total amount of radioactive material and its disintegration products has decreased over time.

    B. The total amount of radioactive material and its disintegration products has increased over time.

    C. The total amount of radioactive material and its disintegration products has stayed essentially the same over time.

    D. The earth will reach a critical mass and explode.

6. Which of the following conditions, if true, would prevent an estimation of the earth's age by Scientist 1's method?

    F. No radioactive disintegration has occurred.

    G. Only some of the radioactive material has disintegrated.

    H. Eighty percent of the radioactive material has disintegrated.

    J. All of the radioactive material has disintegrated.

Game Plan

Quickly Preview the Test Section, but Skip the Directions

Last-minute adjustments to the test format are theoretically (but not practically) possible, so check the subject test before you start to work, especially the number of passages, the number of items, and the time limit. And yes, the test-writers always tell you to "read the directions carefully." But they don't tell you that you have to read them during the test. Instead, become familiar with them <u>before</u> test day. That way, you won't waste 30 seconds or more (enough time to answer an item) re-reading directions you are already familiar with.

Personalize the Passage Order

You are not required to do the passages in the order in which they appear in the test booklet. You can do the first passage second, or fourth, or last; and you can do the last passage first or third. So, you have the flexibility of choosing which ones you will do before the others, and you'll want to do first those passages that seem <u>easier</u>. "Easier," in this context, is really a subjective matter; it means the ones with which you are most comfortable, either because of the type of presentation or the subject matter.

- First, do those passage formats that you find easiest to handle.

- Then, of the remaining passages, do the familiar ones.

- Finally, do the rest of the passages, from the simplest to the most complicated.

Put large numbers in the margins of the test booklet beside each passage to indicate where the passage comes in the order.

Read the Passage

For the Science Test, "reading the passage" means "reading through" the passage. You can't afford to study the passage, and don't forget that this is an "open-book" test. So, learn generally what is going on and where things are located. Then, let the items tell you where to look more carefully.

- Read any introductory paragraph(s). Not only does this material usually explain why an experiment is being conducted or data are being collected, but it often defines a key term that is essential to understanding the connections of the various parts of the passage.

- Examine any diagrams or schematics. The focus of a passage is often a device that includes beakers, tubing, switches, pulleys, test tubes, and other paraphernalia associated with science. Try to understand what the device is designed to accomplish and how the various parts work together.

- Look at the various subparts of the passage. The subparts are things such as experiments that change initial conditions, tables of data, and graphs. Do not try to fully understand these. Just get a general notion of what they do. For example, for a graph, read the title and the labels of the *x*- and *y*-axes. For tables, read the column heads and the titles of the rows. Do not, however, read specific values on a graph or in a table. There are too many of them, and only one or two are likely to be relevant to answering one of the few items based on that passage (compared to all the different questions that the test-writers could have chosen).

Answer the Items

Answer the question that is being asked. One of the most commonly made mistakes is to read the item stem carelessly and then answer the "wrong" question. It's just a matter of inattention, in which you respond to what you think you read rather than what is actually there on the page. Since wrong answers often correspond to wrong readings, if you make this mistake, you are probably going to find a pretty good answer—to the wrong question.

Pay attention to thought-reversers. "Thought-reversers" are words in the item stem like "NOT," "BUT," and "EXCEPT." These words turn the question upside-down. What is normally the right answer is now a wrong answer, and what is normally a wrong answer is the right answer. Circle these words or put stars beside them so that they get your attention again.

Locate the relevant information. The first and often last step in answering an item is to locate the information you need. Most item stems use a key word or phrase to tell you where to look. For example, "in Table 2" tells you that the information you need is located in Table 2; "the troposphere" tells you that you need the graph, table, or description that supplies information about the troposphere; and "lowering the temperature" indicates that the answer is in the subpart of the passage that provides information about temperature.

Use the Answer Choices

Study the answer choices for guidance. The answer choices, like an item stem, can direct you to the subpart of the passage that contains the information you need. Consider the following item, in which only the answer choices are visible:

> **Example:**
>
> A. Sodium
> B. Potassium
> C. Lithium
> D. Oxygen
>
> With this array, you know to look at that table or graph or paragraph that includes that list of terms. The choices will also give you guidance as to what degree of precision is required by the item.

Often, the choices are ranges of values, such as $0.015w$ to $0.018w$, rather than specific values, such as simply $0.018w$. Do not look for more precision than the choices allow.

Read the answer choices carefully. The test-writers love to put in wrong answers that look right. For example, if a particular value doubles with a decrease in temperature from 40°C to 20°C, a question might ask: "Assuming the temperature rises from 20°C to 40°C, what happens to the value?" The correct answer is, of course: "The value is reduced by half." But you can bet that the wrong answers will include ideas like "doubles," "increases by one-fourth," and "decreases by four"—or some other variation on those ideas.

Eliminate Choices, Guess (If Necessary), and Move On

Do NOT spend too much time on any one item. Remember that you get +1 for the hardest item and +1 for the easiest item. The items that correspond to a Science passage tend to be arranged from easiest to most difficult. (This is not an absolute rule; it is just a useful tool.) The first item may ask you to find a single number in a table. The second item may ask for a value that is the largest or smallest in a series. And the third item may require you to interpolate a value. Then, the going might get considerably more difficult. So, try the next item, and if it is totally confusing, skip the rest of the questions and go to the next passage where the difficulty resets to the lowest setting. And don't forget: the ACT test has no penalty for guessing. If you find yourself stuck on a difficult item, eliminate as many choices as possible, guess, and move on!

LESSON

The passages and items in this section accompany the in-class review of the skills and concepts tested by the ACT Science Test. You will work through the items with your instructor in class. Answers are on page 668.

DIRECTIONS: Each passage below is followed by several items. After reading a passage, choose the best answer to each item. You may refer to the passages as often as necessary. You are NOT permitted the use of a calculator.

Data Representation Review and Strategies

Graphs

Graph Reading Strategy

Passage I

The kinetic energy of an object with mass m (measured in grams) after a fall from a height h (measured in centimeters) was recorded for different heights. A graph was made representing the kinetic energy versus height.

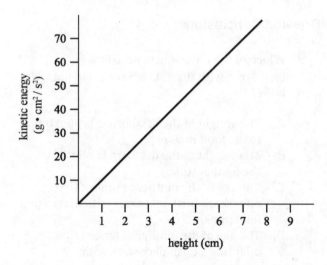

1. In the graph, if the kinetic energy is given in units of $g \cdot cm^2 / s^2$, what units must the slope have?

   A. $g \cdot cm / s$

   B. $g \cdot cm / s^2$

   C. $s \cdot cm / g$

   D. $s^2 / (g \cdot cm)$

2. It is discovered that if the experiment is repeated for an object with twice the mass, the kinetic energy obtained for every height is doubled. The slope of the new set of experiments can be obtained by doing what to the old slope?

   F. Multiplying by 2
   G. Dividing by 2
   H. Squaring
   J. Taking the square root

3. What would be the approximate kinetic energy (in $g \cdot cm^2 / s^2$) of an object of mass m if it were dropped from a height of 4.5 cm?

   A.   4.5
   B.   9.0
   C.   45
   D.   90

Tables

Understanding the Nature of Data

Passage II

A scientist investigated the variables that affect the age at which a female of the animal species *Taedi periculum* first gives birth. Some of the results of this study are summarized in the table below.

EXPERIMENT	TEMPERATURE (°C)	AVERAGE FOOD INTAKE (grams)	AGE WHEN FIRST GAVE BIRTH (months)
1	25	15	7
2	25	30	6
3	25	45	4
4	35	15	5
5	35	30	3
6	35	45	3

4. Which of the following would be good animals to use for the experiment?

    F.   Adult females
    G.   Newborn females
    H.   Newborn males
    J.   Adult males

5. Which of the pairs of experiments listed below would be useful for studying the effect of temperature on the age of first birth?

    A.   1 and 2
    B.   1 and 5
    C.   1 and 4
    D.   2 and 6

Recognizing Trends

6. If all other variables are kept constant, which of the following will result in an increase in the age at which the animals give birth?

    F.   Increase in temperature from 25°C to 35°C
    G.   Increase in food from 15 grams to 45 grams
    H.   Decrease in food from 30 grams to 15 grams
    J.   Increase in temperature from 25°C to 30°C

7. Which of the following experiments was a control for temperature for Experiment 5?

    A.   Experiment 1
    B.   Experiment 2
    C.   Experiment 3
    D.   Experiment 6

8. If an experiment was set up with the temperature set at 30°C and the food intake at 30 grams, which of the following would be a reasonable prediction of the age in months of the animals when they first gave birth?

    F.   7.5
    G.   6.5
    H.   4.5
    J.   2.5

Drawing Conclusions

9. Which of the following conclusions is consistent with the data presented in the table?

    A.   The weight of the firstborn is proportional to the food intake.
    B.   The weight of the firstborn is related to the temperature.
    C.   The age of the mother at time of first offspring's birth increases with decreasing food intake.
    D.   The age of the mother at time of first offspring's birth decreases with decreasing food intake.

Typical Data Representation Items

Passage III

The chart below shows the average blood pressure and relative total surface area associated with the different types of human blood vessels.

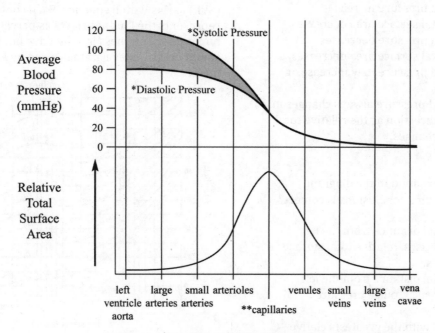

Distance Blood Travels Through the Circulatory System
from the Left Ventricle of the Heart

*Pulse pressure is the difference between systolic and diastolic pressure.
**Blood velocity is lowest in the capillaries (averaging 3 cm/sec).

10. According to the diagram, pulse pressure can be detected:

   F. in large arteries only.
   G. in large arteries as well as in large veins.
   H. in blood vessels between the aorta and the capillaries.
   J. primarily in the arterioles, capillaries, and venules.

11. Based on the information in the diagram, average blood pressure:

   A. decreases with increasing blood vessel distance from the left ventricle.
   B. remains approximately constant regardless of blood vessel distance from the left ventricle.
   C. first increases, then decreases with increasing blood vessel distance from the left ventricle.
   D. is highest in blood vessels with the greatest relative total surface area.

12. Which of the following correctly states the relationship between the relative total surface area of blood vessels and the average blood pressure?

F. As relative total surface area decreases, average blood pressure increases.
G. As relative total surface area decreases, average blood pressure decreases.
H. As relative total surface area decreases, average blood pressure may increase or decrease.
J. Average blood pressure always changes in the opposite direction as the relative total surface area changes.

13. Based on the information in the diagram, which of the following conclusions is correct?

A. As blood vessel distance from the left ventricle increases, relative total surface area decreases.
B. As blood vessel distance from the left ventricle increases, pulse pressure increases.
C. Blood vessels with the greatest relative total surface area have the highest pulse pressure.
D. Blood vessels closest to and farthest from the left ventricle have the smallest relative total surface area.

14. A physician examining a newly discovered tribe of people deep in the Amazon jungles found that the relative total surface area of their capillaries was greater than that previously reported for any other group of people. If the physician were to predict the average velocity of blood through the capillaries of these people, which of the following values would be most reasonable?

F. 2 cm/sec
G. 3 cm/sec
H. 4 cm/sec
J. 5 cm/sec

Passage IV

In 1933, Dr. Fletcher and Dr. Munson of Bell Labs discovered that the sensitivity of the human ear varies with frequency. The Fletcher-Munson equal-loudness contours (Figure 1) show how the human ear's sensitivity to sound pressure level (SPL) varies with frequency. Each contour represents the loudness level as perceived by the human ear. Loudness is subjective but related to sound pressure level as measured by a sound level meter.

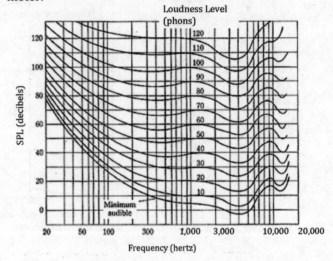

Figure 1

The bottom contour (minimum audible) represents the hearing threshold of the human ear, that is, the minimum SPL of a pure tone that the average human ear with normal hearing can hear with no other sound present. The top contour (120 phons) represents the pain threshold of the human ear, that is, the SPL beyond which sound becomes unbearable to the average listener. Prolonged exposure to sound pressure levels in excess of the pain threshold can cause physical damage, potentially leading to hearing loss.

15. The Fletcher-Munson contours indicate that the human ear is:

A. equally sensitive to all frequencies.
B. less sensitive to low and high frequencies and more sensitive to mid-range frequencies.
C. most sensitive to low and high frequencies and less sensitive to mid-range frequencies.
D. capable of hearing sounds below 20 hertz.

16. The threshold of human hearing:

    F.   does not depend on sound frequency.
    G. is sometimes equal to the threshold of pain.
    H. is based on an average ear with normal hearing.
    J.   is represented by the 10-phon Fletcher-Munson contour.

17. The range of maximum sensitivity for human hearing is approximately:

    A. 50 to 100 hertz.
    B. 100 to 500 hertz.
    C. 500 to 5,000 hertz.
    D. 3,000 to 6,000 hertz.

18. Which of the following is a true statement regarding loudness and SPL?

    F.   Loudness is measured in decibels; SPL is measured in phons.
    G. SPL is a measure of subjective quantity; phons may be measured with a sound level meter.
    H. Loudness is subjective, but related to SPL.
    J.   For any given SPL, loudness remains constant for all frequencies.

19. A 300-hertz sound with an SPL of 15 decibels has a loudness of:

    A. 10 phons.
    B. 20 phons.
    C. 30 phons.
    D. 40 phons.

20. For the human ear to hear a 20-hertz sound at a loudness of 70 phons, the SPL must be:

    F.   50 decibels.
    G. 75 decibels.
    H. 100 decibels.
    J.   110 decibels.

21. For the human ear to hear a minimum audible 30-hertz sound, the SPL must be:

    A. 20 decibels.
    B. 40 decibels.
    C. 60 decibels.
    D. 80 decibels.

22. The perceived loudness of a 300-hertz sound with an SPL of 15 decibels is the same as a 30-hertz sound with an SPL of:

    F.   50 decibels.
    G. 55 decibels.
    H. 62 decibels.
    J.   150 decibels.

Data Representation Strategies

Passage V

Seawater contains dissolved salts. As a result, seawater freezes at a lower temperature than freshwater (Figure 1).

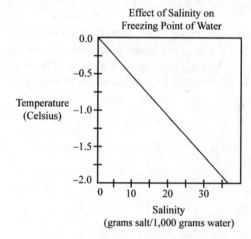

Figure 1

When seawater freezes, as the water molecules begin to form their characteristic ring-like structures, the salt ions, primarily sodium and chloride, are forced out of solution and form pockets of salt. The brine (salty water) leaches out of the bottom of the ice into the water below. Thus, sea ice, when melted, is generally considerably less saline than the original seawater. The solid-line graph below indicates the percentage of salt in a slab of ice that lies over seawater on a cold ocean surface (Figure 2).

Sea Ice Salinity

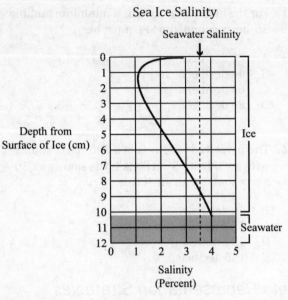

Figure 2

24. Compared to the ocean water below it, the salinity of sea ice in contact with seawater is:

F.   higher than that of the seawater.
G.   about the same as that of the seawater.
H.   lower than that of the seawater.
J.   sometimes lower and sometimes higher than that of the seawater.

25. The salinity of the ice at the surface of the slab is equal to the salinity of the:

A.   sea ice at a depth of approximately 1.5 cm.
B.   sea ice at a depth of approximately 7.0 cm.
C.   sea ice at a depth of approximately 9.0 cm.
D.   water beneath the sea ice.

26. According to Figure 2, the salt content of the sea ice:

F.   equals 0.
G.   is constant at all depths.
H.   decreases, then increases with depth.
J.   increases, then decreases with depth.

23. According to the information provided, the freezing temperature of pure water is approximately:

A.   2 degrees lower than that of seawater.
B.   0.2 degrees lower than that of seawater.
C.   3.5 degrees higher than that of seawater.
D.   2 degrees higher than that of seawater.

27. The researcher takes a 1 gram sample of ice from a depth of 10 cm, and wishes to take a sample of ice from a depth of 1.3 cm that will contain the same weight of total salts. Approximately how large a sample is needed?

A.   0.25 grams
B.   1.0 gram
C.   4.0 grams
D.   10.0 grams

Passage VI

According to the kinetic molecular theory of gases, all gases consist of particles (atoms or molecules) in continuous, random motion. In an ideal gas, particles move freely without interacting with one another except for brief elastic collisions. Particles of a gas at a particular temperature will have a range of different speeds. The distribution of particle speeds, that is, the number of particles moving with a certain speed, is given by the Maxwell-Boltzmann distribution curves. The most probable speed for the particles is represented by the peak of the curve. For a given distribution, the area under the curve corresponds to the total number of particles of a gas sample.

To illustrate how mass affects molecular speed, Figure 1 gives the Maxwell-Boltzmann distributions for the common gases in the table at a fixed temperature (300 K). To illustrate how temperature affects molecular speed, Figure 2 gives the Maxwell-Boltzmann distributions for nitrogen gas (N_2) at several temperatures.

Table 1: Molar Mass of Common Gases (grams/mole)	
H_2 (hydrogen)	2.02
He (helium)	4.00
N_2 (nitrogen)	28.01
O_2 (oxygen)	32.00
Cl_2 (chlorine)	70.91
Kr (krypton)	83.80

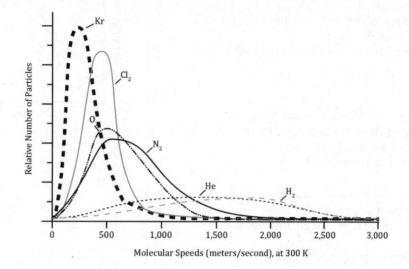

Figure 1

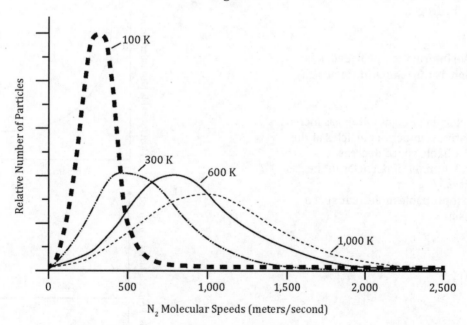

Figure 2

28. A scientist fills one metal cylinder with helium gas and a second metal cylinder with chlorine gas. After the scientist heats both gases to 300 K, which of the following will be true?

    F. The molecules in both gases will have the same most probable speed.

    G. The helium molecules will have the higher most probable speed.

    H. The chlorine molecules will have the higher most probable speed.

    J. The chlorine molecules will have a broader range of speeds.

29. According to the information provided, which one of the following correctly lists, from least to greatest, the gases according to most probable molecular speed at 300 K?

    A. Hydrogen, helium, nitrogen, oxygen, chlorine, krypton

    B. Krypton, chlorine, oxygen, neon, hydrogen, helium

    C. Krypton, chlorine, oxygen, nitrogen, hydrogen, helium

    D. Krypton, chlorine, oxygen, nitrogen, helium, hydrogen

30. Based on the information provided, it is inferable that as the temperature of a gas increases:

    F. The molecular weight of the gas increases.

    G. the relative number of particles at the most probable speed decreases.

    H. the total number of particles in the gas decreases.

    J. the most probable molecular speed decreases.

31. Based on the information provided, which of the following graphs best represents the most probable molecular speed for nitrogen as a function of gas temperature?

A.

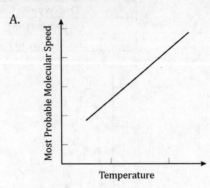

B.

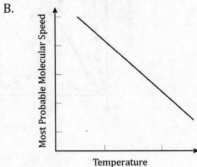

C.

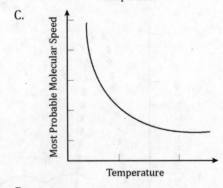

D.

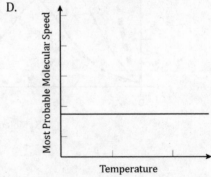

32. Which of the following statements best describes the relationship between nitrogen gas molecule speeds and the temperature of the gas?

    F. As gas temperature increases, the range of molecular speeds increases and the most probable speed decreases.

    G. As gas temperature decreases, the range of molecular speeds decreases and the most probable speed decreases.

    H. As molar mass of gas increases, the range of molecular speeds decreases and the most probable speed decreases.

    J. As molar mass of gas decreases, the range of molecular speeds increases and the most probable speed increases.

33. According to the information provided, as the molar mass of a gas increases:

    A. the number of particles at greater speeds increases.

    B. the number of particles in the gas increases.

    C. the most probable molecular speed decreases.

    D. the most probable molecular speed increases.

34. Argon is a gas with molar mass of 39.95 grams/mole. Based on the information provided, the most probable molecular speed of argon molecules at 100 K is:

    F. less than 300 meters/second.

    G. between 300 and 500 meters/second.

    H. between 500 and 1,000 meters/second.

    J. over 1,000 meters/second.

Passage VII

    Phase diagrams illustrate the relationship between temperature, pressure, and the phases of matter. Each of the three phases—solid, liquid, and gas—is represented by a section of the phase diagram. The curves represent states of equilibrium between two phases—the substance is present in two phases at once as it passes from one phase to the next. All three phases are present at the triple point. For temperatures and pressures both below the triple point, matter passes directly between the solid and gas phases without passing through the liquid phase.

    For pressures and temperatures beyond the critical point, the liquid and gas phases converge and become indistinguishable in what is known as a supercritical fluid. Supercritical fluids can dissolve materials like a liquid and effuse through solids like a gas. Beyond the critical point, no amount of pressure will restore a supercritical fluid to its liquid or solid phase without decreasing the temperature.

    Figure 1 shows the phase diagram for water, a liquid at room temperature (21°C) and atmospheric pressure (1 atm). Figure 2 shows the phase diagram for carbon dioxide, a gas at room temperature and atmospheric pressure.

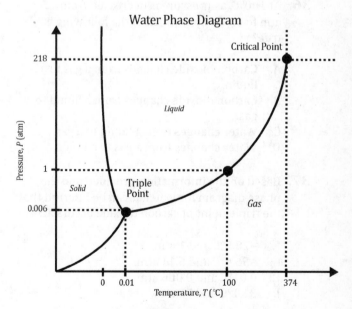

Figure 1

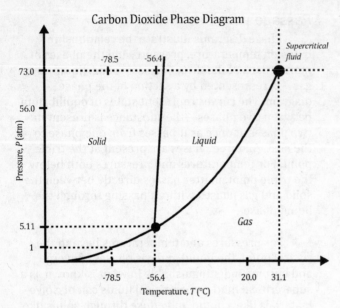

Figure 2

35. According to the information provided and Figure 1, water becomes a supercritical fluid when the temperature and pressure exceed:

F. 0.006°C and 0.01 atm.
G. 0.01°C and 0.006 atm.
H. 218°C and 374 atm.
J. 374°C and 218 atm.

36. At 100°C, as pressure is decreased from 1.5 atm to 0.006 atm, which of the following is true?

A. Carbon dioxide changes from a gas to a liquid.
B. Carbon dioxide changes from a liquid to a gas.
C. Water changes from a liquid to a gas.
D. Water changes from a gas to a liquid.

37. Based on the information provided and the phase diagram for water, it can be inferred that the triple point of carbon dioxide occurs at:

F. −78.5°C and 1 atm.
G. −56.4°C and 5.11 atm.
H. 0.01°C and 0.006 atm.
J. 31.1°C and 73 atm.

38. According to the information provided, both water and carbon dioxide exist solely as liquids at which of the following pressure and temperature combinations?

A. 10°C and 56 atm.
B. 0°C and 1 atm.
C. 30°C and 10 atm.
D. There is no point at which both water and carbon dioxide exist solely as liquids.

39. In Figure 1, the line indicating equilibrium between solid water (ice) and liquid water has a negative slope. This indicates that to maintain equilibrium between the two states:

A. as the temperature is decreased, the pressure must be decreased.
B. as the temperature is increased, the pressure must be decreased.
C. as the temperature is increased, the pressure must remain constant.
D. as the temperature is increased, the pressure must be increased, then decreased.

40. Sublimation occurs when a solid changes to a gas without going through a liquid phase. Under which of the following conditions can sublimation occur?

F. Water at 0°C and 0.80 atm.
G. Water at 80°C and 0.006 atm.
H. Carbon dioxide at −78.5°C and 1 atm.
J. Carbon dioxide at 0°C and 5.11 atm.

Research Summary Review and Strategies

Typical Research Summary Items

Passage VIII

To test the hypothesis that all antibiotics are equally effective in preventing bacterial growth, the following three experiments were carried out using clear plastic plates filled with nutrient agar (a mixture of ingredients that supports the growth of bacteria). When bacteria reproduce successfully, colonies form on the agar, giving it a cloudy appearance.

Experiment 1

Three plates (A, B, and C) of agar were set up, each with an equal amount of bacterial culture (Bacterium X) spread over the agar surface and with a paper disk placed in the center. Plate A's disk was soaked in Antibiotic I; Plate B's disk was soaked in Antibiotic II; Plate C's disk was soaked in plain water. After incubation overnight at 37°C (body temperature), Plates A and B had a clear area, 2" in diameter surrounding the paper disk, but beyond this 2" region, the plates were cloudy. Plate C was entirely cloudy, including the area adjacent to the paper disk.

Experiment 2

Identical procedures were followed except that Plates A, B, and C were incubated overnight at 22°C (room temperature). After incubation, Plate A had a clear area, 2" in diameter, surrounding the paper disk. Plates B and C were entirely cloudy.

Experiment 3

Identical procedures were followed except that the concentrations of Antibiotic I (Plate A) and Antibiotic II (Plate B) were made twice as strong. After incubation overnight at 22°C, Plates A and B both had clear, 2" areas around the paper disk, while Plate C remained entirely cloudy.

41. After incubation, a clear area around a previously soaked paper disk represents a region where:

F. agar had washed away.
G. decomposition had occurred due to high incubation temperatures.
H. bacterial growth did not occur.
J. bacteria grew best.

42. Which of the following results would indicate that the antibiotics being tested have nothing to do with the control of bacterial growth?

A. A clear, 2" region was always observed around the disks soaked in water.
B. All results remained the same at the two experimental temperatures and at the two antibiotic concentration levels.
C. Plates A and B always remained clear.
D. The disks soaked in water were not used in the experiments at all.

43. Which statement is supported by the results of Experiment 1 alone?

F. Antibiotic I, Antibiotic II, and water are equally effective as inhibitors (preventers) of bacterial growth at 37°C.
G. Dry paper disks can be effective in controlling bacterial growth at 37°C.
H. The concentration of an antibiotic may influence its effectiveness in controlling bacterial growth at 37°C.
J. Both Antibiotics I and II can inhibit bacterial growth at 37°C.

44. The results of both Experiment 2 and Experiment 3 lead to which of the following conclusions?

A. Antibiotics I and II have similar effects on bacterial growth, regardless of concentrations.
B. Antibiotic II and water have similar effects on bacterial growth, regardless of concentrations.
C. The effectiveness of Antibiotic I at 22°C depends on its concentration.
D. The effectiveness of Antibiotic II at 22°C depends on its concentration.

45. Which hypothesis best explains the observation that the agar plates never appear clear beyond a 2" area surrounding the soaked paper disks?

F. The bacteria cannot grow well within 2" of any moist paper disks.
G. The antibiotics cannot seep through the agar beyond a distance of 2".
H. At the experimental incubation temperatures used, the two antibiotics interfere with each other's effectiveness.
J. The paper disks can absorb nutrients out of the agar from the distance of 2".

46. If either Antibiotic I or II could be prescribed for internal use to prevent the spread of Bacterium X infections, which recommendation, based on the experimental results, is appropriate if the cost due to the amount of antibiotic used per dose is the most critical factor (the antibiotics are equal in cost for equal concentrations)?

   A. Either Antibiotic I or II can be taken at equal cost.
   B. Antibiotic I would be less expensive.
   C. Antibiotic II would be less expensive.
   D. Neither Antibiotic I nor II would be effective in preventing the spread of Bacterium X.

Passage IX

To investigate the hypothesis that the quality of the detail of a fossil depends on the size of the particles that make up the rock surrounding it, three experiments were performed using a particular type of leaf with many fine veins.

Experiment 1

A leaf was placed on a flat bed made of paste from extrafine grade plaster and then completely covered with more of the same paste. A glass cover with a 5 pound weight was placed on top of the paste for one hour, until the plaster set. The plaster was then baked for 30 minutes at 225°C. When the cast was opened, the imprint of the leaf showed all of the veins, including the finest ones.

Experiment 2

A leaf was placed on a flat bed made of paste from fine grade plaster and then completely covered with more of the same paste. A glass cover with a 5 pound weight was placed on top of the plaster for one hour, until the plaster set. The plaster was then baked for 30 minutes at 225°C. When the cast was opened, all the main veins were visible, but only isolated traces of the finer veins were found.

Experiment 3

A leaf was placed on a flat bed made of paste from coarse grade plaster and then completely covered with more of the same paste. A glass cover with a 5 pound weight was placed on top of the plaster for one hour, until the plaster set. The plaster was then baked for 30 minutes at 225°C. When the cast was opened, only the thickest veins

were visible, and some of the leaf edge was difficult to discern.

47. Should the investigator have used a different type of leaf in each experiment?

   F. Yes: different types of structure could be studied.
   G. Yes: in real life, many different types of fossils are found.
   H. No: the type of leaf served as a controlled variable.
   J. No: the nature of the leaf is not important.

48. When a fossil is formed, the sediment that surrounds it is normally compressed by the tons of earth deposited over it. What part of the model simulates this compressing element?

   A. The 5 pound weight
   B. The glass
   C. The upper layer of paste
   D. The baking oven

49. A fourth experiment was set up the same way as the previous three, except the paste was made by mixing equal amounts of very coarse sand with the extrafine grade plaster. The investigator is likely to discover:

   F. no change from Experiment 1 because only the type of plaster is important.
   G. no change because the same kind of leaf is used.
   H. the imprint is better than Experiment 1 because the sand provides air pockets.
   J. the imprint is worse than Experiment 1 because the average particle size is bigger.

50. Which of the following hypotheses is supported by the results of Experiment 1 alone?

    A. The finer the sediment, the greater the detail of the resulting fossil.
    B. Hardened sediment can preserve the imprint of a specimen.
    C. All fossils must have been baked at high temperatures.
    D. Only organic material can leave imprints in sediment.

51. Which of the following changes in the experiments would have permitted a test of the hypothesis that the quality of a fossil imprint depends on the pressure applied?

    F. Repeat the experiments, except use a 10 pound weight in Experiment 2 and a 20 pound weight in Experiment 3.
    G. Choose one of the plasters, and run experiments using the same plaster in all trials while varying the weights.
    H. Rerun all the experiments without the glass.
    J. Vary the depth of the leaf in each new trial, because, in nature, increased pressure means the fossil is at a greater depth.

Research Summary Strategies

Passage X

Erosion refers to processes that wear down rocks and soil, as well as processes that transport the worn-away materials to other locations. Although these processes usually cause effects gradually (over geologic time), laboratory models can be designed to investigate which environmental factors affect erosion rate.

Three experimental sandboxes were set up that were identical in size (10-by-10-foot), had identical types of soil and rocks, and were filled to equal depths (3 feet). The sandboxes were kept for two weeks in large environmental chambers, each maintained at a constant temperature, with a continuous wind flow of 5 mph.

Sandbox 1

One-half was kept bare (just soil and rocks), while the other half had a variety of grasses and weeds planted among the soil and rocks. After two weeks, the bare half had small channels (ruts) running along its length that averaged 1 inch in width. The planted half had few channels, and those that were found averaged less than 1 inch wide.

Sandbox 2

The conditions were identical to those of Sandbox 1, with the addition that both halves were subjected to light, 15 minute showers of water every twelve hours. After two weeks, the bare half had channels averaging 4 inches wide, while the planted half had fewer channels averaging 2 inches wide.

Sandbox 3

The conditions were identical to those of Sandbox 2, but the entire box was mechanically raised to rest at an angle of 15° to simulate a steep slope. After two weeks, the bare half had channels averaging 7 inches wide, while channels in the planted half were less common and averaged 4 inches in width.

52. Results from all three sandboxes indicate that:

    A. different types of soils and rocks are affected differently by environmental factors.
    B. under all tested conditions, plants reduce erosion.
    C. changing wind and temperature conditions can affect erosion patterns.
    D. water from short periods of rain has little or no effect on erosion patterns.

53. The experimental design and results do NOT support which of the following claims?

    F. Light winds have no erosive effect.
    G. Slopes have more erosion than level surfaces.
    H. Water has major erosive effects.
    J. The effects of changing temperature remain unanswered.

54. Sudden cloudbursts are known to cause more erosion than longer periods of mild rains. How could the present experiments be changed to examine this idea?

A. Raise the angle in Sandbox 3 to produce a steeper slope.
B. Add the "rain conditions" from Sandbox 2 to the conditions in Sandbox 1.
C. Include light, 15 minute showers every six hours instead of every twelve hours.
D. Every twelve hours, allow the same total volume of water to fall in a 5 minute span rather than in a 15 minute span.

55. Should the investigator have used different soil types in each sandbox experiment?

F. Yes, because different soils may erode differently.
G. Yes, because a different group of plants could have been used in each sandbox as well.
H. No, because some soils can be washed completely away within the two week experiment.
J. No, because the soil type was a controlled variable in all three experiments.

56. Sandbox 3 specifically demonstrates the role of which particular variable in the set of experiments?

A. Rain
B. Wind
C. Gravity
D. Temperature

57. If another sandbox were set up, which of the following conditions would probably cause wider and deeper channels in the soil of the new sandbox than those in Sandbox 3?

I. Steeper angles for the sandbox
II. A greater volume of water during the 15 minute showers every twelve hours
III. Removal of plants from soil

F. I only
G. I and II only
H. II and III only
J. I, II, and III

Passage XI

Charles's law states that the volume, V, of a gas at constant pressure is proportional to its absolute temperature T (temperature in kelvins, K):

$$V \propto T \qquad \text{(Equation 1)}$$

Boyle's law states that the volume of a gas at constant temperature is inversely proportional to its pressure P (pressure in pascals, Pa):

$$V \propto 1/P \qquad \text{(Equation 2)}$$

Experiment 1

Students inserted a 30-mL syringe and a thermometer through holes in a rubber stopper. Then they placed the stopper into a flask that had been cooled in an ice bath to 273 K (Figure 1). They then removed the flask from the ice bath and placed it on a hot plate. The gas in the flask expanded as it warmed, slowly pushing the piston up the syringe. Students recorded the temperature and corresponding syringe volume readings as the gas expanded at a constant atmospheric pressure (100 kPa). To obtain the total volume of the gas in the system, they added the volume of the syringe to the volume of the flask. The students then created a graph of the experimental data.

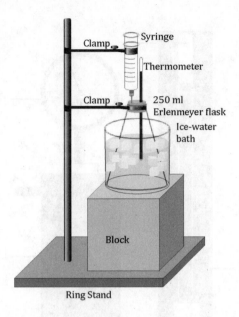

Figure 1

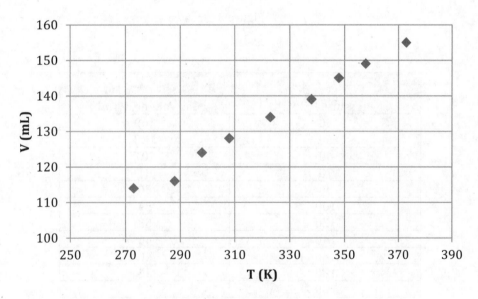

Figure 2

Experiment 2

The students investigated the change in the volume of a gas at room temperature (294 K) at different pressures using the apparatus shown in Figure 3. A glass tube contained a pure nitrogen gas sample (a), and its volume (in mL) was read from the scale. A column of oil (c) transmitted pressure from the reservoir (b), and the pressure value was read on the gauge (d). Table 1 summarizes the data.

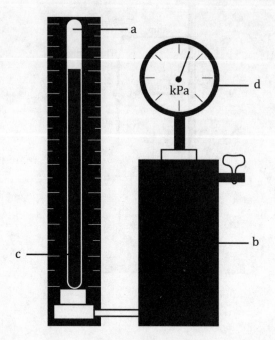

Figure 3

Table 1	
Pressure, P (kPa)	Gas Volume, V (mL)
40	160
50	128
60	107
70	91
80	80
100	64
120	53
140	46
160	40
180	35
200	32

58. Which of the following correctly describes Experiments 1 and 2?

F. Experiment 1 is designed to study Boyle's law and gas temperature is the controlled variable; Experiment 2 is designed to study Charles's law and gas pressure is the controlled variable.

G. Experiment 1 is designed to study Boyle's law and gas pressure is the controlled variable; Experiment 2 is designed to study Charles's law and gas temperature is the controlled variable.

H. Experiment 1 is designed to study Charles's law and gas volume is the controlled variable; Experiment 2 is designed to study Boyle's law and gas pressure is the controlled variable.

J. Experiment 1 is designed to study Charles's law and gas pressure is the controlled variable; Experiment 2 is designed to study Boyle's law and gas temperature is the controlled variable.

59. In the experiment demonstrating Boyle's law, the volume of gas at atmospheric pressure was:

A. 32 mL.
B. 64 mL.
C. 100 mL.
D. Cannot be determined from the given information.

60. In Experiment 2, the function of the column of oil in the experimental apparatus is to:

F. measure the pressure of the air in the glass tube as it expands or contracts.

G. measure the temperature of air in the glass tube as it expands or contracts.

H. transmit pressure from the reservoir to the gas in the glass tube.

J. transmit air to the gas in the glass tube.

61. Does the data graph from Experiment 1 support Charles's law?

A. No; the graph supports Boyle's law because the data demonstrates that volume and temperature are directly proportional.

B. No; the graph does not support Charles's law because the data demonstrates that volume and pressure are inversely proportional.

C. Yes; the graph supports Charles's law because the data demonstrates that volume and temperature are directly proportional.

D. Yes; the graph supports Charles's law because the data demonstrates that volume and temperature are equal.

62. To test the validity of Boyle's law, the students should graph gas volume as a function of:

F. temperature using the data from Experiment 1.

G. temperature using the data from Experiment 2.

H. pressure using the data from Experiment 1.

J. pressure using the data from Experiment 2.

63. Based on the information provided, which of the following is true for the pressure, P, temperature, T, and/or volume, V, of a sample of gas?

A. PV is constant for the same temperature.
B. VT is constant for the same pressure.
C. $\dfrac{V}{P}$ is constant for the same temperature.
D. PVT is constant for all pressures, volumes, and temperatures.

Passage XII

Freezing point depression occurs when a non-volatile solute is added to a pure solvent, resulting in a solution with a lower freezing point than that of the pure solvent. The freezing point depression, ΔT, is roughly proportional to the concentration of the solute in the solution (as measured by molality):

$$\Delta T = -K_f \times m \times i \qquad \text{(Equation 1)}$$

K_f is the freezing point depression constant for the solvent, m is the molality of the solution (moles of solute per kilogram of solvent), and i is the van't Hoff factor, which is equal to the number of particles produced by one molecule of solute.

A chemistry student uses the phenomenon of freezing point depression to determine the molar mass and identification of an unknown substance from Table 1.

Table 1	
Chemical	Molar Mass (grams/mole)
Sodium iodide (NaI)	150
Calcium sulfate (CaSO$_4$)	136
Sodium nitrate (NaNO$_3$)	85
Sodium chloride (NaCl)	58
Sodium fluoride (NaF)	42

Part 1

A test tube filled with distilled water is placed in a salt/ice water bath at below −10°C and constantly stirred until crystals begin to form, at which point the distilled water temperature is recorded.

The procedure is repeated for a sugar-water solution of molality 1.0 m (1.0 mol sugar/1 kg water) and van't Hoff factor of 1. The student uses the freezing point depression for the sugar-water solution to calculate the freezing point depression constant for water (Table 2).

Table 2	
1. Freezing point of distilled water	−0.04°C
2. Freezing point of 1.0 m sugar-water solution	−1.91°C
3. ΔT for sugar-water solution	−1.87°C
4. K_f value for distilled water	1.87°C/(mol/kg)

Part 2

A beaker is weighed before and after the addition of approximately 100 mL of distilled water. The beaker is weighed again after the addition of a sample of an unknown substance from Table 1 known to have a van't Hoff factor of 2. The student calculates the solution concentration (grams of solute per kilogram of water).

The freezing point depression of the unknown solution is determined as in Part 1, and the solution molality is calculated. Finally, the student calculates the molar mass of the unknown solute using Equation 2.

$$\text{molar mass (grams/mole)} = \frac{\text{concentration (grams/kilogram of water)}}{\text{molality (moles/kilogram of water)}}$$

(Equation 2)

The experimental data and calculation results are recorded in Table 3.

Table 3	
1. Mass of empty 250 mL beaker	125.45 g
2. Mass of beaker + water	225.86 g
3. Mass of water in beaker	100.41 g
4. Mass of beaker + water + unknown solute	239.11 g
5. Mass of unknown solute	13.25 g
6. Concentration of unknown solution	131.96 g solute/kg water
7. Freezing point of unknown solution	−8.49°C
8. ΔT for unknown solution	−8.45°C
9. Molality of unknown solution	2.26 mol/kg
10. Molar mass of the unknown solute	?

64. According to the information provided, the ultimate purpose of Part 1 was to experimentally determine:

    F.   the freezing point of distilled water.
    G. the freezing point depression of distilled water.
    H. the freezing point depression constant of sugar-water.
    J.   the freezing point depression constant for distilled water.

65. According to the information provided, which of the following entries in Table 3 were experimental observations?

    A. 1, 2, and 7 only
    B. 1, 2, and 4 only
    C. 1, 2, 4, and 7 only
    D. 1, 2, 3, 4, and 7 only

66. The student repeats Part 1 with a 2.0 m sugar-water solution. Based on the information provided, the student can expect that:

    F.   the freezing point depression for the 2.0 m sugar solution will be half that of the 1.0 m sugar solution.
    G. the freezing point depression for the 2.0 m sugar solution will be twice that of the 1.0 m sugar solution.
    H. the freezing point depression constant for distilled water will be twice that found using the 1.0 m sugar solution.
    J.   freezing point depression constant for distilled water will be half that found using the 1.0 m sugar solution.

67. Based on the information provided, it can be concluded that the unknown solute tested in Part 2 was most likely:

    A. sugar.
    B. calcium fluoride.
    C. sodium chloride.
    D. sodium fluoride.

68. Based on the information provided, decreasing the amount of salt in a salt-water solution will cause the freezing point of the solution to:

    F.   increase only.
    G. decrease only.
    H. decrease, then increase.
    J.   remain the same.

69. The student discovered that the scale was not calibrated properly (set to zero) before it was used in Part 2. Which of the following is the simplest way to correct this mistake?

    A. Determine how much mass was added to the measurements from not zeroing the scale and subtract this value from entry 5 in Table 2.
    B. Determine how much mass was added to the measurements from not zeroing the scale and subtract this value from entries 3 and 5 in Table 2.
    C. Determine how much mass was added to the measurements from not zeroing the scale and subtract this value from entries 1, 2, and 5 and recalculate entries 3 and 5 in Table 2
    D. No correction is necessary because any added mass from not zeroing the balance would cancel out in the calculations leading to entries 3 and 5.

Passage XIII

A useful property of lenses is their ability to form images of objects due to the refraction of light as it passes from one medium to another. If the object and image sizes are h and h', respectively, the magnification of the lens is the ratio of the image size to object size, or:

$$\frac{h'}{h} = -\frac{i}{o}$$

(Equation 1)

Where o represents the distance between the center of the lens and the object and i represents the distance between the center of the lens and the image. The magnification is represented as a negative number to indicate that an inverted image has a negative height and an upright image has a positive height.

Experiment 1

A student places an LED candle 100 centimeters from a thin converging lens. A paper screen on the other side of the lens is moved until a sharply focused image of the candle light appears on the screen (Figure 1). The image distance and height are measured. The candle is moved 20 centimeters closer to the lens and the experiment repeated until an object distance of 20 centimeters is reached. For each data set, the magnification is calculated (Table 1).

Table 1			
Object Distance, o (cm)	Image Distance, i (cm)	Image Height, h' (cm)	Magnification
100.0	11.1	−0.55	−0.11
80.0	11.4	−0.71	−0.14
60.0	12.0	−1.00	−0.20
40.0	13.3	−1.66	−0.33
20.0	20.0	−5.00	−1.00

Experiment 2

The student repeats Experiment 1 after replacing the single lens with two identical lenses side-by-side and in contact with each other. Table 2 summarizes the results.

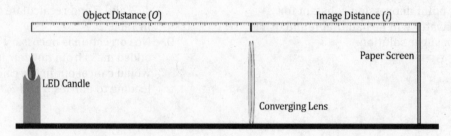

Figure 1

Table 2			
Object Distance, o (cm)	Image Distance, i (cm)	Image Height, h' (cm)	Magnification
100.0	5.3	−0.27	−0.05
80.0	5.3	−0.33	−0.07
60.0	5.5	−0.46	−0.09
40.0	5.7	−0.71	−0.14
20.0	6.7	−1.68	−0.34

Experiment 3

Using a similarly sized waterproofed LED candle and white plastic screen, the student repeats Experiment 1 in a water-filled tank until the length of the tank prevents further measurements. Table 3 summarizes the results.

Table 3			
Object Distance, o (cm)	Image Distance, i (cm)	Image Height, h' (cm)	Magnification
100.0	63.9	−3.20	−0.64
80.0	76.1	−4.76	−0.95
60.0	88.1	−7.34	−1.47

70. Which of the following best describes the purpose of Experiment 3?

F. To study how focal distance is affected by changing the medium surrounding a pair of converging lenses

G. To study how image formation is affected by combining converging lenses

H. To study how image formation is affected by changing the medium surrounding a converging lens

J. To study how image formation is affected by changing the position of an object relative to a converging lens

71. According to the experimental results, for the same object distance, the paired converging lenses in air produces a magnification:

A. less than that of a single converging lens in air.

B. greater than that of a single converging lens in air.

C. equal to that of a single converging lens in air.

D. greater than that of a single converging lens in water.

72. Which of the following graphs best represents the relationship between object distance and image distance for a thin converging lens in air?

F.

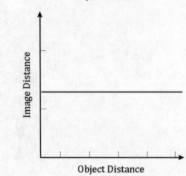

G.

H.

J.

73. Based on the information provided, approximately how tall are the LED candles used in these experiments?

A. 5 cm
B. 10 cm
C. 20 cm
D. Cannot be determined from the given information

74. Focal length is the distance between the center of a lens and the point at which a clear image of a very distant object is formed. . For a thin converging lens in air, the lens formula relates focal length, f, to object distance, o, and image distance, i:

$$\frac{1}{f} = \frac{1}{i} + \frac{1}{o}$$

Using this information, what is the focal length of the lens used in Experiment 1?

F. 33.3
G. 40
H. 10
J. 5

Conflicting Viewpoints Review and Strategies

Typical Conflicting Viewpoints Items

Passage XIV
Theory 1

Early in the twentieth century, many chemists believed that the stability of the molecule methane, CH_4, could be explained by the "octet" rule, which states that stability occurs when the central atom, in this case carbon, is surrounded by eight "valence," or outer, electrons. Four of these originally came from the outer electrons of the carbon itself, and four came from the four surrounding hydrogen atoms (the hydrogen atom was considered an exception to the rule since it was known to favor a closed shell of two electrons as helium has). According to the octet rule, neither CH_3 nor CH_5 should exist as stable compounds, and this prediction has been borne out by experiment.

Theory 2

While the octet rule predicted many compounds accurately, it also had shortcomings. Ten electrons, for example, surround the compound PCl_5. The greatest shock to the octet rule concerned noble gases such as krypton and xenon, which have eight electrons surrounding them in their atomic states, and therefore should not form compounds since no more electrons would be needed to make an octet. The discovery in 1960 that xenon could form compounds such as XeF_4 forced consideration of a new theory, which held that (a) compounds formed when electrons were completely paired, either in bonds or in non-bonded pairs; (b) the total number of shared electrons around a central atom varied, and could be as high as twelve; (c) the shapes of compounds were such as to keep the pairs of electrons as far from each other as possible.

For example, since six electrons in the atomic state surround sulfur, in the compound SF_6 it acquired six additional shared electrons from the surrounding fluorines for a total of twelve electrons. The shape of the compound is "octahedral," as shown in Figure 1, since this conformation minimizes the overlap of bonding pairs of electrons.

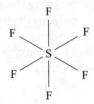

Figure 1

75. According to Theory 1, the compound CH_2Cl_2:

A. should have eight electrons surrounding the carbon atom.
B. cannot exist since the original carbon atom does not have eight electrons.
C. should have eight electrons surrounding each hydrogen atom.
D. requires more electrons for stability.

76. According to Theory 1, the compound XeF_4:

F. exists with an octet structure around the xenon.
G. should not exist since more than eight electrons surround the xenon.
H. will have similar chemical properties to CH_4.
J. exists with the xenon surrounded by twelve electrons.

77. The atom boron has three outer electrons, and in bonding to boron, a fluorine atom has a single, unpaired electron to bond with a boron atom. The BF_3 molecule is known to exist. Which of the following is true?

A. BF₃ obeys Theory 1.
B. The existence of BF₃ contradicts Theory 2.
C. According to Theory 2, the structure of BF₃ is a pyramid:

D. According to Theory 2, the structure of BF_3 is triangular and planar:

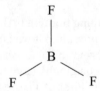

78. A scientist seeking to explain why Theory 2 has more predictive power than Theory 1 might argue that:

F. eight electrons shall represent a "closed shell."
G. while eight electrons represent a "closed shell" for some atoms, for others the closed shell may be six, ten, or twelve.
H. it is incorrect to assume that a given atom always has the same number of electrons around it.
J. CH_4 is not as important a compound as XeF_4.

79. Theory 2 could be threatened by evidence of:

    A. the existence of SF_4.
    B. the existence of XeF_5.
    C. molecules with stable octets.
    D. the existence of SF_6.

Passage XV

Scientist 1

    The atmosphere of Earth was at one time almost totally lacking in oxygen. One piece of evidence supporting this assertion is the very fact that life got started at all. The first chemical reactions that are necessary for the origin of life, the formation of amino acids, require ultraviolet light. Most of the ultraviolet light coming from the Sun is now absorbed by oxygen in the atmosphere. If there were as much oxygen in the atmosphere then as there is now, there would have been too little ultraviolet light available to enable life to begin. Also, the oldest bacteria, the ones that have the shortest DNA, are almost all anaerobes—they either do not need oxygen or die if exposed to oxygen. Most of the oxygen that exists now entered the atmosphere later from volcanic fumes.

Scientist 2

    The prevailing opinion is that the atmosphere, though thicker now than it was in the past, is not essentially different in composition. The argument that Earth must originally have been deficient in oxygen is flawed. First of all, the presence of iron and other oxides in the rocks from this time indicates that there was oxygen available. Secondly, the requirement for a great deal of ultraviolet light holds only if there is a low concentration of the starting materials in the water. If the water in some prehistoric lake began to freeze, the starting materials would be concentrated in a small volume of unfrozen water. The high concentration of the starting materials would offset the so-called deficiency of ultraviolet light, and life could begin.

80. According to the hypothesis of Scientist 1, which of the following would have been among the last living things to evolve?

    F. Anaerobes
    G. Amino Acids
    H. Insects
    J. Viruses

81. According to the information presented by Scientist 1, if his theory of the origin of oxygen in the atmosphere is correct, the total amount of oxygen in the air over the next million years, on the average, should:

    A. decrease, then increase.
    B. increase, then decrease.
    C. increase only.
    D. decrease only.

82. Underlying the argument of Scientist 2 is the assumption that the oxygen in the oxides in the rocks was:

    F. always tied up in the rocks.
    G. involved in biological reactions.
    H. completely gaseous during the early days of the atmosphere.
    J. proportional to the oxygen in the atmosphere at the time.

83. Underlying Scientist 1's suggestion that the evolutionary record supports the idea of an oxygen deficiency on early Earth is the assumption that the oldest living things:

    A. have the shortest DNA.
    B. have the most fragmented DNA.
    C. have changed radically.
    D. must have died out.

84. Which of the following is the strongest argument Scientist 1 could use to counter Scientist 2's suggested mechanism for the origin of life?

F. There was not enough ultraviolet light available.
G. Chemical reactions occurred differently then.
H. The temperature at the surface of Earth at that time was always above 35°C because of geothermal heat release.
J. Most lakes would not have covered large enough areas to guarantee that all the essential building blocks were present.

85. To refute Scientist 1's hypothesis, Scientist 2 might best show that:

A. the amount of oxide in rocks has changed little over the past four billion years.
B. there are ways of making the biologically important molecules without ultraviolet light.
C. there are complex anaerobic bacteria.
D. the atmospheric pressure has not changed over Earth's history.

Conflicting Viewpoints Strategies

Passage XVI

In the 1940s, 1950s, and 1960s, the growing field of animal behavior maintained an ongoing debate about the origin of observed behavior in many different animal species. Two extreme viewpoints were at the center of this "Nature vs. Nurture" debate.

Viewpoint 1 (Nature)

Many behaviors or instincts are literally programmed by one or more genes. Genes serve as "blueprints" that enable an individual to carry out a particular stereotyped behavior (Fixed Action Pattern) as soon as the appropriate stimulus (releaser) is observed. Other individuals do not have to be observed performing the behavior. The releasing stimulus need never have been seen before. At first view of the releaser and every time thereafter, the Fixed Action Pattern will be carried out to completion in the exact same way—even if the releaser is removed before the Fixed Action

Pattern is finished! Examples include: a) the pecking of baby gulls at the red spot on their mother's bill (which causes the mother gull to regurgitate food), b) song birds producing their species song without ever having heard it before, and c) a male stickleback fish defending its territory by attacking anything red because other breeding males always have red underbellies.

Viewpoint 2 (Nurture)

Many behaviors are determined by experience and/or learning during an individual's lifetime. Genes provide the limits of the "blank slate" that each individual starts out as, but then various experiences will determine the actual behavior patterns within the individual genetic range of possibilities. In other words, behavior can be modified. Examples include: a) positive ("reward") reinforcement and punishment causing a behavior to increase and decrease (respectively), and b) songbirds producing their species song only after having heard it performed by other individuals of their species.

86. The red spot on a mother gull's bill is called a(n):

F. Fixed Action Pattern.
G. instinct.
H. releaser.
J. stereotyped response.

87. To refute the strict "genetic blueprint" ideas of Viewpoint 1, a scientist could show that:

A. baby gulls peck at a stick with a red spot.
B. baby gulls will peck at mother gulls' red spot as soon as they hatch out of their eggs.
C. baby gulls pecking at the red spot happens exactly the same way each time.
D. baby gulls' accuracy in pecking at mother gulls' red spot improves with practice.

88. A food-seeking blue jay captured a distinctively colored butterfly that had a bad-tasting substance in its tissues. After spitting out the butterfly, it never again tried to capture a similarly colored butterfly. This incident seems to support:

F. Viewpoint 1.
G. Viewpoint 2.
H. both viewpoints.
J. neither viewpoint (the incident is irrelevant).

89. Which of the following supports Viewpoint 1?

A. A rat reaches the end of a maze by the same route, but finishes faster after each trip.
B. A monkey watches other monkeys wash sweet potatoes before they eat them; then, he washes sweet potatoes before he eats them.
C. A male stickleback fish attacks a picture of a red mailbox held in front of his aquarium.
D. A bird performs its species song after hearing the song only once.

90. If a female goose uses a repeated beak and neck movement to return an egg to her nest, continuing the movement even when the egg slides off course or is removed, then this:

F. supports Viewpoint 1.
G. supports Viewpoint 2.
H. does not refer to behavior.
J. is irrelevant to the Nature vs. Nurture debate.

91. It is thought that some species of birds "learn" to fly. This belief is based on observations of young birds fluttering and flapping their wings at the nest until they reach the age when flight is possible. In Species X, nestlings were kept in harmless, but tight plastic tubes in which they could not carry out such "practice movements." They were released when they reached the age of flight. Viewpoint 1 predicts that the birds will fly:

A. after fluttering their wings for a time.
B. after watching other birds flutter their wings.
C. after watching other birds flutter and fly.
D. immediately.

92. A songbird can sing its species song after it hears other birds of its own species singing. Yet, if it hears the song from another species, the bird will not sing the "foreign" song. This suggests that:

F. genetic "programming" and experience play a role in this species' ability to sing its song.
G. this species' song is a Fixed Action Pattern.
H. song development in this species is strictly a learned behavior with no genetic component.
J. genes appear to be far more important than experience in this example.

Passage XVII

The Sun's atmosphere is divided into three major regions: the photosphere, the chromosphere, and the corona. The photosphere is the visible region of the Sun. Just above the photosphere is the chromosphere which is far less dense, but hotter. Consisting of low-density plasma, the corona is the thin, outermost atmosphere of the sun that extends for millions of kilometers above the Sun's surface.

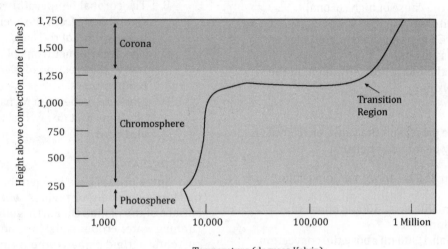

One would expect that the atmosphere of the Sun should become cooler with increasing distance from its surface. To the contrary, as the graph above shows, coronal temperatures increase with increasing distance from the sun's visible photosphere, rising to over a million degrees. The mechanism responsible for this heating remains a fundamental question of modern astrophysics.

Three scientists discuss the heating mechanism.

Scientist 1

Just above the surface of the sun, in the chromosphere, there are approximately 10,000 regions of violently rotating columns of air, or vortices. These vortices are likely produced by magnetic activity within the sun that exerts pressure on the plasma in the atmosphere. Computer simulations suggest that plasma particles trapped within the vortices are accelerated as they spiral toward the corona. The accelerated plasma particles greatly increase the average speed of the coronal particles, which translates into higher coronal temperatures.

Scientist 2

Solar telescopes have detected millions of magnetic patches on the sun's photosphere. The patches, between 50 and 1,000 kilometers wide, are constantly changing in size and shape due to the turbulent movement of the plasma in the chromosphere. The magnetic fields in the sun's corona constantly change as they respond to changes in the photosphere magnetic patches. As magnetic field lines in the corona interact, they undergo a process called reconnection: they snap apart and then reconnect. The reconnection releases a tremendous amount of heat and wave energy, causing the high coronal temperatures.

Scientist 3

Neutrons are produced in the sun's interior through thermonuclear reactions in the core and the stripping of complex particles at the surface. Due to solar flares and other magnetic phenomena, some of these neutrons reach the base of the sun's corona. Free neutrons last about 15 minutes before they undergo radioactive decay, creating electrons as energetic as 0.78 MeV. When these fast moving electrons collide with particles in the corona, they transfer some of their energy, causing the high coronal temperatures.

93. Which of the following best describes the question the three scientists attempt to answer?

A. What is the cause of vortices on the surface of the sun?
B. What is the cause of high coronal temperatures?
C. What are the physical characteristics of the sun's corona?
D. What is the temperature gradient of the sun's corona?

94. Based on the graph and the views of Scientist1, vortices may be found at heights:

F. less than 250 mi above the convection zone.
G. between 250 and 1,300 mi above the convection zone.
H. more than 1,300 mi above the convection zone.
J. more than 10,000 mi above the convection zone.

95. Scientist 2 states that the changing magnetic patches on the sun's photosphere are due to:

A. the radioactive decay of neutrons.
B. plasma particles trapped within vortices.
C. the movement of the plasma in the chromosphere.
D. fast moving electrons colliding with particles in the corona.

96. Magnetism plays a role in the explanation of the coronal heating in the views of:

F. only Scientist 1 and Scientist 2.
G. only Scientist 1 and Scientist 3.
H. only Scientist 2 and Scientist 3.
J. Scientist 1, Scientist 2 and Scientist 3.

97. All three scientists would likely agree with which of the following statements?

A. The energy source for high coronal temperatures in the corona originates near or in the Sun.
B. The coronal temperatures do not vary significantly from the average surface temperature of the Sun.
C. The decay of neutrons plays an important role in the creation of high coronal temperatures.
D. Magnetic-generated tornadoes produce neutrons that decay, creating energetic electrons.

Passage XVIII

Space probes have imaged thousands of gullies on Mars—channels, or ravines, worn into the surface of the planet. On Earth, gullies form as running water erodes soil. Mars, however, is currently a frigid planet without rain or liquid water on the surface. Interestingly, some of the Martian gullies appear to have formed very recently. Three planetary scientists discuss the origins of gullies on Mars.

Scientist 1

Mars contains many deposits of solid carbon dioxide, or dry ice, buried under the dust and sand found on the slopes of hills and craters. When sunlight warms these deposits, the dry ice converts directly into a gas through the process of sublimation. As the carbon dioxide gas blows out of the ground, the surrounding dust and sand flow like a liquid in a process called fluidization.

An experiment conducted on Earth supports this mechanism for gully formation. A tub was filled with Mars-like dust and sand shaped into a small mound. An air pump buried beneath the mound forced air up toward the surface. The dust and sand flowed down the mound, creating gullies similar to those imaged on Mars.

Scientist 2

The gullies on Mars form when water from shallow aquifers seeps onto the surface and flows downslope. Although the surface of Mars is dry today, there is abundant evidence that at one time water flowed on its surface. Some of that water likely still exists in underground aquifers. Liquid water is unstable on the surface of Mars due to low temperatures and low atmospheric pressure.

However, computer models indicate that liquid water could be discharged onto the surface of Mars in two situations: the liquid in a shallow aquifer is water with a temperature of at least 350 K, or if the liquid is a water-based brine with a freezing point of no more than 250 K. In either scenario, the flow of water onto the surface is likely triggered by the melting of surface ice plugs, which otherwise act like caps for the water in the aquifers. Once the ice plugs melt, the sub-surface water gushes to the surface, forming gullies as the water flows downslope.

Scientist 3

The gullies on Mars form when snow packs melt. The melted snow (liquid water) at the bottom of snow packs does not undergo rapid evaporation due to the low atmospheric pressure on Mars. This water carves the gullies as it flows downslope. This theory is supported by the fact that most gullies found on Mars are on the cold, pole-facing slopes of hills and craters. These colder conditions allow for the accumulation of snow on these slopes, which with warmer temperatures, begin to melt, initiating the formation of gullies.

98. According to the information provided, which of the following accurately describes the current environmental conditions on Mars?

   F.   High temperatures and high atmospheric pressure
   G.   High temperatures and low atmospheric pressure
   H.   Low temperatures and high atmospheric pressure
   J.   Low temperatures and low atmospheric pressure

99. Which scientist's argument presents water as the primary agent in gully formation on Mars?

   A.   Scientist 1 only
   B.   Scientist 2 only
   C.   Scientists 1 and 3
   D.   Scientists 2 and 3

100. Which scientist's argument does NOT require the flow of a liquid to explain gully formation on Mars?

   F.   Scientist 1 only
   G.   Scientist 2 only
   H.   Scientist 3 only
   J.   None of the scientists

101. All three scientists agree that gully formation on Mars is triggered by:

   A.   the flow of a liquid on the surface.
   B.   surface warming.
   C.   sublimation of sub-surface ices.
   D.   a drop in atmospheric pressure.

102. Which scientist's argument is best supported by the fact that most gullies on Mars are found on cold, pole-facing slopes?

   F.   Scientist 1
   G.   Scientist 2
   H.   Scientist 3
   J.   All three scientists

103. The gamma ray spectrometer (GRS) on-board the space probe Mars Odyssey detects water on the surface of Mars down to a depth of several meters. A strong correlation is found between areas on Mars where the GRS detected high levels of water and where the majority of gullies are found. That most gullies are found in water-rich areas supports the position(s) of:

   A.   Scientist 1 only.
   B.   Scientist 3 only.
   C.   Scientists 1 and 3.
   D.   Scientists 2 and 3.

QUIZZES

This section contains three Science quizzes. Complete each quiz under timed conditions. Answers are on page 669.

Quiz I

(16 items; 15 minutes)

> **DIRECTIONS:** Each passage below is followed by several items. After reading a passage, choose the best answer to each item. You may refer to the passages as often as necessary. You are NOT permitted the use of a calculator.

Passage I

The ecological pyramid below shows the relative biomass* of organisms at each trophic feeding level of a marine food chain.

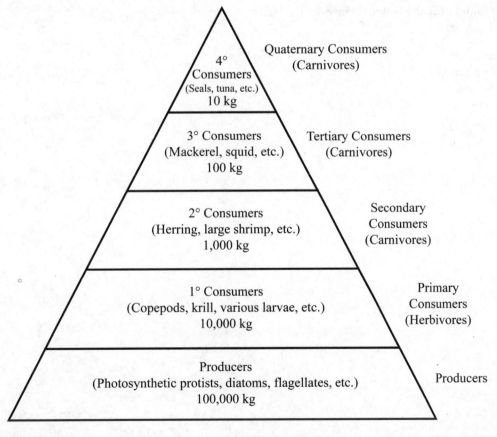

Quaternary Consumers (Carnivores)
4° Consumers (Seals, tuna, etc.) 10 kg

Tertiary Consumers (Carnivores)
3° Consumers (Mackerel, squid, etc.) 100 kg

Secondary Consumers (Carnivores)
2° Consumers (Herring, large shrimp, etc.) 1,000 kg

Primary Consumers (Herbivores)
1° Consumers (Copepods, krill, various larvae, etc.) 10,000 kg

Producers
Producers (Photosynthetic protists, diatoms, flagellates, etc.) 100,000 kg

*Biomass is the total dry weight of organisms (useable chemical energy stored in organic matter) at each trophic level at any given time.

1. According to the diagram, the trophic level with the largest relative biomass is the:

A. 4° consumers.
B. 3° and 2° consumers.
C. 1° consumers.
D. producers.

2. From the information in the diagram, one can conclude that at any given time:

F. 10 seals may be found for every mackerel.
G. the relative dry weight of all carnivores combined is far greater than that of the herbivores alone.
H. only 1 percent of all producers live long enough to be eaten by a mackerel.
J. the relative dry weight of every consumer trophic level is usually less than that of the trophic level on which they feed.

3. Organisms from which trophic level are most likely to be found near the water surface where light can penetrate?

A. 4° consumers
B. 2° consumers
C. 3° consumers
D. producers

4. If there were an additional trophic level of carnivores (5° consumers), its relative biomass at any given time would be approximately:

F.   1 kg.
G.   11 kg.
H.   111 kg.
J.   1,000,000 kg.

5. The best explanation for biomass being measured as dry weight is:

A. if water weight were included, efficiency ratios at each trophic level would be unpredictable.
B. body fluids contribute little to the mass of marine organisms.
C. water molecules contain little or no usable chemical energy.
D. each trophic level contains a different amount of water.

Passage II

The table below shows various characteristics of different layers of the atmosphere.

APPROXIMATE ALTITUDE (KM)	LAYERS OF THE ATMOSPHERE	APPROXIMATE MEAN TEMPERATURE (°C)	CLOUDS
60,000 6,000			
	THERMOSPHERE		
600		1200	
80		–90	
	MESOSPHERE		
50		–3	
	STRATOSPHERE		Cirrus
12		–50	
			Cirrostratus
	TROPOSPHERE		Altostratus
0		18	Nimbostratus

6. Which statement accurately describes the relationship between the approximate altitude and the approximate mean temperature of the layers of the atmosphere?

   F. As altitude increases, temperature increases.
   G. As altitude increases, temperature decreases.
   H. As altitude increases, temperature first decreases then continuously increases.
   J. As altitude increases, temperature first decreases, then increases, then decreases, and then increases.

7. Based on the information in the table, the atmospheric layer with the narrowest range of altitude is the:

   A. thermosphere.
   B. troposphere.
   C. mesosphere.
   D. stratosphere.

8. The type of cloud(s) most likely to consist of ice crystals is (are):

   F. nimbostratus only.
   G. nimbostratus and altostratus.
   H. cirrus and cirrostratus.
   J. cirrostratus only.

9. The absorption of solar heat energy increases as the gases of the atmosphere become less dense, or rarefied. The layer of the atmosphere that appears most rarefied is the:

   A. thermosphere.
   B. mesosphere.
   C. stratosphere.
   D. troposphere.

10. According to the table, which atmospheric layer shows a decrease in temperature of approximately 3°C for every 1 kilometer increase in altitude?

    F. thermosphere
    G. mesosphere
    H. stratosphere
    J. troposphere

Passage III

Using electrical circuits, three experiments were performed to investigate the relationship between voltage (volts), resistance (ohms) (total resistance equals the sum of individual resistances), and current (amperes). Each experiment was set up with the following circuit design:

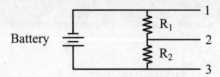

Experiment 1

Using a 6 volt battery (far left), and two 1,000 ohm resistors (R_1 and R_2), the measured voltages between points 1 and 2 and between points 2 and 3 were 3 volts each.

Experiment 2

When the battery voltage was increased to 12 volts, and the resistors were kept the same (1,000 ohms each), the measured voltages between points 1 and 2 and between points 2 and 3 were 6 volts each.

Experiment 3

Using the original 6 volt battery, R_1 was replaced with a 2,000 ohm resistor. The voltages measured between points 1 and 2 and between points 2 and 3 were 4 volts and 2 volts, respectively.

---

11. Judging from the results in Experiment 1 and Experiment 2, if the battery voltage were changed to 1.5 volts and both resistors were 1,000 volts, what voltage would be expected between point 1 and point 2?

   A. 0.75 volts
   B. 1.5 volts
   C. 3.0 volts
   D. 6.0 volts

12. After studying the measurement made in the previous question, as well as those made earlier in Experiments 1, 2, and 3, the experimenter could reasonably hypothesize that:

   F. voltage measured across a resistor is inversely proportional to the value of that resistor.
   G. voltage measured across a resistor is directly proportional to the value of that resistor.
   H. voltage measured across a resistor is not related to the value of that resistor.
   J. voltage measured across a resistor equals the battery voltage.

13. When the experimenter recorded the current in the circuit of Experiment 1, it measured 0.003 amperes. In Experiment 3, however, the current measured 0.002 amperes. These results show that current and total resistances are:

   A. directly proportional.
   B. inversely proportional.
   C. equal.
   D. unrelated.

14. Which of the following formulas for the current in the circuit best summarizes the above results? (The battery voltage is given by V_b and the total resistance is given by R.)

   F. $V_b R$

   G. $\dfrac{R}{V_b}$

   H. $\dfrac{V_b}{R}$

   J. $V_b + R$

15. A new circuit is set up, similar in design to those in the experiments. The battery voltage and the size of the resistors are unknown, but the current measures 0.001 amperes. If the battery voltage is doubled and one of the two resistors is replaced with one having a smaller value, which answer most accurately describes the new current?

A. It will be smaller than 0.001 amperes.
B. It will be unchanged.
C. It will be greater than 0.001 amperes.
D. Cannot be determined from the given information

16. Which of the following single changes to Experiment 2 would produce a current of 0.004 amperes?

F. Decrease the voltage to 8 volts.
G. Increase the resistance to 3,000 ohms.
H. Neither (F) nor (G) will create a current of 0.004 amperes.
J. Either (F) or (G) will create a current of 0.004 amperes.

Quiz II

(16 items; 15 minutes)

DIRECTIONS: Each passage below is followed by several items. After reading a passage, choose the best answer to each item. You may refer to the passages as often as necessary. You are NOT permitted the use of a calculator.

Passage I

The chart below shows in outline form a common means of analyzing a sample solution for various cations (positive ions). Ions above the horizontal arrows are those that are suspected to be present in the sample solution; the substances in the boxes are the reagents added as tests (0.3 M H^+ is acidic, NH_4OH is alkaline); the products shown next to the arrows pointing downward are solid precipitates resulting from the tests. Tests for specific ions need not always start from the beginning of the sequence.

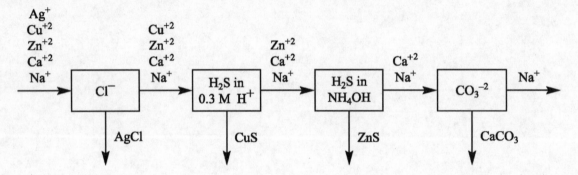

1. According to the chart, which precipitate indicates if silver (Ag) is present in the sample?

   A. AgCl
   B. Ag
   C. CuS
   D. ZnS

2. If a solution containing silver (Ag) nitrate and cupric (Cu) nitrate is tested according to this scheme, an experimenter will:

   F. first observe AgCl on treatment with Cl^-, and next observe CuS on treatment with H_2S.

   G. first observe CuS on treatment with Cl^-, and next observe AgCl on treatment with H_2S.

   H. first observe $CaCO_3$ on treatment with CO_3^{-2}, and next observe AgCl on treatment with Cl^-.

   J. observe no reactions, since the scheme does not test for nitrate.

3. What is the minimum number of tests necessary to confirm the composition of an unknown solution that contains no other positive ions except Cu^{+2} or Zn^{+2}, but not both?

    A. 1
    B. 2
    C. 3
    D. 4

4. Which statement is most correct concerning the separation of Cu^{+2} from Zn^{+2} in the same solution?

    F. Completely different test reagents are used in each of the two steps.
    G. The same test reagents are used in each of the two steps.
    H. The same test reagents are used, but the first step must be in an alkaline environment while the second step must be in an acidic environment.
    J. The same test reagents are used, but the first step must be in an acidic environment while the second step must be in an alkaline environment.

5. A clear solution is found, by a method not discussed here, to contain chloride ion (Cl^-). From the information given here, what ion could not be present in the solution?

    A. Carbonate (CO^{-2})
    B. Cupric (Cu^{+2})
    C. Silver (Ag^+)
    D. Zinc (Zn^{+2})

Passage II

The chart below shows the flavor preferences of mice when offered various fluids to drink at different ages.

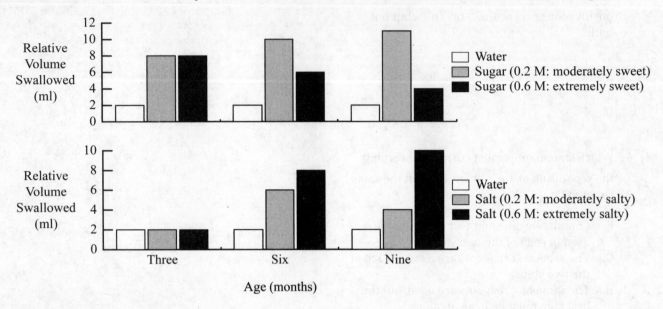

Age (months)

6. Which category on the chart shows no preference between water and the experimental flavor?

- F.   Three months of age/sugar
- G.   Six months of age/salt
- H.   Three months of age/salt
- J.   Nine months of age/sugar

7. Which statement about mice is supported by the information in the chart?

- A.   As age increases, the preference for all tested sugars increases.
- B.   As age increases, the preference for all tested salts increases.
- C.   As age increases, differences between sugars cannot be detected, and differences between salts cannot be detected.
- D.   As age increases, differences between sugars can be detected, and differences between salts can be detected.

8. The flavor preference that fluctuates most irregularly with age is:

- F.   moderately salty.
- G.   moderately sweet.
- H.   extremely salty.
- J.   extremely sweet.

9. Based on the trends shown in the chart, which of the following predictions is most reasonable for one-year-old mice?

- A.   Moderately sweet and moderately salty will be most preferred.
- B.   Extremely sweet and extremely salty will be most preferred.
- C.   Moderately sweet and extremely salty will be most preferred.
- D.   Extremely sweet and moderately salty will be most preferred.

10. Which of the following conclusions about water is NOT consistent with the data in the chart?

    F. Water is never preferred over any tested flavors.

    G. Before the age of six months, mice cannot taste the difference between water and sugar or between water and salt.

    H. At the age of three months, both salty fluids are equal to the water swallowed.

    J. As age increases, the volume of water swallowed remains the same.

Passage III

Approximately 65 million years ago, at the boundary between the Cretaceous and Paleogene geologic periods, a mass extinction of about three-fourths of the Earth's plant and animal species occurred, including all non-flying dinosaurs. Many hypotheses have been proposed to explain the extinction, but only two have received great acceptance: a huge meteorite impact and an episode of intensive volcanism.

Scientist 1
The evidence is overwhelming that a large meteorite hit the earth at the end of the Cretaceous period. Sedimentary rock layers at the 65-million-year mark reveal a high concentration of iridium, which is rare in the Earth's crust but abundant in meteorites. The discovery of the Chicxulub crater in the Gulf of Mexico is further evidence of a major meteor strike. The impact of this meteorite sent up a cloud of particles into the atmosphere, blocking sunlight and drastically reducing solar energy and hence photosynthesis. Plants and marine algae withered and died, followed by the plant-eating herbivores. This reverberated up the food chain to include the predators that depended on the plant-eating animals for food.

Scientist 2
Granted, a meteorite hit the earth 65 million years ago. However, the planet was already an overheated greenhouse snuffing out life before the meteorite's arrival. A major volcanic event occurred around the same time as the Cretaceous-Paleogene boundary extinction. The Deccan Traps in India represent one of the largest volcanic features on the Earth today. Formed between 60 and 68 million years ago from a series of volcanic eruptions, the Deccan Traps consist of multiple layers of solidified basalt lava. It is one of the biggest flood basalts in the history of the planet. The massive release of volcanic gases, particularly carbon dioxide, from the eruptions that created the Deccan Traps caused a greenhouse effect. It heated up the planet and stressed the land-dwelling dinosaurs and many other animal and plant species to extinction. Five major extinctions have occurred in the past 500 million years: the Ordovician, the Devonian, the Permian, the Triassic, and the Cretaceous. All of these extinctions are greenhouse extinctions associated with flood basalts.

11. Which of the following best describes the cause of the Cretaceous-Paleogene boundary extinction according to Scientist 2?

    A. A huge meteorite impact.
    B. An abundance of iridium in the earth's crust.
    C. A massive release of volcanic gases.
    D. A flood covering three-fourths of the earth's surface.

12. According to Scientist 1, a meteorite impact could cause a major extinction due to the resulting:

    F. shockwaves that limited photosynthesis.
    G. sunlight-blocking cloud of particles.
    H. unusually high concentration of the element iridium.
    J. release of toxic gases.

13. According to the information provided, evidence of a meteorite strike at the end of the Cretaceous period includes:

    A. high concentrations of iridium in sedimentary rock.
    B. major extinctions at other times in history.
    C. massive releases of gases, particularly carbon dioxide.
    D. multiple layers of solidified basalt in the Deccan Traps.

14. According to the information provided, both scientists agree that:

F. volcanic activity occurred at the Cretaceous-Paleogene boundary.

G. a meteorite hit the earth 65 million years ago.

H. a meteorite was the cause of the Cretaceous-Paleogene boundary extinction.

J. the Cretaceous-Paleogene boundary extinction is a greenhouse extinction associated with flood basalts.

15. According to Scientist 2, the Deccan Traps:

A. led to a reduction in solar energy and photosynthesis.

B. caused greenhouse warming.

C. resulted from a series of volcanic eruptions.

D. occurred roughly around the same time as the Permian-Triassic boundary extinction.

16. Both scientists would most likely agree that:

F. there were multiple major extinctions throughout history.

G. extinctions impact dinosaurs and other animal species but not plants.

H. the Deccan Traps impacted the major extinction between the Cretaceous and Paleogene periods.

J. a change in Earth's atmosphere led to the extinction between the Cretaceous and Paleogene periods.

Quiz III

(16 items; 15 minutes)

DIRECTIONS: Each passage below is followed by several items. After reading a passage, choose the best answer to each item. You may refer to the passages as often as necessary. You are NOT permitted the use of a calculator.

Passage I

The table below shows the first three ionization energies for the atoms hydrogen through potassium. The first ionization energy, E_1, is the energy (in kilocalories per mole of atoms) that must be added in order to remove the first electron. E_2 is the energy required to remove a second electron once the first has been removed, and E_3 is the energy needed to remove a third electron. If an atom lacks a second or third electron, no value is given in the table.

IONIZATION ENERGIES OF THE ELEMENTS (kcal/mole)				
Atomic No.	Element	E_1	E_2	E_3
1	H	313.6	-	-
2	He	566.8	1254	-
3	Li	124.3	1744	2823
4	Be	214.9	419.9	3548
5	B	191.3	580	874.5
6	C	259.6	562.2	1104
7	N	335.1	682.8	1094
8	O	314	810.6	1267
9	F	401.8	806.7	1445
10	Ne	497.2	947.2	1500
11	Na	118.5	1091	1652
12	Mg	176.3	346.6	1848
13	Al	138	434.1	655.9
14	Si	187.9	376.8	771.7
15	P	241.8	453.2	695.5
16	S	238.9	540	807
17	Cl	300	548.9	920.2
18	Ar	363.4	637	943.3
19	K	100.1	733.6	1100

1. For a given element, which of the following correctly orders the ionization energies from least to most?

   A. E_3, E_2, E_1
   B. E_2, E_1, E_3
   C. E_1, E_2, E_3
   D. Cannot be determined from the given information

2. A student suspects that there may be an atom for which the second ionization energy is roughly twice that of the first, and the third is roughly twice that of the second. Which of the following atoms best fits this relationship?

   F. Be
   G. C
   H. Ne
   J. Ar

3. As atomic number increases, the corresponding value of E_2:

   A. increases only.
   B. decreases only.
   C. increases for a few values, then decreases, followed by another increase, etc.
   D. decreases for a few values, then increases, followed by another decrease, etc.

4. An experimenter has at her disposal a means of providing an atom with any energy up to 200 kcal/mole. From how many different atoms could she remove one electron?

   F. 7
   G. 8
   H. 11
   J. 12

Passage II

A physics student performed two sets of experiments designed to examine the factors that influence the motion of falling objects.

Experiment 1

A stone was dropped from a steep cliff while a camera, mounted on a tripod on the ground, took photographs at 0.1 second intervals. Back in the laboratory, the same procedure was repeated in the absence (nearly) of air inside a huge vacuum chamber.

Experiment 2

The experiments were repeated (on the cliff and inside the vacuum chamber) using a stone and a cork with identical masses dropped at the same time. At the cliff, the stone hit the ground first. In the vacuum chamber, both objects hit the ground together.

5. Assuming that air acts to resist the downward acceleration of the stone, how will the total time required to reach the ground in the vacuum chamber compare to the time required to reach the ground from the cliff?

   A. The time in air is greater than the time in the vacuum chamber.
   B. The time in air is less than the time in the vacuum chamber.
   C. The time is the same in each.
   D. Cannot be determined from the given information

6. If part of Experiment 1 were repeated on the moon, where the pull of gravity is one-sixth that of Earth, the stone's downward speed would increase as it falls (i.e., it would accelerate) but the rate of increase in speed would only be one-sixth as great as on Earth. When the photos taken at 0.1 second intervals on the moon are compared to the photos taken on Earth, the series of moon pictures of the stone will be:

   F. closer together.
   G. farther apart.
   H. identical.
   J. closer at some times and farther apart at others.

7. In Experiment 2, the observed results can be explained by the hypothesis that:

    A. heavier objects fall more rapidly than lighter ones.

    B. a cork of the same mass as a stone is smaller than the stone, and it encounters more air resistance.

    C. a cork of the same mass as a stone is larger than the stone, and it encounters more air resistance.

    D. the gravitational acceleration of objects toward the ground diminishes when air is not present.

8. In Experiment 1, gravity accelerates the stone as it falls from the cliff, causing it to pick up speed as it drops. Which of the following series of pictures most resembles how the stone appears as it drops?

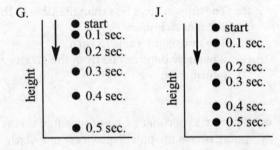

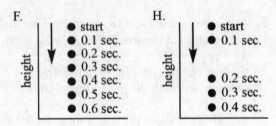

9. The experimenter devises a means of suspending Earth's gravity for short periods of time. Armed with this technique, he drops the stone (on Earth, in air, under conditions of normal gravity), and then suspends gravity 0.2 seconds after the stone has been falling and leaves it off for the next 10 seconds. Recalling that gravity causes the stone's downward speed to increase continually, choose the "photo" that best illustrates, in 0.1 second intervals, this experiment.

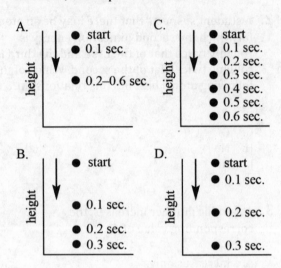

10. If Experiment 2 were repeated on the airless moon, which prediction would be correct?

    F. The cork would fall more slowly than on Earth.

    G. The cork would fall as rapidly as the stone.

    H. Both (F) and (G) are correct.

    J. Neither (F) nor (G) is correct.

Passage III

An object in periodic motion, such as a mass on a spring or a pendulum, vibrates about a fixed position in a regular and repeating fashion. There are two measurable quantities of periodic motion: amplitude and period. The amplitude is the maximum displacement of the object, in either direction, from its resting position. The period is the time it takes the object to complete one cycle of motion: from resting position through the maximum displacement on both sides of the resting position and then back to the resting position. Note that the period does not depend on how far the spring is initially stretched. This independence is a key feature of all systems that undergo periodic motion.

A student investigates the relationships between position, velocity, and acceleration of a vibrating mass-spring system undergoing periodic motion. A motion sensor placed directly below a mass hung from a spring is used to record the vertical position of the mass for 1 second after the spring is stretched (beyond its resting point) and allowed to "spring back." A computer program is used to analyze the data and plot displacement, velocity, and acceleration of the mass-spring system as a function of time (Figure 1).

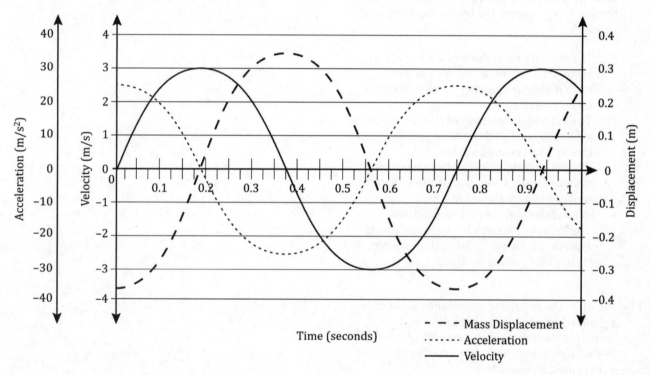

Figure 1

11. In Figure 1, a positive slope for acceleration data indicates that the mass-spring system is:

A. moving upward.
B. moving downward.
C. slowing down.
D. speeding up

12. The period of the mass-spring system is approximately:

F. 0.375 second.
G. 0.75 second.
H. 1 second.
J. Cannot be determined from the given information

13. Negative values of both displacement and velocity indicate that the mass-spring system is:

A. below the resting position and moving upward.
B. moving downward, but speeding up.
C. below the resting position and moving downward.
D. approaching the resting position and moving upward.

14. Which of the following statements about the relationship between displacement and velocity for a mass-spring system in periodic motion is best supported by the experimental results?

F. The velocity magnitude of a mass-spring system decreases as the system moves from maximum positive displacement to its resting position.
G. The velocity magnitude of a mass-spring system is least as the system passes through its resting position.
H. The velocity magnitude of a mass-spring system remains constant as the system moves from maximum negative displacement to its resting position.
J. The velocity magnitude of a mass-spring system is greatest as the system passes through its resting position.

15. Which of the following statements about the relationship between acceleration and displacement for a mass-spring system in periodic motion is best supported by the experimental results?

A. The acceleration of a mass-spring system increases as the system moves from maximum positive displacement to maximum negative displacement.
B. The acceleration of a mass-spring system is least as the system passes through its resting position.
C. The acceleration of a mass-spring system remains constant as the system moves from maximum negative displacement to maximum positive displacement.
D. The acceleration of a mass-spring system decreases each time the system passes through its resting position.

16. The mass-spring system is released from 0.7 meters below its resting position and the experiment repeated. Which of the following results is most likely to occur?

F. The period of the mass-spring system remains unchanged.
G. The period of the mass-spring system doubles.
H. The amplitude of the mass-spring system remains unchanged.
J. The maximum velocity of the mass-spring system decreases by half.

REVIEW

This section contains additional Science items for further practice. Answers begin on page 669.

> **DIRECTIONS:** Each passage below is followed by several items. After reading a passage, choose the best answer to each item. You may refer to the passages as often as necessary. You are NOT permitted the use of a calculator.

Passage I

The graph of the thin line below shows the hearing sensitivity of female moths. The auditory characteristics of certain sounds important to moth survival are also included.

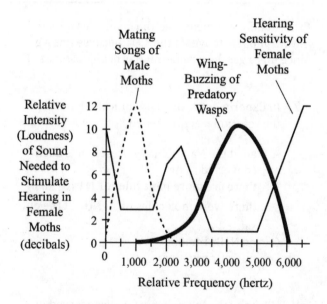

1. According to the graph, female moths are most sensitive to sounds between:

   A. 0–500 hertz.
   B. 500–1,500 hertz.
   C. 2,000–2,500 hertz.
   D. 3,500–5,000 hertz.

2. The nervous system of female moths may be set up to allow them to respond differently to sounds of different frequencies. Based on the information in the graph, which statement best describes the appropriate responses of female moths?

   F. Approach sounds between 500–1,500 hertz, withdraw from sounds between 3,500–5,000 hertz
   G. Approach sounds between 3,500–5,000 hertz, withdraw from sounds between 500–1,500 hertz
   H. Approach sounds between 500–1,500 hertz and 3,500–5,000 hertz
   J. Withdraw from sounds between 500–1,500 hertz and 3,500–5,000 hertz

3. Which of the following statements is supported by the information in the graph?

   A. The wing-buzzing sounds of wasps occur at a narrower range of frequencies than the range of the male moth mating song.
   B. The frequency range of the male moth mating song is narrower than the range of wasp wing-buzzing sounds.
   C. Female moths cannot hear sounds with relative intensities less than 3.
   D. Male moths are less sensitive to sounds than predatory wasps.

4. Which of the following statements accurately describes the relationship between the male moth mating song and female moth hearing sensitivity?

F. The frequency range of the male song coincides with the frequency range at which females are maximally sensitive to any sound.
G. Females need not be maximally sensitive at the frequency range of the male song because of the extremely high intensity of the song.
H. Females cannot hear the male song if its intensity level is less than 10.
J. The male song does not extend to an intensity level above 10.

5. If a new species of wasp were introduced into the moths' environment, which of the following wing-buzzing characteristics would make it the most successful predator of female moths?

A. Extremely high intensity at relative frequencies between 3,500–5,000 hertz
B. An intensity level of 7–8 at relative frequencies between 2,000–2,500 hertz
C. Low intensity at relative frequencies above 6,000 hertz
D. Extremely high intensity at relative frequencies above 6,000 hertz

6. A male is born with a mutation that changes his mating song to a frequency range between 2,000–2,500 hertz and an intensity level of 4. What are his chances of finding a mate?

F. Excellent
G. Poor
H. Good, if no wasps are present
J. Cannot be determined from the given information

Passage II

A chemistry student wishes to study weight relationships between compounds before and after they take part in reactions. Two experiments were conducted to investigate two different reactions. The reactions are shown below, together with the amount (grams) of each substance before and after each reaction has proceeded. Equations are balanced to show the number of each type of atom before and after the reactions.

EXPERIMENT 1				
$NaBr$ +	$AgNO_3$ $\Rightarrow$	$AgBr$ +	$NaNO_3$	
Initial Mass (g)	103	170	0	0
Final Mass (g)	0	0	188	85

EXPERIMENT 2				
Na_2CO_3 + $2HCl$ $\Rightarrow$ $2NaCl$ + $H_2O(g)$ + CO_2				
Initial Mass (g)	106	72	0	0	(?)
Final Mass (g)	0	0	117	18	(?)

(The student has measured the quantities he could, but was unable to weigh the CO_2 because it is a gas. Since it is a gas, he assumes it has negligible mass.)

7. In Experiment 1, the data indicate that after the reaction has proceeded:

A. all of the Na originally present has been converted to Ag.
B. there are more molecules of $NaNO_3$ than there were molecules of $AgNO_3$ at the outset.
C. no NaBr remains.
D. no AgBr remains.

8. Which of the following is (are) conserved in the reaction in Experiment 1?

   I. mass
  II. number of atoms
 III. amount of $AgNO_3$

F. I only
G. I and II only
H. I and III only
J. I, II, and III

9. In Experiment 2, the mass of the weighed products is:

   A. zero.
   B. less than the mass of reactants.
   C. equal to the mass of reactants.
   D. greater than the mass of reactants.

10. Experiment 2 differs from Experiment 1 in that:

   F. the number of atoms is not conserved.
   G. the reaction does not go to completion.
   H. there are no ionic compounds involved.
   J. gas is produced.

11. The student's assumption in neglecting the mass of one of the products in Experiment 2 would most likely lead him to draw which of the following conclusions?

   A. Mass is consumed as the reaction proceeds.
   B. Mass is produced as the reaction proceeds.
   C. Energy is consumed as the reaction proceeds.
   D. Mass is conserved as the reaction proceeds.

12. The student is advised of a means to weigh the CO_2 gas produced in the reaction and finds the mass to be 43 grams. The student can now state that the two experiments:

   F. lead to similar conclusions: neither mass nor atoms are conserved.
   G. lead to similar conclusions: both mass and atoms are conserved.
   H. lead to different conclusions: the number of molecules is not the same for the reactants as for the products.
   J. lead to different conclusions: gases have negligible mass.

Passage III

Jean Baptiste Lamarck hypothesized the process of biological evolution before Charles Darwin was born. Some aspects of Lamarck's ideas and Darwin's ideas are presented below.

Lamarckism

Observations of the fossil record led Lamarck to believe that several lines of descent led to nature's broad diversity of organisms. Old fossils and recent fossils showed patterns leading to the characteristics of modern species. He believed that newer forms were more complex and more "perfectly" adapted to their environment. New adaptations could arise as the environment changed. Body organs that were used to cope with the environment became stronger and larger, while those not used deteriorated. For example, giraffes stretching their necks to reach higher leaves would develop longer necks. In addition, such changes in structure could then be passed on to offspring (these acquired characteristics could be inherited).

Darwinism

Based on the fossil and geologic record, Darwin also came to believe that various modern species were related through descent from common ancestors. He also noted that the great diversity of organisms that he observed during his travels were all very well adapted to their environments. The adaptations, however, did not come about through "coping" or usage. Instead, individuals from a population can each show slight genetic or "heritable" differences (variability) in a trait. If such differences, by chance alone, give the individual some reproductive advantage (he or she can successfully produce more offspring than other members of the population), then more individuals with that trait will make up the next generation. Through this "natural selection" of individuals with characteristics that give them a slight advantage in their particular environment, species appear to become very well-suited to their natural world. However, "perfection" is not a useful term since the environment is constantly changing. The adaptations that are advantageous "today" may not be advantageous "tomorrow" under different conditions.

13. A major difference between Lamarck and Darwin relates to their views on:

   A. the diversity of organisms in the natural world.
   B. the significance of fossils.
   C. the importance of adaptations to the environment.
   D. the way adaptations come about.

14. Which viewpoint supports the idea that present-day species are descended from earlier forms?

   F. Lamarckism
   G. Darwinism
   H. Both viewpoints
   J. Neither viewpoint

15. Which statement might be used by a Darwinist to explain the extinction of a species?

   A. The environment changed, and not enough individuals had traits or adaptations well-suited to the new conditions.
   B. The environment changed, and body parts could not be manipulated enough to adapt to new conditions.
   C. As the environment changed, the individuals present were not "perfect" enough.
   D. As the environment changed, there was no "natural selection."

16. Darwin might dispute the Lamarckian idea of inheriting acquired characteristics by pointing out that:

   F. giraffes with short necks may do just as well as those with long necks.
   G. giraffes that break a leg and walk around on three legs all their lives still do not produce three-legged offspring.
   H. giraffes had shorter necks millions of years ago.
   J. giraffes that break a leg would not be able to reach the highest leaves.

17. Many species of moles live underground in the dark. These species often have small, almost dysfunctional eyes. Which of the following statement(s) would a Lamarckian use to explain this phenomenon?

   I. Moles without eyesight are better adapted for survival underground and therefore produce more offspring.
   II. Disuse of eyes in the dark led to their deterioration in mole species.
   III. Eye deterioration can be transferred to a mole's genes, which are then passed on to the next generation.

   A. I only
   B. II only
   C. II and III only
   D. I, II, and III

18. Which factor is vital to Darwin's ideas, but not to those of Lamarck?

   F. The fossil record
   G. An examination of modern species
   H. The inheritance of adaptations
   J. Chance

19. A few individuals in a population have an adaptation that enables them to tolerate extremely cold temperatures. In their lifetimes, the environment never reaches such extremes. If all other traits are the same among individuals, what would a Darwinist predict about the number of offspring left in the next generation by these individuals, compared to the number left by other members of the population?

   A. These individuals will leave approximately the same number of offspring.
   B. These individuals will leave more offspring.
   C. These individuals will leave fewer offspring.
   D. These individuals will probably not leave any offspring.

Passage IV

Graph I shows the relationship between the relative rates of activity of enzymes A and B and temperature. Graph II shows the relationship between the relative rates of activity of enzymes A and B and pH.

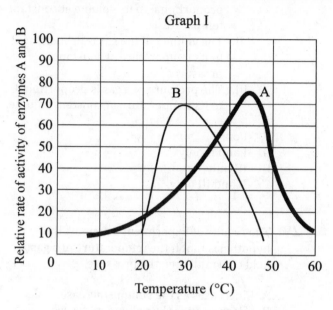

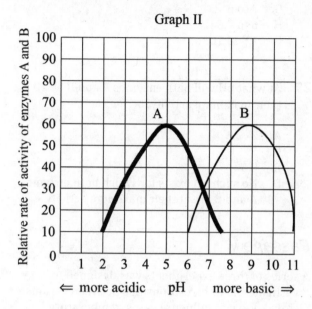

20. Under which conditions is enzyme A most active?

F.   40°C and a pH of 5
G.   45°C and a pH of 5
H.   45°C and a pH of 9
J.   50°C and a pH of 9

21. The optimum environment for enzyme B is:

A.   acidic.
B.   basic.
C.   either acidic or basic.
D.   neutral.

22. At which of the following temperatures do enzymes A and B exhibit approximately the same relative rate of activity?

F.   6.9°C
G.   10°C
H.   37°C
J.   47°C

23. At which pH do both enzymes A and B exhibit approximately the same relative rate of activity?

A.   6.7
B.   10
C.   37
D.   47

24. At what temperature does enzyme A have about half the activity of enzyme B?

F.   20°C
G.   30°C
H.   42°C
J.   53°C

25. At what temperature does enzyme B have about half the activity of enzyme A?

A.   20°C
B.   30°C
C.   42°C
D.   53°C

26. Over which of the following pH ranges will both enzymes A and B be active?

F. 1 to 3
G. 3 to 6
H. 6 to 7.5
J. 7.5 to 10

27. At what pH will both enzymes A and B be at their maximum activity?

A. 2
B. 5
C. 8.5
D. No such pH exists for which both enzymes A and B are at their maximum activity.

Passage V

A series of three experiments was designed to investigate the interrelationships between various factors known to influence gases: temperature (kelvin, K), pressure (atmospheres, atm), volume (liters, L), and the number of moles of gas.

Experiment 1

A gas at 200 K and a volume of 0.30 L was found to have a pressure of 0.40 atm. After the temperature was raised to 400 K while keeping the volume the same, the pressure was found to be 0.80 atm.

Experiment 2

A gas at 200 K had a pressure of 0.50 atm when its volume was 1 L. Its volume was then increased to 2 L at constant temperature. The resulting pressure was 0.25 atm.

Experiment 3

Two moles of a gas were found to occupy 44.8 L at 1 atm and 273 K. Four moles of the same gas are added to the system with temperature and pressure held constant, resulting in a new volume of 134.4 L.

28. Which of the following hypotheses is (are) supported by the results of Experiment 1?

I. The pressure of the gas is proportional to its volume at constant temperature.
II. The volume of the gas is proportional to its temperature at constant pressure.
III. The pressure of a gas is proportional to its temperature at constant volume.

F. I only
G. I and II only
H. III only
J. II and III only

29. The results of Experiment 2 support the hypothesis that if the temperature of a gas is held constant, then the pressure:

A. increases as the volume increases.
B. decreases as the volume increases.
C. does not depend strongly on the volume.
D. Cannot be determined from the given information

30. The result of Experiment 3 supports the hypothesis that if both the pressure and the temperature of a gas are held constant, then the volume:

F. varies inversely with the number of moles of gas.
G. varies directly with the number of moles of gas.
H. is raised to a maximum value of 134.4 L when additional gas is added.
J. does not depend on the number of moles of gas.

31. An experimenter put 0.08 moles of gas into a 4 L flask at 273 K and 0.448 atm. She allowed 0.02 moles of the gas to escape, and she put the remaining gas into a smaller flask that caused the pressure to remain at 0.448 atm, while the temperature was kept constant as well. According to Experiment 3, the volume of the smaller flask must be:

A. 0.06 L.
B. 0.448 L.
C. 3 L.
D. Cannot be determined from the given information

32. Six moles of a gas originally at 0.1 atm and 273 K occupy a volume of 13.4 L. The temperature is then changed to 300 K and the volume changed to 10.0 L. To predict the final pressure on the six moles of gas, a student should use the results of:

    I.   Experiment 1.
   II.   Experiment 2.
  III.   Experiment 3.

F. I only
G. II only
H. I and II only
J. I and III only

33. The final pressure of the gas described in the previous question will be:

A. less than 0.1 atm.
B. equal to 0.1 atm.
C. greater than 0.1 atm.
D. Cannot be determined from the given information

Passage VI

How did life originate on planet Earth? Two opposing views are presented.

Scientist 1

The idea that Earth could have given rise to life independently is mistaken. Life on this planet must have come from elsewhere for several reasons. First of all, complex life appears very suddenly in the geological record. Secondly, all life on Earth has a very similar biochemistry. If life originated on Earth, one would expect regional variations in biochemistry, similar to the variations in species spread over large areas. Finally, the time when life first appeared in the geological record was also a time when large numbers of meteorites struck Earth. The meteorites must have caused life to appear on Earth. The simplest hypothesis is that the meteorites brought life with them.

Scientist 2

Life need not have been imported from outer space. The chemicals required for life existed on the surface of Earth at the time life first appeared. The fact that all life has a similar biochemistry can be explained by considering that any group of chemicals that won the race to life would probably have used the "almost-living" as food. Since we can offer explanations for what happened without relying on a meteorite of unknown composition that might have fallen to Earth, we should stick to hypotheses that have fewer unknowns.

34. Which of the following is an assumption of Scientist 1?

F. Complex life forms can develop quickly.
G. Meteorites burn up as soon as they hit Earth's atmosphere.
H. There is a cause-and-effect relationship between meteors falling and the origin of life.
J. The changes on Earth's surface due to the presence of life attracted meteor showers.

35. Which of the following, if true, most strengthens Scientist 2's argument?

   A. Only five percent more meteors than normal fell on Earth during the time life began.
   B. Only five percent of the meteorites studied contained organic molecules.
   C. A simulation of early Earth chemistry showed the spontaneous formation of complex biomolecules.
   D. Meteorites containing amoebas have been found.

36. Which of the following, if true, most strengthens Scientist 1's argument?

   F. Only five percent more meteors than normal fell on Earth during the time life began.
   G. Only five percent of the meteorites studied contained organic molecules.
   H. A simulation of early Earth chemistry showed the spontaneous formation of complex biomolecules.
   J. Meteorites containing amino acids have been found.

37. With which explanation of the similar biochemistry of all life on Earth would Scientist 1 most likely agree?

   A. A single chemical pathway to life exists.
   B. Life on Earth arose from a single source.
   C. Life on Earth is not varied.
   D. Meteors are simple.

38. With which explanation of the similar biochemistry of all life on Earth would Scientist 2 most likely agree?

   F. A single chemical pathway to life exists.
   G. Life on Earth arose from a single source.
   H. Life on Earth is not varied.
   J. Meteors are simple.

39. Which scientist would be likely to disagree with the idea that life on planets other than Earth could have different biochemistries?

   A. Scientist 1
   B. Scientist 2
   C. Both scientists
   D. Neither scientist

40. Which of the following questions would be the most difficult for Scientist 1 to defend his theory against?

   F. Why was there more meteorite activity earlier in Earth's history?
   G. Why have other meteors not brought other life based on a different biochemistry?
   H. Why did complex life emerge suddenly?
   J. Why should meteor activity have any connection to the origin of life?

41. Could Scientist 2 believe that life exists on other planets without affecting his hypothesis?

   A. Yes, as long as he believes that life elsewhere has a different biochemistry.
   B. Yes, because wherever the chemicals required for life exist, life can begin.
   C. No, because then he has to admit that meteorites brought life from these planets.
   D. No, because then he has to admit that meteorites that came from pieces of similar planets brought life to Earth.

Passage VII

A seismographic station can detect how far away an earthquake occurred, but it cannot determine the direction of the earthquake. Any given station can therefore report that the epicenter of an earthquake occurred somewhere on the circumference of a circle. The map below shows the data recorded for an earthquake at three different seismic stations (A, B, and C). Intersections of the three seismic stations' curves are marked by roman numerals.

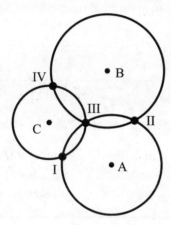

42. Which station was closest to the earthquake epicenter?

    F.   A
    G.   B
    H.   C
    J.   Cannot be determined from the given information

43. Given the information from stations A and B only, which site(s) is (are) possible for the earthquake epicenter?

    A.   I only
    B.   III only
    C.   II and III only
    D.   I and III only

44. Given the information from stations A and C only, which site(s) is (are) possible for the earthquake epicenter?

    F.   I only
    G.   III only
    H.   II and III only
    J.   I and III only

45. Given the information from all three stations, which site(s) is (are) possible for the epicenter?

    A.   I only
    B.   III only
    C.   I and III only
    D.   II and III only

46. If a fourth seismic station gave a report on this earthquake, at what point must its circle meet station A's circle?

    F.   I
    G.   II
    H.   III
    J.   IV

47. If a fourth seismic station gave a report on this earthquake, at what point must its circle meet station C's circle?

    A.   I
    B.   II
    C.   III
    D.   IV

48. What is the minimum number of points where two circumferences from two seismic stations, both measuring the same earthquake, can meet?

    F.   1
    G.   2
    H.   3
    J.   Infinite

Passage VIII

To investigate the factors affecting the rate at which starch is broken down to sugar by the digestive enzyme salivary amylase, two experiments were performed. In both experiments, starch (in the form of a cracker) was mixed in a beaker with the enzyme, and samples were removed every 3 minutes. Special sugar indicators were dipped in the sample to determine the presence of starch (indicating that the cracker had not yet been completely digested).

Experiment 1

To test the effects of different pH levels on enzyme activity rate, one cracker and a standard amount of enzyme were placed in three beakers, each containing buffers of different pH. This procedure was repeated using standard amounts of water in place of the enzyme. All tests were carried out at optimal temperature. Starch and sugar levels (starch/sugar) from selected samples are shown in Table 1.

TABLE 1					
Contents of Beakers	Approximate pH Levels	Levels of Starch/Sugar			
		After 3 minutes	After 9 minutes	After 15 minutes	After 60 minutes
cracker + enzyme + buffer	5	high/none	high/none	high/low	moderate/moderate
	7	moderate/moderate	low/high	none/high	none/high
	9	high/none	high/none	high/low	moderate/moderate
cracker + water + buffer	5	high/none	high/none	high/none	high/none
	7	high/none	high/none	high/none	high/none
	9	high/none	high/none	high/none	high/none

Experiment 2

To test the effects of temperature on enzyme activity rate, one cracker and a standard amount of enzyme were placed in three beakers, each kept at different temperatures. This was also repeated using standard amounts of water in place of the enzyme. All tests were carried out at optimal pH. Starch and sugar levels (starch/sugar) from selected samples are shown in Table 2.

TABLE 2					
Contents of Beakers	Temperatures	Levels of Starch/Sugar			
		After 3 minutes	After 9 minutes	After 15 minutes	After 60 minutes
Cracker + enzyme	25°C	high/none	high/none	high/low	moderate/moderate
	37°C	moderate/moderate	low/high	none/high	none/high
	45°C	high/none	high/none	high/low	moderate/moderate
cracker + water	25°C	high/none	high/none	high/none	high/none
	37°C	high/none	high/none	high/none	high/none
	45°C	high/none	high/none	high/none	high/none

49. Under what conditions does salivary amylase appear to work best?

    A. Any pH level greater than 5 and any temperature greater than 25°C

    B. Any pH level greater than 5 and any temperature less than 45°C

    C. pH level of 9 and temperature equals 37°C

    D. pH level of 7 and temperature equals 37°C

50. The ingredient used as a control for both experiments is the:

    F. cracker.

    G. water.

    H. enzyme.

    J. starch/sugar level.

51. Which of the following hypotheses is supported by the results of Experiment 1?

    A. At the appropriate pH level, water can break down starch, but at a slower rate than salivary amylase can.

    B. After any given time interval, no differences in the effects of the three buffers on salivary amylase activity should be detectable.

    C. Salivary amylase can show activity at each of the three pH levels tested.

    D. The duration of time in which starch and enzyme remain in the beakers should have no effect on the amount of sugar produced.

52. Which of the following experimental designs would test the hypothesis that enzyme concentration can affect the rate of starch digestion?

    F. Using the same pH, temperature, and enzyme levels in all beakers, test additional samples at 90 minutes, 120 minutes, and 240 minutes.

    G. Using different pH, temperature, and enzyme levels in all beakers, test additional samples at 90 minutes, 120 minutes, and 240 minutes.

    H. Using the same pH and temperatures in all beakers, test additional samples with the enzyme at one-half the strength, two times the strength, and four times the strength.

    J. Using the same pH, temperature, and enzyme levels in all beakers, test additional samples after stirring for 3 minutes, 9 minutes, 15 minutes, and 60 minutes.

53. In Experiment 2, an additional beaker was tested at 70°C (cracker + enzyme). After 60 minutes, the sample showed high levels of starch and no sugar. Which of the following best explains this result?

    A. All the starch was destroyed at this high temperature.

    B. The enzyme does not work at all at this high temperature.

    C. Starch cannot be detected at this high temperature.

    D. Iodine and sugar indicators cannot function properly at this high temperature.

54. On the basis of the results of Experiment 1, what would probably occur if Experiment 2 were carried out at a pH level of 5?

    F. Digestion of starch to sugar would slowly begin in the beakers containing crackers plus water.

    G. Overall, digestion of starch to sugar would probably take place less efficiently.

    H. Overall, digestion of starch to sugar would probably take place more efficiently.

    J. The experimental results would not change.

Passage IX

What will the end of the universe be like? Two opposing views are presented.

Scientist 1

The universe will die out with a whimper because the energy of the big bang that created the universe will spread itself out over larger and larger regions of space. Since there is only so much energy in the universe, every cubic foot must hold, on the average, less energy as time goes on. In the end everything will get so cold that all motion will stop. That will be the true end of time.

Scientist 2

The idea that the universe will spread itself too thin and freeze is seriously flawed. Such theories do not take into account the gravitational attractions of the bits of matter in the universe for each other. Gravity can act as a cosmic glue to keep the universe from dissolving into nothingness.

55. Which of the following is a major assumption of Scientist 1?

 A. All matter consists of atoms.
 B. There is a limited amount of energy in the universe.
 C. Gravity does not exist in interstellar space.
 D. The universe is contracting.

56. Which of the following facts, if true, does not help Scientist 2's hypothesis?

 F. It is shown that the galaxies are moving away from each other with a constant speed.
 G. It is shown that the galaxies are moving towards each other with a constant speed.
 H. It is shown that the galaxies are moving towards each other with a constant acceleration.
 J. It is shown that the galaxies are not moving at all relative to each other.

57. It has been calculated that if the universe has a mass greater than or equal to m, then the universe will eventually collapse on itself. Scientist 1 would likely say that the mass of the universe:

 A. is equal to m.
 B. is less than or equal to m.
 C. is greater than m.
 D. is less than m.

58. If Scientist 2 claims that the universe is contracting, what would he expect the average temperature of the universe to be in 10 billion years?

 F. Higher than now
 G. Lower than now
 H. Same as now
 J. No comparison is possible.

59. What must be true about the energy content of the universe if Scientist 1 is correct?

 A. It is increasing.
 B. It is decreasing.
 C. It is a constant.
 D. It increased at the moment of the big bang and decreased afterwards.

60. What would Scientist 1 expect the average temperature of the universe was when it came into existence?

 F. Higher than now
 G. Lower than now
 H. Same as now
 J. No comparison is possible

Passage X

A scientist investigated the number of fossils per cubic foot through several feet in a quarry that has been tectonically stable since deposition. The results are presented below.

LAYER	FISH	SHELLS	PLANTS	LAND REPTILE
1 (TOP)	0	0	3	1
2	0	1	8	2
3	1	10	4	0
4	5	18	1	0
5	7	20	0	0

61. When was the site most likely above water?

    A.   During the formation of Layers 1 and 2
    B.   During the formation of Layers 2 and 3
    C.   During the formation of Layers 1 and 4
    D.   During the formation of Layer 3

62. Was the quarry site most recently above or below water?

    F.   Above
    G.   Below
    H.   Borderline
    J.   Cannot be determined from the given information

63. What assumption is made to relate the fossil record to the surrounding environment?

    A.   No assumption is made.
    B.   Fossils do not affect the environment.
    C.   Fossils are mostly from plants and animals that lived in the region.
    D.   Only animal fossils are important.

64. No trilobite fossils were found. This proves:

    F.   that no trilobites were in the region.
    G.   that the layers were formed before trilobites existed.
    H.   that the layers were formed after the trilobites died out.
    J.   nothing about the presence of the trilobite in the region.

65. A nautilus shell was found in Layer 3. This proves that:

    A.   Layer 3 formed while the nautilus still existed.
    B.   Layer 3 is newer than Layer 2.
    C.   Layer 3 is older than Layer 2.
    D.   the nautilus once lived on land.

66. After quarry excavation is completed, where will the newest layer form?

    F.   Under Layer 4
    G.   Over Layer 1
    H.   Across all the layers
    J.   Layers no longer form.

STRATEGY SUMMARY

General Strategies

Science items test your reasoning skills, not your scientific knowledge. So, most of the passages have all of the information that you will need to answer the items. In some cases, background information at the level of your high school general science courses is required, but do not assume data that is not given. The following are general strategies for the Science Test:

1. Before reading any Science passage, *quickly glance over all of the passages and code them according to passage-type* in order to determine the order in which you will attack them. Identifying and coding the passages should take no more than five seconds each.

2. *Do NOT preview the item stems.* Since the Science item stems tend to be confusing without having first read the corresponding passage, previewing them will only confuse you and slow you down.

3. It is important to only *read the passage thoroughly once*, rather than to skim over it several times. The material can be difficult to understand; thus, it is important to read thoughtfully and carefully. *Be an active reader.* Use your pencil to underline key words and points of information. That way, you will be able to locate them easily when answering the items.

4. When a Science passage includes tables or graphs, make sure that you *read and understand the labels* on axes, columns, and rows. You need to know what information is being presented and what units of measure are being used.

5. Many passages will contain much more information than you need to answer a particular item. In your search for a logical conclusion, *do not be misled by data that does not relate to the item at hand.*

6. In Data Representation passages, tables and graphs present results, often of observations or experiments. Corresponding items will usually ask you to spot patterns in the data, so *look for trends*, such as upward movement, downward movement, inverse variation, etc.

7. The experiments described in Research Summary passages are based on scientific assumptions. However, if an assumption is faulty, the experiment may not prove what it claims, and conclusions drawn from it may therefore be invalid. So, for items that ask about the validity of a scientific conclusion, *consider the validity of any underlying assumptions.*

8. The arguments presented in Conflicting Viewpoints passages are also based on scientific assumptions. Again, *if the assumption is wrong, the entire argument is open to challenge.* Assumptions that are based on scientific fact add strength to an argument; faulty assumptions weaken an argument.

9. Offering the assumptions that you started with as proof of your argument is called circular reasoning, and this type of proof is not acceptable. For that reason, any conclusions discussed in Science passages or offered as answer choices must be based on additional evidence (e.g., experiments) to be valid. *Beware of any conclusions that are nothing more than a restatement of an underlying premise.*

10. All of the information that you need to answer the items is provided in the passage—do not infer any information that is not given or relate any previous experience to the passage. *Pay attention to material noted with an asterisk.*

11. *Transcribe your answers from the test booklet to the answer sheet in groups (by passage).* However, when you arrive at the last passage, transcribe each answer as it is determined.

Strategies for Each Passage-Type

- *Data Representation Passages:* When given data in the form of a graph or a chart, pay particular attention to the scale, units, legend, and other noted information.

- *Research Summary Passages:* When given multiple experiments, identify the controls and variables. Note that the controls must remain the same and that variables can only change one at a time in all experiments.

- *Conflicting Viewpoints Passages:* When given two points of view on a topic, identify the main points of difference and the logical value of each argument. After you understand the nature of the passage, attack the items.

Strategies for Each Item-Type

- *Comprehension Items:* Recognize basic concepts. Read carefully. Make sure that your answers consider appropriate scales and units. Also, note the difference between absolute and percentage changes.

- *Analysis Items:* Identify relationships and trends. Pay particular attention to direct and inverse relationships.

- *Application Items:* Draw conclusions, predict outcomes, and synthesize new information. In answering Application items, beware of the following terms: "all," "none," "always," and "never." Remember that a single case of contradictory evidence is all that is necessary to disprove an absolute theory.

Cambridge Practice Test Reinforcement

Building Basic Skills

Published in *Essential Skills, 13th Edition*

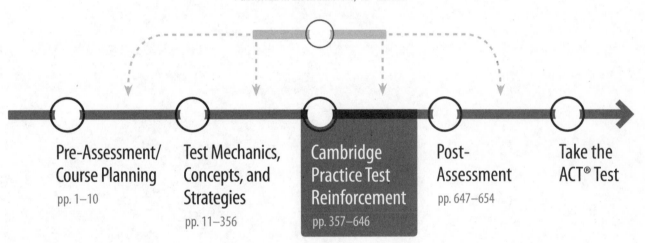

Pre-Assessment/
Course Planning

pp. 1–10

Test Mechanics,
Concepts, and
Strategies

pp. 11–356

Cambridge
Practice Test
Reinforcement

pp. 357–646

Post-
Assessment

pp. 647–654

Take the
ACT® Test

CAMBRIDGE
VICTORY FOR THE
ACT® TEST

Directed Study Practice Test

Outline

I. **Section 1:** English (pp. 361–393)

II. **Section 2:** Mathematics (pp. 394–418)

III. **Section 3:** Reading (pp. 419–434)

IV. **Section 4:** Science (pp. 435–455)

V. **Section 5:** Writing (Optional) (pp. 456–460)

SECTION 1: ENGLISH TEST
75 Items

DIRECTIONS: In the passages below, certain parts of the sentences have been underlined and numbered. In the right-hand column, you will find different ways of writing each underlined part; the original version is indicated by the "NO CHANGE" option. For each item, select the choice that best expresses the intended idea, is most acceptable in standard written English, or is most consistent with the overall tone and style of the passage.

There are also items that ask about a section of the passage or the passage as a whole. These items do not refer to an underlined portion of the passage; these items are preceded by statements that are enclosed in boxes.

Read the passage through once before you begin to answer the accompanying items. Finding the answers to certain items may depend on looking at material that appears several sentences beyond the item. So, be sure that you have read far enough ahead before you select your answer choice.

PASSAGE I

An American Christmas

As befits a nation made up of immigrants from all over the Christian world, Americans have no distinctive Christmas <u>symbols we</u> have taken the
₁
symbols of all the nations and made them our own. The Christmas tree, the holly and the ivy, the mistletoe, the exchange of gifts, the myth of Santa Claus, the carols of all nations, the plum pudding, and the wassail bowl are all elements in the American Christmas of the early

1. **A.** NO CHANGE
   B. symbols but, we
   C. symbols; but we
   D. symbols: but we

1. **(C)** *English/Usage and Mechanics/Punctuation/Semicolons.* The original sentence is incorrect because two independent clauses are spliced together. The two clauses could be split into separate sentences, but if they are going to be a single sentence, they must be joined with a conjunction and appropriate punctuation. (C) uses the second approach. In this case, a semicolon is a good choice for punctuation because the first clause already includes a dependent element joined by a comma. The stronger semicolon will alert the reader to the main break in the logic of the sentence. In (B), a comma, if used, would have to come before, not after, the conjunction "but." (D) is not the appropriate use of a colon.

twenty-first century <u>as we know it today</u>. Though we
₂

have no Christmas symbols of our own, the American

Christmas still has a distinctive aura by virtue of two

<u>character</u> elements.
₃

The first of these <u>is when</u>, as might be expected
₄

in a nation as dedicated to the carrying on of business

as the American nation, the dominant role of the

2. **F.** NO CHANGE
   G. as it is known today
   H. known as it is today
   J. OMIT the underlined portion.

2. **(J)** *English/Rhetorical Skills/Style/Conciseness.*
   The original sentence is incorrect because the
   underlined portion provides information that is
   simply unnecessary. It adds no new or required
   information to the sentence; and, most importantly, the sentence is improved if the underlined
   material is removed. (J) is the correct answer
   choice because it omits the underlined portion.

3. **A.** NO CHANGE
   B. characters
   C. characterized
   D. characteristic

3. **(D)** *English/Usage and Mechanics/Grammar
   and Usage/Adjectives versus Adverbs.* The
   original sentence is incorrect because it includes
   a usage error. As currently written, the sentence
   has "character" (a noun) modifying "elements"
   (a noun). However, a noun cannot modify a
   noun; only an adjective can modify a noun. (D)
   is the correct answer choice because it supplies
   the correct adjective ("characteristic," which
   means "distinctive") for modifying "elements."

4. **F.** NO CHANGE
   G. is that
   H. is which
   J. is where

4. **(G)** *English/Usage and Mechanics/Grammar
   and Usage/Diction.* The original sentence is
   incorrect because it is not idiomatic.
   Specifically, the phrase "is when" is not an
   acceptable idiom. The correct, idiomatic phrase
   is "is that." (G) is the correct answer because it
   supplies the required phrase.

Christmas festivities <u>has come</u> to serve as a stimulus
                       5

to retail business. The themes of Christmas advertising

begin to appear as early as September, and the open

season on Christmas shopping <u>began</u> in November.
                                  6

5. A. NO CHANGE
  B. have come
  C. having come
  D. comes

5. (A) *English/Usage and Mechanics/No Change.*
The original sentence is correct. The singular
verb phrase ("has come") agrees with the
singular subject ("the dominant role") of the
sentence. In addition, the original sentence also
supplies the past tense verb form required here.
(B) is incorrect because a plural verb phrase
("have come") does not agree with a singular
subject ("the dominant role"). (C) is incorrect
because a gerund verb phrase ("having come")
cannot serve as the main verb of an independent
clause. (D) is incorrect because a present tense
verb ("comes") is not needed here; instead, a
past tense verb is required.

6. F. NO CHANGE
  G. beginning
  H. begins
  J. will begin

6. (H) *English/Usage and Mechanics/Grammar
and Usage/Verb Tense.* The original sentence is
incorrect because it includes a verb tense error.
The past tense "began" is inconsistent with the
time frame of the sentence, as indicated by the
present tense "begin" used earlier. (The author is
describing the current situation.) (H) corrects the
error by using the present tense verb "begins."
(J) is incorrect because "will begin" is the future
tense and fails to correct the verb tense
inconsistency. Finally, as for (G), "beginning" is
the participle of the verb "to begin." The
participle, or "-ing" form, cannot be used as the
main verb of the clause.

Fifty years ago, Thanksgiving Day was regarded <u>like it</u>
₇

<u>was</u> the opening day of the season for Christmas
₇

shopping; today, the season opens immediately after

Halloween. Thus, virtually a whole month has been

added to the Christmas <u>season—for</u> shopping purposes.
₈

7. A. NO CHANGE
   B. like as
   C. as
   D. like

7. (C) *English/Usage and Mechanics/Grammar and Usage/Diction.* The original sentence is incorrect because it includes a word choice error. Specifically, "like it was" is an awkward, needlessly wordy, and non-standard phrase that means the same thing as "as." (C) is the correct answer choice because it supplies the simple and more direct word that is required here. As for the other answer choices, (B) and (D) are both incorrect because they are simply not idiomatic phrases; in other words, neither "regarded like" nor "regarded like as" are recognized as acceptable ways of making a comparison.

8. Which of the following would NOT be an acceptable way of punctuating the underlined part?

   F. season—for (NO CHANGE)
   G. season. For
   H. season, for
   J. season for

8. (G) *English/Usage and Mechanics/Sentence Structure/Fragments.* The original sentence is acceptable as are (H) and (J). (G), however, is not acceptable because the period would create a sentence fragment of the word grouping introduced by "For." Notice that each acceptable punctuation alternative gives the sentence a slightly difference emphasis. The dash strongly emphasizes the point that the purpose is "shopping," while no punctuation makes the same point with relatively little emphasis. Using a comma stresses the point to a degree somewhere between the dash and no punctuation at all. All are acceptable with the difference being the author's intended meaning.

Second, the <u>nations</u> season of Christmas
₉

festivities has insensibly combined with the New

Year's celebration into one lengthened period of

Saturnalia. This starts with office parties a few days

before <u>Christmas continues</u> on Christmas Eve, now the
₁₀

occasion in America of one of two large-scale revels

that mark the season; and continues in spirited euphoria

until New Year's Eve, the second of the large-scale

revels. New Year's Day is spent resting, possibly

9. **A.** NO CHANGE
   B. nation's
   C. nations'
   D. nation

9. **(B)** *English/Usage and Mechanics/Punctuation/Apostrophes.* The original sentence is incorrect because it includes a punctuation error. Specifically, an apostrophe is required to show possession. In this instance, the season belongs to the nation. As for the other answer choices, (C) is incorrect because the apostrophe makes "nation" plural when the singular is intended by the author. (D) is incorrect for the same reason as the original—it needs an apostrophe to show possession.

10. **F.** NO CHANGE
    G. Christmas; continues
    H. as Christmas continues
    J. Christmas as continues

10. **(G)** *English/Usage and Mechanics/Punctuation/Commas.* The original sentence is incorrect because it includes a punctuation error. Specifically, the sentence includes a series of singular verbs ("starts … continues … continues") that all agree with the singular subject ("This") of the sentence. The second and third verbs should be preceded by a semicolon. (G) is the correct answer choice because it supplies the required punctuation. As for the other answer choices, (H) and (J) are both incorrect because they result in sentences that are grammatically incorrect as well as incomprehensible.

regretting <u>somebody's</u> excesses, and <u>watching football</u>
                    11   12

<u>games on television</u>.
          12

11. **A.** NO CHANGE
     B. everyone's
     C. someone's
     D. one's

11. **(D)** *English/Usage and Mechanics/Grammar and Usage/Pronoun Usage.* The original sentence is incorrect because it includes a pronoun usage error. Specifically, according to the logic of the sentence, New Year's Day would not be spent regretting the excesses of some unidentified person ("somebody's excesses"); instead, it would be spent regretting one's own excesses ("one's excesses"). (D) is the correct answer choice because it supplies the correct possessive pronoun. As for the other answer choices, (B) and (C) are incorrect for the same reason as the original.

12. **F.** NO CHANGE
     G. watching, football games on television
     H. watching, football games, on television
     J. watching football, games on television

12. **(F)** *English/Usage and Mechanics/Punctuation/No Change.* The original sentence is correct. The comma after "excesses" correctly completes the series. No comma is needed in the underlined portion. (H) is incorrect because the pattern of commas suggests that "football games" is an appositive of "watching," but the two are not synonymous. (G) and (J) are both incorrect because the commas in these choices disrupt the logical flow of the sentence.

PASSAGE II

Scientific Advances Pose Global Risks

[1]

The history of modern pollution problems <u>show</u>
                                                    13
that most have resulted from negligence and ignorance.
We have an appalling tendency to interfere with nature
before all of the possible consequences of our actions

have been studied <u>into completeness</u>. We produce and
                            14
distribute radioactive substances, synthetic chemicals
and fibers, and many other potent compounds before

13. **A.** NO CHANGE
    B. shown
    C. shows
    D. showed

13. **(C)** *English/Usage and Mechanics/Grammar and Usage/Subject-Verb Agreement.* The original sentence is incorrect due to an error involving agreement. The actual subject of the sentence is "history," not "problems." In this sentence, "show" (a plural verb) does not agree with "history" (a singular subject). (C) is the correct answer choice because it supplies a singular verb ("shows") that agrees with the singular subject ("history") of the sentence. As for the other answer choices, (B) and (D) are incorrect because neither a passive, past tense verb ("shown") nor an active, past tense verb ("showed") are appropriate in this context. Only an active, present tense verb ("shows") is appropriate here.

14. **F.** NO CHANGE
    G. as completely as possible
    H. for completeness
    J. a lot

14. **(G)** *English/Rhetorical Skills/Style/Idiomatic Expression.* The original sentence is incorrect because it is not idiomatic. The correct, idiomatic phrase is "as completely as possible." So, (G) is the correct answer choice. As for the other answer choices, (H) is incorrect for the same reason as the original. (J) is incorrect because the phrase "studied a lot" is an example of informal usage.

fully comprehending their <u>effects</u> on living organisms.
15

Synthetic means man-made. Many of today's fashions
16

are made with synthetic fibers. Our education is
16

dangerously incomplete.

15. A. NO CHANGE
    B. effectiveness
    C. affect
    D. affects

15. **(A) *English/Usage and Mechanics/No Change.***
The original sentence is correct. "Effects" is a
plural noun that means "results," and it supplies
the meaning required in this context. As for the
other answer choices, (B) is incorrect because
"effectiveness" means "efficiency," which does
not supply the required meaning. (C) and (D) are
both incorrect because, when used as a noun,
"affect" means "manner" or "attitude"; neither of
those meanings is appropriate here.

16. F. NO CHANGE
    G. Synthetic fibers are man-made.
    H. Many of today's fashions are made with
       synthetic fibers.
    J. OMIT the underlined portion.

16. **(J) *English/Rhetorical Skills/Strategy/Appro-
priate Supporting Material.*** The original
sentence is incorrect because the underlined
portion is redundant. It is made clear in the third
sentence of the passage that "synthetic" means
"artificial" or "man-made" ("We produce …
synthetic chemicals and fibers."); in addition,
there is no logical reason to include the
information about current fashions and synthetic
fibers. (J) is the correct answer choice because it
omits the unnecessary information. As for the
other answer choices, (G) and (H) are both
incorrect for the same reason as the original.

[2]

It will be argued that the purpose of science is to move into unknown <u>territory;</u> to explore, and to discover. It can be said that similar risks have been taken before and that these risks are necessary to

technological progress. 18

17. **A.** NO CHANGE
   B. territory:
   C. territory,
   D. territory

17. **(C)** *English/Usage and Mechanics/Punctuation/Commas.* The original sentence is incorrect because it includes a punctuation error. Specifically, phrases or clauses in a series should be separated by commas unless the phrases or clauses themselves contain commas; in that case, the phrases or clauses should be separated by semicolons. In this sentence, the phrases themselves do not include commas, so commas should be used to separate them. Therefore, (C) is the correct answer choice.

18. The writer could most effectively bolster the essay at this point by:

   F. including an example of one of the risks argued by some to be necessary for technological progress.
   G. adding rhetorical emphasis with the sentence "The risks are necessary."
   H. briefly describing an unknown territory.
   J. defining the word *science.*

18. **(F)** *English/Rhetorical Skills/Strategy/Appropriate Supporting Material.* (F) is the correct answer choice. At this point, it would be best to add a specific example of a risk that it is necessary to undertake in order to achieve technological progress. Such an example would make the author's argument more concrete and vivid for the reader. As for the other answer choices, (G) is incorrect because a rhetorical device would be less effective than a concrete example. (H) is incorrect because the topic at hand is risk and its relationship to technological progress. Finally, (J) is incorrect because the definition of "science" is commonly understood; it is not necessary to define it.

[3]

These arguments overlook <u>an important</u> element.
[19]
In the past, risks taken in the name of scientific

progress were restricted to a small place and brief

period of time. The effects of the processes we now

strive to master are <u>not either</u> localized nor brief. Air
[20]
pollution covers vast urban areas. Ocean pollutants

have been discovered in nearly every part of the world.

Synthetic chemicals spread over huge stretches of

forest and farmland may remain in the soil <u>for decades</u>
[21]
<u>and years to come</u>. Radioactive pollutants will be
[21]
found in the biosphere for generations. The size and

---

19. A. NO CHANGE
  B. a important
  C. importance
  D. important

19. (A) *English/Usage and Mechanics/No Change.*
The original sentence is correct. "An" is used before singular nouns or adjectives that begin with a vowel. (B) is incorrect because "a" is used only before singular nouns or adjectives that begin with consonants. (C) is incorrect because a noun ("importance") cannot modify a noun ("element"). Finally, (D) is incorrect because an adjective that modifies a singular noun must always be preceded by an article (i.e., "a," "an," or "the").

20. F. NO CHANGE
  G. either
  H. not neither
  J. neither

20. (J) *English/Usage and Mechanics/Grammar and Usage/Diction.* The original sentence is incorrect because it is not idiomatic. The correct idiomatic phrase is "neither … nor." So, (J) is the correct answer choice. As for the other answer choices, (G) and (H) are both incorrect for the same reason as the original.

21. A. NO CHANGE
  B. for decades
  C. for years to come in decades
  D. for decades and years

21. (B) *English/Rhetorical Skills/Style/Conciseness.* The original sentence is incorrect because the underlined portion includes redundant information. (B) is the correct answer choice since it eliminates the superfluous phrase. As for the other answer choices, (C) is incorrect for two reasons: first, it is redundant; second, it is grammatically incorrect. (D) is incorrect for the same reason as the original.

persistent of these problems have grown with the
22

expanding power of modern science.

[4]

One might also argue that the hazards of modern

pollutants are small comparison for the dangers
23

associated with other human activity. No estimate of

the actual harm done by smog, fallout, or chemical

residues can obscure the reality that the risks are being

taken before being fully understood.

[5]

The importance of these issues lies in the failure

of science to predict and control. Human intervention
24

into natural processes. The true measure of the danger

is represented by the hazards we will encounter if we

enter the new age of technology without first

evaluating our responsibility to the environment.

22. **F.** NO CHANGE
    G. persistence
    H. persevering
    J. persisting

22. **(G)** *English/Usage and Mechanics/Grammar and Usage/Nouns and Noun Clauses* and *Sentence Structure/Faulty Parallelism.* The original sentence is incorrect due to a lack of parallelism. Specifically, "persistent" (an adjective) is not the same part of speech as "size" (a noun). (G) is the correct answer choice because it makes the needed correction ("The size and persistence of these problems…"). As for the other answer choices, (H) and (J) are incorrect for the same reason as the original.

23. **A.** NO CHANGE
    B. consideration for
    C. comparing with
    D. compared to

23. **(D)** *English/Usage and Mechanics/Grammar and Usage/Diction.* The original sentence is incorrect due to a word choice error. The sentence requires a past tense verb to complete it successfully. (D) is the correct answer choice because it supplies the required verb. As for the other answer choices, (B) and (C) are both incorrect for the same reason as the original.

24. **F.** NO CHANGE
    G. control human
    H. control; human
    J. control and human

24. **(G)** *English/Usage and Mechanics/Sentence Structure/Fragments.* The original is incorrect because the word grouping following the period is a fragment. (G) solves the problem by integrating the fragment into the main part of the sentence as a direct object. As for the other answer choices, (H) is incorrect for the same reason as the original. (J) is incorrect because the conjunction "and" should not appear between a verb phrase and the object of that verb phrase.

Items #25–26 ask about the preceding passage as a whole.

25. Choose the order of paragraph numbers that will make the essay's structure most logical.

A. NO CHANGE
B. 2, 4, 3, 1, 5
C. 1, 3, 2, 4, 5
D. 5, 1, 2, 3, 4

25. **(A) *English/Rhetorical Skills/Organization/ Passage-Level Structure.*** The original order is correct. Paragraph 1 introduces the topic of the entire essay. Only (A) and (C) have Paragraph 1 as the first paragraph, so eliminate (B) and (D). The only difference between (A) and (C) is whether Paragraph 2 or Paragraph 3 should come next. Paragraph 3 begins with "These arguments overlook an important element," so it should be preceded by a paragraph where arguments are made, and this is Paragraph 2. So, (A) is correct.

26. This essay was probably intended for readers who:

F. lack an understanding of the history of technology.
G. are authorities on pollution and its causes.
H. are interested in becoming more aware of our environmental problems and the possible solutions to these problems.
J. have worked with radioactive substances.

26. **(H) *English/Rhetorical Skills/Strategy/Audience.*** (H) is the correct answer choice. The topic of the essay is pollution problems in general, and the level of detail suggests that the essay is aimed at the average reader who is interested in becoming more aware. As for the other answer choices, (F) is incorrect because the topic of the essay is pollution problems in general (and not a history of technology). (G) is incorrect because authorities on this subject would expect a much more technical and specialized level of detail. Finally, (J) is incorrect because the topic of the essay is pollution problems in general (and not just problems related to radioactive substances).

PASSAGE III

The Myth of a Criminal Physique

[1]

Can you spot a criminal by his physical characteristics? [27] When the science of criminology was founded in the nineteenth century, an imaginative Italian observer decided that criminals are

27. Is the use of a question appropriate to begin Paragraph 1?

    A. No, because questions are not used in formal writing.
    B. No, because the question is not answered.
    C. Yes, because it varies sentence structure and interests the reader.
    D. Yes, because an essay should always begin with a question.

27. **(C)** *English/Rhetorical Skills/Strategy/Effective Opening Sentence.* (C) is the correct answer choice. The question clearly introduces the main subject of the essay; in addition, it piques the reader's interest. (A) is incorrect because questions are frequently used in formal writing. (B) is incorrect for two reasons: first, the passage does answer the question asked here; second, even if the passage did not answer the question, formal writing can include unanswered or unanswerable questions. Finally, (D) is incorrect because an essay does not have to begin with a question.

born that way and are distinguished by certainly
                                              28
physical characteristics. They are, he claimed, "a
    28
special species, a subspecies having distinct physical
and mental characteristics. In general, all criminals
have long, large, protruding ears; abundant hair; a thin
beard; prominent front sinuses; a protruding chin; and

28.   F. NO CHANGE
    G. certain physically
    H. certain physical
    J. certainly physically

28. **(H)** *English/Usage and Mechanics/Grammar and Usage/Adjectives versus Adverbs.* The original sentence is incorrect because "certain" is intended to modify the noun phrase "physical characteristics." (H) correctly provides the adjective form "certain." (G) is incorrect because "physical" modifies the noun "characteristics" and so the adjective form is needed. As for (J), it fails to correct the original and changes "physical" to the adverb form "physically."

large cheekbones." According to his <u>theory, murderers</u>
₂₉

<u>have</u> cold, glassy eyes, strong jaws, large cheekbones,
₂₉

and curly hair.

[2]

But the myth did not die <u>easily</u>. During the
₃₀

1930s, a German criminologist, Gustav Aschaffenburg,

declared that stout, squat people with large abdomens

are more <u>like</u> to be occasional offenders, while slender
₃₁

builds and slight muscular development are common

among habitual offenders. In the 1940s, according to

writer Jessica Mitford, a group of Harvard sociologists

---

29. **A.** NO CHANGE.
     B. theory murderers, have
     C. theory, murderers, have
     D. theory, murderers have,

29. (A) *English/Usage and Mechanics/No Change.* The original is correct. (B) is wrong because it deletes the commas used to signal the end of the introductory phrase and it inserts a comma between the subject and the verb (a commonly tested error). (C) also makes this second error. Finally, (D) inserts an unnecessary comma between the verb and the direct object (another commonly tested error).

30. **F.** NO CHANGE
     G. easy
     H. easiest
     J. easier

30. (F) *English/Usage and Mechanics/No Change.* The original sentence is correct. "Easily" is an adverb that properly modifies the verb "die." As for the other answer choices, they are all incorrect because they are adjectives. Adjectives cannot modify verbs, so (G), (H), and (J) must be incorrect.

31. **A.** NO CHANGE
     B. likely
     C. likely apt
     D. possible

31. (B) *English/Usage and Mechanics/Grammar and Usage/Diction.* The original sentence is incorrect due to a diction error. Specifically, "like" means "similar" or "comparable" and does not provide the meaning required here. (B) is the correct answer choice because "likely" provides the required meaning; it means "probable" or "apt." As for the other answer choices, (C) is incorrect because "likely apt" is a redundant phrase; "likely" and "apt" are synonyms, so there is no reason to include both in the same phrase. Finally, (D) is incorrect because "possible" does not provide the required meaning.

who study sociology decided that criminals are most
32

likely to be "mesomorphs," muscular types with large

trunks who walk assertively, talk noisily, and behave

aggressively. The Harvard scholars warned readers to

watch out for people with them.
33

---

32. F. NO CHANGE
G. whom study sociological changes,
H. who studied sociology,
J. OMIT the underlined portion.

32. (J) English/Rhetorical Skills/Style/Conciseness.
The original sentence is incorrect because the
underlined portion is redundant. Sociologists are,
by definition, people who study sociology, so
there is no reason to include the underlined
portion in the sentence. (J) is the correct answer
choice because it makes the required correction.
As for the other answer choices, (G) is incorrect
for three reasons: first, it is incorrect for the
same reason as the original; second, an objective
pronoun ("whom") should not be used when
referring to the subject ("sociologists") in a
sentence; third, the comma after "changes"
introduces a comma splice into the sentence.
Finally, (H) is incorrect for two reasons: first, it
is incorrect for the same reason as the original;
second, the comma after "sociology" introduces
a comma splice into the sentence.

33. A. NO CHANGE
B. them characteristics
C. them kind of characteristics
D. those characteristics

**33. (D) English/Usage and Mechanics/Grammar
and Usage/Pronoun Usage.** The original
sentence is incorrect because the pronoun
"them" does not have a clear antecedent. The
sentence means to refer to the characteristics
listed, and for that the writer needs a plural
reference. The correct choice, (D), uses the
demonstrative adjective "those," which is plural,
to modify the plural "characteristics." (B) and
(C) both use the plural "characteristics" but
exhibit informal usage.

[3]

<u>Around about</u> the turn of the twentieth century, a
34

British physician made a detailed study of the faces of

three thousand convicts and <u>compared</u> them with a like
35

number of English college students, measuring the

<u>noses ears eyebrows and chins</u> of both groups. He
36

could find no correlation among physical types and

criminal behavior.

34. **F.** NO CHANGE
G. At about
H. Around
J. OMIT the underlined portion.

34. **(H)** *English/Rhetorical Skills/Style/Idiomatic Expression.* The original sentence is incorrect because it includes an example of non-standard English. (H) is the correct answer choice because "around" successfully completes the sentence. As for the other answer choices, (G) is incorrect for the same reason as the original. (J) is incorrect because the initial clause would then become a fragment (rather than a fully formed introductory adverbial clause).

35. **A.** NO CHANGE
B. compare
C. compares
D. comparing

35. **(A)** *English/Usage and Mechanics/No Change.* The original sentence is correct. "Compared" (a past tense verb) is consistent with the past tense verb ("made") used earlier in the sentence. As for the other answer choices, they are all incorrect because they are not consistent with the past tense verb used earlier in the sentence.

36. **F.** NO CHANGE
G. noses ears and eyebrows and chins
H. noses; ears; eyebrows and chins
J. noses, ears, eyebrows, and chins

36. **(J)** *English/Usage and Mechanics/Punctuation/Commas.* The original sentence is incorrect due to a punctuation error (the series needs to be separated by commas). (J) is the correct answer choice because it supplies the required punctuation. As for the other answer choices, (G) is incorrect for two reasons: first, it is incorrect for the same reason as the original; second, it inserts "and" between the second and third items in the list, whereas "and" should only appear between the third and fourth items. (H) is incorrect because items in a list should be separated by semicolons only if the items themselves include commas.

Items #37–38 ask about the preceding passage as a whole.

37. This essay was most probably excerpted from a:

   A. college textbook on the history of criminology.
   B. manual of techniques for forensic investigators.
   C. news article on recent discoveries in police science.
   D. biography of Gustav Aschaffenburg.

37. **(A) *English/Rhetorical Skills/Strategy/Audience.*** (A) is the correct answer choice. The level of detail is consistent with a textbook, and the subject is clearly the history of the study of criminals. (B) is wrong because there is not a lot of technical detail in the essay and because the writer discredits the theories discussed. (C) is wrong because the theories discussed are old, not new. (D) is incorrect because the essay focuses on criminology in general and not on Aschaffenburg specifically.

38. Choose the order of paragraph numbers that will make the essay's structure most logical.

   F. NO CHANGE
   G. 3, 2, 1
   H. 1, 3, 2
   J. 2, 3, 1

38. **(H) *English/Rhetorical Skills/Organization/ Passage-Level Structure.*** (H) is the correct answer choice. The most logical ordering of the paragraphs will put them in chronological order. Paragraph 1 refers to the nineteenth century. Paragraph 3 refers to the "turn of the century." Paragraph 2 refers to the 1930s and the 1940s.

PASSAGE IV

The Changing Scientific Workplace

[1]

Many researchers can be of greatest service to a

company by <u>sticking around</u> in the laboratory. A single
₃₉

39. A. NO CHANGE
  B. remaining
  C. remaining around
  D. sticking up

39. (B) *English/Rhetorical Skills/Style/Idiomatic Expression.* The original sentence is incorrect due to an idiomatic expression error. (B) is the correct answer choice because it supplies the word required here. As for the other answer choices, (C) and (D) are incorrect for the same reason as the original.

outstanding discovery <u>may of had</u> a far greater impact
₄₀

on the company's five-year profit picture than the

40. F. NO CHANGE
  G. maybe
  H. might of had
  J. may have

40. (J) *English/Usage and Mechanics/Grammar and Usage/Diction.* The original sentence is incorrect because it confuses "of" with "have." In informal writing, people often make the mistake of saying "I should of stayed in bed" but they mean "I should have stayed in bed." The error is likely due to the similarity of the sounds in spoken English, but it should not be used in written English.

activities of even the <u>most able</u> administrator. It is
₄₁

simply good sense—and good economics—to allow

qualified researchers to continue their work. Granting

these researchers maximum freedom to explore their

scientific ideas is also eminently good sense.

41. A. NO CHANGE
  B. most ablest
  C. more ablest
  D. most abled

41. (A) *English/Usage and Mechanics/No Change.* The original sentence is correct. The correct, superlative form of "able" is "most able." As for the other answer choices, (B), (C), and (D) are all incorrect because they do not supply the correct, superlative form of "able."

[2]

In recent <u>years however</u> this theory has fallen
42

into wide <u>disrepair</u>. Companies find that many
43

researchers continue to be highly productive

throughout their careers. There is every reason to allow

these researchers to continue their pioneering work.

[3]

Some years ago, the theory was rampant that

after the age of about 40, the average researcher

42. F. NO CHANGE
G. years, however
H. years, however,
J. years however,

42. (H) *English/Usage and Mechanics/Punctuation/Commas.* The original sentence is incorrect due to a punctuation error. Specifically, conjunctive phrases ("however," "meanwhile," and "instead") should be set off by commas when they are inserted into the sentence to signal the reader of a continuation or a reversal of thought. As for (G) and (J), they are incorrect because they do not supply the necessary pair of commas.

43. A. NO CHANGE
B. argument
C. ill repute
D. disrepute

43. (D) *English/Usage and Mechanics/Grammar and Usage/Diction.* The original sentence is incorrect due an error involving word choice. Specifically, a word is required here which can be used to describe the status or reputation of an idea ("this theory"). (D) is the correct answer choice because "disrepute" means "having a bad reputation" and is commonly used to describe ideas. As for the other answer choices, (A) is incorrect because "disrepair" is not a word used to describe ideas; instead, it is used to describe physical objects (a building, a bridge, etc.). (B) is incorrect because the phrase "fallen into . . . argument" is simply not idiomatic. Finally, (C) is incorrect because "ill repute" is not a phrase used to describe ideas; instead, it is used to describe people ("a woman of ill repute").

380 CAMBRIDGE PRACTICE TEST REINFORCEMENT

began losing <u>their</u> creative spark. The chance of one
₄₄

making a major discovery was believed to drop off

sharply. Hence, there really wasn't much point to

encouraging a person of 45 or 50 to do research. |45|

[4]

Companies are also convinced that the traditional

guideposts in establishing salaries are not completely

44. **F.** NO CHANGE
    G. its
    H. his or her
    J. theirs

44. **(H)** *English/Usage and Mechanics/Grammar and Usage/Pronoun Usage.* The original sentence is incorrect due to an error in pronoun-antecedent agreement. Specifically, "their" (a plural pronoun) does not agree with "researcher" (a singular noun). (H) is the correct answer choice because it supplies a pair of singular pronouns ("his or her") that agrees with "researcher" (a singular noun). As for the other answer choices, (G) is incorrect because "its" (an impersonal pronoun) does not agree with "researcher" (a personal noun). (J) is incorrect for the same reason as the original.

45. If, at this point in the essay, the writer wanted to increase the information about creative contributions from researchers, which of the following additions would be most relevant to the passage as a whole?

    A. A bibliography of books about retirement
    B. A description of a few of the contributions older researchers have made to science
    C. A list of today's most prominent researchers
    D. A brief description of a model retirement benefits plan

45. **(B)** *English/Rhetorical Skills/Strategy/Appropriate Supporting Material.* (B) is the correct answer choice. In this paragraph, the writer presents a theory related to whether researchers make valuable discoveries after age 40. Therefore, it would be appropriate here to introduce a few contributions that older researchers have made to science. As for the other answer choices, (A) and (D) are both incorrect because they are simply irrelevant. (C) is incorrect because it is too general; again, the paragraph is about older researchers (and not researchers in general).

valid. In former years <u>of previous times</u>, the size of a
46

person's paycheck was determined primarily by the

size of that person's annual budget. On this basis, the

researcher—no matter how <u>brilliant, with</u> only one
47

assistant and a limited budget made an extremely poor

showing. Companies now realize that the two very

important criteria that must also <u>be considerable</u>
48

are a researcher's actual contributions to the company

and creative potential.

[5]

With today's shortage of qualified scientists,

companies have more reason than ever to encourage

scientists to do the work for which they are most

qualified. Companies also have greater reason than

46. **F.** NO CHANGE
   G. of times previous
   H. previously
   J. OMIT the underlined portion.

46. **(J)** *English/Rhetorical Skills/Style/Conciseness.*
   The original sentence is incorrect because the
   underlined portion is redundant. Specifically, "of
   previous times" has a similar meaning to "in
   former years." (J) is the correct answer choice
   because it eliminates this unnecessary phrase. As
   for the other answer choices, (G) and (H) are
   incorrect for the same reason as the original.

47. **A.** NO CHANGE
   B. brilliant with
   C. brilliant—with
   D. brilliant; with

47. **(C)** *English/Usage and Mechanics/Punctua-
   tion/Dashes.* Dashes can be used to set off a
   thought to give it special emphasis. They are not
   used as frequently as comma pairs, but when
   they are used, they also come in pairs. (C)
   correctly provides the following dash for the
   opening dash earlier in the sentence.

48. **F.** NO CHANGE
   G. be considered
   H. most considerable
   J. considerable of

48. **(G)** *English/Usage and Mechanics/Grammar
   and Usage/Diction.* The original sentence is
   incorrect due to a word choice error.
   Specifically, the verb phrase "be considerable"
   has a meaning which is not appropriate in this
   context: "be substantial" or "be large." (G) is the
   correct answer choice since the verb phrase "be
   considered" has the appropriate meaning:
   "thought about" or "taken into account." As for
   the other answer choices, (H) and (J) are
   incorrect because they are not verb phrases ("be
   considered" or "be substantial"); a verb phrase is
   required to complete the sentence successfully.

ever to provide a laboratory environment <u>in which</u> the
49

creative processes of research can be carried out most

effectively.

49. A. NO CHANGE
 B. about which
 C. of which
 D. into which

49. (A) *English/Usage and Mechanics/No Change.*
The original sentence is correct. "In" is the
correct preposition because the creative
processes take place *in* the laboratory environment. (B), (C), and (D) are not correct because
they do not use prepositions that place the action
in the laboratory.

Item #50 asks about the preceding passage as a
whole.

---

50. Choose the order of paragraph numbers that will
make the essay's structure most logical.

 F. NO CHANGE
 G. 1, 2, 4, 3, 5
 H. 1, 2, 3, 5, 4
 J. 3, 2, 1, 4, 5

**50. (J) *English/Rhetorical Skills/Organization/Pas-
sage-Level Structure.*** (J) is the correct answer
choice. The most logical order will involve
presenting the two main topics in a compare-
and-contrast format. Specifically, the most
logical order would present an earlier view of
creativity (Paragraph 3), a contemporary view of
creativity (Paragraphs 2 and 1), an earlier view
of salary guideposts (Paragraph 4), and then a
contemporary view of salary guideposts
(Paragraph 5).

PASSAGE V

Youth Market of Europe

With increasing prosperity, West European

<u>youth am</u> having a fling that is creating distinctive
51

consumer and cultural patterns. The result has been the

increasing emergence in Europe of that phenomenon

well known in America as the "youth market." This

51. **A.** NO CHANGE
    B. youths is
    C. youth be
    D. youth are

51. **(D)** *English/Usage and Mechanics/Grammar and Usage/Subject-Verb Agreement.* The original is incorrect due to an agreement error. Specifically, a third person plural subject ("youth") requires a plural verb that agrees with it. "Am" is a verb that can only be used with first person singular subjects. (D) is the correct choice because it provides the verb that is required here. As for the other answer choices, (B) is incorrect because a plural subject ("youths") does not agree with a singular verb ("is"). (C) is incorrect because it results in a verb phrase ("be having") that is not grammatically correct.

<u>here</u> is a market in which enterprising businesses cater
52

to the demands of teenagers and older youths in all

their rock mania and pop art forms. The evolving

52. **F.** NO CHANGE
    G. here idea
    H. here thing
    J. OMIT the underlined portion.

52. **(J)** *English/Usage and Mechanics/Grammar and Usage/Pronoun Usage* and *Rhetorical Skills/Style/Idiomatic Expression.* The original sentence is incorrect because "this here" is a non-standard variation on the pronoun "this." (J) is the correct answer choice because it eliminates "here" and leaves the correct pronoun. As for the other answer choices, (G) and (H) are incorrect for the same reason as the original.

European youth market has both <u>similarities</u> and
₅₃

differences from the American youth market.

53. **A.** NO CHANGE
    B. similarity
    C. similarities to
    D. similar

53. **(C)** *English/Usage and Mechanics/Grammar and Usage/Diction.* The original sentence is incorrect due to a diction error involving prepositions. As written, "from" completes both "similarities" and "differences." However, "from" is not the proper preposition to use with "similarities." The proper preposition is "to" ("similarities to..."). (C) is correct because it provides the required preposition. As for the other answer choices, (B) is incorrect for two reasons: first, it is incorrect for the same reason as the original; second, the singular noun "similarity" is not parallel with the plural noun "differences." (D) is incorrect for two reasons: first, it is incorrect for the same reason as the original; second, the adjective "similar" is not parallel with the plural noun "differences."

The <u>markets</u> basis is essentially the same—more
₅₄

spending power and freedom to use it in the hands of

teenagers and older youths. Young consumers also

54. **F.** NO CHANGE
    G. markets'
    H. market's
    J. market

54. **(H)** *English/Usage and Mechanics/Punctuation/Apostrophes.* The original sentence is incorrect due to a punctuation error. Specifically, an apostrophe is required in the phrase "the market's basis." An apostrophe should always be used to show possession. Here, the basis belongs to the market, so an apostrophe should be used. As for the other answer choices, (G) is incorrect because the apostrophe is used in the wrong place, indicating plural usage. The "market" is singular; so the apostrophe should appear before the "s." An apostrophe is placed after the "s" only when possession belonging to a plural group is to be established ("After they came in, I cleaned the boys' shoes"). (J) is incorrect for the same reason as the original.

make up an <u>increasing high</u> proportion of the
55

population. Youthful tastes in the United States and

Europe include a similar range of products—MP3

players, CDs, DVD and Blu-ray players, leather

jackets, trendy clothing, cosmetics,

and soft <u>drinks, generally</u> it now is difficult to tell in
56

which direction transatlantic teenage influences are

flowing.

55. **A.** NO CHANGE
 B. increasingly high
 C. increasing higher
 D. high increasing

55. **(B)** *English/Usage and Mechanics/Grammar and Usage/Adjectives versus Adverbs.* The original sentence is incorrect due to a usage error involving modification. Specifically, an adjective ("increasing") cannot modify an adjective ("high"). Only an adverb ("increasingly") can modify an adjective ("high"). (B) is the correct answer because it makes the required correction. As for the other answer choices, (C) and (D) are incorrect for the same reason as the original.

56. **F.** NO CHANGE
 G. drinks. Generally,
 H. drinks, in general
 J. drinks generally

56. **(G)** *English/Usage and Mechanics/Sentence Structure/Run-On Sentences* and *Punctuation/End-Stop Punctuation.* The original sentence is incorrect because it includes a run-on sentence: two or more complete sentences joined together without the necessary punctuation or conjunctions. The first clause in the sentence ("Youthful tastes . . . cosmetics, and soft drinks") is a complete sentence by itself. The second clause ("generally . . . teenage influences are flowing") is also a complete sentence by itself. For the sake of correctness and clarity, it would be best to put a piece of end-stop punctuation at the end of the first clause and then start an entirely new sentence. (G) is the correct answer choice because it accomplishes this task. As for the other answer choices, (H) and (J) are incorrect because they also result in run-on sentences.

As in the United States, where "teen" and

"teenager" <u>becomed</u> merchandising terms,
         57

Europeans also have <u>adapted</u> similar terminology. In
                    58

Flemish and Dutch, it is "tiener" for "teenagers." The

French have simply adopted the English word

"teenager." In Germany, the key word in

advertising addressed to teenagers is "freizeit,"

meaning "holidays" or "time off."

The most obvious difference <u>among</u> the youth
                              59

market in Europe and that in the United States is in

size. In terms of volume and variety of sales, the

market in Europe is only a shadow of its American

57. **A.** NO CHANGE
    B. become
    C. will become
    D. have become

57. **(D)** *English/Usage and Mechanics/Grammar and Usage/Verb Tense*. "Becomed" is neither the past tense nor the past participle of "to become." (D) correctly provides the past tense form ("have become") needed to show the same time frame as "Europeans also have adapted." As for the other answer choices, (B) is the present tense and (C) is the future tense; neither is correct in this case.

58. **F.** NO CHANGE
    G. picked up
    H. added
    J. adopted

58. **(J)** *English/Usage and Mechanics/Grammar and Usage/Diction*. The original sentence is incorrect due to a word choice error. Specifically, "adapted" means "adjusted" or "modified." However, the sentence requires a word that means "to have taken up and used as one's own." (J) is the correct answer choice because "adopted" has that meaning. As for the other answer choices, (G) and (H) are incorrect because they do not provide the required meaning.

59. **A.** NO CHANGE
    B. with
    C. by
    D. between

59. **(D)** *English/Usage and Mechanics/Grammar and Usage/Diction*. The original sentence is incorrect due to a word choice error. Specifically, "among" is only used when describing more than two persons or things ("Her departure caused a stir among the many who were present."). "Between" is used when talking about two persons or things. So, (D) is the correct answer choice. As for (B) and (C), those prepositions have meanings that are not appropriate in this sentence.

counterpart, <u>but it</u> is a growing shadow.
₆₀

60. F. NO CHANGE
    G. it
    H. it being
    J. as it

60. **(F) *English/Usage and Mechanics/No Change.***
    The original is correct as written. There are two
    independent clauses correctly joined by a
    conjunction ("but") and punctuated with a
    comma. (G) and (H) are wrong because they turn
    the word group that follows into a fragment. (J)
    is wrong because "as" creates a dependent clause
    where an independent clause is intended.

Items #61–62 ask about the preceding passage as a whole.

61. Is the author's use of quotation marks appropriate in this essay?

   A. No, because quotation marks are only used to set off a direct quote.
   B. No, because the essay has no dialogue.
   C. Yes, because quotation marks are used to set off words used in a special sense.
   D. Yes, because quotation marks indicate a conversation.

61. **(C)** *English/Usage and Mechanics/Punctuation/Quotation Marks.* (C) is the correct answer. The author uses several words that have meanings specific to the context of this essay. Quotation marks are properly used to set off those words so they are easily identifiable. (A) and (B) are incorrect because quotation marks can be used for several reasons in addition to setting off a direct quote or dialogue. (D) is incorrect because quotation marks are not used in this essay to set off the dialogue in a conversation.

62. This essay was probably written for readers who:

   F. are interested in new trends in the consumer patterns of the world's youth.
   G. are parents of teenagers.
   H. are teenagers.
   J. are interested in the different cultural patterns of Germany.

62. **(F)** *English/Rhetorical Skills/Strategy/Audience.* (F) is the correct answer choice. The passage focuses solely on the topic of youth markets in Western Europe and America; given this single subject, we can assume it was written for readers who are interested in the consumer habits of young people. (G) and (H) are incorrect because there is a level of detail included in the essay that would not be of interest to a general readership such as parents or teenagers in general. (J) is incorrect because the essay discusses the youth market across Europe; in other words, it takes into account more than just cultural patterns within Germany.

PASSAGE VI

An Argument in Favor of Scientific Contributions

[1]

First, what are <u>us of those</u> who have chosen careers
₆₃

in science and engineering able to do about meeting

our current <u>problems?</u>
₆₄

[2]

Second, we can identify the many areas in which

science and technology, more considerately used, can

be of <u>greatest</u> service in the future than in the past to
₆₅

improve the quality of life. While we can make many

speeches and pass many laws, the quality of our

63. **A.** NO CHANGE
B. we
C. we ones
D. us ones

63. **(B)** *English/Usage and Mechanics/Grammar and Usage/Pronoun Usage.* The original sentence is incorrect due to a pronoun error. Instead of an objective pronoun ("us"), a subjective pronoun ("we") should be used. So, (B) is the correct answer choice. (C) and (D) are incorrect because both "we ones" and "us ones" are informal usage.

64. **F.** NO CHANGE
G. problems.
H. problems!
J. problems;

64. **(F)** *English/Usage and Mechanics/No Change.* The original sentence is correct. A question mark should always be used after a direct question. As for the other choices, (G), (H), and (J) are all incorrect because they include incorrect punctuation.

65. **A.** NO CHANGE
B. great
C. more great
D. greater

65. **(D)** *English/Usage and Mechanics/Grammar and Usage/Faulty or Illogical Comparisons* and *Diction.* The original sentence is incorrect due to a word choice error involving a comparison. Specifically, the superlative form of an adjective ("greatest") is not typically used when comparing two ideas or concepts ("service in the future" and "service in the past"). Instead, the comparative form ("greater") is used. (D) is the correct answer choice. (B) is incorrect because it is not the comparative form of an adjective. (C) is incorrect because it is a faulty version of "greater."

environment will be improved only <u>in</u> better
₆₆

knowledge and better application of that knowledge.

[3]

Third, we can recognize that much of the

dissatisfaction we suffer today results from our

successes of former years <u>in the past</u>. We have been so
₆₇

eminently successful in attaining material goals that

we are deeply dissatisfied <u>of the fact that</u> we cannot
₆₈

attain other goals more rapidly. We have achieved a

better life for most people, but we are unhappy that we

have not spread it to all people. We have illuminated

many sources of environmental deterioration, <u>because</u>
₆₉

<u>of</u> we are unhappy that we have not conquered all of
₆₉

66. **F.** NO CHANGE
G. through
H. until
J. inside

66. **(G)** *English/Usage and Mechanics/Grammar and Usage/Diction.* The original sentence is incorrect due to a word choice error. Specifically, the preposition "in" does not fit the context; "through," however, does. Neither "until" nor "inside" has an acceptable meaning.

67. **A.** NO CHANGE
B. of the past
C. being in the past
D. OMIT the underlined portion.

67. **(D)** *English/Rhetorical Skills/Style/Conciseness.* The original sentence is incorrect because the underlined portion is redundant. Specifically, "in the past" has the same meaning as "of former years." (D) is the correct answer choice as it eliminates the unnecessary phrase. (B) and (C) are both incorrect for two reasons: first, they have the same error as the original; second, they both introduce grammatical errors into the sentence.

68. **F.** NO CHANGE
G. in the fact that
H. about
J. that

68. **(J)** *English/Rhetorical Skills/Style/Conciseness.* As written, the original sentence is redundant. The phrase "of the fact" adds no meaning to the sentence; and, in fact, it makes the sentence harder to understand. (J) is the correct answer because it omits the unnecessary language. As for the other answer choices, (G) is incorrect for the same reason as the original. (H) is incorrect because "dissatisfied about" is a non-standard substitute for "dissatisfied that."

69. **A.** NO CHANGE
B. despite
C. but
D. also

69. (C) *English/Usage and Mechanics/Sentence Structure/Problems of Coordination and Subordination* and *Grammar and Usage/ Diction.* The original sentence is incorrect due to a word choice error involving coordination and subordination. Specifically, the phrase "because of" incorrectly suggests that the state of things in the first clause ("We have illuminated…") was motivated by the state of things in the second clause ("we are unhappy…"). In fact, the author intends to suggest a contrast between the two ideas ("We have illuminated … but we are unhappy"). (C) is the correct answer choice because it supplies the required conjunction; the resulting sentence also mirrors the construction of the previous sentence. (B) and (D) are incorrect because they create sentences that include grammatical errors and are not logical.

them. It is our <u>raising</u> expectations rather than our
₇₀

failures that now cause our distress.

[4]

First, we can help destroy the false impression

that science and engineering have caused the current

70. F. NO CHANGE
    G. arising
    H. rising
    J. raised

70. (H) *English/Usage and Mechanics/Grammar and Usage/Diction.* The original sentence is incorrect due to an error involving word choice. Specifically, "raising" cannot be used as an adjective to modify a noun. "Rising," which means "moving upward," can be used as an adjective to modify a noun; in addition, it also supplies the meaning required here. So, (H) is the correct answer choice. As for the other answer choices, (G) is incorrect because "arising" means "as a result of"; it does not provide the required meaning. (J) is incorrect because "raised" means "fully elevated" and incorrectly suggests that expectations have reached their highest levels. As the passage states, though, expectations continue to rise as accomplishments continue to be made; so, "raised" is not the best choice here.

world troubles. <u>To the contrary,</u> science and
₇₁

engineering have made vast contributions to better

71. A. NO CHANGE
    B. Contrary to,
    C. Contrasted with,
    D. In contrast with,

71. (A) *English/Rhetorical Skills/No Change.* The original sentence is correct. The phrase "To the contrary" provides an elegant and grammatically correct transition from the previous sentence.

living for more people.

[5]

Although many of our current problems must

be cured more by social, political, and economic

instruments rather than by science and technology,

science and technology must still be the tools to make

further <u>advances in</u> such things as clean air, clean
⁷³

water, better transportation, better housing, better

medical care, more adequate welfare programs, purer

food, conservation of resources, and many other areas.

(B), (C), and (D) are incorrect because they are incomplete phrases; they require additional language in order to be grammatically and logically correct.

72. Suppose, at this point, that the writer wanted to add more information about the benefits of science and engineering. Which of the following additions would be most relevant?

F. A list of the colleges with the best science and engineering degree programs
G. Specific examples of contributions from the areas of science and engineering that have improved the standard of living
H. A brief explanation of the current world troubles
J. The names of several famous scientists and engineers

72. **(G) *English/Rhetorical Skills/Strategy/Appropriate Supporting Material.*** (G) is the correct answer choice. The writer makes a general claim that science and engineering have helped to improve people's lives. Therefore, it would be appropriate to support that claim with specific examples. As for the other answer choices, (F) and (J) are both incorrect because they are simply irrelevant. (H) is incorrect because it is too general; the paragraph is about only those global problems where science and engineering have made contributions towards improving people's lives (and not global problems in general).

73. A. NO CHANGE
B. advances, in
C. advances. In
D. advances: in

73. **(A) *English/Usage and Mechanics/No Change.*** The original sentence is correct. No punctuation is required between "advances" and "in." (B) is incorrect because the comma disrupts the logical flow of the sentence. (C) is incorrect because "In such things …" would create a sentence fragment. (D) is incorrect because the colon creates a fragment out of the word grouping that follows.

Items #74–75 ask about the preceding passage as a whole.

74. This essay was probably written for readers who:

    F. are retired scientists and engineers.
    G. are interested in a career in the "green" sector of the economy.
    H. are in a career or contemplating a career in science or engineering.
    J. are dissatisfied with the lack of progress in solving various scientific problems.

74. **(H)** *English/Rhetorical Skills/Strategy/Audience.* (H) is the correct answer choice. First, the passage's topic is how science and engineering can help solve the world's problems; this topic would be of interest to scientists, engineers, and anyone considering a career as either. Second, the passage explicitly addresses scientists and engineers. (F) is wrong because the emphasis on making continued efforts doesn't seem to speak to people who are no longer active in the field. (J) is too general; the intended audience is more specific than anyone frustrated by a general lack of progress in the field of science. (G) is incorrect because it is too narrow; the author addresses areas and issues of interest to all scientists and engineers, not just those interested in becoming environmental scientists.

75. Choose the order of paragraph numbers that will make the essay's structure most logical.

    A. NO CHANGE
    B. 1, 4, 2, 3, 5
    C. 5, 4, 2, 3, 1
    D. 4, 2, 3, 1, 5

75. **(B)** *English/Rhetorical Skills/Organization/ Passage-Level Structure.* (B) is correct. Paragraph 1 introduces the passage's main topic. Paragraphs 4, 2, and 3 then begin with "First…," "Second…," and "Third…" respectively. Finally, Paragraph 5 summarizes the author's point of view and provides a conclusion.

SECTION 2: MATHEMATICS TEST
60 Items

DIRECTIONS: Solve each item and choose the correct answer choice. Calculator use is permitted on this test; however, some items are best solved without the use of a calculator.

<u>Note:</u> All of the following should be assumed, unless otherwise stated.

1. Illustrative figures are NOT necessarily drawn to scale.
2. The word *average* indicates arithmetic mean.
3. The word *line* indicates a straight line.
4. Geometric figures lie in a plane.

---

1. What is the additive inverse of $-\dfrac{2}{3}$?

    A. $-\dfrac{3}{2}$

    B. 0

    C. $\dfrac{2}{3}$

    D. 1

    E. $\dfrac{3}{2}$

1. **(C) *Mathematics/Arithmetic/Simple Manipulations.*** Two numbers that add up to zero are additive inverses: $a + (-a) = 0$. The additive inverse is the opposite of the original value: $\dfrac{2}{3}$ is the additive inverse of $-\dfrac{2}{3}$.

2. In the figure below, if O is the center of the circle and $\angle AOC$ is a central angle equal to $70°$, what is the measure of $\angle ABC$?

    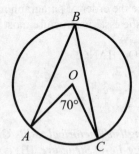

    F. $140°$
    G. $70°$
    H. $50°$
    J. $35°$
    K. $22°$

2. **(J) *Mathematics/Geometry/Lines and Angles* and *Circles.*** A central angle is equal to its intercepted arc, so $\overset{\frown}{AC} = \angle AOC = 70°$. An inscribed angle is equal to one-half the measure of its intercepted arc. Therefore, the measure of $\angle ABC$ is:

    $$\angle ABC = \frac{\overset{\frown}{AC}}{2} = 35°$$

3. Which of the following is a solution to the equation $x^2 + 6x + 8 = 0$?

    A. 8
    B. 6
    C. 4
    D. −2
    E. −8

4. In the figure below $l_1 \parallel l_2$. If $x = 70$ and $y = 105$, what is the value of r?

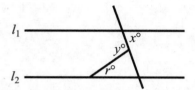

    F. 35
    G. 45
    H. 85
    J. 145
    K. 175

5. $A = \dfrac{2gr}{g + r}$. What is the value of g when $r = 1$ and $A = 4$?

    A. −2
    B. $\dfrac{4}{7}$
    C. $\dfrac{8}{5}$
    D. 2
    E. 4

3. **(D)** *Mathematics/Algebra/Solving Quadratic Equations and Relations.* Factor the quadratic equation:

$$x^2 + 6x + 8 = 0$$
$$(x + 4)(x + 2) = 0$$
$$x + 4 = 0 \text{ or } x + 2 = 0$$

Therefore, $x = -4$ or -2.

4. **(F)** *Mathematics/Geometry/Lines and Angles.* Fill in the given information and label the remaining angles:

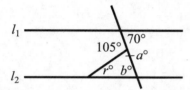

Since $b°$ is an alternate interior angle with $x°$, $b = 70$. And $a = 75$ because it is the supplement of $y°$. The three angles form a triangle: $r + a + b = 180$. Thus:

$$r + 75 + 70 = 180$$
$$r = 35$$

5. **(A)** *Mathematics/Algebra/Manipulating Algebraic Expressions/Evaluating Expressions.* Substitute the given values for A and r and solve for g:

$$A = \frac{2gr}{g + r}$$
$$4 = \frac{2g(1)}{g + 1}$$
$$4(g + 1) = 2g$$
$$4g + 4 = 2g$$
$$2g = -4$$
$$g = -2$$

6. The figure below represents which of the following equations?

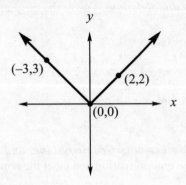

F. $y = x$
G. $y = -x$
H. $y = |x|$
J. $|y| = x$
K. $y = x^2$

6. (H) *Mathematics/Coordinate Geometry/Graphs of Linear Equations.* V-shaped graphs usually indicate absolute value functions. Substitute the given coordinates $(2,2)$, $(0,0)$, and $(-3,3)$ into the answer choices: only $y = |x|$ satisfies all the ordered pairs.

7. Which of the following is an illustration of the distributive property?

A. $(12 \cdot 25)(4) = 12(25 \cdot 4)$
B. $7n + 2 - 3n = 7n - 3n + 2$
C. $(17)(b^2)(5) = (17)(5)(b)^2$
D. $x(x+2) = x^2 + 2x$
E. $ab + ac = ba + ca$

7. (D) *Mathematics/Algebra/Manipulating Algebraic Expressions/Basic Algebraic Manipulations.* The distributive property indicates multiplication over addition $[a(b+c) = ab + ac]$ and multiplication over subtraction $[a(b-c) = ab - ac]$. Thus, $x(x+2) = x^2 + 2x$.

8. Joshua buys a television that costs $600. If the sales tax is 7%, what is the total cost of the purchase?

F. $4.20
G. $42.00
H. $420.00
J. $604.20
K. $642.00

8. (K) *Mathematics/Arithmetic/Common Arithmetic Items/Percents.* The sales tax is 7% of $600: $0.07(600) = \$42$. Thus, the total cost is $\$600 + \$42 = \$642$.

9. What is the value of $-x^2 - 2x^3$ when $x = -1$?

    A. -3
    B. -1
    C. 0
    D. 1
    E. 3

9. **(D)** *Mathematics/Algebra/Expressing and Evaluating Algebraic Functions/Function Notation.* Substitute the value -1 for x:

$$-x^2 - 2x^3 = -(-1)^2 - 2(-1)^3$$
$$= -1 - 2(-1)$$
$$= -1 + 2$$
$$= 1$$

10. What is the average of $n+3$, $2n-1$, and $3n+4$?

    F. $\dfrac{5n+6}{3}$
    G. $2n+2$
    H. $3n+3$
    J. $\dfrac{6n+7}{3}$
    K. $6n+6$

10. **(G)** *Mathematics/Statistics and Probability/Averages.* The average is the sum of the numbers divided by the number of elements:

$$\text{average} = \frac{(n+3) + (2n-1) + (3n+4)}{3}$$
$$= \frac{6n+6}{3}$$
$$= 2n+2$$

11. If $x = 9$, what is the value of $x^0 + x^{\frac{1}{2}} + x^{-2}$?

    A. $77\dfrac{1}{2}$
    B. $76\dfrac{1}{2}$
    C. $5\dfrac{7}{18}$
    D. $4\dfrac{1}{81}$
    E. $3\dfrac{1}{81}$

11. **(D)** *Mathematics/Algebra/Manipulating Algebraic Expressions/Evaluating Expressions.* Substitute 9 for x:

$$x^0 + x^{\frac{1}{2}} + x^{-2} = 9^0 + 9^{\frac{1}{2}} + 9^{-2}$$
$$= 1 + \sqrt{9} + \frac{1}{9^2}$$
$$= 1 + 3 + \frac{1}{81}$$
$$= 4\frac{1}{81}$$

12. $4\sqrt{3} + 3\sqrt{27} = ?$

    F. $10\sqrt{3}$
    G. $13\sqrt{3}$
    H. $7\sqrt{30}$
    J. 63
    K. 108

12. **(G)** *Mathematics/Arithmetic/Simple Manipulations.* To add radicals, rewrite the radicands (the numbers under the radical symbol) in terms of the same number, then combine the coefficients of the terms with the same radicands:

$$4\sqrt{3} + 3\sqrt{27} = 4\sqrt{3} + 3\left(3\sqrt{3}\right)$$
$$= 4\sqrt{3} + 9\sqrt{3}$$
$$= 13\sqrt{3}$$

13. Jessica Dawn received marks of 87, 93, and 86 on 3 successive tests. What grade must she receive on a fourth test in order to have an average grade of 90?

    A. 90
    B. 92
    C. 93
    D. 94
    E. 95

14. In terms of x, what is the total number of cents in $4x$ dimes?

    F. $0.04x$
    G. $0.4x$
    H. $4x$
    J. $40x$
    K. $400x$

15. Which of the following is shown by the graph below?

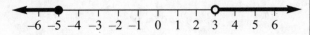

    A. $-5 \le x < 3$
    B. $-5 < x$ or $x < 3$
    C. $-5 \le x$ or $x > 3$
    D. $-5 \le x \le 3$
    E. $-5 \ge x$ or $x > 3$

16. $2\dfrac{2}{5} - 1\dfrac{7}{8} = ?$

    F. $\dfrac{11}{40}$

    G. $\dfrac{19}{40}$

    H. $\dfrac{21}{40}$

    J. $\dfrac{7}{13}$

    K. $1\dfrac{5}{40}$

---

13. **(D)** *Mathematics/Statistics and Probability/Averages.* The average is the sum of the test scores divided by the number of tests:

$$\text{average} = 90 = \frac{87 + 93 + 86 + x}{4}$$
$$4(90) = 87 + 93 + 86 + x$$
$$360 = 266 + x$$
$$x = 94$$

14. **(J)** *Mathematics/Algebra/Manipulating Algebraic Expressions/Creating Algebraic Expressions.* Each dime is 10 cents. Thus, $4x$ dimes would be

$$4x \; \cancel{\text{dimes}} \cdot \frac{10 \text{ cents}}{\cancel{\text{dime}}} = 40x \text{ cents.}$$

15. **(E)** *Mathematics/Arithmetic/Simple Manipulations.* The shaded circle at -5 indicates either $\ge$ or $\le$, and the unshaded circle at 3 indicates either $>$ or $<$, without the equal sign (the $<$ symbol indicates "less than," and the $>$ symbol indicates "greater than"). The graph indicates $x \le -5$ or $x > 3$. The answers are connected by "or," meaning the union of those two sets of numbers. Therefore, the answer is $x \le -5$ or $x > 3$. Note that $x \le -5$ can be rewritten as $-5 \ge x$.

16. **(H)** *Mathematics/Arithmetic/Simple Manipulations.* First, convert the mixed numbers to improper fractions:

$$2\frac{2}{5} - 1\frac{7}{8} = \frac{12}{5} - \frac{15}{8}$$

Since the lowest common denominator is 40, we have:

$$\frac{12}{5} - \frac{15}{8} = \frac{96}{40} - \frac{75}{40} = \frac{21}{40}$$

17. In a circle with a radius of 6, what is the degree measure of an arc whose length is 3π?

    A. 20°
    B. 30°
    C. 60°
    D. 90°
    E. 120°

17. **(D)** *Mathematics/Geometry/Circles.* Use the equation for circumference of a circle:

$$C_{circle} = 2\pi r$$
$$= 2\pi(6)$$
$$= 12\pi$$

Therefore, 3π is $\dfrac{3\pi}{12\pi} = \dfrac{1}{4}$ of the circumference. In turn, the measure (in degrees) of the arc is $\dfrac{1}{4}(360°) = 90°$.

18. If $\dfrac{2x}{3\sqrt{2}} = \dfrac{3\sqrt{2}}{x}$, what is the positive value of x?

    F. $\sqrt{3}$
    G. $\sqrt{6}$
    H. $2\sqrt{3}$
    J. 3
    K. 9

18. **(J)** *Mathematics/Algebra/Solving Algebraic Equations or Inequalities with One Variable/Equations Involving Rational Expressions* and *Equations Involving Radical Expressions.* Solve the equation for x:

$$\frac{2x}{3\sqrt{2}} = \frac{3\sqrt{2}}{x}$$
$$2x(x) = \left(3\sqrt{2}\right)\left(3\sqrt{2}\right)$$
$$2x^2 = 9(2) = 18$$
$$x^2 = 9$$
$$x = \pm 3$$

Therefore, the positive value of x is 3.

19. If $f(x) = 2x - x^2$ and $g(x) = x - 4$, what is the value of $g(f(2))$?

    A. −8
    B. −4
    C. −2
    D.   0
    E.   3

20. What is the solution set of the equation $|5 - 2x| = 7$?

    F. $\{-1, 6\}$
    G. $\{-1\}$
    H. $\{1\}$
    J. $\{6\}$
    K. The empty set

19. **(B)** *Mathematics/Algebra/Expressing and Evaluating Algebraic Functions/Function Notation.* To determine the value of $g(f(2))$, first substitute 2 for x in $f(x)$ and evaluate:

$$f(x) = 2x - x^2$$
$$f(2) = 2(2) - (2)^2 = 4 - 4 = 0$$

Now, substitute this value for x in $g(x)$ and evaluate:

$$g(x) = x - 4$$
$$g(0) = 0 - 4 = -4$$

20. **(F)** *Mathematics/Algebra/Solving Algebraic Equations or Inequalities with One Variable/Equations Involving Absolute Value.* Since $|5 - 2x| = 7$, we know that $5 - 2x = 7$ or $-(5 - 2x) = 7$. Solve each for possible values of x:

$$5 - 2x = 7$$
$$-2x = 2$$
$$x = -1$$

And:

$$-(5 - 2x) = 7$$
$$-5 + 2x = 7$$
$$2x = 12$$
$$x = 6$$

Double-check each possible value for x in the original equation:

$$|5 - 2x| = 7$$
$$|5 - 2(-1)| = 7$$
$$|5 + 2| = 7$$
$$|7| = 7 \checkmark$$

And:

$$|5 - 2x| = 7$$
$$|5 - 2(6)| = 7$$
$$|5 - 12| = 7$$
$$|-7| = 7 \checkmark$$

Therefore, the solution set is $\{-1, 6\}$.

Alternatively, check the answer choice values by plugging them into the equation, starting with (F).

21. When $\dfrac{3-\dfrac{3}{x}}{x(x-1)}$ is defined, it is equivalent to which of the following expressions?

A. $\dfrac{1}{x-1}$

B. $\dfrac{1}{3}$

C. $x+1$

D. $\dfrac{3}{x^2}$

E. 3

22. What is the slope of the line that passes through the points $(-3,5)$ and $(4,7)$?

F. $\sqrt{53}$

G. $\dfrac{7}{2}$

H. 2

J. $\dfrac{1}{2}$

K. $\dfrac{2}{7}$

21. **(D)** *Mathematics/Algebra/Manipulating Algebraic Expressions/Evaluating Expressions.* Multiply the top and bottom of the fraction by the lowest common denominator, which is x:

$$\frac{3-\dfrac{3}{x}}{x(x-1)} = \frac{\dfrac{x}{1}\left(\dfrac{3}{1}\right)-\left(\dfrac{3}{x}\right)}{x(x-1)}$$

$$=\frac{\dfrac{3x}{x}-\dfrac{3}{x}}{x(x-1)}$$

$$=\frac{\dfrac{3(x-1)}{x}}{x(x-1)}$$

$$=\frac{3\cancel{(x-1)}}{x}\cdot\frac{1}{x\cancel{(x-1)}}=\frac{3}{x^2}$$

22. **(K)** *Mathematics/Coordinate Geometry/Slope of a Line.* Use the equation for finding the slope of a line, where m is the slope and (x_1,y_1) and (x_2,y_2) are the two given points:

$$m=\frac{y_2-y_1}{x_2-x_1}$$

$$=\frac{7-5}{4-(-3)}$$

$$=\frac{2}{7}$$

23. In the circle below with center O, diameter $\overline{AB}$ is perpendicular to chord $\overline{CD}$ at point E. If chord $\overline{CD} = 8$ inches and $\overline{OE} = 3$ inches, what is the length of the radius of the circle, in inches, if O is the center of the circle?

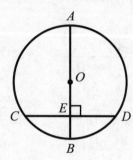

A. $\sqrt{3}$
B. $\sqrt{5}$
C. $\sqrt{7}$
D. $\sqrt{15}$
E. 5

24. In the figure below, the diagonals of parallelogram $ABCD$ intersect at point E. If $\overline{DB} = 4x + 2$ and $\overline{DE} = x + 4$, what is the value of x?

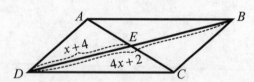

F. 3
G. 2
H. 1
J. $\dfrac{2}{3}$
K. 0

23. (E) *Mathematics/Geometry/Circles* and *Triangles/Pythagorean Theorem.*

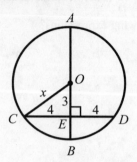

A diameter drawn perpendicular to the chord bisects the chord. Therefore, $\overline{AB}$ bisects $\overline{CD}$. A constructed radius $\overline{OC}$ forms right triangle OEC with $\overline{OC}$ as the hypotenuse. Since $\overline{OE} = 3$ inches and $\overline{CE} = 4$ inches, use the Pythagorean theorem ($a^2 + b^2 = c^2$):

$$(\text{Hypotenuse})^2 = \left(\text{Leg}_1\right)^2 + \left(\text{Leg}_2\right)^2$$
$$\left(\overline{OC}\right)^2 = \left(\overline{OE}\right)^2 + \left(\overline{CE}\right)^2$$
$$x^2 = 3^2 + 4^2$$
$$x^2 = 25$$
$$x = \pm 5$$

Since length must be positive, the radius is 5.

24. (F) *Mathematics/Geometry.* The diagonals of a parallelogram bisect each other. Therefore:

$$\overline{DB} = 2\left(\overline{DE}\right)$$
$$4x + 2 = 2(x + 4)$$
$$4x + 2 = 2x + 8$$
$$2x = 6$$
$$x = 3$$

25. If the measure of the central angle of a sector of a circle is 120°, what is the area, in square units, of the sector if the radius is 6 units long?

    A. 4π

    B. 6π

    C. 8π

    D. 10π

    E. 12π

25. (E) *Mathematics/Geometry/Lines and Angles* and *Circles.* Since a figure isn't provided, draw one:

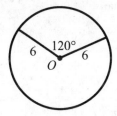

$$x = \text{area of sector}$$
$$\pi r^2 = \text{area of circle}$$

$$\frac{\text{area of sector}}{\text{area of circle}} = \frac{\text{central angle}}{360°}$$

$$\frac{x}{\pi r^2} = \frac{120°}{360°}$$

$$\frac{x}{36\pi} = \frac{1}{3}$$

$$3x = 36\pi$$

$$x = 12\pi$$

26. If the statement "if two triangles are red, then they are equal in area" is true, then which of the following *must* be true?

    F. If the two triangles are not equal in area, then they are not red.

    G. If the two triangles are equal in area, then they are red.

    H. If the two triangles are equal in area, then they are not red.

    J. If the two triangles are not red, then they are not equal in area.

    K. If the two triangles are red, then they are not equal in area.

26. (F) *Mathematics/Arithmetic/Common Arithmetic Items/Sets: Union, Intersection, and Elements.* For all conditional statements, the original statement and its contrapositive are equivalent, "if p, then q" is equivalent to "if not q, then not p."

27. If $\dfrac{a}{b} = \dfrac{r}{t}$, then which of the following is NOT necessarily true?

   A. $\dfrac{a}{r} = \dfrac{b}{t}$

   B. $\dfrac{a}{t} = \dfrac{b}{r}$

   C. $\dfrac{a+b}{b} = \dfrac{r+t}{t}$

   D. $\dfrac{b}{a} = \dfrac{t}{r}$

   E. $at = br$

27. **(B)** *Mathematics/Algebra/Manipulating Algebraic Expressions/Basic Algebraic Manipulations.*
Compare all the answer choices to the original using cross-multiplication. The original is $\dfrac{a}{b} = \dfrac{r}{t} \Rightarrow$ $at = br$.

   A. $\dfrac{a}{r} = \dfrac{b}{t}$
   $at = br$ ✓

   B. $\dfrac{a}{t} = \dfrac{b}{r}$
   $ar = bt$ ✗

   C. $\dfrac{a+b}{b} = \dfrac{r+t}{t}$
   $t(a+b) = b(r+t)$
   $at + bt = br + bt$
   $at = br$ ✓

   D. $\dfrac{b}{a} = \dfrac{t}{r}$
   $at = br$ ✓

   E. $at = br$ ✓

28. If $-2x + 5 = 2 - (5 - 2x)$, then $x = ?$

   F. 6
   G. 5
   H. 4
   J. 3
   K. 2

28. **(K)** *Mathematics/Algebra/Solving Algebraic Equations or Inequalities with One Variable/Simple Equations.* Simply solve the given equation for x:

$$-2x + 5 = 2 - (5 - 2x)$$
$$= 2 - 5 + 2x$$
$$= -3 + 2x$$
$$5 = -3 + 4x$$
$$8 = 4x$$
$$x = 2$$

29. $\dfrac{(1+\sin x)(1-\sin x)}{(1+\cos x)(1-\cos x)}$ is equivalent to which of the following?

    A. $\cos x$
    B. $\tan x$
    C. $\tan^2 x$
    D. $\cos^2 x$
    E. $\cot^2 x$

29. **(E)** *Mathematics/Trigonometry/Trigonometric Relationships.* Use the trigonometric relationships to evaluate the given expression:

$$\frac{(1+\sin x)(1-\sin x)}{(1+\cos x)(1-\cos x)} = \frac{1-\sin x + \sin x - \sin^2 x}{1-\cos x + \cos x - \cos^2 x}$$

$$= \frac{1-\sin^2 x}{1-\cos^2 x}$$

Using the identity $\sin^2 x + \cos^2 x = 1$, we have:

$$\sin^2 x + \cos^2 x = 1$$
$$\cos^2 x = 1-\sin^2 x$$
$$\sin^2 x = 1-\cos^2 x$$

Therefore, by substitution:

$$\frac{1-\sin^2 x}{1-\cos^2 x} = \frac{\cos^2 x}{\sin^2 x} = \cot^2 x$$

30. In the figure below, $\triangle ACB$ is a right triangle. $\overline{CE}$ is the median to hypotenuse $\overline{AB}$, and $\overline{AB} = 14$ centimeters. What is the length, in centimeters, of $\overline{CE}$?

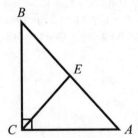

    F. 5
    G. 6
    H. 7
    J. 8
    K. Cannot be determined from the given information

30. **(H)** *Mathematics/Geometry/Triangles/Properties of Triangles.* The median to the hypotenuse of a right triangle is equal in length to half the hypotenuse: $\overline{BE} = \overline{AE} = \overline{CE}$:

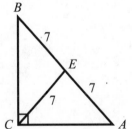

31. If y varies directly as x, and $y = 10$ when $x = \dfrac{1}{5}$, what is the value of y when $x = \dfrac{1}{2}$?

  A. 1
  B. 4
  C. 7
  D. 16
  E. 25

31. **(E) *Mathematics/Arithmetic/Common Arithmetic Items/Proportions and Direct-Inverse Variation.***

Since y varies directly as x, we have: $\dfrac{y_1}{x_1} = \dfrac{y_2}{x_2}$.

Therefore:

$$\frac{10}{\frac{1}{5}} = \frac{y}{\frac{1}{2}}$$
$$10(5) = y(2)$$
$$50 = 2y$$
$$y = 25$$

32. $\dfrac{(-1)(2)(-3)(4)(-5)}{(5)(-4)(3)(-2)(1)} = ?$

  F. −2
  G. −1
  H. 1
  J. 2
  K. 3

32. **(G) *Mathematics/Arithmetic/Complicated Manipulations/Simplifying.*** Cancel like terms until the given expression is simplified:

$$\frac{(-1)(\not2)(-\not3)(\not4)(-\not5)}{(\not5)(-\not4)(\not3)(-\not2)(1)} = \frac{(-1)(\not1)(\not1)}{(\not1)(\not1)} = -1$$

33. How many positive prime factors does the number 36 have?

  A. Two
  B. Three
  C. Four
  D. Five
  E. Six

33. **(A) *Mathematics/Arithmetic/Common Arithmetic Items/Properties of Numbers.*** The factors of 36 are: 1 and 36, 2 and 18, 3 and 12, 4 and 9, 6 and 6. Of those factors, only 2 and 3 are prime numbers. Therefore, 36 has only two positive prime factors.

34. The measure of the vertex angle of an isosceles triangle is 50°. What is the degree measure of each base angle?

    F. 40°
    G. 50°
    H. 65°
    J. 75°
    K. 130°

35. Using the table below, what is the median of the following data?

Score	Frequency
20	4
30	4
50	7

    A. 20
    B. 30
    C. 40
    D. 50
    E. 60

34. **(H)** *Mathematics/Geometry/Triangles/Properties of Triangles* and *Lines and Angles.* An isosceles triangle has two equal sides and two equal base angles:

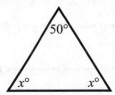

$$50 + x + x = 180$$
$$50 + 2x = 180$$
$$2x = 130$$
$$x = 65$$

35. **(B)** *Mathematics/Statistics and Probability/Median.* The median is the "middle" data element when the data are arranged in numerical order: 20, 20, 20, 20, 30, 30, 30, 30, 50, 50, 50, 50, 50, 50, 50. The "middle" data element is 30.

36. Which of the following number lines represents the solution set of $x^2 - 2x - 3 > 0$?

F.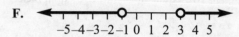

G.

H.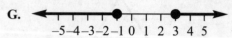

J.

K.

36. **(F)** *Mathematics/Algebra/Solving Quadratic Equations and Relations.* First, rewrite the inequality as an equation, factor, and solve:

$$x^2 - 2x - 3 = 0$$
$$(x-3)(x+1) = 0$$
$$x = 3 \text{ or } x = -1$$

Next, plot -1 and 3 on a number line and test each of the three intervals. Select any value from each of the three intervals, and determine if the inequality holds true.

From the first interval, $x < -1$, test $x = -5$ in the original inequality: $(-5)^2 - 2(-5) - 3 > 0 \Rightarrow 32 > 0$, which is true.

From the second interval, $-1 < x < 3$, test $x = 0$ in the original inequality: $(0)^2 - 2(0) - 3 > 0 \Rightarrow -3 > 0$, which is false.

And from the third interval, $3 < x$, test $x = 6$ in the original inequality: $(6)^2 - 2(6) - 3 > 0 \Rightarrow 21 > 0$, which is true.

Finally, test the values $x = 3$ and $x = -1$: each results in the original inequality being $0 > 0$, which is false, so they are not included in the solution set. Note that "not included" in the solution is indicated by an open circle above a value on the number line.

Therefore, only the first and third intervals satisfy the original inequality.

37. The expression $\sin x + \dfrac{\cos^2 x}{\sin x}$ is equal to which of the following?

    A.   1
    B. $\sin x$
    C. $\cos x$
    D. $\dfrac{1}{\sin x}$
    E. $\dfrac{1}{\cos x}$

37. **(D)** *Mathematics/Trigonometry/Trigonometric Relationships.* To simplify this expression, a common denominator is required. The lowest common denominator is $\sin x$:

$$\frac{\sin x}{1}\left(\frac{\sin x}{\sin x}\right) + \frac{\cos^2 x}{\sin x} = \frac{\sin^2 x}{\sin x} + \frac{\cos^2 x}{\sin x}$$

$$= \frac{\sin^2 x + \cos^2 x}{\sin x}$$

Since $\sin^2 x + \cos^2 x = 1$, the expression reduces to $\dfrac{1}{\sin x}$.

38. The value of $\left(2.5 \times 10^5\right)^2$ is equal to which of the following?

    F. 2.5×10^7
    G. 5×10^7
    H. 6.25×10^7
    J. 2.5×10^{10}
    K. 6.25×10^{10}

38. **(K)** *Mathematics/Arithmetic/Simple Manipulations.* Perform the indicated operations. When in doubt, write it out:

$$\left(2.5 \times 10^5\right)^2 = \left(2.5 \times 10^5\right)\left(2.5 \times 10^5\right)$$

$$= (2.5)^2 \left(10^5\right)^2$$

$$= (2.5)(2.5)\left(10^{5+5}\right)$$

$$= 6.25 \times 10^{10}$$

39. If $f(x) = \dfrac{-2x - x}{-x}$, what is the value of $f(2)$?

    A. -3
    B. -1
    C. 0
    D. 1
    E. 3

39. **(E)** *Mathematics/Algebra/Expressing and Evaluating Algebraic Functions/Function Notation.* Substitute 2 for x in $f(x)$ and evaluate:

$$f(x) = \frac{-2x - x}{-x}$$

$$f(2) = \frac{(-2)(2) - 2}{-2}$$

$$= \frac{-4 - 2}{-2}$$

$$= \frac{-6}{-2}$$

$$= 3$$

40. If one of the roots of the equation $x^2 + kx - 12 = 0$ is 4, what is the value of k?

    F.   −1
    G.   0
    H.   1
    J.   3
    K.   7

40. **(F)** *Mathematics/Algebra/Solving Quadratic Equations and Relations.* Substitute the root for x in the equation and evaluate:

$$x^2 + kx - 12 = 0$$
$$(4)^2 + k(4) - 12 = 0$$
$$16 + 4k - 12 = 0$$
$$4k + 4 = 0$$
$$4k = -4$$
$$k = -1$$

41. In the figure below, D is a point on $\overline{AB}$ and E is a point on $\overline{BC}$ such that $\overline{DE} \parallel \overline{AC}$. If $\overline{DB} = 4$ units long, $\overline{AB} = 10$ units long, and $\overline{BC} = 20$ units long, how many units long is $\overline{EC}$?

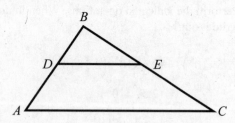

    A.   4
    B.   6
    C.   8
    D.   10
    E.   12

41. **(E)** *Mathematics/Geometry/Triangles/Properties of Triangles.* If $\overline{AB} = 10$ and $\overline{DB} = 4$, then $\overline{DA} = 6$; if $\overline{BC} = 20$ and $\overline{EC} = x$, then $\overline{BE} = 20 - x$.

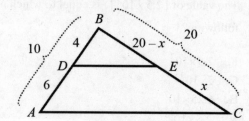

Since $\triangle ABC$ and $\triangle DBE$ are similar triangles, create a proportion between the sides of the two triangles. $\overline{AD} + \overline{DB} = 10 \Rightarrow \overline{AD} + 4 = 10 \Rightarrow \overline{AD} = 6$. Therefore:

$$\frac{\overline{AD}}{\overline{AB}} = \frac{\overline{CE}}{\overline{BC}}$$
$$\frac{6}{10} = \frac{x}{20}$$
$$10x = 120$$
$$x = 12$$

42. $(x+2)(x-4)-(x+4)(x-2) = ?$

   F.   0
   G. $2x^2 + 4x - 16$
   H. $-4x$
   J. $4x$
   K. $-4x - 16$

42. **(H)** *Mathematics/Algebra/Manipulating Algebraic Expressions/Basic Algebraic Manipulations.* Expand each of the binomials in the expression by distribution according to the FOIL method (First, Outer, Inner, Last):

$$(x+2)(x-4) = x^2 - 4x + 2x - 8$$
$$= x^2 - 2x - 8$$

And:

$$(x+4)(x-2) = x^2 - 2x + 4x - 8$$
$$= x^2 + 2x - 8$$

Now, subtract the second expression from the first expression:

$$x^2 - 2x - 8 - (x^2 + 2x - 8) = -2x - 2x = -4x$$

43. If the sum of the measures of the interior angles of a polygon equals the sum of the measures of the exterior angles, how many sides does the polygon have?

   A.   Three
   B.   Four
   C.   Five
   D.   Six
   E.   Seven

43. **(B)** *Mathematics/Geometry/Lines and Angles.* The sum of the measures of the exterior angles of a polygon is 360° for all polygons. The sum of the measures of the interior angles of a polygon can be expressed as $180°(n-2)$, where n is the number of sides. Therefore:

$$180(n-2) = 360$$
$$n - 2 = 2$$
$$n = 4$$

44. If the perimeter of an equilateral triangle is 12 inches, what is its area, in square inches?

    F. $2\sqrt{3}$
    G. $4\sqrt{3}$
    H.   8
    J. $6\sqrt{3}$
    K. $36\sqrt{3}$

44. **(G)** *Mathematics/Geometry/Triangles/Properties of Triangles.* If the perimeter is 12, then each side of the triangle is $\frac{12}{3} = 4$. The area of a triangle is $\frac{bh}{2}$, where b is the base and h is the height. So, draw a figure:

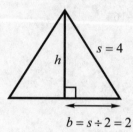

$$b = s \div 2 = 2$$

Use the Pythagorean theorem to solve for h:

$$2^2 + h^2 = 4^2$$
$$h^2 = 16 - 4$$
$$= 12$$
$$h = \pm\sqrt{12} = 2\sqrt{3} \text{ (length is positive)}$$

Therefore:

$$\text{Area}_{\text{triangle}} = \frac{bh}{2}$$
$$= \frac{4\left(2\sqrt{3}\right)}{2}$$
$$= 4\sqrt{3}$$

Alternatively, if you remember the formula for the area of an equilateral triangle, you can use that:

$$\text{Area}_{\text{equilateral triangle}} = \frac{s^2\sqrt{3}}{4}$$
$$= \frac{4^2\sqrt{3}}{4}$$
$$= \frac{16\sqrt{3}}{4}$$
$$= 4\sqrt{3}$$

45. If the ratio of two complementary angles is $8:1$, what is the degree measure of the smaller angle?

    A. $10°$
    B. $20°$
    C. $30°$
    D. $40°$
    E. $80°$

45. **(A)** *Mathematics/Geometry/Lines and Angles.* Let $8x$ equal one angle and x equal the other angle. Since complementary angles add to $90°$, we have:

$$8x + x = 90°$$
$$9x = 90°$$
$$x = 10°$$

46. Given a square, a rectangle, a trapezoid, and a circle, if one figure is selected at random, what is the probability that the figure has four right angles?

    F. 1
    G. $\dfrac{3}{4}$
    H. $\dfrac{1}{2}$
    J. $\dfrac{1}{4}$
    K. 0

46. **(H)** *Mathematics/Statistics and Probability/Probability.* A square has four right angles; a rectangle has four right angles; a trapezoid does not have four right angles; a circle has no angles. Thus, the probability of four right angles is:

$$\frac{\#\,\text{of successes}}{\#\ \text{of possibilities}} = \frac{2}{4} = \frac{1}{2}$$

47. A man travels 320 miles in 8 hours. If he continues at the same rate, how many miles will he travel in the next 2 hours?

    A. 6
    B. 40
    C. 80
    D. 120
    E. 240

47. **(C)** *Mathematics/Arithmetic/Common Arithmetic Items/Proportions and Direct-Inverse Variation.* Set up a direct proportion:

$$\frac{320\ \text{miles}}{x\ \text{miles}} = \frac{8\ \text{hours}}{2\ \text{hours}}$$
$$x\ \text{miles} = \frac{320\ \text{miles} \cdot 2\ \cancel{\text{hours}}}{8\ \cancel{\text{hours}}}$$
$$= 80\ \text{miles}$$

Or, calculate the rate:

$$rt = d$$
$$r(8) = 320$$
$$r = 40\,\text{mph}$$

So, traveling at a rate of 40 mph for 2 hours equals:

$$\left(\frac{40\,\text{miles}}{\cancel{\text{hour}}}\right)\left(\frac{2\ \cancel{\text{hours}}}{2}\right) = 80\,\text{miles}$$

48. $\dfrac{\sin x}{\cos x} + \dfrac{\cos x}{\sin x} = ?$

F. 1

G. $\sin x$

H. $\dfrac{1}{(\sin x)(\cos x)}$

J. $\tan x$

K. $\dfrac{\sin x + \cos x}{(\sin x)(\cos x)}$

48. (H) *Mathematics/Trigonometry/Trigonometric Relationships.* Use the common denominator, $(\sin x)(\cos x)$, to simplify the expression and apply the Pythagorean trigonometric identity:

$$\frac{\sin x}{\cos x}\left(\frac{\sin x}{\sin x}\right) + \frac{\cos x}{\sin x}\left(\frac{\cos x}{\cos x}\right)$$

$$= \frac{\sin^2 x}{(\sin x)(\cos x)} + \frac{\cos^2 x}{(\sin x)(\cos x)}$$

$$= \frac{\sin^2 x + \cos^2 x}{(\sin x)(\cos x)}$$

$$= \frac{1}{(\sin x)(\cos x)}$$

49. The average temperatures for 5 days were 82° F, 86° F, 91° F, 79° F, and 91° F. What is the mode of these temperatures?

A. 79° F

B. 82° F

C. 85.8° F

D. 86° F

E. 91° F

49. (E) *Mathematics/Statistics and Probability/Mode.* The mode is the data element with the greatest frequency: 91° F.

50. A booklet contains 30 pages. If 9 pages in the booklet have drawings, what percentage of the pages in the booklet have drawings?

F. 30%

G. 9%

H. 3%

J. 1%

K. $\dfrac{3}{10}$%

50. (F) *Mathematics/Arithmetic/Common Arithmetic Items/Percents.* Simplify the stem: "9 is what percent of 30?" Set up the "is-over-of" equation and solve for the missing value:

$$\frac{\text{is}}{\text{of}} = \frac{\%}{100}$$

$$\frac{9}{30} = \frac{x}{100}$$

$$x = \frac{9(100)}{30}$$

$$= 30\%$$

51. Which of the following represents $-7t + 6t^2 - 3$ when it is completely factored?

A. $(3t - 1)(2t + 3)$

B. $(3t + 1)(2t - 3)$

C. $(6t - 1)(t + 3)$

D. $(6t + 1)(t - 3)$

E. $(2t - 1)(3t + 3)$

51. (B) *Mathematics/Algebra/Manipulating Algebraic Expressions/Factoring Expressions.* Rearrange the expression and then factor:

$$-7t + 6t^2 - 3 = 6t^2 - 7t - 3$$
$$= (3t + 1)(2t - 3)$$

52. What is the solution set of $2^{x^2 + 2x} = 2^{-1}$?

    F. $\{1\}$
    G. $\{-1\}$
    H. $\{1, -1\}$
    J. $\{2\}$
    K. The empty set

53. Jessica is 3 years younger than Joshua. If x represents Joshua's age now, what was Jessica's age four years ago in terms of x?

    A. $x-1$
    B. $x-3$
    C. $x-4$
    D. $x-6$
    E. $x-7$

54. In a drama club, x students contributed y dollars each to buy an \$18 gift for their advisor. If three more students had contributed, each student could have contributed one dollar less to buy the same gift. Which of the following sets of equations expresses this relationship?

    F. $xy = 18$ and $(x+3)(y-1) = 18$
    G. $xy = 18$ and $(x-3)(y+1) = 18$
    H. $xy = 18$ and $(x+3)(y+1) = 18$
    J. $xy = 18$ and $(x-3)(y-1) = 18$
    K. $xy = 18$ and $(x+1)(y-3) = 18$

52. **(G)** *Mathematics/Algebra/Solving Algebraic Equations or Inequalities with One Variable/Equations Involving Integer and Rational Exponents.* If $2^{x^2 + 2x} = 2^{-1}$, then $x^2 + 2x = -1$. Thus: $x^2 + 2x + 1 = (x+1)(x+1) = 0$. This equation holds true only if $x = -1$.

53. **(E)** *Mathematics/Algebra/Manipulating Algebraic Expressions/Evaluating Expressions.* If Joshua is x years old now and Jessica is 3 years younger, then Jessica is now $x-3$ years old. Four years ago she was $(x-3) - 4 = x - 7$ years old.

54. **(F)** *Mathematics/Algebra/Manipulating Algebraic Expressions/Creating Algebraic Expressions.* The amount collected is equal to the number of students multiplied by the amount that each student contributed. Therefore:

$$x \text{ students} \cdot \frac{y \text{ dollars}}{\text{student}} = \$18$$
$$xy = \$18$$

And adding three more students but each paying one dollar less changes the equation to:

$$(x+3)(y-1) = 18$$

55. $\frac{1}{2}\sqrt{112} - \sqrt{28} + 2\sqrt{63} = ?$

   A. $6\sqrt{7}$
   B. $7\sqrt{7}$
   C. $8\sqrt{7}$
   D. $9\sqrt{7}$
   E. $10\sqrt{7}$

55. **(A)** *Mathematics/Arithmetic/Complicated Manipulations/Simplifying.* First, simplify each radical in the expression:

$$\frac{1}{2}\sqrt{112} = \frac{1}{2}\left(\sqrt{16}\right)\left(\sqrt{7}\right) = \frac{1}{2}(4)\left(\sqrt{7}\right) = 2\sqrt{7}$$

$$\sqrt{28} = \sqrt{4}\sqrt{7} = 2\sqrt{7}$$

$$2\sqrt{63} = 2\left(\sqrt{9}\right)\left(\sqrt{7}\right) = 2(3)\left(\sqrt{7}\right) = 6\sqrt{7}$$

Now, combine the parts as indicated in the stem:

$$\frac{1}{2}\sqrt{112} - \sqrt{28} + 2\sqrt{63} = 2\sqrt{7} - 2\sqrt{7} + 6\sqrt{7} = 6\sqrt{7}$$

56. What is the value of x for the following set of simultaneous equations?

$$\frac{1}{x} + \frac{1}{y} = \frac{1}{4}$$

$$\frac{1}{x} - \frac{1}{y} = \frac{3}{4}$$

   F. 4
   G. 2
   H. $\frac{1}{2}$
   J. $\frac{1}{4}$
   K. -4

56. **(G)** *Mathematics/Algebra/Solving Simultaneous Equations.* Add the two equations:

$$\begin{aligned} \frac{1}{x} + \frac{1}{y} &= \frac{1}{4} \\ + \quad \frac{1}{x} - \frac{1}{y} &= \frac{3}{4} \\ \hline \frac{2}{x} &= 1 \Rightarrow x = 2 \end{aligned}$$

57. Which set could represent the lengths of the sides of a triangle?

   A. $\{1, 3, 6\}$
   B. $\{2, 4, 7\}$
   C. $\{2, 10, 12\}$
   D. $\{4, 6, 8\}$
   E. $\{4, 4, 10\}$

57. **(D)** *Mathematics/Geometry/Triangles/Properties of Triangles.* The sum of the lengths of any two sides of a triangle must be greater than the length of the third side. Check each of the answer choices:

   A. $1 + 3 > 6$ ✗
   B. $2 + 4 > 7$ ✗
   C. $2 + 10 > 12$ ✗
   D. $4 + 6 > 8$
   $\quad\;\; 4 + 8 > 6$
   $\quad\;\; 6 + 8 > 4$ ✓
   E. $4 + 4 > 10$ ✗

58. What is the solution set $\{x,y\}$, in terms of a and b, for the following system of equations?

$$ax + y = b$$
$$2ax + y = 2b$$

F. $\left\{-\dfrac{b}{a}, -1\right\}$

G. $\{-a, b\}$

H. $\left\{\dfrac{b}{a}, 0\right\}$

J. $\left\{\dfrac{b}{a}, \dfrac{a}{b}\right\}$

K. $\left\{\dfrac{2a}{b}, \dfrac{2b}{a}\right\}$

58. (H) *Mathematics/Algebra/Solving Simultaneous Equations.* To eliminate the variable y, multiply the first equation by -1 and add the equations:

$$-ax - y = -b$$
$$+\ \ 2ax + y = 2b$$
$$\overline{\qquad ax = b}$$
$$x = \dfrac{b}{a}$$

Substitute $\dfrac{b}{a}$ for x in the first equation and solve for y:

$$a\left(\dfrac{b}{a}\right) + y = b$$
$$b + y = b$$
$$y = 0$$

The solution set $\{x,y\}$ is $\left\{\dfrac{b}{a}, 0\right\}$.

59. In the figure below, $\sin\theta = \dfrac{r}{4}$. What is the value of $\cos\theta$?

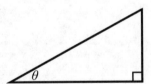

A. $\dfrac{\sqrt{16-r^2}}{4}$

B. $\dfrac{4-r}{4}$

C. $\dfrac{16-r^2}{2}$

D. $\dfrac{4-r}{2}$

E. $\dfrac{16-r^2}{r}$

59. (A) *Mathematics/Trigonometry/Determining Trigonometric Values* and *Geometry/Triangles/Pythagorean Theorem.* Since $\sin\theta = \dfrac{\text{side opposite }\theta}{\text{hypotenuse}}$, we have:

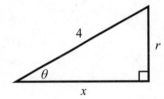

The third side of the triangle, x, is found using the Pythagorean theorem:

$$x^2 + r^2 = 4^2$$
$$= 16$$
$$x^2 = 16 - r^2$$
$$x = \pm\sqrt{16 - r^2}$$
$$= \sqrt{16 - r^2} \ \text{(length is positive)}$$

Since $\cos\theta = \dfrac{\text{side adjacent to }\theta}{\text{hypotenuse}}$, we have:

$$\cos\theta = \dfrac{\sqrt{16 - r^2}}{4}$$

60. If 3 copier machines can copy 300 sheets in 3 minutes, assuming the same rate, how long, in minutes, will it take 6 such copiers to copy 600 sheets?

- F. 2
- G. 3
- H. 4
- J. 6
- K. 9

60. (G) *Mathematics/Arithmetic/Common Arithmetic Items/Proportions and Direct-Inverse Variation.* The number of sheets is directly proportional to the number of machines, as well as directly proportional to the amount of time. Thus:

$$\left(\frac{\text{sheets}}{\text{\# of machines} \cdot \text{time}}\right)_1 = \left(\frac{\text{sheets}}{\text{\# of machines} \cdot \text{time}}\right)_2$$

$$\frac{300}{3(3)} = \frac{600}{6(t)}$$

$$\frac{300}{9} = \frac{600}{6t}$$

$$\frac{100}{3} = \frac{100}{t}$$

$$100t = 300$$

$$t = 3$$

SECTION 3: READING TEST
40 Items

DIRECTIONS: Each passage below is followed by a set of items. Read each passage and choose the best answer for each item. You may refer to the passage as often as necessary to answer the items.

Passage I

PROSE FICTION: This passage is adapted from the short story "Paul's Case: A Study in Temperament" by Willa Cather.

It was Paul's afternoon to appear before the faculty of Pittsburgh High School to account for his various misdemeanors. He had been suspended a week ago. His father had called at the principal's office and
5 confessed his perplexity about his son. Paul entered the faculty room suave and smiling. His clothes were a trifle outgrown. The tan velvet on the collar of his open overcoat was frayed and worn. But for all that there was something of the dandy in him. He wore an opal
10 pin in his neatly knotted black four-in-hand, and a red carnation in his buttonhole. This latter adornment the faculty somehow felt was not properly significant of the contrite spirit befitting a boy under the ban of suspension.

15 Paul was tall for his age and very thin. He had high, cramped shoulders and a narrow chest. His eyes were remarkable for a certain hysterical brilliancy. He continually used them in a conscious, theatrical sort of way, peculiarly offensive in a boy. The pupils were
20 abnormally large, as though he was addicted to belladonna. But there was a glassy glitter about them, which that drug does not produce.

When questioned by the principal as to why he was there Paul stated, politely enough, that he wanted
25 to come back to school. This was a lie, but Paul was quite accustomed to lying; he found it, indeed, indispensable for overcoming friction. His teachers were asked to state their respective charges against him. They did so with such a rancor and aggrievement
30 as evinced that this was not a usual case. Disorder and impertinence were among the offenses named. Yet each of his instructors felt that it was scarcely possible to put into words the real cause of the trouble, which lay in a sort of hysterically defiant manner of the boy's,

35 in the contempt which they all knew he felt for them, and which he seemingly made not the least effort to conceal. Once, when he had been making a synopsis of a paragraph at the blackboard, his English teacher had stepped to his side and attempted to guide his hand.
40 Paul had started back with a shudder and thrust his hands violently behind him. The astonished woman could scarcely have been more hurt and embarrassed had he struck at her. The insult was so involuntary and definitely personal as to be unforgettable. In one way
45 or another he had made all his teachers, men and women alike, conscious of the same feeling of physical aversion. In one class he habitually sat with his hand shading his eyes; in another he always looked out of the window during the recitation; in another he made a
50 running commentary on the lecture, with humorous intention.

His teachers felt this afternoon that his whole attitude was symbolized by his shrug and his flippant red carnation flower. They fell upon him without
55 mercy, his English teacher leading the pack. He stood through it smiling. His pale lips parted over his white teeth. (His lips were continuously twitching, and he had a habit of raising his eyebrows that was contemptuous and irritating to the last degree.) Older
60 boys than Paul had broken down and shed tears under that baptism of fire, but his set smile did not once desert him. His only sign of discomfort was the nervous trembling of the fingers that toyed with the buttons of his overcoat, and an occasional jerking of
65 the other hand that held his hat. Paul was always smiling, always glancing about him, seeming to feel that people might be watching him and trying to detect something. This conscious expression, since it was as far as possible from boyish mirthfulness, was usually
70 attributed to insolence or "smartness."

1. This short story is subtitled "A Study in Temperament," which suggests that the author wants to examine:

    A. a certain type of character.
    B. reactions under pressure.
    C. how people change over time.
    D. people and their settings.

2. The introductory phrases "something of the dandy" (line 9), "hysterical brilliancy" (line 17), and "peculiarly offensive" (line 19):

    I.   describe Paul's reaction to his peers.
    II. show the narrator's distaste for Paul.
    III. reveal Paul as an unpleasant character.

    F. I only
    G. III only
    H. I and II only
    J. II and III only

3. The passage makes it clear in the first paragraph that the faculty of the high school:

    A. is perplexed by Paul's actions.
    B. finds Paul's demeanor inappropriate.
    C. cannot understand Paul's words.
    D. wants only the best for Paul.

1. (A) *Reading/Prose Fiction/Main Idea.* A person's temperament is their usual mood or attitude towards the world, and it is an outgrowth of a person's character. For this reason, (A) is the correct answer choice. Cather's general purpose is to dramatize and examine how a certain type of character, or a person of a certain mood or attitude, responds to the world around him. As for the other answer choices, (B) and (C) are incorrect because they are not broad enough to encompass Cather's general purpose; how a person reacts under pressure, (B), and how a person changes over time, (C), are aspects of temperament, but Cather is interested in more than just these single aspects. Finally, (D) is incorrect because it is too general; as explained above, Cather is interested in a topic much more specific than people in general and their settings.

2. (J) *Reading/Prose Fiction/Implied Idea.* These introductory phrases, as well as several other details throughout the passage, show Paul in a very unsympathetic light. Paul is shown to be an unpleasant character, (III), and the unrelenting nature of the negative description reveals that the narrator finds Paul to be unpleasant as well, (II). These introductory phrases do not describe Paul's reactions to his peers, (I), though, so (J) is the correct answer choice.

3. (B) *Reading/Prose Fiction/Explicit Detail.* At the end of the first paragraph, Cather describes a red carnation that Paul wears in his buttonhole. She says "This latter adornment the faculty somehow felt was not properly significant of the contrite spirit befitting a boy under the ban of suspension" (lines 11–14). In other words, the faculty does not find Paul's demeanor appropriate to the situation at hand. So, (B) is the correct answer choice. As for the other answer choices, (A) is incorrect because it is Paul's father who is described as perplexed (lines 4–5). (C) and (D) are both incorrect because there is simply no evidence to support either idea.

4. The words *hysterical* and *hysterically*, as used in lines 17 and 34, respectively, seem to imply:

F. delirium.
G. raving.
H. uncontrolled behavior.
J. frothing.

5. The author implies that the most serious flaw Paul has is his:

A. inability to complete his work.
B. flippant sense of humor.
C. drug use.
D. failure to hide his contempt for others.

6. In lines 54–55, the author indicates that the faculty behaved like a pack of:

F. cowards.
G. predators.
H. liars.
J. scholars.

7. The author uses the phrase "baptism of fire" (line 61) to denote the:

A. challenge faced by students in a faculty inquisition.
B. youthfulness of Paul and his fellow students.
C. obstacles adolescents confront while growing up.
D. fury with which Paul faced the faculty.

4. **(H)** *Reading/Prose Fiction/Vocabulary.* Although the descriptions in lines 17 and 34 suggest that Paul is unable to control his odd mannerisms, there is no concrete evidence that he suffers from delirium, (F); raving, (G); or frothing, (J). These are all conditions which one normally associates with intense physical illness or psychosis, and these are diagnoses that seem too severe for the behavior that Paul exhibits. So, (H) is the correct answer choice.

5. **(D)** *Reading/Prose Fiction/Implied Idea.* Paul's most serious flaw is vividly described and analyzed in lines 37–51. In these lines, Cather shows Paul's violent interaction with his English teacher, his habit of ignoring teachers during class, and his tendency to mock these teachers who now sit in judgment of him. In short, it is Paul's inability to hide his contempt for others that has landed him in trouble. So, (D) is the correct answer choice. As for the other answer choices, they are all incorrect simply because there is no evidence to support these ideas.

6. **(G)** *Reading/Prose Fiction/Explicit Detail.* In lines 54–55, Cather compares the faculty to a pack of predators. Specifically, she writes that they "fell upon him without mercy, his English teacher leading the pack." So, (G) is the correct answer choice.

7. **(A)** *Reading/Prose Fiction/Implied Idea.* In lines 59–61, Cather writes that "Older boys than Paul had broken down and shed tears under that baptism of fire." The "baptism of fire" is the inquisition performed by the faculty into student misbehaviors. So, (A) is the correct answer choice. As Cather says, most students broke down during such inquisitions. However, Paul manages the entire experience without any visible show of emotion at all.

8. The word *smartness* (line 70) is used to mean:

    F. wit.
    G. intelligence.
    H. impudence.
    J. reasonableness.

9. Which adjective does NOT describe Paul as he is presented in this story?

    A. Defiant
    B. Proud
    C. Flippant
    D. Candid

10. By the end of the selection, we find that the faculty:

    F. resents and loathes Paul.
    G. admires and trusts Paul.
    H. struggles to understand Paul.
    J. is physically revolted by Paul.

8. **(H)** *Reading/Prose Fiction/Vocabulary.* Cather writes that Paul was always smiling, and the faculty attributed his constant smiling to "insolence or 'smartness'" (line 70). "Insolence" means "disrespect" or "rudeness." So, it is logical that "smartness" has a negative connotation in this context. Therefore, (H) is the correct answer choice since "impudence" also means "rudeness" or "disrespect." As for the other answer choices, they are all incorrect because they do not have the negative connotations required here.

9. **(D)** *Reading/Prose Fiction/Implied Idea.* In lines 25–27, Cather focuses on Paul's tendency to lie. As she writes, "Paul was quite accustomed to lying" (lines 25–26). A person who lies cannot be described as "candid" or honest, so (D) is the correct answer choice. As for the other answer choices, Paul is shown to be defiant, (A); proud, (B); and flippant, (C), throughout the passage.

10. **(F)** *Reading/Prose Fiction/Implied Idea.* Although it is evident throughout the passage that Paul's teachers dislike him, it is only in the final paragraph that the ferocity of their hatred for him receives full expression. Cather compares the faculty to a pack of wild wolves that finally "fell upon him without mercy, his English teacher leading the pack" (lines 54–55). The faculty loathes and resents Paul. So, (F) is the correct answer choice. As for the other answer choices, (G) and (H) are incorrect because there is simply no evidence to support either idea. Finally, (J) is incorrect because Paul is physically revolted by the faculty (lines 46–47) and not vice versa.

Passage II

SOCIAL SCIENCE: This passage discusses the history of African Americans in Congress.

Only with the enforcement of the Reconstruction Act of 1867 and the ratification of the Fifteenth Amendment to the Constitution did African Americans first win seats in Congress. Hiram Revels of
5 Mississippi became the first African American to serve. He took his seat in the Senate on February 25, 1870. Joseph Rainey of South Carolina became the first African American member of the House of Representatives later in 1870. In the next 80 years,
10 nearly seventy African Americans served in Congress.

African Americans throughout the South became politically active soon after the close of the Civil War. State conventions and local political groups such as the Union League provided an opportunity for freed
15 African Americans to convey their vision of full participation in the political and economic life of the former slave states. Out of this broad-based mobilization came a generation of African American leaders who nearly all adhered to the Republican Party
20 because it had championed the rights of African Americans. Those elected to Congress during Reconstruction found the legislature an effective forum for the promotion of political equality. Following the end of Reconstruction in 1877, African Americans
25 continued to win election to Congress. Their struggle for civil rights and economic opportunity also continued. The African American congressional representatives of the late nineteenth century were the most prominent indication of the persistence of
30 political organization on a local level in the South.

During the 1890s and early 1900s, no African American won election to Congress. This was in part due to restrictive state election codes in some southern states. During World War I and in the following
35 decade, however, African American migration to northern cities established the foundation for political organization in urban centers. Oscar DePriest's election in 1928 as a representative from Chicago began a slow but steady succession of victories in the North. Over
40 the next three decades African Americans won seats in New York City, Detroit, and Philadelphia. In the wake of the civil rights movement and the Voting Rights Act of 1965, African Americans regained seats in the South. Since the 1930s, nearly all African American
45 representatives have been Democrats.

Since the nineteenth century, African American members of Congress have served as advocates for all African Americans as well as representatives for their constituencies. During Reconstruction and the late
50 nineteenth century, African American representatives called on their colleagues to protect the voting rights of African Americans. These members of Congress, many of them former slaves, also called for more educational opportunities and land grants for freed African
55 Americans. In the mid-twentieth century, African American representatives turned to the needs of urban areas. They asked for improved housing and job training. As the most prominent African American office-holders of the time, these representatives served
60 as defenders of the civil rights movement and proponents of laws to end segregation. In 1971, the formation of the Congressional Black Caucus offered a formal means of representing the combined interests of African Americans. The caucus has shown a special
65 concern for the protection of civil rights: the guarantee of equal opportunity in education, the workplace, and housing, and a broad array of foreign and domestic policy issues.

African Americans in Congress have been further
70 united by their shared experience in the African American community. Many of the early Black representatives were born in slavery. The opportunities of Reconstruction gave these representatives the hope that African Americans might gain genuine equality in
75 American society. However, the opposition of some white Southerners reminded them of the need for federal protection of the liberties won in the aftermath of the Civil War.

Since the victories of the civil rights movement in
80 the 1960s, African American men and women have won election to Congress from more diverse regions of the country. Whether from urban districts, suburban areas, or more recently from rural Mississippi, these members of Congress have kept their common concern
85 with economic issues that affect African Americans and with the protection of civil rights.

The biographies of African Americans who served in the House and Senate provide a unique perspective on the history of the Congress and the role
90 of African Americans in politics. Their stories offer testimony to the long struggle to extend the ideals of the founders to include all citizens of the United States.

11. According to the passage, the first African American to serve in the House of Representatives was:

   A. Hiram Revels.
   B. Joseph Rainey.
   C. from Chicago.
   D. a former slave.

12. The passage suggests that, in contrast to African Americans elected to Congress during and shortly after Reconstruction, African Americans elected to Congress today are more likely to:

   F. be Democrats.
   G. be members of the Republican Party.
   H. work for full political equality for all African Americans.
   J. come from districts in which the majority is African American.

13. One difference between African American congressional representatives in the nineteenth century and those in the mid-twentieth century was:

   A. the political party to which they were likely to belong.
   B. their commitment to education for African Americans.
   C. the strength of their ties to the African American community as a whole.
   D. the extent to which they represented all African Americans and not just their constituents.

14. When the African American representatives "turned to" (line 56) certain issues in the mid-twentieth century, they:

   F. became antagonistic toward those issues.
   G. reversed their positions on those issues.
   H. devoted themselves to those issues.
   J. referred to those issues.

11. **(B)** *Reading/Social Science/Explicit Detail.* The correct answer choice is (B). In lines 7–10, the author says Joseph Rainey was the first African American elected to the House. As for the other answer choices, (A) is incorrect because Hiram Revels was the first African American in the Senate. (C) is incorrect because Joseph Rainey was from South Carolina. (D) is incorrect because there is no evidence in the passage that Rainey was a former slave.

12. **(F)** *Reading/Social Science/Explicit Detail.* The correct answer choice is (F). In the last sentence of the third paragraph, the author states that since "the 1930s, nearly all African American representatives have been Democrats."

13. **(A)** *Reading/Social Science/Explicit Detail.* In lines 17–21, the author says African American leaders after the Civil War "nearly all adhered to the Republican Party." In lines 44–45, the author then says that "Since the 1930s, nearly all African American representatives have been Democrats." So, (A) is the correct answer choice. The other answer choices are all contradicted by the fourth paragraph where the author details the activities of African American members of Congress during both the nineteenth and the twentieth century.

14. **(H)** *Reading/Social Science/Implied Idea.* In lines 55–58, the author writes that "In the mid-twentieth century, African American representatives turned to the needs of urban areas. They asked for improved housing and job training." Given the context of this sentence, it is clear that "turned to" means "concentrated" or "devoted themselves to." So, (H) is correct. (F) and (G) are incorrect because they are the exact opposite of what the author intends to say in the above sentence. (J) is incorrect because the African American representatives did more than just "refer" to these issues; they dedicated themselves and took action to achieve specific goals related to these issues.

15. According to the passage, one reason African Americans began to be elected to Congress from cities in the northern United States after the 1930s was that:

A. more African Americans lived in northern cities at that time than had been the case previously.

B. African Americans in northern cities had better political organizations than did African Americans in the rural South.

C. African American politicians in the North were more likely to be members of the Democratic Party than were those in the South.

D. African American politicians in the North were more likely to focus on voting rights for African Americans than were those in the South.

15. **(A)** *Reading/Social Science/Explicit Detail.* In lines 35–37, the author writes that an "African American migration to northern cities established the foundation for political organization in urban centers" after World War I and in the following decade. So, (A) is the correct answer choice. As for the other answer choices, (B) and (D) are both incorrect because there is no evidence in the passage to support these ideas. (C) is incorrect because lines 44–45 indicate African American representatives from all regions of America were nearly all Democrats.

16. Which one of the following is NOT mentioned in the passage as a common concern of African American congressional representatives?

F. Enforcing voting rights for African Americans

G. Increasing educational opportunities for African Americans

H. Ensuring opportunities for employment for African Americans

J. Protecting people of African descent in other countries

16. **(J)** *Reading/Social Science/Explicit Detail.* Voting rights, (F), are mentioned or implied in lines 26, 51, and 65. Educational opportunities, (G), are mentioned or implied in lines 53 and 66. Finally, employment, (H), is mentioned or implied in lines 57–58 and 66. Only the issue of protecting people of African descent in other countries is not mentioned in the passage. So, (J) is the correct answer choice.

17. One reason cited in the passage for the election of African Americans to Congress from both southern states after Reconstruction and northern states after World War I is the:

A. success of the civil rights movement.
B. passage and enforcement of the Fifteenth Amendment.
C. strength of local African American political organizations.
D. predominance of African Americans in certain districts.

17. **(C)** *Reading/Social Science/Explicit Detail.* In lines 13–17 and lines 27–30, the author discusses the strength of African American political organizations in southern states during the nineteenth century. In lines 34–37, the author mentions the strength of African American political organizations in northern states during the twentieth century. So, (C) is correct. As for the other answer choices, (A) is incorrect because the civil rights movement did not occur until the second half of the twentieth century. (B) is incorrect because, while the Fifteenth Amendment is mentioned in lines 2–3, it is not cited as a reason why African Americans won congressional seats during these two time periods. Finally, (D) is incorrect since there is no evidence to support this idea.

18. According to the passage, the Congressional Black Caucus:

F. focused its attention almost exclusively on domestic issues.
G. was the first organization founded exclusively for African American congressional representatives.
H. was intended to replace local African American political organizations with one large national organization.
J. provided a forum in which African American representatives could deal with issues of concern to all African Americans.

18. **(J)** *Reading/Social Science/Explicit Detail.* In lines 61–68, the author discusses the Congressional Black Caucus. Specifically, the author says that the caucus "offered a formal means of representing the combined interests of African Americans." So, (J) is the correct answer choice. As for the other answer choices, (F) is incorrect because it is contradicted by line 67. (G) and (H) are incorrect because there is no evidence in the passage to support these ideas.

19. The last paragraph suggests that this passage might serve as:

A. a call to political involvement on the part of African Americans.
B. an introduction to biographies of African American members of Congress.
C. the conclusion of a history of African Americans in the United States.
D. part of a longer work on the history of the United States Congress.

19. **(B)** *Reading/Social Science/Main Idea.* In the last paragraph, the author specifically mentions the "biographies of African Americans who served in the House and Senate" (lines 87–88) as well as "their stories" (line 90). Based on these details, it is logical to assume that this passage could serve as the introduction to a collection of biographies of African American members of Congress. So, (B) is the correct answer choice. As for the other answer choices, they are all incorrect because there is no evidence in the final paragraph to support these ideas.

20. The author expresses admiration toward the African American congressional representatives discussed in the passage for their:

F. political acumen.
G. attempts to ensure the rights of all Americans.
H. single-minded devotion to the struggle for civil rights.
J. focus on providing economic opportunity for African Americans.

20. **(G)** *Reading/Social Science/Implied Idea.* In lines 91–92, the author praises African American members of Congress for their "long struggle to extend the ideals of the founders to include all citizens of the United States." In other words, they are praised for their efforts to ensure the rights of all Americans. So, (G) is the correct answer choice. As for the other answer choices, (F) is incorrect because it is never mentioned in the passage. (H) and (J) are incorrect because they are contradicted by the above quotation.

Passage III

HUMANITIES: This passage is adapted from Thomas Bulfinch's *Mythology*.

Minerva was the goddess of wisdom, but on one occasion she did a very foolish thing; she entered into competition with Juno and Venus for the prize of beauty. It happened thus: at the nuptials of Peleus and
5 Thetis all the gods were invited with the exception of Eris, or Discord. Enraged at her exclusion, the goddess threw a golden apple among the guests, with the inscription, "For the fairest." Thereupon Juno, Venus, and Minerva each claimed the apple. Jupiter, not
10 willing to decide in so delicate a matter, sent the goddesses to Mount Ida, where the beautiful shepherd Paris was tending his flocks. To him was committed the decision. The goddesses accordingly appeared before him. Juno promised him power and riches.
15 Minerva promised glory and renown in war. Venus offered the fairest of women for his wife. Each attempted to bias his decision in her own favour. Paris decided in favour of Venus and gave her the golden apple, thus making the two other goddesses his
20 enemies. Under the protection of Venus, Paris sailed to Greece. He was hospitably received by Menelaus, king of Sparta. Now Helen, the wife of Menelaus, was the very woman whom Venus had destined for Paris, the fairest of her sex. She had been sought as a bride by
25 numerous suitors. Before her decision was made known, they all, at the suggestion of Ulysses, one of their number, took an oath that they would defend her from all injury and avenge her cause if necessary. She chose Menelaus, and was living with him happily when
30 Paris became their guest. Paris, aided by Venus, persuaded her to elope with him. He carried her to Troy, whence arose the famous Trojan War, the theme of the greatest poems of antiquity, those of Homer and Virgil.

35 Menelaus called upon his brother chieftains of Greece to fulfill their pledge, and join him in his efforts to recover his wife. They generally came forward, but Ulysses, who had married Penelope, and was very happy in his wife and child, had no disposition to
40 embark in such a troublesome affair. He therefore hung back and Palamedes was sent to urge him. When Palamedes arrived at Ithaca, Ulysses pretended to be mad. He yoked an ass and an ox together to the plough and began to sow salt. Palamedes, to try him, placed
45 the infant Telemachus before the plough, whereupon the father turned the plough aside, showing plainly that he was no madman, and after that could no longer refuse to fulfill his promise. Being now himself gained

for the undertaking, he lent his aid to bring in other
50 reluctant chiefs, especially Achilles. This hero was the son of that Thetis at whose marriage the apple of Discord had been thrown among the goddesses. Thetis was herself one of the immortals, a sea-nymph. Knowing that her son was fated to perish before Troy if
55 he went on the expedition, she endeavored to prevent his going. She sent him away to the court of King Lycomedes, and induced him to conceal himself in the disguise of a maiden among the daughters of the king. Ulysses, hearing he was there, went disguised as a
60 merchant to the palace and offered for sale female ornaments, among which he had placed some arms. While the king's daughters were engrossed with the other contents of the merchant's pack, Achilles handled the weapons and thereby betrayed himself to the keen
65 eye of Ulysses, who found no great difficulty in persuading him to disregard his mother's prudent counsels and join his countrymen in the war.

21. By describing Jupiter as "not willing to decide in so delicate a matter" (lines 9–10), the author implies that:

  A. Jupiter is usually heavy-handed.
  B. any decision is bound to offend someone.
  C. Jupiter is overly sensitive.
  D. the problems are so obscure that no one can judge them.

22. The word *disposition* (line 39) is used to mean:

  F. inclination.
  G. nature.
  H. integrity.
  J. value.

23. All of the following assertions are examples of the author's inserting himself into the narrative EXCEPT:

  A. Minerva did a foolish thing.
  B. The poems of Homer and Virgil were great.
  C. Helen was the fairest of her sex.
  D. The greatest poems of antiquity were about the Trojan War.

24. Ulysses pretended to be mad by planting salt because salt:

  F. does not grow.
  G. is nearly worthless.
  H. was used for money.
  J. is used in battle.

21. **(B)** *Reading/Humanities/Implied Idea.* Jupiter is asked to decide which of three goddesses is the fairest—Juno, Minerva, or Venus. Regardless of which goddess he selects, he will anger the other two because he did not choose them. It is a no-win proposition in that he is bound to offend someone. So, (B) is the correct answer choice. As for the other answer choices, they are all incorrect since there is no evidence to support these ideas.

22. **(F)** *Reading/Humanities/Vocabulary.* The passage tells us that "Ulysses, who had married Penelope, and was very happy in his wife and child, had no disposition to embark in such a troublesome affair" (lines 38–40). Given the context, it is clear that "disposition" means "inclination." In other words, Ulysses had no inclination to embark on the adventure since he is happy at home with his family. So, (F) is the correct answer choice. As for the other answer choices, they are all incorrect because they cannot substitute for "disposition" and create a sentence with the same meaning as the original.

23. **(C)** *Reading/Humanities/Voice.* In lines 1–2, the author asserts that Minerva once did a foolish thing, (A). In lines 33–34, the author asserts that the poems of Homer and Virgil were great, (B), as well as that the greatest poems of antiquity were about the Trojan War, (D). Nowhere in the passage, though, does the author claim that Helen was the fairest of her sex. Instead, it is Venus who identifies Helen as "the fairest of her sex" (lines 23–24) and destines her for a relationship with Paris. So, (C) is the correct answer choice.

24. **(F)** *Reading/Humanities/Implied Idea.* In lines 42–43, the author says "Ulysses pretended to be mad" in order to avoid going off to war. The author then says Ulysses attempted to prove his madness by hitching a mismatched pair of animals together ("an ass and an ox") and sowing into the ground something that could never grow—salt. So, (F) is the correct answer choice. As for the other answer choices, they are all incorrect since there no evidence to support these ideas.

25. When Palamedes tries Ulysses (lines 44–48), he:

    A. finds him guilty.
    B. judges him.
    C. tests him.
    D. attempts to help him.

25. **(C)** *Reading/Humanities/Implied Idea.* In lines 44–48, Palamedes visits Ulysses to take him to war. Ulysses does not wish to go and pretends to be insane. Palamedes is skeptical of Ulysses' act, though, and thinks up a way to test him. He puts Ulysses' child in the path of a sharp plow that Ulysses steers across a field. Ulysses steers the plow so his young child's life is spared, proving that he is indeed sane. (C) is the correct answer choice because Palamedes tries Ulysses in this manner to test him. As for the other answer choices, they are all incorrect because there is no evidence to support these ideas.

26. The author reveals that Thetis is a sea-nymph in order to explain:

    F. why she married Peleus.
    G. why she dislikes the idea of war.
    H. the effect of the apple of Discord.
    J. her ability to predict the future.

26. **(J)** *Reading/Humanities/Implied Idea.* In lines 53–56, the author explains how Thetis, "one of the immortals, a sea nymph" tried to prevent her son Achilles from going off to war because she knew "that her son was fated to perish before Troy if he went on the expedition." Instead of stating explicitly that Thetis could read the future, the author merely mentions her immortal status and expects the reader to understand that this means she can see into the future. So, (J) is the correct answer choice. As for the other answer choices, they are all incorrect because there is no evidence to support these ideas.

27. Among the chieftains of Greece apparently are:

    A. Juno, Venus, and Minerva.
    B. Paris and Lycomedes.
    C. Ulysses, Achilles, and Menelaus.
    D. Eris and Thetis.

27. **(C)** *Reading/Humanities/Explicit Detail.* Juno, Venus, and Minerva, (A), are the goddesses mentioned in the first paragraph. Paris, (B), is "the beautiful shepherd" (line 11) who is asked to decide which of the goddesses is fairest. Eris and Thetis, (D), are the goddess of Discord (line 6) and a sea-nymph (line 53) respectively. Finally, in lines 35–36, the author says "Menelaus called upon his brother chieftains of Greece to fulfill their pledge." The author then explains how Ulysses and Achilles were gathered for the impending war; in other words, they too are chieftains of Greece. So, (C) is the correct answer choice.

28. Why does Ulysses display arms among the ornaments?

    F.   To trick Achilles into revealing himself
    G. As a declaration of war
    H. To mislead the daughters of the king
    J.   To complete his disguise as a merchant

28. **(F)** *Reading/Humanities/Implied Idea.* Readers are expected to understand Ulysses' clever ploy at King Lycomedes' court even though it is not entirely spelled out. In short, Ulysses visits the court because he knows Achilles is hiding there. Ulysses disguises himself as a merchant and pretends to sell "female ornaments" (lines 60–61) to the women at the court. Mixed into this collection of ornaments, though, are several weapons ("some arms"). Now Achilles, who has disguised himself as a woman so he won't be recognized, comes to look through the wares being offered by this new merchant. Achilles looks only at the weapons and ignores the "female ornaments" entirely. In this manner, Achilles betrays himself "to the keen eye of Ulysses" (lines 64–65) and is discovered. (F) is the correct answer choice because, as shown above, the purpose of Ulysses' clever ploy is to trick Achilles into revealing himself.

29. According to the passage, the events described will ultimately lead to:

    I.   the death of Achilles.
    II. the advent of war.
    III. the downfall of Paris.

    A. I only
    B. II only
    C. I and II only
    D. II and III only

29. **(C)** *Reading/Humanities/Development.* In lines 54–55, the passage foreshadows the death of Achilles by telling us that Thetis knows "her son was fated to perish before Troy if he went on the expedition." So, (I) is true. In lines 30–34, the author describes Helen's elopement with Paris to Troy, from "whence arose the famous Trojan War"; in addition, the second paragraph describes the gathering of chieftains in preparation for war. So, (II) is true. Nowhere in the passage, though, is the downfall of Paris mentioned. So, only (I) and (II) are true. Therefore, (C) is the correct answer choice.

30. A reasonable title for this narrative might be:

    F.   "Achilles and Ulysses"
    G. "The Apple of Discord Leads to War"
    H. "Beauty and the Beast"
    J.   "The Pettiness of the Gods"

30. **(G)** *Reading/Humanities/Main Idea.* The correct answer choice is (G). "The Apple of Discord Leads to War" is a title that accurately and fully summarizes all of the events, characters, and themes in this passage. As for the other answer choices, (F) is incorrect because Achilles and Ulysses are only two of several important characters here. (H) is incorrect because it is not clear who "Beauty and the Beast" would be. Finally, (J) is incorrect because the title only relates to part of the passage; in short, the pettiness of the gods precipitates the chain of events in this passage, but much happens in the latter part that is unrelated to the gods' pettiness.

Passage IV

NATURAL SCIENCE: This passage discusses the production of electromagnetic radiation.

When you run a comb through your hair, you disturb electrons in both your hair and the comb, producing static electricity. You can do a simple experiment to confirm this. Stand near an AM radio
5 and comb your hair. You'll hear static. The scientific principle that you've just proved is that whenever you disturb electrons, you generate electromagnetic waves.

The principle also applies to heated objects. The atoms in a heated object are vibrating rapidly, and the
10 hotter the object becomes, the faster the atoms vibrate. The vibrating atoms collide with the electrons in the material. Each time the motion of an electron is disturbed, it emits a photon. Therefore, heated objects emit electromagnetic radiation. This type of radiation,
15 called black body radiation, is very common and is responsible for the light emitted from an ordinary incandescent light bulb.

The light coming from the bulb that your eye can detect is called visible light, but the visible spectrum is
20 just a small segment of the much larger electromag-netic spectrum. The average wavelength of visible light is about 0.0005 mm, so small that 50 light waves could be lined up end to end across the thickness of ordinary plastic wrap. For this reason, scientists measure
25 wavelengths in Angstroms. One Angstrom (Å) is 10^{-10} meters or 0.0000000001 meters.

Visible light ranges from 4,000 Å to 7,000 Å. Light near the short wavelength end of the visible spectrum (4,000 Å) looks violet, and light near the long
30 wavelength end (7,000 Å) looks red. Beyond the red end of the visible spectrum lies infrared radiation, where wavelengths range from 7,000 Å to 1 mm. At wavelengths shorter than violet, there is ultraviolet radiation. These wavelengths range from 4,000 Å down
35 to about 100 Å. At wavelengths shorter than these are X-rays and gamma rays.

Although we cannot see it, our skin senses long wavelength radiation (7,000 Å to 1 mm) as warmth. This is the principle on which heat lamps work. These
40 lower-energy photons can warm us without being dangerous. In contrast, the short wavelengths contain a large amount of energy, and these wavelengths can be quite dangerous.

When a bulb's filament is heated, three sorts of
45 collisions take place among the electrons. Gentle collisions produce low-energy photons with long wavelengths, and violent collisions produce high-energy photons with short wavelengths. Most collisions are of moderate intensity, producing photons of
50 intermediate wavelengths.

The wavelength at which an object emits the maximum amount of energy is called the wavelength of maximum. The wavelength of maximum depends on the object's temperature. As an object is heated, the
55 average collision between electrons becomes more violent, producing high-energy, shorter-wavelength photons. The hotter the object is, the shorter the wavelength of maximum.

This is a very important point in astronomy, since
60 it is possible to determine the temperature of a star from its light. It is also possible to estimate the temperature of a star from the color of light it emits. For a hot star, the wavelength of maximum lies in the ultraviolet spectrum and most of the radiation cannot
65 be seen, but in the visible range, the star emits more blue than red. Thus, a hot star looks blue. In contrast, a cooler star radiates its maximum energy in the infrared. In the visible range of the spectrum it radiates more red than blue and therefore looks red.

31. According to the passage, which of the following types of radiation has the shortest wavelength?

 A. Infrared light
 B. Visible light
 C. Ultraviolet light
 D. X-rays

32. It can be inferred that radiation of very short wavelengths can be dangerous because the radiation:

 F. has no wavelength of maximum.
 G. has very high energy.
 H. originated in a black body.
 J. is visible to the eye.

33. According to the passage, the wavelength of maximum is:

 A. the maximum temperature at which an object emits light.
 B. visible radiation with the longest wavelength.
 C. the wavelength of light at the red end of the spectrum.
 D. the wavelength at which an object emits the maximum amount of energy.

34. The main purpose of the second paragraph is to:

 F. introduce a new theory of electromagnetic radiation.
 G. define the scientific concept of black body radiation.
 H. contrast black body radiation with incandescence.
 J. illustrate the different kinds of radiation that make up the spectrum.

35. According to the passage, ultraviolet radiation has wavelengths:

 A. shorter than 100 Å.
 B. between 100 Å and 4,000 Å.
 C. between 4,000 Å and 7,000 Å.
 D. longer than 7,000 Å.

31. **(D)** *Reading/Natural Science/Explicit Detail.* Lines 35–36 state that X-rays are found at wavelengths shorter than 100 Å, which is the lower end of ultraviolet radiation. The correct answer choice is (D).

32. **(G)** *Reading/Natural Science/Explicit Detail.* Lines 41–43 explain that short wavelengths contain a high amount of energy, which makes them more dangerous than long wavelengths. So, the correct answer choice is (G).

33. **(D)** *Reading/Natural Science/Explicit Detail.* The definition appears in lines 51–53. In short, it is the wavelength at which an object emits the maximum amount of energy. So, (D) is the correct answer choice.

34. **(G)** *Reading/Natural Science/Main Idea.* The last sentence of the second paragraph states the main point of the paragraph, which is to define the concept of black body radiation. So, (G) is the correct answer choice.

35. **(B)** *Reading/Natural Science/Explicit Detail.* According to the fourth paragraph, ultraviolet radiation is the radiation with wavelengths from 4,000 Å down to 100 Å.

36. The passage implies that heat lamps utilize:

   F. X-rays.
   G. gamma rays.
   H. visible wavelengths.
   J. infrared radiation.

36. **(J)** *Reading/Natural Science/Explicit Detail.* In lines 37–41, the passage states that we cannot see the radiation from a heat lamp but do experience it as warmth. Radiation of wavelengths 7,000 Å to 1 mm is infrared radiation. So, (J) is the correct answer choice.

37. An astronomer views two stars of different temperatures. Which is hotter?

   A. The one that is larger.
   B. The one that is smaller.
   C. The one that is redder.
   D. The one that is bluer.

37. **(D)** *Reading/Natural Science/Explicit Detail.* In lines 59–69, the author discusses the temperature of stars. In line 66, the author states that "a hot star looks blue." So, (D) is the correct answer choice.

38. According to the sixth paragraph (lines 44–50), most of the electron collisions in the filament of a light bulb are:

   F. gentle and emit photons with long wavelengths.
   G. violent and emit photons with short wavelengths.
   H. violent and emit photons with long wavelengths.
   J. moderate and emit photons of intermediate wavelengths.

38. **(J)** *Reading/Natural Science/Explicit Detail.* The sixth paragraph describes three types of collisions: gentle, violent, and moderate. Lines 48–50 state that most of the collisions are of moderate intensity and produce photons of intermediate wavelengths. There are fewer gentle, (F), and violent, (G) and (H), collisions.

39. It can be inferred from the information that an incandescent bulb emits light because:

   A. electricity heats the bulb's filament.
   B. high-energy radiation surrounds the filament.
   C. non-visible radiation bombards the filament.
   D. high-energy photons collide with the atoms.

39. **(A)** *Reading/Natural Science/Implied Idea.* The passage states that the incandescent light bulb is a heated object (lines 13–17). The light is emitted when electrons collide in the filament because the filament is heated (lines 44–50). Therefore, answer (A) is correct.

40. According to the passage, the filament of an incandescent bulb produces electromagnetic radiation of:

   F. long wavelengths only.
   G. moderate wavelengths only.
   H. short wavelengths only.
   J. short, moderate, and long wavelengths.

40. **(J)** *Reading/Natural Science/Application.* The information is explicitly stated in lines 44–50. The passage describes how when a bulb's filament is heated, it produces three different electron collisions, which results in three different wavelengths: short, intermediate, and long, (J).

SECTION 4: SCIENCE TEST
40 Items

DIRECTIONS: Each passage below is followed by several items. After reading a passage, choose the best answer for each item. You may refer to the passage as often as necessary. You are NOT permitted the use of a calculator on this test.

Passage I

The solubility of materials in liquids depends not only on the nature of the solute and the solvent, but also on temperature. A graph showing the solubilities of several substances in water is presented below.

Solubility Curves

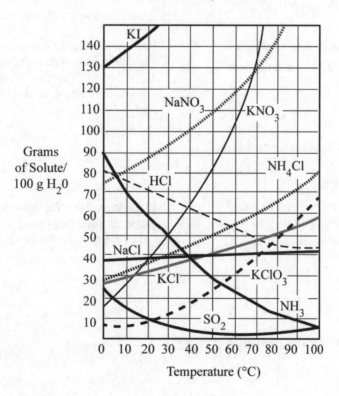

Note: NH_3, SO_2, and HCl are gases at room temperature.

1. Which of the following has the most temperature sensitive solubility in water throughout the range shown?

   A. KNO_3
   B. $NaNO_3$
   C. $NaCl$
   D. NH_3

2. The solubility of sodium (Na) salts is:

   F. high because sodium is an alkali metal.
   G. low because sodium combines with anions to make salts.
   H. dependent on what salt it forms.
   J. always greater than 40 grams per 100 grams of water.

3. A 250 ml alcoholic solution of KNO_3 at 50°C contains how many grams KNO_3 at saturation?

   A. 200
   B. 85
   C. 30
   D. Cannot be determined from the given information

4. An aqueous solution at 100°C containing equal amounts of $NaNO_3$ and KNO_3 is allowed to cool until a white powder begins to appear at the bottom of the flask. That powder is:

   F. KNO_3.
   G. $NaNO_3$.
   H. a mixture of both.
   J. Cannot be determined from the given information

1. **(A)** *Science/Data Representation/Comprehension.* The most sensitive curve will have the steepest slope, suggesting the greatest rate of change. The sharpest sloping curve is for potassium nitrate, KNO_3, answer choice (A).

2. **(H)** *Science/Data Representation/Analysis.* The sodium salts, $NaCl$ and $NaNO_3$, have different solubilities, indicating that solubility depends on more than the nature of sodium. Thus, (F) and (G) must be incorrect. (J) is incorrect because it is not known whether the solubility curves for all sodium compounds have been given. Additionally, the solubility of $NaCl$ is less than 40 grams per 100 grams of water for temperatures lower than 50°C. (H) is correct because it takes into account the differences in solubilities of different sodium salts.

3. **(D)** *Science/Data Representation/Comprehension.* The graph gives data only for aqueous solutions, not alcoholic. Additionally, the question asks about the volume of the solvent while the table indicates the mass of the solvent.

4. **(J)** *Science/Data Representation/Comprehension.* Since the solubility curves cross at approximately 68°C, the temperature needs to be known.

5. The solubility curves of the gases suggest an explanation of why:

    A. divers get the bends (nitrogen bubbles in the blood) if they rise too quickly.
    B. warm soda is less fizzy than cold soda.
    C. warm lemonade is sweeter than cold lemonade.
    D. hot air balloons rise.

5. **(B)** *Science/Data Representation/Application.* According to the graph, the solubilities of gases in aqueous solutions decrease with increasing temperature. Soda loses fizz (carbonation) as gas (carbon dioxide) leaves the liquid (B). The warmer the soda, the faster it loses carbonation. (A) shows the effect of pressure, not temperature, on solubility. (C) shows the effect of temperature on the solubility of a solid (sugar), which has nothing to do with the solubility characteristics of a gas. (D) deals with relative densities of gases, not with solubilities.

Passage II

Part of our understanding of Earth comes from a consideration of its physical properties. Selected properties of Earth are presented in Table 1.

Table 1	
Property	*Value*
Mass	6×10^{24} kg
Radius	6×10^6 m
Orbital Radius	1.5×10^{11} m
Period of Revolution	365.3 days
Period of Rotation	24 hours

Table 2 compares the properties of the other planets of the solar system relative to Earth's properties, shown as a multiple of the same property on Earth.

Table 2								
Property	Mercury	Venus	Earth	Mars	Jupiter	Saturn	Uranus	Neptune
Radius	0.387	0.949	1	0.532	11.21	9.449	4.007	3.86
Mass	0.055	0.815	1	0.107	317.87	95.159	14.536	17.147
Surface Gravity	0.378	0.905	1	0.379	2.53	1.065	0.905	1.14
Volume	0.056	0.857	1	0.151	1,321.37	763.59	63.08	57.74
Average Distance to Sun	0.39	0.723	1	1.524	5.204	9.582	19.201	30.047
Period of Revolution	0.24	0.615	1	1.881	11.862	29.457	84.01	164.79
Period of Rotation	58.79	243.686	1	1.029	0.415	0.445	0.720	0.673

The following are a few basic equations:

(1) $\text{density} = \dfrac{\text{mass}}{\text{volume}}$

(2) $\text{distance} = \text{rate} \cdot \text{time}$

(3) $\text{volume}_{\text{sphere}} = \dfrac{4}{3}\pi r^3$, where r is the radius of the sphere

6. Based on the information given in Table 1 and Table 2, what is the approximate ratio of the period of revolution in days to the period of rotation in days for Mercury?

   F. 240

   G. $\dfrac{3}{2}$

   H. $\dfrac{2}{3}$

   J. $\dfrac{1}{240}$

6. **(G)** *Science/Data Representation/Comprehension.* Mercury's period of revolution equals approximately $0.25 \cdot$ period of Earth's revolution $=$ $0.25 \cdot 365.3$ days ≈ 90 days. Mercury's period of rotation equals approximately $60 \cdot$ period of Earth's rotation $= 60 \cdot 1$ day $= 60$ days. The ratio of Mercury's revolution to rotation is $\dfrac{90}{60} = \dfrac{3}{2}$.

7. Which planet is approximately as dense as Earth?

   A. Mercury
   B. Jupiter
   C. Mars
   D. None

7. **(A)** *Science/Data Representation/Comprehension.* Look for the planet that has a ratio of mass to volume equal to approximately 1 relative to Earth. Of the choices, only Mercury fits.

8. Which planet orbits the sun at the slowest rate?

   F. Mercury
   G. Jupiter
   H. Saturn
   J. Neptune

8. **(J)** *Science/Data Representation/Comprehension.* Rate is distance divided by time. Divide the average distance to the sun by the period of revolution to get the relative rate. The smallest relative rate is the slowest. In this specific case, the planet with the greatest relative period of revolution orbits the sun at the slowest rate: Neptune.

9. Analysis of Table 2 shows that surface gravity most likely depends on:

   A. mass of the planet only.
   B. radius and mass of the planet.
   C. radius of the planet only.
   D. density of the planet and proximity to the sun.

9. **(B)** *Science/Data Representation/Analysis.* Mercury and Mars have the same surface gravity, but not the same mass or radius, so eliminate (A) and (C). Eliminate (D) because proximity to the sun has no correlation to surface gravity (as surface gravity increases, proximity fluctuates). Therefore, (B) is correct. Indeed, gravity depends on both the planet radius and on the mass of the planet. Compare Mars and Mercury to see the effect of volume. Mars is more massive, but the smaller size of Mercury gives it an equivalent surface gravity.

10. Assuming that both Earth and Neptune are spherical, the diameter of Neptune is:

    F. 3.86 times Earth's radius.
    G. 4.007 times Earth's radius.
    H. 7.72 times Earth's radius.
    J. 9.449 times Earth's radius.

10. **(H)** *Science/Data Representation/Comprehension.* Neptune's radius is 3.86 times that of Earth's radius. Therefore:

$$\text{diameter}_{\text{Neptune}} = 2\left((3.86)(\text{radius}_{\text{Earth}})\right) = 7.72(\text{radius}_{\text{Earth}})$$

11. How many meters separate the orbits of the farthest apart planetary consecutive neighbors, based on their average distances to the sun?

    A. 40 times Earth's average distance to the sun.
    B. 11 times Earth's average distance to the sun.
    C. 10 times Earth's average distance to the sun.
    D. 9 times Earth's average distance to the sun.

11. (B) *Science/Data Representation/Comprehension.*
Relative distances to the sun are as follows:

0.39 (Mercury) < 0.723 (Venus) < 1 (Earth) < 1.524 (Mars) < 5.204 (Jupiter) < 9.582 (Saturn) < 19.201 (Uranus) < 30.047 (Neptune)

The largest difference is between Uranus and Neptune: $30 - 19 = 11$ times Earth's average distance to the sun.

Passage III

Medical records for 4,000 men were compiled and analyzed. The men were sorted into four groups based on total blood cholesterol levels. The four groups' histories of illness are recorded below.

Illness	Diagnosis rate, standardized/1,000			
	<160 mg/dL	160–199 mg/dL	200–239 mg/dL	240+ mg/dL
Cancer				
Colon	0.01	0.03	0.04	0.02
Prostate	2.02	0.06	1.03	4.01
Lung	0.03	0.06	0.40	0.20
Coronary				
Thrombosis	5.02	1.01	4.00	10.05
Arrest	6.00	0.98	5.09	11.00
Cardiovascular	5.96	0.65	4.97	9.08
Cerebral Clot	4.01	0.02	0.50	4.01
Depression	5.01	0.30	0.30	0.30

12. Which of the following statements is best supported by the data?

   F. A man with a total blood cholesterol level of less than 160 mg/dL is approximately twice as likely to be diagnosed with prostate cancer as a man with a total blood cholesterol level of 220 mg/dL.

   G. A total blood cholesterol level of 160 mg/dL or more decreases the risk of being diagnosed with all three forms of cancer listed in the table.

   H. Total blood cholesterol level seems unrelated to the probability of being diagnosed with coronary disease.

   J. Cerebral clots are the most prevalent diagnosis among the group with the highest total blood cholesterol level.

12. **(F)** *Science/Data Representation/Analysis.* The prostate cancer diagnosis rate for a man with 200–239 mg/dL total blood cholesterol is 1.03, while that for a man with less than 160 mg/dL total blood cholesterol is 2.02. Thus, (F) is correct. (G) contradicts the data for colon cancer, (H) ignores the direct relationship between coronary diagnoses and cholesterol intake, and cardiac arrest is a more common diagnosis than cerebral clots for men with total blood cholesterol greater than 240 mg/dL.

13. What might one conclude about the relationship between total blood cholesterol levels and depression based on the information above?

   A. Cholesterol causes depression.

   B. Total blood cholesterol level has no effect on the diagnosis of depression.

   C. Lower total blood cholesterol is most effective in combating depression.

   D. Total blood cholesterol of 160–199 mg/dL and 240+ mg/dL are equally effective in reducing the depression diagnosis rate.

13. **(D)** *Science/Data Representation/Analysis.* The depression diagnosis rate for the second, third, and fourth groups is 0.30. This number is lower than for men with less than 160 mg/dL total blood cholesterol, so (A), (B), and (C) are wrong. According to the data, total blood cholesterol of 160–199 mg/dL is just as effective in combating depression as 240+ mg/dL, so (D) is correct.

14. For which of the following illnesses does the highest total blood cholesterol increase the probability of diagnosis most, compared relatively to the lowest total blood cholesterol?

   F. Cerebral clots
   G. Coronary arrest
   H. Cardiovascular disease
   J. Coronary thrombosis

14. **(J)** *Science/Data Representation/Comprehension.* Although having a total blood cholesterol level of 240+ mg/dL increases coronary arrest to the highest absolute diagnosis rate, the percentage increase is less than 100 percent (from 6.00 to 11.00). The percentage increase for coronary thrombosis is greater than 100 percent (from 5.02 to 10.05).

15. For which of the following groups of illnesses does a total cholesterol level of 160–199 mg/dL reduce the probability of diagnosis?

   A. Cerebral clot, coronary thrombosis, and lung cancer
   B. Cerebral clot, depression, and colon cancer
   C. Cerebral clot, coronary arrest, and prostate cancer
   D. Depression, coronary thrombosis, and colon cancer

15. **(C)** *Science/Data Representation/Comprehension.* (C) is the only group in which total blood cholesterol of 160–199 mg/dL decreases the diagnosis rate for all three illnesses. A total blood cholesterol of 160–199 mg/dL raises the probability of diagnosis for lung and colon cancer only. This question is probably best answered by recognizing that fact and eliminating those choices that include either lung or colon cancer, (A), (B), and (D).

16. What might be involved in determining a standardized diagnosis rate for men?

   F. Ignoring diagnoses that do not conform to the average results
   G. Adjusting diagnosis rates according to discrepancies in age
   H. Assuming that the diagnosis rate disregarding effects of aging is 0 diagnoses per 1,000 men
   J. Comparing data with a similar experiment involving women

16. **(G)** *Science/Data Representation/Application.* Standardizing the diagnosis rate involves correcting for variables inherent in the subject groups but not involved in the experiment. Age, weight, and genetic histories are just some of the variables that the scientist must consider. (F) does not correct for intrinsic variables; rather, it ignores results that might not conform to a "neat" result. This does not standardize the diagnosis rate so much as "fudge" it. (H) involves an arbitrary assumption that is in fact incorrect. Assuming a zero diagnosis rate in the male population distorts the result of this experiment and does not correct for variations within the subject groups. (J) is incorrect because this experiment does not consider women at all. It might be valid to compare results with a different experiment involving women, but the actual diagnosis rates for men and women for different diseases are not necessarily similar (e.g., the gender-related differences for breast cancer).

Passage IV

The resistance (R, measured in ohms) of a material is directly proportional ($\propto$) to the resistivity (r, measured in ohm-meters) of the material. The voltage (V, measured in volts) in a circuit is directly proportional to both the resistance and the current (I, measured in amperes). Resistors in series act as one resistor according to the formula:

$$R_s = R_1 + R_2 + R_3 + \ldots$$

and resistors in parallel act as one resistor according to the formula:

$$\frac{1}{R_p} = \frac{1}{R_1} + \frac{1}{R_2} + \frac{1}{R_3} + \ldots$$

The resistivities of several materials at 20°C are listed in Table 1.

Table 1	
Substance	Resistivity, r (ohm-meters)
Aluminum	2.63×10^{-8}
Copper	1.72×10^{-8}
Germanium	6.00×10^{-1}
Silicon	2.30×10^{3}
Silver	1.47×10^{-8}
Sulfur	1.00×10^{15}

17. According to the information provided, the best formula for the voltage in a circuit, where voltage is V, current is I, and resistance is R, is:

    A. $V \propto \dfrac{I}{R}$.

    B. $V \propto I + R$.

    C. $V \propto IR$.

    D. $V \propto I - R$.

17. **(C)** *Science/Data Representation/Analysis.* Since voltage is directly related to current, voltage increases by the same factor as current if other variables are held constant. The same applies for resistance; therefore, the only correct formula is (C).

18. Two resistors with $R = 2$ ohms are placed in series. How does the voltage in the circuit compare with the voltage in a circuit with only one resistor, $R = 2$? (Assume current remains constant.)

   F. The voltage is doubled.
   G. The voltage is halved.
   H. The voltage is the same.
   J. The voltage is zero.

18. (F) *Science/Data Representation/Application.* The total resistance R_s of the series resistors is $R_1 + R_2 = 2 + 2 = 4$. This resistance is double that of the circuit where $R = 2$. If R doubles, then the voltage doubles as long as the current remains the same.

19. According to the information provided, how would the voltage in a circuit with a silver resistor compare to the voltage in a circuit with a germanium resistor of the same length? (Current is the same in both circuits.)

   A. The voltage in the germanium circuit would be greater.
   B. The voltage in the silver circuit would be greater.
   C. The voltage would be the same in both circuits.
   D. Cannot be determined from the given information

19. (A) *Science/Data Representation/Analysis.* The passage states that the voltage is directly proportional to the both the resistance and the current ($V \propto IR$), so the circuit with the greater resistance would have the greater voltage. Since resistance is directly proportional to resistivity, the germanium circuit would have the greater resistance and voltage.

20. A resistor with $R = 4$ ohms is put in parallel with an identical resistor with $R = 4$ ohms. What is R_p?

   F. 0 ohms
   G. $\dfrac{1}{2}$ ohm
   H. 1 ohm
   J. 2 ohms

20. (J) *Science/Data Representation/Application.* Use the given formula for resistors in parallel:

$$\frac{1}{R_p} = \frac{1}{4} + \frac{1}{4}$$
$$= \frac{2}{4}$$
$$= \frac{1}{2}$$
$$R_p = 2$$

21. Power is defined as $P = I^2 R$. If R is a constant, then power would increase _____ with an increase in the current. (Fill in the blank space with the best answer choice.)

   A. exponentially
   B. logarithmically
   C. directly
   D. inversely

21. (A) *Science/Data Representation/Application.* If R is constant, then P increases with I^2; this is the definition of exponential growth.

22. In order to keep the current in a circuit constant, if one increases the voltage, one must:

    F. lengthen the circuit.
    G. shorten the circuit.
    H. decrease the resistance.
    J. increase the resistance.

22. **(J)** *Science/Data Representation/Analysis.* Based on the information given in the passage, we have:

$$V \propto IR$$

$$I \propto \frac{V}{R}$$

Therefore, to keep I constant if V increases, R must be increased.

Passage V

Some reactions occur in a series of steps referred to as a reaction mechanism. In order to discover the steps by which a chemical reaction occurs, the dependence of the initial rate of reaction on the concentration of the reactants is determined. Three experiments exploring the mechanism of a reaction are presented below.

Experiment 1

Chemical A is injected into a rapidly stirred solution of Chemical B in the solvent hexamethyl phosphoramide. As A and B react, they form a compound that has a characteristic absorption at 520 nanometers. The concentration of product, and therefore the rate of reaction, can be calculated by measuring the strength of the absorption. The results are presented in Table 1.

	Table 1		
Trial	Concentration A	Concentration B	Reaction Rate
1	4	4	60
2	2	2	30
3	4	2	30
4	4	8	120

Experiment 2

Chemical A is injected into a rapidly stirred solution of Chemical B in the solvent carbon tetrachloride. The product of the reaction is identical to the product in Experiment 1. The rate of reaction is followed using spectrophotometry as in Experiment 1. The results are presented in Table 2.

	Table 2		
Trial	Concentration A	Concentration B	Reaction Rate
1	3	3	27
2	6	6	108
3	6	3	54
4	12	6	216

Experiment 3

Chemical A is injected into a rapidly stirred solution of Chemical B in a 1:1-by-volume mixture of carbon tetrachloride and hexamethyl phosphoramide. The rate of reaction is followed using spectrophotometry as in Experiment 1. The results are presented in Table 3.

	Table 3		
Trial	Concentration A	Concentration B	Reaction Rate
1	9	9	54
2	9	4.5	27
3	4	4.5	18
4	4	9	36

23. Which of the following statements best describes the effect of the concentration of A on the rate of reaction in Experiment 1?

   A. Rate increases in direct proportion with increasing concentration of A.
   B. Rate increases by the square root of A's concentration.
   C. Rate increases by the square of A's concentration.
   D. Rate is independent of A's concentration.

24. Which of the following statements best describes the effect of the concentration of A on the rate of reaction in Experiment 2?

   F. Rate increases in direct proportion with increasing concentration of A.
   G. Rate increases by the square of A's concentration.
   H. Rate increases by the square root of A's concentration.
   J. Rate is independent of A's concentration.

25. Which of the following statements best describes the effect of Concentration A on the rate of reaction in Experiment 3?

   A. Rate increases in direct proportion with increasing concentration of A.
   B. Rate increases by the square of A's concentration.
   C. Rate increases by the square root of A's concentration.
   D. Rate is independent of A's concentration.

26. What is the likeliest explanation for the results obtained in Experiment 3?

   F. A mechanism intermediates between the ones found in Experiments 1 and 2.
   G. Some of the molecules react by Experiment 1's mechanism, others by Experiment 2's mechanism.
   H. A different mechanism is responsible.
   J. There is an averaging of the mechanisms.

23. (D) *Science/Research Summary/Analysis.* Compare Trials 2 and 3 to see what changing the concentration of only one component has on rate. In this case, there is no change in rate with change in concentration of A, so rate is independent of concentration of A.

24. (F) *Science/Research Summary/Analysis.* Compare Trials 1 and 3 or Trials 2 and 4 to see what changing the concentration of only one component has on rate. In this case, rate increases in direct proportion with increasing concentration of A.

25. (C) *Science/Research Summary/Analysis.* Compare Trials 1 and 4 or Trials 2 and 3 to see what changing the concentration of only one component has on rate. In this case, rate increases by the square root of the concentration of A.

26. (H) *Science/Research Summary/Analysis.* Averaging or intermediate mechanisms do not work because one mechanism (Experiment 1) has no dependence on Concentration A with regard to rate. The likeliest explanation that reconciles Experiment 3 with Experiments 1 and 2 is that a different mechanism causes the reaction.

27. What is the best conclusion that can be drawn from this set of experiments?

    A. Rate is increased by changing solvents.
    B. Reactions may depend on solvent effects as well as on the nature of the reactants.
    C. Mechanisms can always be changed by use of an appropriate solvent.
    D. Reactions depend on solvent effects as well as on the nature of the reactants.

27. **(B)** *Science/Research Summary/Analysis.* This is a subtle question. (C) and (D) are incorrect because they over-generalize from a single case. It cannot be said that mechanisms can always be changed, (C), or that in every case the mechanism depends on solvent effects, (D). (A) is a special case of (D), where the claim is made that all reactions are solvent dependent. (B) alone allows for the possibility that solvents need not have an effect (note the word "may").

Passage VI

Acceleration is defined as the change in the velocity of an object divided by the length of time during which that change took place. In the following sets of experiments, a student studies the motion of bodies on an inclined plane.

For all of the following experiments, time is measured in seconds, distance in feet, and velocity in feet per second. The distance (d) an object travels at a constant acceleration (a) in time (t), assuming it starts from rest, is given by the equation: $d = \frac{1}{2}at^2$.

Experiment 1

A student set up a smooth wooden board at an angle of 30° from horizontal. The board had a length of 10 feet. Using a series of photogates, the student was able to determine the position and velocity of a 100 gram steel ball that was rolled down the incline. The results are presented in Table 1.

Table 1		
Time	Distance (ft)	Instantaneous Velocity (ft/sec)
0	0	0
0.5	0.44	1.75
1.0	1.75	3.50
1.5	3.94	5.25
2.0	7.00	7.00

Experiment 2

The same 10 foot wooden board was used at an angle of 30° from the horizontal. The object used this time was a 100 gram sled made of the same material as the ball in Experiment 1. The photogates were used to determine its position and velocity as it slid down the inclined plane. The results are presented in Table 2.

Table 2		
Time	Distance (ft)	Instantaneous Velocity (ft/sec)
0	0	0
0.5	1.13	2.45
1.0	2.45	4.90
1.5	5.51	7.35
2.0	9.80	9.80

Experiment 3

The same board at the same angle was used in the third experiment as in the previous two. In this experiment, a 100 gram box made of the same material as the ball and the sled was used. The same recording devices were used. The results are presented in Table 3.

Table 3		
Time	Distance (ft)	Instantaneous Velocity (ft/sec)
0	0	0
1.0	0.33	0.66
2.0	1.31	1.32
3.0	2.97	1.98
4.0	5.28	2.64
5.0	8.25	3.30

Experiment 4

The board in the previous experiments was carefully oiled to reduce friction. Once again, the board was placed at an angle of 30° from horizontal. Each of the objects was then allowed to move down the inclined plane, and the time required for each object to reach the bottom of the plane was recorded. Results are presented in Table 4.

Table 4	
Object	Time
sled	2.02
ball	2.39
box	5.50

28. Which object in the first three experiments has the greatest acceleration?

    F. Ball
    G. Sled
    H. Box
    J. The three objects have equal acceleration.

28. (G) *Science/Research Summary/Comprehension.* Since every object starts at 0 ft/sec, compare the instantaneous velocity of each object at a given time ($\frac{\Delta v}{\Delta t}$). For example, at 2 seconds the instantaneous velocity of the ball was 7 ft/sec, the instantaneous velocity of the sled was 9.80 ft/sec, and the instantaneous velocity of the box was 1.32 ft/sec. The sled has the highest instantaneous velocity at 2 seconds, meaning that the $\frac{\Delta v}{\Delta t}$ is highest for the sled, and the sled has the greatest acceleration.

29. The acceleration of the ball relative to that of the sled is due to the ball's:

    A. rolling only.
    B. friction only.
    C. rolling and friction.
    D. having the same mass as the sled and therefore having the same acceleration.

29. (A) *Science/Research Summary/Analysis.* When friction is reduced in Experiment 4, the sled and the ball still travel at about the same accelerations as in the previous experiments. This can be demonstrated by using the equation $d = 0.5at^2$, which relates the distance that an object travels starting from rest to the time (traveling at constant acceleration) it takes to travel the indicated distance. Each object travels the length of the board, 10 feet. Therefore, for the sled:

$$d = \frac{1}{2}at^2$$

$$10 = \frac{1}{2}a(2.02)^2$$

$$10 \approx \frac{1}{2}(a)(4)$$

$$a = 5 \text{ ft/sec}^2$$

For the ball:

$$d = \frac{1}{2}at^2$$

$$10 = \frac{1}{2}a(2.39)^2$$

$$10 \approx \frac{1}{2}(a)(5.7)$$

$$a = 3.5 \text{ ft/sec}^2$$

The ball and sled each travel at about the same accelerations before and after oiling, so the differences in their relative accelerations must be due to something other than friction. The difference is the rolling of the ball.

30. The acceleration of the ball relative to that of the box is due to the ball's:

   F. rolling only.
   G. friction only.
   H. rolling and the box's friction.
   J. having the same mass as the box and therefore having the same acceleration.

30. (H) *Science/Research Summary/Analysis.* Experiment 4 shows that friction affects the relative acceleration between the box and either the sled or ball. Calculate the acceleration for the box:

$$d = \frac{1}{2}at^2$$
$$10 = \frac{1}{2}a(5.50)^2$$
$$10 \approx \frac{1}{2}a(30.25)$$
$$a = 0.661 \text{ ft/sec}^2$$

Because the oiling in Experiment 4 caused a change in the box's acceleration, friction is a factor. Rolling must also be a factor as per the answer explanation to item #29.

31. Based on these four experiments, the ratio of the acceleration of the ball to the acceleration of the sled is:

   A. 1.
   B. $\frac{5}{7}$.
   C. dependent on the amount of friction.
   D. dependent on time.

31. (B) *Science/Research Summary/Comprehension.*
The acceleration of the ball is constant at 3.5 ft/sec^2 (either Experiment 1 or 4). The acceleration of the sled is constant at 4.9 ft/sec^2 (Experiment 2 or 4). Therefore, the ratio of the ball's acceleration to the sled's acceleration is: $\frac{3.5}{4.9} = \frac{5}{7}$.

32. Based on these four experiments, the ratio of the acceleration of the ball to the acceleration of the box is:

   F. 1.
   G. $\frac{5}{7}$.
   H. dependent on the amount of friction.
   J. dependent on time.

32. (H) *Science/Research Summary/Comprehension.*
Although the acceleration of the ball is relatively insensitive to the amount of friction, the acceleration of the box is very sensitive to friction. Therefore, in a ratio, the effect of changing the amount of friction will change the numerator (ball acceleration) only slightly, whereas the denominator (box acceleration) will change significantly depending on friction. (J) is not correct because the acceleration remains constant within each experiment.

Passage VII

What was the fate of Neanderthal man? Two differing views are presented below.

Scientist 1

Whenever two species compete for the same niche, there is a conflict. In this conflict the loser either moves to a different niche or dies out. It is unusual for two species to interbreed. The difference between early modern humans and Neanderthals physically may not appear great to an anatomist, but to the average man on the street, or prehistoric man in the forest, the differences are not subtle. And it was these individuals, not the anatomists, who had to decide whether or not to mate. Even if early modern humans and Neanderthals did mate, the result—us—would look more like a mix of the two rather than like modern humans. Early modern humans and Neanderthals, because they were so close to each other physically, must have been deadly enemies. The population was thinly dispersed at that time because the resources available would not support a greater population density. There literally was not room enough on the planet for the two species. They could not combine because they were so different in appearance, so only one answer remained. We survived because we killed our cousin.

Scientist 2

Neanderthals were very similar to modern humans in appearance. It is true that Neanderthals were somewhat more muscular than modern humans and that the way the muscles seem to have been arranged on the skeleton was, in a few minor ways, different. This we are able to deduce from the places on the surviving bones that mark where the ligaments were once attached. For example, the neck and wrists of Neanderthals were far thicker than is natural to modern humans. Some of the facial structure was also different, especially the protrusion of the brow. But differences between the appearance of Neanderthals and modern humans have been exaggerated since they are based on the skeleton of one individual who was later discovered to have been suffering from severe arthritis. It is likely that, because of the low population density and the nomadic lifestyle that spread the few individuals over ever-larger areas, Neanderthal and early modern humans interbred and eventually merged into one species. The notion that some sort of "war" broke out between these different species (or, more likely, subspecies) of humans is a misguided attempt to look out of early human eyes with a modern perspective.

33. Underlying the hypothesis of Scientist 2 is the assumption that:

    A. Neanderthals were more likely than early modern humans to suffer from diseases such as arthritis.

    B. early modern humans and Neanderthals were sufficiently alike to allow them to interbreed.

    C. Neanderthals and early modern humans lived in geographically distinct regions.

    D. in combat, a group of Neanderthals was likely to defeat a similar grouping of early modern humans.

33. **(B)** *Science/Conflicting Viewpoints/Analysis.* Scientist 2 concludes by saying that Neanderthals and early modern humans merged into a single species by interbreeding, so Scientist 2 assumes that the two groups were sufficiently similar to permit interbreeding of the members. (A) distorts the position of Scientist 2. Scientist 2 says that the picture we have of the Neanderthals is based upon one individual, an individual who was not entirely representative of his species. In other words, the one Neanderthal with arthritis was the exception, not the rule. (C) also misreads the passage. Scientist 2 says that populations were spread out geographically, not that the two groups were separated physically from one another. (Indeed, they must have lived pretty close to each other to permit the interbreeding that Scientist 2 believes occurred.) Finally, as for (D), though Scientist 2 says that Neanderthals were apparently more muscular than early modern humans, this does not automatically mean that they would win a fight. Speed, intelligence, weapons, and a lot of other factors might affect the outcome.

34. Underlying the hypotheses of both scientists is the assumption that:

    F. early modern humans and Neanderthals understood the consequences of their actions.

    G. early modern humans and Neanderthals both lived in exactly the same type of environment.

    H. early modern humans and Neanderthals both lived in the same geographical regions.

    J. early modern humans were more intelligent than Neanderthals.

34. **(H)** *Science/Conflicting Viewpoints/Analysis.* For early modern humans to completely replace Neanderthals, there could not have been a region containing Neanderthals that did not also contain early modern humans.

35. If an isolated community of Neanderthals was discovered, whose hypothesis would be more damaged?

    A. Scientist 2's because his theory does not allow for such a community to survive

    B. Scientist 1's because the descendants of early modern humans inhabit all the earth and therefore there should be no community of Neanderthals

    C. Both hypotheses are disproved.

    D. Neither hypothesis is affected.

35. **(D)** *Science/Conflicting Viewpoints/Analysis.* The discovery of evidence of an isolated community of Neanderthals would not necessarily weaken either hypothesis. When the two scientists talk about populations being dispersed, they are not saying that the individuals were perfectly distributed—like so many salt and chlorine atoms in a water solution. A pocket of Neanderthals here or a concentration of early modern humans there would not be inconsistent with the general distribution pattern described.

36. Which of the following, if true, would most support the hypothesis of Scientist 1?

    F. The camps of early modern humans are often close to the camps of Neanderthals.
    G. The camps of early modern humans are never close to Neanderthal camps.
    H. Bones of Neanderthals and early modern humans are often found near each other.
    J. Chipped Neanderthal bones are found with early modern human weapons.

37. The fact that lions and tigers fight when brought together artificially even though they can be interbred supports which hypothesis to the greater extent?

    A. Scientist 2's hypothesis, because it proves two species can interbreed
    B. Scientist 2's hypothesis, because two species still exist that share the same niche
    C. Scientist 1's hypothesis, because it suggests that two species that can interbreed may not do so under natural conditions
    D. Scientist 1's hypothesis, because lions and tigers fight when brought together artificially

38. According to the hypothesis of Scientist 1, what should be the result of interbreeding lions and tigers?

    F. The offspring should be infertile.
    G. The offspring will resemble one parent only.
    H. The offspring will possess a mixture of traits.
    J. Scientist 1's hypothesis makes no conjectures on the point because lions and tigers would not interbreed.

36. **(J)** *Science/Conflicting Viewpoints/Analysis.* This information suggests that early modern humans killed Neanderthals, which supports Scientist 1.

37. **(C)** *Science/Conflicting Viewpoints/Analysis.* This fact shows that even if two species can breed, they may not do so voluntarily. Scientist 1 can therefore use this case as an example of the fact that two genetically compatible but dissimilar-looking animals choose not to interbreed. (D) is not readily relevant because lions and tigers are brought together artificially. No one disputed the notion that animals can interbreed, so (A) does not enter the argument. (B) is incorrect because lions and tigers do not share the same niche (tigers are solitary forest hunters while lions are group-hunting plains dwellers), and their ranges rarely overlap.

38. **(H)** *Science/Conflicting Viewpoints/Comprehension.* The mixing of traits is part of Scientist 1's objections to Scientist 2's hypothesis.

39. What assumption about Neanderthals and early modern humans is shared by both Scientist 2 and Scientist 1?

    A. Early modern humans were one factor in the disappearance of Neanderthals as a separate species.

    B. Early modern humans were more intelligent than Neanderthals thus enabling humans to prevail.

    C. Early modern humans and Neanderthals differed little from one another in physical appearance.

    D. Neanderthals occupied territories that were not suitable for early modern human habitations.

40. If a burial site containing over one hundred early modern humans and Neanderthal remains was discovered, and if two Neanderthal skeletons were found with early modern human spearpoints in them, which hypothesis would be the most strengthened?

    F. Scientist 2's hypothesis, because spearpoints need not have been what killed the two Neanderthals

    G. Scientist 1's hypothesis, because two Neanderthals were killed by early modern humans

    H. Scientist 1's hypothesis, because the spearpoints prove that the early modern humans had more developed weapons

    J. Scientist 2's hypothesis, because only a couple of the individuals buried together died violently

39. **(A)** *Science/Conflicting Viewpoints/Analysis.* Both hypotheses attribute the disappearance of Neanderthals to early modern humans.

40. **(G)** *Science/Conflicting Viewpoints/Analysis.* (F) is a perfectly logical argument but it does not strengthen the position of Scientist 2. (J) does not strengthen the position of Scientist 2 since there is no way to prove from the given information whether others also died violently (clubs may have been used, or spearpoints that were used may have been valuable and were taken by the victors). Even if (J) is acceptable, it does not strengthen the position of Scientist 2. It only casts doubt on the position of Scientist 1. (H) is true in general. The only possible answer that strengthens a scientist's argument is (G).

DIRECTED STUDY **5 5 5 5 5 5 5 5 5 5 5 5 5**

SECTION 5: WRITING TEST (OPTIONAL)

1 Essay Prompt

DIRECTIONS: Read the prompt carefully and make sure you understand the instructions. A successful essay will have the following features: it will take a position on the issue presented in the writing prompt; it will maintain a consistent focus on the topic; it will use logical reasoning and provide supporting ideas; it will present ideas in an organized manner; and, finally, it will include clear and effective language in accordance with the conventions of standard written English.

Campaign Funding

Political campaigns are part of the fabric of American life, and politicians invite the public to join in the process of selecting those who govern them in a variety of ways, including financial support. Some Americans think that there should be limits to how much any one person, group or corporation may contribute to any particular candidate. This view states that contribution limits allow for more equal participation by all citizens in the electoral process, regardless of their income. Others, however, believe that political campaign contributions should have no limits, that such limitations really abridge freedom of speech and thereby violate constitutionally protected freedoms. Do limits on campaign funding make elections a fairer process in which voters' incomes do not matter, or are such limits unfair to donors who wish to maximize their participation in elections? The issue of campaign funding is a high-profile debate in both state and national elections.

Perspective 1

> Freedom of speech is an essential right for all Americans. The right to allow our hard-earned money to give voice to our choice for governance must be protected.

Perspective 2

> There should be very real limits on the amount of contributions from any one individual or corporation. No one should be allowed to purchase democracy from the people, as self-governance is a right.

Perspective 3

> Democratic participation must be protected at all costs, even if it costs our Treasury. Fair elections must be held on level financial playing fields in order to achieve our dreams. No individual contributions should be allowed, and all campaigns and candidates be funded from public money raised by taxation.

Essay Task

Write a unified, coherent essay in which you evaluate multiple perspectives on the impact of campaign funding. In your essay be sure to:

- Analyze and evaluate perspectives given
- State and develop your own perspective
- Explain the relationship between your perspective and those given

Your perspective may be in full agreement with any of the others, in partial agreement, or wholly different. Whatever the case, support your ideas with logical reasoning and detailed, persuasive examples.

Above Average Response

During each election cycle, billions of dollars are spent on campaigns, and the amount rises every year. Because of this exorbitant spending, there should be limits on how much individuals and corporations can donate to a campaign, and also on the total amount of money a politician can spend on a single campaign. Limits could potentially allow a wider range of candidates to run for office and would decrease donors' influence on campaign proceedings. Furthermore, limits could make the whole campaign process less of a circus and allow politicians to devote more time to their actual jobs.

The high cost of campaigning bars people who are not independently wealthy or well-connected from running for Congress. With expenses such as advertisements, travel, and campaign teams, campaigning is an expensive process, and the cost resembles an arms race, as politicians continue to outspend each other. Those who cannot keep up with their competitors will not be as visible to voters, with fewer ads and public appearances. These campaigns would have made it impossible for many of the people who shaped U.S. history to hold office today. Presidents like Abraham Lincoln would not have been able to rise to prominence from a modest and obscure background. It is true that even with a limit on campaign funding, one would still need to come from an elite background or have powerful, wealthy friends to run for office. However, limitations may open the door a little wider for candidates who are less wealthy.

In addition to restricting who can run for office, campaign spending allows wealthy donors to disproportionately represent politicians' campaigns. Voters, whether rich or poor, will logically support candidates who are the most favorable to their concerns. Therefore, candidates who cater to the wealthy are more likely to receive more campaign funding. This makes it more difficult for lower income voters to elect politicians who will address their concerns. Although one may say that limiting campaign donations is a violation of free speech, I would argue that money is not speech. The high cost of running a campaign may actually limit the range of ideas that can be heard, if people must pay a certain price to gain influence. I do not agree that campaigns should be funded solely by taxpayer money, since this could lead to higher taxes. However, limiting private donations would level the playing field and allow campaigns to be less money-driven.

Finally, limiting spending may force politicians to make their campaigns shorter and less demanding of their time. Politicians who are up for reelection would have more time and energy to focus on fulfilling the duties of their office instead of running for it. It has become a cliché in American politics that the next campaign begins as soon as the previous one ends. For members of Congress who can be reelected for an unlimited number of terms, this means that they are always campaigning or preparing to campaign. However, if politicians could only raise a limited amount of money, their teams would spend less time fundraising, and furthermore, this limited amount of money would force them to shorten their campaigns. Although upper class voters may protest their weakened influence on campaigns, having politicians more focused on their jobs is a change that voters from all social classes and political parties could appreciate.

Although limiting campaign funding would not eliminate the influence of wealth on elections, it would be a step in the right direction. More people could be financially capable of running for office, and wealthy donors would be less likely to have a disproportionate influence on campaigns. Finally, with less emphasis on campaigning, politicians could focus more on what voters elected them to do.

Ideas and Analysis: The writer clearly states his or her thesis in the introduction: limited campaign spending would make campaigns less influenced by money and make politicians less focused on campaigning. The writer argues for Perspective 2 (spending limits for donors) but adds that the total amount of campaign spending per candidate should also be limited.

This essay does not argue for a "compromise" position, except for briefly stating that campaigns should not be solely funded through taxes. The author thoroughly develops three main arguments against campaign spending. However, the author also acknowledges the opposing point of view in Perspective 1 and argues against it.

Development and Support:

- The introduction opens with an attention-grabbing hook (stating the high amount of campaign spending).

- The writer clearly states the thesis in the second sentence of the introduction and previews the three main arguments.

- The body paragraphs begin with topic sentences that state the main point or argument to be made in the paragraph.

- The body paragraphs include a mix of reasoning and examples to support the author's opinion.

  - Body paragraph 1: The writer uses the metaphor of the arms race to explain the increasingly high cost of campaign spending. This metaphor and the example of Abraham Lincoln also demonstrate the writer's historical knowledge.

  - Body paragraph 2: The writer develops lines of reasoning to explain the antidemocratic nature of unlimited campaign spending. Although the reasoning is logical, the paragraph would be stronger with concrete examples.

  - Body paragraph 3: The writer ends with an argument that could appeal to a variety of readers, despite their political opinions: if politicians campaigned less, they would be more focused on their jobs. The writer supports this argument with the concrete example of running for Congress.

Organization:

- The writer introduces each paragraph with a topic sentence.

- The writer uses transitions to connect ideas between and within paragraphs. For example, the first sentence of the second body paragraph ("In addition to restricting who can run for office …") transitions the discussion from wealthy candidates to wealthy donors.

- At the end of the second body paragraph, the two sentences about taxes did not directly relate to the topic (the influence of wealthy donors). Although this part of the paragraph acknowledges Perspective 3, the writer should incorporate the different perspectives into his or her argument, rather than just mentioning them.

Language Use and Conventions: The essay contains at least three principal strengths in this area:

- The essay does not have any mechanics/usage errors. As a result, the reader's attention is not distracted from the substance of the essay.

- The essay does not have any informal language.

- Stylistically, the writer varies sentence structures throughout most of the essay. However, the writer begins two sentences in a row with the transition "although" in the third body paragraph and the conclusion.

Summary and Conclusions: This essay demonstrates writing skills that are well developed and provides several arguments for campaign spending limitations. The writer incorporates Perspectives 1 and 2 into the argument but could develop Perspective 3 more thoroughly. This essay would likely receive a score of 10.

Below Average Response

Campaign spending should be limited because when campaigns are so expensive, only people who are rich or have rich friends can afford to pay for the campaign. This makes government less democratic because it only represents the rich. Also, the expensive campaigns are wasteful. Think of everything else you could do with that money.

The main reason that campaign funding should be limited is that with the current system, you have to be very rich to run for office. If you're opponent can afford to spend millions of dollars on a campaign and you can't, you will be at a disadvantage because you won't be able to afford to promote you're campaign as much. Also, high campaign spending means that people can basically buy influence in government. The more you can pay, the better shot your candidate has at leading a bigger campaign and winning the election.

The money spent on elections is also wasteful imagine what else you could do with it. For example, the billions of dollars used on campaign spending could instead be spent on charities or government programs that the politician supports. This would be a much more constructive use of people's money.

Campaign spending leads to unfair elections where the rich have a lot more influence then the rest of the country. Furthermore, it's just a huge waste of money that could be spent better elsewhere.

Ideas and Analysis: It is clear that the writer is against unlimited campaign spending, but the writer does not use enough reasoning or examples to support his or her argument. The essay develops Perspective 2, but the writer makes no mention of Perspectives 1 and 3. The essay would be stronger if the writer recognized multiple points of view and explained more thoroughly why he or she is against unlimited campaign spending.

Development and Support:

- The introduction previews the writer's opinions, but the writer only presents two main arguments against campaign spending, and the second argument is not well developed. Furthermore, the writer does not specify how campaign spending should be limited.

- In the body paragraphs, the writer does not use concrete examples to support his or her arguments.

- In the first body paragraph, the writer argues how unlimited campaign spending favors the rich. Although the reasoning is logical, the paragraph would be stronger with concrete examples, rather than just the writer's opinions.

- In the second body paragraph, the writer has a valid point when he or she says that campaign spending is a waste of money. However, the argument is not plausible. One cannot assume that the money a corporation or individual donor would have spent on a campaign would be used "constructively."

Organization:

- The writer states his or her opinions in the introduction but does not combine these arguments into a clear thesis.

- The topic sentences should have transitions to introduce new ideas in the following paragraph.

- The first body paragraph should have a topic sentence that is more general. The topic sentence just mentions that you must be rich to run for office, but the paragraph discusses the advantages of being a rich politician and a rich donor. Another solution would be to write one paragraph about politicians' wealth and a separate paragraph about donors' wealth.

Language Use and Conventions: The essay contains several weaknesses in this area:

- The essay contains some usage and mechanics errors.

- o Body paragraph 1: "you're opponent" and "you're campaign" should be changed to "your opponent" and "your campaign."

- Conclusion: "a lot more influence then the rest of the country" should be changed to "than the rest of the country." The word "than" should be used for comparison.

- The use of informal language is one of the main problems in this essay. The writer expresses a few ideas that could be turned into strong arguments if they were worded more carefully. For example, in the introduction, the phrase "you have to be very rich to run for office" could be reworded as "you must be wealthy to run for office." It might help to read this essay and reword phrases with slang or informal language.

Summary and Conclusions: The writer's opinion is clear and consistent, but not all of the main arguments are well developed, and the second body paragraph does not use logical reasoning. Furthermore, the writer does not consider the opposing viewpoints. This essay would likely receive a score of 5.

Practice Test I

Outline

I.   **Section 1:** English (pp. 464–476)

II. **Section 2:** Mathematics (pp. 478–497)

III. **Section 3:** Reading (pp. 498–507)

IV. **Section 4:** Science (pp. 509–522)

V.   **Section 5:** Writing (Optional) (p. 523)

DIRECTIONS

Practice Test I includes five subject tests: English, Mathematics, Reading, Science, and Writing. Calculator use is permitted on the Mathematics Test only.

Cambridge offers several services for schools utilizing our practice tests. Ask your teacher whether your school has decided to send your answers to Cambridge for scoring or to score your answers at your school. If Cambridge is scoring your test, you will use a Scantron™ form provided by your teacher, or you will enter your answers online. If your school is scoring your test, you may use a Scantron™ form provided by your teacher, or you may write your answers on paper.

If you are entering your test answers on a Scantron™ form, please be sure to include the following information on the Scantron™:

Book and edition	*Victory for the ACT Test, 13th Edition*
Practice Test Number	**Practice Test I**

If you are only completing a single section of this practice test, make sure to also include the following information:

Subject	**English**, **Mathematics**, **Reading** or **Science**
Section Number	**Section 1, 2, 3** or **4**

The items in each multiple-choice test are numbered and the answer choices are lettered. The Scantron™ form has numbered rows that correspond to the items on the test. Each row contains lettered ovals to match the answer choices for each item on the test. Each numbered row has a corresponding item on the test.

For each item, first decide on the best answer choice. Then, locate the row number that corresponds to the item. Next, find the oval in that row that matches the letter of the chosen answer. Then, use a soft lead pencil to fill in the oval. DO NOT use a ballpoint pen.

Mark only one answer for each item. If you change your mind about an answer choice, thoroughly erase your first mark before marking your new answer.

Note that only responses marked on your Scantron™ form or written on your paper will be scored. Your score on each test will be based only on the number of items that are correctly answered during the time allowed for that test. You will not be penalized for guessing. Therefore, it is in your best interest to answer every item on the test, even if you must guess.

On the Writing Test, write your response to the prompt using the essay response sheets or loose-leaf paper provided by your teacher. Your teacher might also direct you to enter your essay response online. (Note that the Writing Test is optional.)

You may work on each test only during the time allowed for that test. If you finish a test before time is called, use the time to review your answer choices or work on items about which you are uncertain. You may not return to a test on which time has already been called, and you may not preview another test. You must lay down your pencil immediately when time is called at the end of each test. You may not for any reason fill in or alter ovals for a test after time has expired for that test. Violation of these rules will result in immediate disqualification from the exam.

GO ON TO THE NEXT PAGE.

| PRACTICE TEST I | **1 1 1 1 1 1 1 1 1 1 1** |

SECTION 1: ENGLISH TEST
45 Minutes—75 Items

DIRECTIONS: In the passages below, certain parts of the sentences have been underlined and numbered. In the right-hand column, you will find different ways of writing each underlined part; the original version is indicated by the "NO CHANGE" option. For each item, select the choice that best expresses the intended idea, is most acceptable in standard written English, or is most consistent with the overall tone and style of the passage.

There are also items that ask about a section of the passage or the passage as a whole. These items do not refer to an underlined portion of the passage; these items are preceded by statements that are enclosed in boxes.

Read the passage through once before you begin to answer the accompanying items. Finding the answers to certain items may depend on looking at material that appears several sentences beyond the item. So, be sure that you have read far enough ahead before you select your answer choice. Answers are on page 673.

PASSAGE I

Basic Principles of Nuclear Weapons

The challenge <u>to start to begin to make</u> timely
₁

progress toward removing the threat of nuclear war is

the most important challenge in international relations

today. Three general principles guide our defense

and negotiation policies toward such a goal, principles

based on the technical realities of nuclear war.

First, nuclear weapons are <u>fundamentally</u>
₂

<u>different than</u> non-nuclear weapons. These weapons of
₂

mass destruction <u>that could do a lot of harm</u> have a
₃

1. **A.** NO CHANGE
   B. to begin making
   C. to begin the making of
   D. of beginning the making of

2. **F.** NO CHANGE
   G. different than fundamentally
   H. different from fundamentally
   J. fundamentally different from

3. **A.** NO CHANGE
   B. (and they could also do a great deal of harm)
   C. (owing to the fact that they could do a lot of harm)
   D. OMIT the underlined portion.

GO ON TO THE NEXT PAGE.

long and deadly radioactive <u>memory, the</u> unknowns of
₄

nuclear conflict dwarf the predictable consequences.

The number of deaths resulting <u>from injuries and the</u>
₅

<u>unavailability of medical care</u> and the economic
₅

damage <u>as a result from</u> disruption and disorganization
₆

<u>would be even more devastating than</u> the direct loss of
₇

life and property. [8]

Second, <u>the sole purpose</u> of nuclear weapons
₉

must be to deter nuclear <u>war, it is</u> neither a substitute
₁₀

for maintaining adequate conventional military forces

4. F. NO CHANGE
   G. memory. The
   H. memory the
   J. memory and the

5. A. NO CHANGE
   B. from injuries and also from the unavailabil-
      ity of medical care
   C. from the unavailability of injuries and medi-
      cal care
   D. both from injuries and also from the un-
      availability of medical care as well

6. F. NO CHANGE
   G. as a result to
   H. resulting from
   J. with a result of

7. A. NO CHANGE
   B. is even more devastating than
   C. are even more devastating as
   D. might be more devastating even as

8. Which of the following would be an appropriate
   final sentence for this paragraph?

   F. And so I believe nuclear weapons to be a
      challenge.
   G. Nuclear war could have no winners.
   H. Nuclear conflict is very dangerous.
   J. Nuclear conflict would be rather wasteful.

9. A. NO CHANGE
   B. solely, the purpose
   C. the solely purpose
   D. the purpose solely

10. F. NO CHANGE
    G. war. They are
    H. war they are
    J. war; it is

GO ON TO THE NEXT PAGE.

to meet vital national security goals <u>but</u> an effective
¹¹
defense against the almost total mutual annihilation and

devastation that results from a full-scale nuclear war.

<u>Third,</u> arms control is an essential part of our national
¹²
security. Thus far, we have had no effective controls on

offensive nuclear weaponry, and it is clear that each

step forward in the arms race toward more and

improved weapons <u>has made less</u> our security. Before
¹³

deploying additional weapons, <u>they must develop</u> a
¹⁴
coherent arms control strategy.

11. **A.** NO CHANGE
    B. and
    C. nor
    D. including

12. **F.** NO CHANGE
    G. Third
    H. (Begin a new paragraph) Third
    J. (Begin a new paragraph) Third,

13. **A.** NO CHANGE
    B. has lessened
    C. have lessened
    D. have made less of

14. **F.** NO CHANGE
    G. the development is necessary of
    H. it is necessary to develop
    J. it is necessarily to be developed,

Items #15–16 ask about the preceding passage as
a whole.

---

15. Which of the following best describes the overall
    structure of the essay?

    A. A three-part argument
    B. A two-part narrative
    C. A three-part comparison
    D. A four-part argument

16. Which of the following is the thesis of this
    essay?

    F. Nuclear weapons are fundamentally
        different from non-nuclear weapons.
    G. The sole purpose of nuclear weapons must
        be to deter nuclear war.
    H. There are three principles that guide our
        effort to remove the threat of nuclear war.
    J. Nuclear war is a frightening possibility.

GO ON TO THE NEXT PAGE.

PASSAGE II

Education for a New Republic

The founders of the Republic <u>viewing their</u>
₁₇

revolution primarily in political terms <u>rather as</u> in
₁₈

economic terms. <u>Therefore,</u> they viewed the kind of
₁₉
education needed for the new Republic largely in

political terms instead of <u>as a means to</u> academic
₂₀

excellence or individual self-fulfillment. <u>Talking about</u>
₂₁
education as a bulwark for liberty, equality, popular

consent, and devotion to the public <u>good goals</u> that
₂₂

<u>took precedence over</u> the uses of knowledge for self-
₂₃
improvement or occupational preparation. Over and

over again, the Revolutionary generation, both liberal

and conservative in <u>outlook—assert their</u> faith that the
₂₄
welfare of the Republic rested upon an educated

citizenry.

17. **A.** NO CHANGE
    B. having viewed its
    C. viewed its
    D. viewed their

18. **F.** NO CHANGE
    G. rather than
    H. but
    J. OMIT the underlined portion.

19. **A.** NO CHANGE
    B. Since
    C. However
    D. On the contrary

20. **F.** NO CHANGE
    G. as a means or a way to
    H. to
    J. as

21. **A.** NO CHANGE
    B. Talking
    C. They talked about
    D. With the talking about

22. **F.** NO CHANGE
    G. good. Goals
    H. good, goals
    J. good; goals

23. **A.** NO CHANGE
    B. precede
    C. precede over
    D. took precedence on

24. **F.** NO CHANGE
    G. outlook, asserted its
    H. outlook; asserted its
    J. outlook asserts their

GO ON TO THE NEXT PAGE.

All agreed that the principal ingredients of a civic education <u>was</u> literacy and inculcation of patriotic and
₂₅

25. A. NO CHANGE
    B. being
    C. were
    D. were like

moral <u>virtues some</u> others added the study of history
₂₆
and the study of the principles of the republican government itself. The founders, as was the case of almost all their successors, were long on exhortation and rhetoric regarding the value of civic <u>education;</u>
₂₇
<u>since</u> they left it to the textbook writers to distill the
₂₇
essence of those values for school children. Texts in American history and government appeared as early as the 1790s. The textbook writers <u>turned out being</u> very
₂₈
largely of conservative persuasion, more likely

26. F. NO CHANGE
    G. virtues—some
    H. virtues, some
    J. virtues; some

27. A. NO CHANGE
    B. education. And
    C. education. Since
    D. education, but

28. F. NO CHANGE
    G. turned out to be
    H. turning out to be
    J. having turned out to be

Federalist in outlook than Jeffersonian, and <u>universally</u>
₂₉
<u>almost agreed</u> that political virtue must rest upon moral
₂₉
and religious precepts. Since most textbook writers were New Englanders, this meant that the texts had a decidedly Federalist slant.

In the first half of the Republic, civic education in the schools emphasized the inculcation of civic values, put less emphasis on political knowledge, and <u>no attempt to develop</u> political skills. The development
₃₀
of political skills was left to the local parties, town meetings, churches, coffeehouses, and ale houses

29. A. NO CHANGE
    B. almost, agreed universally
    C. almost universally agreed
    D. almost universally, agreed

30. F. NO CHANGE
    G. made no attempt to develop
    H. none at all on the development of
    J. none was put at all on developing

GO ON TO THE NEXT PAGE.

where men gathered to talk. [31]

31. Which of the following correctly describes how the last paragraph of the essay functions?

    A. It contradicts much of what was said before.
    B. It continues the logical development of the essay.
    C. It reiterates what was said in the first paragraph.
    D. It is a transitional paragraph to introduce a new topic.

Item #32 asks about the preceding passage as a whole.

---

32. This essay would most likely be published in a:

    F. history textbook.
    G. political science journal.
    H. journal for educators.
    J. biography of Jefferson.

PASSAGE III

Women and World War I

[1]

The contribution of women on the home front
        33

during World War I was varied. It included a large

range of activities—from knitting and the operation of
               34

drill presses—and engaged a cross section of the

female population, from housewives to society girls.

World War I marked the first time in the history of the
           35

United States that a systematic effort was made,

through organizations like the League for Women's

33. **A.** NO CHANGE
    B. Women, their contribution
    C. The contribution of woman
    D. Woman's contribution

34. **F.** NO CHANGE
    G. from knitting with the operation of
    H. from knitting and operating
    J. from knitting to operating

35. **A.** NO CHANGE
    B. has marked the first time
    C. is the first time it is marked
    D. was marked, the first time

GO ON TO THE NEXT PAGE.

Service, to utilize the capabilities of women in all
36

regions of the country.

[2]

While much of this volunteer work falls within
37

the established bounds of women's club work, many

women entered areas of industrial work previously
38

reserved by the male population. Women put on the
38

uniforms of elevator operators, streetcar conductors,

postmen, and industrial workers. However, they were
39

employed in aircraft and munitions plants as well as in
39

shipbuilding yards and steel mills.

[3]

Much of the work fell into the traditional realm

of volunteer activity knitting garments for the boys
40

overseas, canning for Uncle Sam, planting Victory

gardens, etc. Through these activities, every

homemaker could demonstrate their patriotism while
41

still fulfilling her role as homemaker. Women with

more time volunteered to hostess at canteens: make
42

bandages, and organize food and clothing drives. The

Women's Land Army, dressed in bloomer uniforms

and armed with such slogans as "The Woman with the

36. F. NO CHANGE
    G. being able to utilize
    H. utilizing
    J. and utilize

37. A. NO CHANGE
    B. fell within
    C. having fallen within
    D. fell in

38. F. NO CHANGE
    G. having previously been reserved
    H. previously reserved for
    J. reserved previous to then

39. A. NO CHANGE
    B. workers. They were employed
    C. workers, but they were employed
    D. workers. Since they were employed

40. F. NO CHANGE
    G. activity; knitting
    H. activity: knitting
    J. activity, knitting

41. A. NO CHANGE
    B. be demonstrating
    C. have demonstrated their
    D. demonstrate her

42. F. NO CHANGE
    G. canteens make
    H. canteens, make
    J. canteens; make

GO ON TO THE NEXT PAGE.

Hoe Must Defend the Man with the <u>Musket," was</u>
₄₃

<u>dispatched</u> to assist farmers in processing crops.
₄₃

[4]

Women performed ably during the war and <u>laid</u>
₄₄

<u>the foundation</u> for more specialized jobs, increased
₄₄

wages, better working conditions, and a more

competitive job status in the labor market.

43. A. NO CHANGE
    B. Musket," which was then dispatched
    C. Musket," and it was dispatched
    D. Musket," and it got dispatched

44. F. NO CHANGE
    G. the foundation was laid
    H. the foundation was lain
    J. laying the foundation

Items #45–46 ask about the preceding passage as a whole.

---

45. Which of the following represents the most logical order for the paragraphs?

    A. 1, 4, 3, 2
    B. 1, 3, 4, 2
    C. 1, 3, 2, 4
    D. 2, 4, 3, 1

46. Is the use of the sample slogan appropriate to the essay?

    F. Yes, because it helps the reader to understand one of the points being made.
    G. Yes, because all general statements should be illustrated with an example.
    H. No, because it does not help the reader to understand the point being made.
    J. No, because it is needlessly distracting.

PASSAGE IV

Democracy in Japan

Following the end of World War II, substantial

changes <u>undertaken</u> in Japan to liberate the individual
₄₇

from authoritarian restraints. The new democratic

47. A. NO CHANGE
    B. will be undertaken
    C. have been undertaken
    D. were undertaken

GO ON TO THE NEXT PAGE.

value system was <u>acceptable by</u> many teachers,
48

48. **F.** NO CHANGE
    G. excepted to
    H. excepted by
    J. accepted by

students, intellectuals, and old <u>liberals, and</u> it was not
49

immediately embraced by the society as a whole.

49. **A.** NO CHANGE
    B. liberals, since
    C. liberals, but
    D. liberals; consequently

<u>Japanese traditions were dominated by group values,</u>
50

and notions of personal freedom and individual rights

50. **F.** NO CHANGE
    G. Dominated by group values were the Japanese traditions
    H. Group values were always dominating the Japanese traditions
    J. Dominating Japanese traditions were group values

<u>being</u> unfamiliar.
51

51. **A.** NO CHANGE
    B. were
    C. was
    D. are

<u>Today, the triumph of</u> democratic processes
52

52. **F.** NO CHANGE
    G. (Do NOT begin a new paragraph) Today the triumph, of
    H. Today, the triumph, of
    J. (Do NOT begin a new paragraph) Today, owing to the fact that

<u>is clear</u> evident in the widespread participation of the
53

53. **A.** NO CHANGE
    B. is
    C. is clear and also
    D. are clearly

Japanese in social and political life. <u>Furthermore,</u>
54

there is no universally accepted and stable value

54. **F.** NO CHANGE
    G. Therefore,
    H. So,
    J. Yet,

<u>system, values being</u> constantly modified by strong
55

infusions of Western ideas. School textbooks expound

55. **A.** NO CHANGE
    B. system with that values are
    C. system since that values are
    D. system since values are

GO ON TO THE NEXT PAGE.

democratic <u>principles, and so emphasizing</u> equality
                        56

over hierarchy and rationalism over tradition, but in

practice, these values <u>are often sometimes</u>
                        57

<u>misinterpreted and distorted</u>, particularly by the
 57

youth <u>that translated</u> the individualistic and humanistic
       58

goals of democracy into egoistic and materialistic

ones.

56. F. NO CHANGE
      G. principles, emphasizing
      H. principles and the emphasis of
      J. principles with the emphasis that

57. A. NO CHANGE
      B. had been misinterpreted and distorted often
      C. often misinterpreted and distorted
      D. are often misinterpreted and distorted

58. F. NO CHANGE
      G. that translate
      H. who translate
      J. translate

59. What type of discussion might logically follow
      this last paragraph?

      A. A discussion of goals of Japanese youth
      B. A discussion of democratic principles
      C. A discussion of Western education
      D. A discussion of World War II

PASSAGE V

Zoological Nature

From the beginning, humankind <u>always has</u>
                                   60

<u>shared</u> some sort of link with the animal world. The
 60

earliest and most primitive was surely that of hunter

and prey—with humans possibly playing the fatal role

of victim. Later, of course, humans reversed the roles

as they became more skillful <u>and intelligenter</u>.
                                61

60. F. NO CHANGE
      G. have always shared
      H. is always sharing
      J. has always shared

61. A. NO CHANGE
      B. so intelligent
      C. and more intelligent
      D. but intelligent

GO ON TO THE NEXT PAGE.

The later domestication of certain animals and also the
62
discovery of agriculture, made for a more settled and

stable existence and was an essential step in the not-so-

orderly and very chaotic process of becoming civilized.
63
However, the intellectual distance between regarding

an animal as the source of dinner or of material

comfort and to consider them a worthy subject for
64
study is considerable.

   Not until Aristotle did the animal world become

a subject for serious scientific study. Although he
65
seemingly writes on every subject, Aristotle's work in
65   66
zoology—studying animals as animals—is considered

his most successful. He seemed to have had a natural

affinity for and curiosity about all the living creatures

of the world, and he took special interest in marine life.
67
   Aristotle's zoological writings reveal him to be a

remarkably astute observer of the natural world,

wedding his observations to what might be called
68
speculative reason. He was therefore a theorist as well.

His overall theory was simple. In the works of
69
Nature," he said, "purpose and not accident is

predominant." A thing is known then when we know

62. F. NO CHANGE
    G. animals, also
    H. animals, along with
    J. animals; along with

63. A. NO CHANGE
    B. (and very chaotic)
    C. yet very chaotic
    D. OMIT the underlined portion.

64. F. NO CHANGE
    G. considering it
    H. considering them
    J. then to consider them

65. A. NO CHANGE
    B. he wrote (seemingly) on
    C. writing seemingly on
    D. he wrote on seemingly

66. F. NO CHANGE
    G. subject; Aristotles work
    H. subject Aristotles' work
    J. subject: Aristotle's work

67. A. NO CHANGE
    B. so
    C. but
    D. because

68. F. NO CHANGE
    G. who was wedded to
    H. in that he wedded
    J. with the wedding of

69. A. NO CHANGE
    B. simple—in
    C. simple. "In
    D. simply. "In

GO ON TO THE NEXT PAGE.

PRACTICE TEST I • 475

what it is for. He linked <u>and combined</u> theory and
₇₀

practice by saying that interpretation of an observed

phenomenon must always be made <u>in light of its</u>
₇₁

<u>purpose</u>. His zoological theory was thus a reflection
₇₁

of the essentially teleological nature of his overall

philosophy. ☐72

70. F. NO CHANGE
G. combining
H. to combine
J. OMIT the underlined portion.

71. A. NO CHANGE
B. always keeping its purpose in mind
C. without ever forgetting what its purpose is
D. given an understanding of what its purpose is

72. Is the quote from Aristotle in the last paragraph appropriate?

F. Yes, because it is important to quote the works of people you are talking about.
G. Yes, because it is a succinct statement of Aristotle's theory.
H. No, because the quote is irrelevant to what the author is talking about in that paragraph.
J. No, because it is wrong to quote when you can express the idea in your own words.

Items #73–75 ask about the preceding passage as a whole.

---

73. The author probably had which of the following audiences in mind for this essay?

A. Zoologists
B. Students who are studying Aristotle
C. The average person interested in science
D. Teachers of marine biology

GO ON TO THE NEXT PAGE.

74. What is the actual thesis of this essay?

    F. People have always liked animals.
    G. Animals and people reversed roles.
    H. Aristotle was interested in the natural world.
    J. The animal world became a source of
       serious study because of Aristotle.

75. How does the first paragraph of this essay
    function?

    A. It poses questions to be answered.
    B. It provides general background for the rest
       of the passage.
    C. It introduces an argument.
    D. It provides an anecdote related to the rest of
       the passage.

END OF TEST 1

NO TEST MATERIAL ON THIS PAGE

PRACTICE TEST I

2 2 2 2 2 2 2 2 2 2 2 2

SECTION 2: MATHEMATICS TEST

60 Minutes—60 Items

DIRECTIONS: Solve each item and choose the correct answer choice. Then, fill in the corresponding oval on the bubble sheet.

Allocate time wisely. Try to solve as many items as possible, returning to skipped items if time permits.

Calculator use is permitted on this test; however, some items are best solved without the use of a calculator.

Note: All of the following should be assumed, unless otherwise stated.

1. Illustrative figures are NOT necessarily drawn to scale.
2. The word *average* indicates arithmetic mean.
3. The word *line* indicates a straight line.
4. Geometric figures lie in a plane.

Answers are on page 680.

---

1. If $\dfrac{1}{x} + \dfrac{1}{x} = 8$, then $x = $?

   A. $\dfrac{1}{4}$

   B. $\dfrac{1}{2}$

   C. 1

   D. 2

   E. 4

2. If $x = 2$ and $y = -1$, then $3x - 4y = $?

   F. -5

   G. -1

   H. 0

   J. 2

   K. 10

DO YOUR FIGURING HERE.

GO ON TO THE NEXT PAGE.

3. In a certain school, there are 600 boys and 400 girls. If 20% of the boys and 30% of the girls are on the honor roll, how many of the students are on the honor roll?

    A. 120
    B. 175
    C. 240
    D. 250
    E. 280

4. If p, q, r, s, and t are whole numbers, the expression $t[r(p+q)+s]$ must be an even number when which of the five numbers is even?

    F. p
    G. q
    H. r
    J. s
    K. t

5. A student conducting a lab experiment finds that the population of flies in a bottle increases by the same multiple from week to week. If the pattern shown in the table continues, how many flies can the student expect to find in the bottle in Week 5?

Results of Biology Project Conducted by Student X					
Week	1	2	3	4	5
# of flies in bottle	3	12	48	192	?

    A. 195
    B. 240
    C. 384
    D. 564
    E. 768

DO YOUR FIGURING HERE.

GO ON TO THE NEXT PAGE.

6. At a school assembly, 3 students are each scheduled to give a short speech. In how many different orders can the speeches be scheduled?

   F. 12
   G. 9
   H. 6
   J. 4
   K. 3

DO YOUR FIGURING HERE.

7. If points P and Q lie in the xy-plane and have the coordinates shown below, what is the midpoint of $\overline{PQ}$?

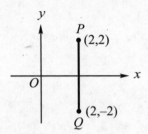

   A. $(-2,0)$
   B. $(-2,2)$
   C. $(0,2)$
   D. $(2,0)$
   E. $(2,2)$

8. If $xy = |xy|$ and $xy \neq 0$, which of the following CANNOT be true?

   F. $x > y > 0$
   G. $y > x > 0$
   H. $x > 0 > y$
   J. $0 > x > y$
   K. $0 > y > x$

GO ON TO THE NEXT PAGE.

9. In the scale drawing of the floor of a rectangular room shown below, the scale used was 1 cm = 4 m. What is the actual area, in square meters, of the floor of the room?

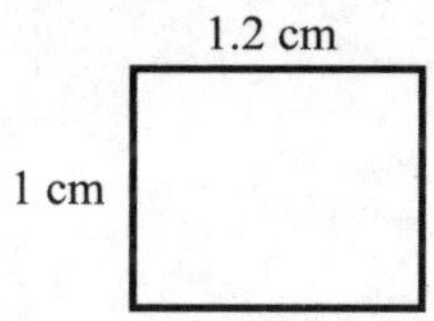

DO YOUR FIGURING HERE.

1.2 cm

1 cm

A. 9.6
B. 13.6
C. 15
D. 19.2
E. 38.4

10. If $30,000 \times 20 = 6 \times 10^n$, then $n = $?

F. 4
G. 5
H. 6
J. 7
K. 8

11. Karen purchased 4 pounds of candy, which was a mix of chocolates and caramels. If chocolates cost \$3 per pound and caramels cost \$2 per pound, and if Karen spent a total of \$10.00, how many pounds of chocolates did she buy?

A. 1
B. 2
C. 2.5
D. 3
E. 3.5

12. The average of Al's scores on 3 tests was 80. If the average of his scores on the first 2 tests was 77, what was his score on the third test?

F. 86
G. 83
H. 80
J. 77
K. 74

GO ON TO THE NEXT PAGE.

13. A book contains 10 photographs, some in color and some in black-and-white. Which of the following CANNOT be the ratio of color to black-and-white photographs?

A. 9 : 1
B. 4 : 1
C. 5 : 2
D. 3 : 2
E. 1 : 1

DO YOUR FIGURING HERE.

14. If $\dfrac{4}{5} = \dfrac{x}{4}$, then $x = ?$

F. 5

G. $\dfrac{16}{5}$

H. $\dfrac{5}{4}$

J. $\dfrac{4}{5}$

K. $\dfrac{5}{16}$

15. In the figure below, three equilateral triangles have a common vertex. What is the degree measure of $x + y + z$?

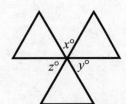

A. 60°
B. 90°
C. 120°
D. 180°
E. 240°

GO ON TO THE NEXT PAGE.

16. Peter spent $\frac{1}{4}$ of his allowance on Monday and $\frac{1}{3}$ of the remainder on Tuesday. What part of the allowance does Peter still have?

DO YOUR FIGURING HERE.

   F. $\frac{1}{12}$

   G. $\frac{1}{4}$

   H. $\frac{1}{2}$

   J. $\frac{3}{4}$

   K. $\frac{11}{12}$

17. If 100 identical bricks weigh p pounds, then how many pounds do 20 of the identical bricks weigh in terms of p?

   A. $\frac{p}{20}$

   B. $\frac{p}{5}$

   C. $20p$

   D. $\frac{5}{p}$

   E. $\frac{20}{p}$

GO ON TO THE NEXT PAGE.

18. If the distances between points P, Q, and R are equal, which of the following could be true?

    I. P, Q, and R are points on a circle with center O.

    II. P and Q are points on a circle with center R.

    III. P, Q, and R are vertices of an equilateral triangle.

  F. I only
  G. I and II only
  H. I and III only
  J. II and III only
  K. I, II, and III

DO YOUR FIGURING HERE.

19. In the table below, the percentage increase in the price of the item was greatest during which of the following periods?

Year	1980	1985	1990	1995	2000	2005
Price	$2	$4	$7	$12	$20	$30

  A. 1980–1985
  B. 1985–1990
  C. 1990–1995
  D. 1995–2000
  E. 2000–2005

20. Which of the following is a factorization of $x^2 + 4x - 12$?

  F. $(x-2)(x+6)$
  G. $(x-4)(x+3)$
  H. $(x-6)(x+2)$
  J. $(x+2)(x+6)$
  K. $(x+3)(x+4)$

GO ON TO THE NEXT PAGE.

21. Two cartons weigh $3x-2$ and $2x-3$ pounds, respectively. If the average weight of the cartons is 10 pounds, the heavier carton weighs how many more pounds than the lighter carton?

   A. 2
   B. 4
   C. 5
   D. 6
   E. 10

22. A group of 15 students took a test that was scored from 0 to 100. If 10 students scored 75 or more on the test, what is the lowest possible value for the average score of all 15 students?

   F. 25
   G. 50
   H. 70
   J. 75
   K. 90

23. For all real numbers x, 16^x is equal to which of the following expressions?

   A. x^{16}
   B. 2^{3x}
   C. 4^{2x}
   D. 8^{2x}
   E. 8^{4x}

24. If the figure below is a square, what is the perimeter of the figure?

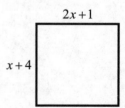

   F. 28
   G. 16
   H. 9
   J. 3
   K. 2

DO YOUR FIGURING HERE.

GO ON TO THE NEXT PAGE.

25. If a certain rectangle has a length that is 2 times its width, what is the ratio of the area of the rectangle to the area of an isosceles right triangle with a hypotenuse equal to the width of the rectangle?

    A. $\dfrac{1}{8}$

    B. $\dfrac{1}{4}$

    C. $\dfrac{1}{2}$

    D. $\dfrac{4}{1}$

    E. $\dfrac{8}{1}$

26. In the coordinate plane, what is the shortest distance between the point with (x, y) coordinates $(1, 3)$ and the line with the equation $x = -2$?

    F. 1
    G. 3
    H. 4
    J. 6
    K. 9

27. If 5 pounds of coffee cost \$12, how many pounds of coffee can be purchased for \$30?

    A. 7.2
    B. 10
    C. 12.5
    D. 15
    E. 18

DO YOUR FIGURING HERE.

GO ON TO THE NEXT PAGE.

28. If the 2 triangles below are equilateral, what is the ratio of the perimeter of the smaller to that of the larger?

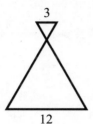

F. $\dfrac{1}{36}$

G. $\dfrac{1}{15}$

H. $\dfrac{1}{9}$

J. $\dfrac{1}{4}$

K. $\dfrac{1}{3}$

29. If $f(x) = -3x^3 + 3x^2 - 4x + 8$, then $f(-2) = ?$

A. 16
B. 22
C. 28
D. 36
E. 52

30. A merchant pays $60 wholesale for a dress and then adds a 40% markup. Two months later, the dress is put on sale at 30% off the retail price. What is the sale price of the dress?

F. $70.00
G. $64.70
H. $58.80
J. $56.30
K. $42.00

DO YOUR FIGURING HERE.

GO ON TO THE NEXT PAGE.

31. If $\frac{1}{3}$ of a number is 2 more than $\frac{1}{5}$ of the number, then which of the following equations can be used to find the number x?

A. $\frac{1}{3}x - \frac{1}{5}x = 2$

B. $\frac{1}{3}x - \frac{1}{5}x = -2$

C. $\frac{1}{3}x - 2 = -\frac{1}{5}x$

D. $\frac{1}{3}x + 2 = -\frac{1}{5}x$

E. $5\left(\frac{1}{3}x + 2\right) = 0$

DO YOUR FIGURING HERE.

32. In the figure below, the triangle is equilateral and has a perimeter of 12 centimeters. What is the perimeter, in centimeters, of the square?

F. 9
G. 12
H. 16
J. 20
K. 24

33. If one solution of the equation $12x^2 + kx = 6$ is $\frac{2}{3}$, then $k = ?$

A. 1

B. $\frac{3}{2}$

C. 2
D. 5
E. 9

GO ON TO THE NEXT PAGE.

34. If a 6-sided polygon has 2 sides of length $x - 2y$ each and 4 sides of length $2x + y$ each, what is its perimeter?

  F. $6x - 6y$
  G. $6x - y$
  H. $5x$
  J. $6x$
  K. $10x$

35. At the first stop on her route, a driver unloaded $\dfrac{2}{5}$ of the packages in her van. After she unloaded another 3 packages at her next stop, $\dfrac{1}{2}$ of the original number of packages in the van remained. How many packages were in the van before the first delivery?

  A. 10
  B. 20
  C. 25
  D. 30
  E. 50

36. For all x and y, $12x^3y^2 - 8x^2y^3 = ?$

  F. $2x^2y^2(4x - y)$
  G. $4x^2y^2(2xy)$
  H. $4x^2y^2(3xy)$
  J. $4x^2y^2(3x - 2y)$
  K. $x^3y^3(12xy - 8xy)$

DO YOUR FIGURING HERE.

GO ON TO THE NEXT PAGE.

37. When $\dfrac{1}{1+\dfrac{1}{x}}$ is defined, it is equivalent to which

of the following expressions?

  A. $x+1$

  B. $\dfrac{1}{x+1}$

  C. $\dfrac{x}{x+1}$

  D. $\dfrac{x+1}{x}$

  E. x^2+x

38. If S is 150% of T, what percentage of $S+T$ is T?

  F. $33\dfrac{1}{3}\%$

  G. 40%

  H. 50%

  J. 75%

  K. 80%

39. In $\triangle PQR$, the lengths of $\overline{PQ}$ and $\overline{QR}$ are equal, and the measure of $\angle Q$ is 3 times that of $\angle P$. What is the measure of $\angle R$?

  A. 24°

  B. 30°

  C. 36°

  D. 45°

  E. 60°

DO YOUR FIGURING HERE.

GO ON TO THE NEXT PAGE.

40. If the cost of b books is d dollars, which of the following equations can be used to find the cost, C, in dollars, of x books at the same rate?

F. $\ C = xd$

G. $\ C = \dfrac{dx}{b}$

H. $\ C = \dfrac{bd}{x}$

J. $\ C = bx$

K. $\ C = \dfrac{bx}{d}$

41. An article is on sale for 25% off its regular price of $64. If the merchant must also collect a 5% sales tax on this reduced price, what is the total cost of the article including sales tax?

A. $42.10
B. $44.20
C. $49.60
D. $50.40
E. $56.70

42. If $\dfrac{x}{z} = k$ and $\dfrac{y}{z} = k - 1$, then $x = $?

F. $\ \dfrac{y}{z}$

G. $\ z - y$

H. $\ y - 1$

J. $\ y + 1$

K. $\ y + z$

43. If x is 25% of y, then y is what percentage of x?

A. 400%
B. 300%
C. 250%
D. 125%
E. 75%

DO YOUR FIGURING HERE.

GO ON TO THE NEXT PAGE.

44. If x is an integer that is a multiple of both 9 and 5, which of the following *must* be true?

      I. x is equal to 45.
     II. x is a multiple of 15.
   III. x is odd.

  F. I only
  G. II only
  H. III only
  J. II and III only
  K. I, II, and III

45. If each edge of a cube is 2 units long, what is the distance from any vertex (corner of the cube) to the cube's center?

  A. $\dfrac{\sqrt{2}}{2}$

  B. $\sqrt{3}$
  C. $2\sqrt{2}$
  D. $2\sqrt{3}$

  E. $\dfrac{3}{2}$

46. The figure below shows 2 circular cylinders, C and C'. If $r = kr'$ and $h = kh'$, what is the ratio of the volume of C' to the volume of C?

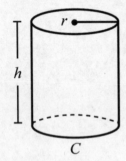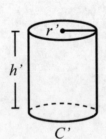

  F. $1 : \pi$
  G. $\pi : 1$
  H. $k\pi : 1$
  J. $1 : k^3$
  K. $k^3 : 1$

DO YOUR FIGURING HERE.

GO ON TO THE NEXT PAGE.

47. In the figure below, if the triangle has an area of 1 square unit, what is the area of the circle, in square units?

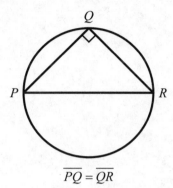

$$\overline{PQ} = \overline{QR}$$

- **A.** π
- **B.** 2π
- **C.** $2\sqrt{3}\pi$
- **D.** 4π
- **E.** $4\sqrt{3}\pi$

48. In the figure below, P and Q are the centers of their respective circles and the radius of each circle is 1 inch. What is the perimeter, in inches, of the shaded part of the figure?

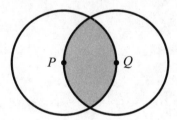

- **F.** $\dfrac{4\pi}{3}$
- **G.** π
- **H.** $\dfrac{2\pi}{3}$
- **J.** $\dfrac{\pi}{3}$
- **K.** $\dfrac{\pi}{6}$

DO YOUR FIGURING HERE.

GO ON TO THE NEXT PAGE.

DO YOUR FIGURING HERE.

49. A student's final grade in a certain course is the average of his scores on 10 tests graded on a scale of 0 to 100, inclusive. For the first 6 tests, the student's scores averaged 83. If x is the student's final grade for the course, then which of the following is true?

   A. $8.3 \leq x \leq 83.0$
   B. $49.8 \leq x \leq 83.0$
   C. $49.8 \leq x \leq 89.8$
   D. $54.7 \leq x \leq 89.8$
   E. $83.0 \leq x \leq 89.8$

50. What is the multiplicative inverse of the complex number $2 - i$?

   F. $2 + i$
   G. $i - 2$
   H. $\dfrac{2 + i}{3}$
   J. $\dfrac{2 - i}{3}$
   K. $\dfrac{2 + i}{5}$

51. $\log_3 \sqrt{3} = ?$

   A. -1
   B. $\dfrac{1}{3}$
   C. $\dfrac{1}{2}$
   D. $\dfrac{2}{3}$
   E. 2

52. If $f(x) = (x - 1)^2 + 2$, then what value for x creates the minimum value for $f(x)$?

   F. -3
   G. -2
   H. 0
   J. 1
   K. 2

GO ON TO THE NEXT PAGE.

53. If $2^n + 2^n + 2^n + 2^n = x(2^{n+1})$, then $x = ?$

    A. 2
    B. 4
    C. 2^n
    D. 2^{2n}
    E. 2^{n+1}

54. If $f(k) = k^2 + 2k + 1$, then what is the set of all k for which $f(k) = f(-k)$?

    F. {0}
    G. {1}
    H. {2}
    J. {1, 2}
    K. All real numbers

55. The limit of a function, $\lim_{x \to a} f(x)$, denotes the value $f(x)$ approaches for values of x approaching a. What is $\lim_{x \to 1} \dfrac{x^2 - 1}{x - 1}$?

    A. -1
    B. 0
    C. 1
    D. 2
    E. The limit does not exist.

56. If $0 \le x \le \pi$ and $\cos x = -1$, then $\cos \dfrac{x}{2} = ?$

    F. $-\dfrac{\sqrt{3}}{2}$
    G. $-\dfrac{1}{2}$
    H. 0
    J. $\dfrac{1}{2}$
    K. $\dfrac{\sqrt{3}}{2}$

DO YOUR FIGURING HERE.

GO ON TO THE NEXT PAGE.

57. Which of the following defines the range of the function $f(x) = \dfrac{1-x}{x}$?

   A. All real numbers
   B. All real numbers except -1
   C. All real numbers except 0
   D. All real numbers except 1
   E. All real numbers greater than -1

DO YOUR FIGURING HERE.

58. Which of the following graphs represents the equations $x = 3(\sin\theta)$ and $y = 2(\cos\theta)$?

F.
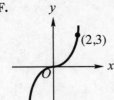

J.
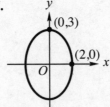

G.
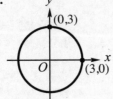

K.
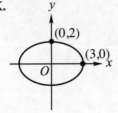

H.
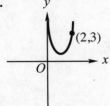

59. For all θ such that $0° < \theta < 90°$, which of the following is equal to $(\sin\theta)(\csc\theta)$?

   A. 1
   B. $\sqrt{2}$
   C. $\tan\theta$
   D. $\cot\theta$
   E. $\sec\theta$

GO ON TO THE NEXT PAGE.

60. In the figure below, how many units long is $\overline{BC}$?

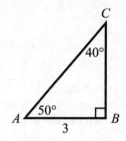

DO YOUR FIGURING HERE.

F. 4
G. 5
H. $\sin 10°$
J. $3(\tan 50°)$
K. $3(\tan 40°)$

END OF TEST 2
STOP! DO NOT TURN THE PAGE UNTIL TOLD TO DO SO.
DO NOT RETURN TO THE PREVIOUS TEST.

PRACTICE TEST I   3 3 3 3 3 3 3 3 3 3 3 3 3

SECTION 3: READING TEST
35 Minutes—40 Items

DIRECTIONS: Each passage below is followed by a set of items. Read each passage and choose the best answer for each item. Fill in the corresponding oval on your bubble sheet. You may refer to the passage as often as necessary to answer the items. Answers are on page 691.

Passage I

PROSE FICTION: In this passage, a young country man, alone in town for the first time, tries to find a relative, Major Molineux.

It was near nine o'clock of a moonlit evening, when a boat crossed the ferry with a single passenger, who had obtained his conveyance at that unusual hour by the promise of extra fare. He was a youth of barely
5   eighteen years, evidently country-bred, and now upon his first visit to town. The youth finally drew from his pocket a little province bill of five shillings, which, in depreciation in that sort of currency, satisfied the ferry-man's demand with the addition of a hexagonal piece
10 of parchment, valued at three pence. He then walked forward into the town with as light a step as if his day's journey had not already exceeded thirty miles and with as eager an eye as if he were entering London city, instead of the little metropolis of a New England
15 colony. However, before Robin had proceeded far, it occurred to him that he knew not whither to direct his steps; so he paused and looked up and down the narrow street, scrutinizing the small and mean wooden buildings that were scattered on either side.

20   "This low hovel cannot be my kinsman's dwelling," thought he, "nor yonder old house; and truly I see none hereabouts that might be worthy of him. It would have been wise to inquire my way of the ferryman, and doubtless, he would have gone with me
25 and earned a shilling from the Major for his pains. But the next man I meet will do as well."

He resumed his walk and was glad to perceive that the street now became wide, and the houses were more respectable in their appearance. He soon

30 discerned a figure moving on moderately in advance, and he hastened his steps to overtake it. Robin laid hold of the skirt of the man's old coat, just when the light from the open door and windows of a barber's shop fell upon both their figures.

35   "Good evening to you, honored sir," said he, making a low bow and still retaining hold of the skirt. "I pray you tell me whereabouts is the dwelling of my kinsman, Major Molineux."

The citizen answered him in a tone of excessive
40 anger and annoyance. "Let go my garment, fellow! I tell you, I know not the man you speak of. What! I have the authority, I have—hem, hem—authority; and if this be the respect you show for your betters, your feet shall be brought acquainted with the stocks by
45 daylight, tomorrow morning!"

Robin released the old man's skirt and hastened away, pursued by an ill-mannered roar of laughter from the barber's shop. He was at first considerably surprised by the result of his question, but, being a
50 shrewd youth, he soon thought himself able to account for the mystery.

"This is some country representative," was his conclusion, "who has never seen the inside of my kins-man's door and lacks the breeding to answer a stranger
55 civilly. Ah, Robin, Robin! Even the barber's boys laugh at you for choosing such a guide! You will be wiser in time, friend Robin."

GO ON TO THE NEXT PAGE.

1. In the final paragraph, the young man is talking to:

   A. the Major.
   B. the man in the coat.
   C. the barbers.
   D. himself.

2. The total cost of the young man's passage on the ferryboat was:

   F. five shillings.
   G. three pence.
   H. five shillings less three pence.
   J. five shillings plus three pence.

3. The young man believes that his relative is a:

   A. barber.
   B. wealthy person.
   C. constable.
   D. builder.

4. The incidents described in the passage take place:

   F. in the late morning.
   G. in the early afternoon.
   H. in the late afternoon.
   J. at night.

5. The passage suggests that thirty miles is:

   A. a long distance to travel in one day.
   B. easily traveled in a single day.
   C. easily traveled in an hour.
   D. a long ferryboat ride.

6. The young man believes that the barbers laughed at him because:

   F. his clothes clearly show that he is from the country.
   G. he asked a question of a stranger who obviously would not know the answer.
   H. he badly needs a haircut and a shave.
   J. the stranger he questioned is actually the man he is looking for.

7. The scenes in the passage are most likely set in which of the following time periods?

   A. Eighteenth century
   B. Nineteenth century
   C. Early twentieth century
   D. Present time

8. The young man approaches the stranger in the coat:

   F. respectfully.
   G. rudely.
   H. coyly.
   J. stealthily.

9. The young man is the only passenger on the ferryboat because:

   A. he paid the ferryman extra for a private charter.
   B. no one else was traveling at that hour.
   C. the Major had sent the boat especially for him.
   D. the ferryman was a good friend of the young man.

10. Just after he gets off the ferry, the young man finds himself in a:

    F. poorer neighborhood.
    G. wealthy neighborhood.
    H. forest.
    J. large city.

GO ON TO THE NEXT PAGE.

Passage II

SOCIAL SCIENCE: These passages discuss Frederick Turner's hypothesis of the American frontier.

Passage A

In 1893, Frederick Jackson Turner presented a paper to a group of historians convening in Chicago during the Columbian Exposition. Entitled "The Significance of the American Frontier in History,"
5 Turner's paper drew little immediate reaction. Yet, no theory of history has had a greater influence on the direction and methodology of inquiry and the issues of debate in American history. Later historians took issue with some of Turner's interpretations; even some of his
10 own students were among those whose research proved some of his views to be wrong. However, these debates merely serve to illustrate the importance of Turner's hypothesis.

Turner's argument was a grand hypothesis about
15 how the settlement of the frontier had shaped the American experience and character. As with all general hypotheses in any field of study, it gave a coherent interpretation to many facts that had been largely ignored by historians up to that time.

20 Turner used statistical evidence from the 1880 census as the basis for a startling conclusion: Prior to 1880 there had been a frontier to be settled. By 1890, Turner pointed out, there was no longer any area of wilderness completely untouched by settlements. The
25 frontier had disappeared. The passing of the frontier, Turner concluded, was a historic moment.

Turner further claimed that the frontier experience had produced a distinctively American character, which was not explainable simply as the
30 predictable behavioral traits molded by English political institutions. Frontier settlers developed inquisitiveness, inventiveness, energy, and a great passion for freedom. These attributes defined a new American character—one evidenced in nationalism,
35 independence, and democracy. This new sense of national identity derived from the fact that people from every section of the country mixed at the Western frontier. Economic independence could be traced to the fact that the settlers no longer depended on England for
40 goods but had become self-sufficient. In addition, the frontier settlers, whose basic social unit was the family, enjoyed freedom from direct governmental interference. Frontier life thus reinforced the fundamental ideals of populist democracy.

45 In addition, Turner argued that the frontier fostered democracy in the cities of the East. The availability of free land at the frontier provided a "safety-valve" against possible social unrest: those discontented with social inequities and economic
50 injustice could strike out and settle the free land that was available in frontier territories.

Turner's thesis was thus original in both what it said and in the methodology that Turner used in formulating it. Up to the time of Turner's essay, history
55 had been essentially the history of politics. A Midwesterner, Turner challenged this traditional approach of Eastern historians by incorporating techniques of the social sciences, showing how factors of geography, economics, climate, and society
60 influenced the development of the American West. Although now common among historians, at the time this interdisciplinary approach was novel.

Passage B

Three years before Turner put forth the frontier thesis, the U.S. Census Bureau had announced the
65 disappearance of a contiguous frontier line. For Turner, the significance of the frontier was its effect on the American character. According to Turner, uniquely American traits were developed by the frontier culture, including a can-do problem-solving attitude, a nervous
70 energy, and rugged individualism.

Turner's essay reached triumphant heights in his belief that the promotion of individualistic democracy was the most important consequence of the frontier. Individuals, forced to rely on their own wits and
75 strength, were necessarily skeptical of hierarchies and fearful of centralized authority.

Turner's thesis that the frontier is the key to American history as a whole has rightfully been abandoned. There is too much evidence for the critical
80 influence of factors like slavery and the Civil War, immigration, and the development of industrial capitalism. But even as an account of the West and frontier, Turner's thesis was lacking.

Turner's formulation of "free land" ignored the
85 presence of the numerous Indian peoples whose subjugation was required by the nation's westward march. The many Indian wars started by American expansion belie Turner's argument that the American frontier, in sharp contrast to European borders between
90 nation-states, was "free land."

More fundamentally, the very concept of a frontier is dubious, because it applies to too many disparate places and times to be useful. How much do

GO ON TO THE NEXT PAGE.

Puritan New England and the California of the
95 transcontinental railroad really have in common? Many
such critics have sought to replace the idea of a moving
frontier with the idea of the West as a distinctive
region, much like the American South.

Additionally, cooperation and communities of
100 various sorts, not isolated individuals, made possible
the absorption of the West into the United States. Most
migrant wagon trains, for example, were composed of
extended kinship networks. Moreover, the role of the
federal government and large corporations grew
105 increasingly important. Corporate investors built the
railroads; government troops defeated Indian nations;
even cowboys, enshrined in popular myth as rugged
loners, were generally low-level employees of cattle
corporations.

11. According to Passage A, Turner's methodology
was original in its:

   A. reliance on the history of politics to explain
the American experience.

   B. use of an interdisciplinary approach to study
a historical question.

   C. reliance on a presentation at a professional
conference to announce a theory.

   D. suggestion that key terms like "frontier" have
to be more clearly defined.

12. The phrase "even some of his own students"
(lines 9–10) implies that students are:

   F. not necessarily familiar with the most recent
scholarly work.

   G. ordinarily sympathetic to the views of one of
their professors.

   H. not likely to accept a theory until it has been
studied for some time.

   J. disposed to propose new theories that have
little merit.

13. The attitude of the author of Passage A toward
Turner's work can best be described as:

   A. suspicious.

   B. condescending.

   C. undecided.

   D. approving.

14. In this context, "grand" (line 14) means:

   F. incorrect.

   G. comprehensive.

   H. lavish.

   J. tentative.

15. The author of Passage B lists the "factors" in
lines 80–82 in order to show that:

   A. Turner's thesis did not adequately explain
the history of the frontier.

   B. historians prior to Turner had tended to focus
on only a single explanatory factor.

   C. the frontier was only one of many important
factors in American history.

   D. different regions of America had different
experiences of the frontier.

16. The author of Passage B mentions wagon trains
(line 102) in order to show that:

   F. frontier land had previously been inhabited
by indigenous peoples.

   G. groups were as important in the westward
expansion as individuals.

   H. government army troops were needed to
secure the safety of settlers.

   J. groups from different regions came into
contact at the frontier.

17. It can be inferred that the author of Passage B
believes that:

   A. Turner's thesis is still generally valid.

   B. Turner's thesis had very limited usefulness.

   C. Turner was intellectually dishonest.

   D. Turner intentionally ignored evidence.

18. In context, "belie" (line 88) means:

   F. tell an untruth about.

   G. conceal a flaw in.

   H. prove to be false.

   J. retract a point.

GO ON TO THE NEXT PAGE.

19. Both passages mention all of the following as elements of Turner's view regarding the American character EXCEPT:

   A. practical inventiveness.
   B. pro-democracy attitude.
   C. skepticism toward authority.
   D. nationalistic feelings.

20. The evidence that frontier land was not free (lines 84–90) most undermines what aspect of Turner's thesis as explained in Passage A?

   F. Safety-valve theory
   G. Census data of 1880
   H. Claim of self-sufficiency
   J. Mixing at the frontier

GO ON TO THE NEXT PAGE.

Passage III

HUMANITIES: In this passage, the author expresses his opinion regarding the role of philosophy.

The service of philosophy towards the human spirit is to startle it into sharp and eager observation. Every moment, and for that moment only, some form grows perfect in hand or face; some tone on the hills or
5 the sea is choicer than the rest. Not the fruit of experience, but experience itself is the end. Only a counted number of pulses are given to us of a variegated, dramatic life. How shall we pass most quickly from point to point and be present always at
10 the focus where the greatest number of vital forces unite in their purest energy?

To burn always with this hard, gemlike flame, to maintain this ecstasy, is success in life. It is only the roughness of the eye that makes any two persons,
15 things, or situations seem alike. While all melts under our feet, we may well catch at any exquisite passion, or any knowledge that seems by a lifted horizon to set the spirit free for a moment, or any stirring of the senses, strange dyes, strange colors, curious odors, or work of
20 the artist's hands or the faces of one's friends. Not to discriminate every moment some passionate attitude in those about us, and in the brilliancy of their gifts some tragic dividing of forces of their ways is, on this short day of the frost and sun, to sleep before evening. With
25 this sense of the splendor of our experience and of its awful brevity, gathering all we are into one desperate effort to see and touch, we shall hardly have time to make theories about the things we see and touch.

We are all under sentence of death but with a sort
30 of indefinite reprieve; we have an interval and then our place knows us no more. Some spend this interval in listlessness, others in high passions, the wisest—at least among the "children of this world"—in art and song. Our one chance lies in expanding this interval—
35 in getting as many pulsations as possible into the given time. Great passions may give us this quickened sense of life, ecstasy, sorrow, and love, the various forms of enthusiastic activity. Of this wisdom, the poetic passion, the desire of beauty, the love of art for art's
40 sake has most; for art comes to you professing frankly to give nothing but the highest quality to your moments as they pass, and simply for the sake of those moments.

21. Which of the following best describes the overall structure of the passage?

   A. The author raises a question and then provides an answer.
   B. The author presents a theory, which he then proves.
   C. The author studies a widely held belief and then rejects it.
   D. The author defines a term and then provides examples.

22. In the passage, the author uses the word *pulsations* (line 35) to mean:

   F. children.
   G. lives.
   H. death.
   J. experiences.

23. According to the author, the function of art is to:

   A. depict reality accurately.
   B. stimulate strong emotions.
   C. encourage social reform.
   D. express the artist's feelings.

24. With which of the following statements would the author most likely agree?

   F. A person's lifetime is merely preparation for what comes after death.
   G. Only an artist can truly enjoy life.
   H. The original experience is more important than the memory of it.
   J. A perceptive person understands that all experience is repetitious.

25. The tone of the passage can best be described as:

   A. impassioned.
   B. scholarly.
   C. informative.
   D. speculative.

GO ON TO THE NEXT PAGE.

26. In the context of this passage, the phrase "short day of the frost and sun" (lines 23–24) refers to:

F. the transient effect of poetry.
G. a brief moment of passion.
H. the life of a person.
J. stimulation of the senses.

27. The phrase "awful brevity" (line 26) means that:

A. philosophy is not really useful.
B. art may not satisfy everyone.
C. life is short.
D. passion is the greatest virtue.

28. The "children of this world" (line 33) are NOT:

F. passionate.
G. wise.
H. lovers of art and song.
J. listless.

29. According to the author, the greatest passion is the love of:

A. beauty.
B. one's spouse.
C. wealth.
D. security.

30. The phrase "then our place knows us no more" (lines 30–31) means that we:

F. move to another town.
G. have children.
H. die.
J. divorce.

GO ON TO THE NEXT PAGE.

Passage IV

NATURAL SCIENCE: This passage explains how energy becomes usable through photosynthesis.

Every living cell must acquire energy in a usable form. According to the First Law of Thermodynamics, energy, which is the capacity for doing work, can be converted from one form into another without any net
5 gain or loss. An organism must have an outside source of usable energy. The Second Law of Thermodynamics states that every energy transformation reduces the free (usable) energy of the system. Living cells primarily use chemical energy derived from complex organic
10 compounds.

Photosynthesis is the process by which green plants transform sunlight into a usable energy source. Green plants utilize the energy of light to combine carbon dioxide with water to form organic material
15 (sugar) and oxygen.

$$6CO_2 + 12H_2O + light \overset{chlorophyll}{\Rightarrow} 6O_2 + C_6H_{12}O_6 + 6H_2O$$

Photosynthesis is a reduction reaction. Reduction is the addition of one or more electrons to an atom or molecule. Oxidation is the removal of electrons from
20 an atom or molecule. Reduction stores energy, while oxidation releases it. Biological systems rely on the addition or removal of an electron from hydrogen. Photosynthesis is based on two key processes. Light energy is trapped and stored, and hydrogen atoms are
25 transformed from water to carbon dioxide to form carbohydrate.

Photosynthesis takes place within the chloroplasts. The pigments within the chloroplasts are precisely arranged within the membranes of flattened
30 sacs called thylakoids. Thylakoids often lie close together in sacks called grana. The light reactions of photosynthesis take place within the thylakoid membranes, while the dark reactions take place in the colorless matrix (stroma) surrounding the thylakoids.

35 Different wavelengths of light, especially red and blue light, are trapped by various pigment molecules contained within chloroplasts. When a photon of light strikes a pigment molecule and is absorbed, the energy is transferred to an electron, which is raised to a high-
40 energy state. A specialized form of chlorophyll passes the energized electron to an acceptor molecule, X,

which has a high affinity for electrons. X passes the electron to a series of acceptor molecules, each at a slightly lower energy level. After being passed from
45 molecule to molecule, the electron may return to the chlorophyll from which it started. Some of the energy released as the electron is passed down the energy gradient is used to synthesize the compound ATP from ADP and inorganic phosphate.

50 ATP is a universal energy packet used by cells to do work. ATP is synthesized from ADP and inorganic phosphate in a process called phosphorylation. Phosphorylation is a very high energy-demanding process. *Cyclic photophosphorylation* occurs when the
55 energy used for ATP synthesis comes from light-energized electrons as they are returned to the chlorophyll molecules from which they originated.

Another process that occurs in green plants is noncyclic photophosphorylation. In this reaction, some
60 electrons are passed from the chlorophyll to a different type of acceptor molecule called $NAPD_{ox}$, which retains the electron and is therefore reduced to become $NAPD_{re}$.

The ATP and $NAPD_{re}$ produced in the light
65 reaction are used to reduce carbon dioxide to carbohydrate in a series of reactions called the *Calvin cycle* (dark reaction). Basically, a five-carbon sugar, ribulose diphosphate (RuDP), is combined with CO_2. This process is called carboxyilation. The products are
70 then phosphorylated by ATP and reduced by $NAPD_{re}$ to form PGAL, a three-carbon sugar.

Under certain conditions, the very same enzyme that under more agreeable conditions would facilitate its carboxyilation oxidizes RuDP. This process, called
75 photorespiration, is seemingly a wasteful process since no ATP is created. Photorespiration predominates over photosynthesis when CO_2 levels are low and O_2 levels are high.

Some tropical angiosperm plants have a unique
80 leaf structure known as *Kranz* anatomy (C_4 plants). In Kranz plants, the bundle-sheath cells have numerous chloroplasts (other plants usually do not), and the mesophyll cells are clustered in a ring-like arrangement around the bundle sheath. These plants can carry out
85 photosynthesis under conditions of high temperature and concentrated light, when loss of water induces closure of the stomata. When the stomata close, the concentration of CO_2 in the air spaces inside the leaf

GO ON TO THE NEXT PAGE.

falls, and the concentration of O_2 rises. Under these
90 conditions most plants (C_3) would experience a net
loss of CO_2 because of photorespiration. Kranz plants
(C_4) do not because of their specialized way of initially
fixing CO_2. They combine CO_2 with a three-carbon
compound in the mesophyll cells to form a four-carbon
95 compound that passes into the bundle-sheath cells,
where the CO_2 is regenerated. Therefore, Kranz plants
can maintain a CO_2 level in the bundle-sheath cells
that allows carboxyilation of RuDP in the Calvin cycle
to predominate over its oxidation in photorespiration.

31. According to this passage, "the capacity for doing work" (line 3) is the definition of:

    A. photosynthesis.
    B. energy.
    C. oxidation.
    D. thermodynamics.

32. In the equation in line 16, $C_6H_{12}O_6$ apparently names:

    F. oxygen.
    G. carbon dioxide.
    H. a sugar.
    J. photosynthesis.

33. Which of these could be considered the reverse of reduction?

    A. Oxidation
    B. Photosynthesis
    C. Transformation
    D. Phosphorylation

34. Which of the following conclusions is (are) suggested by the third paragraph?

    I. Photosynthesis involves the addition of electrons.
    II. Photosynthesis involves action on hydrogen.
    III. Photosynthesis is a form of energy release.

    F. I only
    G. II only
    H. III only
    J. I and II only

35. The fifth paragraph deals mainly with:

    A. defining terms related to plant growth.
    B. comparing one reduction reaction to another.
    C. explaining the process of photosynthesis.
    D. expressing the author's opinion.

36. Which of the following statements is NOT true about ATP?

    F. It mixes with phosphate to make ADP.
    G. It is created through phosphorylation.
    H. It serves a purpose in the Calvin cycle.
    J. It is used by cells to do work.

37. The Calvin cycle involves:

    A. the combination of carbon dioxide and a five-carbon sugar, with a three-carbon sugar as the result.
    B. the combination of oxygen and a three-carbon sugar, with a five-carbon sugar as the result.
    C. a mix of ATP and sugar to create carbon dioxide.
    D. a reduction of carbohydrate to form carbon dioxide.

GO ON TO THE NEXT PAGE.

38. By "more agreeable conditions" (line 73), the author probably means:

    F. conditions that produce higher levels of oxygen.
    G. conditions that produce higher levels of CO_2.
    H. conditions with higher temperatures.
    J. conditions with longer growing periods.

39. Which of the following statements names a difference between photorespiration and photosynthesis?

    I.   Photorespiration involves RuDP.
    II.   In photosynthesis, ATP is synthesized.
    III.   Photorespiration is a reduction reaction.

    A. I only
    B. I and II only
    C. II and III only
    D. I, II, and III

40. Unlike the preceding paragraphs, the final paragraph discusses:

    F. plants that do not photosynthesize.
    G. living matter other than plants.
    H. plants with an unusual structure.
    J. plants that transform carbon dioxide into carbohydrate.

END OF TEST 3
STOP! DO NOT TURN THE PAGE UNTIL TOLD TO DO SO.
DO NOT RETURN TO THE PREVIOUS TEST.

NO TEST MATERIAL ON THIS PAGE

PRACTICE TEST I

4 4 4 4 4 4 4 4 4 4 4 4 4

SECTION 4: SCIENCE TEST
35 Minutes—40 Items

DIRECTIONS: Each passage below is followed by several items. After reading a passage, choose the best answer for each item. Fill in the corresponding oval on your bubble sheet. You may refer to the passage as often as necessary. You are NOT permitted the use of a calculator on this test. Answers are on page 695.

Passage I

Alkanes are open-chain organic compounds that have the general chemical formula C_nH_{2n+2}. For example, propane has the following structural formula:

$$CH_3 — CH_2 — CH_3$$

For propane, $n = 3$ (the number of carbon atoms), and $2(3) + 2 = 8$ (the number of hydrogen atoms). The series of linked carbon atoms is called the carbon backbone of the compound, and the number of carbon atoms in the backbone gives the compounds their different names. Alkanes that differ by one carbon atom differ in molecular mass by 14u (one carbon atom of mass 12u and two hydrogen atoms of mass 1u each).

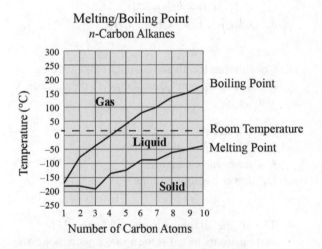

Melting/Boiling Point
n-Carbon Alkanes

Physical Properties of Straight-Chain Alkanes					
Name	# of Carbons	Boiling Point (°C)	Melting Point (°C)	Molecular Mass (atomic mass unit, u)	Flash Point (°C)	Density (g/cm³ at 290°C)
methane	1	−162	−183	16	–	0.466
ethane	2	−89	−183	30	–	0.572
propane	3	−42	−188	44	–	0.585
butane	4	0	−138	58	–	0.601
pentane	5	36	−130	72	−49	0.626
hexane	6	69	−95	86	−22	0.660
heptane	7	98	−91	100	−4	0.684
octane	8	126	−57	114	13	0.703
nonane	9	151	−54	128	31	0.718
decane	10	174	−30	142	46	0.730

GO ON TO THE NEXT PAGE.

1. According to the table, as the number of carbon atoms in the backbone of the alkane molecule increases, the:

    A. molecular mass decreases.
    B. boiling point increases.
    C. melting point decreases.
    D. density at 290°C decreases.

2. Which of the following is the structural formula for butane?

    F. CH_3—CH_3—CH_3—CH_3
    G. CH_2—CH_3—CH_3—CH_2
    H. CH_3—CH_2—CH_2—CH_3
    J. CH_{12}—CH_{10}—CH_{10}—CH_{12}

3. Considering the alkanes listed, if alkane X has a higher boiling point than alkane Y, then alkane X also has:

    A. a lower flash point.
    B. a lower molecular mass.
    C. more carbon atoms.
    D. fewer hydrogen atoms.

4. The alkane undecane has a backbone of 11 carbon atoms. What is the approximate molecular mass of the compound?

    F. 154
    G. 155
    H. 156
    J. 157

5. The alkane dodecane has a backbone of 12 carbon atoms. The compound has how many hydrogen atoms?

    A. 14
    B. 24
    C. 26
    D. 28

6. Which of the following is not a gas at room temperature?

    F. Methane.
    G. Ethane.
    H. Butane.
    J. Hexane.

GO ON TO THE NEXT PAGE.

7. Which of the following graphs most accurately depicts the density of the first ten alkanes as a function of the number of atoms in the carbon backbone in the alkanes?

A.

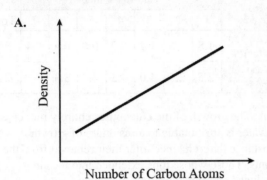

B.

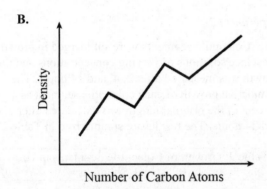

C.

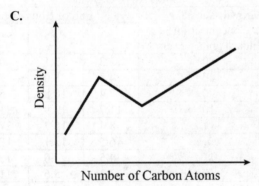

D.

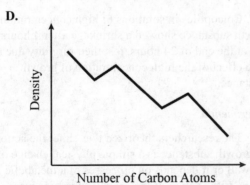

Passage II

The protective sheath that covers the emerging shoot tip of monocotyledons, such as grasses, is called the coleoptile. Coleoptiles consist of specialized cells that do not divide but increase in size as they accumulate water. When the coleoptile pushes above the soil surface, it stops growing as the flag leaves emerge from it and continue to grow.

Figure 1

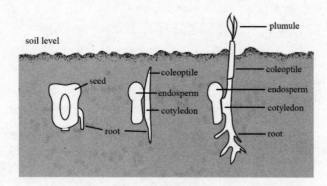

To study the impact of conditions on the growth rate of coleoptiles, *Avena* (oats) plants were grown in sand in the dark at 25°C and 85–90% relative humidity and harvested when 4 days old. Shoot tips 3 to 5 millimeters long were removed from the plants 2 hours before being immersed in water or growth solutions prepared from the fungus *Rhizopus suinus*. Growth substance concentrations were measured in standard units per cubic centimeter.

Experiment 1

Coleoptile segments were immersed in pure water and the growth measured at the end of each hour for 7 hours. The test was repeated with the tops of the segments above the water surface. The growth of each coleoptile segment per hour as a percent of the original length was calculated. The averages across all segments for both tests are summarized in Table 1.

Table 1: Growth of Coleoptile Segments in Water								
Average Growth per Hour as a Percent of Original Length								
Test	End of Hour *n*							
	1	2	3	4	5	6	7	Total
1 (tops in water)	1.8	1.5	1.2	0.7	0.6	0.4	0.4	6.6
2 (tops in air)	2.5	2.5	4.0	4.3	4.7	3.3	--	21.3

The growth of the coleoptiles entirely immersed in water is attributable to a residuum of growth substance that remained after their removal from the plants. Those whose tops extended into the air produced additional growth substance.

Experiment 2

Coleoptile segments were submerged in growth substance solutions of varying concentrations and the growth was measured after 2, 4, and 24 hours. The cumulative growth of each coleoptile segment as a percent of the original length was calculated after 2, 4, and 24 hours. The results are summarized in Table 2.

Table 2: Growth of Coleoptile Segments in Growth Substance Solutions			
Cumulative Growth			
Growth Substance Concentration (standard units per cm³)	End of Hour *n*		
	2	4	24
80	3.3	2.1	0.4
40	4.3	8.0	7.2
20	7.4	10.8	15.4
10	11.7	19.9	31.0
1	8.4	15.7	27.0
0.1	6.5	12.1	17.5
0.01	4.5	7.0	15.5
0	3.3	5.6	11.9

Coleoptiles in solutions of high concentrations of growth substance showed a shrinkage after 4 hours and, at the end of 24 hours, lost their turgidity due to a toxic effect of the high concentration of growth substance.

Experiment 3

The researchers theorized that either the action of the growth substance is a simple physical change of the cell wall or it depends on processes of a metabolic nature. If the action of the growth substance were a

GO ON TO THE NEXT PAGE.

simple physical change, then it would not be affected by the presence of cyanide. If, however, it depends on metabolic processes, cyanide should inhibit the action of the growth substance. A series of tests were conducted to determine the impact of potassium cyanide (KCN) on the growth of coleoptile segments. Table 3 summarizes the results.

Table 3: Inhibition of Growth of Coleoptile Segments by KCN	
Solution	Total Percent Growth
Growth substance alone	23
Growth substance + 2×10^{-4} M KCN	5
Growth substance + 1×10^{-3} M KCN	2
Growth substance + 2×10^{-3} M KCN	–4
Growth substance + 2×10^{-2} M KCN	–3
Water + 2×10^{-2} M KCN	–4

8. The "flag leaves" referred to in the introductory paragraph of the passage correspond to which of the features shown in Figure 1?

   F. Plumule.
   G. Endosperm.
   H. Coyledon.
   J. Root.

9. According to the information provided, the greater growth rate recorded in Test 2 in Experiment 1 is explained by the:

   A. addition of growth substance to the water used to immerse the coleoptiles.
   B. production by the coleoptiles of additional growth substance following clipping.
   C. retention by the coleoptiles of growth substance already present in the plants.
   D. metabolism by the coleoptiles of a growth substance present in the air.

10. Which of the three experiments used water and no growth solution?

    F. Experiment 1 only
    G. Experiment 2 only
    H. Experiments 1 and 2 only
    J. Experiments 2 and 3 only

GO ON TO THE NEXT PAGE.

11. Which of the following graphs most accurately represents the average growth of the coleoptile segments as a percent of original length for Test 1 in Experiment 1?

A.

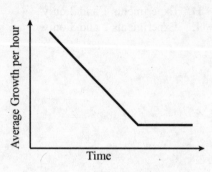

B.

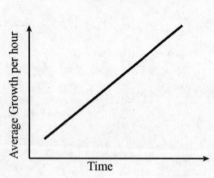

C.

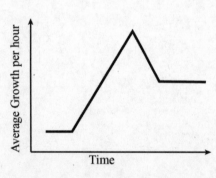

D.

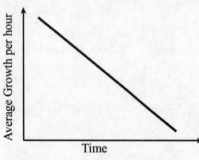

12. According to the data provided, the greatest growth of the coleoptile segments after 24 hours was for which concentration of growth substance in solution (in standard units per cubic centimeter)?

F. 0
G. 1
H. 10
J. 80

13. According to the data provided, the lowest concentration of growth substance in solution (in standard units per cubic centimeter) that resulted in shrinkage of coleoptile segments was:

A. 0
B. 1
C. 40
D. 80

14. The hypothesis that the action of the growth substance depends on metabolic processes is:

F. disproved by the data in Table 3.
G. weakened slightly by the data in Table 3.
H. weakly supported by the data in Table 3.
J. strongly supported by the data in Table 3.

GO ON TO THE NEXT PAGE.

Passage III

Osmosis is the spontaneous movement of solvent molecules through a semi-permeable membrane into a region of higher solute concentration. The molecules move in the direction that tends to equalize solute concentration on both sides of the membrane.

The following figure shows a semi-permeable membrane between two sugar solutions of different concentrations. Osmosis occurs as the water molecules pass through the membrane to the side with higher sugar concentration; the sugar molecules cannot pass through the membrane.

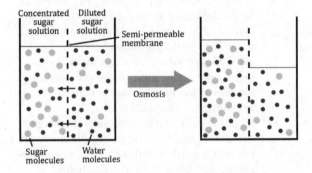

To observe the effect of osmosis, a group of students conducts experiments using plant tissues. In the experiments, the walls of the cells in the plant tissues function as the semi-permeable membrane separating regions of different solution concentrations.

Experiment 1

The students prepare shallow dishes with sugar solutions of varying concentrations. Using tweezers, the students gently pull off small strips of tissue, 3 to 10 millimeters in length and one cell layer thick, from the outer layer of an onion. Each strip is submerged in one of the prepared dishes.

After 45 minutes, the students mount the strips on slides and, using a microscope, examine the tissues for evidence of plasmolysis—the shrinkage of a cell's protoplasm and separation from the cell wall due to water loss from the cell. Forty to sixty-five cells from each onion strip are analyzed and scored as either plasmolyzed or not plasmolyzed. Any cells not clearly plasmolyzed are classified as not plasmolyzed. Table 1 summarizes the experimental results.

Table 1: Plasmolyzed Onion Cell Counts			
Sugar Solution Concentration (mol/kg)*	Number of Cells Analyzed	Number of Plasmolyzed Cells	Percentage of Plasmolyzed Cells
0.55	50	50	100
0.50	50	46	92.0
0.45	64	50	78.1
0.40	64	44	68.8
0.35	50	25	50.0
0.30	62	12	19.4
0.25	48	5	10.4
0.20	55	3	5.5
0.15	57	2	3.5
0.10	41	1	2.4
0.05	40	0	0.0
0.00	50	0	0.0

*moles of sugar per kilogram of water

Experiment 2

The students conduct a second experiment with beets. Beakers are prepared with sugar solutions of the same concentrations as in Experiment 1. Using an 8-millimeter diameter cork borer, cylinders of tissue are extracted from the beets. The tissue cylinders are sliced into disks approximately 3 millimeters thick. Each disk is weighed before being submerged in one of the prepared beakers.

After 75 minutes, the students extract, blot dry, and weigh each of the disks. The percentage of weight change in the disks are calculated. Table 2 summarizes the experimental results.

Table 2: Changes in Beet Tissue Weights			
Sugar Solution Concentration (mol/kg)	Original Weight (g)	Final Weight (g)	Percentage of Weight Change
0.55	2.865	2.460	−14.14
0.50	2.732	2.407	−11.90
0.45	2.807	2.666	−5.02
0.40	2.474	2.422	−2.10
0.35	3.101	3.152	+1.64
0.30	3.060	3.118	+1.90
0.25	2.549	2.642	+3.65
0.20	2.801	2.889	+3.50
0.15	2.357	2.428	+3.01
0.10	2.675	2.754	+2.95
0.05	2.413	2.528	+4.77
0.00	2.880	3.060	+6.25

GO ON TO THE NEXT PAGE.

15. In Experiment 1, osmosis proceeds due to the cell wall permitting:

    A. sugar molecules but not water molecules to pass.

    B. water molecules but not sugar molecules to pass.

    C. neither sugar nor water molecules to pass.

    D. certain water and certain sugar molecules to pass.

16. The purpose of Experiment 1 is to measure the:

    F. solute concentrations of the solutions in which the onion strips are submerged.

    G. quantity of water gained or lost by the onion cells due to osmosis.

    H. number of cells plasmolyzed due to the effect of osmosis.

    J. solute concentration threshold at which osmosis is triggered in onion cells submerged in a sugar solution.

17. Which of the following best explains why the students analyze 40 to 65 cells from each onion strip in Experiment 1?

    A. The number of plasmolyzed cells in an onion strip ranges from 40 to 65 cells.

    B. A sampling adequate to determine the effect of osmosis on onion cells requires 40 to 65 cells.

    C. The average number of cells in an onion strip is 40 to 65 cells.

    D. The unanalyzed cells of the onion strips do not show the effects of osmosis.

18. Which of the following best explains why no plasmolyzed cells are observed for the 0.05 mol/kg sugar solution?

    F. The concentration of sugar inside the cells is greater than 0.05 mol/kg.

    G. The concentration of sugar inside the cells is less than 0.05 mol/kg.

    H. The concentration of sugar inside the cells is greater than 0.55 mol/kg.

    J. The concentration of sugar inside the cells is less than 0.55 mol/kg.

19. The students identify the same number of plasmolyzed cells in both samples from the onion strips submerged in the 0.55 mol/kg and the 0.45 mol/kg sugar solutions yet calculate a value of "Percentage of Plasmolyzed Cells" of 100 percent for the 0.55 mol/kg solution but only 78.1 percent for the 0.45 mol/kg solution. This difference in percentage of plasmolyzed cells is due to the fact that:

    A. the cells plasmolyzed by the 0.45 mol/kg solution are less completely depleted than those plasmolyzed by the 0.55 mol/kg solution.

    B. the students analyze 50 cells from the onion strip submerged in the 0.55 mol/kg solution and 64 cells from the onion strip submerged in the 0.45 mol/kg solution.

    C. the 0.55 mol/kg solution acts more vigorously on the onion cells, accelerating the rate of plasmolysis on the cells submerged in that solution.

    D. all of the cells in the onion strip submerged in the 0.45 mol/kg solution are plasmolyzed but only a portion of those in the onion strip submerged in the 0.55 mol/kg are are plasmolyzed.

20. Which of the following best explains the change in weight of the beet disk before and after submersion in the beaker containing the 0.00 mol/kg sugar solution?

    F. The disk is dehydrated, causing it to absorb water while submerged in the solution.

    G. The disk has a sugar concentration greater than 0.00 mol/kg of water, causing it to absorb water while submerged in the solution due to osmosis.

    H. The disk has a sugar concentration less than 0.00 mol/kg of water and loses water while submerged in the solution due to osmosis.

    J. No sugar molecules are available in the 0.00 mol/kg solution to migrate across the semi-permeable membranes of the cells in the beet disk.

GO ON TO THE NEXT PAGE.

21. Which of the following graphs best represents the percentage of weight change for the beet disks in Experiment 2?

A.

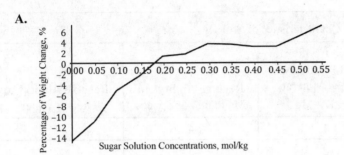

B.

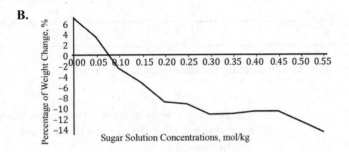

C.

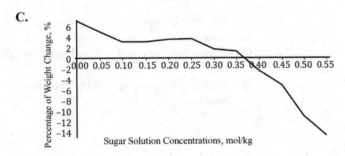

D.

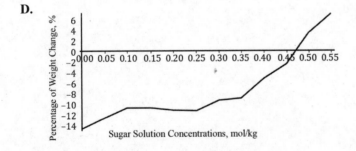

22. It can be inferred from the results of Experiment 2 that the average concentration of sugar per kilogram of water in the sampled beets is:

F. 0.45–0.50 moles.
G. 0.40–0.45 moles.
H. 0.35–0.40 moles.
J. 0.30–0.35 moles.

GO ON TO THE NEXT PAGE.

Passage IV

The chart below shows various physical characteristics of different types of soil.

		Physical Characteristics of Soil		
Types of Soil	Diameter of Particles, d (μm)	Relative Ability* to Hold Positively Charged Minerals (Ca^{+2}, K^+, Mg^{+2})	Relative Ability* to Maintain Air Spaces	Relative Ability* to Retain Water
Clay	$d < 2$	1	4	1
Silt	$2 \leq d < 20$	2	3	2
Sand	$20 \leq d < 200$	3	2	3
Coarse Sand	$200 \leq d \leq 2,000$	4	1	4

*Relative abilities are rated from 1, indicating the most able, to 4, indicating the least able.

23. The soil type that is LEAST able to hold substances such as magnesium (Mg^{+2}) is:

A. sand.
B. coarse sand.
C. silt.
D. clay.

24. Based on the information in the chart, which of the following statements best describes the relationship between a soil's particle size and its other physical characteristics?

F. As particle size increases, the ability to hold positively charged minerals increases.
G. As particle size decreases, the ability to retain water decreases.
H. As particle size decreases, the ability to maintain air spaces increases.
J. As particle size increases, the ability to retain water decreases.

25. The size of particles in the soil type that is neither most able nor least able for any of the listed abilities must be:

A. less than 20 μm.
B. greater than or equal to 20 μm.
C. greater than or equal to 2 and less than 200 μm.
D. greater than or equal to 2 and less than or equal to 2,000 μm.

GO ON TO THE NEXT PAGE.

26. Loam is a type of soil that is mostly clay, but it also contains some sand and silt particles. Which prediction is most likely to be accurate about the ability of loam to support plant growth?

   F. Plants will grow well because loam primarily has small particles that can hold minerals and retain water, yet it also has enough large particles to provide air spaces containing oxygen.
   G. Plants will grow well because loam primarily has large particles that can provide air spaces containing oxygen, yet it also has enough small particles that can hold minerals and retain water.
   H. Plants will not grow well because although loam is excellent at maintaining air spaces for oxygen, it will not hold enough minerals or water.
   J. Plants will not grow well because although loam has enough minerals and air spaces for oxygen, it cannot retain enough water.

27. Based on the information provided in the chart, which of the following conclusions about soil types is NOT correct?

   A. Soils most able to retain water are also most able to hold positively charged minerals.
   B. No two soil types have the exact same combination of relative abilities.
   C. Clay and coarse sand are the soil types that are most different in every physical characteristic.
   D. No soil type is best for more than one category of relative ability.

GO ON TO THE NEXT PAGE.

Passage V

Theory 1

The rate of a chemical reaction is defined as the number of moles of a specified product formed per unit of time. Reactants must collide in order for a reaction to occur, so it might seem that rates would depend upon the concentration of reactants—the more reactants that are present, the greater the likelihood of a collision. In fact, this is the case; a concrete example makes this clear. For the reaction:
$Mg + 2HCl \Rightarrow MgCl_2 + H_2$, the rate is proportional to the amount of Mg and HCl present. This fact is expressed in the following "rate law":

rate $= k[Mg]^1 [HCl]^2$, where k is the rate constant, and the exponents reflect the coefficients in front of the reactants in the reaction. The relationship between numbers of reactant molecules and exponents in the rate law is a general one.

Theory 2

Theory 1 is very often true, for it expresses the reasonable insight that the greater the concentration of reactants, the greater the likelihood of a reaction. It has a great shortcoming, however, in its assumption that all reactions proceed in one fell swoop rather than in several skirmishes.

For example, let letters A, B, and C stand for molecules. In the reaction $A + 2B \Rightarrow C$, Theory 1 predicts a rate law as follows: rate $= k[A][B]^2$. However, if the reaction actually proceeds in two stages, the first one would be $A + B \Rightarrow AB$ and the second one would be $AB + B \Rightarrow C$.

Thus, Theory 2 implies that one must understand the details of the reaction, including the relative speeds of the sub-reactions, in order to predict a rate law. For example, if in a three-stage reaction stage 1 and stage 2 are completed in seconds and stage 3 requires several hours to complete, then the reaction rate is primarily determined by the reaction rate of stage 3. Theory 1 is not completely wrong, just incomplete.

28. Theory 1 relates:

    F. reaction rate to the concentration of products.
    G. reaction rate to the concentration of reactants.
    H. the relative amounts of products to one other.
    J. reaction rate to the individual rates of various stages of the reaction.

29. According to a proponent of Theory 2, Theory 1:

    A. can never give a correct prediction for a rate law.
    B. will give a correct result if the reactant coefficients are all equal to 1.
    C. will give a correct result for a single-stage reaction.
    D. is in error because it claims that collisions are required for reactions to occur.

30. According to Theory 1, the rate of the reaction $3M + 2N \Rightarrow 4P$ will be given by:

    F. $k[M][N]$.
    G. $k[M]^3[N]^2$.
    H. $k[M]^3[N]^2[P]^4$.
    J. $k([M]^3 + [N]^2)$.

31. A chemist studies the rate of the reaction $2NO_2 + F_2 \Rightarrow 2NO_2F$. According to Theory 1, the rate of the reaction is proportional to:

    A. the first power of $[NO_2]$ and the first power of F_2.
    B. the second power of $[NO_2]$ and the second power of $[NO_2F]$.
    C. the second power of $[NO_2]$ and the second power of $[F_2]$.
    D. the second power of $[NO_2]$ and the first power of $[F_2]$.

GO ON TO THE NEXT PAGE.

32. Supporters of Theory 2 would best be able to defend their positions if:

   F. they could show that a chemical reaction occurs in more than one stage.
   G. they could show that the rate of reaction speeds up with increasing concentration of products.
   H. they sped the reaction up with additional heat.
   J. they eliminated all collisions.

33. According to Theory 2, if in a two-stage reaction Stage 1 is much slower than Stage 2, then the overall reaction rate will be:

   A. primarily determined by the rate of Stage 1.
   B. primarily determined by the rate of Stage 2.
   C. undeterminable unless all collisions are counted.
   D. undeterminable unless the rate law is measured experimentally.

34. When discussing the rates of reactions that have more than one stage, Theory 2 would not be necessary if:

   F. all stages went quickly.
   G. all stages had different rates.
   H. the sum of the rates of each stage always equaled the rate of the reaction as a whole.
   J. the sum of the rates of each stage was never equal to the rate of the reaction as a whole.

GO ON TO THE NEXT PAGE.

Passage VI

Closely related species of butterflies are often found living in very different environments. A pair of experiments was performed in which butterfly species previously captured in either desert areas or mountain areas were tested in laboratory incubators to determine the conditions at which they could carry out important life functions such as mating, oviposition (egg-laying), and pupation (the stage in which the stationary cocoon undergoes its final development into an adult).

Experiment 1

Under conditions of 100% relative humidity (maximum moisture content of the air), 100 desert butterflies (Species D) and 100 mountain butterflies (Species M) were tested at temperature intervals of 2°C (from 0°C to 40°C) to determine if they could mate, oviposit, and pupate. Each species achieved at least 90% success at the following ranges of temperatures:

Table 1			
	Temperature Ranges (°C)		
	Mating	Oviposition	Pupation
Species D	26–36	28–36	4–38
Species M	24–34	29–33	4–34

Experiment 2

The experiment was repeated at 50% relative humidity. Each species achieved at least 90% success at the following ranges of temperatures:

Table 2			
	Temperature Ranges (°C)		
	Mating	Oviposition	Pupation
Species D	26–36	28–36	4–38
Species M	24–32	29–32	4–28

35. Results of Experiments 1 and 2 indicate that the life function with the narrowest range of temperature at which both species achieve 90% success is:

   A. mating.
   B. oviposition.
   C. pupation.
   D. different in Experiment 1 than it is in Experiment 2.

36. Which condition hadecreases the success of Species M in mating, oviposition, and pupation?

   F. 100% relative humidity at low temperatures
   G. 100% relative humidity at high temperatures
   H. 50% relative humidity at low temperatures
   J. 50% relative humidity at high temperatures

37. A third experiment was conducted at 100% relative humidity in which the temperature range for caterpillar survival (another life function) was tested in Species D and Species M. Species D achieved 90% success at 12–36 (°C), while Species M achieved 90% success at 8–30 (°C). Which temperature range is a good prediction of survival in Species D at 50% relative humidity?

   A. 8°C–30°C
   B. 8°C–24°C
   C. 12°C–36°C
   D. 12°C–30°C

38. If an investigator wanted to set up an experiment to determine the effects of light and dark on mating ability in Species D and Species M at 100% relative humidity, which set of conditions would provide the most complete results?

   F. Test both species at 20°C in the light and 20°C in the dark.
   G. Test both species at 30°C in the light and 30°C in the dark.
   H. Test both species at 34°C in the light and 34°C in the dark.
   J. Test both species at 34°C in the light and 30°C in the dark.

GO ON TO THE NEXT PAGE.

39. Which hypothesis is NOT supported by the results of Experiment 1 and Experiment 2?

   A. For all tested life functions, 50% relative humidity only affects Species M at the high end of its temperature ranges.
   B. For all tested life functions, 50% relative humidity has no effect on the temperature ranges of the desert species.
   C. Species D does better than Species M at high temperatures in all tested life functions.
   D. Species M does better than Species D at low temperatures for pupation.

40. Which of the following statements best explains the broad range of temperatures for pupation observed in both butterfly species?

   F. Since the cocoon is stationary, it must be able to survive changing temperature conditions until the adult butterfly emerges.
   G. Deserts can get very hot and mountains can get very cold.
   H. Mountain butterflies would not survive long in the desert, and desert butterflies would not survive long in the mountains.
   J. The stationary cocoon must be able to survive under light and dark conditions until the adult butterfly emerges.

END OF TEST 4
STOP! DO NOT TURN THE PAGE UNTIL TOLD TO DO SO.
DO NOT RETURN TO THE PREVIOUS TEST.

PRACTICE TEST I

5 5 5 5 5 5 5 5 5 5 5 5

SECTION 5: WRITING TEST (OPTIONAL)
40 Minutes—1 Essay Prompt

DIRECTIONS: You have 40 minutes to plan and write an essay. Read the prompt carefully and make sure you understand the instructions. A successful essay will have the following features: it will take a position on the issue presented in the writing prompt; it will maintain a consistent focus on the topic; it will use logical reasoning and provide supporting ideas; it will present ideas in an organized manner; and, finally, it will include clear and effective language in accordance with the conventions of standard written English. Sample essay responses begin on page 699.

Plastic Bag Use

Some countries and states have banned free plastic bags at grocery stores because of the environmental problems they cause. Plastic bags worsen communities' litter problems and can suffocate animals that come into contact with them. Some bags are also non-biodegradable and accumulate in landfills. Because of these environmental risks, some governments have required stores to sell paper or reusable bags to customers, instead of providing plastic bags for free. However, some argue that banning bags is impractical and would inconvenience customers. As more cities and states debate whether to ban free plastic bags, this issue will potentially affect millions of shoppers.

Perspective 1

It is impractical to ban free plastic bags in stores, and it will inconvenience shoppers who forget to bring reusable bags with them. Plastic bags can also be reused as trash bags at home.

Perspective 2

Free plastic bags should be banned, but stores should have more paper or more durable plastic bags available for sale. Having to pay for bags will encourage shoppers to reuse them, either at home or on their next shopping trip.

Perspective 3

Plastic bags should be banned at all stores, and shoppers should either buy recyclable paper bags or bring their own reusable bags. Although this may initially annoy consumers, the environmental risks outweigh the convenience of free plastic bags.

Essay Task

Write a unified, coherent essay in which you evaluate multiple perspectives on the issue of plastic bag use in grocery stores. In your essay be sure to:

- Analyze and evaluate perspectives given
- State and develop your own perspective
- Explain the relationship between your perspective and those given

Your perspective may be in full agreement with any of the others, in partial agreement, or wholly different. Whatever the case, support your ideas with logical reasoning and detailed, persuasive examples.

END OF TEST 5
STOP! DO NOT RETURN TO ANY OTHER TEST.

Practice Test II

Outline

I.   **Section 1:** English (pp. 528–540)

II. **Section 2:** Mathematics (pp. 542–559)

III. **Section 3:** Reading (pp. 560–567)

IV. **Section 4:** Science (pp. 568–580)

V.   **Section 5:** Writing (Optional) (p. 582)

DIRECTIONS

Practice Test II includes five subject tests: English, Mathematics, Reading, Science, and Writing. Calculator use is permitted on the Mathematics Test only.

Cambridge offers several services for schools utilizing our practice tests. Ask your teacher whether your school has decided to send your answers to Cambridge for scoring or to score your answers at your school. If Cambridge is scoring your test, you will use a Scantron™ form provided by your teacher, or you will enter your answers online. If your school is scoring your test, you may use a Scantron™ form provided by your teacher, or you may write your answers on paper.

If you are entering your test answers on a Scantron™ form, please be sure to include the following information on the Scantron™:

Book and edition	*Victory for the ACT Test, 13th Edition*
Practice Test Number	**Practice Test II**

If you are only completing a single section of this practice test, make sure to also include the following information:

Subject	**English**, **Mathematics**, **Reading** or **Science**
Section Number	**Section 1**, **2**, **3** or **4**

The items in each multiple-choice test are numbered and the answer choices are lettered. The Scantron™ form has numbered rows that correspond to the items on the test. Each row contains lettered ovals to match the answer choices for each item on the test. Each numbered row has a corresponding item on the test.

For each item, first decide on the best answer choice. Then, locate the row number that corresponds to the item. Next, find the oval in that row that matches the letter of the chosen answer. Then, use a soft lead pencil to fill in the oval. DO NOT use a ballpoint pen.

Mark only one answer for each item. If you change your mind about an answer choice, thoroughly erase your first mark before marking your new answer.

Note that only responses marked on your Scantron™ form or written on your paper will be scored. Your score on each test will be based only on the number of items that are correctly answered during the time allowed for that test. You will not be penalized for guessing. Therefore, it is to your best advantage to answer every item on the test, even if you must guess.

On the Writing Test, write your response to the prompt using the essay response sheets or loose-leaf paper provided by your teacher. Your teacher might also direct you to enter your essay response online. (Note that the Writing Test is optional.)

You may work on each test only during the time allowed for that test. If you finish a test before time is called, use the time to review your answer choices or work on items about which you are uncertain. You may not return to a test on which time has already been called, and you may not preview another test. You must lay down your pencil immediately when time is called at the end of each test. You may not for any reason fill in or alter ovals for a test after time has expired for that test. Violation of these rules will result in immediate disqualification from the exam.

GO ON TO THE NEXT PAGE.

PRACTICE TEST **II**   1 1 1 1 1 1 1 1 1 1 1 1 1

SECTION 1: ENGLISH TEST
45 Minutes—75 Items

DIRECTIONS: In the passages below, certain parts of the sentences have been underlined and numbered. In the right-hand column, you will find different ways of writing each underlined part; the original version is indicated by the "NO CHANGE" option. For each item, select the choice that best expresses the intended idea, is most acceptable in standard written English, or is most consistent with the overall tone and style of the passage.

There are also items that ask about a section of the passage or the passage as a whole. These items do not refer to an underlined portion of the passage; these items are preceded by statements that are enclosed in boxes.

Read the passage through once before you begin to answer the accompanying items. Finding the answers to certain items may depend on looking at material that appears several sentences beyond the item. So, be sure that you have read far enough ahead before you select your answer choice. Answers are on page 705.

PASSAGE I

The Philosophy of Botany

[1]

Botany is surely <u>the more gentler of</u> sciences.
¹

The careful observation of a flower is a calm,

1. **A.** NO CHANGE
   B. the most gentle of
   C. the gentler of
   D. the gentlest in the

<u>ostentatious</u> action—the peaceful contemplation of a
²

2. **F.** NO CHANGE
   G. unobtrusive
   H. violent
   J. chaotic

beautiful object. Reduced to its <u>essentials, it</u> requires
³

3. **A.** NO CHANGE
   B. essentials; it
   C. essentials, botany
   D. essentials; botany

no laboratory <u>and the natural world is needed</u>, a few
⁴

tools and the naked eye. Botany in its most scientific or

4. **F.** NO CHANGE
   G. but you do need the natural world
   H. but the natural world
   J. but the natural world is necessary

GO ON TO THE NEXT PAGE.

purest form <u>consists about</u> seeking to know more about
                         5
the plant simply for the sake of that knowledge. Plants

have not always been regarded as worthy <u>of knowing</u>
                                                  6
or studying in and of themselves, not on their merits

as sources of food or drugs but as life-forms. In fact,

the history of botany can be viewed in terms of

repeated rediscoveries of this one theme—that plants

are worthy of study <u>in and of themselves</u>, quite apart
                             7
from any use they might have for mankind.

[2]

8 The practical motives behind plant study should

not be <u>disparaging—the</u> bulk of our medical history,
               9
for instance, is made up of accounts of herbal remedies.

<u>Nonetheless,</u> the study of the medicinal properties of
        10
plants contained a self-limiting mechanism: if a plant

seemed to have no utilitarian value, it was disregarded,

and no further study of it <u>is made</u>. The Renaissance
                                   11
attitude towards nature changed this overly practical

bent and initiated the scientific study of plants.

5. A. NO CHANGE
    B. consists of
    C. consists in
    D. consist of

6. F. NO CHANGE
    G. for knowledge
    H. of knowledge
    J. to know

7. A. NO CHANGE
    B. by themselves
    C. themselves
    D. by and for themselves

8. Beginning Paragraph 2 with which of the follow-
    ing might make the transition from Paragraph 1
    to Paragraph 2 clearer?

    F. Since
    G. Heretofore
    H. However,
    J. Hence

9. A. NO CHANGE
    B. disparaged—the bulk
    C. disparaged; the bulk
    D. disparaging, the bulk

10. F. NO CHANGE
    G. Consequently
    H. Thus
    J. Moreover

11. A. NO CHANGE
    B. had been made
    C. was made
    D. were made

GO ON TO THE NEXT PAGE.

[3]

Botany, as a pure science, has certain characteristics and makes certain assumptions that prove thought provoking and interesting. One of its unspoken or basic assumptions is an implicit respect
12
and regard for all living things. The botanist who

studies a plant's structure or tries to have understood
13
their functions confronts nature on its own terms.
13
Investigations of how a plant thrives or reproduces, or studies of the purposefulness of a flower's coloration and structure, are almost implicitly egalitarian and tautological. The botanist studies the flower because they exist, but because it exists, it is worthy of study.
14

12. **F.** NO CHANGE
    G. because
    H. and thus
    J. yet

13. **A.** NO CHANGE
    B. to understand its
    C. understanding their
    D. having understood its

14. **F.** NO CHANGE
    G. it exists, but
    H. it exists and
    J. it exists, and

Item #15 asks about the preceding passage as a whole.

---

15. The last sentence of the essay is actually a restatement of which of the following ideas?

    A. The study of the medicinal properties of plants has a self-limiting mechanism.
    B. The botanist who tries to understand a plant's function confronts nature on its own terms.
    C. The study of plants and flowers is tautological.
    D. Botany is a gentle science.

GO ON TO THE NEXT PAGE.

PASSAGE II

Poverty in America

The main characteristic of poverty is, <u>of course,</u>
₁₆
lack of money. A family is defined as poor when its

16. The use of the phrase "of course" is:

    F. appropriate because it is not obvious that someone who is poor lacks money.

    G. appropriate because it disrupts the flow of the sentence.

    H. appropriate because someone who is poor obviously lacks money.

    J. questionable since someone might be poor in spirit.

annual income <u>falls below a certain dollar amount,</u>
₁₇
calculated by the US Federal Government to be the

17. A. NO CHANGE

    B. falls and is under a certain dollar amount,

    C. is under a certain specified dollar amount,

    D. OMIT the underlined portion.

minimum a family of <u>their</u> size would need to
₁₈
maintain a minimally decent standard of living. In

18. F. NO CHANGE

    G. there

    H. its

    J. it's

certain areas of rural America, <u>consequently,</u> poverty
₁₉
is the rule rather than the exception. As many as 50

19. A. NO CHANGE

    B. and therefore, as a result of this,

    C. moreover, due to this fact,

    D. OMIT the underlined portion.

percent of the families may earn <u>less than</u> the poverty
₂₀
level, and some may manage to subsist somehow on

amounts even less than half the official poverty level

income. $\boxed{21}$

20. F. NO CHANGE

    G. lower than

    H. less as

    J. lower as

21. The first paragraph provides which of the following?

    A. An argument

    B. A comparison

    C. A definition

    D. A narrative

GO ON TO THE NEXT PAGE.

Although lack of money is the defining
22

characteristic of poverty, poverty is more than simply

lack of money. Poverty is an entire complex of

symptoms. Low levels of formal schooling among

adults parallel low-income levels. Additionally, in
23

families below the poverty level, the number of

children and elderly who depend on those who work is,

in general, higher than the national average for all

families. As a consequence, fewer workers support a
24

greater number of non-workers than in other, more

prosperous families.

Often, the schooling provided in low-income

areas are as inadequate like incomes. In particular,
25

rural children get poorer schooling than city children,

and many rural poor are severely handicapped by it.
26

The general rural average is only 8.8 years of school

completed. Moreover, low educational levels seem to

just keep repeating and repeating themselves. If the
27

head of a rural poor family have little schooling, the
28

children are often handicapped in their efforts to get an

education. It is especially difficult for people who are

handicapped educationally to acquire new skills, get

new jobs, or otherwise adjust to an increasingly

22. **F.** NO CHANGE
    G. (Do NOT begin a new paragraph) Although
    H. Since
    J. (Do NOT begin a new paragraph) Since

23. **A.** NO CHANGE
    B. go along with
    C. are a lot like
    D. very often go together with

24. **F.** NO CHANGE
    G. However,
    H. Surprisingly,
    J. Fortunately,

25. **A.** NO CHANGE
    B. is—like family income, inadequate
    C. is so inadequate as family income
    D. is, like family income, inadequate

26. **F.** NO CHANGE
    G. education
    H. their education
    J. their lack of education

27. **A.** NO CHANGE
    B. be self-perpetuating of themselves
    C. be self-perpetuating
    D. cause the same thing to happen all over
    again

28. **F.** NO CHANGE
    G. have had
    H. has had
    J. was to have

GO ON TO THE NEXT PAGE.

urbanized society. This is as true on the farm <u>rather</u>
₂₉

<u>than</u> in urban industry, since modern farming <u>of the</u>
₂₉   ₃₀

<u>present day</u> requires skills that <u>poor educated</u> people
₃₀   ₃₁

lack. Lacking in education, the rural poor either take

low-paying jobs on the farm or elsewhere in rural areas

or swell the ranks of the unemployed or under-

employed.

29. **A.** NO CHANGE
    B. rather as
    C. as they are
    D. as it is

30. **F.** NO CHANGE
    G. of the present
    H. presently
    J. OMIT the underlined portion.

31. **A.** NO CHANGE
    B. poorly educated
    C. educated poor
    D. poor education

Item #32 asks about the preceding passage as a whole.

32. The author does NOT use which of the following in the development of the essay?

    F. Definitions
    G. Personal experience
    H. Statistics
    J. Explanation

PASSAGE III

School Dropouts

One out of every four children who entered the

fifth grade in the fall of 1966 <u>fail to graduate</u> with his
₃₃

or her class. The total number <u>that should of</u> graduated
₃₄

was 4.1 million, but approximately 900,000 fell by

the wayside.

33. **A.** NO CHANGE
    B. failed to graduate
    C. failed graduation
    D. fails to graduate

34. **F.** NO CHANGE
    G. that should of been
    H. who should of
    J. who should have

GO ON TO THE NEXT PAGE.

Those who do not make it are called school dropouts. (Official statistics define a dropout as a person who has not yet attained the age of 16 and leaves school before graduation for any reason except transfer.) School officials who work with dropouts who leave school say a student will usually starting thinking about dropping out about two years before
₃₅ ₃₆
₃₆

35. A.	NO CHANGE
B.	who have left school
C.	who are leaving school
D.	OMIT the underlined portion.

36. F.	NO CHANGE
G.	usually will be starting thinking
H.	starts usually thinking
J.	usually starts to think

he or she ceases to attend school: roughly at age 14.
₃₇
Absenteeism, class cutting, lack of motivation, and

37. A.	NO CHANGE
B.	school but roughly
C.	school and roughly
D.	school, roughly

lack of interest in school is often early signs of the
₃₈

38. F.	NO CHANGE
G.	is oftentimes
H.	are often
J.	were often

potential dropout. Also, many students drop out
₃₉
mentally very early in their school career, despite their physical presence until graduation.

39. A.	NO CHANGE
B.	dropout also
C.	dropout many
D.	dropout but also

The dropout is most often a boy who mostly,
₄₀
frequently leaves school at the age of 16 while in the
₄₀

40. F.	NO CHANGE
G.	frequently and often
H.	frequently
J.	sometimes often

tenth grade. He is most likely than those who stay in
₄₁
school to score low on an intelligence test and is likely

41. A.	NO CHANGE
B.	more likely than those
C.	most likely as one
D.	more likely than one

GO ON TO THE NEXT PAGE.

to be failing in school at the time <u>of him dropping out</u>.
₄₂

Yet most dropouts <u>are really not less bright than</u>
₄₃

<u>students who remain</u> in school until graduation. The
₄₃

dropout typically comes from the lower-income class

and most often leaves school for financial reasons. His

absences from school <u>increasing noticeably</u> during the
₄₄

eighth grade and he participates little <u>or none</u> in extra-
₄₅

curricular activities. The reasons a student drops out of

school <u>goes deeper as</u> a mere desire to be rid of school.
₄₆

Dropping out is a symptom; the roots of the problem

are usually below the surface. ☐47

42. **F.** NO CHANGE
    G. he drops out
    H. of his having dropped out
    J. he dropped out

43. **A.** NO CHANGE
    B. really they are no less bright than are the students who remain
    C. are, than the students who remain, really no less bright
    D. than the students who remain are really no less bright

44. **F.** NO CHANGE
    G. increase so that
    H. increase noticeably
    J. increased to the point where it was noticed

45. **A.** NO CHANGE
    B. and not at all
    C. or not much
    D. or not at all

46. **F.** NO CHANGE
    G. go more deeply than
    H. go deeper as
    J. go deeper than

47. A logical continuation of the essay would be a discussion of:

    A. the financial reasons a student might leave school.
    B. a student's lack of motivation.
    C. possible extracurricular activities.
    D. why students might drop out of school.

GO ON TO THE NEXT PAGE.

536 • CAMBRIDGE PRACTICE TEST REINFORCEMENT

Item #48 asks about the preceding passage as a whole.

48. Is the use of the official definition of dropout in the second paragraph appropriate?

   F. Yes, because without a definition, the article would not be understandable.
   G. Yes, because the nature of a "dropout" is one of the central themes of the passage.
   H. No, because the definition has nothing to do with what the author is discussing in the second paragraph.
   J. No, because the author then redefines the word.

PASSAGE IV

Wind Machines

The idea of generating electricity with wind power is not new. But the kind of attention that idea is getting today, in terms of research and development, are both new and encouraging to planners looking for

renewable energy sources satisfying growing national demands. An effort is being made in the United States to use one of humankind's oldest energy sources to

49. A. NO CHANGE
   B. development, is
   C. developing, is
   D. development are

50. F. NO CHANGE
   G. that would have satisfied
   H. to satisfy
   J. with the satisfaction of

GO ON TO THE NEXT PAGE.

solve one of <u>its</u> most modern <u>problems, to find</u> reliable
₅₁ ₅₂

and cost-effective ways to harness the wind to produce

electricity.

Wind machines are not the simple devices <u>that</u>
₅₃

<u>they may be appearing to be</u>, and the lessons they
₅₃

teach seldom come easy. <u>On the other hand,</u> the
₅₄

potential reward to a nation that needs more energy

from a renewable source is beyond calculation.

Rewards for using wind power <u>have been gathered</u> by
₅₅

civilizations and cultures since early in recorded

history.

No record survives of the earliest wind machine.

It <u>may have been built</u> in China more than three
₅₆

thousand years ago. It may have been built on the

windy plains of Afghanistan. History hints at some

sort of wind power used in the Pharaoh's Egypt <u>for the</u>
₅₇

<u>drawing of water</u> for agriculture, long before the birth
₅₇

of Christ. Hammurabi may have taken time out from

developing a legal code about 2,000 BCE to sponsor

development of some sort of wind machine. The

earliest confirmed wind machines are in that same

51. A. NO CHANGE
    B. their
    C. it's
    D. your

52. F. NO CHANGE
    G. problems: to find
    H. problems, finding
    J. problems. To find

53. A. NO CHANGE
    B. they may be
    C. it may seem to be
    D. they may appear to be

54. F. NO CHANGE
    G. Therefore,
    H. As a consequence
    J. This means that

55. A. NO CHANGE
    B. has been gathering
    C. is gathering
    D. will have been gathered

56. F. NO CHANGE
    G. may have been
    H. was being built
    J. has been building

57. A. NO CHANGE
    B. to draw water
    C. in order that water be drawn
    D. in order to draw water

GO ON TO THE NEXT PAGE.

region. Persian writers described gardens irrigated
₅₈

through the means of wind-driven water lifts several
₅₈   ₅₉

centuries BCE. Ultimately, we can only guess at the
₆₀

origin of the windmill.
₆₀

      Persian machines were horizontal devices,
₆₁

carousel-like contraptions that revolved around a center

pole and caught the wind with bundles of reeds. The

carousel is perhaps the more simple design for
₆₂

capturing the wind; it cares nothing for the direction of
₆₂

the breeze, but revolves no matter where on the

compass the wind may originate. From the Middle

East, wind-machine technology may have been carried

to Europe by returning Crusaders. Accurate records do

not exist, but soon after the Crusades, windmills

appeared in northern Europe and soon were found on

the British Isles.

58. **F.** NO CHANGE
   G. irrigated by means of
   H. which were then irrigated by means of
   J. irrigated by

59. **A.** NO CHANGE
   B. lifts several,
   C. lifts but several
   D. lifts and several

60. **F.** NO CHANGE
   G. the origin of the windmill can only be guessed at
   H. the origin of the windmill can only be guessed at by us
   J. the origin of the windmill could only be guessed at

61. **A.** NO CHANGE
   B. (Do NOT begin a new paragraph) Persian machines were horizontal devices,
   C. Since Persian machines were
   D. It was discovered that Persian machines were horizontal devices,

62. **F.** NO CHANGE
   G. most simplest design for capturing
   H. simpler design to capture
   J. simplest design for capturing

GO ON TO THE NEXT PAGE.

For a while, windmills flourished in Europe, but

with the advent of steam power, they <u>come close to</u>
₆₃

63. **A.** NO CHANGE
    B. came close to
    C. are coming closer to
    D. come close upon

extinction, for the wind is <u>real iffy</u>. It can fail to blow
₆₄

64. **F.** NO CHANGE
    G. likely to blow sometimes and not to others
    H. here today and gone tomorrow
    J. capricious

just when it is needed the most, or it can <u>rage into a</u>
₆₅

<u>gale</u> when it is not needed at all.
₆₅

65. The author's use of the phrase "rage into a gale" is:

    A. inappropriate because images are out of place in scientific writing.
    B. inappropriate because wind is sometimes calm.
    C. appropriate because it creates a vivid image.
    D. appropriate because it minimizes the importance of weather.

PASSAGE V

The Development of Television Programming

Television and its programs do not just happen.

<u>It is</u> planned products of a huge, wealthy, and highly
₆₆

competitive commercial enterprise. The television

industry, which includes stations, networks, production

companies, actors, and <u>writers, are</u> responsible for
₆₇

selecting, creating, and distributing programs. The

66. **F.** NO CHANGE
    G. They are
    H. They would be
    J. It was

67. **A.** NO CHANGE
    B. writers, is
    C. writers are
    D. writers—is

three most popular programs are the <u>episodic series, the</u>
₆₈

made-for-television movie, and the mini-series.

68. **F.** NO CHANGE
    G. episodic series the
    H. episodic, series the
    J. episodic series the,

GO ON TO THE NEXT PAGE.

In the 1970s, the episodic series, both dramatic

and comic, <u>was the most</u> popular of these. <u>With the</u>
       69   70

<u>advent</u> of cable and pay television and of video disks
 70

and tapes, the television movie <u>is rapidly gaining in</u>
                                      71

popularity. The past ten years <u>have seen</u> several
                                 72

changes in television drama. The action-adventure

police drama has lost and the situation comedy <u>has</u>
                                           73

<u>grew</u> in popularity. Topics previously considered
 73

taboo <u>emerged. Unmarried</u> couples living together,
                74

divorce, and single parents. Even topics that are

<u>politically controversy</u> can now be the focus of
          75

programs.

69. **A.** NO CHANGE
    B. was the more
    C. were the most
    D. were the more

70. **F.** NO CHANGE
    G. Including the advent
    H. Notwithstanding the advent
    J. With the beginning of the advent

71. **A.** NO CHANGE
    B. has rapidly gained in
    C. is rapidly gaining
    D. will rapidly gain in

72. **F.** NO CHANGE
    G. see
    H. will see
    J. would be seeing

73. **A.** NO CHANGE
    B. has grown
    C. grew
    D. grow

74. **F.** NO CHANGE
    G. emerged, unmarried
    H. emerged unmarried
    J. emerged: unmarried

75. **A.** NO CHANGE
    B. politically controversial
    C. politics controversy
    D. political controversy

END OF TEST 1
STOP! DO NOT TURN THE PAGE UNTIL TOLD TO DO SO.

NO TEST MATERIAL ON THIS PAGE

SECTION 2: MATHEMATICS TEST
60 Minutes—60 Items

DIRECTIONS: Solve each item and choose the correct answer choice. Then, fill in the corresponding oval on the bubble sheet.

Allocate time wisely. Try to solve as many items as possible, returning to skipped items if time permits.

Calculator use is permitted on this test; however, some items are best solved without the use of a calculator.

Note: All of the following should be assumed, unless otherwise stated.

1. Illustrative figures are NOT necessarily drawn to scale.
2. The word *average* indicates arithmetic mean.
3. The word *line* indicates a straight line.
4. Geometric figures lie in a plane.

Answers are on page 712.

DO YOUR FIGURING HERE.

1. $121,212 + \left(2 \times 10^4\right) = ?$

    A. 121,232
    B. 121,412
    C. 123,212
    D. 141,212
    E. 312,212

2. If $6x + 3 = 21$, then $2x + 1 = ?$

    F. 1
    G. 2
    H. 3
    J. 6
    K. 7

3. At a recreation center, it costs $3 per hour to rent a ping pong table and $12 per hour to rent a bowling lane. At the same cost as renting a bowling lane for 2 hours, for how many hours is possible to rent a ping pong table?

    A. 4
    B. 6
    C. 8
    D. 18
    E. 36

GO ON TO THE NEXT PAGE.

4. If q, r, s, and t are natural numbers and $q < r < s < t$, which of the following could be true?

    F. $r = r + s$
    G. $q = s + t$
    H. $q + r = s + t$
    J. $q + r + t = s$
    K. $q + t = r + s$

5. Which of the following is greater than $\dfrac{1}{2}$?

    A. $\dfrac{6}{11}$
    B. $\dfrac{9}{19}$
    C. $\dfrac{7}{15}$
    D. $\dfrac{4}{9}$
    E. $\dfrac{3}{7}$

6. Out of a group of 360 students, exactly 18 are on the track team. What percent of the students are on the track team?

    F. 5%
    G. 10%
    H. 12%
    J. 20%
    K. 25%

DO YOUR FIGURING HERE.

GO ON TO THE NEXT PAGE.

7. In the figure below, 3 lines intersect as shown. Which of the following *must* be true?

DO YOUR FIGURING HERE.

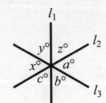

  I. $a = x$
  II. $y + z = b + c$
  III. $x + a = y + b$

A. I only
B. II only
C. I and II only
D. I and III only
E. I, II, and III

8. In the figure below, $x = ?$

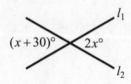

F. 15
G. 30
H. 45
J. 60
K. 90

9. Which of the following is the prime factorization of 60?

A. (2)(3)(10)
B. (3)(4)(5)
C. (2)(2)(3)(5)
D. (2)(2)(3)(6)
E. (3)(3)(3)(5)

GO ON TO THE NEXT PAGE.

10. The average height of 4 buildings is 20 meters. If 3 of the buildings are each 16 meters tall, what is the height, in meters, of the fourth building?

   F. 32
   G. 28
   H. 24
   J. 22
   K. 18

DO YOUR FIGURING HERE.

11. In the figure below, what is the value of x?

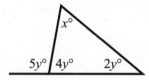

   A. 15
   B. 20
   C. 30
   D. 45
   E. 60

12. In the figure below, what is the length of $\overline{PQ}$?

   F. 0.09
   G. 0.11
   H. 0.12
   J. 0.13
   K. 0.16

13. What is the perimeter of the rectangle below?

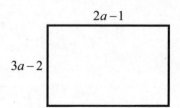

   A. $10a - 6$
   B. $10a - 3$
   C. $6a - 3$
   D. $5a - 6$
   E. $5a - 3$

GO ON TO THE NEXT PAGE.

14. If the average of x, x, x, 56, and 58 is 51, then
$x = ?$

    F. 43
    G. 47
    H. 49
    J. 51
    K. 53

15. How many integers can x be if $-2 \le 2x \le 2$?

    A. 1
    B. 2
    C. 3
    D. 4
    E. 5

16. For all real numbers x, 8^x equals which of the
following?

    F. $8x$
    G. x^8
    H. 2^{2x}
    J. $x^{\frac{2}{3}}$
    K. 2^{3x}

17. What is the sum of the areas of 2 squares with
sides of 2 and 3 unit lengths, respectively?

    A. 1
    B. 5
    C. 13
    D. 25
    E. 36

DO YOUR FIGURING HERE.

GO ON TO THE NEXT PAGE.

18. If the rectangular solid shown below has a volume of 54 cubic inches, what is the value of x, in inches?

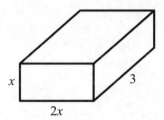

F. 2
G. 3
H. 6
J. 9
K. 12

19. If x is 80% of y, then y is what percent of x?

A. $133\frac{1}{3}\%$
B. 125%
C. 120%
D. 90%
E. 80%

20. From which of the following statements can it be deduced that $m > n$?

F. $m+1=n$
G. $2m=n$
H. $m+n>0$
J. $m-n>0$
K. $mn>0$

21. If $f(x) = x^2 + x$, then what is the value of $f(f(2))$?

A. 42
B. 38
C. 32
D. 18
E. 4

GO ON TO THE NEXT PAGE.

22. The circle below with center O has a radius with a length of 2. If the total area of the shaded regions is 3π, then $x = ?$

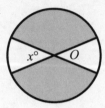

F. 270

G. 180

H. 120

J. 90

K. 45

DO YOUR FIGURING HERE.

23. If a bar of metal alloy consists of 100 grams of tin and 150 grams of lead, what percent of the entire bar, by weight, is tin?

A. 10%

B. 15%

C. $33\dfrac{1}{3}\%$

D. 40%

E. $66\dfrac{2}{3}\%$

24. If $\dfrac{1}{x}+\dfrac{1}{y}=\dfrac{1}{z}$, then $z = ?$

F. $\dfrac{1}{xy}$

G. xy

H. $\dfrac{x+y}{xy}$

J. $\dfrac{xy}{x+y}$

K. $\dfrac{2xy}{x+y}$

GO ON TO THE NEXT PAGE.

25. $|-5| + |-12| - |-2| + (-6) = ?$

   A. 2
   B. 3
   C. 6
   D. 9
   E. 14

DO YOUR FIGURING HERE.

26. If the average of $2x$, $2x+1$, and $2x+2$ is $x-1$, which of the following equations could be used to find x?

   F. $6x + 3 = x - 1$
   G. $6x + 3 = 3(x - 1)$
   H. $3(6x + 3) = x - 1$
   J. $(6x + 3) + (x - 1) = 3$
   K. $(6x + 3)(x - 1) = 3$

27. Participants in a community service project purchase boxes of candy for $1 each and sell them for $2 each. If no other expenses are incurred, how many boxes of candy must they sell to earn a net profit of $500?

   A. 250
   B. 500
   C. 1,000
   D. 1,500
   E. 2,000

28. $(-2)^2 - (-2)^3 = ?$

   F. 16
   G. 12
   H. 2
   J. −2
   K. −8

GO ON TO THE NEXT PAGE.

DO YOUR FIGURING HERE.

29. The sum, the product, and the average of 3 different integers are equal. If 2 of the integers are x and $-x$, the third integer is:

   A. $\dfrac{x}{2}$
   B. $2x$
   C. -1
   D. 0
   E. 1

30. In a school with a total enrollment of 360, 90 students are seniors. What percent of all students enrolled in the school are seniors?

   F. 25%
   G. $33\dfrac{1}{3}\%$
   H. 50%
   J. $66\dfrac{2}{3}\%$
   K. 75%

31. The perimeter of the square below is:

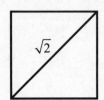

   A. 1
   B. $\sqrt{2}$
   C. 4
   D. $4\sqrt{2}$
   E. 8

GO ON TO THE NEXT PAGE.

32. If 2 straight line segments intersect as shown, what is the value of x?

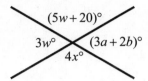

$3w°$ $(5w+20)°$ $(3a+2b)°$ $4x°$

- F. 15
- G. 30
- H. 45
- J. 60
- K. 75

DO YOUR FIGURING HERE.

33. The figure below is a scale drawing of the floor of a dining hall. If 1 centimeter on the drawing represents 5 meters, what is the area, in square meters, of the floor?

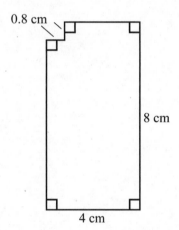

0.8 cm

8 cm

4 cm

- A. 144
- B. 156
- C. 784
- D. 796
- E. 844

GO ON TO THE NEXT PAGE.

34. One side of a triangle has a length of 4 and another side has a length of 11. What are the *greatest* and *least* possible integer values for the length of the remaining side?

DO YOUR FIGURING HERE.

- **F.** 7 and 4
- **G.** 11 and 4
- **H.** 14 and 8
- **J.** 15 and 7
- **K.** 16 and 7

35. Which of the following is the solution set for the function $-x^2 = 3 - 4x$?

- **A.** $\{-3, -1\}$
- **B.** $\{-3, 1\}$
- **C.** $\{1, 3\}$
- **D.** $\{1, 4\}$
- **E.** $\{3, 5\}$

36. The Global Exchange Club spends $\frac{2}{5}$ of its budget for one project and $\frac{1}{3}$ of what remains for another project. If the club's entire budget is $300, how much of the budget is left after the two projects?

- **F.** $60
- **G.** $90
- **H.** $120
- **J.** $180
- **K.** $240

GO ON TO THE NEXT PAGE.

37. If the cost of n nails is c cents, which of the following equations could be used to determine d, the cost in dollars, of x nails?

    A. $d = 100cnx$

    B. $d = 100\dfrac{cx}{n}$

    C. $d = \dfrac{100nx}{c}$

    D. $d = \dfrac{nx}{100c}$

    E. $d = \dfrac{cx}{100n}$

38. If a, b, and c are real numbers and $a^2b^3c < 0$, which of the following inequalities *must* be true?

    F. $b^3 < 0$
    G. $b^2 < 0$
    H. $b < 0$
    J. $c < 0$
    K. $bc < 0$

39. If the figure below is an equilateral triangle, what is its perimeter?

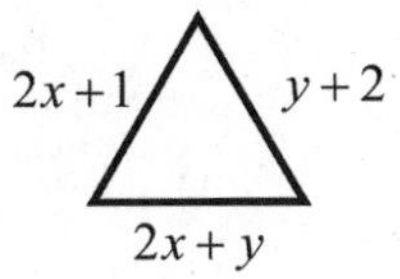

    A. 1
    B. 3
    C. 9
    D. 12
    E. 15

40. In the coordinate plane, what is the distance between the point with (x, y) coordinates $(2,1)$ and the point with (x, y) coordinates $(5,5)$?

    F. $\sqrt{3}$
    G. $2\sqrt{3}$
    H. $3\sqrt{2}$
    J. 5
    K. 6

DO YOUR FIGURING HERE.

GO ON TO THE NEXT PAGE.

41. $\sqrt{45} - \sqrt{20} + \sqrt{5} = ?$

    A. $2 - \sqrt{5}$
    B. 0
    C. $2 + \sqrt{5}$
    D. $2\sqrt{5}$
    E. 10

DO YOUR FIGURING HERE.

42. What is the least positive integer x for which $12 - x$ and $15 - x$ will yield non-zero results with opposite signs?

    F. 3
    G. 4
    H. 11
    J. 12
    K. 13

43. The solution set to the pair of equations $mx + ny = 15$ and $nx + my = 13$ is $x = 3$ and $y = 1$. What are the values of m and n?

    A. $m = 5$; $n = 3$
    B. $m = 4$; $n = 3$
    C. $m = 3$; $n = 4$
    D. $m = 3$; $n = 5$
    E. $m = 2$; $n = 6$

44. In the figure below, line segments intersecting each other at 90° join equally spaced points. If the total length of all the small line segments joining two of these equally spaced points in the figure is 24, what is the area of the shaded part?

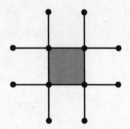

    F. 1
    G. 4
    H. 8
    J. 12
    K. 16

GO ON TO THE NEXT PAGE.

45. All of the following are true for all real numbers EXCEPT:

- A. $|a-b| = -|b-a|$
- B. $|a-b| = |b-a|$
- C. $|a-b| \leq |a| + |b|$
- D. $|a+b| \leq |a| + |b|$
- E. $|a| = |-a|$

DO YOUR FIGURING HERE.

46. $\text{Arccos}\left(\cos\dfrac{\pi}{2}\right) = ?$

- F. 0
- G. $\dfrac{\pi}{4}$
- H. $\dfrac{\pi}{2}$
- J. π
- K. $\dfrac{3\pi}{2}$

47. $\triangle ABC$ has coordinates $A\ (-1,-2)$, $B\ (0,4)$, and C $(3,-1)$. If $\triangle A'B'C'$ is the reflection of $\triangle ABC$ across the line $y = -x$, which of the following provides the coordinates of $\triangle A'B'C'$, respectively?

- A. $(2,1),\ (-4,0),\ (1,-3)$
- B. $(1,2),\ (0,-4),\ (-3,1)$
- C. $(2,1),\ (4,0),\ (1,-3)$
- D. $(3,2),\ (5,1),\ (2,-2)$
- E. $(4,0),\ (3,-1),\ (-1,-2)$

48. If $\sin x = \cos x$, then x terminates only in:

- F. quadrant I
- G. quadrant I or quadrant III
- H. quadrant II
- J. quadrant II or quadrant III
- K. quadrant II or quadrant IV

GO ON TO THE NEXT PAGE.

DO YOUR FIGURING HERE.

49. If the line $x = k$ is tangent to the circle $(x-2)^2 + (y+1)^2 = 4$, then which of the following is the point of tangency?

    A. $(-6,-1)$ or $(2,-1)$
    B. $(-2,-1)$ or $(6,-1)$
    C. $(0,-1)$ or $(4,-1)$
    D. $(0,1)$ or $(4,1)$
    E. $(2,1)$ or $(6,1)$

50. What is the last term in the expansion of $(2x + 3y)^4$?

    F. y^4
    G. $9y^4$
    H. $27y^4$
    J. $81y^4$
    K. $(xy)^4$

51. Which of the following could be a graph of the equation $y = ax^2 + bx + c$, where $b^2 - 4ac = 0$?

A.

D.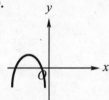

B.

E.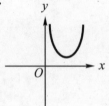

C.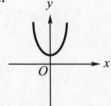

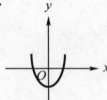

GO ON TO THE NEXT PAGE.

52. For any acute angle θ, which of the following is equal to $\dfrac{\sin\theta}{\cos\theta}$?

   F. $\tan\theta$
   G. $\cot\theta$
   H. $\sec\theta$
   J.   1
   K.   0.5

53. An angle that measures $\dfrac{3}{2}\pi$ radians measures how many degrees?

   A.   60
   B.   90
   C.   120
   D.   180
   E.   270

54. What is the solution set for $|2x-1| = 3$?

   F.   All real numbers
   G.   The empty set
   H. $\{-1\}$
   J. $\{2\}$
   K. $\{-1, 2\}$

55. The end points of a line segment have coordinates $(2,5)$ and $(2,-4)$. What are the coordinates of the midpoint of the line segment?

   A. $(0,1)$
   B. $\left(2,\dfrac{1}{2}\right)$
   C. $(2,1)$
   D. $(2,9)$
   E. $(4,9)$

DO YOUR FIGURING HERE.

GO ON TO THE NEXT PAGE.

56. What is the slope of the line $2x + 3y - 2 = 0$?

DO YOUR FIGURING HERE.

F. $-\dfrac{3}{2}$

G. $-\dfrac{2}{3}$

H. $\dfrac{2}{3}$

J. 4

K. 6

57. $\dfrac{1}{\sqrt{3}-1} = ?$

A. $\dfrac{\sqrt{3}-1}{4}$

B. $\dfrac{\sqrt{3}-1}{3}$

C. $\dfrac{\sqrt{3}-1}{2}$

D. $\dfrac{\sqrt{3}+1}{2}$

E. $\sqrt{3}+1$

58. $(-2)^2 - 2^{-2} = ?$

F. -5

G. -3

H. 3

J. $3\dfrac{3}{4}$

K. $4\dfrac{1}{4}$

GO ON TO THE NEXT PAGE.

59. $\dfrac{-3 + \sqrt{5}}{2}$ is one root of the equation

$x^2 + 3x + 1 = 0$. What is the other root?

A. $\dfrac{-3 - \sqrt{5}}{2}$

B. $\dfrac{3 - \sqrt{5}}{2}$

C. $\dfrac{3 + \sqrt{5}}{2}$

D. $3 - \dfrac{\sqrt{5}}{2}$

E. $3 + \dfrac{\sqrt{5}}{2}$

DO YOUR FIGURING HERE.

60. The figure below represents which of the following equations?

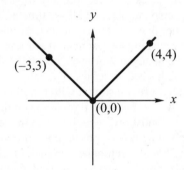

F. $y = x$
G. $y = -x$
H. $y = |x|$
J. $y = 2x$
K. $y = x^2$

END OF TEST 2
STOP! DO NOT TURN THE PAGE UNTIL TOLD TO DO SO.
DO NOT RETURN TO THE PREVIOUS TEST.

PRACTICE TEST II **3 3 3 3 3 3 3 3 3 3 3 3 3**

SECTION 3: READING TEST
35 Minutes—40 Items

DIRECTIONS: Each passage below is followed by a set of items. Read each passage and choose the best answer for each item. Fill in the corresponding oval on your bubble sheet. You may refer to the passage as often as necessary to answer the items. Answers are on page 720.

Passage I

PROSE FICTION: In this excerpt from Herman Melville's short story *Bartleby, the Scrivener*, the narrator shares his exasperation with and sympathy for an employee.

Turkey was a short, pursy Englishman, of about my own age—that is, somewhere not far from sixty. In the morning, one might say, his face was of a fine florid hue. But after twelve o'clock, meridian—his

5 dinner hour—it blazed like a grate full of Christmas coals; and continued blazing—but, as it were, with a gradual wane—till six o'clock p.m., or thereabouts; after which, I saw no more of the proprietor of the face, which, gaining its meridian with the Sun, seemed to set

10 with, to rise, culminate, and decline the following day, with the like regularity and undiminished glory. There are many singular coincidences I have known in the course of my life. Not the least among these was the fact that, exactly when Turkey displayed his fullest

15 beams from his red and radiant countenance, just then, too, at that critical moment, began the daily period when I considered his business capacities as seriously disturbed for the remainder of the twenty-four hours.

Not that he was absolutely idle, or averse to

20 business then. Far from it. The difficulty was he was apt to be altogether too energetic. There was a strange, inflamed, flurried, flighty recklessness of activity about him. He would be incautious in dipping his pen into his inkstand. All his blots upon my documents were

25 dropped there after twelve o'clock, meridian. Indeed, not only would he be reckless, and sadly given to making blots in the afternoon, but, some days, he went further, and was rather noisy. At such times, too, his face flamed with augmented blazonry, as if cannel coal

30 had been heaped upon anthracite. He made an unpleasant racket with his chair; spilled his sand box;

in mending his pens, impatiently split them all to pieces, and threw them on the floor in a sudden passion; stood up, and leaned over his table, boxing the

35 papers about in a most indecorous manner, very sad to behold in an elderly man like him.

Nevertheless, he was in many ways a most valuable person to me, and all the time before twelve o'clock, meridian, was the quickest, steadiest creature,

40 too, accomplishing a great deal of work in a style not easily to be matched. For these reasons, I was willing to overlook his eccentricities. Though, indeed, occasionally, I remonstrated with him. I did this very gently, however, because, though the civilest, nay, the

45 blandest and most reverential of men in the morning, in the afternoon he was disposed, upon provocation, to be slightly rash with his tongue—in fact, insolent. Now, valuing his morning services as I did, and resolved not to lose them—yet, at the same time, made

50 uncomfortable by his inflamed ways after twelve o'clock—and being a man of peace, unwilling by my admonitions to call forth unseemly retorts from him, I took upon me, one Saturday noon (he was always worse on Saturdays) to hint to him, very kindly, that

55 perhaps, now that he was growing old, it might be well to abridge his labors; in short, he need not come to my chambers after twelve o'clock, but, dinner over, had best go home to his lodgings, and rest himself till teatime. But no; he insisted upon his afternoon

60 devotions. His countenance became intolerably fervid. He oratorically assured me—gesticulating with a long ruler at the other end of the room—that if his services in the morning were useful, how indispensable, then, in the afternoon?

65 "With submission, sir," said Turkey, on this occasion, "I consider myself your right-hand man. In the morning I but marshal and deploy my columns; but in the afternoon I put myself at their head, and gallantly

GO ON TO THE NEXT PAGE.

charge the foe, thus"—and he made a violent thrust
70 with the ruler.

"But the blots, Turkey," intimated I.

"True; but, with submission sir, behold these
hairs! I am getting old. Surely, sir, a blot or two of a
warm afternoon is not to be severely urged against gray
75 hairs. Old age—even if it blot the page—is honorable.
With submission, sir, we *both* are getting old."

This appeal to my fellow-feeling was hardly to be
resisted. At all events, I saw that go he would not. So, I
made up my mind to let him stay. I resolved,
80 nevertheless, to see to it that, during the afternoon, he
had to do with my less important papers.

1. The narrator is Turkey's:

    A. older brother.
    B. physician.
    C. co-worker.
    D. employer.

2. The passage suggests that Turkey is a:

    F. copyist.
    G. painter.
    H. fencing instructor.
    J. sales clerk.

3. A logical explanation for Turkey's behavior is
    that he:

    A. becomes fatigued.
    B. is growing old.
    C. drinks alcohol.
    D. dislikes the narrator.

4. The fellow-feeling mentioned in the final
    paragraph is based on the fact that:

    F. Turkey is the narrator's right-hand man.
    G. Turkey and the narrator are the same age.
    H. the narrator also makes ink blots.
    J. the ink blots are not very serious.

5. The narrator's final resolution of the problem is
    to:

    A. find a replacement for Turkey.
    B. give Turkey Saturdays off.
    C. give Turkey afternoons off.
    D. give Turkey less important work after noon.

6. According to the narrator, Turkey's face is
    reddest:

    F. in early morning.
    G. shortly after noon.
    H. in midafternoon.
    J. in early evening.

7. It can be inferred that when cannel coal is heaped
    on anthracite, a fire:

    A. burns more intensely.
    B. burns less intensely.
    C. goes out altogether.
    D. begins to sputter and spit.

8. The narrator's attitude toward Turkey's afternoon
    behavior is one of:

    F. amusement.
    G. discomfort.
    H. indifference.
    J. outrage.

9. The narrator finds Turkey's work in the mornings
    to be:

    A. entirely satisfactory.
    B. frequently unsatisfactory.
    C. almost always unsatisfactory.
    D. inconsistent.

10. Which of the following does NOT characterize
    Turkey's behavior in the afternoon?

    F. Frenzied activity
    G. Excessive carelessness
    H. Idleness
    J. Verbal insolence

GO ON TO THE NEXT PAGE.

Passage II

SOCIAL SCIENCE: This passage discusses punishment for individuals who have violated the law.

Justice in society must include both a fair trial for the accused and the selection of an appropriate punishment for those proved guilty. Because justice is regarded as one form of equality, we find in its earlier
5   expressions the idea of a punishment equal to the crime. Recorded in the Old Testament is the expression "an eye for an eye, and a tooth for a tooth." That is, the individual who has done wrong has committed an offense against society. To atone for this offense,
10   society must get even. Only inflicting an equal injury upon him can do this. This conception of retributive justice is reflected in many parts of the legal codes and procedures of modern times. It is illustrated when we demand the death penalty for a person who has
15   committed murder.

The German idealist, Hegel, supported this philosophy of punishment. He believed that society owed it to the criminal to administer a punishment equal to the crime committed. The criminal has by his
20   own actions denied his true self, and it is necessary to do something to restore the self that has been denied. To the murderer, nothing less than giving up his own life will pay his debt. The exaction of the death penalty is a right the state owes the criminal, and it should not
25   deny him his due.

Modern jurists have tried to replace retributive justice with the notion of corrective justice. The aim of the latter is not to abandon the concept of equality but to find a more adequate way to express it. It tries to
30   preserve the ideal of equal opportunity for each individual to realize the best that is in him. The criminal is regarded as being socially ill and in need of treatment that will enable him to become a normal member of society. Before treatment can be adminis-
35   tered, the causes that led to antisocial behavior must be found. If the causes can be removed, provisions must be made to have this done.

Only those criminals who are incurable should be permanently separated from the rest of society. This
40   does not mean that criminals will escape punishment or be quickly returned to take up careers of crime. It means that justice is to heal the individual, not simply to get even with him. If severe punishment is the only adequate means for accomplishing this, it should be

45   administered. However, the individual should be given every opportunity to assume a normal place in society. His conviction of crime must not deprive him of the opportunity to make his way in the society of which he is a part.

11. The best title for this selection is:

    A. Fitting Punishment to the Crime.
    B. Approaches to Just Punishment.
    C. Improvement in Legal Justice.
    D. Attaining Justice in the Courts.

12. Hegel would view the death sentence for murder as:

    F. inadequate justice.
    G. the best way for society to get revenge.
    H. the most efficient method of removing a known danger.
    J. an inalienable right of the murderer.

13. The passage implies that the basic difference between retributive justice and corrective justice is:

    A. the type of crime that was committed.
    B. the severity of the punishment.
    C. the reason for the sentence.
    D. the outcome of the trial.

14. The punishment that would be most inconsistent with the views of corrective justice is:

    F. forced brain surgery.
    G. solitary confinement.
    H. life imprisonment.
    J. the electric chair.

GO ON TO THE NEXT PAGE.

15. The Biblical expression "an eye for an eye, and a tooth for a tooth" was presented in order to:

   A. justify the need for punishment as a part of law.
   B. give moral backing to retributive justice.
   C. show that humanity has long been interested in justice as a form of equality.
   D. indicate the lack of social development during Biblical times.

16. The concept of retributive justice still reflected in many modern legal codes is:

   F. giving the accused a fair trial.
   G. rehabilitating the criminal.
   H. separating incurable criminals from the rest of society.
   J. inflicting equal injury on the criminal.

17. A major goal of modern jurists is to:

   A. ensure that criminals do not escape punishment.
   B. preserve the notion of equality.
   C. restore states' rights.
   D. select an appropriate punishment for a crime.

18. Under the notion of corrective justice, assuming "a normal place in society" (line 46) most likely means:

   F. acting in one's best interests.
   G. denying one's true self.
   H. curing antisocial behavior.
   J. accepting punishment.

19. The author's tone in the passage is best described as:

   A. argumentative.
   B. sympathetic.
   C. explanatory.
   D. conciliatory.

20. According to the author, criminals cannot be treated until:

   F. they have been punished properly for their crime.
   G. they have received a fair trial.
   H. a legal code for treatment has been established.
   J. the causes of antisocial behavior have been found.

GO ON TO THE NEXT PAGE.

Passage III

HUMANITIES: This passage describes events leading to and the effects of World War I.

The event that touched off World War I occurred in Sarajevo, the capital of the Austro-Hungarian province of Bosnia, on June 28, 1914. There the Archduke Francis Ferdinand, the Hapsburg heir to the
5 throne of the Austro-Hungarian Empire, was shot and killed by a young Serbian nationalist seeking revenge against the Austrians for their annexation of Bosnia. Austria issued an ultimatum to Serbia. The Serbians acquiesced, in an attempt to stave off war. Austria,
10 however, was intent on exacting retribution. In July of that year it declared war on Serbia.

For almost a century, since the Congress of Vienna in 1815, European diplomats had prevented any real threat to the delicate balance of power achieved by
15 the Congress. This time, though, they seemed power-less to stop the movement toward war. The assassina-tion caused a fateful series of failed diplomatic attempts that led Russia to mobilize its armed forces as Serbia's ally. Austria sought and gained the
20 mobilization aid of its ally Germany. The other members of the Triple Entente, France and Great Britain, soon joined their ally Russia against Austria. In 1917, the United States was drawn into the battle as an ally of France and Great Britain.

25 World War I was unlike any other war fought before or since. The profound shock it generated dramatically affected life in Europe and America and changed the course of world politics. Moreover, the war shocked millions of people throughout Europe into
30 confronting the terrible losses and the grim and brutal realities of modern war. The few wars that had been fought since 1815 were distant colonial wars. Europeans had always been victorious. The battles seemed nothing more than skirmishes that offered
35 chances to experience adventure and to demonstrate bravery and heroism. The trenches and battlefields of Europe introduced millions of young men and women to a world of pain and death that they had never imagined.

40 The war altered the social sensibility of the people of Europe. It destroyed the spirit of optimism that had prevailed in the nineteenth century. Civilized, polite behavior now seemed archaic and hypocritical. Moreover, the impression that there appeared to be no

45 sane way to end the carnage only added to the sense of futility. The war changed relationships between members of the same social class. Before the war, the upper classes of Europe felt a bond that united them across national borders. After the war, national
50 boundaries defined social consciousness in a way that destroyed the solidarity of class.

World War I produced several dramatic changes in the political landscape of Europe. The breakup of the Austro-Hungarian, Russian, and German empires led to
55 the reemergence of the state of Poland. It also brought about the formation of new nation states in Europe. The war acted as a catalyst for European revolutionar-ies. The Russian Revolution of 1917 set the stage for the Bolshevik seizure of power. Total power was
60 achieved by the Communist party. Stalin became the absolute dictator of the Russian state (renamed the Union of Soviet Socialist Republics). World War I bore bitter fruit in Central and Southern Europe as well. The rise of Nazism in Germany and fascism in Italy led
65 many historians to conclude that World War II, which was begun by Nazi Germany in 1939, was in fact the continuation of the Great War that destroyed the social fabric of Europe in 1914.

21. The precipitating cause of World War I was:

   A. an assassination.
   B. a coronation.
   C. a rebellion.
   D. a plebiscite.

22. The event occurred in the city of:

   F. Sarajevo in Bosnia.
   G. Vienna in Austria.
   H. Trieste in Italy.
   J. Budapest in Hungary.

23. Before World War I, a balance of power had existed for:

   A. nearly 15 years.
   B. almost a quarter century.
   C. almost 100 years.
   D. nearly 10 years.

GO ON TO THE NEXT PAGE.

24. The chief reason European countries other than Austria and Serbia were drawn into the conflict was that they:

   F. were members of the two alliance systems to which the combatants belonged.
   G. feared the Hapsburgs.
   H. wanted to ensure freedom of the seas.
   J. wanted the land of neighboring countries.

25. Mobilization for war resulted swiftly when:

   A. the United States declared war.
   B. attempts at diplomacy failed.
   C. Russia refused to help Serbia.
   D. Italy joined the conflict.

26. The way in which class relationships changed as a result of the outbreak of World War I suggests that:

   F. nationalism might have weakened had the war never occurred.
   G. the middle classes had no real love of country.
   H. the upper classes had eagerly anticipated war.
   J. everyone sanctioned the war.

27. The forces of militant nationalism that were unleashed during World War I culminated in the breakup of the Russian Empire and the German Empire. The political regimes that came to power in Germany and the Soviet Union before World War II were:

   A. democracies that isolated themselves from world politics.
   B. ruthless dictatorships dedicated to world conquest.
   C. weak states allied with the United States.
   D. members of a Europe-wide common market.

28. The sense of futility felt throughout Europe during and after World War I would be evident in a study of:

   F. American investment policies.
   G. statistics concerning foreign language study in America.
   H. the number of transatlantic voyages between 1920 and 1930.
   J. European literature of the 1920s, 1930s, and 1940s.

29. World War I and its aftermath suggest the idea that:

   A. nationalism has little to do with world conflict.
   B. war feeds on nationalist sympathies.
   C. the cause of peace is best aided by reinvigorating the spirit of nationalism.
   D. diplomacy never works.

30. Archduke Francis Ferdinand, as the heir to the Austro-Hungarian Empire, was a member of the:

   F. Hohenzollern family.
   G. Hanover family.
   H. Hapsburg family.
   J. Stuart family.

GO ON TO THE NEXT PAGE.

Passage IV

NATURAL SCIENCE: This selection discusses the information gathered about the planet Uranus by the Voyager 2 spacecraft.

When the Voyager 2 spacecraft flew past Uranus and its moons in 1986, it gathered startling new information about these extraordinary celestial objects. Uranus had long been known to be different from all
5 the other planets in one important respect: it lies tipped over on its side, and instead of spinning like a top, it rolls like a ball along the path of its orbit. Its geographic poles, instead of being on the top and bottom of the planet as Earth's are, are located on
10 either side, one facing the Sun and one facing away— as if they were the ends of a gigantic axle. Voyager found another oddity: Uranus' magnetic poles, instead of lying close to the geographic poles as Earth's do, are located not far from the planet's equator, 60° away
15 from the geographic poles. Still another discovery is that the clouds in the Uranian atmosphere move in the same direction as the planet rotates; that is, from top to bottom and back to top, rather than horizontally, as Earth's clouds move.

20 The Uranian moons proved to have equally striking features. Miranda, the moon nearest the planet, bears tremendous markings where terrains of completely different types appear to have been wedged together. On Ariel, the next moon out, the landscape
25 has been stretched apart, creating huge faults where the ground has broken apart and sunk inward. However, there is no evidence of any geological activity. Umbriel, the third moon, seems to be "painted" with some dark substance. On one side of Umbriel is a
30 large, round bright marking called the "donut." It is presumably some type of impact crater. Each of Uranus' other seven moons is equally odd and unique in its own way. Furthermore, between the orbit of Miranda and Uranus' surface are up to one hundred
35 charcoal-colored rings, ringlets, and bands of dust, and between some of these rings are still more tiny moonlets.

The moons and rings of Uranus are odd in still another way. Like the clouds in the planet's atmos-
40 phere, they circle Uranus in the same direction as the planet rotates. That is, they orbit over the top and bottom of the planet rather than around the sides, as Earth's moon does.

31. Because of the odd way in which Uranus rotates, one geographic pole:

   A. alternates between daylight and darkness.
   B. receives only indirect sunlight.
   C. varies between heat from the Sun and cold.
   D. is always in darkness.

32. The warmest spot on Uranus would most likely be located at:

   F. one of the magnetic poles.
   G. the equator.
   H. one of the geographic poles.
   J. a spot midway between a geographic pole and the equator.

33. On Uranus, a surface location that receives sunlight:

   A. will alternate between daylight and darkness.
   B. will always be in daylight.
   C. will occasionally be in darkness.
   D. must be near one of the magnetic poles.

34. The Uranian equator extends:

   F. around the planet horizontally, as Earth's does.
   G. around the planet through the geographic poles.
   H. around the planet from top to bottom.
   J. around the planet through the magnetic poles.

35. An observer at the Uranian equator would most likely experience:

   A. a regular succession of days and nights.
   B. constant, indirect sunlight.
   C. a regular succession of warmth and cold.
   D. only darkness.

GO ON TO THE NEXT PAGE.

36. Auroras are sky phenomena that generally appear near a planet's magnetic poles. On Earth, auroras can be seen at extreme north or south latitudes. On Uranus, auroras would most likely:

    F. be visible near the planet's geographic poles.
    G. never be visible.
    H. be visible not far from the planet's equator.
    J. be visible from everywhere on the planet's surface.

37. On Earth, atmospheric circulation patterns are largely controlled by the varying amounts of sunlight received at different latitudes. On Uranus:

    A. atmospheric circulation functions in an identical way.
    B. there is no atmospheric circulation.
    C. the atmosphere circulates from one geographic pole to the other.
    D. some other factor besides sunlight controls atmospheric circulation.

38. It has been suggested that the moon Miranda was shattered into pieces by a collision with some other object. Gravity then caused the pieces to reassemble; however, great "seam" marks most likely remained because:

    F. the gravitational forces involved were weak.
    G. the lack of atmosphere meant that no erosion ever took place.
    H. the second object remained nearby, exerting gravitational pull.
    J. the force of the collision was so great.

39. The great faults observed on the moon Ariel could have been caused by:

    A. moonquakes.
    B. continental drift.
    C. the gravitational pull of other nearby moons.
    D. volcanic activity.

40. Uranus has how many moons?

    F. 3
    G. 7
    H. 10
    J. 12

END OF TEST 3
STOP! DO NOT TURN THE PAGE UNTIL TOLD TO DO SO.
DO NOT RETURN TO THE PREVIOUS TEST.

SECTION 4: SCIENCE TEST
35 Minutes—40 Items

DIRECTIONS: Each passage below is followed by several items. After reading a passage, choose the best answer for each item. Fill in the corresponding oval on your bubble sheet. You may refer to the passage as often as necessary. You are NOT permitted the use of a calculator on this test. Answers are on page 723.

Passage I

The table below shows selected elements from the periodic table, together with atomic radii in angstrom units (Å) and electronegativities (second number).

H 0.37 Å 2.20						
Li 1.52 Å 0.98	Be 1.12 Å 1.57	B 0.85 Å 2.04	C 0.77 Å 2.55	N 0.75 Å 3.04	O 0.73 Å 3.44	F 0.72 Å 3.98
Na 1.86 Å 0.93	Mg 1.60 Å 1.31	Al 1.43 Å 1.61	Si 1.18 Å 1.90	P 1.10 Å 2.19	S 1.03 Å 2.58	Cl 1.00 Å 3.16
K 2.27 Å 0.82						Br 1.14 Å 2.96
Rb 2.48 Å 0.82						I 1.33 Å 2.66

When two atoms of the same element form a covalent bond, the approximate bond length may be calculated by adding together the two atomic radii.

The electronegativity has important chemical significance. If two atoms form a bond, the difference in the two electronegativities indicates the degree to which the bond is covalent (indicated by a small difference) or ionic (indicated by a large difference).

GO ON TO THE NEXT PAGE.

1. Which of the following occur when moving down a column in the table?

   A. Radii decrease; electronegativities decrease or stay the same.
   B. Radii increase; electronegativities increase or stay the same.
   C. Radii decrease; electronegativities increase or stay the same.
   D. Radii increase; electronegativities decrease or stay the same.

2. The greatest electronegativity in the table is for the element:

   F. fluorine (F).
   G. chlorine (Cl).
   H. rubidium (Rb).
   J. hydrogen (H).

3. The bond length in a P-P bond is:

   A. 0.55 Å.
   B. 1.21 Å.
   C. 2.20 Å.
   D. 4.40 Å.

4. The bond between which of the following elements is likely to have the most covalent character?

   F. Sodium (Na) and iodine (I)
   G. Magnesium (Mg) and oxygen (O)
   H. Sulfur (S) and oxygen (O)
   J. Carbon (C) and nitrogen (N)

5. When the element fluorine (F) bonds with a second element in the table shown, the resulting bond generally has a greater ionic character:

   A. the closer the second element is to fluorine in the same row.
   B. the closer the second element is to fluorine in the same column.
   C. the farther the second element is from fluorine in the same row.
   D. the farther the second element is from fluorine in both a different row and a different column.

6. The element astatine (At) lies directly below iodine (I) in the periodic table. The electronegativity difference in HAt is likely to be:

   F. less than 0.46.
   G. greater than 0.46.
   H. equal to 0.46.
   J. Cannot be determined from the given information

GO ON TO THE NEXT PAGE.

Passage II

A set of experiments was carried out to investigate the relative sizes of the planets of our solar system and the relative distances from the Sun. Table 1 was given to all students performing the experiments.

Experiment 1

Using a compass, ruler, and poster board (22 inches by 28 inches), students were asked to compare the sizes of the planets. Calling the size of Earth 1.00 (Earth diameter = 1 inch), a circle was made by inserting the point of the compass in the center of the poster board. The circle had a radius of 0.5 inches to produce a circle with a diameter of 1 inch representing the Earth. All other planets were drawn to scale based on the size of their diameters relative to one Earth diameter (Table 1).

Table 1		
Planet	Approximate Diameter (in Earth diameters)	Approximate Distance from the Sun (A.U.)
Mercury	0.38	0.40
Venus	0.95	0.70
Earth	1.00	1.00
Mars	0.54	1.50
Jupiter	11.20	5.20
Saturn	9.50	9.50
Uranus	4.01	19.20
Neptune	3.88	30.00

Experiment 2

Using the equipment from Experiment 1, students were also asked to compare planetary distances from the Sun. The Earth is 93 million miles from the Sun. This distance is called 1.00 astronomical unit (1 A.U. = 1 inch), and it was used as a reference distance when the other planets were drawn at their proper distances (Table 1) from the Sun (a planet twice as far as the Earth is from the Sun would be drawn 2 A.U., or 2.0 inches, from the Sun).

7. In Experiment 1, the two planets represented by circles most similar in size on the paper are:

   A. Earth and Venus.
   B. Mars and Mercury.
   C. Mars and Venus.
   D. Saturn and Jupiter.

8. In Experiment 2, if the poster board were held the "long way" (landscape) and the left-hand edge represented the Sun, which planet(s) would not fit on the paper?

   F. Saturn, Uranus, and Neptune
   G. Uranus and Neptune
   H. Neptune only
   J. All planets would fit on the paper.

9. Which of the following statements is supported by the data in Table 1?

   A. The larger the planet, the greater is its distance from the Sun.
   B. The smaller the planet, the greater is its distance from the Sun.
   C. Only planets larger than the Earth are farther away from the Sun.
   D. There is no consistent pattern between a planet's size and its distance from the Sun.

10. A planet's "year" is how long it takes to orbit the Sun, and it is related to the distance of that planet from the Sun. If asteroids are found 2.8 A.U. from the Sun, an "asteroid year" should be:

   F. longer than an "Earth year" but shorter than a "Mars year."
   G. longer than a "Jupiter year" but shorter than a "Mars year."
   H. longer than a "Mars year" but shorter than a "Jupiter year."
   J. longer than a "Neptune year" but shorter than a "Saturn year."

GO ON TO THE NEXT PAGE.

11. In Experiment 1, how large would a circle
    representing the Sun be if its diameter is
    approximately 110 times greater than that of
    Earth?

    A. It would have a radius of approximately 55
    inches.
    B. It would have a diameter of approximately
    55 inches.
    C. It would have a radius of approximately 5.5
    inches.
    D. It would have a diameter of approximately
    5.5 inches.

12. A third experiment was conducted in which the
    mass of each planet was described relative to the
    mass of Earth (Jupiter had the greatest mass,
    Saturn had the next largest mass, Mercury and
    Mars had the smallest masses). If the planets were
    placed in an order based on how they compared
    to Earth for the variables measured in all three
    experiments, which two orders would be expected
    to be most similar?

    F. Diameter and distance from the Sun
    G. Mass and distance from the Sun
    H. Diameter and mass
    J. All three orders would be similar.

GO ON TO THE NEXT PAGE.

Passage III

During photosynthesis, leaf pigments absorb light energy. Eventually, this process results in the production of glucose and other carbohydrates to be used by the green plant. Oxygen gas (O_2) is also produced during the process. Various factors affecting the rate of photosynthesis were investigated by counting the number of oxygen bubbles produced under the conditions described in the following three experiments.

Experiment 1

A sample of leaf extract (a mixture of pigments previously separated from other leaf components) from the pond plant *Elodea* was placed in a beaker containing water and a standard concentration of carbon dioxide (CO_2), both necessary ingredients for photosynthesis. Light of varying intensity was used to illuminate the beaker, and the number of oxygen bubbles emitted by the plant each minute was recorded. The results are summarized in Figure 1.

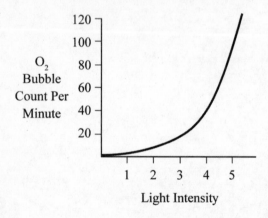

Figure 1

Experiment 2

An identical experiment was conducted in which the concentration of leaf extract was reduced four-fold (the mixture was one-fourth as concentrated as in Experiment 1). The results are summarized in Figure 2.

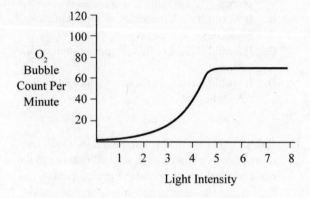

Figure 2

Experiment 3

Visible light consists of many different colors, or light wavelengths. Only those wavelengths that are absorbed by leaf pigments can provide the energy to maintain photosynthesis in the leaf. Different light wavelengths were used separately to illuminate two samples of leaf extract, each containing a different *Elodea* leaf pigment. Oxygen (O_2) bubbles were counted again as a measure of the rate of photosynthesis. The results are summarized in Figure 3.

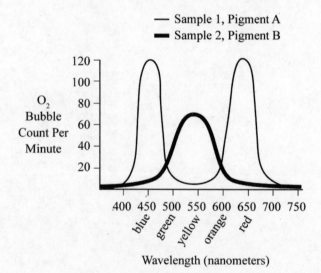

Figure 3

GO ON TO THE NEXT PAGE.

13. Which of the following changes in Experiment 1 would test the hypothesis that the level of carbon dioxide affects the rate of photosynthesis?

   A. Repeat the experiment, using the same concentration of carbon dioxide in the beaker of water, but with different species of green plants.
   B. Repeat the experiment, using no carbon dioxide as well as varying concentrations of carbon dioxide in the beaker of water.
   C. Repeat the experiment using different levels of water in the beaker containing a standard concentration of carbon dioxide.
   D. Repeat the experiment using additional light intensities.

14. The results from Experiments 1 and 2 demonstrate that maintaining a continued increase in the photosynthesis rate requires adequate amounts of:

   F. light.
   G. carbon dioxide.
   H. oxygen.
   J. leaf pigments.

15. Based on the information in Figure 3, which of the following statements is correct?

   A. Pigment A primarily absorbs light at 450 and 650 nanometers, while Pigment B absorbs light at 500–575 nanometers.
   B. Pigment B primarily absorbs light at 450 and 650 nanometers, while Pigment A absorbs light at 500–575 nanometers.
   C. Pigment A can influence the rate of photosynthesis, while Pigment B cannot.
   D. Pigment B can influence the rate of photosynthesis, while Pigment A cannot.

16. If the concentration of *Elodea* leaf extract were increased in Experiment 2, which of the following results could be expected?

   F. A decrease in the number of oxygen bubbles
   G. An increase in the number of oxygen bubbles
   H. No change in the number of oxygen bubbles
   J. A gradual dimming of light intensity

17. In Experiments 1 and 2, approximately how many oxygen bubbles per minute were produced at a light intensity level of 4?

   A. 0
   B. 20
   C. 40
   D. 80

18. According to the information in Figure 3, if an additional experiment were conducted, which condition would be LEAST effective in maintaining photosynthetic rate in *Elodea*?

   F. Using blue light only
   G. Using red light only
   H. Using yellow light only
   J. Using orange light only

GO ON TO THE NEXT PAGE.

Passage IV

The accompanying figure shows how the world records for various footraces have improved during a portion of the twentieth century. Speeds are given in both meters per minute and minutes per mile.

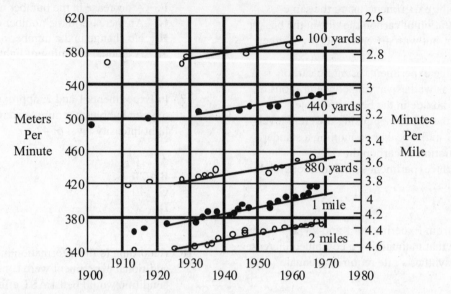

Modified from H.W. Ryder, H.J. Carr, and P. Herget, "Future performance in footracing," *Sci. Amer.* 234 (6): 109–114, 1976.

19. In what race and in what year was the greatest speed in meters per minute achieved?

  A. The 440 yard dash in 1900
  B. The 100 yard dash in 1930
  C. The 100 yard dash in 1962
  D. The 1 mile run in 1947

20. The trend in the graph of speed for the various distances shows:

  F. roughly a linear increase.
  G. roughly a linear decrease.
  H. a linear increase for short distances and a linear decrease for long distances.
  J. no systematic pattern.

21. For 1960, the ratio of speed in minutes per mile for the 1 mile run to speed in minutes per mile for the 440 yard dash is approximately:

  A. 3/4.
  B. 4/5.
  C. 5/5.
  D. 4/3.

22. The increase in speed, in meters per minute, for the 2 mile run from 1925 to 1967 is approximately:

  F. 0.3.
  G. 10.
  H. 30.
  J. 100.

23. If the trends shown can be expected to hold for later years, then the value of minutes per mile for the 880 yard run in 1980 is expected to be:

  A. 3.5.
  B. 3.8.
  C. 420.
  D. 460.

GO ON TO THE NEXT PAGE.

Passage V

Two experiments were performed in which constant amounts of heat were added continuously to samples over a defined period of time. The temperatures of the samples were monitored while the heat was added. The results from the two experiments are shown below.

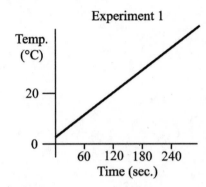

Experiment 1

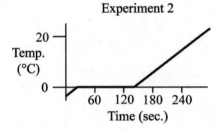

Experiment 2

24. The results of Experiment 1 may be interpreted to show that:

   F. it takes longer to heat a hot sample than a cold one.
   G. the temperature of the sample rises proportionately with time as heat is applied.
   H. temperature is not related to heat.
   J. temperature and time measure the same thing.

25. Experiment 2 differs from Experiment 1 in that:

   A. only the starting temperature is different in the two experiments.
   B. since the graph in Experiment 2 is not a straight line, there must have been experimental error.
   C. Experiment 2 has a lower starting temperature and a time period when the temperature does not rise.
   D. in Experiment 2, the heat was off for a while in the middle of the experiment.

26. The experimenter wants to explain the flat part of the graph from Experiment 2. It could represent:

   F. a period when the clock was turned off but heat was added as in Experiment 1.
   G. a period when the heat was turned off but the clock continued to run.
   H. a period when heat was added but some process occurred that did not occur in Experiment 1.
   J. a period when less heat was added but the clock continued to run.

27. The "phase" of the sample changes (an example of a phase change is the melting of a solid, or the boiling of a liquid) in conjunction with the flat part of the graph in Experiment 2. From the temperature data given, the phase change might be:

   A. the melting of ice.
   B. the boiling of water.
   C. the condensation of steam.
   D. the freezing of water.

28. The results of these experiments demonstrate that:

   F. heat and temperature are basically the same.
   G. heat and temperature are not the same.
   H. a pause in heating can lead to a pause in temperature change.
   J. constant heating leads to constant change.

GO ON TO THE NEXT PAGE.

29. If the experimenter extends Experiment 2 to higher temperatures, using a sample with a phase change at 0°C and 100°C, which graph best illustrates the expected results?

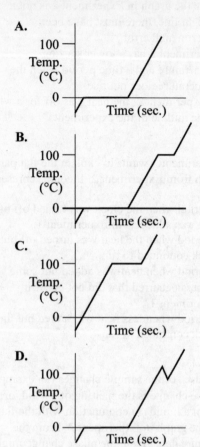

A.

100
Temp.
(°C)
0
Time (sec.)

B.

100
Temp.
(°C)
0
Time (sec.)

C.

100
Temp.
(°C)
0
Time (sec.)

D.

100
Temp.
(°C)
0
Time (sec.)

Passage VI

The following chart shows the generalized sequence of early developmental stages (terms in boxes) observed in most vertebrates.

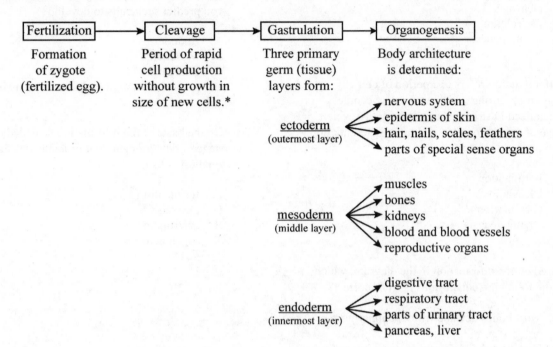

*New cells form as the zygote and its subsequent daughter cells divide and re-divide.

GO ON TO THE NEXT PAGE.

30. According to the chart, the stage of development when the three primary tissue layers form is:

    F. fertilization.
    G. cleavage.
    H. gastrulation.
    J. organogenesis.

31. Differentiation refers to a period of cell maturation during which time cells become specialized in structure and function. At which stage of development would most differentiation be expected to occur?

    A. Fertilization
    B. Cleavage
    C. Gastrulation
    D. Organogenesis

32. Based on the information in the diagram, which of the following conclusions is NOT correct?

    F. Most bones develop from the innermost primary germ layer.
    G. Vertebrates develop three primary germ layers.
    H. Diverse structures such as scales, feathers, and hair always develop from the same primary germ layer.
    J. Before an organism can form different primary tissue layers, it must go through a period of rapid cell production.

33. If a species of monkey were found to have extraordinary vision due to special receptor cells that were highly sensitive to different colors of light, from which primary germ layer(s) would you predict such cells to develop?

    A. Endoderm
    B. Mesoderm
    C. Ectoderm
    D. A combination of endoderm and mesoderm

34. On the basis of the information provided, the stage of development that probably has the smallest cells is:

    F. fertilization.
    G. cleavage.
    H. gastrulation.
    J. organogenesis.

GO ON TO THE NEXT PAGE.

Passage VII

The following are two theories regarding the proportions of chemicals that will react to form products.

Theory 1

Although a chemical reaction is more than simple mixing, the two are similar in that any amounts of reactants may be brought together to form chemical products that contain the same elements as the reactants. For example, in the chemical reaction " hydrogen + oxygen ⇒ water ," we may use 1 mole of hydrogen and 1 mole of oxygen, or 2 to 1, or 1 to 2, etc. The reaction will adjust to the proportions given.

Theory 2

Only certain proportions of reactants will combine chemically. For example, when hydrogen and oxygen are reacted, the amounts that will combine will be *exactly* 2 grams of hydrogen for every 32 grams of oxygen. We can show, using molecular weights, that these weights of reactants (which correspond to 2 moles of hydrogen and 1 mole of oxygen), imply the following reaction:

$$2H_2 + O_2 \Rightarrow 2H_2O$$

From this statement about the proportions of hydrogens and oxygens that react with each other, we can conclude that two hydrogen molecules must react with a single oxygen molecule to form two molecules of water.

35. Theory 1 does NOT predict that:

    A. 2 moles of zinc will react completely with 2 moles of sulfur.

    B. 2 moles of zinc will react completely with 3 moles of sulfur.

    C. 7 moles of zinc will react completely with 4 moles of sulfur.

    D. if 3 moles of zinc were mixed with 4 moles of sulfur, then 1 mole of sulfur would be left unreacted.

36. According to Theory 1, how many moles of water would be produced by the reaction of 2 moles of hydrogen and 1 mole of oxygen?

    F. 1

    G. 2

    H. 4

    J. Cannot be determined from the given information

Items #37–38 refer to the following:

An experimenter finds that when 170 grams of $AgNO_3$ is reacted with 58.5 grams of NaCl to form products, none of the original reactants remain in appreciable amounts. When the original amount of $AgNO_3$ is increased to 175 grams, then all of the NaCl is used up, but 5 grams of $AgNO_3$ remains.

37. The result described above is:

    A. consistent with Theory 1.

    B. consistent with Theory 2.

    C. consistent with both Theory 1 and Theory 2.

    D. not consistent with either theory.

38. According to Theory 2, how might the remaining 5 grams of $AgNO_3$ be used up?

    F. Add more of the reactant NaCl.

    G. Remove some of the reactant NaCl.

    H. Add even more of the reactant $AgNO_3$.

    J. There is no mechanism for using the 5 grams of $AgNO_3$.

GO ON TO THE NEXT PAGE.

39. An experimenter wishes to determine which theory better fits her data for an experiment in which iron is chemically combined with oxygen. She finds that 2 moles of iron will react completely with 2 moles of oxygen; she also finds that 2 moles of iron will react completely with 3 moles of oxygen. At this point she is confident that Theory 1, which is in opposition to the idea of "definite proportions," is correct. What further experiment might she do to test the success of Theory 1 over Theory 2?

   A. Add 1 mole of iron to 1 mole of oxygen.
   B. Add 2 moles of iron to 4 moles of oxygen.
   C. Add 3 moles of iron to 4.5 moles of oxygen.
   D. Add 4 moles of iron to 4 moles of oxygen.

40. According to Theory 1, the product of the reaction of hydrogen and oxygen:

   F. is H_2O.
   G. could be anything.
   H. must contain hydrogen and oxygen, but lacks a specific formula.
   J. has a definite proportion of hydrogen to oxygen.

END OF TEST 4
STOP! DO NOT TURN THE PAGE UNTIL TOLD TO DO SO.
DO NOT RETURN TO THE PREVIOUS TEST.

NO TEST MATERIAL ON THIS PAGE

SECTION 5: WRITING TEST (OPTIONAL)
40 Minutes—1 Essay Prompt

DIRECTIONS: You have 40 minutes to plan and write an essay. Read the prompt carefully and make sure you understand the instructions. A successful essay will have the following features: it will take a position on the issue presented in the writing prompt; it will maintain a consistent focus on the topic; it will use logical reasoning and provide supporting ideas; it will present ideas in an organized manner; and, finally, it will include clear and effective language in accordance with the conventions of standard written English. Sample essay responses begin on page 727.

Social Activism Online

With the viral nature of online information, especially through social media, many people use social media to raise awareness or express support for various causes. Often, people post articles or sign online petitions to protest injustices. Others may start online campaigns about various social causes, encouraging people to spread the information or to donate to an organization. However, some call this form of activism "slacktivism," comparing it negatively to actions that require more time, effort, and sometimes risk, such as volunteering or protesting. Opponents of online activism question whether such activities really make a difference; furthermore, they argue that it could be counterproductive because "slacktivists" feel like they've done their part without ever leaving their chairs. As more citizens address social causes online, it is important to evaluate whether online activism can generate true social engagement.

Perspective 1

Online activism does not make people truly involved in social causes because it requires minimal time or effort and does not generate concrete results. It allows participants to feel involved in issues while doing little to nothing to help people who are suffering.

Perspective 2

Online activism can be effective when it is combined with more direct forms of activism. For example, one could advertise activist organizations on social media to attract volunteers and increase donations.

Perspective 3

Supporting or advertising a cause online is a valuable way to generate support for pressing social issues. When significant amounts of people are aware of social problems, it is more likely that governments or other organizations will address them.

Essay Task

Write a unified, coherent essay in which you evaluate multiple perspectives on the issue of social activism online. In your essay be sure to:

- Analyze and evaluate perspectives given
- State and develop your own perspective
- Explain the relationship between your perspective and those given

Your perspective may be in full agreement with any of the others, in partial agreement or wholly different. Whatever the case, support your ideas with logical reasoning and detailed, persuasive examples.

END OF TEST 5
STOP! DO NOT RETURN TO ANY OTHER TEST.

Practice Test III

Outline

I. **Section 1:** English (pp. 586–600)

II. **Section 2:** Mathematics (pp. 602–621)

III. **Section 3:** Reading (pp. 622–631)

IV. **Section 4:** Science (pp. 633–644)

V. **Section 5:** Writing (Optional) (p. 646)

DIRECTIONS

Practice Test III includes five subject tests: English, Mathematics, Reading, Science, and Writing. Calculator use is permitted on the Mathematics Test only.

Cambridge offers several services for schools utilizing our practice tests. Ask your teacher whether your school has decided to send your answers to Cambridge for scoring or to score your answers at your school. If Cambridge is scoring your test, you will use a Scantron™ form provided by your teacher, or you will enter your answers online. If your school is scoring your test, you may use a Scantron™ form provided by your teacher, or you may write your answers on paper.

If you are entering your test answers on a Scantron™ form, please be sure to include the following information on the Scantron™:

Book and edition	*Victory for the ACT Test, 13th Edition*
Practice Test Number	**Practice Test III**

If you are only completing a single section of this practice test, make sure to also include the following information:

Subject	**English**, **Mathematics**, **Reading**, or **Science**
Section Number	**Section 1**, **2**, **3**, or **4**

The items in each multiple-choice test are numbered and the answer choices are lettered. The Scantron™ form has numbered rows that correspond to the items on the test. Each row contains lettered ovals to match the answer choices for each item on the test. Each numbered row has a corresponding item on the test.

For each item, first decide on the best answer choice. Then, locate the row number that corresponds to the item. Next, find the oval in that row that matches the letter of the chosen answer. Then, use a soft lead pencil to fill in the oval. DO NOT use a ballpoint pen.

Mark only one answer for each item. If you change your mind about an answer choice, thoroughly erase your first mark before marking your new answer.

Note that only responses marked on your Scantron™ form or written on your paper will be scored. Your score on each test will be based only on the number of items that are correctly answered during the time allowed for that test. You will not be penalized for guessing. Therefore, it is to your best advantage to answer every item on the test, even if you must guess.

On the Writing Test, write your response to the prompt using the essay response sheets or loose-leaf paper provided by your teacher. Your teacher might also direct you to enter your essay response online. (Note that the Writing Test is optional.)

You may work on each test only during the time allowed for that test. If you finish a test before time is called, use the time to review your answer choices or work on items about which you are uncertain. You may not return to a test on which time has already been called, and you may not preview another test. You must lay down your pencil immediately when time is called at the end of each test. You may not for any reason fill in or alter ovals for a test after time has expired for that test. Violation of these rules will result in immediate disqualification from the exam.

GO ON TO THE NEXT PAGE.

PRACTICE TEST III **1 1 1 1 1 1 1 1 1 1 1 1 1 1**

SECTION 1: ENGLISH TEST

45 Minutes—75 Items

DIRECTIONS: In the passages below, certain parts of the sentences have been underlined and numbered. In the right-hand column, you will find different ways of writing each underlined part; the original version is indicated by the "NO CHANGE" option. For each item, select the choice that best expresses the intended idea, is most acceptable in standard written English, or is most consistent with the overall tone and style of the passage.

There are also items that ask about a section of the passage or the passage as a whole. These items do not refer to an underlined portion of the passage; these items are preceded by statements that are enclosed in boxes.

Read the passage through once before you begin to answer the accompanying items. Finding the answers to certain items may depend on looking at material that appears several sentences beyond the item. So, be sure that you have read far enough ahead before you select your answer choice. Answers are on page 733.

PASSAGE I

Trade in the Northwest Territory

[1]

In 1849, San Francisco became the first official

port of entry on the Pacific Coast. In 1851, <u>on account</u>
₁

<u>of</u> the rapid growth of the lumber industry and a
₁

corresponding expansion of population in the

Northwest Territory, the government established the

Puget Sound District of the Bureau of Customs.

<u>Nonetheless,</u> smuggling grew rapidly, fostered by the
₂

tempting proximity of British havens and the natural

cover afforded by vast forested areas and by the coves

and inlets of <u>countless heavy</u> timbered islands.
₃

1. A. NO CHANGE
   B. since
   C. because of
   D. for

2. F. NO CHANGE
   G. Therefore,
   H. Consequently,
   J. On the contrary,

3. A. NO CHANGE
   B. countless, heavy
   C. countless, heavily
   D. countlessly heavy

GO ON TO THE NEXT PAGE.

[2]

Such fears were <u>well foundationed</u>. In 1851, US
                    4

customs officers <u>seize</u> the Hudson Bay Company's
                  5

steamer *Beaver* <u>for a technical violation of the revenue</u>
                                                        6

<u>laws</u>. This incident signaled an end to the era of
6

unrestricted trade in the Pacific Northwest and drove

some traders on both sides of the international border

into illicit commercial arrangements. British wool,

blankets, and liquor <u>were the principle articles</u> of this
                      7

trade. <u>In fact,</u> so much British wool was smuggled into
        8

the San Juan Islands <u>selling</u> as domestic wool by
                      9

American <u>sheepmen one</u> naive textbook writer credited
          10
San Juan sheep with a world's record annual

production of 150 pounds of wool per animal.

4. **F.** NO CHANGE
    G. well founded
    H. founded well
    J. well found

5. **A.** NO CHANGE
    B. seized
    C. were seizing
    D. have seized

6. **F.** NO CHANGE
    G. on account of violating the revenue laws
    H. for technically being in violation of the revenue laws
    J. in that they were in technical violation of the revenue laws

7. **A.** NO CHANGE
    B. was the principle article
    C. were the principal articles
    D. was the principal article

8. **F.** NO CHANGE
    G. Furthermore,
    H. Moreover,
    J. On the contrary,

9. **A.** NO CHANGE
    B. to sell
    C. and sold
    D. and would be sold

10. **F.** NO CHANGE
    G. sheepmen, one
    H. sheepmen that one
    J. sheepmen, and a

GO ON TO THE NEXT PAGE.

[3]

Although American settlers in the Northwest
11

11. A. NO CHANGE
     B. Since
     C. Therefore
     D. Thus

Territory welcomed the assertion of national control to
12

the forty-ninth parallel, they were less amenable to

restrictions on trade with Vancouver Island. They

wanted the duty-free rum and woolens offered by the

British but were fearing that the imposition and
13

enforcement of permanent tariffs on goods from British

North America might be resulting in the losing of
14

British markets for American products.

12. F. NO CHANGE
     G. welcoming
     H. would welcome
     J. were welcomed by

13. A. NO CHANGE
     B. and were fearing
     C. and was fearful
     D. but feared

14. F. NO CHANGE
     G. might result in the losing
     H. might result in the loss
     J. results in the loss

Items #15–16 ask about the preceding passage as
a whole.

15. Which of the following represents the most
     logical order of the three paragraphs?

     A. 1, 2, 3
     B. 1, 3, 2
     C. 2, 3, 1
     D. 3, 1, 2

16. Which of the following does NOT represent a
     technique used in the development of the essay?

     F. Narrative
     G. Example
     H. Statistics
     J. Quotations

GO ON TO THE NEXT PAGE.

PASSAGE II

Mapping the Cosmos

One of the beauties of astronomy <u>is that one does not have to be an expert to enjoy it</u>. Anyone can step outside on a clear, moonless night, gaze at thousands

of stars shining across the vast interstellar <u>spaces, and then one can become</u> intoxicated by a heady mix of grandeur and existential chill. The same questions come to mind time and <u>again, how</u> far away are the stars? How many are there? Are they strewn endlessly through space, or are we a part of an island universe of suns <u>ending</u> abruptly somewhere out there in the black ocean of space?

It has been the sometimes heroic and often frustrating task of astronomers since the dawn of science <u>to chart</u> our position in the cosmic ocean. In

the twentieth century, significant progress <u>had been made</u> in constructing an accurate map of the cosmos. We know, for example, that our solar system is part of a much larger system of hundreds of billions of stars.

17. A. NO CHANGE
   B. is the not having to be an expert to enjoy it
   C. is that the enjoying of it does not have to be done by an expert
   D. is that one doesn't necessarily have to be an expert in order to derive some enjoyment from it

18. F. NO CHANGE
   G. spaces—and became
   H. spaces, and become
   J. spaces and becomes

19. A. NO CHANGE
   B. again and how
   C. again how
   D. again. How

20. F. NO CHANGE
   G. that end
   H. that ends
   J. ended

21. A. NO CHANGE
   B. charting
   C. having charted
   D. who charted

22. F. NO CHANGE
   G. was made
   H. is made
   J. will be made

GO ON TO THE NEXT PAGE.

As such, this system is the Milky Way Galaxy, a huge
23

disk of stars and gas. We also know that ours is not the

only galaxy in the universe. As far as the largest

telescopes in the world can see, there are galaxies in

every direction. The nearest galaxies to our own are the
24

Magellanic Clouds; the "crown jewels" of the southern
25

skies.

    Since they are so near, they offer a laboratory in

which astronomers can study the evolution of stars and

galaxies. The nearest large galaxy to the Milky Way is

the Andromeda Galaxy, which is about two million

light years away. It is a giant spiral galaxy, much like
26

our own in size, shape, and number and type of stars.

This nearby sister galaxy provides to us an opportunity
27

to get a bird's eye view of a galaxy much like our

own—in effect, to see ourselves as others do.
28

23. **A.** NO CHANGE
    B. Obviously, this
    C. Doubtless, this
    D. This

24. **F.** NO CHANGE
    G. These
    H. (Begin a new paragraph here rather than after "skies") The
    J. (Begin a new paragraph here rather than after "skies") As the

25. **A.** NO CHANGE
    B. Clouds, the crown jewels
    C. Clouds which is the "crown jewels"
    D. Clouds, the "crown jewels"

26. **F.** NO CHANGE
    G. much as
    H. like much
    J. much the same like

27. **A.** NO CHANGE
    B. provides us
    C. provide us
    D. providing to us

28. **F.** NO CHANGE
    G. to see ourselves the way other people tend to see us
    H. so that we would be seeing ourselves the way other people would be seeing us
    J. so that in this way we would see ourselves as others do

GO ON TO THE NEXT PAGE.

Item #29 asks about the preceding passage as a whole.

29. Which of the following is NOT one of the reasons the author poses a series of questions in the first paragraph?

    A. To give the reader a sense of the "grandeur and existential chill"
    B. To stimulate the reader's interest in astronomy
    C. To give specific examples of questions about the cosmos that are still unanswered
    D. To alert the reader that answers to these questions will follow later in the passage

---

PASSAGE III

A Brief History of the Mercury Space Program

The first astronauts entered the Mercury program in April 1959. They were volunteer, military <u>pilots, graduated</u> of test pilot schools. Each <u>were required having</u> a bachelor's degree in engineering (or its equivalent) and at least 1,500 hours of jet time. Of the first group of sixty candidates called to Washington to hear about the program, more than 80 percent volunteered. Only seven <u>got</u> chosen. (Officials assumed that no more than seven men would have the

30. **F.** NO CHANGE
    G. pilots graduates
    H. pilots; graduates
    J. pilots, graduates

31. **A.** NO CHANGE
    B. was required to have
    C. required having
    D. had been required to have

32. **F.** NO CHANGE
    G. were
    H. had been
    J. has been

GO ON TO THE NEXT PAGE.

opportunity to fly.) [33] These men were true

33. Is the second use of parentheses in the first paragraph appropriate?

    A. Yes, because the information contained in the parentheses is irrelevant to the passage.

    B. Yes, because the information explains something the author said but is not vital to the understanding of the passage.

    C. No, because the material is vital to the understanding of the author's main argument.

    D. No, because an entire sentence should never be placed in parentheses.

<u>pioneers, they</u> volunteered at a time when the plans
34

for space travel were only on paper and no one knew

what the chance of success was.

34. F. NO CHANGE

    G. pioneers but

    H. pioneers yet

    J. pioneers. They

    <u>Scientists</u> were able to learn from each failure.
    35

35. Which of the following phrases would best replace the word *scientists* to provide a transition from the first to the second paragraph?

    A. It was lucky that the men volunteered because scientists

    B. There were failures as well as successes in the Mercury program, but scientists

    C. Since the chances for success were unknown, scientists

    D. Since the volunteers were also engineers, scientists

<u>Fortunately they had these failures</u> early in the
36

program. The astronauts and the animal passengers as

36. F. NO CHANGE

    G. Fortunately, they had these failures occurring

    H. These failures occurred fortunately

    J. Fortunately, these failures occurred

well were flown without mishap when <u>their time came</u>
37

<u>for them.</u>
37

37. A. NO CHANGE

    B. the time for them finally came

    C. their time finally came for them

    D. their time came

GO ON TO THE NEXT PAGE.

The most spectacular failure in the Mercury program came to be known as the "tower flight." [38] The escape tower, the parachutes, and the peroxide fuel were all deployed on the launching pad in front of the domestic and international press. A <u>relatively simple</u> ground-circuit defect in the Redstone launch vehicle caused the main rocket engine to ignite <u>and then</u> <u>shutting</u> down immediately after liftoff from the launching pad. The "flight" lasted only a second and covered a distance of only two inches. [41]

<u>One of the requirements</u> of the Mercury program

---

38. Is the use of the word *spectacular* in the first sentence of the third paragraph appropriate?

    F. Yes, because the author obviously disapproves of the Mercury program.
    G. Yes, because the author is using the word in an ironic sense.
    H. No, because the reader might be misled about the goals of the Mercury program.
    J. No, because the failure cited was caused by a simple defect.

39. **A.** NO CHANGE
    B. relative and simple
    C. relative simple
    D. simple relatively

40. **F.** NO CHANGE
    G. and then will shut
    H. and then they shut
    J. and then to shut

41. The author put the word *flight* in quotation marks because:

    A. the author believes a flight must last for many miles.
    B. there was no real flight at all.
    C. the word is a technical term used by astronauts.
    D. the word is often repeated in the passage.

42. **F.** NO CHANGE
    G. (Do NOT begin a new paragraph) One of the requirements
    H. (Do NOT begin a new paragraph) One requirement
    J. (Do NOT begin a new paragraph) A requirement

GO ON TO THE NEXT PAGE.

was that an animal <u>had to precede man into space</u>. The
₄₃

flight of Ham, the chimpanzee, was a major milestone

in the program. Again, there were some problems. The

pickup of the spacecraft was delayed, and <u>water had</u>
₄₄

<u>leaked into</u> the capsule. Ham, however, was eventually
₄₄

rescued <u>unharmed</u>.
₄₅

     Sending a man into zero gravity was among the

greatest medical experiments of all time. Fortunately,

all astronauts found the weightlessness to be no

problem. All <u>returning</u> to Earth with no medical
₄₆

difficulties whatsoever. In this area, the only question

left unanswered by the Mercury program was how long

man <u>will tolerate</u> weightlessness. It <u>seemed like,</u>
₄₇   ₄₈

however, that longer flights would require only that

43. **A.** NO CHANGE
     B. had to be the one to precede man in space
     C. was going to have to go into space before man
     D. needed to be the one to go into space before man did

44. **F.** NO CHANGE
     G. water leaked into
     H. water leaks in
     J. leaking water into

45. The best placement for the underlined portion would be:

     A. where it is now.
     B. before the word *was*.
     C. before the word *eventually*.
     D. before the word *rescued*.

46. **F.** NO CHANGE
     G. return
     H. returned
     J. will return

47. **A.** NO CHANGE
     B. will be able to tolerate
     C. was able to tolerate
     D. could tolerate

48. **F.** NO CHANGE
     G. seemed,
     H. seemed as,
     J. seemed to be,

GO ON TO THE NEXT PAGE.

astronauts <u>to have</u> suitable methods of exercise and
        49

nutrition. ⬚50

49. **A.** NO CHANGE
    B. have
    C. had had
    D. are sure to have

50. Which of the following might be an appropriate concluding sentence for the essay?

    F. Although the Mercury program had some failures, it was on the whole a successful part of the space program.
    G. Although the Mercury program had some successes, it was on the whole a failure.
    H. Many people have objected to the use of animals in testing programs.
    J. Science fiction writers have often written about space travel.

PASSAGE IV

Advances in Modern Medicine

It was not until the nineteenth century that

medicine was able, in any broad and real <u>way, to help</u>
                                            51

the suffering individual. During this century, technical

51. **A.** NO CHANGE
    B. way of help
    C. way to help
    D. way, of helping

advances aided the diagnostician <u>and also</u> the surgeon,
                                    52

and the beginnings of an understanding of the

52. **F.** NO CHANGE
    G. as well as
    H. with
    J. as opposed to

fundamental mechanisms of disease <u>had been</u>
                                    53

<u>emerging</u>. All aspects of medicine—from the research
  53

53. **A.** NO CHANGE
    B. was emerging
    C. were emerging
    D. emerged

laboratory to the operating table—<u>was enjoying</u> the
                                    54

benefits of the rigorous application of the scientific

method.

54. **F.** NO CHANGE
    G. were enjoying
    H. is enjoying
    J. enjoys

GO ON TO THE NEXT PAGE.

By the end of the nineteenth century, a person's chances were fairly good that a doctor could not only give a name to his medical complaint <u>yet probably had</u>[55] an elementary understanding of what it was and how it progressed. With somewhat more luck, the doctor could select the proper treatment <u>and he could also</u>[56] <u>mitigate</u>[56] the symptoms if not cure the disease altogether.

This transition to modern medicine depended on three important advances. First, it required an understanding of the true nature and origin of disease. Second, it required that an organized body of standard medical practice <u>be available to</u>[57] guide physicians in the diagnosis and treatment of disease. Last, <u>it presupposes</u>[58] a degree of medical technology never before available.

<u>Among the more dramatic</u>[59] nineteenth-century medical advances were those in the field of human

55. **A.** NO CHANGE
    B. but probably had
    C. consequently probably has
    D. but, probably would have

56. **F.** NO CHANGE
    G. but could mitigate
    H. and mitigate
    J. and can mitigate

57. **A.** NO CHANGE
    B. was available to
    C. is available for
    D. be available as

58. **F.** NO CHANGE
    G. it is presupposed
    H. it presupposed
    J. they presuppose

59. **A.** NO CHANGE
    B. (Do NOT begin a new paragraph) Among the more dramatic
    C. Since
    D. (Do NOT begin a new paragraph) Since

GO ON TO THE NEXT PAGE.

physiology. [60] In 1822, an obscure American army

camp surgeon practicing medicine <u>near where the</u>
₆₁

<u>Canadian frontier is</u> was transformed almost overnight
₆₁

into a specialist on the mechanism of human digestion.

The physician, William Beaumont, was called to treat

a young trapper who had been accidentally shot in the

stomach. <u>Beaumont's operating skill</u> saved the boy's life
₆₂

but the patient was left with an abnormal opening

leading to the stomach. To Beaumont's credit, he

recognized this unique opportunity to study the human

digestive <u>process, but</u> for the next 10 years he conducted
₆₃

hundreds of experiments with the reluctant cooperation

of his not-so-willing patient.

   From his experiments, Beaumont was able to

describe the physiology of digestion, demonstrating

---

60. Which of the following correctly describes the function of the first sentence of this paragraph?

   F. It introduces a topic that has nothing to do with the material discussed in the first three paragraphs.
   G. It introduces material that will contradict what was discussed in the first three paragraphs.
   H. It provides a transition that sets up a contrast to the material that came before.
   J. It provides a transition that moves from a general discussion to a more specific yet related topic.

61. A. NO CHANGE
   B. near where the Canadian frontier is,
   C. near where the Canadian frontier was
   D. near the Canadian frontier

62. F. NO CHANGE
   G. (Begin a new paragraph) Beaumont's operating skill
   H. The skill of Beaumont at operating
   J. (Begin a new paragraph) The skill of Beaumont at operating

63. A. NO CHANGE
   B. process, and
   C. process,
   D. process. But

GO ON TO THE NEXT PAGE.

the characteristics of gastric motility <u>and describe</u> the
properties of gastric juice. He determined that the
stomach contained hydrochloric acid and that it broke
down food by a chemical process and not by
maceration or putrefaction. Beaumont's pioneering
work made him a famous man. The young trapper did
not fare as well; he was forced to tour medical schools
as "the man with the window in his stomach."

64. **F.** NO CHANGE
   G. to describe
   H. that describe
   J. and describing

PASSAGE V

All About Babies

Newborn babies are not the passive creatures
most people assume <u>him to be</u>. Recent research shows

65. **A.** NO CHANGE
   B. he was
   C. them to be
   D. it is

that the newborn comes well-endowed <u>of</u> charm and
full potential for social graces. His eyes are equipped
with surprisingly good vision. Shortly after birth, he
begins to watch his mother's face, which he soon
comes to recognize. He also learns to know her voice

66. **F.** NO CHANGE
   G. for
   H. with
   J. by

and will turn toward her when he hears <u>it. This</u> is about
the time when affection begins. The infant's cry alerts

67. **A.** NO CHANGE
   B. it, this
   C. it this
   D. it

the mother and causes a biological <u>including</u> an
emotional reaction. The infant's ability to cling and

68. **F.** NO CHANGE
   G. and
   H. with
   J. but

GO ON TO THE NEXT PAGE.

cuddle communicates a pleasurable warmth to the

mother, and the infant's odor is pleasant and uniquely

its own. The newborn also smiles. The human infant,

unfortunately, is in possession of attributes that
_____ _____
69   70

are guaranteeing its attractiveness.
_____
71

69. **A.** NO CHANGE
     B. on the other hand
     C. nevertheless
     D. in fact

70. **F.** NO CHANGE
     G. possessed
     H. possesses
     J. are in possession of

71. **A.** NO CHANGE
     B. guaranteed
     C. guarantee
     D. guarantees

Although there is some argument about whether

the child sparks the development of love or whether or
                                    _____
                                    72

not a special physiological state of the mother prompts
___
72

72. **F.** NO CHANGE
     G. or whether
     H. and whether if
     J. or whether if

her to interact with the new infant. But most
                           _____
                            73

researchers agree that the newborn does mold or trigger

adult behavior. The neonate organizes the mother's

behavior by crying and by eye-to-eye contact. The

newborn is not a passive creature at all.

73. **A.** NO CHANGE
     B. infant: but most
     C. infant. Most
     D. infant, most

GO ON TO THE NEXT PAGE.

Items #74–75 ask about the preceding passage as a whole.

74. Which of the following best describes the function of the last sentence of the essay?

    F. It introduces a new topic for the reader to investigate.

    G. It contradicts everything that was said before.

    H. It reiterates the main theme of the passage.

    J. It establishes the author as an authority.

75. Which of the following best describes the overall development of the essay?

    A. A comparison and contrast using anecdotes

    B. A narrative using examples

    C. A description using statistics

    D. An argument using examples

END OF TEST 1

STOP! DO NOT TURN THE PAGE UNTIL TOLD TO DO SO.

NO TEST MATERIAL ON THIS PAGE

PRACTICE TEST **III**   **2 2 2 2 2 2 2 2 2 2 2 2**

SECTION 2: MATHEMATICS TEST
60 Minutes—60 Items

DIRECTIONS: Solve each item and choose the correct answer choice. Then, fill in the corresponding oval on the bubble sheet.

Allocate time wisely. Try to solve as many items as possible, returning to skipped items if time permits.

Calculator use is permitted on this test; however, some items are best solved without the use of a calculator.

<u>Note:</u> All of the following should be assumed, unless otherwise stated.

1. Illustrative figures are NOT necessarily drawn to scale.
2. The word *average* indicates arithmetic mean.
3. The word *line* indicates a straight line.
4. Geometric figures lie in a plane.

Answers are on page 743.

---

1. Amanda has to arrange the five shapes below in a row. How many arrangements can Amanda make if the circle cannot be placed at the beginning or end of the row?

   A.   5
   B.   24
   C.   36
   D.   72
   E.   120

2. John is now three times Pat's age. Four years from now, John will be x years old. In terms of x, how old is Pat now?

   F. $\dfrac{x+4}{3}$
   G. $3x$
   H. $x+4$
   J. $x-4$
   K. $\dfrac{x-4}{3}$

DO YOUR FIGURING HERE.

GO ON TO THE NEXT PAGE.

3. If $\frac{3}{4}$ of x is 36, then $\frac{1}{3}$ of $x = ?$

DO YOUR FIGURING HERE.

   A.   9
   B.   12
   C.   16
   D.   24
   E.   42

4. In the figure below, what is the value of $x + y$?

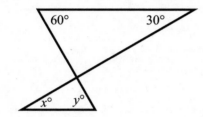

   F.   45
   G.   60
   H.   75
   J.   90
   K.   120

5. If n is a multiple of 3, which of the following expressions is also a multiple of 3?

   A. $2 + n$
   B. $2 - n$
   C. $2n - 1$
   D. $2n + 1$
   E. $2n + 3$

6. Which of the following is NOT equal to the ratio of 2 whole numbers?

   F. $\left(\frac{1}{5}\right)^2$
   G. 5%
   H. $\frac{1}{5}$
   J. 0.25
   K. $\frac{\sqrt{5}}{1}$

GO ON TO THE NEXT PAGE.

7. Nine playing cards from the same deck are placed as shown in the figure below to form a large rectangle of area 180 sq. in. What is the perimeter, in inches, of this large rectangle?

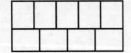

DO YOUR FIGURING HERE.

A. 29
B. 58
C. 64
D. 116
E. 210

8. A train running between two towns arrives at its destination 10 minutes late when it travels at a constant rate of 40 miles per hour and 16 minutes late when it travels at a constant rate of 30 miles per hour. What is the distance, in miles, between the two towns?

F. $8\frac{6}{7}$
G. 12
H. 192
J. 560
K. 720

9. What is the greatest factor of the expression $3x^2y^3z + 6x^3yz^3 + 2xy^2z^2$?

A. $3x^2y^2z^2$
B. $2x^2y^2z^2$
C. $x^3y^3z^3$
D. xyz
E. xz

10. Depending on the value of k, the expression $3k + 4k + 5k + 6k + 7k$ may or may not be divisible by 7. Which of the terms, when eliminated from the expression, guarantees that the resulting expression is divisible by 7 for every positive integer k?

F. $3k$
G. $4k$
H. $5k$
J. $6k$
K. $7k$

GO ON TO THE NEXT PAGE.

11. If $\dfrac{1}{3} < x < \dfrac{3}{8}$, which of the following is a possible value of x?

   A. $\dfrac{3}{16}$

   B. $\dfrac{17}{48}$

   C. $\dfrac{9}{24}$

   D. $\dfrac{5}{12}$

   E. $\dfrac{1}{2}$

12. If $x^2 - y^2 = 3$ and $x - y = 3$, then $x + y = ?$

   F. 0
   G. 1
   H. 2
   J. 3
   K. 9

13. If n is a positive integer, which of the following *must* be an even integer?

   A. $n+1$
   B. $3n+1$
   C. $3n+2$
   D. $n^2 + 1$
   E. $n^2 + n$

14. If the area of a square inscribed in a circle is 16 square centimeters, what is the area of the circle, in square centimeters?

   F. 2π
   G. 4π
   H. 8π
   J. 16π
   K. 32π

DO YOUR FIGURING HERE.

GO ON TO THE NEXT PAGE.

15. Ellen bought a CD player on sale for 25% off the usual price of $120. If the store also collected an 8% sales tax on the sale price of the CD player, how much did Ellen pay for the CD player, including sales tax?

    A. $106.30
    B. $101.40
    C. $97.20
    D. $95.10
    E. $88.44

16. A certain mixture of gravel and sand consists of 2.5 kilograms of gravel and 12.5 kilograms of sand. What percentage of the mixture, by weight, is gravel?

    F. 10%
    G. $16\frac{2}{3}\%$
    H. 20%
    J. 25%
    K. $33\frac{1}{3}\%$

17. The figure below is the top-view of a folding room divider, hinged at P and Q. If sections $\overline{PR}$ and $\overline{QS}$ are moved as shown until R and S meet, what will be the enclosed area, in square feet? (Ignore the thickness of the hinges and the screen's sections.)

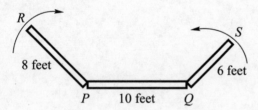

    A. 6
    B. 12
    C. 6π
    D. 24
    E. 12π

DO YOUR FIGURING HERE.

GO ON TO THE NEXT PAGE.

18. Motorcycle A averages 40 kilometers per liter of gasoline while Motorcycle B averages 50 kilometers per liter. If the cost of gasoline is $2 per liter, what will be the difference in the cost of operating the two motorcycles for 300 kilometers?

DO YOUR FIGURING HERE.

    F. $3
    G. $6
    H. $12
    J. $15
    K. $20

19. If $f(x) = x^2 - 2x + 1$, then what is $f(f(3))$?

    A. 3
    B. 9
    C. 14
    D. 27
    E. 39

20. If $N! = N(N-1)(N-2) \ldots [N-(N-1)]$, what does $\dfrac{N!}{(N-2)!}$ equal?

    F. $N^2 - N$
    G. $N^5 + N^3 - N^2 + \dfrac{N}{N^2}$
    H. $N + 1$
    J. 1
    K. 6

21. Mailing a letter costs x cents for the first ounce and y cents for every additional ounce or fraction of an ounce. What is the cost, in cents, to mail a letter weighing a whole number of ounces, w?

    A. $w(x + y)$
    B. $x(w - y)$
    C. $x(x-1) + y(w-1)$
    D. $x + wy$
    E. $x + y(w-1)$

GO ON TO THE NEXT PAGE.

22. $\left|-3\right| \cdot \left|2\right| \cdot \left|-\dfrac{1}{2}\right| + (-4) = ?$

    F. −1
    G. 0
    H. 1
    J. $\dfrac{3}{2}$
    K. 4

23. In the figure below, the area of the square *OPQR* is 2 square inches, what is the area of the circle with center *O* (in square inches)?

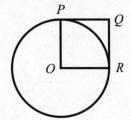

    A. $\dfrac{\pi}{4}$
    B. $\pi\sqrt{2}$
    C. 2π
    D. $2\pi\sqrt{2}$
    E. 4π

24. Which of the following *must* be an odd number?

    I.   The product of a prime number and another prime number
    II. The sum of a prime number and another prime number
    III. The product of an odd number and another odd number

    F. I only
    G. III only
    H. I and II only
    J. II and III only
    K. I, II, and III

GO ON TO THE NEXT PAGE.

25. What is the area of the shaded portion of the figure below, expressed in terms of *a* and *b*?

DO YOUR FIGURING HERE.

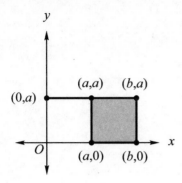

A. $a(b-a)$
B. $a(a-b)$
C. $b(a-b)$
D. $b(b-a)$
E. ab

26. $\sqrt{(43-7)(29+7)} = ?$

F. $3\sqrt{3}$
G. 6
H. 36
J. 42
K. 1,296

27. A concrete mixture contains 4 cubic yards of cement for every 20 cubic yards of grit. If a mason orders 50 cubic yards of cement, how much grit (in cubic yards) should he order if he is to use all of the cement?

A. 250
B. 200
C. 100
D. 80
E. 10

GO ON TO THE NEXT PAGE.

28. In the figure below, $\overline{QT} = \overline{QR}$. If $x = 150$, then $y = ?$

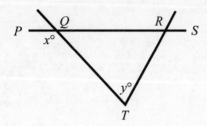

F. 30
G. 60
H. 75
J. 90
K. 120

29. If $\dfrac{x}{y} = -1$, then $x + y = ?$

A. 2
B. 1
C. 0
D. −1
E. −2

30. According to the table below, which fabric costs the LEAST per yard?

Fabric	Cost
F	3 yards for $8
G	2 yards for $6
H	4 yards for $9
J	5 yards for $7
K	8 yards for $10

F. F
G. G
H. H
J. J
K. K

DO YOUR FIGURING HERE.

GO ON TO THE NEXT PAGE.

31. In $\triangle PQR$ below, if $\overline{PQ} \parallel \overline{ST}$, then $y = ?$

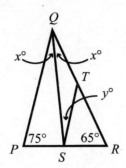

A. 20
B. 40
C. 45
D. 50
E. 55

32. $\dfrac{10^3 \left(10^5 + 10^5\right)}{10^4} = ?$

F. $2\left(10^2\right)$

G. 10^4

H. $2\left(10^4\right)$

J. 10^6

K. $2\left(10^9\right)$

33. What is the solution set for the following equation: $x^2 - 5x + 4 = 0$?

A. $\{-4, -1\}$
B. $\{-3, -1\}$
C. $\{-1, 3\}$
D. $\{1, 4\}$
E. $\{2, 3\}$

GO ON TO THE NEXT PAGE.

34. The average of seven different positive integers is 12. What is the greatest that any one integer could be?

    F. 19
    G. 31
    H. 47
    J. 54
    K. 63

35. If $x = b + 4$ and $y = b - 3$, then in terms of x and y, $b = $?

    A. $x + y - 1$
    B. $x + y + 1$
    C. $x - y - 1$
    D. $\dfrac{x + y + 1}{2}$
    E. $\dfrac{x + y - 1}{2}$

36. If $5x = 3y = z$, and x, y, and z are positive integers, all of the following must be an integer EXCEPT:

    F. $\dfrac{z}{xy}$
    G. $\dfrac{z}{5}$
    H. $\dfrac{z}{3}$
    J. $\dfrac{z}{15}$
    K. $\dfrac{x}{3}$

37. What is the width of a rectangle with an area of $48x^2$ and a length of $24x$?

    A. 2
    B. $2x$
    C. $24x$
    D. $2x^2$
    E. $3x^2$

GO ON TO THE NEXT PAGE.

DO YOUR FIGURING HERE.

38. If $x = \dfrac{1}{y+1}$ and $y \neq -1$, then $y = ?$

    F. $x+1$

    G. x

    H. $\dfrac{x+1}{x}$

    J. $\dfrac{x-1}{x}$

    K. $\dfrac{1-x}{x}$

39. In the figure below, if the area of the triangle is 54, then $x = ?$

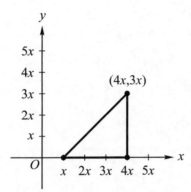

    A. $3\sqrt{3}$

    B. $2\sqrt{3}$

    C. 3

    D. 2

    E. $\sqrt{2}$

40. A drawer contains 4 green socks, 6 blue socks, and 10 white socks. If socks are pulled out of the drawer at random and not replaced, what is the minimum number of socks that must be pulled out of the drawer to *guarantee* that 2 of every color have been pulled out of the drawer?

    F. 6

    G. 7

    H. 11

    J. 12

    K. 18

GO ON TO THE NEXT PAGE.

DO YOUR FIGURING HERE.

41. In the figure below, the circle with center O has a radius that is 4 units long. If the area of the shaded region is 14π square units, what is the value of x?

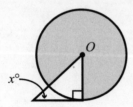

    A. 55
    B. 50
    C. 45
    D. 40
    E. 35

42. In the figure below, a circle is inscribed in a square that is in turn inscribed in a larger circle. What is the ratio of the area of the larger circle to the area of the smaller circle?

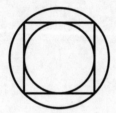

    F. $8:1$
    G. $4:1$
    H. $2\sqrt{2}:1$
    J. $2:1$
    K. $\sqrt{2}:1$

43. $2^0 + 2^3 - 2^{-2} = ?$

    A. 4
    B. $6\dfrac{1}{4}$
    C. 7
    D. $8\dfrac{3}{4}$
    E. $9\dfrac{3}{4}$

GO ON TO THE NEXT PAGE.

44. The graph of $y = x^2 - 3$ is a parabola with the axis of symmetry given by the equation $x = 0$. Which of the following are the (x, y) coordinates of the point on the parabola that is symmetric, with respect to the axis of symmetry, to the point with coordinates $(-1, -2)$?

F. $(-2, -1)$
G. $(-1, 2)$
H. $(0, -3)$
J. $(1, -2)$
K. $(1, 2)$

45. If two lines with equations $y = m_1 x + b_1$ and $y = m_2 x + b_2$ are perpendicular, which of the following *must* be true?

A. $m_1 = m_2$
B. $m_1 m_2 = 1$
C. $m_1 m_2 = -1$
D. $b_1 = b_2$
E. $b_1 b_2 = -1$

46. The figure below has lengths as marked, in units. What is the area, in square units, of the figure?

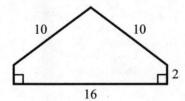

F. 36
G. 48
H. 56
J. 64
K. 80

DO YOUR FIGURING HERE.

GO ON TO THE NEXT PAGE.

DO YOUR FIGURING HERE.

47. For all $x > 0$ and $y > 0$, $\dfrac{\sqrt{x}}{2\sqrt{x} - \sqrt{y}}$ is equivalent to which of the following expressions?

A. $\dfrac{2x + \sqrt{xy}}{4x - y}$

B. $\dfrac{4x + \sqrt{xy}}{4x - y}$

C. $\dfrac{2\sqrt{x} + \sqrt{y}}{4xy}$

D. $\dfrac{2\sqrt{x} + \sqrt{xy}}{2x - y}$

E. $\dfrac{2\sqrt{x} - \sqrt{y}}{2}$

48. In the figure below, if $l_1 \parallel l_2$, then $x = ?$

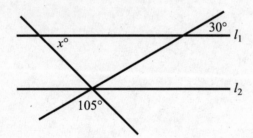

F. 20
G. 30
H. 45
J. 65
K. 130

49. The graph of $y = 2\cos(2x) + 2$ intersects the y-axis where $y = ?$

A. 0
B. 2
C. 3
D. 4
E. 5

GO ON TO THE NEXT PAGE.

50. In the figure below, *PQRS* is a square, and each of the 4 circles has a radius of *r*. What fractional part of the area of the square is shaded?

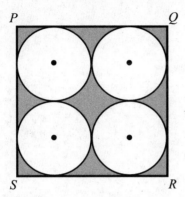

F. $\dfrac{\pi - 4}{2}$

G. $\dfrac{4 - \pi}{4}$

H. $\dfrac{\pi}{4}$

J. $\dfrac{4}{\pi}$

K. π

51. If $0° < \theta < 90°$, $\dfrac{\sin^2 \theta + \cos^2 \theta}{\sin \theta}$ is equivalent to:

A. $\sin \theta$
B. $\cos \theta$
C. $\csc \theta$
D. $\sec \theta$
E. $\cot \theta$

GO ON TO THE NEXT PAGE.

52. In the figure below, ABC is a right triangle. If $\sin 35° \approx 0.57$ and $\tan 55° \approx 1.4$, which of the following is the best approximation of the length of $\overline{AC}$?

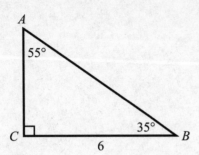

F. 3.42
G. 4.28
H. 8.57
J. 10.50
K. 12.25

53. For what value(s) of x is $\dfrac{x(x+3)}{(x-1)(x+2)}$ undefined?

A. $\{-3\}$
B. $\{-2\}$
C. $\{1\}$
D. $\{-2, 1\}$
E. $\{-3, -2, 1\}$

54. What is the maximum value of $3y$ for x and y satisfying the system of inequalities below?

$$x \geq 0$$
$$y \geq 0$$
$$x + y \leq 6$$

F. -3
G. 0
H. 6
J. 12
K. 18

DO YOUR FIGURING HERE.

GO ON TO THE NEXT PAGE.

55. Which of the following graphs correctly shows the points on the graph of $y(x) = \left| x^2 - 3 \right|$ for $x = -1, 0,$ and 1?

DO YOUR FIGURING HERE.

A.

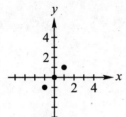

B.

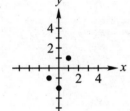

C.

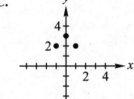

D.

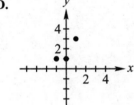

E.

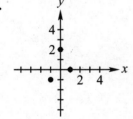

GO ON TO THE NEXT PAGE.

56. The figure below is a graph of which of the following equations?

DO YOUR FIGURING HERE.

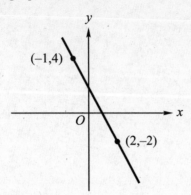

F. $y = -3x + 5$

G. $y = -2x + 2$

H. $y = -\dfrac{3}{2}x - 2$

J. $y = \dfrac{2}{3}x + 3$

K. $y = x + 2$

57. The roots of equation $ax^2 + bx + c = 0$ are $\dfrac{-3 + \sqrt{5}}{2}$ and $\dfrac{-3 - \sqrt{5}}{2}$. Which of the following could be the equation?

A. $x^2 + 3x + 1 = 0$

B. $x^2 - 3x + 1 = 0$

C. $x^2 + 3x - 1 = 0$

D. $x^2 - 3x - 1 = 0$

E. $-x^2 + 3x + 1 = 0$

58. The relation defined by the set of ordered pairs $\{(0,3), (2,1), (3,0), (-1,2), (0,5), (-2,5)\}$ is NOT a function. Deleting which of the ordered pairs will make the resulting set a function?

F. $(0,3)$

G. $(2,1)$

H. $(3,0)$

J. $(-1,2)$

K. $(-2,5)$

GO ON TO THE NEXT PAGE.

59. Trapezoid *ABCD* has lengths, in units, and angle measures as marked in the figure below. What is the area of the trapezoid *ABCD*?

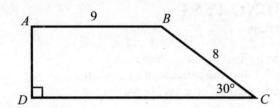

A. $18 + 8\sqrt{2}$
B. $18 + 8\sqrt{3}$
C. 42
D. $36 + 8\sqrt{2}$
E. $36 + 8\sqrt{3}$

60. What is $\tan\theta$ if $\sin\theta = \dfrac{3}{5}$ and $\cot\theta = \dfrac{4}{3}$?

F. $\dfrac{3}{4}$

G. $\dfrac{4}{5}$

H. $\dfrac{7}{8}$

J. $\dfrac{5}{3}$

K. $\dfrac{20}{9}$

DO YOUR FIGURING HERE.

END OF TEST 2
STOP! DO NOT TURN THE PAGE UNTIL TOLD TO DO SO.
DO NOT RETURN TO THE PREVIOUS TEST.

PRACTICE TEST III 3 3 3 3 3 3 3 3 3 3 3 3 3

SECTION 3: READING TEST
35 Minutes—40 Items

DIRECTIONS: Each passage below is followed by a set of items. Read each passage and choose the best answer for each item. Fill in the corresponding oval on your bubble sheet. You may refer to the passage as often as necessary to answer the items. Answers are on page 754.

Passage I

PROSE FICTION: Passage A is adapted from Henry David Thoreau's *Walden* (1854) in which the author discusses his life of solitude in the New England woods. Passage B is adapted from *Public Opinion*, published in 1922 by Walter Lippman, a noted journalist and commentator.

Passage A

I am sure that I never read any memorable news in a newspaper. If we read of one man robbed or murdered or killed by accident, or one steamboat blown up, or one mad dog killed, or one lot of
5 grasshoppers in the winter—we never need read of another. One is enough. If you are acquainted with the principle, what do you care for a myriad instances and applications? All news, as it is called, is gossip, even though many people insist on hearing it. If I should pull
10 the bell-rope of the local church to sound a fire alarm, almost everyone in the entire area would stop everything and come running, not mainly to save property from the flames but to see the blaze, especially if it were the parish church itself on fire.
15 After a night's sleep the news is as indispensable to most people as breakfast: "Pray tell me everything important that has happened anywhere on this globe." They read over coffee and rolls that a man has had his eyes gouged out the previous evening on the Wachito
20 River. There was such a rush the other day at the railway office to learn the foreign news by the last arrival, that several large squares of plate glass were broken—news that I seriously think a ready wit might have written a year or twelve years earlier with
25 surprising accuracy. As for Spain, for instance, if you know how to throw in Don Carlos and the Infanta or

Don Pedro and Seville and Granada from time to time in the right proportions—they may have changed the names a little since I last saw the papers—and serve up
30 a bull-fight when other entertainments fail, it will be true to the letter and give as good an idea of the exact state of ruin of things in Spain as the most succinct and lucid reports under this head in the newspapers. And as for England, almost the last significant scrap of news
35 from that quarter was the revolution of 1649; and if you have learned the history of her crops for an average year, you never need attend to that thing again, unless your speculations are of a merely pecuniary character. If one may judge who rarely looks into the
40 newspapers, nothing new does ever happen in foreign parts, a French revolution not excepted.

Passage B

There is an island in the ocean, where in 1914 a few Englishmen, Frenchmen, and Germans lived. The island was not served by telegraph, and the British mail
45 steamer came once every sixty days. On a day in mid-September, they learned of the start of the war and that for over six weeks those of them who were English and those of them who were French had acted as if they were friends with those of them who were Germans,
50 when in fact they were enemies.
Their plight was not so different from that of most of the population of Europe. They had been mistaken for six weeks. There was a moment when the picture of Europe on which business was conducted as
55 usual, and it did not correspond in any way to the Europe that was about to make a jumble of so many lives. All over the world as late as July 25th people were making goods that they would not be able to ship, and buying goods that they would not be able to
60 import. Then, over four years later, on a Thursday

GO ON TO THE NEXT PAGE.

morning, came the news of an armistice, and people
gave vent to their unutterable relief that the slaughter
was over. Yet, in the five days before the real armistice
came, though the end of the war had been celebrated,
65 several thousand young men died on the battlefields.

Looking back, we can see how indirectly we
know the environment in which we live. We can see
that the news of it comes to us sometimes quickly,
sometimes slowly, but whatever we believe to be a true
70 picture, we treat as if it were the environment itself. It
is harder to remember that about the beliefs upon
which we are now acting, but in respect to other
peoples and other ages, we flatter ourselves that it is
easy to see when they were in deadly earnest about
75 ludicrous pictures of the world. We insist, because of
our superior hindsight, that the world as they needed to
know it and the world as they did know it were often
two quite contradictory things. We can see, too, that
while they governed and fought, traded and reformed
80 in the world as they imagined it to be, they produced
results, or failed to produce any, in the world as it was.
They started for the Indies and found America.

1. The newspaper report that a man has had his eyes
   gouged out is included by the author of Passage A
   as an example of:

   A. a local event that affects people's lives
      directly.
   B. an insignificant incident that does not affect
      the reader.
   C. an unusual occurrence that merits special
      coverage.
   D. an international incident that warrants
      detailed description.

2. The author mentions Don Carlos and the Infanta
   in order to:

   F. demonstrate a thorough familiarity with
      current events in Spain.
   G. familiarize the reader with recent events that
      occurred in Spain.
   H. explain how events in Europe affect people
      all over the world.
   J. illustrate the point that news from Spain
      repeats itself.

3. The attitude of the author of Passage A towards
   the news is:

   A. ridicule.
   B. admiration.
   C. indifference.
   D. confidence.

4. As used in this context, "attend to" (line 37)
   means:

   F. be present at.
   G. be ignorant of.
   H. be concerned with.
   J. grow weary of.

5. The author adds "especially if it were the parish
   church" (line 14) in order to:

   A. emphasize that people are fascinated by the
      bizarre.
   B. prove that citizens do not care about public
      property.
   C. show that residents take an interest in local
      events.
   D. stress the importance of the church to
      community.

6. According to the author of Passage B, the people
   on the island "acted as if they were friends"
   (lines 48–49) because they:

   F. originally came from European countries.
   G. were isolated from the rest of the world.
   H. disagreed over the outcome of the trial.
   J. did not realize that war had started.

7. The "plight" to which the author refers in line 51
   was:

   A. incorrect reporting about the progress of the
      war.
   B. lack of accurate information about current
      conditions.
   C. an inability to obtain reports on a regular
      basis.
   D. slanted war news from the European front.

GO ON TO THE NEXT PAGE.

8. In line 82, the author implies that people of another time:

    F. accomplished something significant based upon wrong information.

    G. failed to realize that the information available was wrong.

    H. could have foreseen that America lay between Europe and India.

    J. realized only in hindsight that they had landed in America.

9. Which of the following best summarizes the different points of view of the two passages?

    A. The author of Passage B believes that news is important while the author of Passage A believes it is irrelevant.

    B. The author of Passage A believes that news is unreliable while the author of Passage B believes that it is accurate.

    C. The author of Passage A believes that newspapers provide critical information while the author of Passage B believes newspapers are too slow.

    D. The author of Passage A believes that news coverage could be improved while the author of Passage B believes that it is already adequate.

10. If the two authors had been able to write about the internet, they likely would:

    F. say that their points apply to the news content on the worldwide web.

    G. acknowledge that the new media makes reporting more relevant and more reliable.

    H. insist that newspapers remain a better source of information than electronic media.

    J. conclude that global news coverage gives readers a more accurate view of the world.

GO ON TO THE NEXT PAGE.

Passage II

SOCIAL SCIENCE: This passage discusses the regulation of corporate takeovers.

American financial markets are regulated by the federal government through the Securities and Exchange Commission and by various state agencies. In recent years, there has been considerable discussion
5 of the need for more regulation due to the increased number of corporate takeovers. Many argue that much of this activity has had harmful effects not only on stockholders but also on the economy as a whole.

Many corporate takeovers are hostile; that is, an
10 outside group or company tries to seize control of an existing company whose management opposes the takeover. Most hostile takeovers begin with a tender offer in which the outside raiders offer to buy a sufficient amount of the company's outstanding stock
15 at a stated price—usually well above the current market price. Another takeover strategy is to orchestrate a proxy battle in which a vote of shareholders of record on a specific date is taken to approve or reject a new slate of directors put forth by
20 the raiders. The raiders generally argue that the new directors will make the company more profitable and thereby enhance the value of the stock for the existing stockholders.

Regardless of the takeover strategy employed,
25 most raiders must purchase a significant portion of the company's stock at a price above its current market value. Outsiders usually finance such large purchases of stock through the sale of bonds that pay a very high rate of interest. The raiders argue that the debt to be
30 incurred can easily be paid off by selling parts of the targeted company or by drawing on the additional profits that the new management insists it can make.

In 1986 and 1987, charges emerged that individuals within Wall Street firms specializing in
35 raising capital for corporate takeovers were, in fact, selling inside information about future takeover attempts. Some of the individuals involved were sentenced to jail terms. In addition, such scandals have added to pressure on Congress and the Securities and
40 Exchange Commission to provide more effective regulation of the financial aspects of attempted corporate takeovers.

Critics of hostile corporate takeovers believe that the managers of the company to be taken over usually
45 engage in short-term activities that have very negative long-term effects. In order to avoid hostile takeovers, managers of companies generally take measures to make the takeovers less desirable. For instance, they may insert a *golden parachute clause* in employment
50 contracts. This clause requires a company to pay very large bonuses to any management members who are fired after a takeover. Another tactic, the *poison pill,* restructures the financial base of the corporation so that a takeover would make the company less profitable.
55 Yet another anti-raid tactic is to pay *greenmail* to the raiders; that is, the target of the takeover pays the raiders to sell their shares back to the targeted company at a much higher price. This prevents the takeover, but it usually adds a large sum to the company's debt.

60 Supporters of corporate raiders counter-argue that, in fact, it is the threat of a takeover that makes managers more efficient. For instance, it may cause managers to sell parts of the company that they are not managing well in order to raise the money to fend off
65 the takeover. In addition, those who believe that takeovers are good argue that the existing shareholders always do better in a hostile takeover since they end up getting a higher price for each share of stock than the current market value.

11. Which statement expresses the main idea of this passage?

   A. The government is regulating the financial aspects of corporate takeovers adequately.
   B. There has been recent debate over the need for additional government regulation of corporate takeovers.
   C. Hostile corporate takeovers are beneficial to the targeted corporation.
   D. Trading insider secrets has become a common problem in hostile corporate takeovers.

GO ON TO THE NEXT PAGE.

12. A corporation's board of directors votes to approve a new company policy. According to the plan, each member of the board and of upper management would receive severance of two to five years' pay if the new owner fired the member after a corporate takeover. This action would be considered:

    F. a poison pill.
    G. a golden parachute.
    H. greenmail.
    J. a hostile takeover.

13. What is the most important difference between a hostile and a non-hostile takeover?

    A. In a hostile takeover, stockholders must pay greenmail to the existing directors.
    B. In a non-hostile takeover, raiders sell bonds with high interest rates.
    C. In a hostile takeover, the existing management is opposed to the takeover.
    D. In a non-hostile takeover, the existing management uses golden parachutes.

14. According to the passage, which of the following parties in a hostile takeover will likely incur new debt?

    F. The raiders, because they need money to buy large blocks of stock
    G. The Securities and Exchange Commission, because it must oversee the transactions more closely
    H. The stockholders, because they must furnish additional funds
    J. The critics of hostile takeovers, because they make less money in the stock market

15. According to the passage, a poison pill strategy involves:

    A. paying the raiders high prices to buy back the company's stock from them.
    B. paying high bonuses to the members of the old management who are fired by the new management.
    C. more regulation by the Securities and Exchange Commission.
    D. restructuring the financial base of the company so that it will be less profitable or valuable to the raiders.

16. According to the passage, supporters of corporate takeovers believe that:

    F. the shareholders always lose money because a takeover profits only the raiders.
    G. fear of being targeted for a takeover makes managers more efficient.
    H. insider trading should be made legal.
    J. a proxy fight is the best way to win control.

17. According to the passage, in a proxy fight:

    A. the raiders sell bonds to buy the targeted company's stock.
    B. the raiders offer to buy stock at a higher-than-market price.
    C. insider information is traded illegally.
    D. the shareholders vote for approval or rejection of a new board of directors put forth by the raiders.

18. The management of a business recently targeted for takeover decides to sell two of its unprofitable subsidiaries to raise cash and cut expenses. Supporters of corporate takeovers would say that this action:

    F. is an example of how the greenmail strategy works.
    G. is an example of how a golden parachute strategy works.
    H. is an example of how the fear of a takeover makes managers more efficient.
    J. is an example of how the poison pill strategy works.

GO ON TO THE NEXT PAGE.

19. The Securities and Exchange Commission is a:

    A. state regulatory agency that polices financial markets.
    B. federal regulatory agency that polices financial markets.
    C. source of funding for hostile takeovers.
    D. board of business executives who promote fair business practices.

20. Some individuals working on Wall Street have been sentenced to jail terms for:

    F. attempting to greenmail other companies.
    G. forcing companies to swallow a poison pill.
    H. selling inside information about takeover attempts.
    J. agreeing to pay greenmail to corporate raiders.

GO ON TO THE NEXT PAGE.

Passage III

HUMANITIES: This passage explores the contributions of Josquin des Prez to Western music.

Until Josquin des Prez (1440–1521), Western music was liturgical, designed as an accompaniment to worship. Like the intricate gargoyles perched atop medieval cathedrals beyond sight of any human, music
5   was composed to please God before anyone else; its main theme was reverence. Emotion was there, but it was the grief of Mary standing at the foot of the Cross, the joy of the faithful hailing Christ's resurrection. Even the secular music of the Middle Ages was tied to
10   predetermined patterns that sometimes seemed to stand in the way of individual expression.

While keeping one foot firmly planted in the divine world, Josquin stepped with the other into the human world. He scored magnificent masses, but also
15   newly expressive motets such as the lament of David over his son Absalom or the *Deploration d'Ockeghem*, a dirge on the death of Ockeghem, the greatest master before Josquin. This motet was written all in black notes and was one of the most profoundly moving
20   scores of the Renaissance. Josquin was the first composer to set psalms to music. But alongside *Benedicite omnia opera Domini Domino* ("Bless the Lord, all ye works of the Lord") he put *El Grillo* ("The cricket") and *Allegez moy* ("Solace me"). Martin Luther praised
25   Josquin, for his music blends respect for tradition with a rebel's willingness to risk the horizon. What Galileo was to science, Josquin was to music. While preserving their allegiance to God, both asserted a new importance for man.

30   Why then should Josquin languish in obscurity? The answer has to do with the separation of concept from performance in music. In fine art, concept and performance are one; both the art lover and the art historian have thousands of years of paintings and
35   sculptures to study and enjoy. Similarly with literature: poetry, fiction, and criticism survive on the printed page or in manuscript for judgment and admiration by future generations. But musical notation on a page is not art, no matter how lofty or excellent the composer's
40   conception; it is, crudely put, a set of directions for making art.

Being highly symbolic, musical notation requires training before it can even be read, let alone performed. Moreover, because the musical conventions of other
45   days are not ours, translation of a Renaissance score into modern notation brings difficulties of its own. For example, the Renaissance notation of Josquin's day did not provide the tempo at which the music should be played or sung. It did not indicate all flats or sharps;
50   these were sounded in accordance with musician rules, which were capable of changing major to minor, minor to major, diatonic to chromatic sound, and thus affect melody, harmony, and musical expression. A Renaissance composition might include several parts—
55   but it did not tell which were to be sung or played, or whether instruments were to be used at all.

Thus, Renaissance notation permits many interpretations. A creative musician may give an interpretation that is a revelation. But no matter how
60   creative, few modern musicians can offer any interpretation of Renaissance music. The public need for it is small, limiting the number of musicians who can afford to learn, rehearse, and perform it. Most of those who attempt it at all are students organized in
65   *collegia musica* whose memberships have a habit of changing every semester. This prevents directors from maintaining the year-in, year-out continuity required to achieve excellence of performance. Finally, the instruments used in Renaissance times—krummhorns,
70   rauschpfeifen, shawms, sackbuts—must be specially procured.

21. The primary purpose of the passage is to:

   A. introduce the reader to Josquin and account for his relative obscurity.
   B. describe the main features of medieval music and show how Josquin changed them.
   C. place Josquin's music in an historical context and show its influence on later composers.
   D. enumerate the features of Josquin's music and supply critical commentary.

GO ON TO THE NEXT PAGE.

22. The passage contains information that would help answer all of the following items EXCEPT:

    F. What are the titles of some of Josquin's secular compositions?
    G. What are the names of some Renaissance musical instruments?
    H. Who was the greatest composer before Josquin?
    J. What are the names of some of Josquin's most famous students?

23. It can be inferred from the passage that modern musical notation has which of the following characteristics?

    I. The tempo at which a composition is to be played is indicated in the notation.
    II. Whether a note is a sharp or a flat is indicated in the notation.
    III. The notation indicates which parts of the music are to be played by which instruments.

    A. I only
    B. II only
    C. I and III only
    D. I, II, and III

24. The author would most likely agree with which of the following statements?

    F. Music is a better art form than painting or sculpture.
    G. Music can be said to exist only when it is being performed.
    H. Josquin was the greatest composer of the Middle Ages.
    J. Renaissance music is superior to music produced in modern times.

25. The passage leads most logically to a proposal to:

    A. establish more *collegia musica*.
    B. study Josquin's compositional techniques in greater detail.
    C. include Renaissance music in college studies.
    D. provide funds for musicians to study and play Josquin.

26. The author cites all of the following as reasons for Josquin's relative obscurity EXCEPT:

    F. the difficulty one encounters in attempting to read his musical notation.
    G. the inability of modern musicians to play instruments of the Renaissance.
    H. the difficulty of procuring the unusual instruments needed to play the music.
    J. the lack of public interest in Renaissance music.

27. The author's attitude toward Galileo can best be described as:

    A. admiring.
    B. critical.
    C. accepting.
    D. analytical.

28. Which of the following statements about liturgical music is consistent with the selection?

    F. It is lacking in any emotion.
    G. It is written to entertain people.
    H. It is intended to be reverential.
    J. It treats primarily nonreligious themes.

29. Which of the following is NOT an example of fine art as that term is used in the passage?

    A. A ballet
    B. A novel
    C. A poem
    D. A mural

30. Josquin des Prez is important in the history of music because he:

    F. wrote motets using only black notes.
    G. wrote only nonliturgical music.
    H. wrote both liturgical and nonliturgical music.
    J. invented new musical instruments for his music.

GO ON TO THE NEXT PAGE.

Passage IV

NATURAL SCIENCE: This passage discusses supernova explosions and their effects.

About twice every century, the light reaches us from one of the massive stars in our galaxy that blew apart millions of years ago in a supernova explosion, a type of explosion that sends massive quantities of
5   radiation and matter into space and generates shock waves that sweep through the arms of the galaxy. The shock waves heat the interstellar gas, evaporate small clouds, and compress larger ones to the point at which they collapse under their own gravity to form new
10 stars. The general picture that has been developed for the supernova explosion and its aftermath goes something like this. Throughout its evolution, a star is much like a leaky balloon; it keeps its equilibrium figure through a balance of internal pressure against the
15 tendency to collapse under its own weight. The pressure is generated by nuclear reactions in the core of the star that must continually supply energy to balance the energy that leaks out in the form of radiation. Eventually, the nuclear fuel is exhausted, and the
20 pressure drops in the core. With nothing to hold it up, the matter in the center of the star collapses inward, creating higher and higher densities and temperatures, until the nuclei and electrons are fused into a super-dense lump of matter known as a neutron star.

25   As the overlying layers rain down on the surface of the neutron star, the temperature rises until, with a blinding flash of radiation, the collapse is reversed. A thermonuclear shock wave runs through the now expanding stellar envelope, fusing lighter elements into
30 heavier ones and producing a brilliant visual outburst that can be as intense as the light of 10 billion suns. The shell of matter thrown off by the explosion plows through the surrounding gas, producing an expanding bubble of hot gas, with gas temperatures in the millions
35 of degrees. This gas will emit most of its energy at X-ray wavelengths, so it is not surprising that X-ray observatories have provided some of the most useful insights into the nature of the supernova phenomenon. More than twenty supernova remnants have now been
40 detected in X-ray studies.

Recent discoveries of meteorites with anomalous concentrations of certain isotopes indicate that a supernova might have precipitated the birth of our solar system more than four and a half billion years ago.
45 Although the cloud that collapsed to form the Sun and

the planets was composed primarily of hydrogen and helium, it also contained carbon, nitrogen, and oxygen, elements essential for life as we know it. Elements heavier than helium are manufactured deep in the
50 interior of stars and would, for the most part, remain there if it were not for the cataclysmic supernova explosions that blow giant stars apart. Additionally, supernovas produce clouds of high-energy particles called cosmic rays. These high-energy particles
55 continually bombard the Earth and are responsible for many of the genetic mutations that are the driving force of the evolution of species.

31. According to the passage, we can expect to observe a supernova in our galaxy about:

   A. twice each year.
   B. 100 times each century.
   C. once every 50 years.
   D. once every other century.

32. According to the passage, all of the following are true of supernovas EXCEPT:

   F. they are extremely bright.
   G. they are an explosion of some sort.
   H. they are emitters of large quantities of X-rays.
   J. they are caused by the collision of large galaxies.

33. The author employs which of the following to develop the first paragraph?

   A. Analogy
   B. Irony
   C. Statistics
   D. Example

GO ON TO THE NEXT PAGE.

34. It can be inferred from the passage that the meteorites mentioned by the author (line 41):

    F. contain dangerous concentrations of radioactive materials.
    G. give off large quantities of X-rays.
    H. include material not created in the normal development of our solar system.
    J. are larger than the meteorites normally found in a solar system like ours.

35. The author implies that:

    A. it is sometimes easier to detect supernovas by observation of the X-ray spectrum than by observation of visible wavelengths of light.
    B. life on Earth is endangered by its constant exposure to radiation forces that are released by a supernova.
    C. recently discovered meteorites indicate that the Earth and other planets of our solar system survived the explosion of a supernova several billion years ago.
    D. lighter elements are formed from heavier elements during a supernova as the heavier elements are torn apart.

36. According to the passage, what is the first event in the sequence that leads to the occurrence of a supernova?

    F. An ordinary star begins to emit tremendous quantities of X-rays.
    G. A superheated cloud of gas envelops a neutron star.
    H. An imbalance between light and heavy elements causes an ordinary star to collapse.
    J. An ordinary star exhausts its supply of nuclear fuel and begins to collapse.

37. According to the passage, a neutron star is:

    A. a gaseous cloud containing heavy elements.
    B. an intermediate stage between an ordinary star and a supernova.
    C. the residue that is left by a supernova.
    D. the core of an ordinary star that houses the thermonuclear reactions.

38. The author is primarily concerned with:

    F. speculating about the origins of our solar system.
    G. presenting evidence proving the existence of supernovas.
    H. discussing the nuclear reaction that occurs in the core of a star.
    J. describing a theory about the causes and effects of supernovas.

39. How long ago was our galaxy formed?

    A. 100 million years
    B. 1 billion years
    C. 2 billion years
    D. Over 4.5 billion years

40. What is the connection between supernovas and the evolution of species on Earth?

    F. There is no connection.
    G. Cosmic radiation from supernovas retards evolution.
    H. Cosmic radiation from supernovas drives evolution.
    J. Evolution makes future supernovas possible.

END OF TEST 3
STOP! DO NOT TURN THE PAGE UNTIL TOLD TO DO SO.
DO NOT RETURN TO THE PREVIOUS TEST.

NO TEST MATERIAL ON THIS PAGE

SECTION 4: SCIENCE TEST
35 Minutes—40 Items

DIRECTIONS: Each passage below is followed by several items. After reading a passage, choose the best answer for each item. Fill in the corresponding oval on your bubble sheet. You may refer to the passage as often as necessary. You are NOT permitted the use of a calculator on this test. Answers are on page 758.

Passage I

Before making their historic first powered flight, the Wright Brothers made extensive lift tests in 1901 using a glider. Their data differed from that obtained twelve years earlier by the German, Otto Lilienthal.

Results of both tests (Wright: thin line; Lilienthal: thick line) are shown below. "Lift" is the force that pulls the wing away from the earth, in a direction perpendicular to the flight path, and the "angle of incidence" is the angle that the flight path makes with the horizon.

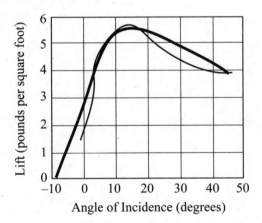

Modified from Culick, F.E.C, "The Wright 'Flyer' was the outcome of an intensive program of research." *Sci. Amer. 241* (1): 86–100, 1979.

1. The two curves differ chiefly in that:

   A. the Wrights' data were more accurate.
   B. lift was generally greater in Lilienthal's experiments.
   C. lift was generally greater in the Wrights' experiments.
   D. the peak value for lift was greater in Lilienthal's experiments.

2. In the Wrights' experiments, the greatest lift occurred at an angle of incidence of about:

   F. −5.5 degrees.
   G.   0 degrees.
   H. 14 degrees.
   J. 46 degrees.

3. At an angle of incidence of 50 degrees, by how much would you expect the two experiments to show a difference in lift?

   A. 0–1 pounds per square foot.
   B. 1–2 pounds per square foot.
   C. 2–3 pounds per square foot.
   D. 3–4 pounds per square foot.

4. The two sets of experiments differed most in lift at which of the following angles?

   F. 10 degrees
   G. 15 degrees
   H. 30 degrees
   J. 40 degrees

GO ON TO THE NEXT PAGE.

5. The widest range of angles, in degrees, over
   which the Lilienthal values for lift continuously
   exceeded the Wrights' values was:

   A. 43.
   B. 25.
   C. 19.
   D. 10.

Passage II

Two experiments were performed to determine the effects of temperature on the rate of cellular respiration* in germinating peas.

*Summary Equation:

consumed   produced

$$C_6H_{12}O_6 + 6O_2 \Rightarrow 6CO_2 + 6H_2O$$

(glucose)   (oxygen)   (carbon dioxide)   (water)

Experiment 1

A simple respirometer was used, primarily consisting of a large test tube partially filled with germinating peas. The peas were covered with a layer of cotton and a small amount of potassium hydroxide (KOH), a substance that can absorb and remove carbon dioxide from the tube. The remainder of the tube, with its starting volume of air sealed inside, was closed to the outside with a rubber stopper. Attached was a meter designed to detect and measure any changes in pressure in the tube during the experiment. The experiment was conducted at room temperature (22°C), and the respirometer was monitored for 15 minutes. At the end of 15 minutes, the pressure inside the tube had *decreased* from its starting pressure of 760 torr to 722 torr.

Experiment 2

An identical experiment was conducted at 30°C. At this temperature, the pressure inside the tube after 15 minutes had decreased from 786 torr (starting pressure) to 707 torr.

6. Separate control experiments were performed alongside Experiments 1 and 2. The control contained plastic beads (the same size as peas) instead of germinating peas. All other conditions were identical. Any decrease in pressure inside the control tube would suggest that:

   F. plastic beads utilize oxygen at approximately the same rate as germinating peas.
   G. plastic beads produce carbon dioxide at about the same rate as germinating peas.
   H. plastic beads carry out all aspects of cellular respiration at approximately the same rate as germinating peas.
   J. factors having nothing to do with cellular respiration must be responsible.

7. In both experiments, the decrease in pressure in the tube was mainly due to a change in the volume of what specific gas?

   A. Oxygen
   B. Carbon dioxide
   C. Potassium hydroxide
   D. All of the above

8. If potassium hydroxide (KOH) were not included in the tubes, what would happen to the pressure during each experiment?

   F. Final pressure would approximately be the same as starting pressure.
   G. Final pressure would be higher than starting pressure.
   H. Final pressure would decrease faster than what was observed in Experiments 1 and 2.
   J. Results would not be different from what was observed in Experiments 1 and 2.

9. Experiment 2 showed a greater decrease in pressure in the tube because:

   A. at higher temperatures, peas use oxygen slower.
   B. at higher temperatures, potassium hydroxide absorbs and removes carbon dioxide slower.
   C. at higher temperatures, peas use oxygen faster.
   D. at lower temperatures, peas use oxygen slower than they produce carbon dioxide.

GO ON TO THE NEXT PAGE.

10. An additional set of experiments with germinating peas is conducted in the dark at 22°C and 30°C. All other conditions are identical to those in Experiments 1 and 2. After 15 minutes, if the final pressure inside the tube at 22°C is 722 torr, and the final gas volume inside the tube at 30°C is 707 torr, which hypothesis best explains the results?

    F. Darkness affects cellular respiration in germinating peas the same way that a rise in temperature affects cellular respiration in germinating peas.

    G. Light/dark conditions have little or no effect on cellular respiration in germinating peas.

    H. Cellular respiration in germinating peas occurs faster in the light than in the dark.

    J. Cellular respiration in germinating peas occurs faster in the dark than in the light.

11. The summary equation in the passage shows that during cellular respiration, germinating peas must consume glucose. In Experiments 1 and 2, glucose molecules:

    A. were in the peas.
    B. were not available.
    C. were consumed at equal rates.
    D. were available but not consumed at all.

GO ON TO THE NEXT PAGE.

Passage III

Two different views of the earth's past are presented below.

Scientist 1

The history of our planet has been marked by sudden spectacular events that have no counterpart in the natural processes observed today (catastrophism). Today's valleys formed during periods of downward slippage by fragments of the earth's crust. Mountains rose due to gigantic upheavals of land during the earth's beginnings. The three major types of rock formed when one worldwide ocean precipitated out great masses of different materials during three sudden and separate events. Substances such as granite were precipitated first (today's igneous rocks), while materials in the flat upper layers precipitated last (today's sedimentary rocks). This was followed by the disappearance of much of this great ocean's water (perhaps by evaporation during years of intensive heat). Distinct assemblages of animal and plant fossils, found in successive rock layers of a region, can be explained by local catastrophic events, such as massive fires or floods. Old forms were wiped out, and eventually new forms replaced them as foreign species immigrated from other geographic areas.

Scientist 2

Processes now in operation are adequate to account for changes in the earth's past (principle of uniform change). Although today's processes seem to have negligible effects on the landscape, great changes can result from ongoing processes, if given long enough periods of time. Valleys form as flowing water cuts through the sides and bottom of the land and rock they pass across. Rocks and mountains can be formed, destroyed and reformed by processes still going on today. Volcanic activity, heat and pressure under the earth's surfaces, erosion, weathering, and even shifts and movements can lift massive areas below the land and ocean surfaces to high elevations. Different fossil types in successive layers of rocks represent the changes in form that can take place among related organisms as a result of evolutionary processes over vast periods of time.

12. One major difference between the views of Scientist 1 and Scientist 2 relates to:

   F. where fossils are found.
   G. when the processes that shaped the earth took place.
   H. the size of mountain ranges.
   J. whether water played a role in forming any of the earth's characteristics.

13. Which of the following provides the strongest evidence against Scientist 1's point about mountain formation?

   A. The beginnings of the earth are not well documented.
   B. Floods and fires have never been massive enough to eliminate fossils from all mountain areas.
   C. Volcanic activity, weathering, and erosion are believed to be less common today than in years past.
   D. Fossils of recent sea creatures can be found in rocks on mountain peaks.

GO ON TO THE NEXT PAGE.

14. Which of the following best characterizes the main difference between catastrophism and the principle of uniform change?

   F. Catastrophism maintains that violent changes in the relatively recent past shaped the earth's landscape while the principle of uniform change holds that gradual changes over an enormous span are responsible.
   G. Catastrophism predicts that sudden, violent events will soon reshape the earth's landscape while the principle of uniform change expects the landscape to remain mostly unchanged.
   H. Catastrophism theorizes that the landscape was largely shaped by cataclysmic events in the distant past while the principle of uniform change holds that the landscape is the result of a steady transformation over a long time.
   J. Catastrophism holds that relatively recent events of enormous magnitude created the landscape while the principle of uniform change holds that the landscape has remained relatively unchanged since the earth's formation.

15. According to Scientist 1, which of the major types of rocks should be found at the lowest levels?

   A. Igneous (granite)
   B. Metamorphic (marble)
   C. Sedimentary (limestone)
   D. Cannot be determined from the given information

16. According to the views of Scientist 1, the number of major rock types will most likely:

   F. remain unchanged.
   G. decrease.
   H. increase.
   J. Cannot be determined from the given information

17. To refute Scientist 2's point of view about strictly uniform processes of change, Scientist 1 could argue that:

   A. the streams of today are not measurably effective in cutting through the sides and bottoms of rock they pass across.
   B. fossils are not found everywhere today.
   C. at some early point in time, the actual formation of the earth had to involve very different processes than those now in evidence.
   D. no mountain ranges have formed in our lifetime.

18. Which argument does NOT support the views of Scientist 2?

   F. There are many regions of lava where no volcanoes are present today.
   G. There are three major types of rock that exist today.
   H. Many rivers today are flowing far below their former channels.
   J. Distinctive fossils in upper layers of rock show similarities to those in lower layers, yet they are never found in any other geographic areas.

GO ON TO THE NEXT PAGE.

Passage IV

Cold-blooded animals cannot regulate their body temperatures internally. Their body temperature varies as the environmental temperature varies. Consequently, the rates of many bodily processes also vary as outside temperatures change (as environmental temperatures increase, body temperature as well as the rates of bodily processes may also increase). Warm-blooded animals, on the other hand, can maintain their body temperatures internally. Therefore, the rates of their bodily processes can remain relatively stable when environmental temperatures change.

Experiments were set up to determine how heart rate, a bodily process, may be affected by different temperatures in two species of live laboratory animals.

Experiment 1

In this experiment, 10 individuals from Species A and 10 individuals from Species B were kept in 20 separate containers at room temperature (22°C) for 30 minutes. Their heart rates (heart beats/minute) were recorded every 10 minutes starting 10 minutes into the experiment. Average heart rates for the entire experiment were calculated for each species: Species A had an average heart rate of 150 beats/minute, while Species B averaged 100 beats/minute.

Experiment 2

Identical procedures were used to repeat the original experiment except that the containers holding the individuals of each species were placed in an incubator set at 35°C. At the end of 30 minutes, the average heart rate for both species was 148 beats/minute.

19. How many values were used to calculate the average heart beats for each species in each of these experiments?

   A. 1
   B. 10
   C. 20
   D. 30

20. Which of the following hypotheses is supported by the results of both experiments?

   F. Species A is most likely cold-blooded.
   G. Species B is most likely cold-blooded.
   H. Both species are most likely cold-blooded.
   J. Neither species is cold-blooded.

21. Which of the following statements best explains why 10 individuals of each species were used in each of the experiments?

   A. In case a few died, there would still be others available for testing.
   B. If only one individual was used, it would be lonely.
   C. An average value for 10 individuals reduces the chance of getting an extreme value based on any one individual.
   D. If only one individual was chosen from each species, it would be difficult to show differences.

22. If a third experiment were conducted at 6°C, which set of results for average heart rates (in beats/minute) is closest to what might be expected?

   F. Species A: 146; Species B: 146
   G. Species A: 50; Species B: 146
   H. Species A: 50; Species B: 50
   J. Species A: 146; Species B: 50

23. Which statement is accurate concerning Species A and Species B?

   A. At 22°C, Species A has a higher average heart rate than Species B.
   B. Species A has a larger average size than Species B.
   C. As environmental temperature increases, average heart rate increases more for Species A than Species B.
   D. As environmental temperature decreases, average heart rate increases more for Species A than Species B.

GO ON TO THE NEXT PAGE.

24. If the average body temperature for 10 individuals of each species were recorded during Experiments 1 and 2, which results would be expected?

    F. Species A: Temperature stays the same in both experiments. Species B: Temperature increases in Experiment 2.

    G. Species A: Temperature increases in Experiment 2. Species B: Temperature stays the same in both experiments.

    H. Both Species: Temperature increases in Experiment 2.

    J. Both Species: Temperature stays the same in both experiments.

Passage V

The chart below shows a set of "energy levels" that an electron in molecule X can occupy. The value of the energy in each level is shown to the right.

Energy Level	Energy Value
E_5 ------	2.07 eV
E_4 ------	1.75 eV
E_3 ------	1.52 eV
E_2 ------	1.20 eV
E_1 -------	0.60 eV

An electron can move from one level to the next (transition) in two ways:

(1) The molecule can absorb a particle of light, called a "photon," of just the right energy to lift the electron to a higher level. For example, an electron in level 4 can be raised to level 5 if the molecule absorbs a photon whose energy is 0.32 eV.

(2) The molecule can emit, or give off, a photon of just the right energy necessary to lower an electron to another level. For example, an electron in level 4 can move to level 2 if the molecule emits a photon whose energy is 0.55 eV.

25. A sample containing many X molecules absorbs light, each photon of which carries 0.60 eV. As each photon is absorbed an electron moves from:

    A. level 1 to level 2.
    B. level 2 to level 4.
    C. level 2 to level 1.
    D. level 4 to level 2.

26. A sample containing many X molecules emits light, each photon of which carries 0.32 eV. As each photon is emitted, an electron moves from:

    F. level 3 to level 2.
    G. level 2 to level 3.
    H. level 5 to level 4.
    J. level 3 to level 2 or from level 5 to level 4.

27. A sample of molecule X emits light, each photon of which carries 0.92 eV. As each photon is emitted an electron moves from:

    A. level 5 to level 2.
    B. level 1 to level 5.
    C. level 1 to level 3.
    D. level 3 to level 1.

28. Suppose that in a sample containing many X molecules, all of the electrons are in level 5. Based on the information in the chart, the sample could emit photons of how many different energies, if each emission resulted in an electron transitioning to a new level?

    F. One
    G. Two
    H. Three
    J. Four

29. Assume that each of the molecules in a sample containing many X molecules has two electrons, and those two electrons are on the same level, but the level is not known. Light is passed through the sample, and photons, each of energy 0.23 eV, are absorbed. A very short time later, photons of the same energy are emitted. It is likely that:

    A. electrons are moving from level 1 to level 2.
    B. electrons are moving from level 4 to level 3, then back again to level 4.
    C. electrons are moving from level 3 to level 4, then back again to level 3.
    D. electrons are moving from level 5 to level 4.

30. If photons whose individual energies are each 2.07 eV encounter a sample containing many X molecules, then:

    F. electrons will be promoted from level 1 to level 5.
    G. electrons will be promoted from all levels to level 5.
    H. electrons will drop from level 5 to level 1.
    J. no electron transitions will occur between levels 1 and 5.

GO ON TO THE NEXT PAGE.

Passage VI

A student performs three experiments in which a light beam passes through water and air. The "refraction angles" are the angles that the light beam makes with a line perpendicular to the surface of the water or air. In the water, this angle is called θ_1. When the beam leaves the water and passes into air, a second angle, θ_2, can be measured. Figure 1 illustrates θ_1 and θ_2.

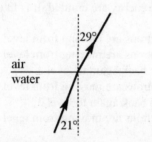

Figure 1

Experiment 1

The entry angle, θ_1, and the exit angle, θ_2, are both equal to zero.

Experiment 2

The angles observed are shown in Figure 2.

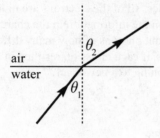

Figure 2

Experiment 3

The angles observed are shown in Figure 3.

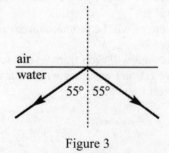

Figure 3

31. Which of the following diagrams could represent the observations of Experiment 1?

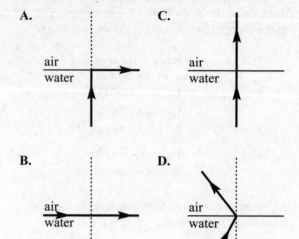

32. The student attempts to draw a conclusion from Experiments 1 and 2 that may apply to all other measurements as well. Which of the following is justified by the data?

   F. Refraction angles in water are greater than those in air.
   G. Refraction angles in water are less than those in air.
   H. Refraction angles are equal in air and in water.
   J. Refraction angles in water are equal to or less than those in air.

33. In Experiment 3, the beam travels through the water and:

   A. is reflected back down from the surface of the water.
   B. enters the air.
   C. is absorbed completely.
   D. is reflected back on itself.

GO ON TO THE NEXT PAGE.

34. An observer in the air attempts to see the beam of light in Experiments 2 and 3. She will:

   F. be able to observe the light in each experiment, provided she is in the right place.
   G. be unable to observe the light in either experiment, regardless of position.
   H. be able to observe the light in Experiment 2 but not Experiment 3.
   J. be able to observe the light in Experiment 3 but not Experiment 2.

35. A student attempts to summarize the results of all three experiments. Which of the following is most consistent with the observations?

   A. The angle of refraction in water is less than that in air.
   B. The angle of refraction in air is less than that in water.
   C. The angle of refraction in water is less than or equal to that in air, but at high angles in the water, the light is reflected back into the water.
   D. The angle of refraction in water is less than or equal to that in air.

GO ON TO THE NEXT PAGE.

Passage VII

The table below presents the results of a study in which butterflies of different size and color were captured in flight for marking with a chemical, and then recaptured in flight a few weeks later.

Size	White		Tan		Dark Brown	
	Marked	Recaptured	Marked	Recaptured	Marked	Recaptured
Small (less than 20 mm)	35	30	40	10	20	10
Medium (20–40 mm)	30	15	40	20	20	10
Large (greater than 40 mm)	50	25	60	30	30	10

36. For all sizes of butterflies, the color that seems most difficult to capture for marking is:

    F. white.
    G. tan.
    H. dark brown.
    J. Both tan and dark brown are almost equally difficult

37. The specific type of butterfly that is easiest to recapture after being marked is:

    A. between 10–20 mm and tan.
    B. greater than 40 mm and tan.
    C. greater than 40 mm and dark brown.
    D. less than 20 mm and white.

38. Based on the information in the table, which statement best represents the relationship between a butterfly's size and its tendency to be captured for marking?

    F. The larger the butterfly, the harder it is to be captured for marking.
    G. The larger the butterfly, the easier it is to be captured for marking.
    H. Medium-sized butterflies are consistently the easiest to capture for marking.
    J. The smaller the butterfly, the easier it is to be captured for marking.

39. The chemical used to mark all the butterflies was found to be poisonous to one specific type because it was being absorbed through the wings. Based on the data in the table, which type of butterfly appears most likely to have suffered from the effects of the marking chemical?

    A. Greater than 40 mm and white
    B. Less than 20 mm and tan
    C. Greater than 40 mm and dark brown
    D. Less than 20 mm and white

40. Which conclusion is correct concerning the information in the table?

    F. For tan butterflies, the proportion of individuals that are recaptured always stays the same.
    G. For medium-sized butterflies, the proportion of individuals that are recaptured always stays the same.
    H. For small-sized butterflies, the proportion of individuals recaptured always stays the same.
    J. For all sizes of butterflies, the darker the color the easier it is to recapture an individual.

END OF TEST 4
STOP! DO NOT TURN THE PAGE UNTIL TOLD TO DO SO.
DO NOT RETURN TO THE PREVIOUS TEST.

NO TEST MATERIAL ON THIS PAGE

PRACTICE TEST III **5 5 5 5 5 5 5 5 5 5 5 5 5**

SECTION 5: WRITING TEST (OPTIONAL)
40 Minutes—1 Essay Prompt

DIRECTIONS: You have 40 minutes to plan and write an essay. Read the prompt carefully and make sure you understand the instructions. A successful essay will have the following features: it will take a position on the issue presented in the writing prompt; it will maintain a consistent focus on the topic; it will use logical reasoning and provide supporting ideas; it will present ideas in an organized manner; and, finally, it will include clear and effective language in accordance with the conventions of standard written English. Sample essay responses begin on page 762.

Online Voting Systems

Homes, schools, libraries, and churches all have Internet access. With the broad availability of Internet access, the problem of voter turnout can be addressed and effectively solved. In America's last national election, less than 40% of the eligible voters cast ballots. Internet access can be used to theoretically double voter turnout and maybe even increase it to 100%. The technology exists to allow each American to register and vote from a computer terminal of his or her choosing. Such a move would certainly increase democratic voice and popular participation in our elections, but would it lead to more voters who are uninformed about candidates and issues? It is important to address this controversy, as future generations of voters will be increasingly technology-oriented.

Perspective 1	Perspective 2	Perspective 3
Informed voters are the heart of democracy. Simply providing mechanical solutions that add quantity to the voter turnout would not necessarily lead to an educated electorate to shape our future.	This type of voting system is risky because it will be difficult to determine who will monitor the electronic machines that are used. We cannot trust the security systems to protect our most precious right when these very same systems regularly fail to protect our credit cards.	Voter turnout is supremely important to a democracy. A country needs the participation of its citizens to realize its fondest hopes and dreams. We need to get more people to vote to help America reach its potential.

Essay Task

Write a unified, coherent essay in which you evaluate multiple perspectives on the issue of online voting systems. In your essay be sure to:

- Analyze and evaluate perspectives given
- State and develop your own perspective
- Explain the relationship between your perspective and those given

Your perspective may be in full agreement with any of the others, in partial agreement, or wholly different. Whatever the case, support your ideas with logical reasoning and detailed, persuasive examples.

END OF TEST 5
STOP! DO NOT RETURN TO ANY OTHER TEST.

Post-Assessment

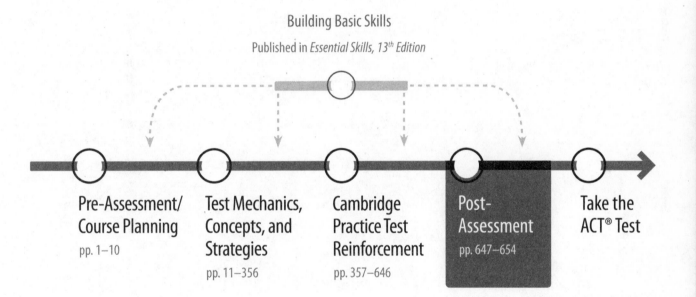

Building Basic Skills

Published in *Essential Skills, 13th Edition*

Pre-Assessment/
Course Planning

pp. 1–10

Test Mechanics,
Concepts, and
Strategies

pp. 11–356

Cambridge
Practice Test
Reinforcement

pp. 357–646

Post-
Assessment

pp. 647–654

Take the
ACT® Test

CAMBRIDGE
VICTORY FOR THE
ACT® TEST

POST-ASSESSMENT

ADMINISTRATION

At the end of the course, you will take a post-assessment. This post-assessment consists of an ACT, Inc. ACT practice exam. When you take the post-assessment, you should bring the following items to the classroom, in addition to anything else your teacher instructs you to bring:

1. Sharpened, soft-lead No. 2 pencils

2. A calculator that is approved for use on the test. This includes any four-function, scientific, or graphing calculator, except for the following:

   - Devices with built-in computer algebra systems

   - Pocket organizers or PDAs

   - Handheld, laptop, or tablet computers

   - Electronic writing pad or pen-input devices

   - Calculators built into any electronic communication device, such as a cell phone

   - Models with a QWERTY (typewriter) keypad (Calculators with letters on the keys are permitted as long as the keys are not arranged in a QWERTY keypad.)

   You may use the following types of calculators if you make appropriate modifications:

   - Calculators that can hold programs or documents—remove all documents and remove all programs that have computer algebra system functionality

   - Models with paper tape: the paper must be removed.

   - Models that make noise: the sound feature must be turned off.

   - Models that have an infrared data port: the port must be covered with duct tape, electrician's tape, or another heavy, opaque material.

   - Models that have a power cord: the power cord must be removed.

   (For more detailed information on calculator usage, go to www.actstudent.org/faq/calculator.html.)

3. A watch (to pace yourself as you work through each test section)

HOW TO USE THE POST-ASSESSMENT REPORTS

You will receive the results of your post-assessment in the form of Student Summary and Student Item Analysis reports approximately six days after taking the test. These reports provide details about your performance and will help you to determine where to focus your efforts from now until your test date by targeting those skills, concepts, and strategies that will help you to improve in your areas of weakness. Just as you did with the pre-assessment, review the details of the sample reports on pages 5–6 of this book so that you are familiar with their contents.

Once you have received your post-assessment reports, you can develop a Personal Action Plan. Make connections between the reports and the specific skills, concepts, and strategies that you need to study, then complete the "to do" list on the following page.

TOPIC	START DATE	DATE TO BE COMPLETED	DATE COMPLETED

PLANNING FOR FURTHER STUDY

You have received the results of your post-assessment. You have finished the Cambridge *Victory for the ACT® Test* program. Now what?

In most cases you will have some spare time before the test day, so planning a study schedule for the time between the post-assessment and the real test is critical to reinforce and maintain the skills, concepts, and strategies that you have learned throughout the course. Below are three steps that will help you make the most of your time.

Take the Practice Tests

Most students grasp knowledge of the subjects, but many struggle with time management. If you have not yet done so, take Practice Tests I–III (pp. 461–646) included in the Cambridge Practice Test Reinforcement part of this book. These practice tests:

1. reinforce skills and strategies,

2. simulate the experience of the real test by using time restrictions to emphasize time management, and

3. are an excellent guide to targeting your study plan.

Create a Written Study Plan

Use the results of your post-assessment and the Practice Tests to determine a day-by-day schedule that will give you a clear and dependable guide for study. Create this plan based on the amount of time you have before the test day.

Several weeks before test day:

- Plan to review all material equally.

- As the test date approaches, devote your time to any particular areas of weakness.

Remember: picking a few subjects to focus on each week will help you manage your time between now and the test.

A few days before test day:

- Focus on core subjects that are giving you difficulty, or areas in which you would like to improve.

- Divide your time proportionally among these subjects based on your assessment of their difficulty.

Determine the topics you will study each day and allot the proper amount of time to study those sections of the book and complete relevant exercises.

Stick to the Plan

Once you have determined your rubric for study, stick to it without fail. Such discipline will surely reward you on the day of the test. Follow these helpful hints:

- Ask your teacher for insight. He or she can help you set goals for each core subject and may be able to suggest further strategies or a re-allotment of your time.

- Do not study too much. An hour or two of studying each day will be more productive than a severe study schedule.

- Practice every day.

Appendix A:
Answers and Explanations

Building Basic Skills

Published in *Essential Skills, 13th Edition*

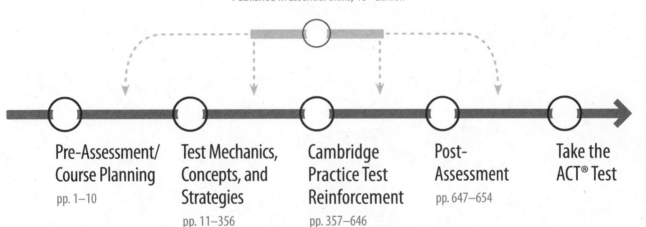

Pre-Assessment/
Course Planning

pp. 1–10

Test Mechanics,
Concepts, and
Strategies

pp. 11–356

Cambridge
Practice Test
Reinforcement

pp. 357–646

Post-
Assessment

pp. 647–654

Take the
ACT® Test

ENGLISH

Lesson (p. 25)

1. A	22. F	43. A	64. K	85. A	106. G	127. G
2. G	23. E	44. K	65. A	86. K	107. B	128. C
3. B	24. H	45. D	66. H	87. B	108. J	129. G
4. H	25. E	46. H	67. B	88. H	109. B	130. E
5. D	26. J	47. C	68. H	89. A	110. J	131. J
6. G	27. A	48. H	69. E	90. H	111. A	132. B
7. C	28. G	49. D	70. J	91. B	112. H	133. J
8. H	29. A	50. H	71. B	92. H	113. A	134. B
9. B	30. J	51. A	72. G	93. E	114. K	135. F
10. F	31. B	52. F	73. D	94. K	115. *	136. B
11. A	32. J	53. D	74. H	95. B	116. D	137. F
12. K	33. A	54. F	75. A	96. H	117. J	138. D
13. E	34. J	55. A	76. H	97. D	118. D	139. H
14. F	35. D	56. G	77. C	98. K	119. G	140. A
15. D	36. G	57. C	78. K	99. D	120. B	141. F
16. G	37. D	58. G	79. B	100. G	121. F	142. B
17. D	38. J	59. C	80. H	101. A	122. B	143. J
18. H	39. B	60. H	81. B	102. F	123. J	144. D
19. C	40. F	61. B	82. K	103. B	124. A	145. H
20. J	41. B	62. K	83. E	104. J	125. F	
21. C	42. G	63. B	84. K	105. C	126. B	

*115. On Monday, Mark received a letter of acceptance from State College. He immediately called his mother—herself a graduate of State College—to tell her about his acceptance. When he told her he had also been awarded a scholarship, she was very excited. After hanging up, Mark's mother decided to throw a surprise party for Mark. She telephoned his brother, his sister, and several of his friends. Because the party was supposed to be a surprise, she made them all promise not to say anything to Mark. Mark, however, had a similar idea: a party for his mother to celebrate his acceptance at her alma mater. He telephoned his brother, his sister, and several of his parents' friends to invite them to a party at his house on Saturday night, and he made them all promise to say nothing to his mother. On Saturday night, both Mark and his mother were surprised.

Quizzes (p. 47)

Quiz I		Quiz II		Quiz III		Quiz IV
1. B	17. B	1. D	17. D	1. B	17. C	1. C
2. F	18. H	2. F	18. F	2. H	18. J	2. J
3. B	19. C	3. D	19. C	3. B	19. C	3. E
4. F	20. J	4. J	20. G	4. F	20. F	4. H
5. C	21. C	5. C	21. A	5. C	21. A	5. D
6. F	22. F	6. F	22. J	6. F	22. G	6. J
7. D	23. A	7. B	23. B	7. C	23. A	7. D
8. J	24. G	8. G	24. H	8. H	24. G	8. H
9. A	25. B	9. A	25. D	9. D	25. A	9. C
10. J	26. H	10. F	26. H	10. J	26. H	10. G
11. C	27. D	11. B	27. D	11. C	27. C	11. E
12. J	28. G	12. F	28. F	12. G	28. J	12. F
13. B	29. C	13. B	29. B	13. A	29. A	13. B
14. H	30. G	14. G		14. F	30. G	14. G
15. A	31. B	15. D		15. C	31. B	15. D
16. J	32. H	16. F		16. J		16. F
						17. D
						18. H
						19. D
						20. K

Review (p. 69)

1. A	8. F	15. A	22. G	29. B	36. G	43. C
2. J	9. D	16. G	23. B	30. H	37. C	44. H
3. B	10. H	17. B	24. J	31. B	38. G	45. A
4. H	11. A	18. G	25. A	32. H	39. A	46. F
5. A	12. F	19. D	26. H	33. A	40. F	47. B
6. F	13. A	20. G	27. A	34. G	41. A	48. H
7. A	14. J	21. D	28. F	35. D	42. H	

READING

Lesson (p. 97)

1. C	23. A	45. D	67. D	89. B	111. C	133. B
2. F	24. G	46. F	68. J	90. F	112. G	134. H
3. A	25. A	47. C	69. C	91. D	113. C	135. D
4. J	26. F	48. H	70. G	92. J	114. H	136. F
5. B	27. A	49. A	71. D	93. C	115. B	137. A
6. J	28. H	50. J	72. F	94. G	116. J	138. J
7. C	29. C	51. B	73. B	95. D	117. B	139. A
8. H	30. F	52. G	74. H	96. F	118. J	140. J
9. D	31. A	53. C	75. A	97. B	119. D	141. C
10. J	32. G	54. G	76. J	98. J	120. H	142. G
11. A	33. D	55. B	77. C	99. B	121. D	143. B
12. J	34. G	56. H	78. J	100. F	122. H	144. G
13. A	35. D	57. D	79. D	101. D	123. B	145. D
14. H	36. J	58. H	80. F	102. G	124. J	146. G
15. C	37. C	59. A	81. D	103. A	125. C	147. C
16. G	38. J	60. H	82. H	104. F	126. H	148. H
17. D	39. A	61. D	83. A	105. B	127. B	
18. F	40. F	62. G	84. H	106. J	128. J	
19. D	41. B	63. A	85. C	107. B	129. C	
20. H	42. F	64. J	86. G	108. J	130. F	
21. B	43. D	65. C	87. B	109. C	131. D	
22. G	44. J	66. F	88. G	110. H	132. H	

Quizzes (p. 131)

Quiz I	Quiz II	Quiz III	Quiz IV	
1. A	**1.** B	**1.** A	**1.** D	**19.** A
2. H	**2.** G	**2.** J	**2.** J	**20.** F
3. A	**3.** B	**3.** C	**3.** C	**21.** A
4. G	**4.** F	**4.** G	**4.** J	**22.** H
5. A	**5.** D	**5.** C	**5.** A	**23.** B
6. H	**6.** H	**6.** G	**6.** G	**24.** G
7. D	**7.** A	**7.** B	**7.** D	**25.** A
8. J	**8.** F	**8.** J	**8.** H	**26.** F
9. B	**9.** C	**9.** D	**9.** A	**27.** B
10. J	**10.** G	**10.** J	**10.** H	**28.** F
11. D	**11.** D	**11.** D	**11.** A	**29.** D
12. F	**12.** G	**12.** H	**12.** F	
13. D	**13.** B	**13.** D	**13.** D	
14. H	**14.** H	**14.** H	**14.** J	
15. D	**15.** A	**15.** A	**15.** A	
16. H	**16.** J	**16.** G	**16.** G	
17. C	**17.** C	**17.** B	**17.** C	
18. G		**18.** G	**18.** F	

Review (p. 153)

1. D	**8.** J	**15.** B	**22.** J	**29.** C	**36.** H	**43.** D
2. G	**9.** B	**16.** F	**23.** C	**30.** J	**37.** D	**44.** H
3. C	**10.** J	**17.** C	**24.** G	**31.** A	**38.** G	**45.** D
4. J	**11.** B	**18.** G	**25.** C	**32.** J	**39.** B	**46.** F
5. A	**12.** F	**19.** D	**26.** J	**33.** D	**40.** F	
6. F	**13.** C	**20.** F	**27.** A	**34.** F	**41.** B	
7. C	**14.** F	**21.** D	**28.** J	**35.** D	**42.** H	

WRITING

Lesson (p. 177)

Sample Essay Outline

I. Introduction

    A. My three supporting arguments relate to technology making it easier and faster to communicate, lack of meaningful content in quick, impersonal communication, and the need to use technology with care.

    B. Thesis statement: Technological advances have opened many possibilities for communication and are professionally and socially indispensable in today's world; however, one must use this technology wisely in order to build meaningful relationships.

II. Online communication has revolutionized professional and personal interactions, and it is essential for maintaining relationships in today's globalized society.

    A. Ease of communication for personal and business purposes

    B. You can keep in contact with people if you have to move

    C. You can learn about a greater diversity of people and places

III. There are some potential drawbacks of online communication.

    A. Since information is shared so quickly, there is a greater chance that it might not be accurate or express complex viewpoints

    B. In the workplace, close relationships are important for some tasks

IV. One can benefit the most from online communication by using it cautiously.

    A. Verify online information with other sources

    B. Use forms of technology that require closer communication, such as video chatting

V. Conclusion

    A. Restatement of thesis: To avoid the risks of online communication, one must assess the value of the information received and use technologies that allow for more personal interaction.

Sample Essay—Above Average Response

Thanks to online communication, you can share news, conduct meetings, or make friends across the globe. Technologies such as email and video chats allow you to contact others instantaneously and cheaply. However, some argue that the low cost of online communication isn't the only thing that's "cheapened" by the use of these technologies. When online interactions are quick and easy, they can lack deep and meaningful information and be insufficient to build relationships. Technological advances have opened many possibilities for communication and are professionally and socially indispensable in today's world; however, one must use this technology wisely in order to build meaningful relationships.

Online communication has revolutionized professional and personal interactions in the twenty-first century, and in today's increasingly globalized society, it is essential for maintaining relationships. As Perspective 3 states, communication has become instantaneous. Instead of waiting days or paying expensive phone bills to reach colleagues and friends abroad, businesses can hold online meetings between London and New York, and you can chat with a friend on another continent. Moving to another country or even another state used to isolate you from the people you had met, but now, it is possible to stay in close contact with people you cannot see on a regular basis. Furthermore, even if you never leave your hometown, you can be exposed to a diverse array of cultures and opinions across the globe.

Although technology has had a positive impact on the ease of communication, it comes with some potential dangers. For example, when information or opinions can be shared instantaneously, there is a temptation to post information without thoroughly checking for accuracy or developing a nuanced viewpoint. This leads to what Perspective 1 calls "fast food" information that is "empty of real depth." Additionally, it is harder to build significant, lasting relationships with people you only meet online. In a professional context, weak relationships could cause problems when one needs to negotiate with colleagues abroad. And while social networking allows one to have a wide range of personal contacts, commenting on someone's post or browsing through a friend's online photos does not require direct contact.

One can optimize the benefits of online communication by using it cautiously. For example, instead of reading news updates on social media and believing them at face value, one should verify the information with other sources. Furthermore, the type of technology that one uses can make a huge difference in the quality of communication. As Perspective 2 argues, "We have a need for closer contact with the people we know." Some technologies, such as video chats, facilitate closer communication. While talking to someone important, such as a colleague or a close friend, it is better to use this type of technology, rather than relying on instant messaging or social media.

Technology has made it easier to maintain communication that is crucial for conducting business and establishing relationships. However, reliance on these instantaneous interactions can compromise the accuracy of information shared, as well as the depth of one's relationships. To avoid these risks, one must assess the value of the information received and use technologies that allow for more personal interaction. And if it is possible, one should make an effort to see friends in person from time to time.

Sample Essay—Below Average Response

I agree with the third perspective that online communication is a positive change. You can read information from all over the world and keep in touch with family and friends who live far away. Some people argue that online communication is not real communication, I disagree.

When my family and I moved to another state, I was afraid that I would lose touch with all of my friends from home. However, thanks to email, and Facebook, we have stayed in contact. I think the smartphone is the most important piece of technology for staying connected with other people because you can take it with you everywhere. No matter where I am. I can text my friends, send them photos through Instagram, or see what their up to on social media. I know that commenting one someone's Twitter post isn't enough to stay friends with them, but for people who I really care about, I can always message them directly or video chat with them. The video chat makes it very easy to have a conversation.

Online communication also makes it easier to get information from all over the world. For example, if you need to do business with people from another country, you can contact them right away instead of waiting several days for a response. It's also easier to learn about global topics because there's so much information on the internet.

It's true that I would feel lonely, as perspective 2 says, if I only talked to people online. However, online communication makes it easier to talk to people who I can't see face to face.

Quizzes (p. 179)

Quiz I

Sample Essay—Above Average Response

With fuel to heat our homes and run our cars, our need for fossil fuels will not disappear any time soon. However, because of the environmental risks involved, fracking should be undertaken with caution, and the long-term focus should be on renewable energy sources. The methods used through fracking to extract natural gas could cause environmental problems, such as pollution or even earthquakes. Companies, therefore, should be required to follow strict environmental and safety regulations and to cooperate with nearby communities. Furthermore, fracking should not detract from long-term goals of developing renewable energy sources.

Although the debate is controversial, critics of fracking argue that it causes serious environmental problems, such as air and water pollution and instability of the earth's crust. The process of fracking involves drilling at least a few thousand feet below the earth's surface, as well as drilling horizontally. A combination of water and chemicals is poured down the drill at an extremely high pressure, which fractures shale rocks and releases natural gas. Studies in communities near fracking sites reported higher amounts of methane in well water, which could endanger the local population. Critics also argue that because fracking wells run thousands of feet deeper than wells for more traditional methods of natural gas extraction, fracking could destabilize the earth's crust and cause earthquakes.

However, because renewable energy sources are not sufficiently developed to replace fossil fuel consumption, it is important to find additional sources of fossil fuels. Fracking, therefore, should be undertaken with caution. Governmental agencies should regulate which chemicals can be used during fracking and should require companies to construct wells in ways that would minimize the risk of natural gas leakage. Additionally, companies should be required to drill at a safe distance from surrounding communities, to eliminate health risks involved with fracking. Although fracking could bring many economic benefits, especially greater energy independence for the US, the process should not jeopardize local ecosystems and the health of surrounding communities.

Furthermore, fracking is not a permanent solution because it extracts a nonrenewable resource. It should not compromise efforts to develop renewable sources of energy. Although developing equipment and researching safe methods for fracking will be an extremely expensive endeavor, it should not cripple government and private funding for development of other sources of energy, such as wind or solar energy. Renewable energy sources will have a greater long-term impact on energy independence and will be safer for the environment than fracking.

Despite the environmental problems that it can cause, fracking is currently a necessary risk, until renewable energy resources are more developed and widely available. However, companies should be required to follow strict regulations to minimize risks for the surrounding communities. Economic gains from fracking should not come at the expense of environmental and health disasters.

Sample Essay—Below Average Response

Fracking can be a dangerous process, causing pollution and other environmental problems. It can even cause health issues for people who live nearby. However, we use fossil fuels for so many things, like heating and driving, so we have no choice but to do it.

People who argue against fracking argue that it causes environmental problems. For example, if the well used for drilling isn't built correctly, gas and chemicals could leak out and pollute the surrounding community. I even heard that it could cause earthquakes because you have to dig so deeply underground.

These environmental problems can be harmful for the surrounding communities. Water pollution can kill animals that live nearby and can also cause health problems for humans. Wouldn't want to live in a community that was harmed by fracking. Just look at past oil spills to see how much damage drilling can do. For example, the Gulf of Mexico oil spill in 2010 killed workers, destroyed local ecosystems, and is still contaminating the water.

However, the reality is that we still need fossil fuels, so fracking might be a good thing. Communities might need to move away from fracking cites if they're unsafe, and unfortunately, our energy needs make us cause environmental problems.

Quiz II

Sample Essay—Above Average Response

With educational games on computers and tablets, technology can enhance students' learning experiences in Pre-K classrooms. Pre-K programs should foster a balance between technology-based and technology-free learning to develop different forms of creativity in children. Computer-based learning can make academic concepts fun for students and can make technology use intuitive for them, and technology in the classroom can be made more affordable through grants and educational discounts. However, it is important that they learn to appreciate other forms of entertainment and learning.

Learning basic concepts such as numbers and the alphabet may frustrate or bore children, but computer programs can make this process seem like a game. While parents may complain about their children's addiction to video games, educational games can harness the addicting nature of technology for a useful purpose. As Perspective 2 argues, when students are engaged with the graphics, characters, or story of a computer game, learning will seem like play, rather than a chore. Furthermore, computer games can be easily adapted to students' abilities, which can help teachers with a range of skill levels in the class. As a child, I enjoyed learning independently with computer games, which stimulated my curiosity and love of learning. Games helped me work with numbers and learn new words, and when I was a little older, they also introduced me to different historical periods and parts of the world.

In addition to engaging children in academic subjects, computer programs teach students another important skill: the use of technology. While I disagree with the idea of preparing four-year-olds for the workplace, as Perspective 3 mentions, children may have an educational disadvantage if they enter elementary school without basic technological skills. At the Pre-K level, it is more likely for technology use to become intuitive and habitual for children. One objection to technology in the classroom is its price, as Perspective 1 argues, but schools may be eligible for government grants, and companies often offer educational discounts for computers and software. Although technology changes rapidly, schools could invest in versatile devices such as desktops, laptops, or tablets that are still useful even if one does not own the latest version.

However, I also think preschools should give children time away from technology so that they do not become dependent on it for entertainment or creative stimulation. I have seen children who become bored or even angry when they do not have access to laptops or tablets. Although the addicting nature of computer games can be used to promote learning, children must also be able to put down their games and focus on other activities. Technology may stimulate children's minds, but it is important for their physical health to exercise and play outside, and they should also be offered more hands-on creative activities, such as art projects.

If used in moderation, technology can expand students' educational opportunities and make them excited about concepts such as numbers and letters. If schools have access to funding, the skills that students gain can outweigh the cost of computers. However, it is important to remember that technology can be "too much of a good thing" and that students must learn to function without it.

Sample Essay—Below Average Response

Technology has no place in pre-K classrooms. Children this young cannot use technology properly, and they will only break expensive products like computers and tablets. Technology actually might harm children's development. It can stifle kids creativity and individuality and makes them greedier and unable to work in groups.

I agree with Perspective 1 I think that the biggest reason not to use technology in the classroom is that it's too expensive and can brake easily. A desktop costs hundreds of dollars, and even though tablets are a little cheaper, they still cost at least $100. Kids are too young to appreciate how expensive these things are and can't learn to use them properly. Since it's impossible for a teacher to supervise so many students at once, kids might misuse and damage the technology, and it would be really expensive to repair or replace it.

Perspectives 2 and 3 argue that technology is good for making kids learn, but I think that it can actually make kids less creative. It might help them learn a certain skill, like counting, but it can stop kids from thinking for themselves. They depend on computers to create games for them, instead of using their imaginations and thinking of their own games.

I also think that technology is bad for kids' social skills. Instead of playing games with others, they are all alone on a computer game. They don't learn important skills like sharing and how to act in groups. This could make kids more materialistic they take technology for granted and expect their parents to buy them these expensive things.

Although I see how technology can be helpful in the classroom, I think it's better for older kids. Pre-K students are too young to use technology properly and should focus instead on building their creativity and social skills.

Quiz III

Sample Essay—Above Average Response

A quick glance at an online forum or a website's comment section reveals the offensive, and often abusive language that is sometimes used online. Website moderators should be allowed to monitor commenters' language on their sites, and threatening comments that would have legal repercussions in real life should have legal consequences online. Eliminating profanity and threatening speech would allow the website to foster respectable dialogue and would provide its writers with a safe space to express their opinions. Furthermore, by taking online threats as seriously as "real life" threats, law enforcement could prevent serious crimes.

Although one may argue that filtering offensive language is an attack on free speech online, forcing people to speak respectfully would actually help build constructive debate. I agree with Perspective 1 that filtering language is a slippery slope and should not lead to narrowing of opinions expressed online. However, there is a difference between censoring ideas and setting guidelines for how they are expressed. A website, for example, could set up a program that blocks posts with certain profane words. This would allow for debate without regressing to obscenity. I am not arguing for a universal ban on profanity on the Internet, but I think that individual websites should have the discretion to monitor their users' language. Just as print media have the right to choose whether to print letters to the editor, online media should have the right to choose what appears on their websites.

Furthermore, abusive language online could actually curb writers' freedom of speech. As Perspective 2 argues, writers could be intimidated into silence by threats from commenters, which would stifle certain viewpoints and limit the diversity of writers. For example, recent articles about online harassment have reported that many female bloggers quit writing because of sexual harassment and even death threats from their readers. Also, as said in Perspective 3, the anonymity of posting online may allow commenters to speak more offensively than they would in person. Certain websites should be safe spaces where writers can share a variety of ideas without worrying about threats. In "real life," free speech does not allow for bullying and harassment, and these behaviors should not be protected online.

Finally, people's language should be held to the same legal standards online as it would be in personal interactions. If writers receive violent threats, those threats should be investigated. I also think that, in general, police should investigate threats that Internet users make on platforms such as forums or social media because such investigations should prevent violent crime. Last year, two female students were murdered at the University of California Santa Barbara, and the murderer had posted online videos where he threatened to kill women. If his online actions had legal consequences, his victims might still be alive. I recognize that this legal issue is not black and white; for example, I don't think that someone who writes a violent work of fiction and posts it online must be investigated. However, cases that could clearly be interpreted as threats should be reported to the police.

Monitoring speech online is a complicated issue, but I think that certain forms of speech can be limited without censoring ideas. Eliminating profane and vulgar language online could promote a respectful exchange of ideas and make writers feel safe to express a variety of opinions. Furthermore, law enforcement could prevent tragedies by investigating online threats.

Sample Essay—Below Average Response

I agree with Perspectives 2 and 3 and agree that certain types of speech should be limited online. Mean speech online is called cyber-bullying and can cause lots of harm for it's victims. If certain websites are dominated by hateful speech, people might be afraid to express controversial ideas. Parents should also monitor their children's behavior online.

On websites, it is easy to bully others because you do not have to reveal your identity. Even if you do not know who your attacker is, cyber-bullying can have harmful consequences, just like being bullied in person. Online, you can also insult people unfairly for everything from their opinions to their appearance, in the past, this has led to depression or eating disorders.

Offensive language on websites could also scare writers into not expressing their believes. Sometimes, people say really angry things in the comments section and even threaten writers if they don't agree with what they said. I'm not saying that people shouldn't be able to argue back at what the writer says, but they should argue in a polite way. The website should be able to remove comments with things like swear words or insults to the writer that have nothing to do with the article.

Parents should supervise their children's behavior online. Kids sometimes go onto websites where theirs a lot of offensive language, and they learn to speak like that. Teenagers especially sometimes say violent things online, and if parents find this, they should figure out what is causing this behavior.

The Internet could be a safer place for everyone if people limited offensive speech, especially cyber-bullying, and if parents watched their kids' behavior.

MATHEMATICS

Calculator Exercise (p. 198)

1. D; 1   **3.** B; 2   **5.** A; 1   **7.** D; 3   **9.** E; 3

2. K; 2   **4.** F; 3   **6.** H; 2   **8.** F; 3   **10.** H; 3

Lesson (p. 201)

#		#		#		#		#		#		#	
1.	C	**28.**	H	**55.**	E	**82.**	J	**109.**	B	**136.**	H	**163.**	C
2.	J	**29.**	D	**56.**	H	**83.**	B	**110.**	K	**137.**	B	**164.**	G
3.	D	**30.**	H	**57.**	D	**84.**	G	**111.**	C	**138.**	H	**165.**	C
4.	J	**31.**	C	**58.**	H	**85.**	D	**112.**	H	**139.**	A	**166.**	G
5.	C	**32.**	F	**59.**	C	**86.**	F	**113.**	D	**140.**	K	**167.**	C
6.	F	**33.**	C	**60.**	F	**87.**	C	**114.**	K	**141.**	B	**168.**	F
7.	E	**34.**	G	**61.**	A	**88.**	J	**115.**	C	**142.**	F	**169.**	D
8.	H	**35.**	C	**62.**	J	**89.**	D	**116.**	F	**143.**	D	**170.**	K
9.	D	**36.**	J	**63.**	D	**90.**	J	**117.**	A	**144.**	G	**171.**	C
10.	F	**37.**	A	**64.**	H	**91.**	E	**118.**	K	**145.**	C	**172.**	J
11.	D	**38.**	K	**65.**	A	**92.**	J	**119.**	D	**146.**	G	**173.**	D
12.	J	**39.**	A	**66.**	J	**93.**	C	**120.**	F	**147.**	D	**174.**	G
13.	D	**40.**	J	**67.**	A	**94.**	H	**121.**	C	**148.**	K	**175.**	C
14.	J	**41.**	D	**68.**	K	**95.**	D	**122.**	F	**149.**	C	**176.**	H
15.	E	**42.**	H	**69.**	E	**96.**	K	**123.**	A	**150.**	K	**177.**	C
16.	J	**43.**	D	**70.**	K	**97.**	B	**124.**	K	**151.**	C	**178.**	K
17.	C	**44.**	G	**71.**	C	**98.**	J	**125.**	A	**152.**	K	**179.**	B
18.	K	**45.**	D	**72.**	K	**99.**	D	**126.**	F	**153.**	B	**180.**	J
19.	C	**46.**	K	**73.**	B	**100.**	F	**127.**	D	**154.**	G	**181.**	B
20.	G	**47.**	E	**74.**	K	**101.**	D	**128.**	G	**155.**	B	**182.**	H
21.	D	**48.**	J	**75.**	C	**102.**	K	**129.**	B	**156.**	F	**183.**	E
22.	H	**49.**	C	**76.**	H	**103.**	D	**130.**	J	**157.**	B	**184.**	K
23.	B	**50.**	J	**77.**	A	**104.**	J	**131.**	C	**158.**	K	**185.**	B
24.	H	**51.**	B	**78.**	F	**105.**	D	**132.**	J	**159.**	A	**186.**	K
25.	D	**52.**	K	**79.**	C	**106.**	H	**133.**	D	**160.**	K	**187.**	A
26.	K	**53.**	D	**80.**	K	**107.**	D	**134.**	H	**161.**	D	**188.**	F
27.	E	**54.**	J	**81.**	B	**108.**	F	**135.**	B	**162.**	H	**189.**	A

190. H	**201.** C	**212.** H	**223.** C	**234.** J	**245.** C	**256.** G
191. D	**202.** H	**213.** E	**224.** G	**235.** E	**246.** G	**257.** B
192. H	**203.** A	**214.** K	**225.** A	**236.** F	**247.** C	**258.** G
193. D	**204.** G	**215.** C	**226.** H	**237.** D	**248.** H	**259.** D
194. K	**205.** C	**216.** K	**227.** D	**238.** H	**249.** E	**260.** J
195. C	**206.** H	**217.** C	**228.** J	**239.** D	**250.** G	
196. J	**207.** A	**218.** H	**229.** B	**240.** F	**251.** E	
197. E	**208.** H	**219.** D	**230.** G	**241.** E	**252.** J	
198. K	**209.** E	**220.** H	**231.** C	**242.** F	**253.** B	
199. C	**210.** J	**221.** D	**232.** H	**243.** D	**254.** G	
200. H	**211.** E	**222.** G	**233.** E	**244.** K	**255.** A	

Quizzes (p. 251)

Quiz I

1. A	**11.** D		
2. K	**12.** J		
3. D	**13.** D		
4. H	**14.** F		
5. D	**15.** A		
6. J	**16.** G		
7. E	**17.** E		
8. J	**18.** J		
9. B	**19.** C		
10. H	**20.** J		

Quiz II

1. C	**11.** D
2. F	**12.** J
3. C	**13.** D
4. G	**14.** K
5. C	**15.** E
6. H	**16.** H
7. B	**17.** B
8. J	**18.** G
9. A	**19.** E
10. H	**20.** K

Quiz III

1. C	**11.** D
2. F	**12.** F
3. E	**13.** A
4. G	**14.** F
5. D	**15.** C
6. G	**16.** G
7. B	**17.** C
8. F	**18.** G
9. D	**19.** E
10. J	**20.** H

Quiz IV

1. C	**14.** J
2. F	**15.** B
3. E	**16.** H
4. H	**17.** B
5. D	**18.** F
6. F	**19.** E
7. D	**20.** F
8. G	**21.** C
9. E	**22.** H
10. H	**23.** A
11. A	**24.** J
12. G	**25.** C
13. D	

Review (p. 269)

1. D	**6.** J	**11.** A	**16.** K	**21.** B	**26.** F	**31.** E
2. H	**7.** B	**12.** J	**17.** D	**22.** H	**27.** E	**32.** K
3. C	**8.** F	**13.** C	**18.** G	**23.** B	**28.** J	
4. K	**9.** C	**14.** F	**19.** D	**24.** J	**29.** D	
5. D	**10.** J	**15.** B	**20.** H	**25.** B	**30.** H	

SCIENCE

Lesson (p. 295)

1. B	17. D	33. C	49. D	65. C	81. C	97. A
2. F	18. H	34. F	50. G	66. G	82. J	98. J
3. C	19. A	35. J	51. B	67. C	83. A	99. D
4. G	20. J	36. C	52. G	68. F	84. H	100. F
5. C	21. C	37. G	53. A	69. D	85. B	101. B
6. H	22. H	38. A	54. J	70. H	86. H	102. H
7. D	23. D	39. B	55. D	71. A	87. D	103. D
8. H	24. F	40. H	56. H	72. G	88. G	
9. C	25. B	41. C	57. D	73. A	89. C	
10. H	26. H	42. F	58. J	74. H	90. F	
11. A	27. C	43. D	59. B	75. A	91. D	
12. H	28. G	44. J	60. H	76. G	92. F	
13. D	29. D	45. B	61. C	77. D	93. B	
14. F	30. G	46. F	62. J	78. G	94. G	
15. B	31. A	47. C	63. A	79. B	95. C	
16. H	32. G	48. F	64. J	80. H	96. J	

Quizzes (p. 325)

Quiz I

1. D	12. G
2. J	13. B
3. D	14. H
4. F	15. C
5. C	16. J
6. J	
7. B	
8. H	
9. A	
10. G	
11. A	

Quiz II

1. A	12. G
2. F	13. A
3. A	14. G
4. J	15. C
5. C	16. J
6. H	
7. D	
8. F	
9. C	
10. G	
11. C	

Quiz III

1. C	12. G
2. G	13. C
3. C	14. J
4. F	15. B
5. A	16. F
6. F	
7. C	
8. G	
9. B	
10. H	
11. B	

Review (p. 341)

1. D	11. A	21. B	31. C	41. B	51. C	61. A
2. F	12. G	22. H	32. H	42. H	52. H	62. F
3. B	13. D	23. A	33. C	43. C	53. B	63. C
4. G	14. H	24. G	34. H	44. J	54. G	64. J
5. C	15. A	25. C	35. C	45. B	55. B	65. A
6. G	16. G	26. H	36. J	46. H	56. F	66. G
7. C	17. C	27. D	37. B	47. C	57. D	
8. G	18. J	28. H	38. G	48. F	58. F	
9. B	19. A	29. B	39. D	49. D	59. C	
10. J	20. G	30. G	40. G	50. G	60. F	

PRACTICE TEST I

Multiple-Choice Answer Keys

DIRECTIONS: For the correct answer, check the corresponding unshaded box. Then, total the number of checkmarks for each of the content areas, and add these totals to determine the raw score for that test.

Section 1: *English* (Student Text, p. 464)

	UM	RH			UM	RH			UM	RH			UM	RH			UM	RH
1. B				16. H				31. B				46. F				61. C		
2. J				17. D				32. H				47. D				62. H		
3. D				18. G				33. A				48. J				63. D		
4. G				19. A				34. J				49. C				64. G		
5. A				20. F				35. A				50. F				65. D		
6. H				21. C				36. F				51. B				66. F		
7. A				22. H				37. B				52. F				67. A		
8. G				23. A				38. H				53. B				68. F		
9. A				24. G				39. B				54. J				69. C		
10. G				25. C				40. H				55. D				70. J		
11. C				26. J				41. D				56. G				71. A		
12. J				27. D				42. H				57. D				72. G		
13. B				28. G				43. A				58. H				73. B		
14. H				29. C				44. F				59. A				74. J		
15. A				30. G				45. C				60. J				75. B		

Usage and Mechanics (UM): _____ /44   Rhetorical Skills (RH): _____ /31   Raw Score (UM + RH): _____ /75

Section 2: *Mathematics* (Student Text, p. 478)

	EA	AG	GT			EA	AG	GT			EA	AG	GT			EA	AG	GT
1. A					16. H					31. A					46. J			
2. K					17. B					32. H					47. A			
3. C					18. K					33. A					48. F			
4. K					19. A					34. K					49. C			
5. E					20. F					35. D					50. K			
6. H					21. D					36. J					51. C			
7. D					22. G					37. C					52. J			
8. H					23. C					38. G					53. A			
9. D					24. F					39. C					54. F			
10. G					25. E					40. G					55. D			
11. B					26. G					41. D					56. H			
12. F					27. C					42. K					57. B			
13. C					28. J					43. A					58. K			
14. G					29. E					44. G					59. A			
15. D					30. H					45. B					60. J			

Pre-Algebra/Elementary Algebra (EA): _____ /30   Plane Geometry/Trigonometry (GT): _____ /17

Int. Algebra/Coordinate Geometry (AG): _____ /13   Raw Score (EA + AG + GT): _____ /60

Section 3: Reading (Student Text, p. 498)

		SS	AL
1.	D		
2.	J		
3.	B		
4.	J		
5.	A		
6.	G		
7.	A		
8.	F		
9.	B		
10.	F		

		SS	AL
11.	B		
12.	G		
13.	D		
14.	G		
15.	C		
16.	G		
17.	B		
18.	H		
19.	D		
20.	F		

		SS	AL
21.	A		
22.	J		
23.	B		
24.	H		
25.	A		
26.	H		
27.	C		
28.	J		
29.	A		
30.	H		

		SS	AL
31.	B		
32.	H		
33.	A		
34.	J		
35.	C		
36.	F		
37.	A		
38.	G		
39.	B		
40.	H		

Social Studies/Sciences (SS): _____ /20   Arts/Literature (AL): _____ /20   Raw Score (SS + AL): _____ /40

Section 4: Science (Student Text, p. 509)

		B	C	P	ES
1.	B				
2.	H				
3.	C				
4.	H				
5.	D				
6.	J				
7.	A				

		B	C	P	ES
8.	F				
9.	B				
10.	F				
11.	B				
12.	H				
13.	C				
14.	J				

		B	C	P	ES
15.	B				
16.	H				
17.	B				
18.	F				
19.	B				
20.	G				
21.	C				
22.	H				

		B	C	P	ES
23.	B				
24.	J				
25.	C				
26.	F				
27.	D				

		B	C	P	ES
28.	G				
29.	C				
30.	G				
31.	D				
32.	F				
33.	A				
34.	H				

		B	C	P	ES
35.	B				
36.	J				
37.	C				
38.	G				
39.	D				
40.	F				

Biology (B): _____ /21   Chemistry (C): _____ /14   Raw Score (B + C + ES): _____ /40

Earth/Space Sciences (ES): _____ /5

Multiple-Choice Explanations

Section 1: *English*

1. **(B)** (p. 464) *English/Rhetorical Skills/Style/Conciseness.* The original sentence is needlessly repetitious: "to begin" means "to start." (B) eliminates the unnecessary repetition.

2. **(J)** (p. 464) *English/Usage and Mechanics/Grammar and Usage/Diction.* The original sentence contains an error of diction. The correct word for making the comparison intended by the original is "from," not "than." ("Than" is a conjunction, and conjunctions are used to introduce clauses. What follows the underlined part of the sentence is a noun phrase, not a clause.) (G) fails to make the needed correction. (H) makes the needed correction but introduces a new error. In general, a modifier should be placed as close as possible to what it modifies. Here, "fundamentally" must modify "are different," but the placement of "fundamentally" after "from" suggests that it is intended to modify "weapons." Thus, (H) would result in an ambiguous sentence.

3. **(D)** (p. 464) *English/Rhetorical Skills/Style/Conciseness.* The underlined material is needlessly repetitious. A weapon of "mass destruction" is one "that could do a lot of harm." Eliminate the surplus material.

4. **(G)** (p. 465) *English/Usage and Mechanics/Sentence Structure/Run-On Sentences.* The original sentence is a run-on sentence. (G) solves the problem by starting a new sentence at an appropriate point. Neither (H) nor (J) solve the problem of the run-on sentence.

5. **(A)** (p. 465) *English/Rhetorical Skills/No Change.* The original sentence is correct. (B) destroys the logic of the sentence. (C) ambiguously implies that injuries are unavailable. (D) is needlessly wordy.

6. **(H)** (p. 465) *English/Usage and Mechanics/Grammar and Usage/Diction.* The original sentence is not idiomatic. (H) is idiomatic with "resulting from." (G) and (J) are not idiomatic.

7. **(A)** (p. 465) *English/Usage and Mechanics/No Change.* The original sentence is correct as written. The use of the subjunctive "would" correctly suggests that a nuclear war might or might not occur. (B) and (C) are both wrong because the indicative mood ("is" and "are") does not have this meaning. Additionally, (B) must be wrong because the subject of the sentence is the compound subject "number of deaths . . . and economic damage," and a compound subject requires a plural verb. (C) is also wrong because "as" makes the answer unidiomatic. In (D), although "might" preserves the element of contingency suggested by the subjunctive "would," the phrasing "more devastating even as" is not idiomatic.

8. **(G)** (p. 465) *English/Rhetorical Skills/Strategy/Effective Concluding Sentence.* In the second paragraph, the author is arguing that nuclear weapons are fundamentally different from conventional weapons because of their massive destructive power on multiple levels. (G) correctly summarizes this point.

9. **(A)** (p. 465) *English/Usage and Mechanics/No Change.* The original sentence is correct. The other choices introduce errors in modification.

10. **(G)** (p. 465) *English/Usage and Mechanics/Sentence Structure/Run-On Sentences* and *Grammar and Usage/Pronoun Usage.* The original sentence has two mistakes. First, it is a run-on sentence. Also, "it" is singular but refers to "weapons," which is plural. (G) makes both the needed corrections.

11. **(C)** (p. 466) *English/Usage and Mechanics/Grammar and Usage/Diction.* The original sentence is not idiomatic as written. The correct idiom is "neither . . . nor," not "neither . . . but."

12. **(J)** (p. 466) *English/Rhetorical Skills/Organization/Paragraph-Level Structure.* The original sentence is incorrect because a new paragraph should begin here. In the opening paragraph, the author announces that he or she will make three points. The second paragraph is devoted to the first point—the other two points should be presented in separate paragraphs.

13. **(B)** (p. 466) *English/Rhetorical Skills/Style/Conciseness.* The original sentence is awkward. (B) is more concise and reads better than the original sentence. (C) is incorrect because the subject of the sentence is the singular noun "step," so the singular verb "has," not the plural verb "have," is needed. (D) has the errors of the original sentence and inappropriately includes a plural verb.

14. **(H)** (p. 466) *English/Usage and Mechanics/Grammar and Usage/Pronoun Usage.* The ubiquitous "they" makes the original sentence ambiguous. Who are they? The other choices eliminate the ambiguous pronoun, but (H) is the most direct and concise.

15. **(A)** (p. 466) *English/Rhetorical Skills/Organization/Passage-Level Structure.* In the initial paragraph, the author announces that three considerations should guide our formulation of a defense policy. The author then proceeds to address each consideration.

16. **(H)** (p. 466) *English/Rhetorical Skills/Strategy/Main Idea.* Again, the author argues that three principles should guide our defense policy.

17. **(D)** (p. 467) *English/Usage and Mechanics/Sentence Structure/Fragments.* The original sentence lacks a main verb. (C) and (D) supply the verb, but (B) does not. ("Having viewed" is a participle form and cannot be a main verb.) In (C), "its" is intended to refer to "founders," but "founders" is plural, so the plural "their" is needed.

18. **(G)** (p. 467) *English/Usage and Mechanics/Grammar and Usage/Diction.* The original sentence is not idiomatic. The correct idiom is "rather than," not "rather as." Both (H) and (J) are wrong because they too are not idiomatic.

19. **(A)** (p. 467) *English/Rhetorical Skills/Strategy/Effective Transitional Sentence.* This question tests understanding of the relationship between ideas in the passage. The idea discussed in the second sentence of the passage is the result or effect of the idea discussed in the first sentence. "Therefore" is then the best choice to show this relationship.

20. **(F)** (p. 467) *English/Usage and Mechanics/No Change.* The original sentence is correct as written. (G) is needlessly wordy, so the original sentence is preferable. (H) destroys the logical structure of the sentence. (J) changes the intended meaning of the sentence by implying that the founders could have chosen to view education "as" academic excellence, rather than "as a means to" academic excellence.

21. **(C)** (p. 467) *English/Usage and Mechanics/Sentence Structure/Fragments.* The problem with the sentence as originally written is that it lacks a conjugated or main verb. "Talking" is a participle and cannot function as a main verb. Only (C) supplies a conjugated verb form.

22. **(H)** (p. 467) *English/Usage and Mechanics/Punctuation/Commas.* The original sentence is not punctuated correctly. "Goals" is an appositive that refers to "liberty," "equality," etc. The correct punctuation is a comma preceding the appositive. (G) is wrong because the period completely isolates the appositive from the sentence that supports it and turns everything following the comma into a sentence fragment. (J) is also incorrectly punctuated. The semicolon is too powerful—it signals that an independent clause will follow. An appositive, however, is dependent for its existence on the nouns that come before it, so a comma provides enough separation from the main body of the sentence without being too powerful.

23. **(A)** (p. 467) *English/Usage and Mechanics/No Change.* The original sentence is correct as written. To "take precedence over" is an English idiom meaning to be more important than something else. (B) distorts

the intended meaning of the original sentence. To "precede" means to come before in time, so the resulting sentence would make no sense. (C) and (D) are simply not idiomatic.

24. **(G)** (p. 467) *English/Usage and Mechanics/Punctuation/Commas* and *Grammar and Usage/Subject-Verb Agreement* and *Pronoun Usage.* The original sentence contains three errors. First, a comma, not a dash, must close the parenthetical expression signaled by the comma following "generation." (Dashes or commas may be used to set off such remarks, but not a mixture of both.) Second, the subject of the sentence is "generation," which is singular. So, the plural noun "assert" is wrong. Third, "their" refers to "generation" and so fails to agree in number with its referent. (G) makes all three changes. (H) makes two of the changes, but the semicolon is a mistake. The semicolon would be used to separate two clauses, but what follows the semicolon used in (H) is not a clause. Finally, (J) fails to correct the third error mentioned above and is incorrectly punctuated (a second comma is needed). Additionally, (J) uses the present tense verb "asserts," which is inconsistent with the other verbs in the selection.

25. **(C)** (p. 468) *English/Usage and Mechanics/Grammar and Usage/Subject-Verb Agreement.* The verb "was" is singular and fails to agree with its plural subject, "ingredients." (C) corrects this problem. (B) eliminates the problem of agreement. "Being" is a participle and does not show number. Unfortunately, since "being" is a participle, the resulting construction lacks a main verb, and the sentence becomes a sentence fragment. Finally, (D) distorts the intended meaning of the original sentence. The author does not mean to say that the principal ingredients of a civic education were similar to literacy and inculcation of patriotic and moral virtues.

26. **(J)** (p. 468) *English/Usage and Mechanics/Sentence Structure/Run-On Sentences.* The original sentence is a run-on, with two clauses that run together without any punctuation or conjunction. (J) is one way of solving the problem: use a semicolon to separate the two clauses. (A comma and a coordinate conjunction such as "and" could also be used.) The dash cannot be used to separate two clauses, so (G) is wrong. As for (H), a comma by itself is just not strong enough to do the job.

27. **(D)** (p. 468) *English/Usage and Mechanics/Sentence Structure/Problems of Coordination and Subordination.* The original sentence contains an error of illogical subordination, compounded by a punctuation mistake. The two ideas joined at the underlined part have equal importance. One should not be subordinated to the other, but "since" always signals a subordinate idea. Additionally, a semicolon cannot be used to join a subordinate clause to an independent or main clause. (B) solves the subordination problem, but "and" signals a continuation of a thought. The second idea here contrasts with the first and should be signaled by a word like "but." (C) eliminates the punctuation mistake but creates a sentence fragment in the second half of the sentence. "Since" introduces a subordinate clause that must be joined to an independent or main clause.

28. **(G)** (p. 468) *English/Usage and Mechanics/Grammar and Usage/Diction.* The original sentence is not idiomatic. The correct idiom requires the use of the infinitive "to be" rather than the gerund "being." (H) and (J) both correct this error, but they also eliminate the only conjugated verb in the clause. The result is a fragment rather than a complete sentence. (G) correctly uses "to be" without introducing another error.

29. **(C)** (p. 468) *English/Usage and Mechanics/Grammar and Usage/Diction.* The placement of "almost" is not idiomatic. Given its proximity to "agreed," "almost" seems to modify "agreed" rather than "universally." The intended meaning of the sentence is that "almost" modifies "universally." (C) provides the correct and idiomatic placement of "almost." (B) is also not idiomatic. As for (D), although the words are in the correct order, the comma between "universally," an adverb, and the word it modifies, "agreed," disrupts the logical flow of the sentence.

30. **(G)** (p. 468) *English/Usage and Mechanics/Sentence Structure/Faulty Parallelism.* The underlined part is incorrect because it destroys the parallelism of the sentence. The sentence has a series of three elements: "emphasized," "put," and "attempt." However, the third element is a noun rather than a verb. (G) restores

the parallelism of the sentence by supplying a verb. (H) fails to provide a verb. Finally, although (J) includes a verb, it also includes a subject. The result is a clause that is not parallel to the verb forms.

31. **(B)** (p. 469) *English/Rhetorical Skills/Organization/Paragraph-Level Structure.* The final paragraph contains a new thought that extends the logical development of the essay.

32. **(H)** (p. 469) *English/Rhetorical Skills/Strategy/Audience.* The passage is a discussion of old textbooks. Surely educators would be most interested in old textbooks.

33. **(A)** (p. 469) *English/Rhetorical Skills/No Change.* The original sentence is correct. (B) destroys the logic of the sentence. (C) and (D) are illogical because the sentence intends to refer generally to "the contribution of women" as a whole—not to the contribution of any particular individual.

34. **(J)** (p. 469) *English/Usage and Mechanics/Grammar and Usage/Diction.* The original sentence is non-idiomatic. (J) provides the correct idiom: "range . . . from . . . to." (G) and (H) fail to correct the problem, though (H) does change the noun "operation" to the verb "operating," creating parallelism with "knitting."

35. **(A)** (p. 469) *English/Rhetorical Skills/No Change.* The original sentence is correct as written. It is idiomatic, and the past tense verb "marked" is consistent with the other past tense verbs in the selection. (B) is wrong because the present perfect "has marked" implies an action that began in the past but continues into the present. (C) is wordy and awkward. As for (D), the use of the passive voice completely destroys the logic of the sentence.

36. **(F)** (p. 470) *English/Usage and Mechanics/No Change.* The original sentence is correct as written: "effort was made . . . to utilize." (G) and (H) are not idiomatic—"effort was made . . . being able to utilize" and "effort was made . . . utilizing." Finally, (J) destroys the logical structure of the sentence: "effort was made . . . and utilize."

37. **(B)** (p. 470) *English/Usage and Mechanics/Grammar and Usage/Sequence and Verb Tense.* The original sentence uses an incorrect verb tense. The present tense "falls" conflicts with the other past tense verbs of the selection. (B) and (D) both make the needed correction, but (D) is not idiomatic in this context. The correct idiom is "falls within" a category. (C) is grammatically incorrect because it eliminates the only conjugated verb in the clause introduced by "while."

38. **(H)** (p. 470) *English/Usage and Mechanics/Grammar and Usage/Diction.* The original sentence is not idiomatic. The correct idiom is "reserved for," not "reserved by." "Reserved by" has a meaning that is not appropriate here. (G) is needlessly wordy and ambiguous because it is not clear what the phrase is intended to modify. It seems to modify "women," but the intent of the sentence is for the phrase to modify "work." (J) is also wordy and awkward.

39. **(B)** (p. 470) *English/Usage and Mechanics/Sentence Structure/Unintended Meanings.* The original sentence uses an illogical transition word. "However" is used to signal a contrast, but the sentence that is introduced by "however" is actually a continuation of the thought contained in the previous sentence. (B) is correct; since there is no transition word, the reader will naturally assume that the next sentence will continue the train of thought. (C) is wrong because the use of "but" tells the reader to expect a contrasting thought. Finally, (D) is a fragment rather than a complete sentence.

40. **(H)** (p. 470) *English/Usage and Mechanics/Punctuation/Colons.* The original sentence is incorrectly punctuated. Since there is no punctuation between "activity" and "knitting," a reader will not pause after "activity." Consequently, "knitting" seems to be a participle that somehow modifies "activity." The author intends for "knitting" to be a gerund in the series including "knitting," "canning," and "planting." The correct punctuation in this series is the colon.

41. **(D)** (p. 470) ***English/Usage and Mechanics/Grammar and Usage/Pronoun Usage.*** The original sentence contains an error of pronoun usage. The pronoun "their" refers to "homemaker"—the singular "her" should be used. (B) eliminates the problem by using no pronoun at all. The resulting structure is a bit awkward ("could be demonstrating patriotism") but not incorrect. However, the verb in (B) is not acceptable. "Could be demonstrating" is inconsistent with the other verbs in the paragraph. (C) is incorrect—the verb "could have demonstrated" implies that a woman might or might not have demonstrated her patriotism, but this is not the intended meaning. The author means to assert definitely that women did demonstrate their patriotism. (C) is also wrong because it fails to correct the pronoun problem.

42. **(H)** (p. 470) ***English/Usage and Mechanics/Punctuation/Commas.*** The original sentence is incorrectly punctuated. The colon seems to signal a clarification of the idea of hostessing at canteens. Instead, hostessing is one of a group of activities women volunteered to do. The correct punctuation is a comma.

43. **(A)** (p. 471) ***English/Rhetorical Skills/No Change.*** The material between the commas is an adjective phrase: "Army, dressed . . . and armed . . . 'with the Musket,' was dispatched." The other choices destroy this logic.

44. **(F)** (p. 471) ***English/Usage and Mechanics/No Change.*** The original sentence is correct as written. The other choices disrupt the parallelism of the sentence. Since the two verbs "performed" and "laid" have a similar function in the sentence, they should both have similar forms. (G) and (H) use the passive voice and are not parallel to the active voice "performed." (J) is the participle and is not parallel to "performed," a conjugated verb.

45. **(C)** (p. 471) ***English/Rhetorical Skills/Organization/Passage-Level Structure.*** A way to fix the order of the paragraphs is to recognize that neither [2] nor [3] can be the first paragraph. "This" in the first sentence of [2] clearly refers to something that has come before.

Similarly, the phrase "much of the work" in the first sentence of [3] also refers to something that has come before. [1] appears to be the best choice for the first paragraph because [4] seems to be a summary or conclusion. Only (C) has [4] as the conclusion, so it is the correct answer.

As for [2] and [3], [2] must follow [3] because [2] is intended to contrast with [3]: most of the work was traditional, but some was not. A reader cannot understand the importance of the contrast suggested by [2] without the information provided by [3].

46. **(F)** (p. 471) ***English/Rhetorical Skills/Strategy/Appropriate Supporting Material.*** Examples are often helpful, as they enable readers to understand a general point in a more concrete fashion. In this instance, the slogan helps the reader understand the motivation and purpose behind the Women's Land Army.

47. **(D)** (p. 471) ***English/Usage and Mechanics/Sentence Structure/Fragments.*** "Undertaken" is the past participle of the verb "to undertake." A past participle is not itself a complete verb. (D) solves this problem by creating a sentence that uses the passive voice: "changes were undertaken."

48. **(J)** (p. 472) ***English/Usage and Mechanics/Grammar and Usage/Diction.*** The original sentence is not idiomatic. The sentence means to say that some people embraced the new values, and that is the sense of (J). (G) introduces an error in diction, substituting "excepted" for the intended word choice "accepted," as well as using the wrong preposition for "excepted." (H) is wrong for the same first reason that (G) is wrong.

49. **(C)** (p. 472) ***English/Usage and Mechanics/Sentence Structure/Problems of Coordination and Subordination.*** The two ideas joined at the underlined part contrast with each other: these did something; the others did not. To signal this contrast, something other than "and" must be used. "But" is an acceptable choice, so (C) is correct. (B) and (D) are incorrect because "since" and "consequently" signal a relationship in which one idea follows from or is the consequence of another.

50. **(F)**(p. 472) *English/Rhetorical Skills/No Change.* The original sentence is correct. By comparison, the other choices are needlessly wordy and awkward.

51. **(B)** (p. 472) *English/Usage and Mechanics/Sentence Structure/Fragments.* The comma and the conjunction "and" signal that the last half of the sentence is a clause. Yet, the original contains no main verb. (B) supplies a main verb in the right tense that also agrees in number with its subject, "notions."

52. **(F)**(p. 472) *English/Rhetorical Skills/No Change.* The original sentence is correct. This is the proper place at which to begin a new paragraph since the author is shifting from talking about the past to a discussion of the present. Since a new paragraph is needed here, (G) and (J) are wrong. (J) is wrong for two additional reasons: "Today, owing to the fact that . . . political life" is an incomplete sentence; and the use of "owing to the fact that" makes "democratic processes" the new subject, which will no longer agree with the verb "is." "Triumph" is the necessary subject. Finally, (H) illogically isolates the subject of the sentence from its verb.

53. **(B)** (p. 472) *English/Rhetorical Skills/Style/Conciseness.* In the original sentence, "clear" is intended to modify "evident." However, that is a job that can be done only by the adverb "clearly." In any event, "clear" and "evident" are synonyms, so both are not needed. (B) is the best choice because it eliminates the redundant term "clear."

54. **(J)** (p. 472) *English/Rhetorical Skills/Strategy/Effective Transitional Sentence.* The transitional word must signal a contrast between two ideas. The best choice is "yet."

55. **(D)** (p. 472) *English/Rhetorical Skills/Style/Conciseness.* "Being" is a participle that can function as an adjective. However, there is no noun that can logically be modified by "being." What the sentence means to assert is that the lack of a stable value system is due to the influence of Western ideas. The word "since" in (D) is sufficient by itself to give the reason for the preceding part of the sentence. Both (B) and (C) are wrong because they are awkward.

56. **(G)** (p. 473) *English/Usage and Mechanics/Sentence Structure/Unintended Meanings.* "And so" distorts the logical structure of the sentence. It seems to introduce another clause, but what follows lacks a main verb. By eliminating "and so," (G) allows "emphasizing," a participle, to function as an adjective modifying "principles." (H) results in a sentence that is distorted because "and" seems to join another verb to the first verb, "expound." However, "emphasis" is a noun, so the sentence reads: "textbooks expound . . . and the emphasis." In (J), "that" seems to introduce a relative clause, but no verb follows.

57. **(D)** (p. 473) *English/Rhetorical Skills/Style/Conciseness.* "Often sometimes" is not a possible phrase because the words have contradictory meanings. One of the words must be eliminated. All of the choices make this correction. (B), however, uses a verb tense that is inconsistent with the other tenses in the paragraph. In (C), "misinterpreted" and "distorted" are past participles and cannot stand alone. They require another verb such as "are."

58. **(H)** (p. 473) *English/Usage and Mechanics/Grammar and Usage/Sequence and Verb Tense* and *Pronoun Usage.* The original sentence contains two errors. The past tense "translated" is inconsistent with the present tense verbs in the rest of the paragraph. Also, "who" should replace "that" since the author is referring to people. Only (H) makes both corrections.

59. **(A)** (p. 473) *English/Rhetorical Skills/Strategy/Appropriate Supporting Material.* At the end, the author introduces the topic of Japanese youth; it would be appropriate for the discussion to continue along these lines.

60. **(J)** (p. 473) *English/Usage and Mechanics/Grammar and Usage/Diction.* The original sentence does not contain a grievous error, but it is not as idiomatic as (J). The placement of "always" directly before the main element of the verb, instead of before "has," is preferable to the original. (G) is wrong because "have" does

not agree with the singular "humankind." (H) is wrong as the present tense is inconsistent with the introductory phrase "from the beginning."

61. **(C)** (p. 473) ***English/Usage and Mechanics/Grammar and Usage/Faulty or Illogical Comparisons.*** In English, if an adjective has more than one syllable, the comparative is formed by using "more" rather than by adding "-er."

62. **(H)** (p. 474) ***English/Usage and Mechanics/Punctuation/Commas.*** The comma following "agriculture" has no logical function in the sentence. (H) solves this problem by allowing the comma to mark the close of a parenthetical expression introduced by the first comma in front of "along." (G) attempts the correction but is wrong because the resulting phrase has no clear logical connection with the rest of the sentence. (H) does not have this problem. In (H), the noun "discovery" is the object of a preposition, and the prepositional phrase is connected to the rest of the sentence as a modifier of "domestication." (J) destroys the logical structure of the sentence by isolating the subject from the verb. The semicolon is too strong.

63. **(D)** (p. 474) ***English/Rhetorical Skills/Style/Conciseness.*** The underlined material is repetitious and therefore should be omitted.

64. **(G)** (p. 474) ***English/Usage and Mechanics/Sentence Structure/Faulty Parallelism*** and ***Grammar and Usage/Pronoun Usage.*** The original sentence contains two errors. First, it lacks parallelism. As written, it reads: "between regarding . . . and to consider." Second, the pronoun "them" does not agree in number with its antecedent, "animal." Only (G) corrects both of these problems. (H) solves the problem of parallelism but fails to eliminate the wrong pronoun. (J) does not correct either mistake.

65. **(D)** (p. 474) ***English/Usage and Mechanics/Sentence Structure/Misplaced Modifiers*** and ***Grammar and Usage/Sequence and Verb Tense.*** The original sentence contains two errors. First, the placement of "seemingly" is incorrect. It is intended to modify "every," which in turn modifies "subject." However, its placement in front of the verb seems to suggest that Aristotle "seemingly" wrote. Second, the present tense "writes" is inconsistent with the other verbs in the paragraph (e.g., "seemed" and "took"). (Note: The present tense verbs are used to describe our attitudes today. Although Aristotle wrote in the past, we currently have certain attitudes about those writings.) (B) corrects the second problem but not the first. Simply putting "seemingly" into parentheses does not clarify what the word is supposed to modify. As for (C), while it eliminates the problem of verb tense by reducing the verb to a participle modifying "Aristotle," there is still the ambiguity created by "seemingly."

66. **(F)** (p. 474) ***English/Usage and Mechanics/No Change.*** The original sentence is correct as written. The comma following "subject" marks the end of the introductory dependent clause. Since punctuation is needed at that point, (H) is wrong. The correct punctuation is a comma. The semicolon and the colon are both too powerful, so (G) and (J) are wrong as well. (H) also uses the possessive apostrophe incorrectly and (G) is missing it altogether.

67. **(A)** (p. 474) ***English/Usage and Mechanics/Sentence Structure/Problems of Coordination and Subordination.*** The transition word here must connect the two ideas: Aristotle was interested in all life; he was particularly interested in marine life. "And" correctly coordinates these two ideas. Had the passage gone on to discuss marine life in particular, then the contrast set up by "but" in (C) would make it the better choice.

68. **(F)** (p. 474) ***English/Rhetorical Skills/No Change.*** The original sentence is correct as written. "Wedding" is a participle that modifies "observer." (G) distorts the intended meaning by suggesting that Aristotle himself was joined to something. The sentence means to say that Aristotle joined two ideas. (H) is needlessly wordy and awkward. Finally, (J) creates a prepositional phrase that does not clearly modify any other element in the sentence.

69. **(C)** (p. 474) *English/Usage and Mechanics/Punctuation/Quotation Marks.* The original sentence is incorrectly punctuated. Quotation marks must be used to indicate the start of the quotation. (B) fails to make this correction and makes another error of punctuation. A dash cannot be used instead of a period. (D) is wrong because the adverb "simply" cannot be used as a predicate complement; that is, "simply" cannot modify the subject of the sentence.

70. **(J)** (p. 475) *English/Rhetorical Skills/Style/Conciseness.* The underlined material is repetitious and therefore should be omitted.

71. **(A)** (p. 475) *English/Rhetorical Skills/No Change.* The original sentence is correct. By comparison, the other choices are needlessly wordy and awkward.

72. **(G)** (p. 475) *English/Rhetorical Skills/Strategy/Appropriate Supporting Material.* The author's use of Aristotle's own words is particularly forceful. It lets Aristotle make the point for himself.

73. **(B)** (p. 475) *English/Rhetorical Skills/Strategy/Audience.* The passage is expository but not overly technical, so (A) and (D) are wrong. Since the main topic is Aristotle, (B) is the best choice.

74. **(J)** (p. 476) *English/Rhetorical Skills/Strategy/Main Idea.* As stated in the first sentence of the second paragraph of the passage, the essay intends to show how the animal world became a source of serious study because of Aristotle.

75. **(B)** (p. 476) *English/Rhetorical Skills/Organization/Paragraph-Level Structure.* The first paragraph doesn't pose any questions, (A); introduce an argument, (C); or provide an anecdote, (D). Its function is to place Aristotle in a certain context. It gives a kind of history of the link between humans and animals that segues into Aristotle's interest in the subject.

Section 2: *Mathematics*

1. **(A)** (p. 478) *Mathematics/Algebra/Solving Algebraic Equations or Inequalities with One Variable/Equations Involving Rational Expressions.* Solve for x: $\frac{1}{x}+\frac{1}{x}=8 \Rightarrow \frac{2}{x}=8 \Rightarrow x=\frac{1}{4}$. Alternatively, one can reason that $\frac{1}{x}$ and $\frac{1}{x}$ are equal, and since their sum is 8, $\frac{1}{x}$ equals 4. Thus, $x=\frac{1}{4}$.

2. **(K)** (p. 478) *Mathematics/Algebra/Expressing and Evaluating Algebraic Functions/Function Notation.* Substitute the given values for x and y: $3x-4y=3(2)-4(-1)=6+4=10$.

3. **(C)** (p. 479) *Mathematics/Arithmetic/Common Arithmetic Items/Percents.* First, 20% of 600 boys equals $0.20(600)=120$ boys on the honor roll. Second, 30% of 400 girls equals $0.30(400)=120$ girls on the honor roll. Therefore, there are $120 \text{ boys}+120 \text{ girls}=240$ students on the honor roll.

4. **(K)** (p. 479) *Mathematics/Arithmetic/Common Arithmetic Items/Properties of Numbers.* Since the variable t is outside the brackets and parentheses, it must be multiplied by everything within the brackets and parentheses. And since an even number times any other whole number yields an even number, t must be even. None of the other letters being even guarantees an even result.

5. **(E)** (p. 479) *Mathematics/Statistics and Probability/Data Representation/Tables.* The data in the table represents an arithmetic sequence: the number of flies in each successive week is four times the number in the previous week. The final count should be $4 \cdot 192=768$.

6. **(H)** (p. 480) *Mathematics/Arithmetic/Simple Manipulations* **and** *Statistics and Probability.* Use the formula for finding the number of permutations: $3!=3 \cdot 2 \cdot 1=6$.

7. **(D)** (p. 480) ***Mathematics/Coordinate Geometry/The Coordinate System.*** Since the *x*-coordinate of both points is 2, the line runs parallel to the *y*-axis, and the *x*-coordinate of the midpoint will also be 2. As for the *y*-coordinate, the midpoint is halfway between 2 and −2 : 0.

8. **(H)** (p. 480) ***Mathematics/Algebra/Solving Algebraic Equations or Inequalities with One Variable/Equations Involving Absolute Value.*** Since the absolute value of *xy* is positive, *xy* itself must be positive (since $|xy| = xy$). Therefore, both *x* and *y* have the same sign: they might both be positive, or they might both be negative, so (F), (G), (J), and (K) can all be true. However, (H) cannot be true because *x* and *y* cannot have different signs, as a positive times a negative yields a negative result.

   Alternatively, substitute some numbers. If $x > 0 > y$, then *x* could be 1 and *y* could be −1, and $(1)(-1) = -1$.

9. **(D)** (p. 481) ***Mathematics/Geometry/Rectangles and Squares.*** Convert the dimensions shown to real dimensions. Since 1 centimeter is equal to 4 meters, the width of the room is 4 meters and the length is 4.8 meters. Thus, the area of the room is $4 \cdot 4.8 = 19.2$ square meters.

10. **(G)** (p. 481) ***Mathematics/Algebra/Manipulating Algebraic Expressions/Basic Algebraic Manipulations.*** First, perform the indicated multiplication: $30,000 \times 20 = 600,000$. And convert 600,000 to scientific notation by increasing the power of 10 once for each zero to the right of the leading digit before the decimal place: $600,000 = 6 \times 10^5$.

11. **(B)** (p. 481) ***Mathematics/Arithmetic/Complicated Arithmetic Application Items*** and ***Algebra/Solving Simultaneous Equations.*** Use simultaneous equations to solve this problem. If *x* is the quantity of chocolates and *y* is the quantity of caramels, then $x + y = 4$ and 3*x* + 2*y* = 10. Substitute 4 − *x* for *y* in the second equation and solve for *x*: $y = 4 - x \Rightarrow 3x + 2(4-x) = 10 \Rightarrow 3x + 8 - 2x = 10 \Rightarrow x = 10 - 8 = 2$.

   Alternatively, test the answer choices, starting with (C). If Karen bought 2.5 pounds of chocolates, she bought $4 - 2.5 = 1.5$ pounds of caramels and the total cost is $(2.5 \cdot 3) + (1.5 \cdot 2) = 7.50 + 3 = \$10.50$. This is too much money. Since chocolates are more expensive than caramels, Karen bought less than 2.5 pounds of chocolates. Try (B): 2 pounds of chocolates and 2 pounds of caramels cost $(2 \cdot 3) + (2 \cdot 2) = 6 + 4 = 10$.

12. **(F)** (p. 481) ***Mathematics/Statistics and Probability/Averages.*** Set up an equation for the average and solve for the missing element. Since the average of two of the tests is 77, they can both be set equal to 77 in the average for all three: $\dfrac{77 + 77 + x}{3} = 80 \Rightarrow x = 86$.

13. **(C)** (p. 482) ***Mathematics/Arithmetic/Common Arithmetic Items/Ratios.*** Only the ratio in (C), $5:2$, is impossible because the number of photographs, 10, would not be evenly divisible by the total number of ratio parts: 5 + 2 = 7.

14. **(G)** (p. 482) ***Mathematics/Algebra/Solving Algebraic Equations or Inequalities with One Variable/Simple Equations.*** Solve for *x*: $\dfrac{4}{5} = \dfrac{x}{4} \Rightarrow 4(4) = 5x \Rightarrow x = \dfrac{16}{5}$.

15. **(D)** (p. 482) ***Mathematics/Geometry/Lines and Angles*** and ***Triangles/Properties of Triangles.*** Label the unlabeled angles:

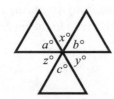

Since the measure of the degrees in a circle is 360, the sum of x, y, and z plus the sum of a, b, and c is 360. What is the value of the angles inside the triangles? Since they are equilateral triangles, each angle is 60°: $3(60) + x + y + z = 360 \Rightarrow x + y + z = 180$.

Alternatively, since you can determine from the given figure that the unlabeled angles each measure 60 and therefore total 180, you can use vertical angles to solve this item. After labeling the unlabeled angles, as done above, simply recognize that $a° = y°$, $b° = z°$, and $c° = x°$. So, $x + y + z = a + b + c = 180$.

16. **(H)** (p. 483) ***Mathematics/Arithmetic/Complicated Arithmetic Application Items.*** If Peter spent $\frac{1}{4}$ of his allowance on Monday, he had $\frac{3}{4}$ of his allowance left. Then, he spent $\frac{1}{3}$ of that $\frac{3}{4}$ on Tuesday: $\frac{1}{3} \cdot \frac{3}{4} = \frac{1}{4}$. After spending the additional $\frac{1}{4}$, he was left with $\frac{3}{4} - \frac{1}{4} = \frac{1}{2}$ of the original allowance. Substitution of numbers would also work, but the arithmetic would be the same.

17. **(B)** (p. 483) ***Mathematics/Arithmetic/Common Arithmetic Items/Proportions and Direct-Inverse Variation.*** There are three ways to solve the problem. The simplest and most direct is to reason that if 100 bricks weigh p pounds, 20 bricks, which is $\frac{1}{5}$ of 100, must weigh $\frac{1}{5}$ of p. This same reasoning can be expressed using a direct proportion. The fewer the bricks, the lesser the weight, so:
$\frac{x}{p} = \frac{20}{100} \Rightarrow 100x = 20p \Rightarrow x = \frac{20p}{100} \Rightarrow x = \frac{p}{5}$.

Alternatively, substitute some numbers. Assume that 100 bricks weigh 100 pounds, which is 1 pound each, so 20 bricks weigh 20 pounds. Only the correct formula will generate the number 20 when 100 is substituted for p in the answer choices.

18. **(K)** (p. 484) ***Mathematics/Geometry/Circles*** and ***Triangles/Properties of Triangles.*** The following drawings show that (I), (II), and (III) are all possible:

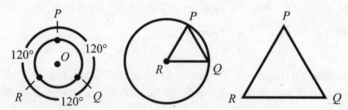

19. **(A)** (p. 484) ***Mathematics/Statistics and Probability/Data Representation/Tables*** and ***Arithmetic/Common Arithmetic Items/Percents.*** This problem can be solved with the "change-over" principle, but that would require five different calculations. It is always easier and faster to find the greatest ratio of the increased value to the original value. Therefore, look at the successive ratios. The price doubles during the first 5-year period. However, it less than doubles during each of the other periods. Thus, the answer is (A).

20. **(F)** (p. 484) ***Mathematics/Algebra/Manipulating Algebraic Expressions/Factoring Expressions.*** The easiest approach is to multiply the binomials given in the answer choices to find the one that is equivalent to the given expression:

F. $(x-2)(x+6) = x^2 + 4x - 12$ ✓

G. $(x-4)(x+3) = x^2 - x - 12$ ✗

H. $(x-6)(x+2)=x^2-4x-12$ ✘

J. $(x+2)(x+6)=x^2+8x+12$ ✘

K. $(x+3)(x+4)=x^2+7x+12$ ✘

21. **(D)** (p. 485) *Mathematics/Algebra/Solving Algebraic Equations or Inequalities with One Variable/Simple Equations.* Since the average of $3x-2$ and $2x-3$ is 10, the sum is 20: $3x-2+2x-3=20\Rightarrow 5x-5=20\Rightarrow 5x=25\Rightarrow x=5$. One package weighs $3(5)-2=13$ pounds and the other package weighs $2(5)-3=7$ pounds. The weight difference is $13-7=6$ pounds.

22. **(G)** (p. 485) *Mathematics/Statistics and Probability/Averages.* This question is a variation on the theme of an average with missing elements. Since 10 students have scores of 75 or more, the total of their scores is at minimum $10\cdot75=750$. Then, even assuming the other 5 students each scored zero, the average for the 15 would be at least $750\div15=50$.

23. **(C)** (p. 485) *Mathematics/Algebra/Manipulating Algebraic Expressions/Manipulating Expressions Involving Exponents.* Since $16=4^2$, $16^x=\left(4^2\right)^x=4^{2x}$. This problem is also solvable by assuming a value for x. If $x=1$, $16^x=16^1=16$. The correct answer choice will yield the value 16 when 1 is substituted for x:

A. $1^{16}=1$ ✘

B. $2^{3(1)}=2^3=8$ ✘

C. $4^{2(1)}=4^2=16$ ✔

D. $8^{2(1)}=8^2=64$ ✘

E. $8^{4(1)}=8^4=4,096$ ✘

24. **(F)** (p. 485) *Mathematics/Geometry/Rectangles and Squares.* The figure is a square, so the two sides are equal: $2x+1=x+4\Rightarrow x=3$. One side is $x+4=3+4=7$. Since all four sides are equal, the perimeter is $4\cdot7=28$.

25. **(E)** (p. 486) *Mathematics/Geometry/Rectangles and Squares and Triangles/45º-45º-90º Triangles and Properties of Triangles.* If w is the width of the rectangle, the length is $2w$ and the rectangle has an area of $w\cdot2w=2w^2$. Then, w is also the length of the hypotenuse of a 45°-45°-90° triangle. Each of the other two sides forming the right angle (which also represent the altitude and base) is $\frac{1}{2}\cdot w\cdot\sqrt{2}=\frac{\sqrt{2}w}{2}$. The area of the triangle is $\frac{1}{2}\cdot$ altitude $\cdot$ base $=\frac{1}{2}\cdot\frac{\sqrt{2}w}{2}\cdot\frac{\sqrt{2}w}{2}=\frac{1}{2}\cdot\frac{2w^2}{4}=\frac{w^2}{4}$. The ratio of the area of the rectangle to that of the triangle is $\dfrac{2w^2}{\frac{w^2}{4}}=\dfrac{2}{\frac{1}{4}}=\dfrac{8}{1}$.

The above explanation is difficult to follow without a diagram, so draw one:

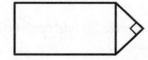

The explanation will not only be easier to follow, but it can be dispensed with altogether. The rectangle is obviously bigger than the triangle, so eliminate (A), (B), and (C). Adding to the figure shows that the area of the triangle is less than $\frac{1}{4}$ of the area of the rectangle. Approximating all of the triangles shows it is $\frac{1}{8}$ the area:

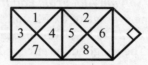

26. **(G)** (p. 486) ***Mathematics/Coordinate Geometry/The Coordinate System.*** No diagram is provided, so sketch one:

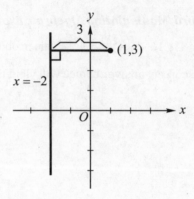

27. **(C)** (p. 486) ***Mathematics/Arithmetic/Common Arithmetic Items/Proportions and Direct-Inverse Variation.*** Determine how much coffee costs per pound: $\frac{\$12}{5\text{ pounds}} = \$2.40$ per pound. Therefore, $30 buys

$$\frac{\$30}{\$2.40\,/\,\text{pound}} = 12.5 \text{ pounds}.$$

Alternatively, the process can be represented in a single direct proportion:

$$\frac{\text{Cost }X}{\text{Cost }Y} = \frac{\text{Pounds }X}{\text{Pounds }Y} \Rightarrow \frac{\$30}{\$12} = \frac{x}{5} \Rightarrow 12x = 150 \Rightarrow x = \frac{150}{12} = 12.5.$$

28. **(J)** (p. 487) ***Mathematics/Geometry/Triangles/Properties of Triangles.*** Since the triangles are equilateral, the ratio of their perimeters is the same as the ratio of their sides. Thus, the ratio of their perimeters is also $\frac{3}{12} = \frac{1}{4}$.

Alternatively, find the perimeter of each triangle. Since the triangles are equilateral, the smaller one has a perimeter of $3+3+3=9$, and the larger one has a perimeter of $12+12+12=36$. Therefore, the ratio is $\frac{9}{36} = \frac{1}{4}$.

29. **(E)** (p. 487) ***Mathematics/Algebra/Expressing and Evaluating Algebraic Functions/Function Notation.*** Substitute -2 for x in the given function:

$$f(-2) = -3(-2)^3 + 3(-2)^2 - 4(-2) + 8 = -3(-8) + 3(4) - (-8) + 8 = 24 + 12 + 8 + 8 = 52.$$

30. (H) (p. 487) *Mathematics/Arithmetic/Common Arithmetic Items/Percents.* Add 40 percent to the $60 wholesale price: $60 + (0.40 \cdot \$60) = \$60 + \$24 = \$84$. Then, find the sale price: $\$84 - (0.30 \cdot \$84) = \$84 - \$25.20 = \$58.80$.

31. (A) (p. 488) *Mathematics/Algebra/Manipulating Algebraic Expressions/Evaluating Expressions.* $\frac{1}{3}$ of the number equals $\frac{1}{5}$ of the number plus 2: $\frac{1}{3}x = \frac{1}{5}x + 2 \Rightarrow \frac{1}{3}x - \frac{1}{5}x = 2$.

32. (H) (p. 488) *Mathematics/Geometry/Complex Figures* and *Triangles/Properties of Triangles* and *Rectangles and Squares.* This is a composite figure. One side of the equilateral triangle is also a side of the square. The triangle has a perimeter of 12, so each side is 4. If the square has a side of 4, then the perimeter is $4 + 4 + 4 + 4 = 16$.

33. (A) (p. 488) *Mathematics/Algebra/Manipulating Algebraic Expressions/Evaluating Expressions.* Substitute $\frac{2}{3}$ for x in the expression and solve for k:

$$12\left(\frac{2}{3}\right)^2 + k\left(\frac{2}{3}\right) = 6 \Rightarrow 12\left(\frac{4}{9}\right) + k\left(\frac{2}{3}\right) = 6 \Rightarrow 4\left(\frac{4}{3}\right) + k\left(\frac{2}{3}\right) = 6 \Rightarrow \frac{16}{3} + k\left(\frac{2}{3}\right) = 6 \Rightarrow k\left(\frac{2}{3}\right) = \frac{18}{3} - \frac{16}{3} = \frac{2}{3} \Rightarrow k = 1.$$

34. (K) (p. 489) *Mathematics/Geometry.* The perimeter is equal to the sum of the lengths of the sides: $2(x - 2y) + 4(2x + y) = 2x - 4y + 8x + 4y = 10x$.

Alternatively, substitute some numbers. Assume that $x = 3$ and $y = 1$. The two short sides are each $3 - 2(1) = 1$, for a total of 2. The four long sides are $2(3) + 1 = 7$, for a total of 28. The perimeter is $28 + 2 = 30$. Thus, if $x = 3$ and $y = 1$, the correct formula will generate the number 30. Only (K) produces the correct value.

35. (D) (p. 489) *Mathematics/Arithmetic/Complicated Arithmetic Application Items.* Let x be the number of packages in the van before the first delivery:

$$\left(x - \frac{2}{5}x\right) - 3 = \frac{1}{2}x \Rightarrow \frac{3}{5}x - 3 = \frac{1}{2}x \Rightarrow \frac{3}{5}x - \frac{1}{2}x = 3 \Rightarrow \frac{1}{10}x = 3 \Rightarrow x = 30.$$

36. (J) (p. 489) *Mathematics/Algebra/Manipulating Algebraic Expressions/Evaluating Expressions.* Perform the indicated operations in the answer choices to determine which one is equal to the expression in the stem $\left(12x^3 y^2 - 8x^2 y^3\right)$:

F. $2x^2 y^2 (4x - y) = 8x^3 y^2 - 2x^2 y^3$ ✘

G. $4x^2 y^2 (2xy) = 8x^3 y^3$ ✘

H. $4x^2 y^2 (3xy) = 12x^3 y^3$ ✘

J. $4x^2 y^2 (3x - 2y) = 12x^3 y^2 - 8x^2 y^3$ ✓

K. $x^3 y^3 (12xy - 8xy) = 12x^4 y^4 - 8x^4 y^4$ ✘

37. (C) (p. 490) *Mathematics/Algebra/Manipulating Algebraic Expressions/Basic Algebraic Manipulations.* The fastest way to solve this problem is to simply rewrite the expression:

$$\frac{1}{1 + \frac{1}{x}} = \frac{1}{\frac{x+1}{x}} = 1\left(\frac{x}{x+1}\right) = \frac{x}{x+1}.$$

Alternatively, substitute numbers into the expression. If $x = 1$, then: $\dfrac{1}{1 + \dfrac{1}{x}} = \dfrac{1}{1 + \dfrac{1}{1}} = \dfrac{1}{1+1} = \dfrac{1}{2}$. If $x = 1$, both

(B) and (C) generate $\dfrac{1}{2}$. Therefore, try another number. If $x = 2$, the correct answer should generate the

value $\dfrac{2}{3}$; (B) is eliminated and (C) must be correct.

38. **(G)** (p. 490) ***Mathematics/Arithmetic/Common Arithmetic Items/Percents.*** Use S and T as unknowns.
Since S is 150 percent of T, S equals $1.5T$. Substitute $1.5T$ for S: $\dfrac{T}{1.5T + T} = \dfrac{T}{2.5T} = \dfrac{1}{2.5} = 40$ percent.

Alternatively, substitute real numbers. Let S be 15 and T be 10; then, $\dfrac{T}{S + T} = \dfrac{10}{10 + 15} = \dfrac{10}{25} = 40\%$.

39. **(C)** (p. 490) ***Mathematics/Geometry/Lines and Angles.*** No figure is provided, so sketch one:

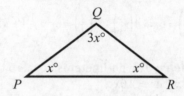

$x° + x° + 3x° = 180° \Rightarrow 5x° = 180° \Rightarrow x = 36$.

40. **(G)** (p. 491) ***Mathematics/Arithmetic/Common Arithmetic Items/Proportions and Direct-Inverse Variation.*** Use a direct proportion: $\dfrac{C}{x} = \dfrac{d}{b} \Rightarrow Cb = dx \Rightarrow C = \dfrac{dx}{b}$.

41. **(D)** (p. 491) ***Mathematics/Arithmetic/Common Arithmetic Items/Percents.*** First, find the reduced price:
$\$64 - (25\% \text{ of } \$64) = \$64 - (0.25 \cdot \$64) = \$64 - \$16 = \$48$. Next, calculate the sales tax on \$48:
$5\% \text{ of } \$48 = 0.05 \cdot \$48 = \$2.40$. Now, find the total cost: $\$48.00 + \$2.40 = \$50.40$.

42. **(K)** (p. 491) ***Mathematics/Algebra/Solving Simultaneous Equations.*** Use the method for solving
simultaneous equations: $\dfrac{y}{z} = k - 1 \Rightarrow k = \dfrac{y}{z} + 1$. Since $\dfrac{x}{z} = k$: $\dfrac{x}{z} = \dfrac{y}{z} + 1 \Rightarrow x = z\left(\dfrac{y}{z} + 1\right) = y + z$.

43. **(A)** (p. 491) ***Mathematics/Algebra/Solving Algebraic Equations with Two Variables.*** If $x = 0.25y$, then
$y = \dfrac{x}{0.25} = 4x$. Thus, y is 400 percent of x.

44. **(G)** (p. 492) ***Mathematics/Arithmetic/Common Arithmetic Items/Properties of Numbers.*** Since 3 is a
factor of 9 and 5 is a factor of 5, any multiple of both 9 and 5 will be a multiple of $3(5) = 15$; (II) belongs in
the correct choice. (I), however, is not correct. x could be any multiple of 45, e.g., 90, which also proves that
(III) does not belong in the correct choice.

45. **(B)** (p. 492) ***Mathematics/Geometry/Complex Figures*** and ***Triangles/Pythagorean Theorem.*** The neat
thing about a cube is that if given any one feature (e.g., volume, edge, diagonal of a face, diagonal of the cube,
surface area), every other feature can be calculated. This is why cubes are often the focus of test problems.
The edge has a length of 2, so use the Pythagorean theorem to find the length of the diagonal of a face:

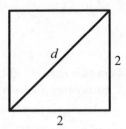

$d^2 = 2^2 + 2^2 = 4 + 4 = 8 \Rightarrow d = 2\sqrt{2}$. Now, find the length of the diagonal of the cube:

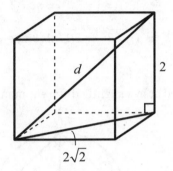

$d^2 = 2^2 + \left(2\sqrt{2}\right)^2 = 4 + 8 = 12 \Rightarrow d = 2\sqrt{3}$. That is the length of the entire diagonal of the cube. The point that is the center of the cube is the midpoint of the diagonal of the cube and is $\sqrt{3}$ units of length from each vertex.

46. **(J)** (p. 492) *Mathematics/Geometry.* $\text{Volume}_{\text{cylinder}} = \pi r^2 h$. Redefine the dimensions of the smaller cylinder in terms of r and h: $r = kr'$ so $r' = \dfrac{r}{k}$ and $h = kh'$ so $h' = \dfrac{h}{k}$.

$\text{Volume}_{\text{smaller cylinder}} = \pi\left(\dfrac{r}{k}\right)^2 \left(\dfrac{h}{k}\right) = \dfrac{\pi r^2 h}{k^3}$. The ratio is $\dfrac{\dfrac{\pi r^2 h}{k^3}}{\pi r^2 h} = \dfrac{1}{k^3}$. Therefore, the correct answer is (J), $1 : k^3$.

Alternatively, assume some numbers. Let the radius and height of the larger cylinder be 4 and 4, and those of the smaller cylinder be 2 and 2. Since $r = kr'$ and $h = kh'$, k must be 2.
$\text{Volume}_{\text{larger cylinder}} = \pi(4)^2(4) = 64\pi$. $\text{Volume}_{\text{smaller cylinder}} = \pi(2)^2(2) = 8\pi$. The ratio 8π to 64π is 1 to 8 or $\dfrac{1}{8}$. Use $k = 2$ to find the answer that has a value of $\dfrac{1}{8}$:

F. $1 : \pi = \dfrac{1}{\pi}$ ✖

G. $\pi : 1 = \dfrac{\pi}{1} = \pi$ ✖

H. $k\pi : 1 = \dfrac{k\pi}{1} = 2\pi$ ✖

J. $1 : k^3 = \dfrac{1}{k^3} = \dfrac{1}{2^3} = \dfrac{1}{8}$ ✔

K. $k^3 : 1 = \dfrac{k^3}{1} = \dfrac{2^3}{1} = \dfrac{8}{1} = 8$ ✗

47. **(A)** (p. 493) ***Mathematics/Geometry/Complex Figures*** and ***Triangles/Pythagorean Theorem*** and ***Circles.*** This is a right triangle, so $\angle PQR$ intercepts an arc of 180°. (The inscribed angle $\angle PQR$ is equal to half its intercepted arc.) Because the arc is 180°, the hypotenuse of the triangle, $\overline{PR}$, is also the diameter of the circle. From any bit of information about a right isosceles triangle (e.g., either side lengths, the hypotenuse, or the area), the other information can be found. Using the two adjacent sides as the altitude and the base, we have: $\text{area}_{\text{triangle}} = \dfrac{1}{2}(s)(s) \Rightarrow 1 = \dfrac{1}{2}s^2 \Rightarrow s^2 = 2$. Now, use the Pythagorean theorem to solve for $\overline{PR}$: $s^2 + s^2 = \overline{PR}^2 \Rightarrow 2 + 2 = \overline{PR}^2 \Rightarrow 4 = \overline{PR}^2 \Rightarrow \overline{PR} = 2$. Since $\overline{PR} = 2$, the radius of the circle is 1, and $\text{area}_{\text{circle}} = \pi(1)^2 = \pi$.

The same conclusion can be arrived at in a slightly different manner:

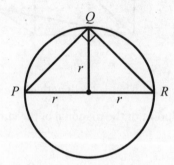

Based on the figure, r is the length of the altitude of the triangle and $2r$ is the length of the base, so $\text{area}_{\text{triangle}} = \dfrac{1}{2}(2r)(r) = r^2$ and $r^2 = 1 \Rightarrow r = 1$. Thus, $\text{area}_{\text{circle}} = \pi r^2 = \pi(1)^2 = \pi$.

Finally, a little common sense can solve this problem without any math. The triangle, which has an area of 1, takes up slightly less than half the circle:

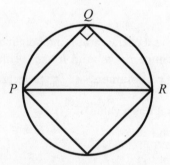

The correct answer must be a bit larger than 2, and only one choice qualifies: (A) is π and π is slightly larger than 3. Therefore, (A) is reasonable. All of the other choices are more than 6 and so are too large to be reasonable.

48. **(F)** (p. 493) ***Mathematics/Geometry/Complex Figures*** and ***Circles.*** This is a good exercise in organized problem-solving. Look at the figure and ask what is known: the radius of the circle and the perimeter of the shaded area consist of two arcs. There must be some way to use the information about the radius to find the length of the arcs. Arcs can be measured in terms of length or in terms of degrees.

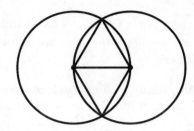

Since the sides of the triangles are all radii, the triangles must be equilateral, and the degree measure of each arc is 120. The circles have radii of 1, so they have circumferences of $2\pi(1) = 2\pi$. Each arc is a third of that length: $\frac{2\pi}{3}$. Since there are two such arcs, the perimeter of the shaded area is $2 \cdot \frac{2\pi}{3} = \frac{4\pi}{3}$.

49. **(C)** (p. 494) ***Mathematics/Statistics and Probability/Averages.*** For the first six tests, the student has a total point count of $(6)(83) = 498$. If the student scores a 0 on each of the remaining four tests, the total point count will remain 498 and the average will be $\frac{498}{10} = 49.8$. If the student scores 100 on each of the four remaining tests, the total point count will be 898 and the average will be $\frac{898}{10} = 89.8$.

50. **(K)** (p. 494) ***Mathematics/Arithmetic/Common Arithmetic Items/Complex Numbers.*** Let x be the multiplicative inverse of $2 - i$: $x(2 - i) = 1 \Rightarrow x = \frac{1}{2 - i} \Rightarrow x = \frac{1}{2 - i} \cdot \frac{2 + i}{2 + i} = \frac{2 + i}{4 - i^2}$. $i = \sqrt{-1}$, so $i^2 = -1$. Thus,

$$x = \frac{2 + i}{4 - (-1)} = \frac{2 + i}{5}.$$

51. **(C)** (p. 494) ***Mathematics/Arithmetic/Simple Manipulations.*** From the exponential concept of logarithms, if $a^x = b$, then the equation can be written in logarithmic form as $\log_a b = x$. Let $\log_3 \sqrt{3} = x$; then

$$3^x = \sqrt{3} \Rightarrow 3^x = 3^{\left(\frac{1}{2}\right)}.$$ Thus, $x = \frac{1}{2}$.

52. **(J)** (p. 494) ***Mathematics/Algebra/Expressing and Evaluating Algebraic Functions/Function Notation.*** Study the structure of f. When will the function be at its minimum value? This is like asking for the minimum value of $(x - 1)^2$. Squaring any positive number yields a positive number; squaring any negative number yields a positive number; and squaring zero yields zero. Since zero is less than any positive number, we want $x - 1$ to equal zero, and this occurs when $x = 1$. Now, plug in 1 for x in the given function and solve to find the minimum value of the function: $f(1) = (x - 1)^2 + 2 = (1 - 1)^2 + 2 = 2$.

Alternatively, test the answer choices. Plug each answer choice into the given function; the correct choice will be the lowest value:

F. $(-3 - 1)^2 + 2 = (-4)^2 + 2 = 16 + 2 = 18$ ✗
G. $(-2 - 1)^2 + 2 = (-3)^2 + 2 = 9 + 2 = 11$ ✗
H. $(0 - 1)^2 + 2 = (-1)^2 + 2 = 1 + 2 = 3$ ✗
J. $(1 - 1)^2 + 2 = (0)^2 + 2 = 0 + 2 = 2$ ✓
K. $(2 - 1)^2 + 2 = (1)^2 + 2 = 1 + 2 = 3$ ✗

Finally, if you recognized the function $f(x)=(x-1)^2+2$ as a parabolic equation in the form $(x-h)^2+k$ with a vertex of (h, k), you could simply plug in the values of h and k to determine the vertex: (1,2). Which means $x = 1$ is the minimum value of x.

53. **(A)** (p. 495) ***Mathematics/Algebra/Manipulating Algebraic Expressions/Manipulating Expressions Involving Exponents.*** Simply use the rules for working with exponents to solve the given equation for x:

$$2^n + 2^n + 2^n + 2^n = x(2^{n+1}) \Rightarrow (4)(2^n) = x\left(2^{n+1}\right) \Rightarrow (2)\left(2^1\right)\left(2^n\right) = x\left(2^{n+1}\right) \Rightarrow 2\left(2^{n+1}\right) = x\left(2^{n+1}\right) \Rightarrow 2 = x.$$

54. **(F)** (p. 495) ***Mathematics/Algebra/Expressing and Evaluating Algebraic Functions/Function Notation.*** $f(k)$ will equal $f(-k)$ when $(k)^2 + 2(k) + 1 = (-k)^2 - 2k + 1 \Rightarrow k^2 + 2k + 1 =$
$k^2 - 2k + 1 \Rightarrow 2k = -2k \Rightarrow 4k = 0 \Rightarrow k = 0$.

Another approach is to work backward from the answer choices. First, use the value 0: $(0)^2 + 2(0) + 1 =$ $(-0)^2 - 2(0) + 1 \Rightarrow 1 = 1$. Thus, 0 is part of the solution set; eliminate (G), (H), and (J). The only question that remains is whether the correct answer is (K). Take another value, say 1. If $k = 1$, $f(1) = (1)^2 + 2(1) + 1 = 4$ and $f(-1) = (-1)^2 - 2(1) + 1 = 0$, so $f(1) \ne f(-1)$, and (K) is eliminated. This proves that the answer is (F).

55. **(D)** (p. 495) ***Mathematics/Algebra/Manipulating Algebraic Expressions/Factoring Expressions.*** Factor the expression: $\dfrac{x^2 - 1}{x - 1} = \dfrac{(x+1)(x-1)}{x-1} = x + 1$. Therefore, as x approaches 1, $x + 1$ approaches 2.

56. **(H)** (p. 495) ***Mathematics/Trigonometry/Determining Trigonometric Values.*** Given the restrictions on x and since $\cos x = -1$, x must equal π and $\cos\dfrac{\pi}{2} = 0$.

Alternatively, visualize the graph of the cosine function (or graph it on a calculator).

57. **(B)** (p. 496) ***Mathematics/Algebra/Expressing and Evaluating Algebraic Functions/Concepts of Domain and Range.*** The domain of a function is the set of all possible x values; the range of a function is the set of all possible y values. Sketch (or use a calculator to graph) the function:

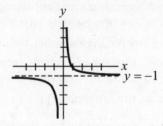

From the graph, it is obvious that the y-values both approach, but never actually reach, –1. Therefore, the range is defined by all real numbers except –1.

Alternatively, this item can be solved algebraically by solving for x. Since $f(x) = \dfrac{1-x}{x}$, $x[f(x)] = 1 - x \Rightarrow$

$x[f(x)] + x = 1 \Rightarrow x[f(x) + 1] = 1 \Rightarrow x = \dfrac{1}{f(x) + 1}$. The range of the function is the set of all possible values for $f(x)$. Since division by zero is undefined, $f(x) + 1 \ne 0 \Rightarrow f(x) \ne -1$. Thus, $f(x)$ can be any value except –1.

58. **(K)** (p. 496) ***Mathematics/Trigonometry/Trigonometric Relationships.*** $x = 3(\sin\theta)$ and $y = 2(\cos\theta)$; thus, $\sin\theta = \dfrac{x}{3}$ and $\cos\theta = \dfrac{y}{2}$. $\sin^2\theta + \cos^2\theta = 1$; thus, $\left(\dfrac{x}{3}\right)^2 + \left(\dfrac{y}{2}\right)^2 = 1 \Rightarrow \dfrac{x^2}{9} + \dfrac{y^2}{4} = 1$ is the equation of an ellipse with center (0,0) that passes through the points (3,0) and (0,2).

Alternatively, plug in values for θ. For $\theta = 0$, $x = 3[\sin(0)] = 3(0) = 0$. For $\theta = \dfrac{\pi}{2}$, $x = 3\left(\sin\dfrac{\pi}{2}\right) = 3(1) = 3$ and $y = 2\left(\cos\dfrac{\pi}{2}\right) = 2(0) = 0$. Therefore, the graph must include the points (3,0) and (0,2). The only graph given that contains both of these points is (K).

59. **(A)** (p. 496) ***Mathematics/Trigonometry/Definitions of the Six Trigonometric Functions.*** Sine and cosecant are reciprocal functions, so the product of the sine of any angle and the cosecant of that angle is 1. This fact can quickly be derived from the definitions of sine and cosecant. Given a triangle with sides a and b and hypotenuse c, let θ be opposite side b. $\sin\theta = \dfrac{b}{c}$ and $\csc\theta = \dfrac{c}{b}$. Therefore, $\sin\theta \cdot \csc\theta = 1$.

60. **(J)** (p. 497) ***Mathematics/Trigonometry/Trigonometry as an Alternative Method of Solution.*** There are several different ways of expressing the length of $\overline{BC}$: as a number, as a function of $\angle ACB$, and as a function of $\angle CAB$. "Testing-the-test" is the easiest option, and some exam wisdom will help. First, do not fall for (F) or (G). Test-takers are not expected to know values of trigonometric functions at particular angles. Since 40° and 50° are not easily remembered values, the answer is not going to be 4 or 5. The answer will be expressed using a trigonometric function. (J) is correct:

$$\tan A = \dfrac{\overline{BC}}{\overline{AB}} \Rightarrow \overline{BC} = \overline{AB}(\tan A) = 3(\tan 50°).$$

Section 3: Reading

1. **(D)** (p. 499) ***Reading/Prose Fiction/Implied Idea.*** In the final paragraph, the young man, Robin, is trying to explain to himself why the barbers laughed at him. Thus, he is talking to himself.

2. **(J)** (p. 499) ***Reading/Prose Fiction/Explicit Detail.*** The five shillings were not enough to satisfy the ferryman for having to make a special trip. The young man was forced to pay an additional three pence, bringing the total fare to five shillings and three pence.

3. **(B)** (p. 499) ***Reading/Prose Fiction/Implied Idea.*** Just after the young man gets off the ferryboat, he finds himself in a neighborhood of hovels and old houses that, he concludes, could not belong to his relative. Therefore, the young man must think his relative is well-to-do.

4. **(J)** (p. 499) ***Reading/Prose Fiction/Implied Idea.*** The scene is at night: the boat crosses at nine o'clock in the evening, the lights are on in the barber shop, and the stranger in the coat threatens to have the young man put in the stocks by morning.

5. **(A)** (p. 499) ***Reading/Prose Fiction/Implied Idea.*** In the first paragraph, the narrator remarks that the young man sets off on foot with a light step—as though he had not already traveled more than thirty miles. Thus, thirty miles is a long way to travel in a day.

6. **(G)** (p. 499) ***Reading/Prose Fiction/Explicit Detail.*** The young man finally concludes that the barbers laugh at him for approaching the stranger in the coat because it should have been obvious to him that the stranger in the coat would not know the Major.

7. **(A)** (p. 499) ***Reading/Prose Fiction/Implied Idea.*** The currency used to pay the ferryman and the length of a day's journey is suggestive. The reference to a "New England colony" clearly places the action some time before the end of the eighteenth century.

8. **(F)** (p. 499) ***Reading/Prose Fiction/Implied Idea.*** The young man bows to the stranger and addresses him as "honored sir" in order to show respect.

9. **(B)** (p. 499) ***Reading/Prose Fiction/Implied Idea.*** The passage states that nine o'clock in the evening was an "unusual hour." Such language implies that nine o'clock was an unusual time for anyone to be using the ferryboat. This is why the young man was its only passenger.

10. **(F)** (p. 499) ***Reading/Prose Fiction/Implied Idea.*** The phrase "small and mean wooden buildings" characterizes the neighborhood near the ferry landing. The next paragraph also mentions a hovel and an old house.

11. **(B)** (p. 501) ***Reading/Social Science/Explicit Detail.*** In the last paragraph, and the last sentence in particular, the author of the first passage states that the interdisciplinary approach used by Turner was a new technique. (B) best captures this idea. As for (A), the same paragraph states specifically that the reliance on political history was characteristic of history prior to Turner. As for (C), although Turner made the original presentation at a conference, the passage does not say that presenting was a technique of study. While Turner used the opportunity to present his new theory, he could equally well have published an article or made an informal presentation to colleagues. As for (D), the first passage doesn't enter into such a debate, though you will find some mention of this in the second passage. But because the information appears in the second passage, it cannot be an answer to this Explicit Detail item about the first passage.

12. **(G)** (p. 501) ***Reading/Social Science/Implied Idea.*** Passage A notes even some students of Turner demonstrated that some of his points were wrong. There would have been no reason to use "even" unless one would ordinarily expect for students to support the work of a professor. And in the development of the passage, the author is pointing out that even though Turner's thesis was criticized by some scholars who might otherwise have been supporters, the thesis still remains important. As for (F), the passage implies that the students did scholarly work on the thesis, not that they were ignorant of it. As for (J), there is no support for this conclusion in the text. (H) is wrong because there is nothing to support this conclusion.

13. **(D)** (p. 501) ***Reading/Social Science/Voice.*** The author of Passage A evidently approves of Turner's work. The passage says that it had great influence, that it was original, and that it used a novel approach. That's a pretty good review. As for (A), while the author allows that Turner's thesis was not immune to debate or even criticism, this does not mean that the author was "suspicious" of the work itself. After all, it could turn out to be that Turner's conclusions are ultimately false, but the groundbreaking approach and radical theory would still have value. As for (B), the thesis is not treated negatively, so "condescending" can't be used to express the author's attitude. Finally, as for (C), the author takes a pretty strong position, so "undecided" is not a good description.

14. **(G)** (p. 501) ***Reading/Social Science/Vocabulary.*** Because "grand" is a word with some common meanings, you can pretty much discount any choices that use these more common synonyms. That would certainly eliminate (H). Instead, the author is using the word "grand" in a derivative sense to mean large or great or overall. Turner's thesis did try to be comprehensive, accounting for the uniquely American character. As for (F), though the author allows that Turner's thesis was not perfect, line 14 is not where that discussion occurs. And (J) must be wrong since Turner's thesis was not tentative.

15. **(C)** (p. 501) ***Reading/Social Science/Development.*** The author of Passage B discusses the limitations of Turner's theory, and one of the most important of these is its attempt to explain everything American in terms of the frontier. At the referenced lines, the author lists some other very important historical factors in order to show that the frontier could not have been the entire story. As for (A), this is the topic introduced at the end of that paragraph and developed in the following paragraphs, but it is not an answer to this

question. As for (B), even granting that this statement is correct, it is not an answer to this question. For example, the author mentions the Civil War in order to show that Turner's thesis was too limited, not that traditional histories were too limited. As for (D), this is a point that is raised in the fifth paragraph, so it is not an answer to the question asked about the third paragraph.

16. **(G)** (p. 501) ***Reading/Social Science/Development.*** At the end of the third paragraph, the author of Passage B states that Turner's thesis, in addition to failing as a comprehensive theory of American history, does not do an adequate job of explaining the frontier. The next three paragraphs are the specific points to support this argument: (i) land wasn't free, (ii) frontier is a dubious concept, and (iii) groups as well as individuals were important. The information about wagon trains supports this last point: it was groups, not loners, who moved into the westward regions and stayed. As for (F), (H), and (J), these are ideas that are mentioned, but they do not explain the significance of the wagon trains.

17. **(B)** (p. 501) ***Reading/Social Science/Voice.*** The author of Passage B is critical of the frontier thesis, but you'll notice that the criticisms all deal with Turner's ideas. For example, Turner thought that the frontier offered free land, but the author of Passage B argues that he was wrong because the land was already used by indigenous peoples. So, while the passage criticizes Turner's idea, it doesn't criticize Turner himself. Thus, (C) and (D) are wrong, and (B) is correct. As for (A), the author says that the thesis has "rightfully" been abandoned because of its weaknesses.

18. **(H)** (p. 501) ***Reading/Social Science/Vocabulary.*** You get the information you need to answer the question from the discussion about the significance of the Indian Wars. Turner claimed that the land was free, but in reality, it was necessary to pursue a policy of military aggression to secure the land. So, when the author writes that the wars "belie" the free land theory, the author means "prove false." (F) is a distracting choice, but don't be misled by the superficial connection between "lie" and "untruth." In this context, the phrase is "prove to be false," not "lie about." As for (G) and (H), while these are phrases that relate generally to the idea of debating the merits of a theory, they don't focus on the connection between the wars and the free land thesis.

19. **(D)** (p. 502) ***Reading/Social Science/Explicit Detail.*** The key word other than "EXCEPT" in this item is "both;" therefore, the correct answer choice is the only one that is *not* mentioned in *both* passages. Both authors mention (A), (B), and (C). However, "nationalism" is only mentioned in the first passage.

20. **(F)** (p. 502) ***Reading/Social Science/Application.*** To a certain extent, any weakening of Turner's theory would have implications for all aspects of the theory. So, you might argue that the referenced evidence, in some way, tends to show that people from different regions did not mix at the frontier because the frontier was not quite as well-defined as Turner thought. But that's a pretty feeble point, and so (J) is wrong. You can apply similar reasoning to (G) and (H). The best answer here is (F). The "safety valve" point, as explained in Passage A, maintained that people who were dissatisfied with life in the urban areas could simply pack up and move to the country because there was land for the claiming. If the "free land" thesis is false, then the "safety valve" thesis must also be false.

21. **(A)** (p. 503) ***Reading/Humanities/Development.*** At the end of the first paragraph, the author raises a question, which he then proceeds to answer. (A) describes this development. (B) is incorrect because the author does not present a theory as such. A theory is a hypothetical explanation of phenomena; the author instead presents his viewpoint about what is important in life. Also, while the author offers many opinions, none "prove" his viewpoint. As for (C), the author does not contrast his own views with other views. As for (D), the author does not define a term.

22. **(J)** (p. 503) ***Reading/Humanities/Vocabulary.*** In the final paragraph, the author explains that life is much too short. The author introduces the discussion by stating that experience is the end goal of life—to get the most out of life, one must pack it with "as many pulsations as possible." One can infer that the author means experiences.

23. **(B)** (p. 503) *Reading/Humanities/Explicit Detail.* The discussion of art is found in the closing sentences of the passage. Having said that the best life is one packed with experiences (pulsations), the author goes on to say how one can have these intense experiences. This is one function of art, he says—to do nothing but provoke feelings—not to depict reality, (A); not to encourage reform, (C); not as a means of expression, (D).

24. **(H)** (p. 503) *Reading/Humanities/Application.* Experience is everything according to the author, so he would probably agree with (H). It is the feeling of the moment that is important, not the memory of the feeling. Once the feeling is past, you should be looking for new feelings, not thinking about past ones.

25. **(A)** (p. 503) *Reading/Humanities/Voice.* The writing is highly impassioned. The intensity of the writing is evident in every sentence. The issues are those of life and death. The author uses phrases such as "passionate attitude," "tragic dividing," "awful brevity," and "splendor of our experience."

26. **(H)** (p. 504) *Reading/Humanities/Implied Idea.* In the second paragraph, the author argues that the best life is one filled with experiences of every sort. Not to seek after a variety of experiences is, in the author's words, "on this short day of the frost and sun, to sleep before evening." The phrase "to sleep before evening" must mean to stop living even before death. Thus, the "short day of the frost and sun" refers to a person's life.

27. **(C)** (p. 504) *Reading/Humanities/Implied Idea.* The author emphasizes the importance of living life to the fullest. In line 26, "awful brevity" refers to the shortness of life.

28. **(J)** (p. 504) *Reading/Humanities/Explicit Detail.* In the final paragraph, the author contrasts those who are listless with those who are the children of the world. The children of the world are high in passion, wise, and in love with art and song.

29. **(A)** (p. 504) *Reading/Humanities/Implied Idea.* Lines 36–42 say that the desire for beauty has the most power to quicken our sense of life.

30. **(H)** (p. 504) *Reading/Humanities/Implied Idea.* The author says that we are all under a sentence of death with an indefinite reprieve, meaning that we are all mortal. We have an "interval," meaning our life; and then "our place knows us no more," meaning we are gone from the earth; that is, we are dead.

31. **(B)** (p. 506) *Reading/Natural Science/Explicit Detail.* Line 3 reads, in part: "energy, which is the capacity for doing work."

32. **(H)** (p. 506) *Reading/Natural Science/Explicit Detail.* The second paragraph states that the result of the process is a mix of sugar and oxygen. O_2 names oxygen, and H_2O names water, so $C_6H_{12}O_6$ names a sugar.

33. **(A)** (p. 506) *Reading/Natural Science/Explicit Detail.* Lines 17–21 define both terms. Reduction is the addition of electrons, and oxidation is the removal of electrons.

34. **(J)** (p. 506) *Reading/Natural Science/Explicit Detail.* Lines 17–19 state that photosynthesis involves the addition of electrons, making (I) correct. Lines 23–26 state that photosynthesis involves action on hydrogen, meaning that (II) is also correct. Lines 20–21 state that "Reduction stores energy, while oxidation releases it," and line 17 states that "Photosynthesis is a reduction reaction." So, (III) cannot be correct. Since (I) and (II) are correct, the answer is (J).

35. **(C)** (p. 506) *Reading/Natural Science/Main Idea.* The fifth paragraph gives a systematic analysis of the process defined in preceding paragraphs, which is photosynthesis.

36. **(F)** (p. 506) *Reading/Natural Science/Explicit Detail.* (G) is supported by lines 51–52, (H) is supported by lines 64–67, and (J) is stated in lines 50–51. (F) states the reverse of the truth; it is ADP that is mixed with phosphate to form ATP (see lines 51–52).

37. **(A)** (p. 506) *Reading/Natural Science/Implied Idea.* A careful reading of lines 64–71 can lead to no other conclusion. A five-carbon sugar (RuDP) is combined with carbon dioxide (CO_2), ultimately resulting in the formation of a three-carbon sugar (PGAL).

38. **(G)** (p. 507) *Reading/Natural Science/Implied Idea.* Growing periods, (J), are never discussed. Higher temperatures, (H), as indicated in the final paragraph, can lead to disagreeable conditions. Lines 72–78 state that the photorespiration, with its seemingly wasteful result, occurs when CO_2 levels are low, suggesting that a higher level of CO_2 would be a more agreeable condition. Also, more agreeable conditions facilitate carboxyilation. This process involves combining CO_2. Therefore, more CO_2 means an increase in carboxyilation.

39. **(B)** (p. 507) *Reading/Natural Science/Explicit Detail.* As stated in line 17, photosynthesis is a reduction reaction, which makes (III) an incorrect choice. Lines 67–69 and lines 72–75 indicate that RuDP is used in carboxyilation and photorespiration, making (I) correct. Another difference, as stated in lines 75–76, is that no ATP is created via photorespiration, (II).

40. **(H)** (p. 507) *Reading/Natural Science/Main Idea.* The angiosperm plants discussed in the final paragraph *do* photosynthesize, so (F) is incorrect. They do it in an unusual way, using their specialized leaf structure (H). According to the paragraph, Kranz plants have a method of maintaining carbon dioxide levels; they do not transform carbon dioxide into carbohydrate.

Section 4: Science

1. **(B)** (p. 510) *Science/Data Representation/Comprehension.* As the table shows, with each additional carbon atom, the boiling point of the compound increases. For example, from methane (1 carbon atom) to ethane (2 carbon atoms), the boiling point increases from –162°C to –89°C, and from ethane to propane (3 carbon atoms), from –89°C to –42°C.

2. **(H)** (p. 510) *Science/Data Representation/Analysis.* Butane has four carbon atoms. This means it has ten hydrogen atoms. Both (G) and (H) have chains with ten hydrogen, but only (H) is similar to the propane example, with CH_3 on the end and CH_2 in the middle.

3. **(C)** (p. 510) *Science/Data Representation/Application.* This item is answered by looking at the values in the table. Boiling points for the compounds shown increase as the number of carbon atoms increase.

4. **(H)** (p. 510) *Science/Data Representation/Application.* This item tests information provided in the passage. The passage states that alkanes that differ by one carbon atom differ in molecular mass by 14u: 142 + 14 = 156.

5. **(C)** (p. 510) *Science/Data Representation/Application.* According to the passage, the number of hyrdrogen atoms can be found using the formula $2n + 2$, where n is the number of carbon molecules: 2(12) + 2 = 26.

6. **(J)** (p. 510) *Science/Data Representation/Application.* The graph shows that the boiling points of the first four alkanes are below room temperature (about 20°C). So methane, ethane, propane, and butane are all gases at that temperature. Hexane, however, is still a liquid. It boils and becomes a gas between 50°C and 100°C.

7. **(A)** (p. 511) *Science/Data Representation/Analysis.* The graph in (A) shows the correct values for density; as the number of atoms in the carbon backbone increases, the density of the alkane increases. The relationship is most closely approximated by a straight line since the increment each time is not always constant.

8. **(F)** (p. 513) *Science/Research Summary/Comprehension.* According to the explanation provided in paragraph one, the flag leaves penetrate the top of the coleoptile once it has reached the surface and continue to grow. The feature corresponding to that description is the plumule.

9. **(B)** (p. 513) *Science/Research Summary/Comprehension.* The paragraph following Table 1 states that the greater growth rate for the coleoptiles with tips exposed to the air is explained by the production of additional growth substance. Those coleoptiles completely immersed in water had available only the growth substance left over from before the clipping.

10. **(F)** (p. 513) *Science/Research Summary/Comprehension.* The first experiment immersed the coleoptiles in water, though in the second test the tops were allowed to extend into the air. But in neither test was anything but water used. Experiments 2 and 3 used growth solution.

11. **(B)** (p. 514) *Science/Research Summary/Analysis.* The numbers in the table represent increments of growth. The cumulative growth is the result of adding the increments. Each increment shows some growth, so the line which continues to increase at every time point represents the correct cumulative growth, (B).

12. **(H)** (p. 514) *Science/Research Summary/Comprehension.* The greatest cumulative growth after 24 hours was 31.0 percent, associated with a concentration of 10 units per cm^3.

13. **(C)** (p. 514) *Science/Research Summary/Analysis.* Table 2 shows that the solution of 40 units grew 8.0% longer than the original length after 4 hours, but after 24 hours it had only grown 7.2% longer than the original length. Therefore, it showed shrinkage.

14. **(J)** (p. 514) *Science/Research Summary/Application.* The introductory material for Table 3 explains that cyanide would interfere with a metabolic process. The data in the table clearly shows that the greater the concentration of KCN, the lower the growth rate.

15. **(B)** (p. 516) *Science/Research Summary/Comprehension.* According to the introductory paragraph, osmosis occurs when solvent molecules pass through a semi-permeable membrane to dilute the solute concentration on the other side of the membrane. In Experiment 1, the water (solvent) passes through the membrane from the side with lower sugar concentration to the side with higher sugar concentration—no sugar (solute) molecules pass through the membrane. This is also explained in the second paragraph, which introduces the figure illustrating the process of osmosis with sugar solutions.

16. **(H)** (p. 516) *Science/Research Summary/Comprehension.* The purpose of Experiment 1 is to determine how many cells in a representative sample undergo plasmolysis—an effect of osmosis—after being submerged in sugar solutions of varying solute concentrations, (H). The solute concentrations of the solutions, (F), is a controlled variable. The quantity of water lost due to osmosis, (G), is beyond the scope of the experiment. Finally, although the data do show the threshold at which osmosis is first observed, (J), locating that point is not the purpose of the experiment.

17. **(B)** (p. 516) *Science/Research Summary/Comprehension.* The description of Experiment 1 states that "[f]orty to sixty-five cells from each onion strip are analyzed and scored." The statement is part of the experimental setup and not tied with any experimental outcome. The best approach to an item like this is to eliminate the wrong choices. Nothing is known about the number of cells, plasmolyzed (A) or average total (C), in an onion strip—what is known is the number of plasmolyzed cells in a sample consisting of 40 to 65 cells. As for (D), nothing can be known about the unanalyzed cells of the onion strips simply because they are unanalyzed. Therefore, by the process of elimination, the correct choice must be (B). Indeed, the purpose of analyzing 40 to 65 cells from each strip is to provide a representative snapshot of the cells in an onion without having to count endlessly.

18. **(F)** (p. 516) *Science/Research Summary/Analysis.* According to the passage, osmosis is the movement of solvent (e.g., water) from an area of lesser solute (e.g., sugar) concentration to one of higher concentration. In Experiment 1, osmosis results in plasmolyzed cells because the cells lose water (solvent) to regions of

higher sugar (solute) concentration. When immersed in the 0.05 mol/kg sugar solution, the cells do no lose water—that is, there is no evidence of plasmolysis—because the sugar concentration inside the cells is greater than that of the surrounding solution.

19. **(B)** (p. 516) ***Science/Research Summary/Analysis.*** The difference in percentage of plasmolyzed cells is accounted for by the number of cells analyzed in each case. For the onion strip submerged in the 0.55 mol/kg sugar solution, 50 of the 50 analyzed cells are plasmolyzed: $\frac{50}{50} = 100\%$. For the onion strip submerged in the 0.45 mol/kg sugar solution, 50 of the 64 analyzed cells are plasmolyzed: $\frac{50}{64} \approx 78.1\%$.

20. **(G)** (p. 516) ***Science/Research Summary/Analysis.*** According to Table 2, the beet disk submerged in the 0.00 mol/kg sugar solution increases in weight. A solution concentration of 0.00 moles of sugar per kilogram of water indicates that there is no sugar in the solution—the beaker contains only water. Therefore, any sugar in the cells of the beet disk triggers osmosis and water molecules moved across the semi-permeable cell walls into the beet cells, adding weight to the disk.

21. **(C)** (p. 517) ***Science/Research Summary/Application.*** According to Table 2, as the sugar solution concentration increases, the percentage of weight change decreases. Therefore, eliminate (A) and (D). The graphs in (B) and (C) are similar for high and low values but different for values in the middle of the graph, so compare the values in Table 2 for a sugar solution concentration of 0.25 mol/kg. According to the table, the percentage of weight change in the disk submerged in the 0.25 mol/kg sugar solution is +3.65%, so (C) is the correct choice.

22. **(H)** (p. 517) ***Science/Research Summary/Analysis.*** According to Table 2, the beet disk submerged in the 0.35 mol/kg sugar solution increases in weight, while the beet disk submerged in the 0.40 mol/kg sugar solution decreases in weight. Thus, the concentration of sugar in the beet cells must be between 0.35 moles and 0.40 moles per kilogram of water.

23. **(B)** (p. 518) ***Science/Data Representation/Comprehension.*** Magnesium is a positively charged mineral (Mg^{+2}). The soil that has the worst relative ability to hold such minerals is coarse sand.

24. **(J)** (p. 518) ***Science/Data Representation/Analysis.*** As particles get larger (from less than 2 micrometers to 200–2,000 micrometers), their relative ability to retain water decreases (from 1 to 4).

25. **(C)** (p. 518) ***Science/Data Representation/Comprehension.*** Soils that are neither most able nor least able for any ability cannot be ranked 1 or 4. The only soils that are never ranked 1 or 4 are silt (greater than or equal to 2 μm and less than 20 μm) and sand (greater than or equal to 20 μm and less than 200 μm). The total size range, therefore, is greater than or equal to 2 μm and less than 200 μm.

26. **(F)** (p. 519) ***Science/Data Representation/Application.*** Since loam is mostly clay, it primarily has small particles that hold minerals and water well. The larger silt and sand particles in loam are adequate at maintaining air spaces containing oxygen. None of the other predictions fit the data in the chart.

27. **(D)** (p. 519) ***Science/Data Representation/Analysis.*** (A), (B), and (C) are all true. However, (D) is NOT true: Clay is most able (relative ability: l) to both hold positively charged minerals and retain water, so there is a soil type that is best for more than one category of relative ability.

28. **(G)** (p. 520) ***Science/Conflicting Viewpoints/Comprehension.*** Concentrations of reactants, not products, determine rate in both theories.

29. **(C)** (p. 520) ***Science/Conflicting Viewpoints/Comprehension.*** This question tests critical comprehension of the passage, and it requires an understanding of the relationship between the two theories. According to the passage, Theory 2 explains that Theory 1 is based upon an incomplete understanding of the details of

chemical reactions, assuming that all reactions operate by a single-step mechanism. Therefore, one can conclude that a proponent of Theory 2 believes that Theory 1 can be used for single step reactions, but should not be used for more complex reactions.

30. **(G)** (p. 520) *Science/Conflicting Viewpoints/Comprehension.* This question tests understanding of the relation of numbers of reactants in the overall equation to exponents in the rate law. For the reaction $Mg + 2HCl \Rightarrow MgCl_2 + H_2$, Theory 1 states that $rate = k[Mg]^1[HCl]^2$, where k is the rate constant and the exponents are the coefficients in front of the reactants in the reaction. Using this formula, the rate equation for $3M + 2N \Rightarrow 4P$ must be $k[M]^3[N]^2$.

31. **(D)** (p. 520) *Science/Conflicting Viewpoints/Analysis.* The coefficients of the reactants determine their exponents in the rate law.

32. **(F)** (p. 521) *Science/Conflicting Viewpoints/Analysis.* This question tests understanding of the differences between the theories. Theory 2 disagrees with Theory 1 on the grounds that chemical reactions do not all occur in one stage. Therefore, Theory 2 may be best supported by evidence that proves that some reactions occur in more than one stage.

33. **(A)** (p. 521) *Science/Conflicting Viewpoints/Comprehension.* If the first stage is very slow and the second stage is much quicker, the overall rate is essentially that of the first stage.

34. **(H)** (p. 521) *Science/Conflicting Viewpoints/Analysis.* If the sum of the rates of each stage always equaled the rate of the reaction taken as a whole, there would be no need to analyze each sub-reaction.

35. **(B)** (p. 522) *Science/Research Summary/Comprehension.* Temperature range for a life function is the high temperature minus the low temperature. For both species and both humidity conditions, oviposition always has the narrowest range.

36. **(J)** (p. 522) *Science/Research Summary/Comprehension.* For each life function, Species M achieved 90% success at the same low temperatures in either humidity. At high temperatures, however, 50% humidity was detrimental. (Under 50% humidity, 90% success was not achieved at the same high temperatures as 100% relative humidity.)

37. **(C)** (p. 522) *Science/Research Summary/Analysis.* Since humidity levels had no effect on Species D for mating, oviposition, or pupation, it is likely that 50% relative humidity will have little effect on caterpillar survival in Species D as well. The temperature range would, therefore, be the same as observed at 100% relative humidity: 12°C–36°C.

38. **(G)** (p. 522) *Science/Research Summary/Analysis.* Mating success in the light and in the dark should be compared at the same temperature. It should be a temperature at which both species can successfully mate. Otherwise, additional variables confuse the issue. (30°C is an optimum temperature for both species under all conditions presented.)

39. **(D)** (p. 523) *Science/Research Summary/Analysis.* Species M and Species D are both equally successful at low temperatures for pupation.

40. **(F)** (p. 523) *Science/Research Summary/Analysis.* (G) and (H) are not relevant to the question. (J) only refers to light conditions. (F) is a hypothesis supported by the results.

Sample Essay Responses and Analyses

Section 5: Writing (p. 524)

Above Average Response

If you walk through a suburban parking lot, on a city street, or even along a beach, you are likely to see grocery bags littering the ground. Because of the environmental risks they pose, free plastic and paper bags should be eliminated and be replaced with cloth bags or purchased bags that are designed for reuse. Non-reusable bags have a harmful impact on the environment, and consumers needlessly accumulate them. Although eliminating free grocery bags would be an unwelcome change for some consumers and manufacturers, it is a long-term change that needs to be made for the good of the environment.

The production and use of both plastic and paper bags have a negative impact on the environment. As litter, plastic bags are more dangerous than paper because often, they are not biodegradable. They accumulate in landfills and can kill animals that attempt to eat them or that become entangled in them and suffocate. Plastic bags can be especially harmful in coastal cities because they can float into bodies of water, where they are difficult to recover and can kill marine life. Paper bags, however, require more energy to manufacture, which produces more greenhouse gases. Unless paper bags are made from recycled material, trees must be cut down to manufacture them. Paper bags are also harder to reuse because some plastic bags are waterproof and more durable. Because both types of cause environmental problems, it is best to shop with reusable, cloth bags.

Grocery bags are also an example of waste because Americans accumulate more bags than necessary. One may argue that some sources of pollution, such as gasoline, cannot be eliminated because there is no widely available substitute. However, paper and plastic bags can easily be replaced with more environmentally-friendly products. It is wasteful to manufacture a product that harms the environment and that is used for about 20 minutes before being thrown out. Because these bags are so rapidly disposed, they accumulate in shoppers' homes, or worse, outside. Some California cities, for example, have banned plastic bags because of the pollution they cause when they accumulate in natural environments. Stores should cut down on the number of non-reusable bags they distribute by charging for paper and plastic bags and also by having cloth bags available for sale.

Opponents of banning plastic bags claim that a ban would be inconvenient for consumers and would harm manufacturers. For consumers, however, the ban would cease to be an annoyance once they adjusted to bringing their own bags. Shoppers could keep bags in their cars or backpacks for last-minute trips to the store, and initially, stores could reward customers who bring their own bags. For example, some stores enter shoppers with their own bags in a raffle for free groceries. Some consumers argue that they reuse plastic bags for garbage; however, they would still be able to purchase durable plastic bags at a low cost. The biggest challenge to eliminating plastic bags would be the threat to bag manufacturers. In California, a statewide ban was delayed because it would have eliminated manufacturers' jobs. Before implementing a ban, states should devise plans to minimize job loss; for example, factories could transition into making fewer, more durable bags.

Although eliminating free grocery bags would be an adjustment for many Americans, it would be worth the long-term environmental benefits. The large quantities of bags that Americans currently use is wasteful, and their convenience does not justify the threat they pose for the environment.

Ideas and Analysis: The writer clearly states his or her thesis in the introduction: free, non-reusable shopping bags are a threat to the environment and should be banned. The writer's thesis largely agrees with Perspective 2, but the writer adds that paper bags can also harm the environment. The author addresses Perspective 3's argument by arguing that both paper and plastic bags can be harmful, and the quantity of bags overall should be reduced. The essay also counters Perspective 1's claim that the convenience of free bags makes them necessary for consumers.

Development and Support:

- The introduction opens with a hook, and the description of litter in different environments illustrates that it is a widespread problem.

- The writer clearly states the thesis in the second sentence of the introduction and previews the three main arguments.

- The body paragraphs begin with topic sentences that state the main point or argument to be made in the paragraph.

- The body paragraphs include concrete examples to support the writer's opinions.

   o Body paragraph 1: The writer describes specific effects of both paper and plastic bags on the environment.

   o Body paragraph 2: The writer argues that the accumulation of non-reusable bags is harmful and unnecessary and uses the California ban to illustrate this claim.

   o Body paragraph 3: The writer acknowledges the opposing viewpoint. Although the writer does not have specific, proven examples of how to prevent job loss when fewer bags are manufactured, he or she provides practical advice on how to make the transition easier for consumers.

Organization:

- The writer introduces each paragraph with a topic sentence.

- The writer uses transitions to connect ideas between and within paragraphs. See, for example, the first sentence of the second body paragraph: "Grocery bags are also an example of waste because Americans accumulate more bags than necessary."

- The main ideas are arranged in a logical progression:

1) Non-reusable bags are harmful for the environment.

2) These risks are unnecessary because non-reusable bags can be replaced with products that are more environmentally friendly.

3) Consumers and companies can think of solutions to make the elimination of non-reusable bags easier for customers and manufacturers.

- The second body paragraph becomes slightly repetitive because both the first and second body paragraphs mention the accumulation of paper and plastic bags.

Language Use and Conventions: The essay contains at least three principal strengths in this area:

- The essay does not have any mechanics/usage errors. As a result, the reader's attention is not distracted from the substance of the essay.

- The essay does not have any informal language.

- Stylistically, the writer varies sentence structures throughout most of the essay.

Summary and Conclusions: This essay demonstrates writing skills that are well developed and provides arguments, as well as practical suggestions for eliminating non-reusable shopping bags. The writer also addresses all three perspectives throughout the essay. This essay would likely receive a score of 10.

Below Average Response

Eliminating paper and plastic bags might be good for the environment but its just not doable in America. Shopping bags are really convenient for shoppers and can be used around the house. Also, we do other things also have a bad affect on the environment, so I don't see why people have to care so much about plastic bags.

Shopping bags are very convenient, and it would be too much of a burden on customers if they were eliminated. Often, my parents just stop by the store on the way home from work to pick up a few things they need. They would never remember to bring a reusable bag with them to work in case they needed to go shopping afterwards. I think it would be unfair to consumers to have to buy bags every single time they went shopping because the reality is that shoppers aren't used to bringing bags with them, and it would take a long time for them to get used to this.

Also, plastic bags can be used around the house. I often use them as trash bags, since they're waterproof, they're very useful for this purpose. Sometimes when it's raining, I also use them to protect my books and my calculator because my backpack isn't completely waterproof.

Also, it is impossible not to harm the environment. So many things that we do harm the environment, like driving, taking long showers, and using gas stoves. However, theres never going to be a law banning these activities, so why should shopping bags be banned?

Although in an ideal world we'd be able to ban non-reusable shopping bags, this wouldn't work in the US. It would be too hard for Americans to adjust to the change.

Ideas and Analysis: The writer has a clear thesis and three main supporting arguments. However, while the essay defends Perspective 1, it does not take into account the opposing arguments in Perspectives 2 and 3. The writer's analysis of the situation is weak because he or she claims to speak for all "Americans" but only offers arguments and examples from his or her personal life. The essay would be stronger if it analyzed a wider range of viewpoints, instead of relying on generalizations.

Development and Support:

- The writer states his or her thesis in the first sentence of the introduction, and the introduction also previews the three main supporting arguments.

- In the body paragraphs, the writer uses several personal examples, but he or she generalizes from these examples and claims that banning plastic bags would be difficult for everyone.

- The second body paragraph does not develop the writer's argument well. The writer provides two examples of uses of plastic bags but does not explain that these activities make plastic bags a less wasteful product.

- The third body paragraph, in particular, contains a superficial argument. The writer does not acknowledge that activities like driving and cooking are necessary parts of one's daily life, whereas there is a feasible alternative to using plastic bags.

Organization:

- The organization of the essay is clear and easy to follow. The writer states his or her thesis in the introduction, and each body paragraph has a topic sentence.

- The writer uses transitions, but the transitions sometimes sound repetitive and awkward. For example, both the second and third body paragraphs begin with the transition "also." The writer needs to vary transitions to make the essay flow more smoothly.

Language Use and Conventions: The essay contains several weaknesses in this area:

- The essay contains some usage and mechanics errors.

    o Introduction: In the first sentence, "its" should be changed to "it's." (Explain that "its" is the possessive form, and "it's" means "it is.")

    o Introduction: In the last sentence, "affect" should be changed to "effect." (Explain that usually, "affect" is a verb and "effect" is a noun.)

    o Body paragraph 2: The second sentence has a comma splice. (I often use them as trash bags, since they're waterproof, they're very useful for this purpose.) The writer should begin a new sentence after "bags" or replace the comma with a semicolon.

    o Body paragraph 3: In the final sentence, "theres" should be changed to "there's."

- The essay contains many examples of informal language. For example, in the conclusion, the writer says, "this wouldn't work in the US." Instead, the writer should say, "banning non-reusable bags would not be practical in the US."

- The essay also uses repetitive language. For example, the introduction states that "Shopping bags are really convenient for shoppers." The writer should use a synonym for "shoppers," such as "consumers," to avoid sounding repetitive.

Summary and Conclusions: The essay has a clear thesis and three main arguments. However, the writer does not use developed reasoning or a variety of examples to support these arguments. Furthermore, the writer does not consider the opposing viewpoints. This essay would likely receive a score of 5.

PRACTICE TEST II

Multiple-Choice Answer Keys

DIRECTIONS: For the <u>correct</u> answer, check the corresponding unshaded box. Then, total the number of checkmarks for each of the content areas and add these totals to determine the raw score for that test.

Section 1: English (Student Text, p. 528)

	UM RH		UM RH		UM RH		UM RH		UM RH
1. B		16. H		31. B		46. J		61. A	
2. G		17. A		32. G		47. D		62. J	
3. C		18. H		33. B		48. G		63. B	
4. H		19. D		34. J		49. B		64. J	
5. B		20. F		35. D		50. H		65. C	
6. F		21. C		36. J		51. A		66. G	
7. A		22. F		37. D		52. H		67. B	
8. H		23. A		38. H		53. D		68. F	
9. C		24. F		39. A		54. F		69. A	
10. F		25. D		40. H		55. A		70. F	
11. C		26. J		41. B		56. F		71. B	
12. J		27. C		42. G		57. B		72. F	
13. B		28. H		43. A		58. J		73. B	
14. J		29. D		44. H		59. A		74. J	
15. C		30. J		45. D		60. F		75. B	

Usage and Mechanics (UM): _____/45   Rhetorical Skills (RH): _____/30   Raw Score (UM + RH): _____/75

Section 2: Mathematics (Student Text, p. 542)

	EA AG GT		EA AG GT		EA AG GT		EA AG GT
1. D		16. K		31. C		46. H	
2. K		17. C		32. G		47. A	
3. C		18. G		33. C		48. G	
4. K		19. B		34. H		49. C	
5. A		20. J		35. C		50. J	
6. F		21. A		36. H		51. A	
7. C		22. K		37. E		52. F	
8. G		23. D		38. K		53. E	
9. C		24. J		39. C		54. K	
10. F		25. D		40. J		55. B	
11. E		26. G		41. D		56. G	
12. K		27. B		42. K		57. D	
13. A		28. G		43. B		58. J	
14. G		29. D		44. G		59. A	
15. C		30. F		45. A		60. H	

Pre-Algebra/Elementary Algebra (EA): _____/27   Plane Geometry/Trigonometry (GT): _____/17

Int. Algebra/Coordinate Geometry (AG): _____/16   Raw Score (EA + AG + GT): _____/60

Section 3: Reading (Student Text, p. 560)

#	Ans	SS	AL
1.	D	■	
2.	F	■	
3.	C	■	
4.	G	■	
5.	D	■	
6.	G	■	
7.	A	■	
8.	G	■	
9.	A	■	
10.	H	■	

#	Ans	SS	AL
11.	B		■
12.	J		■
13.	C		■
14.	J		■
15.	C		■
16.	J		■
17.	B		■
18.	F		■
19.	C		■
20.	J		■

#	Ans	SS	AL
21.	A	■	
22.	F	■	
23.	C	■	
24.	F	■	
25.	B	■	
26.	F	■	
27.	B	■	
28.	J	■	
29.	B	■	
30.	H	■	

#	Ans	SS	AL
31.	D		■
32.	H		■
33.	B		■
34.	H		■
35.	B		■
36.	H		■
37.	D		■
38.	G		■
39.	C		■
40.	H		■

Social Studies/Sciences (SS): _____ /20   Arts/Literature (AL): _____ /20   Raw Score (SS + AL): _____ /40

Section 4: Science (Student Text, p. 568)

#	Ans	B	C	P	ES
1.	D	■		■	■
2.	F	■		■	■
3.	C	■		■	■
4.	J	■		■	■
5.	D	■		■	■
6.	F	■		■	■

#	Ans	B	C	P	ES
7.	A	■	■	■	
8.	H	■	■	■	
9.	D	■	■	■	
10.	H	■	■	■	
11.	A	■	■	■	
12.	H	■	■	■	

#	Ans	B	C	P	ES
13.	B		■	■	■
14.	J		■	■	■
15.	A		■	■	■
16.	G		■	■	■
17.	C		■	■	■
18.	J		■	■	■

#	Ans	B	C	P	ES
19.	C	■	■		■
20.	F	■	■		■
21.	D	■	■		■
22.	H	■	■		■
23.	A	■	■		■

#	Ans	B	C	P	ES
24.	G	■		■	■
25.	C	■		■	■
26.	H	■		■	■
27.	A	■		■	■
28.	G	■		■	■
29.	B	■		■	■

#	Ans	B	C	P	ES
30.	H		■	■	■
31.	D		■	■	■
32.	F		■	■	■
33.	C		■	■	■
34.	G		■	■	■

#	Ans	B	C	P	ES
35.	D	■		■	■
36.	J	■		■	■
37.	B	■		■	■
38.	F	■		■	■
39.	B	■		■	■
40.	H	■		■	■

Biology (B): _____ /11   Physics (P): _____ /5   Raw Score (B + C + P + ES): _____ /40

Chemistry (C): _____ /18   Earth/Space Sciences (ES): _____ /6

Multiple-Choice Explanations

Section 1: *English*

1. **(B)** (p. 528) *English/Usage and Mechanics/Grammar and Usage/Faulty or Illogical Comparisons.* The original sentence is incorrect for two reasons. First, the phrase "more gentler" is wrong. "More" is redundant of the "-er" suffix. Second, the rest of the passage makes it clear that the author means to say that botany is the most gentle of sciences. (C) is wrong because the passage makes it clear that the author intends the superlative "most." (D) is not idiomatic.

2. **(G)** (p. 528) *English/Usage and Mechanics/Grammar and Usage/Diction.* The word "ostentatious" means "showy" and is not appropriate here. "Unobtrusive" is a better fit.

3. **(C)** (p. 528) *English/Usage and Mechanics/Grammar and Usage/Pronoun Usage.* The original sentence is incorrect because the pronoun "it" does not have a clear and unambiguous referent. Although it must refer to "botany," on first reading it seems that it might refer to "flower." (C) eliminates the potential for misreading. (B) and (D) are incorrectly punctuated.

4. **(H)** (p. 528) *English/Rhetorical Skills/Style/Conciseness.* The original sentence is incorrect because the phrasing is awkward and wordy. (H) provides the most direct and concise phrasing: "but the natural world." (G) and (J) are incorrect for the same reason as the original.

5. **(B)** (p. 529) *English/Usage and Mechanics/Grammar and Usage/Diction.* The original sentence is not idiomatic. The correct idiom is "consists of," not "consists about." (C) is wrong because it is not idiomatic. (D) is wrong because it uses a plural verb with a singular subject.

6. **(F)** (p. 529) *English/Usage and Mechanics/No Change.* The original sentence is correct as written. The other choices are not idiomatic and destroy the parallelism between "knowing" and "studying."

7. **(A)** (p. 529) *English/Rhetorical Skills/No Change.* The original sentence is the best phrasing. The phrase "in and of themselves" serves to emphasize the thought that plants are intrinsically worth studying.

8. **(H)** (p. 529) *English/Rhetorical Skills/Strategy/Effective Transitional Sentence.* The second paragraph sets up a contrast with the first. In the first paragraph, the author states that plants are intrinsically worthy of study. Here, the author says that we should not entirely discount their practical value.

9. **(C)** (p. 529) *English/Usage and Mechanics/Grammar and Usage/Verb Tense* and *Punctuation/Semicolons.* The original sentence contains two errors. First, the past participle "disparaged" is needed rather than the present participle following "should." Second, the dash disrupts the logical flow of the sentence. It seems to signal an aside or a clarifying remark, but what follows is actually another clause. (C) is the best choice; it uses the correct verb form, and the semicolon is a correct choice of punctuation to separate two clauses when no coordinate conjunction is used. (B) corrects the verb but not the punctuation error. (D) contains both errors.

10. **(F)** (p. 529) *English/Rhetorical Skills/No Change.* "Nonetheless" sets up a contrast between the idea that plants have practical value and the idea that this very fact imposes limits on the study of plants.

11. **(C)** (p. 529) *English/Usage and Mechanics/Grammar and Usage/Sequence and Verb Tense.* The present tense conflicts with the other verbs in the sentence. They are all in the simple past tense. Only (C) makes the required change. (B) is wrong because there is no reason to use the past perfect. ("Had been made" suggests that one past event occurred and was completed before another past event, but

that is not the intended meaning of the original.) (D) is wrong because the subject is "study," a singular noun.

12. **(J)** (p. 530) *English/Usage and Mechanics/Sentence Structure/Problems of Coordination and Subordination.* "Or" implies that the two ideas are alternatives. However, an assumption can be basic and still unspoken. What the author intends to say is that these ideas are very basic but no one ever makes them explicit.

13. **(B)** (p. 530) *English/Usage and Mechanics/Grammar and Usage/Sequence and Verb Tense* and *Pronoun Usage.* The original sentence contains two mistakes. First, "to have understood" is inconsistent with the other verb forms in the paragraph, for it suggests something that will occur at a future time before some other action. (e.g., John hopes to have finished his homework before his mother comes home.) Additionally, "their" is a plural pronoun and cannot substitute for the singular "plant." (B) makes both of the needed corrections.

14. **(J)** (p. 530) *English/Usage and Mechanics/Grammar and Usage/Pronoun Usage* and *Sentence Structure/Problems of Coordination and Subordination.* The original sentence contains two errors. First, "they" is a plural pronoun and cannot substitute for the singular noun "flower." Second, "but" illogically suggests a contrast where none is intended. Only (J) corrects both of these problems without creating new ones. (G) fails to correct the second problem. (H) corrects both problems but is incorrectly punctuated. Without a comma ("it exists, and") the result is a run-on sentence.

15. **(C)** (p. 530) *English/Rhetorical Skills/Strategy/Main Idea.* The author states that one must study plants simply because they exist, and further, that simply because they exist they are worthy of study. This circularity is characteristic of a tautology.

16. **(H)** (p. 531) *English/Rhetorical Skills/Strategy/Appropriate Supporting Material.* The author inserts "of course" to acknowledge that the point being made is an obvious one: of course, poverty means lack of money.

17. **(A)** (p. 531) *English/Rhetorical Skills/No Change.* The original sentence is correct. (B) and (C) are awkward or wordy by comparison. (D) destroys the structure of the sentence.

18. **(H)** (p. 531) *English/Usage and Mechanics/Grammar and Usage/Pronoun Usage.* The original sentence contains an error of pronoun usage. "Their" is intended to refer to "family," which might be either plural or singular. However, there is already another pronoun in the sentence that refers to "family," and it is singular. Thus, the first "its" determines that the author will treat "family" as a singular noun. (G) is wrong because "there" is not a pronoun. Finally, (J) is the contraction for "it is" and not a pronoun at all.

19. **(D)** (p. 531) *English/Rhetorical Skills/Strategy/Effective Transitional Sentence.* The logic of the sentence does not support the use of the transitional word "consequently." "Consequently" is used to show that one idea follows logically from another idea or that one event follows from another event as a matter of causality. Neither of these notions is implied by the sentence. The author has not yet explained why one would find more poverty in rural America than in other regions. The best course is simply to drop the word entirely.

20. **(F)** (p. 531) *English/Usage and Mechanics/No Change.* The original sentence is correct as written. (G) is wrong because "lower" cannot be substituted for "less." The phrase "may earn lower than" is not idiomatic. (H) is wrong because the correct idiom for making a comparison like this is "less than," not "less as." Finally, (J) combines the errors of both (G) and (H).

21. **(C)** (p. 531) *English/Rhetorical Skills/Organization/Paragraph-Level Structure.* In the first paragraph, the author provides the definition of "poor."

22. **(F)** (p. 532) *English/Rhetorical Skills/No Change.* The original sentence is correct as written. A new paragraph is needed here because the author is taking up a new topic. Thus, (G) and (J) are wrong. As for (H), "since" destroys the logic of the sentence.

23. **(A)** (p. 532) *English/Rhetorical Skills/No Change.* The single word "parallel" nicely expresses the thought that lack of education is associated with low income. By comparison, the alternatives are wordy. Notice also that the wrong choices use phrases that would seem out of place given the formal style of the passage.

24. **(F)** (p. 532) *English/Rhetorical Skills/No Change.* The last sentence of the paragraph expresses an idea that follows from, or is the result of, the idea that precedes it. The phrase "as a consequence" signals the reader that the second idea is the result of the first.

25. **(D)** (p. 532) *English/Usage and Mechanics/Grammar and Usage/Subject-Verb Agreement* **and** *Diction.* The original sentence contains two errors. First, the plural verb "are" does not agree with its subject, "schooling." Second, the phrase "as inadequate like" is not idiomatic. (B) corrects both errors but is punctuated incorrectly. One can treat the phrase "like family income" as an aside, but the limits of the aside cannot be marked with one dash and one comma. Either two dashes or two commas must be used. (C) is guilty of illogical expression, because it seems to imply that schooling is supposed to function "as" family income. (D) is the right choice because it corrects the problems of the original and is correctly punctuated.

26. **(J)** (p. 532) *English/Usage and Mechanics/Grammar and Usage/Pronoun Usage.* "It" has no antecedent. (J) corrects this by supplying a noun. (G) and (H) make illogical statements.

27. **(C)** (p. 532) *English/Rhetorical Skills/Style/Conciseness.* The original sentence is needlessly wordy. (C) is more concise and more in keeping with the formal tone of the selection.

28. **(H)** (p. 532) *English/Usage and Mechanics/Grammar and Usage/Subject-Verb Agreement.* The original sentence is incorrect because the plural verb "have" does not agree with its singular subject, "head." (G) fails to correct this problem. (H) and (J) are both singular verbs, but "was to have" in (J) implies a condition that was never fulfilled. This suggestion of an unfulfilled condition is out of place here. (H) is the correct choice. The present perfect is acceptable because it indicates an action that occurred at some unspecified time in the past (the head of the family had some schooling). It would also be acceptable to use the present tense: "If the head...has little schooling, the children are...."

29. **(D)** (p. 533) *English/Usage and Mechanics/Grammar and Usage/Diction.* The original sentence is incorrect because the expression "as...rather than in" is not idiomatic. An idiomatically correct alternative is supplied by (D): "is as true...as." (B) fails to correct the problem of the original sentence. Although (C) is idiomatic, "they" does not agree with the demonstrative pronoun, "this," to which it refers.

30. **(J)** (p. 533) *English/Rhetorical Skills/Style/Conciseness.* The underlined phrase is redundant of "modern." Just omit it.

31. **(B)** (p. 533) *English/Usage and Mechanics/Grammar and Usage/Adjectives versus Adverbs.* The original sentence is incorrect because the adjective "poor" cannot be used to modify another adjective (educated). The adverb "poorly" is needed for that. (B) makes the correction. (C) is wrong because it changes the intended meaning of the sentence. The author is talking about poor people who are not well educated, not "educated poor people." Finally, (D) is grammatically incorrect. The noun "education" cannot modify a noun.

32. **(G)** (p. 533) *English/Rhetorical Skills/Organization/Passage-Level Structure.* The author supplies a definition and statistics in the first paragraph. Throughout the selection the author offers explanations.

33. **(B)** (p. 533) *English/Usage and Mechanics/Grammar and Usage/Sequence and Verb Tense.* The original sentence is wrong because the present tense "fail" is not consistent with the other verb in the sentence. The other verb describes a past action. Additionally, "fail" is a plural verb, but the subject of the sentence is "one," a singular noun. (B) corrects the problem of tense (and the problem of agreement since there is only one form in the simple past). (C) makes the needed corrections, but the resulting phrase is not idiomatic. Finally, (D) addresses the problem of agreement, but there is still the problem of tense.

34. **(J)** (p. 533) *English/Usage and Mechanics/Grammar and Usage/Pronoun Usage* **and** *Diction.* The original sentence contains two errors. First, it uses "that" rather than "who" to refer to people. Second, it is not idiomatic. The correct idiom is "should have," not "should of." "Should of" is never correct diction because "of" is not a verb. (G) corrects neither of these errors. (H) corrects the first but not the second. Only (J) corrects both errors.

35. **(D)** (p. 534) *English/Rhetorical Skills/Style/Conciseness.* The underlined phrase is redundant of "dropouts." It should be deleted.

36. **(J)** (p. 534) *English/Usage and Mechanics/Grammar and Usage/Verb Tense* **and** *Diction.* The original sentence is both grammatically incorrect and not idiomatic. First, "will starting" is not an English verb form at all. Second, an infinitive is used after a verb ending in "-ing" rather than the gerund. Thus, "starting to think" is more idiomatic than "starting thinking." (J) corrects both the problems of the original sentence. (G) does not solve the idiom problem, and (H) is ambiguous. The placement of "usually" suggests that it is intended to modify "thinking" rather than "starts."

37. **(D)** (p. 534) *English/Usage and Mechanics/Punctuation/Commas.* The original sentence is incorrectly punctuated; if, for clarity, the final prepositional phrase is set apart, a comma must be used. The colon is too powerful and isolates the prepositional phrase from the rest of the sentence. (B) and (C) are wrong because connecting the prepositional phrase to the rest of the sentence with a coordinate conjunction gives it an importance equal to that of the verb: "he or she ceases...and roughly at age 14."

38. **(H)** (p. 534) *English/Usage and Mechanics/Grammar and Usage/Subject-Verb Agreement.* The original sentence is incorrect because the singular verb "is" does not agree with its subject. The subject is a compound subject (a series of elements joined by "and"), which is plural. (G) fails to correct this mistake. (H) and (J) correct the error, but the use of the past tense in (J) is incorrect. The author is describing a current problem using the present tense.

39. **(A)** (p. 534) *English/Usage and Mechanics/No Change.* The original sentence is correct. Each of the wrong answer choices creates a run-on sentence. In general, when there are two independent clauses, one of three things is done: the clauses are joined together using a comma and a coordinate conjunction such as "and" or "but"; the clauses are joined together using a semicolon; or the clauses are put in separate sentences.

40. **(H)** (p. 534) *English/Rhetorical Skills/Style/Conciseness.* "Most often" and "mostly" have the same meaning. (H) eliminates the needless repetition.

41. **(B)** (p. 534) *English/Usage and Mechanics/Grammar and Usage/Faulty or Illogical Comparisons.* The original sentence contains a grammatical mistake. It uses "most" rather than "more" to compare two things. Both (B) and (D) make the needed correction. (D) is wrong, however, because the singular "one" does not agree with its verb "stay."

42. **(G)** (p. 535) *English/Usage and Mechanics/Grammar and Usage/Pronoun Usage.* The original sentence is wrong for two reasons. First, it uses the objective case pronoun "him" to modify the gerund "dropping." Instead, the possessive case "his" must be used. Second, the use of the gerund is awkward. It is much more direct to simply say "at the time he drops out." (G) corrects the original sentence and is

more direct and concise as well. (J) would be correct except that it uses the past tense. The author uses present tense verbs to describe an ongoing problem, so the present tense should also be used here.

43. **(A)** (p. 535) *English/Rhetorical Skills/No Change.* The original sentence is the best version. The other choices are awkward and wordy.

44. **(H)** (p. 535) *English/Usage and Mechanics/Sentence Structure/Fragments.* The original sentence is incorrect because the sentence lacks a conjugated or main verb. "Increasing" is a participle and cannot function as a main verb. Each of the other choices uses a conjugated form of "to increase" and so avoids this error. (G), however, is incorrect because "so that" seems to introduce a clause, but what follows is not a clause: "so that during the eighth grade...." (J) is wordy and indirect. Additionally, the past tense in (J) is inconsistent with the other verbs in this paragraph.

45. **(D)** (p. 535) *English/Usage and Mechanics/Grammar and Usage/Diction.* In the original sentence, "none" is a pronoun. What is required, however, is an adverb to explain how the dropout participates in activities: not at all. (B) uses the correct idiom, but the "and" results in a contradictory statement. How could one participate a little and not at all? (C) is incorrect because "not much" is equivalent to "little," so the resulting statement does not create the either/or situation intended by the original sentence.

46. **(J)** (p. 535) *English/Usage and Mechanics/Grammar and Usage/Subject-Verb Agreement* **and** *Diction.* The original sentence contains two errors. First, "goes" is a singular verb and does not agree with the subject of the sentence, "reasons." Second, the phrase "goes deeper as" is not idiomatic. (J) corrects both of these problems. (G) and (H) do correct the problem of subject-verb agreement, but they are not idiomatic.

47. **(D)** (p. 535) *English/Rhetorical Skills/Strategy/Appropriate Supporting Material.* In the final sentence, the author notes that dropping out is a symptom that has other root causes. It would be appropriate for the author to continue talking about those causes.

48. **(G)** (p. 536) *English/Rhetorical Skills/Strategy/Appropriate Supporting Material.* The word "dropout" is familiar, so the passage would not be incomprehensible without the definition. However, the definition serves to tighten up the discussion.

49. **(B)** (p. 536) *English/Usage and Mechanics/Grammar and Usage/Subject-Verb Agreement.* In the original sentence, the verb "are" does not agree with its subject, "kind." Both (B) and (C) make the needed correction, but (C) makes a change that disrupts the parallelism of the sentence: "research and developing." Since "research" and "development" have similar functions in the sentence (they are both objects of the preposition "of"), the noun "development" should be used.

50. **(H)** (p. 536) *English/Usage and Mechanics/Grammar and Usage/Diction.* The original sentence is not idiomatic. The correct idiom is "look for something to do something" (to satisfy), not "look for something doing something." (G) is incorrect because the subjunctive "would have" suggests that an anticipated past event did not occur because of some other event. (John would have come to the party, but he was taken ill.) Finally, (J) is ambiguous. "With the satisfaction of" is a prepositional phrase, but it is not clear what the phrase is supposed to modify.

51. **(A)** (p. 537) *English/Usage and Mechanics/No Change.* The original sentence is correct as written. "Its" refers to "humankind." (B) is incorrect because "humankind" is singular. (C) is wrong because "it's" is the contraction of "it is" and is not a pronoun at all. Finally, "your" cannot be substituted for "humankind."

52. **(H)** (p. 537) *English/Usage and Mechanics/Grammar and Usage/Diction.* In the original sentence, the infinitive "to find" does not have a clear logical relationship to any other part of the sentence. (H) solves this problem by turning "to find" into "finding," which can then function as an appositive for "one" ("one

of the problems"). (G) doesn't solve the problem of the orphaned phrase and, if anything, makes matters worse since a colon is more powerful than a comma. Finally, (J) just creates a sentence fragment of everything that follows the period.

53. **(D)** (p. 537) *English/Rhetorical Skills/Style/Conciseness.* The original sentence is wordy. (D) is more concise and more direct. (B) is very concise, but (B) destroys the sense of the sentence: what may they be? (C) is wrong because "it" is a singular pronoun and cannot refer to "machines."

54. **(F)** (p. 537) *English/Rhetorical Skills/Strategy/Effective Transitional Sentence.* The author intends here to contrast two ideas: wind is difficult to harness, but it is valuable. (G), (H), and (J) signal a cause-effect relationship, when a contrast is needed instead.

55. **(A)** (p. 537) *English/Usage and Mechanics/No Change.* The original sentence is correct as written. (B) is wrong because the singular "has" does not agree with the subject "rewards." (C) is wrong for this reason and also because the author clearly intends to make a statement about the past, not the present. Finally, (D), which uses the future tense, must be wrong as well.

56. **(F)** (p. 537) *English/Usage and Mechanics/No Change.* The original sentence is correct. Notice how the next sentence parallels the structure of this sentence. (G) is wrong because it eliminates this stylistic feature and also because the resulting sentence is ambiguous. Does the author mean to say the machine was located in China, was built in China, or was simply in China one day passing through? (H) is wrong for the same reasons as (G) and also because the verb tense is illogical. Finally, (J) is wrong because "has" switches to the active voice and implies that the machine was building something.

57. **(B)** (p. 537) *English/Rhetorical Skills/Style/Conciseness.* The original sentence does not contain a grammatical mistake, but it is awkward. By comparison, (B) is more concise and more direct than any of the other choices.

58. **(J)** (p. 538) *English/Rhetorical Skills/Style/Conciseness.* The original sentence does not contain an error but is needlessly wordy. By substituting "by" for "through the means of," the thought can be rendered more concisely and directly.

59. **(A)** (p. 538) *English/Rhetorical Skills/No Change.* The original sentence is correct. (B) is wrong because the comma separates the adjective "several" from the noun it modifies, "centuries." (C) is wrong because "but" suggests a contrast that is not intended by the author. Finally, (D) is wrong because the use of "and" suggests that what follows is similar to what comes before. However, "water lift" is not like "centuries."

60. **(F)** (p. 538) *English/Rhetorical Skills/No Change.* The original sentence is correct as written. It uses the active voice and is more direct than the alternatives, which use the passive voice.

61. **(A)** (p. 538) *English/Rhetorical Skills/No Change.* The original sentence is correct. The author takes up a new topic at this point, so a new paragraph is appropriate and (B) is wrong. (C) is wrong because it creates a sentence fragment from what is otherwise a complete sentence. (D) is wrong because it is needlessly wordy.

62. **(J)** (p. 538) *English/Usage and Mechanics/Grammar and Usage/Faulty or Illogical Comparisons.* The original sentence is incorrect because it implies a comparison of two machines. In fact, the author means to compare one machine with all other such machines; therefore, the superlative "most" should be used. (G) does use the superlative, but "most simplest" is redundant. Use one or the other, but not both. (H) fails to correct the problem of the original sentence.

63. **(B)** (p. 539) *English/Usage and Mechanics/Sentence Structure/Faulty Parallelism.* The original sentence suffers from a lack of parallelism. The second in the series of two verbs should have the same form as the first: "flourished" and "came." Only (B) makes the needed correction.

64. **(J)** (p. 539) *English/Rhetorical Skills/Style/Idiomatic Expression.* The phrase "real iffy" is an example of informal usage that should not be included in formal writing. (G) and (H) are needlessly wordy. "Capricious" solves both of these problems.

65. **(C)** (p. 539) *English/Rhetorical Skills/Strategy/Appropriate Supporting Material.* The phrase "rage into a gale" has an appropriate meaning for the sentence and helps to maximize the importance of the weather by creating vivid imagery.

66. **(G)** (p. 539) *English/Usage and Mechanics/Grammar and Usage/Pronoun Usage.* The original sentence contains an error of pronoun usage. It refers to both "television" and "products," so a plural pronoun is required. (J) fails to make the needed correction. Both (G) and (H) make the correction, but (H) introduces a new error. The use of the subjunctive "would be" implies that an event is contingent upon the occurrence of some other event. However, there is no such other event mentioned in the selection.

67. **(B)** (p. 539) *English/Usage and Mechanics/Grammar and Usage/Subject-Verb Agreement.* The original sentence contains an error of subject-verb agreement. The subject of the sentence is "industry," so the verb should be singular: "industry is." The relative clause introduced by "which" is not part of the simple subject. (C) fails to make the needed correction. (D) corrects the original sentence but is incorrectly punctuated. The relative clause should be marked with two commas, not one comma and a dash.

68. **(F)** (p. 539) *English/Usage and Mechanics/No Change.* The original sentence is correctly punctuated. (G) is incorrect because a comma must be used to separate the first two elements in a series of three or more elements. (H) is wrong because the comma separates an adjective from the noun that it modifies. Finally, (J) is wrong because it separates the definite article "the" from the noun that it modifies.

69. **(A)** (p. 540) *English/Usage and Mechanics/No Change.* The original sentence is correct. The subject of the verb is "the episodic series," a singular noun. Since three items are being compared, "most" is the correct choice.

70. **(F)** (p. 540) *English/Rhetorical Skills/No Change.* The original sentence is correct as written. "With the advent of" is an idiom that identifies a certain point in time. The remaining choices are simply not idiomatic.

71. **(B)** (p. 540) *English/Usage and Mechanics/Grammar and Usage/Sequence and Verb Tense.* The original sentence uses the wrong verb tense. The phrase "with the advent of" pegs the time as belonging to the past. Some form of the past tense is needed. Only (B) supplies a verb that refers to a past event.

72. **(F)** (p. 540) *English/Usage and Mechanics/No Change.* The original sentence is correct as written. The verb "have" correctly agrees with its plural subject. Also, some form of the past tense is required here since the sentence obviously refers to events that belong to the past. Thus, the other choices are incorrect.

73. **(B)** (p. 540) *English/Usage and Mechanics/Grammar and Usage/Verb Tense.* The past participle of "to grow" is "grown." (B) makes the needed change. (C) and (D) are incorrect because their forms are not parallel to the other verb form, "has lost."

74. **(J)** (p. 540) *English/Usage and Mechanics/Sentence Structure/Fragments.* In the original underlined portion, everything following the period is a sentence fragment—there is no main verb. (J) uses a colon

to introduce the list. (G) is wrong because the comma incorrectly suggests that the elements of the list will be verbs. (H) is wrong because it fails to mark the transition from the main part of the sentence to the list.

75. **(B)** (p. 540) ***English/Usage and Mechanics/Grammar and Usage/Adjectives versus Adverbs.*** The original sentence is incorrect because "controversy" is intended to be an adjective that modifies "topics." However, "controversy" is a noun—not an adjective. (B) makes the needed correction.

Section 2: Mathematics

1. **(D)** (p. 542) ***Mathematics/Arithmetic/Simple Manipulations.*** Perform the indicated operations: $2 \times 10^4 = 20,000$, and $121,212 + 20,000 = 141,212$.

2. **(K)** (p. 542) ***Mathematics/Algebra/Manipulating Algebraic Expressions/Factoring Expressions.*** Recognize that $6x + 3$ can be factored and rewrite the equation as: $3(2x + 1) = 21 \Rightarrow 2x + 1 = 7$.

   Alternatively, if you failed to see the shortcut, solve the given equation for x: $6x + 3 = 21 \Rightarrow 6x = 18 \Rightarrow x = 3$. Therefore, $2x + 1 = 2(3) + 1 = 7$.

3. **(C)** (p. 542) ***Mathematics/Arithmetic/Common Arithmetic Items/Proportions and Direct-Inverse Variation.*** The cost of renting a bowling lane for 2 hours is $2 \cdot \$12 = \$24$. For \$24, a ping pong table can be rented for $\$24 \div \$3 = 8$ hours.

4. **(K)** (p. 543) ***Mathematics/Arithmetic/Common Arithmetic Items/Properties of Numbers.*** (F) is incorrect since a natural number cannot equal the sum of itself and a number greater than itself. Similar reasoning applies to (G), (H), and (J). (K) is the only choice that could be true: for example, if q is 5 and r is 10, and if s is 15 and t is 20, then $5 + 20 = 10 + 15$.

5. **(A)** (p. 543) ***Mathematics/Arithmetic/Complicated Manipulations/Decimal-Fraction Equivalents.*** Use $\frac{1}{2}$ as a benchmark. Reason in this way: eliminate (C)—since $\frac{7}{14}$ is $\frac{1}{2}$, $\frac{7}{15}$ is less than $\frac{1}{2}$. Continue eliminating choices until only the correct answer, (A), is left.

   Alternatively, you can use a calculator to determine which answer choice has a decimal equivalent that is greater than the decimal equivalent of $\frac{1}{2}$, or 0.5.

6. **(F)** (p. 543) ***Mathematics/Arithmetic/Common Arithmetic Items/Percents.*** Use the "is-over-of" equation: $\dfrac{is}{of} = \dfrac{\text{students on track team}}{\text{total students}} \Rightarrow \dfrac{18}{360} = \dfrac{1}{20} = 0.05 = 5\%$.

7. **(C)** (p. 544) ***Mathematics/Geometry/Lines and Angles.*** (I) must be true because a and x are vertically opposite each other. Similarly, (II) must be true because y and b are equal and z and c are equal. (III), however, is not necessarily true. x and a are equal and y and b are equal, but there is no information on which to base a conclusion about the relationship between x and y or the relationship between a and b.

8. **(G)** (p. 544) ***Mathematics/Geometry/Lines and Angles.*** Vertical angles have equal measures. so $x + 30 = 2x \Rightarrow x = 30$.

9. **(C)** (p. 544) ***Mathematics/Arithmetic/Complicated Manipulations/Factoring.*** Eliminate choices (A), (B), and (D) since they contain numbers that are not prime. Then, calculate the remaining choices:

C. $2 \cdot 2 \cdot 3 \cdot 5 = 60$ ✓
E. $3 \cdot 3 \cdot 3 \cdot 5 = 135$ ✗

10. **(F)** (p. 545) ***Mathematics/Statistics and Probability/Averages.*** Use the method for finding the missing element of an average. Since the average height of all four buildings is 20, the sum of the heights of all four is $4 \cdot 20 = 80$. The three known heights total $3 \cdot 16 = 48$. Therefore, the missing value is $80 - 48 = 32$.

11. **(E)** (p. 545) ***Mathematics/Geometry/Lines and Angles.*** The angles labeled $4y$ and $5y$ form a straight line, so $5y + 4y = 180 \Rightarrow 9y = 180 \Rightarrow y = 20$. Next, the angles of a triangle total $180°$, so
$4y + 2y + x = 180 \Rightarrow 6y + x = 180 \Rightarrow 6(20) + x = 180 \Rightarrow 120 + x = 180 \Rightarrow x = 60$.

12. **(K)** (p. 545) ***Mathematics/Arithmetic/Simple Manipulations.*** Each of the marks between the numbered marks is $\frac{1}{5}$ of the distance between the numbered marks. The distance between each numbered mark is 0.1, so each of the others is worth $0.1 \div 5 = 0.02$. Thus, $\overline{PQ} = 0.02 + 0.1 + 2(0.02) = 0.16$.

13. **(A)** (p. 545) ***Mathematics/Geometry/Rectangles and Squares.*** The perimeter is:
$2(3a - 2) + 2(2a - 1) = 6a - 4 + 4a - 2 = 10a - 6$.

Alternatively, assume a value for a. For example, if $a = 1$, then the length of the figure is $3(1) - 2 = 1$, and the width of the figure is $2(1) - 1 = 1$. The perimeter would be $4 \cdot 1 = 4$. Substituting 1 for a into the correct formula yields the value 4.

14. **(G)** (p. 546) ***Mathematics/Statistics and Probability/Averages.*** The average of the five numbers is 51, so their sum is $5 \cdot 51 = 255$. The two known values total 114. Therefore, the remaining three numbers total $255 - 114 = 141$. And $\frac{141}{3} = 47$.

15. **(C)** (p. 546) ***Mathematics/Algebra/Solving Algebraic Equations or Inequalities with One Variable.***
$-2 \leq 2x \leq 2 = -1 \leq x \leq 1$, so x could be -1, 0, or 1.

16. **(K)** (p. 546) ***Mathematics/Algebra/Manipulating Algebraic Expressions/Manipulating Expressions Involving Exponents.*** $8 = 2^3$, so $8^x = \left(2^3\right)^x = 2^{3x}$.

17. **(C)** (p. 546) ***Mathematics/Geometry/Rectangles and Squares.*** One square has an area of $2 \cdot 2 = 4$, the other an area of $3 \cdot 3 = 9$, and the sum of their areas is $4 + 9 = 13$.

18. **(G)** (p. 547) ***Mathematics/Geometry.*** Set up an equation:
$x(2x)(3) = 54 \Rightarrow 2x^2 = 18 \Rightarrow x^2 = 9 \Rightarrow x = \sqrt{9} = \pm 3 = 3$. (Remember that distances are always positive.)

Alternatively, "test-the-test" by trying each answer choice until one generates a volume of 54.

19. **(B)** (p. 547) ***Mathematics/Algebra/Solving Algebraic Equations with Two Variables.*** Since x is 80 percent of y, $x = 0.8y$, and $y = \frac{x}{0.8} = 1.25x$. So, y is 125% of x.

20. **(J)** (p. 547) ***Mathematics/Algebra/Manipulating Algebraic Expressions/Evaluating Expressions.***
Rewrite $m - n > 0$ by adding n to both sides: $m > n$. Now consider each answer choice. As for (F), it proves that $m < n$. As for (G), it proves nothing about m and n since m and n might be either negative or positive. The same is true of (H), which is equivalent to $m > -n$. As for (K), it proves nothing because it provides neither relative values for m and n nor their signs.

21. **(A)** (p. 547) ***Mathematics/Algebra/Expressing and Evaluating Algebraic Functions/Function Notation.*** First, find $f(2)$: $f(2) = (2)^2 + 2 = 4 + 2 = 6$. Next, find $f(6)$: $f(6) = (6)^2 + 6 = 36 + 6 = 42$. Thus, $f(f(2)) = 42$.

22. **(K)** (p. 548) ***Mathematics/Geometry/Complex Figures*** and ***Lines and Angles*** and ***Circles.*** First, find the area of the circle: $\pi r^2 = \pi (2)^2 = 4\pi$. Since the shaded area is equal to 3π, it accounts for $\dfrac{3\pi}{4\pi} = \dfrac{3}{4}$ of the circle. Thus, the unshaded area is $\dfrac{1}{4}$ of the circle. Therefore, $\angle x$ plus the angle vertically opposite x are equal to $\dfrac{1}{4}(360°) = 90°$. Thus, $2x = 90$ and $x = 45$.

23. **(D)** (p. 548) ***Mathematics/Arithmetic/Common Arithmetic Items/Percents.*** Solve using the "is-over-of" equation: $\dfrac{\text{is}}{\text{of}} = \dfrac{\text{tin}}{\text{entire bar}} = \dfrac{100}{100 + 150} = \dfrac{100}{250} = \dfrac{2}{5} = 40\%$.

24. **(J)** (p. 548) ***Mathematics/Algebra/Manipulating Algebraic Expressions/Basic Algebraic Manipulations.*** $\dfrac{1}{x} + \dfrac{1}{y} = \dfrac{1}{z} \Rightarrow \dfrac{y+x}{xy} = \dfrac{1}{z} \Rightarrow z \cdot \dfrac{y+x}{xy} = 1 \Rightarrow z = \dfrac{xy}{y+x} = \dfrac{xy}{x+y}$.

Alternatively, assume some values. Assume that $x = 1$ and $y = 1$. On that assumption, $z = \dfrac{1}{2}$. Substitute 1 for x and 1 for y into the choices. Only (J) generates the value $\dfrac{1}{2}$.

25. **(D)** (p. 549) ***Mathematics/Arithmetic/Common Arithmetic Items/Absolute Value.*** $|-5| = 5$, $|-12| = 12$, and $|-2| = 2$. Thus, the expression is equal to $5 + 12 - 2 + (-6) = 15 - 6 = 9$.

26. **(G)** (p. 549) ***Mathematics/Statistics and Probability/Averages.*** Add the three elements and divide by 3: $\dfrac{2x + 2x + 1 + 2x + 2}{3} = x - 1 \Rightarrow \dfrac{6x + 3}{3} = x - 1 \Rightarrow 6x + 3 = 3(x - 1)$.

27. **(B)** (p. 549) ***Mathematics/Arithmetic/Complicated Arithmetic Application Items.*** The profit on each box of candy is $\$2 - \$1 = \$1$. To earn a total profit of $\$500$, it will be necessary to sell $\dfrac{\$500}{\$1} = 500$ boxes.

28. **(G)** (p. 549) ***Mathematics/Arithmetic/Simple Manipulations.*** $(-2)^2 - (-2)^3 = 4 - (-8) = 12$.

29. **(D)** (p. 550) ***Mathematics/Arithmetic/Common Arithmetic Items/Properties of Numbers.*** If the sum and average of 3 different integers are equal, one of the integers must be 0: $x - x + y = \dfrac{x - x + y}{3} \Rightarrow y = \dfrac{y}{3}$ can only be true if $y = 0$.

30. **(F)** (p. 550) ***Mathematics/Arithmetic/Common Arithmetic Items/Percents.*** Use the "is-over-of" strategy: $\dfrac{is}{of} = \dfrac{seniors}{total} = \dfrac{90}{360} = \dfrac{1}{4} = 25\%$.

31. **(C)** (p. 550) ***Mathematics/Geometry/Complex Figures*** and ***Rectangles and Squares*** and ***Triangles/45º-45º-90º Triangles.*** The diagonal of a square creates an isosceles right triangle. Since this is a 45°-45°-90° right triangle, each side of the square is equal to $\dfrac{\sqrt{2}}{\sqrt{2}} = 1$. Alternatively, designate the length of a side of the square as x. From the Pythagorean theorem, $x^2 + x^2 = \left(\sqrt{2}\right)^2 \Rightarrow 2x^2 = 2 \Rightarrow x^2 = 1 \Rightarrow x = \pm 1 = 1$ (since length is positive). Therefore, the perimeter of the square is $4(1) = 4$.

32. **(G)** (p. 551) ***Mathematics/Geometry/Lines and Angles.*** The angles labeled $3w$ and $(5w + 20)$ form a straight line segment, so $3w + (5w + 20) = 180 \Rightarrow 8w + 20 = 180 \Rightarrow 8w = 160 \Rightarrow w = 20$. The angles labeled $3w$ and $4x$ also form a straight line segment:
$3w + 4x = 180 \Rightarrow 3(20) + 4x = 180 \Rightarrow 60 + 4x = 180 \Rightarrow 4x = 120 \Rightarrow x = 30$.

33. **(C)** (p. 551) ***Mathematics/Geometry/Rectangles and Squares.*** If the floor were a perfect rectangle, it would have a width of $4 \cdot 5 = 20$ meters, a length of $8 \cdot 5 = 40$ meters, and a total area of $20 \cdot 40 = 800$ square meters. However, the floor is not a perfect rectangle. Its actual area is smaller. Subtract the area of the missing "corner," which is a square since its sides are the same length. Each side is $0.8 \cdot 5 = 4$ meters. Therefore, the corner's area is $4 \cdot 4 = 16$ square meters, and $800 - 16 = 784$ square meters.

34. **(H)** (p. 552) ***Mathematics/Geometry/Triangles/Properties of Triangles*** and ***Arithmetic/Common Arithmetic Items/Properties of Numbers.*** The sum of the lengths of any two sides of a triangle must be greater than the length of the third side. If x is the length of the third side, then $x + 4 > 11 \Rightarrow x > 7$, and the smallest integer value for x is 8. Also, $4 + 11 > x \Rightarrow 15 > x$, and the largest integer value for x is 14.

35. **(C)** (p. 552) ***Mathematics/Algebra/Solving Quadratic Equations and Relations.*** Put the function in standard form, factor, and solve for x: $-x^2 = 3 - 4x \Rightarrow$
$0 = 3 - 4x + x^2 \Rightarrow x^2 - 4x + 3 = 0 \Rightarrow (x - 3)(x - 1) = 0$. Therefore, either $x - 3 = 0$ and $x = 3$ or $x - 1 = 0$ and $x = 1$. The solution set is {1, 3}.

36. **(H)** (p. 552) ***Mathematics/Arithmetic/Complicated Arithmetic Application Items.*** The club spent $\dfrac{2}{5}$ of the budget on the first project and was left with $\dfrac{3}{5}$ of \$300 = \$180. Then, $\dfrac{1}{3}$ of \$180 was spent, leaving $\dfrac{2}{3}$ of \$180 = \$120.

37. **(E)** (p. 553) ***Mathematics/Algebra/Manipulating Algebraic Expressions/Creating Algebraic Expressions.*** Since n nails cost c cents, each nail will cost $\dfrac{c}{n}$ cents. Then, x nails will cost $x\left(\dfrac{c}{n}\right)$ or $\dfrac{cx}{n}$ cents. A dollar contains 100 cents, so the cost of x nails in dollars is $d = \dfrac{cx}{100n}$.

Alternatively, use the technique of assuming some values for the variables. For example, assume that nails cost 5 cents each and 20 are to be purchased. On that assumption, the cost is \$1. If $n = 1$, $c = 5$, and $x = 20$, then $d = 1$:

A. $1 = 100(5)(1)(20)$ ✗

B. $1 = \dfrac{100(5)(20)}{1}$ ✗

C. $1 = \dfrac{100(1)(20)}{5}$ ✗

D. $1 = \dfrac{(1)(20)}{100(5)}$ ✗

E. $1 = \dfrac{(5)(20)}{100(1)}$ ✓

38. **(K)** (p. 553) ***Mathematics/Algebra/Manipulating Algebraic Expressions/Basic Algebraic Manipulations.*** For all real numbers, a^2 is greater than 0, so b^3c must be less than 0. However, $b^3c = b^2bc$, and b^2 is greater than 0. Therefore, bc must be less than 0, and the answer is (K). (Note that either b or c is less than 0, but not both.)

39. **(C)** (p. 553) ***Mathematics/Geometry/Triangles/Properties of Triangles.*** Since this is an equilateral triangle, the sides are equal. Set up equations: $2x + 1 = 2x + y$, so $y = 1$. Therefore, side $y + 2 = 1 + 2 = 3$. The perimeter of the triangle is $3(3) = 9$.

40. **(J)** (p. 553) ***Mathematics/Coordinate Geometry/Distance Formula.*** Use the distance formula or the Pythagorean theorem.

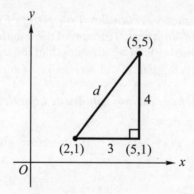

Using the distance formula, we have: $d = \sqrt{(5-2)^2 + (5-1)^2} = \sqrt{3^2 + 4^2} = \sqrt{9 + 16} = \sqrt{25} = 5$. Or, using the Pythagorean theorem, we have: $d^2 = 3^2 + 4^2 = 25 \Rightarrow d = 5$.

41. **(D)** (p. 554) ***Mathematics/Arithmetic/Complicated Manipulations/Factoring.*** The key to combining the expressions is recognizing that 45 and 20 are both multiples of 5: $\sqrt{9 \cdot 5} - \sqrt{4 \cdot 5} + \sqrt{5} = 3\sqrt{5} - 2\sqrt{5} + \sqrt{5} = 2\sqrt{5}$.

42. **(K)** (p. 554) ***Mathematics/Arithmetic/Simple Manipulations.*** This is a good item for testing the answer choices:

F. $12 - 3 = 9$ and $15 - 3 = 12$ ✗

G. $12 - 4 = 8$ and $15 - 4 = 11$ ✗

H. $12 - 11 = 1$ and $15 - 11 = 4$ ✗

J. $12 - 12 = 0$ and $15 - 12 = 3$ ✗

K. $12 - 13 = -1$ and $15 - 13 = 2$ ✓

43. **(B)** (p. 554) ***Mathematics/Algebra/Solving Simultaneous Equations.*** First, substitute the values for x and y into the equations. Then, solve the simultaneous equations $3m+n=15$ and $3n+m=13$. Use the first equation to solve for n: $n=15-3m$. Substitute this expression for n in the second equation: $3(15-3m)+m=13 \Rightarrow 45-9m+m=13 \Rightarrow 8m=32 \Rightarrow m=4$. Only (B) has $m=4$. You can double-check (B) by substituting $m=4$ and $n=3$ into one of the original equations.

44. **(G)** (p. 554) ***Mathematics/Geometry/Rectangles and Squares.*** The total length of all 12 of the small line segments is 24. Thus, the length of each small line segment is $24 \div 12=2$. So, $\text{area}_{\text{square}}=2^2=4$.

    Alternatively, the four large segments total 24, so each large segment is 6 units long. Each of these segments is divided into 3 equal parts, so each part is 2 units long. The shaded area is bounded by a square with sides of 2. Therefore, the area of the shaded part is $2 \cdot 2=4$.

45. **(A)** (p. 555) ***Mathematics/Arithmetic/Common Arithmetic Items/Absolute Value.*** $|a-b|=-|b-a|$ only when $a-b=0$. Substituting numbers for a and b works as well: $|3-2|=-|2-3| \Rightarrow |1|=-|-1| \Rightarrow 1 \neq -1$.

46. **(H)** (p. 555) ***Mathematics/Trigonometry/Trigonometric Relationships.*** The easiest method is to recognize that the arccosine is the inverse function of the cosine. For all inverse functions f and f', $f'(f(x))=x$. Therefore, $\arccos\left(\cos\dfrac{\pi}{2}\right)=\dfrac{\pi}{2}$.

47. **(A)** (p. 555) ***Mathematics/Coordinate Geometry.*** A reflection across the line $y=-x$ maps a point P with coordinates (x,y) onto point P' with coordinates $(-y,-x)$:

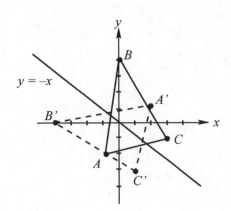

	(x,y)			$(-y,-x)$
A	$(-1,-2)$	$\rightarrow$	A'	$(2,1)$
B	$(0,4)$	$\rightarrow$	B'	$(-4,0)$
C	$(3,-1)$	$\rightarrow$	C'	$(1,-3)$

48. **(G)** (p. 555) ***Mathematics/Trigonometry/Determining Trigonometric Values.*** Visualize the graph of the sine and cosine functions:

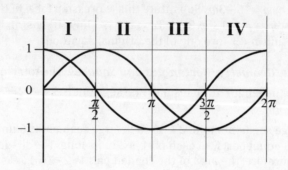

Alternatively, recall that in quadrant I, at the coordinate $\frac{\pi}{4}$, both sine and cosine values are the same:

$\frac{\sqrt{2}}{2}$. Now, look at the same relative coordinates in the other quadrants. In quadrant II, sine values are positive, but cosine values are negative. In quadrant IV, sine values are negative, while cosine values are positive. And in quadrant III, both sine and cosine values are negative and they are the same at the coordinate $\frac{3\pi}{4}$. Therefore, $\sin x = \cos x$ in quadrants I and III.

49. **(C)** (p. 556) ***Mathematics/Coordinate Geometry/Graphs of Quadratic Equations and Relations.*** The general form of the equation of a circle is: $(x-h)^2 + (y-k)^2 = r^2$, where (h,k) is the center of the circle and r its radius. The circle described in the question stem has a radius of 2 and has its center at $(2,-1)$:

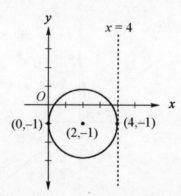

If a line of the form $x = k$ (a vertical line) is tangent to this circle, it passes through points $(0,-1)$ or $(4,-1)$.

50. **(J)** (p. 556) ***Mathematics/Algebra/Manipulating Algebraic Expressions/Evaluating Expressions.*** According to the binomial theorem, the last term in the expansion of a binomial having the form $(a+b)^n$ is b^n. Therefore, the last term of the expansion will be $(3y)^4 = 81y^4$.

51. **(A)** (p. 556) ***Mathematics/Coordinate Geometry/Graphs of Quadratic Equations and Relations.*** The quadratic formula: $x = \dfrac{-b \pm \sqrt{b^2 - 4ac}}{2a}$ is used to find the roots of a quadratic equation having the form $ax^2 + bx + c$. $b^2 - 4ac$ is called the discriminant because it discriminates among three possibilities:

1. When $b^2 - 4ac = 0$, the equation has one root.

2. When $b^2 - 4ac > 0$, the equation has two unequal real roots.

3. When $b^2 - 4ac < 0$, the equation has no real roots.

Therefore, for the equation given in the question stem, $ax^2 + bx + c = 0$, has only one root. The graph given in (A) is the only one that has only one point on the x-axis (where $y = 0$).

52. **(F)** (p. 557) ***Mathematics/Trigonometry/Trigonometric Relationships.*** This is a standard quotient

identity: $\dfrac{\sin\theta}{\cos\theta} = \tan\theta$. This fact can be easily derived. Given a right triangle with sides a and b and

hypotenuse c, let θ be the angle opposite side b. Since $\sin\theta = \dfrac{\text{side opposite }\theta}{\text{hypotenuse}} = \dfrac{b}{c}$ and

$\cos\theta = \dfrac{\text{side adjacent to }\theta}{\text{hypotenuse}} = \dfrac{a}{c}$, $\dfrac{\sin\theta}{\cos\theta} = \dfrac{b}{c} \div \dfrac{a}{c} = \dfrac{b}{c} \cdot \dfrac{c}{a} = \dfrac{b}{a}$. For θ: $\dfrac{b}{a} = \dfrac{\text{side opposite }\theta}{\text{side adjacent to }\theta} = \tan\theta$.

53. **(E)** (p. 557) ***Mathematics/Geometry/Lines and Angles.*** Since 2π radians equals 360°, use a simple

proportion, putting the unknown in the numerator: $\dfrac{x°}{360°} = \dfrac{\frac{3}{2}\pi}{2\pi} \Rightarrow x = \dfrac{\frac{3}{2}\pi}{2\pi}(360°) \Rightarrow x = \dfrac{3}{4}(360°) = 270°$.

54. **(K)** (p. 557) ***Mathematics/Algebra/Solving Algebraic Equations or Inequalities with One Variable/Equations Involving Absolute Value.*** $|2x - 1| = 2x - 1$ or $|2x - 1| = -(2x - 1) = -2x + 1$ since $|n| = n$ or $|n| = -n$, whichever possibility is greater. Thus:

$$
\begin{array}{ll}
2x - 1 = 3 & -(2x - 1) = 3 \\
\quad 2x = 4 \quad \text{or} & \quad -2x + 1 = 3 \\
\quad\quad x = 2 & \quad\quad -2x = 2 \\
& \quad\quad\quad x = -1
\end{array}
$$

Check all absolute value equations or inequalities. Substituting the two solutions into the original equations confirms that both are actual solutions.

55. **(B)** (p. 557) ***Mathematics/Coordinate Geometry/Distance Formula.*** Since the two points have the same x-coordinate, the line segment is parallel to the y-axis and the midpoint will have an x-coordinate of 2. The y-coordinate of the midpoint is the average of the two y-coordinates. The midpoint formula is

$(x_m, y_m) = \left(\dfrac{x_1 + x_2}{2}, \dfrac{y_1 + y_2}{2} \right)$, so $(x_m, y_m) = \left(2, \dfrac{5 + (-4)}{2} \right) = \left(2, \dfrac{1}{2} \right)$.

Alternatively, the line segment length is $5 - (-4) = 9$, half of which is $4\dfrac{1}{2}$. The y-coordinate of the

midpoint is $5 - 4\dfrac{1}{2} = \dfrac{1}{2}$.

56. **(G)** (p. 558) ***Mathematics/Coordinate Geometry/Slope of a Line.*** To find the slope, rewrite the equation in the form $y = mx + b$, where m is the slope and b is the y-intercept:

$2x + 3y - 2 = 0 \Rightarrow 3y = -2x + 2 \Rightarrow y = \dfrac{-2x + 2}{3} = -\dfrac{2}{3}x + \dfrac{2}{3}$, so $m = -\dfrac{2}{3}$.

57. **(D)** (p. 558) ***Mathematics/Arithmetic/Complicated Manipulations/Simplifying.*** Rationalize the fraction by using the conjugate to remove the radical from the denominator:

$$\frac{1}{\sqrt{3}-1} \cdot \frac{\sqrt{3}+1}{\sqrt{3}+1} = \frac{\sqrt{3}+1}{(\sqrt{3}+1)(\sqrt{3}+1)} = \frac{\sqrt{3}+1}{3+\sqrt{3}-\sqrt{3}-1} = \frac{\sqrt{3}+1}{2}.$$

58. **(J)** (p. 558) ***Mathematics/Arithmetic/Simple Manipulations.*** Perform the indicated operations:

$$(-2)^2 - 2^{-2} = 4 - \frac{1}{2^2} = 4 - \frac{1}{4} = 3\frac{3}{4}.$$

59. **(A)** (p. 559) ***Mathematics/Algebra/Solving Quadratic Equations and Relations.*** One way to find the roots or solutions of a quadratic equation of the form $ax^2 + bx + c = 0$ is to use the quadratic formula:

$x = \frac{-b \pm \sqrt{b^2 - 4ac}}{2a}$. For $x^2 + 3x + 1 = 0$, the roots are $\frac{-3 \pm \sqrt{5}}{2}$. The root given in the question stem has the "plus" form of the "plus or minus" formula. Therefore, the other root will have the "minus" form.

60. **(H)** (p. 559) ***Mathematics/Coordinate Geometry/Graphs of Linear Equations.*** When a graph appears to be a "V" or a rotated "V," you should suspect that the graph is an absolute value graph. One way to solve this problem is to examine each answer choice to determine what the graph would look like. The graph of $y = x$ is a straight line passing through the origin with a slope of +1. The graph of $y = -x$ is a straight line passing through the origin with a slope of –1. The graph of $y = |x|$ will look like the graph of $y = x$ for all $x \ge 0$ and will look like the graph of $y = -x$ for all $x \le 0$. That is the correct answer. The graph of the equation $y = 2x$ is a straight line passing through the origin with a slope of +2. The graph of $y = x^2$ is a parabola.

Alternatively, plug x-coordinates of points in the graph, such as $x = 4$ and $x = -3$, into the equations in the answer choices. Only the equation $y = |x|$ will return values for y that correspond to the graphed points (4,4) and (–3,3).

Section 3: Reading

1. **(D)** (p. 561) ***Reading/Prose Fiction/Implied Idea.*** The passage never specifically describes the relationship between Turkey and the narrator, but it does suggest that it is an employee/employer relationship. The narrator is judging Turkey in his professional capacity and apparently has the authority to discharge him (if necessary), as shown in lines 78–79.

2. **(F)** (p. 561) ***Reading/Prose Fiction/Implied Idea.*** Turkey uses pen and ink and has a bad habit of spilling ink during the afternoons. That is indicative of a copyist.

3. **(C)** (p. 561) ***Reading/Prose Fiction/Implied Idea.*** The explanation that Turkey gives to the narrator for his eccentric behavior is age, but the behavior is more than coincidental. After his lunch, Turkey's face becomes a brilliant red, he becomes careless in his work, and his behavior becomes erratic. All of these facts suggest the conclusion that Turkey consumes alcohol at lunchtime.

4. **(G)** (p. 561) ***Reading/Prose Fiction/Implied Idea.*** In the preceding paragraph, Turkey asks the narrator to excuse his behavior on account of his age and reminds the narrator that he too is growing older. (The narrator has said that he and Turkey are the same age.) Thus, the "fellow-feeling" refers to the similarity of their ages.

5. **(D)** (p. 561) *Reading/Prose Fiction/Explicit Detail.* In the final paragraph, the narrator decides to continue to employ Turkey, but resolves that he will deal with the narrator's "less important papers."

6. **(G)** (p. 561) *Reading/Prose Fiction/Explicit Detail.* In the first paragraph, the narrator says Turkey's face veritably blazes "after twelve o'clock, meridian" during his lunch hour.

7. **(A)** (p. 561) *Reading/Prose Fiction/Implied Idea.* The narrator compares the increased redness of Turkey's face to dropping cannel coal on anthracite. Thus, the result is a more intense fire.

8. **(G)** (p. 561) *Reading/Prose Fiction/Implied Idea.* The narrator says that although Turkey works well in the morning, his afternoon antics cause the narrator to feel uncomfortable.

9. **(A)** (p. 561) *Reading/Prose Fiction/Implied Idea.* The narrator refers to Turkey of the morning as quick and steady and a valuable asset.

10. **(H)** (p. 561) *Reading/Prose Fiction/Explicit Detail.* The narrator says that Turkey does not become lethargic in the afternoon. Rather, he seems to become overly active.

11. **(B)** (p. 562) *Reading/Social Science/Main Idea.* (B) is the best title for this selection: it discusses two different approaches to punishment—retributive and corrective. (A) is incorrect because it is basically concerned with the retributive punishment and not with corrective punishment. The answers represented by (C) and (D) are not at all appropriate to the subject of the selection.

12. **(J)** (p. 562) *Reading/Social Science/Explicit Detail.* The last sentence of the second paragraph clearly illustrates that the death penalty is a right of the murderer. The author's discussion of Hegel's views further substantiates this argument. (F) and (G) are in opposition to Hegel's views. (H), although a good answer and acceptable to Hegel, does not indicate the death penalty as a murderer's right and is therefore insufficient.

13. **(C)** (p. 562) *Reading/Social Science/Implied Idea.* (C) is the best choice for this question. The philosophy of equal injury in retributive justice differs from the philosophy in corrective justice of treating the criminal to conform with normal society. The reason for each type of justice, therefore, is quite different. (A) is wrong because both kinds of justice can be applied to any type of crime. (D) has no bearing on the question. (B) is incorrect because the severity of punishment can be the same with either form of justice.

14. **(J)** (p. 562) *Reading/Social Science/Application.* The philosophy behind corrective justice is one of treatment and rehabilitation, not death. (F), (G), and (H), although forms of varying degrees of punishment, do not result in death, so they would be consistent with the philosophy of corrective justice; therefore, they are wrong. (J) is the answer that should be selected, as the electric chair results in death and is therefore inconsistent with the philosophy of corrective justice.

15. **(C)** (p. 563) *Reading/Social Science/Implied Idea.* In line 7, the author uses the Biblical expression "an eye for an eye, and a tooth for a tooth" to show that the idea of justice as "one form of equality" (line 4) is expressed as early as in the Bible.

16. **(J)** (p. 563) *Reading/Social Science/Explicit Detail.* The answer to this item is clear from the sixth sentence of the first paragraph: "Only inflicting an equal injury upon him can do this." A fair trial, (F), rehabilitation, (G), and separation, (H) are concepts associated with corrective justice rather than retributive justice.

17. **(B)** (p. 563) *Reading/Social Science/Implied Idea.* The key is in the third paragraph (lines 26–31). None of the other answers are inferable from the passage.

18. **(F)** (p. 563) *Reading/Social Science/Implied Idea.* Denying the true self, (G), and accepting punishment, (J), are parts of the retributive justice code. Curing antisocial behavior, (H), is a means of enabling the criminal to act in his own best interests. (F) best embodies the notion of "normal" in corrective justice systems.

19. **(C)** (p. 563) *Reading/Social Science/Voice.* The author aims to explain the differences between ancient and modern systems of justice.

20. **(J)** (p. 563) *Reading/Social Science/Explicit Detail.* The last sentence of the third paragraph states this explicitly. A fair trial, (G), and a legal code, (H), do not apply to treating the criminal. Punishment, (F), is a last resort of the corrective justice system. (J) is the most appropriate answer.

21. **(A)** (p. 564) *Reading/Humanities/Explicit Detail.* The precipitating cause of World War I was the assassination of Archduke Francis Ferdinand, the heir to the Austro-Hungarian Empire throne, by a Serbian nationalist on June 28, 1914, as stated in the first paragraph of the passage.

22. **(F)** (p. 564) *Reading/Humanities/Explicit Detail.* The assassination occurred in the city of Sarajevo in Bosnia. Claimed by Serbia, Bosnia was annexed by Austria, provoking the rage of the government and the people of Bosnia and Serbia.

23. **(C)** (p. 564) *Reading/Humanities/Explicit Detail.* Before the outbreak of WWI, a balance of power had existed for almost a century, or 100 years. As stated in the first sentence of the second paragraph of the passage, WWI shattered the balance of power that had been established by the Congress of Vienna in 1815.

24. **(F)** (p. 565) *Reading/Humanities/Explicit Detail.* Russia, the protector of Serbia, and Austria were members of competing alliance systems. When war broke out between them, the member states of their alliances were drawn into the conflict. Germany intervened on the side of Austria, its alliance member, and Great Britain and France joined forces with Russia, with which both countries were allied.

25. **(B)** (p. 565) *Reading/Humanities/Explicit Detail.* The second paragraph describes how suspicions enkindled by the failure of diplomacy sparked the order to mobilize the Russian armed forces. German mobilization was ordered after the Russian order was issued.

26. **(F)** (p. 565) *Reading/Humanities/Implied Idea.* A spirit of nationalism, not class solidarity, animated the people of the individual nation states that fought against one another in World War I. No longer did the upper classes of Europe act as a unified class. Instead, they joined with their compatriots of the middle and lower classes to wage war against people in other countries with whom they had once shared values, beliefs, and a way of life.

27. **(B)** (p. 565) *Reading/Humanities/Explicit Detail.* The Nazi regime that came to power in Germany in 1933 and the regime of Stalin that tyrannized the Soviet people from 1927 to 1953 were ruthless dictatorships dedicated to world conquest.

28. **(J)** (p. 565) *Reading/Humanities/Application.* The sense of futility felt throughout Europe during and after World War I would be evident in European literature of the 1920s, 1930s, and 1940s. It is a fair assumption that the literature of a particular period mirrors, as well as illuminates, the spirit of the age.

29. **(B)** (p. 565) *Reading/Humanities/Implied Idea.* World War I and its aftermath suggest the idea that war feeds on nationalist sympathies. The sense of affront felt by the Austrian people when the heir to the throne of their empire was assassinated did not allow the Austrian leaders to adopt a moderate stance in their dealings with the government of Serbia (lines 9–10). The passage states that in the aftermath of the war, "national boundaries defined social consciousness" (lines 49–50).

30. **(H)** (p. 565) ***Reading/Humanities/Explicit Detail.*** As noted in lines 4–5, Archduke Francis Ferdinand, as the heir to the Austro-Hungarian Empire, was a member of the Hapsburg family.

31. **(D)** (p. 566) ***Reading/Natural Science/Explicit Detail.*** Since Uranus "rolls like a ball along the path of its orbit" with the geographic poles located like axles on either side, one pole is always in direct sunlight and the other is always in darkness.

32. **(H)** (p. 566) ***Reading/Natural Science/Implied Idea.*** The warmest location on Uranus would be the one that receives the most direct sunlight. Of the choices, the one with the most direct sunlight would be the geographic pole in the center of the planet's daylight side.

33. **(B)** (p. 566) ***Reading/Natural Science/Implied Idea.*** Because of the way Uranus rotates, one side is always in daylight and the other is always in darkness. A location on the daylight side is not necessarily near the magnetic poles, which lie in indirect sunlight near the planet's equator.

34. **(H)** (p. 566) ***Reading/Natural Science/Explicit Detail.*** A planet's equator is by definition located midway between the geographic poles. Since on Uranus these are on the sides of the planet, the equator must ring the planet from top to bottom.

35. **(B)** (p. 566) ***Reading/Natural Science/Application.*** The Uranian equator, ringing the planet from top to bottom, is located at the juncture of the planet's daylight and dark sides. An observer at the equator would most likely experience constant indirect sunlight.

36. **(H)** (p. 567) ***Reading/Natural Science/Application.*** Auroras appear near a planet's magnetic poles. On Uranus, these are near the equator and nowhere near the geographic poles, so the equator would be the most likely place to see auroras.

37. **(D)** (p. 567) ***Reading/Natural Science/Implied Idea.*** On Uranus, the daylight side receives varying amounts of sunlight at different latitudes. However, this appears to have no effect on atmospheric circulation, which instead flows along the equator around the top and bottom of the planet. Clearly, some other factor besides sunlight is in operation.

38. **(G)** (p. 567) ***Reading/Natural Science/Application.*** Lack of an atmosphere to create erosion is the only possible choice. Gravity was obviously strong enough to reassemble the planet, and in any case, gravity cannot wear away surface features. As for the possibility that the second object remained nearby, any collision strong enough to shatter Miranda most likely destroyed that object; in any case, the passage makes no mention of it.

39. **(C)** (p. 567) ***Reading/Natural Science/Application.*** (C) is the only possibility since the passage states that there is no evidence of geological activity on Ariel.

40. **(H)** (p. 567) ***Reading/Natural Science/Explicit Detail.*** The second paragraph mentions three moons by name—Miranda, Ariel, and Umbriel—and then notes that there are seven other moons.

Section 4: Science

1. **(D)** (p. 569) ***Science/Data Representation/Analysis.*** Consider the first column: the radii increase (0.37 Å, 1.52 Å, 1.86 Å, etc.) and the electronegativities decrease or stay the same (2.20, 0.98, 0.93, etc.) as one moves down the column.

2. **(F)** (p. 569) ***Science/Data Representation/Comprehension.*** Remember that the second number means electronegativity. The greatest value shown is for fluorine (F): 3.98.

3. **(C)** (p. 569) *Science/Data Representation/Comprehension.* According to the passage, bond length is the sum of the bonded atoms' radii. So for P-P, the bond length is 1.10 + 1.10 = 2.20 Å.

4. **(J)** (p. 569) *Science/Data Representation/Comprehension.* Carbon and nitrogen have the smallest electronegativity difference, 0.49.

5. **(D)** (p. 569) *Science/Data Representation/Analysis.* According to the passage, ionic character increases as the difference in electronegativity increases. In the table, the difference in electronegativity between fluorine and the other elements in the table generally increases the farther the second element is from fluorine in both a different row and a different column.

6. **(F)**(p. 569) *Science/Data Representation/Analysis.* Several choices include the value 0.46, which is the electronegativity difference in HI. Since At is below I, it may be expected to have an electronegativity below the value of 2.66, which is found for I, a prediction that leads to an electronegativity difference for HAt that is less than 0.46.

7. **(A)** (p. 570) *Science/Research Summary/Comprehension.* Venus is only 0.05 units smaller in diameter than Earth (0.95 Earth diameters).

8. **(H)** (p. 570) *Science/Research Summary/Comprehension.* One astronomical unit equals 1 inch in the scale used in Experiment 2. The poster board is only 28 inches long. Neptune's distance is 30 A.U. (30 inches) and would not fit on the paper.

9. **(D)** (p. 570) *Science/Research Summary/Analysis.* As planets get farther from the Sun (A.U. column), some are larger than Earth (Jupiter and Saturn have larger diameters), while others are smaller than Earth (Mars has a smaller diameter).

10. **(H)** (p. 570) *Science/Research Summary/Application.* If the asteroids are 2.8 A.U. away from the Sun, they would be found between Mars and Jupiter. Thus, an asteroid year is longer than that on Mars but shorter than that on Jupiter.

11. **(A)** (p. 571) *Science/Research Summary/Analysis.* If the Sun's diameter is 110 times greater than that of the Earth, its diameter would be $110 \cdot 1 \text{ inch} = 110 \text{ inches}$ (Experiment 1 uses a scale where 1 Earth diameter = 1 inch). Therefore, its radius would be 55 inches.

12. **(H)** (p. 571) *Science/Research Summary/Application.* The relative mass information given in the question is very similar to the order of planets based on their relative diameters (Table 1: Earth diameters column).

13. **(B)** (p. 573) *Science/Research Summary/Analysis.* If carbon dioxide is the variable in question, all factors except carbon dioxide should remain fixed. Only then can the effects of various carbon dioxide levels be evaluated.

14. **(J)** (p. 573) *Science/Research Summary/Analysis.* The only difference between Experiments 1 and 2 is that the concentration of leaf extract (containing a mixture of pigments) was reduced in Experiment 2. Using the lower concentration of pigments, the rate of photosynthesis leveled off, suggesting that the amount was inadequate to maintain the previously observed continued increase in rate.

15. **(A)** (p. 573) *Science/Research Summary/Analysis.* The description of Experiment 3 states that certain wavelengths must be absorbed to maintain photosynthesis (which is measured by counting oxygen bubbles). The bubble counts (and therefore peak absorption) for Pigment A are at approximately 450 and 650 nanometers. For Pigment B, peak count is between 500 and 575 nanometers.

16. **(G)** (p. 573) *Science/Research Summary/Analysis.* Since the reduced concentration of pigments in Experiment 2 led to a leveling off in bubble count, an increase in pigment concentration should lead to an increase in the rate of photosynthesis and an associated increase in bubble count.

17. **(C)** (p. 573) *Science/Research Summary/Comprehension.* In Figures 1 and 2, use a straight edge and follow the graphs up from a light intensity of 4—the graphs indicate an oxygen bubble count of approximately 40 bubbles per minute.

18. **(J)** (p. 573) *Science/Research Summary/Analysis.* Figure 3 shows that at 600 nm (orange light), both Pigments A and B show very little absorption, as measured by the low oxygen bubble count. Since light must be absorbed to provide energy for photosynthesis, orange light would be least effective.

19. **(C)** (p. 574) *Science/Data Representation/Comprehension.* The meters per minute scale increases from bottom to top. The highest point on the chart shows the fastest speed to be approximately 590–600 meters per minute for the 100 yard dash in 1962.

20. **(F)** (p. 574) *Science/Data Representation/Analysis.* The lines represent the best-fitting slopes of points, which show how running speed has increased.

21. **(D)** (p. 574) *Science/Data Representation/Comprehension.* In 1960, the speed for the 1 mile run was approximately 4 minutes/mile, while the speed for the 440 yard dash was approximately 3 minutes/mile. Therefore, the ratio is 4/3.

22. **(H)** (p. 574) *Science/Data Representation/Comprehension.* The speeds for the 2 mile run are all between 345 and 375 meters per minute. Since $375 - 345 = 30$, the gain in speed must be closest to the "30 meters per minute" choice.

23. **(A)** (p. 574) *Science/Data Representation/Analysis.* This problem, requiring the right-hand scale, asks for an extrapolation beyond the given data. The 880 yard line, when extrapolated in the graph, crosses the 1980 axis at approximately 3.5 minutes per mile.

24. **(G)** (p. 575) *Science/Research Summary/Analysis.* The results from Experiment 1 show temperature rising at an even rate during the time that the sample is heated.

25. **(C)** (p. 575) *Science/Research Summary/Analysis.* Experiment 1 starts above 0°C, whereas Experiment 2 starts below 0°C. In addition, the temperature in Experiment 2 stabilizes along the "x-axis" for a while.

26. **(H)** (p. 575) *Science/Research Summary/Analysis.* The passage states that constant amounts of heat were added continuously to samples over a defined period of time. Assuming that all of these given conditions remain unchanged, (F), (G), and (J) can be eliminated. Therefore, another process is the best explanation for the flat part of the graph, since it is not a given condition.

27. **(A)** (p. 575) *Science/Research Summary/Application.* Ice melts at 0°C. This is the temperature at which the graph temporarily levels off.

28. **(G)** (p. 575) *Science/Research Summary/Analysis.* The experiment utilized constant heating. Yet, temperature change was not constant. Therefore, heat and temperature are not the same thing.

29. **(B)** (p. 576) *Science/Research Summary/Analysis.* At the two phase changes (0°C and 100°C), the graph should be flat, corresponding to the heat absorbed by the solid or liquid.

30. **(H)** (p. 578) *Science/Data Representation/Comprehension.* An examination of the diagram reveals that primary tissue layers and primary germ layers are names for the same developing parts. This information is part of the description of the gastrulation stage.

31. **(D)** (p. 578) *Science/Data Representation/Application.* The diagram arrows show the changes that occur as each developmental stage follows the previous one. The greatest amount of differentiation in structure and function occurs during organogenesis as the primary germ layers formed in gastrulation become the many specialized systems, organs, and related structures of the organism.

32. **(F)** (p. 578) *Science/Data Representation/Analysis.* (G), (H), and (J) can be verified from the given chart. As for (F), under the organogenesis stage, arrows show that the body's bones develop from the middle primary germ layer (mesoderm), not the innermost layer (endoderm).

33. **(C)** (p. 578) *Science/Data Representation/Application.* Structures (receptor cells) that contribute to visual abilities in the monkey would develop as parts of the eye, "a special sense organ." The arrows show that parts of the special sense organs arise from the ectoderm.

34. **(G)** (p. 578) *Science/Data Representation/Comprehension.* The chart indicates that during the cleavage stage, the many new cells that form from the zygote and its materials do not grow. Thus, as the zygote's material is simply subdivided, the resulting cells must be extremely small.

35. **(D)** (p. 579) *Science/Conflicting Viewpoints/Comprehension.* Theory 1 states that, "[t]he reaction will adjust to the proportions given." Therefore, all proportions of reactants will be used. (D) does not follow this guideline.

36. **(J)** (p. 579) *Science/Conflicting Viewpoints/Comprehension.* Theory 1 simply states that any proportion of reactants may mix. It does not explain the relation of the amounts of reactants to the amounts of product produced by the reaction.

37. **(B)** (p. 579) *Science/Conflicting Viewpoints/Analysis.* Theory 2 states that a certain proportion of reactants will react; otherwise, one or another reactant will fail to react completely.

38. **(F)** (p. 579) *Science/Conflicting Viewpoints/Analysis.* Theory 2 states that both reactants must be in the appropriate proportions to be used in the process of forming more product, so adding more NaCl is the only way to use up the leftover $AgNO_3$.

39. **(B)** (p. 580) *Science/Conflicting Viewpoints/Analysis.* Adding 2 moles of iron to 4 moles of oxygen is the only response that provides a ratio of iron to oxygen that is different from the two ratios that proved successful in the experiment.

40. **(H)** (p. 580) *Science/Conflicting Viewpoints/Comprehension.* Theory 1 only states that products contain the original elements.

Sample Essay Responses and Analyses

Section 5: Writing (p. 582)

Above Average Response

Online activism can be a helpful way to engage with a social issue, depending on the situation, but supporting an issue online does not necessarily need to change. Online support is truly activism when people's words have direct consequences, such as a journalist who can influence his or her readers or an organization that uses social media to fundraise. However, people who merely express support for a cause online without risking anything or devoting time to the cause cannot call themselves activists.

Expressing one's opinion online can be an effective way to generate support for a cause and can sometimes even put you at risk. It is hard to generalize about online activism because its use around the world varies so greatly. In repressive regimes that prohibit freedom of speech or of the press, online activism may be a courageous way to express or gain support for a cause. For example, during the Arab Spring, social media was crucial for generating support among youth. Recently, a blogger in Saudi Arabia was arrested and condemned to receive 1,000 lashes for promoting religious tolerance online. Even in countries like the United States where freedom of speech is promoted, expressing one's opinion online can still be a brave act for some. Someone might be ostracized for supporting gay rights in a homophobic community or for posting something about his or her faith in an anti-religious community. If one's words or actions online are intended to have consequences, that person is engaging in activism.

Online activism is also a useful tool for journalists or charity organizations to gain support for a cause. In the case of the blogger in Saudi Arabia, journalists worldwide published articles protesting the injustice of his punishment, and their readers spread information on social media. Because of international attention and pressure from foreign governments, the Saudi Arabian government said it would review the case. This is an example of how the viral nature of online information can influence important causes. Online activism can also raise money for charities. For example, in 2014, the ALS Association raised millions of dollars to fund research on the disease because of the "Ice Bucket Challenge" fundraiser on social media. Participants posted a video in which they dumped a bucket of ice on their head, and each participant nominated three other people to post their own video and/or donate to the ALS Association. This example shows how online activism can generate popularity in an entertaining way, yet support a serious cause.

Despite these cases of effective online activism, millions of people engage in "slacktivism," in which they express their support for an issue without causing change or risking any consequences for themselves. After a natural disaster, for example, someone may post an article about the tragedy on social media, but never donate or volunteer his or her own time to help the victims. One could argue that the "slacktivist" is raising awareness about an issue, but if the issue has already received media attention, posting an article about it does not make a difference. Internet users who post such articles might feel like better citizens by doing so, but if nothing is at stake in their actions, they cannot call themselves activists.

It is not easy to generalize about online activism because of the many forms it can take. However, internet users are truly activists if their words put them at risk or lead to direct action. People who merely repost information online have the right to express their opinions in this way, but they are not engaging in activism.

Ideas and Analysis: The writer develops a nuanced perspective on online activism, acknowledging that it is difficult to generalize about the subject because it comes in many different forms. The writer develops criteria to determine whether online "activists" are truly engaged in a cause: Are they taking a risk, or do they intend for their online actions to have consequences? The essay considers multiple points of view, but the writer's own viewpoint is consistent.

Although the writer does not adopt one of the three perspectives, he or she addresses them throughout the essay. For example, the first and second body paragraphs argue that online activism can cause change (Perspective 3), but only in certain situations (Perspective 2). The third paragraph acknowledges that there are many cases in which online "activists" make no difference and are not truly involved in a cause (Perspective 1).

Development and Support: The introduction states the thesis and previews the arguments that will support it. The writer presents these arguments in a thorough and logical manner with many supporting examples:

- The writer states his or her thesis in the first sentence of the introduction: Online activism can be a helpful way to engage with a social issue, depending on the situation, but supporting an issue online does not always make someone an activist. The essay could be stronger, however, if the writer began with a "hook" to grab the reader's attention and stated the thesis in the second sentence.

- The writer previews the main arguments of the essay throughout the remainder of the introduction.

- Each body paragraph begins with a clear topic sentence.

- The writer uses concrete examples to support each argument:

  o Body paragraph 1: The examples show how online activism can be just as risky as more traditional forms of activism, and the writer draws from current events, rather than only providing hypothetical examples. The paragraph could be stronger, though, if the writer elaborated on one or two examples rather than mentioning several examples.

  o Body paragraph 2: The writer chooses two very different examples, which is an effective way to show how online activism can work in a variety of situations.

  o Body paragraph 3: The writer uses a hypothetical example to show how online activism is not always effective. This paragraph would be stronger with a concrete, real-life example.

Organization:

- The writer previews the main ideas in the introduction and begins each body paragraph with a topic sentence.

- The writer uses transitions to begin new paragraphs. For example, the third paragraph begins with "despite" because it introduces an opposing idea.

- The writer organizes the main ideas in a logical order, in order to defend online activism in certain situations. The first two body paragraphs describe legitimate cases of online activism, while the last body paragraph acknowledges that not all online activists are truly engaged in the causes that they claim to support.

Language Use and Conventions:

- The essay does not have any mechanics/usage errors. As a result, the reader's attention is not distracted from the substance of the essay.

- The essay does not have any informal language.

- In the first body paragraph, however, the writer inconsistently uses "one" and "you": "Expressing **one's** opinion online can be an effective and way to generate support for a cause and can sometimes even put **you** at risk."

Summary and Conclusions: The writer develops a nuanced viewpoint on the issue and incorporates all three perspectives into his or her argument. Even though the author examines multiple opinions, he or she maintains a consistent argument throughout the essay. The essay would likely receive a score of 10.

Below Average Response

Online activism is a useful tool because it raises awareness and gaining support for important causes. It is unfair to call this "slacktivism" because even though it is different than traditional forms of activism, it is still an important activity.

Sharing information online can make more people care about an issue. Information gets spread so quickly online, which makes it easier to gain the attention of thousands and even millions of people. By sharing an article about an event that happened in another country, you can make your friends aware of the issue. Then if they share the article, their friends can also read about the issue. This seems like the most efficient way to spread information.

Online activism is also useful because it shows when large amounts of people care about an issue. For example, when I signed an online petition for Congress, I saw that over 100,000 people had also signed it. When Congress sees that so many people care about that issue, will be more likely to listen to us. This would not be possible without a website where you could see how many people in your country or worldwide support a cause.

Online activism is also practical because you can become involved with many causes at once. If you are volunteering for a local cause, it takes up all of your time and you don't have time to learn about anything else. However, when I use the internet to learn about social causes, I can learn about what's happening in many places that are thousands of miles away from me. I feel more involved in the world this way.

As these situations show, online activism is a useful tool for raising awareness of issues and getting many people involved. With the internet, people care about a lot more issues than they used to.

Ideas and Analysis: The writer clearly states his or her opinion, and the body paragraphs all support this opinion. However, the writer does not take any opposing arguments into account. Students should know that it is possible to write an essay that firmly supports one side instead of developing a "compromise" position, but such an essay should mention the opposing viewpoint and argue against it.

Furthermore, the writer's analysis contains few concrete examples and is often weak. The main point of the third paragraph, in particular, is not logical. The writer seems to misunderstand the prompt and argues that learning about an issue while not taking any action is a form of activism.

Development and Support:

- The writer states his or her thesis in the introduction. However, the introduction does not preview the essay's main arguments.

- The writer should use more examples in the body paragraphs. The second body paragraph is the most effective, with the example of petitioning Congress. However, the first and third body paragraphs only use hypothetical examples or generalizations.

- The argument in the third body paragraph does not develop the essay or show, concretely, how online activism makes a difference. In fact, the writer's description in this paragraph is a perfect example of the "slacktivism" that Perspective 1 criticizes.

Organization:

- The writer should preview his or her main arguments in the introduction.

- Sometimes, the writer uses repetitive transitions. For example, both the second and third body paragraphs begin with "Online activism is also."

- The wording in the conclusion is too similar to the wording in the introduction. The writer should restate his or her thesis in the conclusion, but the wording should not be exactly the same.

Language Use and Conventions: The essay contains several weaknesses in this area:

- The essay contains some usage and mechanics errors.

  o Introduction: The first sentence does not use parallel verb structure: "Online activism is a useful tool because it **raises** awareness **and gaining** support for important causes." The sentence should either say, "Online activism is a useful tool because it **raises** awareness **and gains** support for important causes" or "Online activism is a useful tool for **raising** awareness **and gaining** support for important causes."

  o Body paragraph 2: "When Congress sees that so many people care about that issue, will be more likely to listen to us." This is not a complete sentence because it is missing a subject. The writer could say, for example, "When Congress sees that so many people care about that issue, **lawmakers** will be more likely to listen to us."

- The essay contains many examples of informal language. For example, in the third body paragraph, the writer says that he or she can learn about "what's happening" in many places. Instead, the writer should use a formal, more concrete word, such as "current events."

Summary and Conclusions: The essay has a clear thesis and three main arguments. However, the writer does not consider the opposing viewpoints in Perspectives 1 and 2, and the essay contains faulty reasoning and weak examples. This essay would likely receive a score of 5.

PRACTICE TEST III

Multiple-Choice Answer Keys

DIRECTIONS: For the <u>correct</u> answer, check the corresponding unshaded box. Then, total the number of checkmarks for each of the content areas, and add these totals to determine the raw score for that test.

Section 1: English (Student Text, p. 586)

	UM RH		UM RH		UM RH		UM RH		UM RH
1. C		16. J		31. B		46. H		61. D	
2. F		17. A		32. G		47. D		62. F	
3. C		18. H		33. B		48. G		63. B	
4. G		19. D		34. J		49. B		64. J	
5. B		20. H		35. B		50. F		65. C	
6. F		21. A		36. J		51. A		66. H	
7. C		22. G		37. D		52. G		67. A	
8. F		23. D		38. G		53. D		68. G	
9. C		24. H		39. A		54. G		69. D	
10. H		25. D		40. J		55. B		70. H	
11. A		26. F		41. B		56. H		71. C	
12. F		27. B		42. F		57. A		72. G	
13. D		28. F		43. A		58. H		73. D	
14. H		29. D		44. G		59. A		74. H	
15. B		30. J		45. A		60. J		75. D	

Usage and Mechanics (UM): _____/46   Rhetorical Skills (RH): _____/29   Raw Score (UM + RH): _____/75

Section 2: Mathematics (Student Text, p. 602)

	EA AG GT		EA AG GT		EA AG GT		EA AG GT
1. D		16. G		31. A		46. K	
2. K		17. D		32. H		47. A	
3. C		18. F		33. D		48. H	
4. J		19. B		34. K		49. D	
5. E		20. F		35. E		50. G	
6. K		21. E		36. F		51. C	
7. B		22. F		37. B		52. G	
8. G		23. C		38. K		53. D	
9. D		24. G		39. B		54. K	
10. G		25. A		40. K		55. C	
11. B		26. H		41. C		56. G	
12. G		27. A		42. J		57. A	
13. E		28. H		43. D		58. F	
14. H		29. C		44. J		59. E	
15. C		30. K		45. C		60. F	

Pre-Algebra/Elementary Algebra (EA): _____/26   Plane Geometry/Trigonometry (GT): _____/18

Int. Algebra/Coordinate Geometry (AG): _____/16   Raw Score (EA + AG + GT): _____/60

Section 3: Reading (Student Text, p. 622)

#	Ans	SS	AL
1.	B	▪	
2.	J	▪	
3.	A	▪	
4.	H	▪	
5.	A	▪	
6.	J	▪	
7.	B	▪	
8.	F	▪	
9.	A	▪	
10.	F	▪	
11.	B		▪
12.	G		▪
13.	C		▪
14.	F		▪
15.	D		▪
16.	G		▪
17.	D		▪
18.	H		▪
19.	B		▪
20.	H		▪
21.	A	▪	
22.	J	▪	
23.	D	▪	
24.	G	▪	
25.	D	▪	
26.	G	▪	
27.	A	▪	
28.	H	▪	
29.	A	▪	
30.	H	▪	
31.	C		▪
32.	J		▪
33.	A		▪
34.	H		▪
35.	A		▪
36.	J		▪
37.	B		▪
38.	J		▪
39.	D		▪
40.	H		▪

Social Studies/Sciences (SS): _____ /20   Arts/Literature (AL): _____ /20   Raw Score (SS + AL): _____ /40

Section 4: Science (Student Text, p. 633)

#	Ans	B	C	P	ES
1.	B	▪	▪		▪
2.	H	▪	▪		▪
3.	A	▪	▪		▪
4.	H	▪	▪		▪
5.	B	▪	▪		▪
6.	J		▪	▪	▪
7.	A		▪	▪	▪
8.	F		▪	▪	▪
9.	C		▪	▪	▪
10.	G		▪	▪	▪
11.	A		▪	▪	▪
12.	G	▪	▪	▪	
13.	D	▪	▪	▪	
14.	H	▪	▪	▪	
15.	A	▪	▪	▪	
16.	F	▪	▪	▪	
17.	C	▪	▪	▪	
18.	G	▪	▪	▪	
19.	D		▪	▪	▪
20.	G		▪	▪	▪
21.	C		▪	▪	▪
22.	J		▪	▪	▪
23.	A		▪	▪	▪
24.	F		▪	▪	▪
25.	A	▪		▪	▪
26.	J	▪		▪	▪
27.	D	▪		▪	▪
28.	J	▪		▪	▪
29.	C	▪		▪	▪
30.	J	▪		▪	▪
31.	C	▪	▪		▪
32.	J	▪	▪		▪
33.	A	▪	▪		▪
34.	H	▪	▪		▪
35.	C	▪	▪		▪
36.	H		▪	▪	▪
37.	D		▪	▪	▪
38.	G		▪	▪	▪
39.	B		▪	▪	▪
40.	G		▪	▪	▪

Biology (B): _____ /17   Physics (P): _____ /10   Raw Score (B + C + P + ES): _____ /40

Chemistry (C): _____ /6   Earth/Space Sciences (ES): _____ /7

Multiple-Choice Explanations

Section 1: English

1. **(C)** (p. 586) *English/Usage and Mechanics/Grammar and Usage/Diction.* The original sentence is not idiomatic. "On account of" cannot be used as a substitute for "because of." (C) is the correct answer because it makes the needed correction. As for the other answer choices, (B) is wrong because "since" is a conjunction that can only be used to introduce a dependent clause; however, the material that follows is not a clause since it does not include a verb. As for (D), "for" can be a preposition; however, its meaning is not appropriate in this context.

2. **(F)** (p. 586) *English/Rhetorical Skills/No Change.* The original sentence is correct. "Nonetheless" provides the meaning required in this context since it means "in spite of this." As for the other answer choices, (G) and (H) are wrong because the author means to say that smuggling grew in spite of government efforts (not because of government efforts). As for (J), "on the contrary" generally means "in opposition to what has been stated"; however, it does not provide the precise meaning ("in spite of this") that is required here.

3. **(C)** (p. 586) *English/Usage and Mechanics/Grammar and Usage/Adjectives versus Adverbs* and *Punctuation/Commas.* The original sentence contains two errors. First, an adjective cannot modify an adjective ("heavy timbered islands"). Only an adverb can modify an adjective ("heavily timbered islands"). Second, a comma is needed after "countless" ("countless, heavily timbered islands") to make it clear that "countless" modifies "islands" (and not "heavily timbered"). (C) is the correct answer choice because it makes both of these corrections.

4. **(G)** (p. 587) *English/Usage and Mechanics/Grammar and Usage/Diction.* The original sentence, (H), and (J) are all incorrect because they are not idiomatic. The correct idiomatic phrase is "well founded."

5. **(B)** (p. 587) *English/Usage and Mechanics/Grammar and Usage/Sequence and Verb Tense.* The original sentence is incorrect because "seize" (a present tense verb) is inconsistent with the past tense verbs used throughout the rest of the paragraph. Past events are being described here, so "seized" (a past tense verb) is the correct answer choice. As for the other answer choices, (C) and (D) refer to past events; however, they provide meanings that are inappropriate in this context. First, "were seizing" (a progressive past tense verb) implies an action that occurred over and over again in the past (e.g., "during this period, customs officials were seizing tons of wool each month"). Second, "have seized" (a present perfect tense verb) implies an action that began in the past but that also continues into the present (e.g., "the British have repeatedly seized our ships and continue to do so"). Neither of these meanings is appropriate here, so both (C) and (D) are incorrect.

6. **(F)** (p. 587) *English/Rhetorical Skills/No Change.* The original sentence is correct. As for the other answer choices, both (G) and (J) are awkward and needlessly wordy compared to the original sentence. (H) is incorrect because it misconstrues the meaning of the original sentence. Specifically, the original states that the *Beaver* was seized because of a "technical violation"; in contrast, (H) says the *Beaver* was seized "for technically being in violation" of the law, which incorrectly suggests that the author believes the violation was minor or perhaps even non-existent.

7. **(C)** (p. 587) *English/Usage and Mechanics/Grammar and Usage/Diction.* The original sentence is incorrect because it includes an incorrect word choice. "Principle" is a noun which means "rule" or "belief," and it cannot modify the plural noun "articles." The word required here is the adjective "principal," which means "main" or "important." Therefore, (C) is the correct answer choice. As for the other answer choices, (B) is wrong for two reasons. First, it does not fix the original, incorrect word choice. Second, it introduces a singular verb ("was"), which does not agree with the plural subject

("British wool, blankets, and liquor") of the sentence. (D) is also incorrect because it introduces a singular verb, "was," which does not agree with the plural subject of the sentence.

8. **(F)** (p. 587) ***English/Rhetorical Skills/No Change.*** The original sentence is correct. "In fact" is used to introduce a sentence that illustrates or emphasizes a point made in the previous sentence. In this paragraph, the sentence about British wool being smuggled into the San Juan Islands illustrates the point made in the previous sentence—namely, that British wool was a principal article of illicit trade. So, "in fact" is correctly used here. As for the other answer choices, (G) and (H) are wrong for the same reason. "Furthermore" and "moreover" are used to introduce a sentence that includes an idea similar to (but that is not an illustration of) an idea from the previous sentence. In this paragraph, though, the sentence about British wool being smuggled into the San Juan Islands is an illustration of an idea in the previous sentence; so, both "furthermore" and "moreover" are incorrect answer choices. Finally, (J) is incorrect because "on the contrary" is used to signal that a contrasting idea will be introduced; however, the author does not introduce a contrasting idea.

9. **(C)** (p. 587) ***English/Usage and Mechanics/Grammar and Usage/Verb Tense.*** The original sentence is incorrect because it includes an incorrect verb form. A passive past tense verb ("was smuggled") is used earlier in the sentence, and another passive past tense verb ("and sold") is needed to agree with it. So, (C) is the correct answer choice. As for the other answer choices, they are all incorrect because they do not provide the required passive past tense verb.

10. **(H)** (p. 587) ***English/Usage and Mechanics/Grammar and Usage/Diction.*** The original sentence is incorrect because it sets up an idiom ("so much...that") but does not successfully complete it. (H) is the correct answer choice because it successfully completes the idiomatic phrase. As for the other answer choices, they are all incorrect because they do not complete the idiomatic phrase.

11. **(A)** (p. 588) ***English/Rhetorical Skills/No Change.*** The original sentence is correct. In the sentence, there is a contrast between how settlers welcomed national control and how they resented the accompanying restrictions on trade. "Although" is the right word for introducing this type of contrast. As for the other answer choices, none of them would be appropriate for introducing the type of contrast discussed in this sentence.

12. **(F)** (p. 588) ***English/Usage and Mechanics/No Change.*** The original sentence is correct. The simple past tense verb ("welcomed") is consistent with the other verb in this sentence ("they <u>were</u> less amenable") as well as the other past tense verbs in the passage. As for the other answer choices, (G) is incorrect because it eliminates the only conjugated verb ("welcomed") in the clause; as a result, the sentence becomes a sentence fragment. (H) is wrong because "would welcome" is inconsistent with the past tense verbs in the paragraph. (J) is incorrect because it creates a completely illogical sentence; in short, an "assertion of national control" cannot welcome people.

13. **(D)** (p. 588) ***English/Usage and Mechanics/Grammar and Usage/Diction.*** The original sentence is incorrect because it includes an incorrect verb form. An active past tense verb ("They wanted") is used earlier in the sentence, and another active past tense verb ("but feared") is needed here to agree with it. So, (D) is the correct answer choice. As for the other answer choices, (A) and (B) are incorrect because "were fearing" is not an idiomatic expression; the correct idiomatic expression is "were fearful." (C) is incorrect because, although it uses the correct idiomatic phrase ("was fearful"), the singular verb ("was") does not agree with the plural subject ("they") of the sentence.

14. **(H)** (p. 588) ***English/Usage and Mechanics/Grammar and Usage/Sequence and Verb Tense*** and ***Diction.*** The original sentence includes two errors. First, the underlined portion includes a verb phrase ("might be resulting") that is awkward and needlessly wordy; it should be replaced by the more accurate and succinct verb phrase "might result." Second, the underlined portion includes a prepositional phrase ("in the losing of") that is non-idiomatic; the correct idiomatic phrase is "in the loss of." (H) is the correct

answer choice because it makes both of these corrections. As for the other answer choices, (G) is incorrect because it only makes one of these corrections. (J) is incorrect because a present tense verb ("results") does not suggest the element of uncertainty or contingency required here. Verb phrases such as "might result" or "would result" accomplish this task. However, a present tense verb ("results") does not.

15. **(B)** (p. 588) ***English/Rhetorical Skills/Organization/Passage-Level Structure.*** The paragraphs need to be in chronological order. Therefore, (B) is the correct answer choice here. Paragraph 1 is first because it describes the earliest event (the opening of the customs office). Paragraph 3 is next because it describes events that followed (the settlers' concerns about the new office). Paragraph 2 is last because it describes events that occurred last (the Americans' concerns turned out to be true).

16. **(J)** (p. 588) ***English/Rhetorical Skills/Organization/Passage-Level Structure.*** The author does not provide any quotations in the essay. So, (J) is correct. (F) is incorrect because the author describes or provides a narrative of several events. (G) is incorrect because the author gives specific examples in the essay. (H) is incorrect because the author provides statistics related to the production of wool.

17. **(A)** (p. 589) ***English/Rhetorical Skills/No Change.*** The original sentence is the best choice. In comparison, the other answer choices are awkward and needlessly wordy.

18. **(H)** (p. 589) ***English/Usage and Mechanics/Sentence Structure/Faulty Parallelism.*** The original sentence is incorrect due to a lack of parallelism. All three verbs in the sentence ("step," "gaze," and "become") are governed by the first instance of "can," which establishes the present tense. It is unnecessary for another instance of "can" to appear in the sentence. However, the original sentence has an instance of "can" before "become." As a result, a series is created in which the elements are not parallel or do not have exactly the same form. (H) is the correct answer choice because it eliminates the problem and brings the third verb into line with the other two. As for the other answer choices, (G) is incorrect because a past tense verb ("became") destroys the parallelism needed here. (J) is incorrect because the verb ("becomes") does not agree in number with the subject ("anyone") of the sentence.

19. **(D)** (p. 589) ***English/Usage and Mechanics/Sentence Structure/Comma Splices.*** The original sentence is incorrect because it is a run-on sentence. A run-on sentence is two or more complete sentences joined together without the necessary punctuation or conjunctions. For example, the first clause in the sentence ("The same questions come to mind time and again") is a complete sentence by itself. For the sake of correctness and clarity, it would be best to put a piece of end-stop punctuation at the end of this clause and then start an entirely new sentence. (D) is the correct answer choice because it accomplishes this task. As for the other answer choices, (B) and (C) are incorrect because they also result in run-on sentences.

20. **(H)** (p. 589) ***English/Usage and Mechanics/Sentence Structure/Misplaced Modifiers.*** The original sentence is incorrect because it is too ambiguous. Specifically, "ending" seems to modify "suns"; however, the author intends for it to modify "island universe." The ambiguity is eliminated by replacing the ambiguous "ending" with the relative clause "that ends…." It is now clear that the relative clause modifies "island universe." So, (H) is correct. (G) creates the appropriate relative clause to modify "island universe"; however, the plural verb "end" does not agree in number with the singular noun antecedent of the relative clause ("island universe"). Finally, (J) is incorrect because it suffers from the same defect as the original; "ended" seems to modify "suns" rather than "island universe."

21. **(A)** (p. 589) ***English/Usage and Mechanics/No Change.*** The original sentence is correct. Standard written English requires the infinitive "to chart" in this context. (B) and (C) are incorrect because standard written English does not allow for participles ("charting" or "having charted") in this context. (D) is incorrect because it creates a sentence that is illogical and impossible to understand.

22. **(G)** (p. 589) *English/Usage and Mechanics/Grammar and Usage/Verb Tense.* The original sentence is incorrect because it includes an incorrect verb tense. The past perfect tense ("progress had been made") implies that progress was actually made *before* the twentieth century. Of course, the author intends to say that progress was made "in the twentieth century," so a simple past tense verb ("was made") is needed. Therefore, (G) is the correct answer choice. (H) is incorrect because a present tense verb form ("is made") fails to communicate that progress has already been made during the twentieth century. (J) is incorrect because a future tense verb form ("will be made") incorrectly suggests that progress has not yet been made at all.

23. **(D)** (p. 590) *English/Rhetorical Skills/Strategy/Effective Transitional Sentence.* The original sentence is incorrect because it begins with a misleading introductory phrase. "As such" is a phrase which suggests a connection between two events or ideas. For example, "He is the head of security. As such, he helped develop the emergency response procedures." So, because he is head of security he helped develop the procedures. As for this particular sentence, though, it is certainly not the case that the Milky Way was so named because our solar system was discovered to be part of it. In fact, there is not a cause-and-effect relationship between the name of the Milky Way and our solar system's relationship to it. (D) is the correct answer choice here because it eliminates any suggestion that there is any relationship of this type. As for the other answer choices, (B) and (C) are both incorrect because it is not clear why the statement made is obvious or beyond doubt.

24. **(H)** (p. 590) *English/Rhetorical Skills/Organization/Paragraph-Level Structure.* The original sentence is incorrect because the material in it belongs in the next paragraph. Therefore, the original sentence should actually be the first sentence of the following paragraph. It should then be immediately followed (i.e., without a break for a new paragraph) by the sentence that used to begin that paragraph ("Since they are so near..."). Both (H) and (J) make the required changes. However, (J) is incorrect because "As" would turn the sentence into a dependent clause that did not have a supporting independent clause. (H) does not introduce this error. So, (H) is the correct answer choice.

25. **(D)** (p. 590) *English/Usage and Mechanics/Punctuation/Commas.* The original sentence is incorrect because only a comma or a dash (and not a semicolon) should be used to separate an appositive phrase ("the 'crown jewels' of the southern skies") from the main part of the sentence. (D) is the correct answer choice because it provides the appropriate punctuation. As for the other answer choices, (B) also provides the appropriate punctuation. However, it improperly removes the quotation marks from "crown jewels." The phrase is an example of words that are used in an uncommon, unusual, or unfamiliar way (i.e., the galaxies are not literally jewels); as a result, the phrase needs to appear inside quotation marks. (C) is incorrect because a singular verb ("is") does not agree with a plural noun ("Magellanic Clouds").

26. **(F)** (p. 590) *English/Usage and Mechanics/No Change.* The original sentence is correct. As for the other answer choices, they are either not idiomatic or not grammatically correct.

27. **(B)** (p. 590) *English/Rhetorical Skills/Style/Conciseness.* The original sentence is incorrect because the "to" in the underlined portion is unnecessary and makes the phrasing stilted. Both (B) and (C) make the needed correction. However, (C) is incorrect because a plural verb ("provide") does not agree with the singular subject ("galaxy") of the sentence.

28. **(F)** (p. 590) *English/Rhetorical Skills/No Change.* The original sentence is the best choice. In comparison, the other answer choices are awkward and needlessly wordy.

29. **(D)** (p. 591) *English/Rhetorical Skills/Organization/Paragraph-Level Structure.* (A), (B), and (C) are incorrect because the author does pose questions for these very reasons in the essay. (D) is the correct answer choice because the author does not promise that answers will be provided later in the essay to

what are, simply, many unanswerable questions (i.e., How many stars are there? Where and how does the universe end?).

30. (J) (p. 591) *English/Usage and Mechanics/Grammar and Usage/Diction.* The original sentence is incorrect because it includes an improperly formed appositive. The final phrase in the sentence ("graduated of test pilot schools") is meant to be an appositive for "volunteer, military pilots." To properly form the appositive, simply rewrite the final phrase as "graduates of test pilot schools." (J) is the correct answer choice because it makes this revision. As for the other answer choices, both (G) and (H) are wrong because an appositive can be set off only by a comma or a dash.

31. (B) (p. 591) *English/Usage and Mechanics/Grammar and Usage/Subject-Verb Agreement* **and** *Diction.* The original sentence is incorrect for two reasons. First, a plural verb ("were") does not agree with the singular subject ("each") of the sentence. Second, the use of a present participle ("having") here is not idiomatic. (B) is the correct answer choice because it corrects both of these errors. As for the other answer choices, (C) does not correct the second error. (D) corrects both errors, but the past perfect "had been required" is inconsistent with the past tense verbs in the rest of the paragraph.

32. (G) (p. 591) *English/Rhetorical Skills/Style/Idiomatic Expression.* The original sentence is incorrect because it includes informal usage. Specifically, it is not acceptable standard written English to use "got" when forming a passive verb form. Instead, use a form of the verb "to be" (e.g., "was," "were," etc.). (G) is the correct answer choice because it makes the needed correction. As for the other answer choices, (H) is a form of the passive voice; however, the past perfect "had been chosen" is inconsistent with the past tense verbs in the rest of the paragraph. (J) is incorrect for two reasons. First, the present perfect "has been" is not consistent with the past tense verbs in the rest of the paragraph. Second, a singular verb ("has") does not agree with the plural subject ("seven") of the sentence.

33. (B) (p. 592) *English/Rhetorical Skills/Strategy/Appropriate Supporting Material.* The information contained in the parentheses explains why only seven astronauts were chosen. However, this information is not vital to the development of the passage. By placing the explanation in parentheses, the author signals to the reader that the information is not vital.

34. (J) (p. 592) *English/Usage and Mechanics/Sentence Structure/Comma Splices.* The original sentence is incorrect because it is a run-on sentence. A run-on sentence is two or more complete sentences joined together without the necessary punctuation or conjunctions. For example, the first clause in the sentence ("These men were true pioneers") is a complete sentence by itself. For the sake of correctness and clarity, it would be best to put a piece of end-stop punctuation at the end of this clause and then start an entirely new sentence. (J) is the correct answer choice because it accomplishes this task. As for the other answer choices, (G) and (H) are incorrect because they also result in run-on sentences.

35. (B) (p. 592) *English/Rhetorical Skills/Strategy/Effective Transitional Sentence.* The topic of the second paragraph is the failures experienced during the early days of the Mercury space program. (B) is the correct answer choice because it provides the best signal to the reader that this will be the topic of the paragraph.

36. (J) (p. 592) *English/Usage and Mechanics/Grammar and Usage/Pronoun Usage.* The original sentence is incorrect for two reasons. First, the subject ("they") of the original sentence is too ambiguous. Who were "they"? The scientists? The pilots? The full scientific staff? It is not clear. Second, "fortunately" should be set off from the rest of the sentence by a comma. (J) is the correct answer choice because it eliminates both of these errors. As for the other answer choices, (G) is incorrect because it does not correct the first error. (H) is incorrect because "fortunately" is improperly placed in the sentence; as a result, it almost sounds as if "fortunately" were intended to modify "early."

37. **(D)** (p. 592) *English/Rhetorical Skills/Style/Conciseness.* (A), (B), and (C) are all incorrect because they are needlessly wordy. (D) is the correct answer choice because it is succinct and to the point.

38. **(G)** (p. 593) *English/Rhetorical Skills/Strategy/Appropriate Supporting Material.* When the author uses the word "spectacular" to describe a failure during a rocket flight, the reader is led to expect sensational, extraordinary, and quite likely terrifying details. However, as the author quickly points out, the details of this "spectacular" failure were instead quite mundane and pathetic. In short, after all the preparation leading up to the launch, the rocket only traveled two inches due to a circuit error. This is a classic case of irony, where there is a great incongruity or difference between anticipated and actual results.

39. **(A)** (p. 593) *English/Usage and Mechanics/No Change.* The original sentence is correct. Only an adverb ("relatively") can modify an adjective ("simple"). As for the other answer choices, (B) is incorrect because "relative" is intended to modify "simple" in this context; and, as stated above, only an adverb can modify an adjective. (D) is incorrect because an adjective cannot modify an adverb.

40. **(J)** (p. 593) *English/Usage and Mechanics/Sentence Structure/Faulty Parallelism.* The original sentence is incorrect because the underlined verb ("shutting") is not parallel with the other verb ("to ignite") in the sentence. (J) is the correct answer choice because it makes the needed correction ("to ignite and then to shut down"). As for the other answer choices, neither (G) nor (H) solves the original problem. In addition, (H) suffers from the further defect that "they" does not have a referent; in other words, it is not at all clear who or what "they" are.

41. **(B)** (p. 593) *English/Usage and Mechanics/Punctuation/Quotation Marks.* This is another example of irony. The rocket never really launched, and it never achieved true flight. In fact, as the passage tells us, the rocket only moved two inches. So, the quotation marks signal that the word "flight" is being used in a non-standard way.

42. **(F)** (p. 593) *English/Rhetorical Skills/No Change.* The original sentence is correct. A new topic is being introduced (i.e., the role of animals in the Mercury space program), so a new paragraph should be started. As for the other answer choices, they are all incorrect because they do not introduce a change in paragraphs to signal the change in topics.

43. **(A)** (p. 594) *English/Rhetorical Skills/No Change.* The original sentence is correct. In comparison with the other answer choices, it is the most concise and least awkward.

44. **(G)** (p. 594) *English/Usage and Mechanics/Grammar and Usage/Sequence and Verb Tense.* The original sentence is incorrect because it includes a verb tense error. The "delay" in picking up the spacecraft and the "leak" of water into the capsule belong to the same time frame. So, they should be expressed in the same verb tense. The "delay" is expressed in the past tense ("The pickup…was delayed"), so the "leak" should also be expressed in the past tense ("water leaked into the capsule"). For this reason, (G) is the correct answer choice.

45. **(A)** (p. 594) *English/Usage and Mechanics/No Change.* The original sentence is correct. As for the other answer choices, none of the other suggested positions for "unharmed" are idiomatic.

46. **(H)** (p. 594) *English/Usage and Mechanics/Sentence Structure/Fragments.* The original sentence is incorrect because "returning" is not a conjugated verb and, thus, cannot be the main verb of a sentence. (H) is the correct answer choice because it provides a conjugated verb that is consistent with the other past tense verbs in the paragraph. As for the other answer choices, (G) and (J) are incorrect because neither a present tense verb ("return") nor a future tense verb ("will return") are consistent with the past tense verbs in the paragraph.

47. (D) (p. 594) *English/Usage and Mechanics/Grammar and Usage/Sequence and Verb Tense.* The original sentence is incorrect because it includes a verb tense error. The question of how long an astronaut could tolerate weightlessness was unanswered at the time. So, a verb is required here that reflects that uncertainty. (D) is the correct answer choice because it provides the appropriate verb ("could tolerate"). As for the other answer choices, they are all incorrect because they do not supply a verb which suggests the degree of uncertainty required here.

48. (G) (p. 594) *English/Usage and Mechanics/Grammar and Usage/Diction.* The original sentence is incorrect because it includes language that is both superfluous and not idiomatic. Specifically, in the underlined portion, "like" is not grammatically required and also makes the sentence sound stilted. (G) is the correct answer choice because it eliminates this unnecessary word. As for the other answer choices, (H) and (J) are both incorrect because they introduce new language that is similarly superfluous and not idiomatic.

49. (B) (p. 595) *English/Usage and Mechanics/Grammar and Usage/Verb Tense.* The original sentence is incorrect because it includes a grammar error. Specifically, the underlined portion is an infinitive verb ("to have"). However, an infinitive verb cannot serve as the main verb for a clause. (B) is the correct answer choice because it supplies a main verb for the clause ("astronauts have...methods...") that is consistent with the verb tenses in the rest of the paragraph. As for the other answer choices, (C) is incorrect because the past perfect tense ("had had") suggests a sequence of events not supported by the meaning of the sentence. (D) is incorrect because the phrase "are sure to" is unnecessary before "have," and it creates a sentence that is not idiomatic.

50. (F) (p. 595) *English/Rhetorical Skills/Strategy/Effective Concluding Sentence.* Over the course of the passage, the author emphasizes the successes of the Mercury space program and downplays its failures. (F) is the correct answer choice because it best reflects the general theme and argument of the essay.

51. (A) (p. 595) *English/Usage and Mechanics/No Change.* The original sentence is correct. As for the other answer choices, (B) is incorrect for two reasons. First, it omits a required comma; specifically, both the beginning and the end of an aside ("in any broad and real way") must be marked with a comma. Second, the phrase "of help" is simply not idiomatic or grammatically correct. (C) is incorrect because it too omits the required comma that is mentioned above. Finally, (D) is incorrect because the phrase "of helping" is not idiomatic or grammatically correct.

52. (G) (p. 595) *English/Rhetorical Skills/Style/Conciseness.* The original sentence is incorrect because it is needlessly wordy. "And" and "also" mean the same thing, so it is redundant to include both. (G) is the correct answer choice because it replaces the redundant phrase ("and also") with "as well as," a phrase which means "and." As for the other answer choices, (H) is incorrect because "with" does not provide the meaning required in this context. (J) is incorrect because "as opposed to" signals a contrast between two ideas; however, the author does not intend to contrast two ideas.

53. (D) (p. 595) *English/Usage and Mechanics/Grammar and Usage/Sequence and Verb Tense.* The original sentence is incorrect because it includes a verb tense error. Earlier in the sentence, a simple past tense verb ("aided") is used. For the sake of consistency, another simple past tense verb ("emerged") should be used here. (D) is the correct answer choice because it is the only option that provides the appropriate verb form.

54. (G) (p. 595) *English/Usage and Mechanics/Grammar and Usage/Subject-Verb Agreement.* The original sentence is incorrect because it includes an error of subject-verb agreement. The plural subject of the sentence ("All aspects of medicine") requires a plural verb ("were enjoying"). (G) is the correct answer choice because it supplies the appropriate verb form. As for the other answer choices, (H) and (J) are incorrect because they do not supply plural verbs.

55. (B) (p. 596) *English/Usage and Mechanics/Grammar and Usage/Diction.* The original sentence is incorrect because it includes an expression that is not idiomatic. The correct idiom is "not only this but that." (B) is the correct answer choice because it provides the language needed to complete the idiom correctly. As for the other answer choices, (C) is incorrect because "not only this consequently that" is not a correct idiom. (D) supplies the correct idiom ("not only this but that"), but it includes a new error. Specifically, the comma after "but" is illogical and grammatically incorrect.

56. (H) (p. 596) *English/Usage and Mechanics/Sentence Structure/Run-On Sentences.* The original sentence is incorrect because it is a run-on sentence. A run-on sentence is two or more complete sentences joined together without the necessary punctuation or conjunctions. For example, the first clause ("With somewhat more luck, the doctor could select the proper treatment") is a complete sentence by itself. Similarly, the following clause ("he could also mitigate the symptoms...") is also a complete sentence by itself. Usually, there are two ways to fix a run-on sentence. First, it could be divided into two separate and correctly punctuated sentences. Second, it could be fixed by supplying the punctuation and conjunction needed between the two clauses. Since neither option is offered here, review the answer choices for the best solution possible. (H) is the correct answer choice because it rewrites the underlined portion so there is only one subject in the sentence ("the doctor"); as a result, the sentence is no longer a run-on sentence. As for the other answer choices, (G) is incorrect because "but" signals a contrast; however, a contrast is not then introduced. (J) is incorrect because it creates a sentence where the verbs are not parallel ("the doctor could select...and can mitigate...").

57. (A) (p. 596) *English/Usage and Mechanics/No Change.* The original sentence is correct. The subjunctive verb form ("be available") is the appropriate verb form in this context. As for the other answer choices, (B) is incorrect because the past tense ("was available") is not required here. (C) is incorrect for two reasons. First, a present tense verb ("is available") is inconsistent with the past tense verbs in the rest of the paragraph. Second, "for" does not have the same meaning as "to"; as a result, the sentence becomes grammatically incorrect. Finally, (D) is wrong because "as" does not have the same meaning as "to"; as a result, the sentence again becomes grammatically incorrect.

58. (H) (p. 596) *English/Usage and Mechanics/Grammar and Usage/Sequence and Verb Tense.* The original sentence is incorrect because a present tense verb ("presupposes") is not consistent with the past tense verbs in the rest of the paragraph. (H) is the correct answer choice because it provides the past tense verb required here. As for the other answer choices, (G) is incorrect because the passive verb form ("it is presupposed") is inconsistent with the past tense verbs in the rest of the paragraph and also creates a sentence that is grammatically incorrect. (J) is incorrect for two reasons. First, a present tense verb ("presuppose") is not consistent with the past tense verbs in the rest of the paragraph. Second, a plural subject ("they") is not consistent with the singular subject ("it") used in the rest of the paragraph.

59. (A) (p. 596) *English/Rhetorical Skills/No Change.* The original sentence is correct. A new topic is being introduced, so a new paragraph should be started. As for the other answer choices, (B) and (D) are incorrect because they do not introduce a change in paragraphs to signal the change in topics. (C) is incorrect because it results in a subordinate or dependent clause that does not have a supporting independent clause.

60. (J) (p. 597) *English/Rhetorical Skills/Organization/Sentence-Level Structure.* The first three paragraphs are a general discussion of medical advances during the nineteenth century. The last two paragraphs are about a specific example of this progress. As for the first sentence of the fourth paragraph, it serves as a transition from the general discussion to a more detailed look at the specific example. So, (J) is the correct answer choice.

61. (D) (p. 597) *English/Rhetorical Skills/Style/Conciseness.* The original sentence, (B), and (C) are all awkward and needlessly wordy. (B) and (C) also introduce grammatical errors into the sentence. (D) is the correct answer choice here because it concisely and clearly conveys the idea; in addition, it also does not introduce any new errors.

62. **(F)** (p. 597) *English/Rhetorical Skills/No Change.* The original sentence is correct. The underlined portion is clear, concise, and contains no errors. As for the other answer choices, (H) is incorrect because it is awkward and needlessly wordy. (G) and (J) are both wrong because they incorrectly start a new paragraph—a new paragraph should not be started because this portion of the essay continues to be about Dr. Beaumont. (J) is also incorrect for the same reason as (H).

63. **(B)** (p. 597) *English/Usage and Mechanics/Sentence Structure/Problems of Coordination and Subordination.* The original sentence is incorrect because it includes a logical error. The conjunction "but" should only be used to introduce an idea that modifies or contrasts with another idea. For example, "It was sunny, but clouds were approaching." In this sentence, though, "but" introduces a clause ("for the next 10 years he conducted hundreds of experiments...") that in no way modifies or contrasts with the earlier part of the sentence. So, it is a logical error to use "but" here. (B) is the correct answer because "and" correctly signals that the following clause continues and elaborates upon information from the earlier part of the sentence. As for the other answer choices, (C) is incorrect because it creates a run-on sentence. (D) is incorrect for the same reason as (A).

64. **(J)** (p. 598) *English/Usage and Mechanics/Sentence Structure/Faulty Parallelism.* The original sentence is incorrect because it includes an example of faulty parallelism. The forms of "demonstrate" and "describe" have the same function in this sentence, and they should be expressed in the same or parallel verb forms. "Demonstrating" is a present participle, so the present participle of "describe" must also be used. Therefore, (J) is the correct answer choice. As for the other answer choices, (G) and (H) are both wrong because they do not create the required parallelism.

65. **(C)** (p. 598) *English/Usage and Mechanics/Grammar and Usage/Pronoun Usage.* The original sentence is incorrect because it includes an error of pronoun usage. The subject of the sentence ("Newborn babies") is a plural noun. So, any pronoun used in its place must also be plural. (C) is the correct answer choice because it provides the appropriate plural pronoun. As for the other answer choices, (B) and (D) are incorrect for the same reason as the original. (B) and (D) are also incorrect because they introduce singular verbs ("was" and "is") that do not agree with the plural subject of the sentence.

66. **(H)** (p. 598) *English/Usage and Mechanics/Grammar and Usage/Diction.* The original sentence is incorrect because it is not idiomatic. The correct idiom is "endowed with." As for the other answer choices, (G) is incorrect because it is not idiomatic in any context. (J) is incorrect because, although the phrase "endowed by" is idiomatic, it is not appropriate in this context. It would be appropriate in other contexts (i.e., "...endowed by their Creator with certain inalienable rights"), but it is not correct here.

67. **(A)** (p. 598) *English/Usage and Mechanics/No Change.* The original sentence is correct. As for the other answer choices, (B) and (C) both create run-on sentences. (D) is incorrect because it removes the subject ("This") of the second clause; as a result, the reader is left with a hybrid of the two sentences that is illogical, grammatically incorrect, and nearly impossible to understand.

68. **(G)** (p. 598) *English/Usage and Mechanics/Sentence Structure/Problems of Coordination and Subordination.* The original sentence is incorrect because it includes an error related to word choice. The author intends to say that an infant's cry causes two parallel reactions—a biological reaction as well as an emotional reaction. As the sentence is currently written, though, "including" illogically implies that the emotional reaction is a part or a component of the biological reaction. (G) is the correct answer choice because "and" is a conjunction that allows the reader to understand that the author is talking about two distinct and parallel reactions. Neither (H) nor (J) accomplishes the same task.

69. (D) (p. 599) *English/Rhetorical Skills/Strategy/Effective Transitional Sentence.* The original sentence is incorrect because "unfortunately" has a meaning that is not appropriate here. In the last sentence of this paragraph, the author intends to make a statement that summarizes the details provided earlier in the paragraph. The word "unfortunately" is only used when introducing information that contradicts or contrasts with earlier information. For example, "He is very handsome; unfortunately, he is also unfriendly." (D) is the correct answer choice here because the phrase "in fact" can be used to introduce an idea that complements or is related to earlier ideas. As for the other answer choices, (B) and (C) are incorrect for the same reason as the original.

70. (H) (p. 599) *English/Rhetorical Skills/Style/Conciseness.* The original sentence is incorrect because the underlined portion is needlessly wordy. (H) is the correct answer choice because it clearly and concisely summarizes the underlined portion in one word. As for the other answer choices, (G) is incorrect because a past tense verb ("possessed") is inconsistent with the present tense verbs in the paragraph. (J) is incorrect for the same reason as the original; in addition, a plural verb ("are") does not agree with the singular subject ("the human infant") of the sentence.

71. (C) (p. 599) *English/Usage and Mechanics/Grammar and Usage/Verb Tense.* The original sentence is incorrect because it includes a verb tense error. A present progressive verb ("are guaranteeing") is used to describe and emphasize activity happening at this very moment. However, the author is speaking in broad terms about babies in general; the author is not talking about a specific baby and what that particular baby is doing at this very moment. (C) is the correct answer choice here because a simple present tense verb ("guarantee") is consistent with the other simple present tense verbs in the rest of the paragraph. As for the other answer choices, (B) is incorrect because a past tense verb is not consistent with the present tense verbs in the rest of the paragraph. (D) is incorrect because a singular verb ("guarantees") does not agree with its plural subject ("attributes").

72. (G) (p. 599) *English/Usage and Mechanics/Grammar and Usage/Diction.* The original sentence is incorrect because it is not idiomatic. The correct idiom required here is "whether *this*... or whether *that*..." The phrase "whether or not" is another English idiom, but its use here is not appropriate. As for the other answer choices, (H) and (J) are both incorrect because "whether if" is not idiomatic in any context.

73. (D) (p. 599) *English/Usage and Mechanics/Sentence Structure/Fragments.* The original sentence is incorrect because the period after "infant" turns the first clause into a dependent clause without a supporting independent clause; in other words, it turns the dependent clause into a sentence fragment. (D) is the correct answer choice because it connects the initial dependent clause to a supporting independent clause, combines them in one sentence, and does so without introducing any grammatical or punctuation errors. As for the other answer choices, (B) and (C) are incorrect for the same reason as the original.

74. (H) (p. 600) *English/Rhetorical Skills/Organization/Sentence-Level Structure.* The final sentence summarizes the author's main point in an emphatic way. So, (H) is the correct answer choice. As for the other answer choices, they are all incorrect because they are simply not true.

75. (D) (p. 600) *English/Rhetorical Skills/Organization/Passage-Level Structure.* The passage is an argument. The author makes a claim (i.e., newborn infants are not passive creatures) and then supports the claim with several examples of how newborn infants actively engage with their worlds and their caregivers. So, (D) is the correct answer choice. As for the other answer choices, (A) is incorrect for two reasons: first, the author does not provide contrasting information in an attempt to disprove the main argument; second, the author does not supply any anecdotes or specific stories. (B) is incorrect because this essay is not a narrative or story filled with examples or anecdotes about specific newborn infants. Finally, (C) is incorrect because the author never uses statistics.

Section 2: *Mathematics*

1. **(D)** (p. 602) ***Mathematics/Arithmetic/Simple Manipulations.*** Since there is a restriction on the placement of the circle, the counting principal must be modified. Four shapes can be placed as normal, so the total number of arrangements including only these four shapes is $4! = 4 \cdot 3 \cdot 2 \cdot 1 = 24$. The restriction on the circle limits it to the 3 center places, so there are a total of $24 \cdot 3 = 72$ different arrangements of the five shapes that meet the stated condition.

2. **(K)** (p. 602) ***Mathematics/Algebra/Manipulating Algebraic Expressions/Creating Algebraic Expressions.*** Let J be John's age and P be Pat's age. John is 3 times as old as Pat: $J = 3P$. In four years, John's age will be: $x = J + 4$. Substitute $3P$ for J: $x = 3P + 4 \Rightarrow x - 4 = 3P \Rightarrow \dfrac{x-4}{3} = P$.

    Alternatively, plug in numbers: if Pat is 9 years old, then John is 27 years old; in 4 years, John will be 31. "Test-the-test" by plugging 31 into the given formulas to produce an answer of 9, (K).

3. **(C)** (p. 603) ***Mathematics/Algebra/Manipulating Algebraic Expressions/Evaluating Expressions.*** This question really just tests fractions. If $\dfrac{3}{4}$ of x equals 36, then: $\dfrac{3}{4}x = 36 \Rightarrow x = 36 \cdot \dfrac{4}{3} = 48$ and $\dfrac{1}{3}x = \dfrac{1}{3}(48) = 16$.

4. **(J)** (p. 603) ***Mathematics/Geometry/Lines and Angles.*** The measure of the unlabeled angle in the top triangle is 90°. The angle vertically opposite it in the bottom triangle is also equal to 90°. Therefore, $x + y + 90° = 180°$ and $x + y = 90°$.

5. **(E)** (p. 603) ***Mathematics/Arithmetic/Common Arithmetic Items/Properties of Numbers.*** There are two ways to attack this question. One is to reason as follows:

    A. $2 + n$ cannot be a multiple of 3: since n is a multiple of 3, when $2 + n$ is divided by 3 there will be a remainder of 2.
    B. $2 - n$ cannot be a multiple of 3: since n is a multiple of 3, when $2 - n$ is divided by 3 there will be a remainder of 1.
    C. $2n - 1$ cannot be a multiple of 3: since n is a multiple of 3, $2n$ will also be a multiple of 3, and $2n - 1$ cannot be a multiple of 3.
    D. $2n + 1$ cannot be a multiple for the same reason that $2n - 1$ cannot be a multiple of 3.
    E. $2n + 3$ is a multiple of 3: $2n$ is a multiple of 3; 3 is a multiple of 3; thus, $2n + 3$ is a multiple of 3.

    Alternatively, substitute an assumed value into the choices. For example, let $n = 3$:

    A. $2 + n = 2 + 3 = 5$ ✘ (Not a multiple of 3)
    B. $2 - n = 2 - 3 = -1$ ✘ (Not a multiple of 3)
    C. $2n - 1 = 2(3) - 1 = 6 - 1 = 5$ ✘ (Not a multiple of 3)
    D. $2n + 1 = 2(3) + 1 = 6 + 1 = 7$ ✘ (Not a multiple of 3)
    E. $2n + 3 = 2(3) + 3 = 6 + 3 = 9$ ✓ (A multiple of 3)

6. **(K)** (p. 603) ***Mathematics/Arithmetic/Common Arithmetic Items/Ratios.*** A ratio is just another way of writing a fraction. Simply inspect each of the answer choices. As for (F), $\left(\dfrac{1}{5}\right)^2$ is equal to $\dfrac{1}{25}$, and both 1 and 25 are whole numbers. Choice (G) is not the correct because 5% can be written as $\dfrac{5}{100}$, or

$\frac{1}{20}$, which is a ratio of two whole numbers. As for (J), 0.25 is equal to $\frac{1}{4}$, the ratio of two whole

numbers. As for (H), $\frac{1}{5}$ is the ratio of 1 to 5, so (H) is a ratio of two whole numbers. Only (K) is not a

ratio of two whole numbers.

7. **(B)** (p. 604) *Mathematics/Geometry/Rectangles and Squares.* Let L equal the length and W equal the
width of each playing card. The area of the large rectangle is equal to the sum of the areas of the nine
playing cards: $\text{area}_{\text{rectangle}} = 9(\text{area}_{\text{card}}) \Rightarrow 180 = 9(LW) \Rightarrow LW = 20$. Both $5W$ and $4L$ are equal to the
length of the large rectangle, and $L + W$ is equal to its width:

$$\text{area}_{\text{rectangle}} = \left(\text{length}_{\text{rectangle}}\right)\left(\text{width}_{\text{rectangle}}\right) \Rightarrow 180 = (5W)(L+W) = 5LW + 5W^2 \Rightarrow LW + W^2 = 36 \Rightarrow$$

$W^2 = 36 - 20 \Rightarrow W = \sqrt{16} \Rightarrow W = 4$. Since $5W = 4L$, $L = 5$. Therefore, the perimeter of the large rectangle
is: $2[5W + (L+W)] = 2(20+9) = 58$.

8. **(G)** (p. 604) *Mathematics/Algebra/Solving Algebraic Equations or Inequalities with One Variable.*
Let t be the train's scheduled arrival time. If the train travels at 40 mph, the journey takes $t + \frac{10}{60} = t + \frac{1}{6}$

hours; if it travels at 30 mph, the journey takes $t + \frac{16}{60} = t + \frac{4}{15}$ hours. Since the distance traveled is the
same in each case, write an equation equating the two distances, where the distances are written in
terms of the travel time and the train speed. When formulating the equation, make sure that the units on
each side of the equality are equivalent and that the final answer will be in miles.

$$\left(\frac{40 \text{ miles}}{\text{hour}}\right)\left(t + \frac{1}{6} \text{ hour}\right) = \left(\frac{30 \text{ miles}}{\text{hour}}\right)\left(t + \frac{4}{15} \text{ hour}\right) \Rightarrow 40t + \frac{40}{6} = 30t + \frac{30 \cdot 4}{15} \Rightarrow$$

$10t = \frac{120}{15} - \frac{40}{6} = 1\frac{1}{3}$ hours $= 80$ minutes $\Rightarrow t = 8$ minutes. Therefore, the distance between the two

towns is: $d = \left(\frac{40 \text{ miles}}{\text{hour}}\right)\left(\frac{8}{60} \text{ hour} + \frac{10}{60} \text{ hour}\right) = (40 \text{ miles})\left(\frac{18}{60}\right) = 12 \text{ miles}$.

9. **(D)** (p. 604) *Mathematics/Algebra/Manipulating Algebraic Expressions/Factoring Expressions.* The
coefficients are 3, 6, and 2: 1 is the only common factor of those numbers. The smallest term containing
the variable x is simply x. The same is true for the terms containing y and z. Therefore, the greatest
common factor is xyz.

10. **(G)** (p. 604) *Mathematics/Arithmetic/Common Arithmetic Items/Properties of Numbers.* The sum of
$3k$, $4k$, $5k$, $6k$, and $7k$ is $25k$, which is divisible by 7 if the value of k is divisible by 7. If, however, the
coefficient of k were divisible by 7, then that number would be divisible by 7 regardless of the value of k.
Dropping the term $4k$ from the group, the sum of the remaining terms is $21k$. Since 21 is divisible by 7,
$21k$ will be divisible by 7, regardless of the value of k.

11. **(B)** (p. 605) *Mathematics/Arithmetic/Complicated Manipulations/Decimal-Fraction Equivalents.*
Use a benchmark or approximate to eliminate the wrong answer choices. First, eliminate (E): $\frac{1}{2}$ is more

than $\frac{3}{8}$. Next, eliminate (A): $\frac{3}{15}$ is equal to $\frac{1}{3}$, so $\frac{3}{16}$ is smaller than $\frac{1}{3}$. As for (C), $\frac{9}{24}$ is equal to $\frac{3}{8}$, not less than $\dfrac{3}{8}$. As for (D), $\dfrac{5}{12}$ is equal to $\dfrac{10}{24}$, and $\dfrac{3}{8}$ is equal to $\dfrac{9}{24}$. Only (B) is a possible value for x: $\dfrac{17}{48}$ is close to and slightly less than $\dfrac{18}{48} = \dfrac{3}{8}$.

Alternatively, express each fraction as a decimal and compare the answer choices to find a value between $\dfrac{1}{3} \approx 0.333$ and $\dfrac{3}{8} = 0.375$:

A. $\dfrac{3}{16} = 0.1875$

B. $\dfrac{17}{48} \approx 0.3542$

C. $\dfrac{9}{24} = 0.375$

D. $\dfrac{5}{12} \approx 0.4167$

E. $\dfrac{1}{2} = 0.5$

Only (B) is between $\dfrac{1}{3}$ (approximately 0.333) and $\dfrac{3}{8}$ (0.375).

12. **(G)** (p. 605) *Mathematics/Algebra/Manipulating Algebraic Expressions/Factoring Expressions.*
Simply factor the expression as the difference of two squares: $x^2 - y^2 = (x+y)(x-y) = 3$. Since $x - y = 3$, then $(x+y)(3) = 3 \Rightarrow x+y = 1$.

13. **(E)** (p. 605) *Mathematics/Arithmetic/Common Arithmetic Items/Properties of Numbers.* As for (A), whether $n+1$ is odd or even will depend on whether n is odd or even. The same is true for (B) and (C) since whether $3n$ is odd or even will depend on whether n is odd or even. As for (D), n^2 will be odd or even depending on whether n is odd or even. However, (E) is even regardless of whether n is odd or even: $n^2 + n$ can be factored as $n(n+1)$, and since either n or $n+1$ is even, the product must be even.

14. **(H)** (p. 605) *Mathematics/Geometry/Complex Figures* and *Rectangles and Squares* and *Circles.* For any square with a side of x, the diagonal of that square is equal to $x\sqrt{2}$. Since the square has an area of 16, it has a side of 4 and a diagonal of $4\sqrt{2}$. The diagonal of the square is also the diameter of the circle. Therefore, the circle has a diameter of $4\sqrt{2}$ and a radius of $2\sqrt{2}$. Finally, a circle with a radius of length $2\sqrt{2}$ has an area of $\pi r^2 = \pi \left(2\sqrt{2}\right)^2 = 8\pi$.

15. **(C)** (p. 606) *Mathematics/Arithmetic/Common Arithmetic Items/Percents.* First, calculate the sale price of the CD player that Ellen bought: $\$120 - (25\% \text{ of } \$120) = \$120 - (0.25 \cdot \$120) = \$120 - \$30 = \$90$. Next, calculate the sales tax: $\text{tax} = 8\% \text{ of } \$90 = 0.08 \cdot \$90 = \$7.20$. Therefore, the total price was $\$90 + \$7.20 = \$97.20$.

16. **(G)** (p. 606) *Mathematics/Arithmetic/Complicated Arithmetic Application Items* and *Common Arithmetic Items/Percents.* Use the "is-over-of" equation. The "of," which is the denominator of the fraction, is the mixture. There is a total of $2.5 + 12.5 = 15$ kilograms of mixture. The word "is," which is

the numerator of the fraction, is the 2.5 kilograms of gravel. Thus:

$$\frac{\text{is}}{\text{of}} = \frac{\%}{100} \Rightarrow \frac{2.5}{15} = \frac{\%}{100} \Rightarrow \frac{250}{15} = 16\frac{2}{3}\%.$$

17. **(D)** (p. 606) *Mathematics/Geometry/Triangles/Properties of Triangles.* The triangle has sides of 6, 8, and 10 (multiples of 3, 4, and 5). Therefore, the triangle is a right triangle. The sides of 6 and 8 form the right angle, so they can be used as altitude and base for finding the area:

$$\text{area}_{\text{triangle}} = \frac{1}{2} \cdot \text{altitude} \cdot \text{base} = \frac{1}{2} \cdot 6 \cdot 8 = 24.$$

18. **(F)** (p. 607) *Mathematics/Arithmetic/Common Arithmetic Items/Proportions and Direct-Inverse Variation.* First, determine the amount of fuel used by Motorcycle A using a direct proportion:

$$\frac{\text{Fuel Used } X}{\text{Fuel Used } Y} = \frac{\text{Kilometers Driven } X}{\text{Kilometers Driven } Y} \Rightarrow \frac{1}{x} = \frac{40}{300} \Rightarrow 40x = 300 \Rightarrow x = 7.5.$$ Thus, Motorcycle A uses 7.5 liters of fuel for the 300-kilometer trip. Now, do the same for Motorcycle B:

$$\frac{1}{x} = \frac{50}{300} \Rightarrow 50x = 300 \Rightarrow x = 6.$$ Therefore, Motorcycle B uses 6 liters. Since Motorcycle A uses

$7.5 - 6 = 1.5$ liters more than Motorcycle B, the fuel for Motorcycle A costs $1.5 \text{ liters} \cdot \dfrac{\$2}{\text{liter}} = \$3$ more.

19. **(B)** (p. 607) *Mathematics/Algebra/Expressing and Evaluating Algebraic Functions/Function Notation.* First, substitute 3 for x in $f(x)$: $f(3) = 3^2 - 2(3) + 1 = 9 - 6 + 1 = 4$. Now, substitute 4 for x in $f(x)$: $f(4) = 4^2 - 2(4) + 1 = 16 - 8 + 1 = 9$. Therefore, $f(f(3)) = 9$.

20. **(F)** (p. 607) *Mathematics/Algebra/Manipulating Algebraic Expressions/Factoring Expressions.*

$$\frac{N!}{(N-2)!} = \frac{N(N-1)(N-2)(N-3)(N-4)...[N-(N-1)]}{(N-2)(N-3)(N-4)...[N-(N-1)]}.$$ Canceling like factors in the numerator and the denominator leaves only $\dfrac{N(N-1)}{1} = N(N-1) = N^2 - N$.

21. **(E)** (p. 607) *Mathematics/Algebra/Manipulating Algebraic Expressions/Creating Algebraic Expressions.* The formula will be x, the cost for the first ounce, plus some expression to represent the additional postage for each additional ounce over the first ounce. The postage for the additional weight is y cents per ounce, and the additional weight is w minus the first ounce, or $w - 1$. Therefore, the additional postage is $y(w - 1)$, and the total postage is $x + y(w - 1)$.

Alternatively, assume some numbers. For ease of calculations, assume that the first ounce costs 1 cent and every additional ounce is 2 cents. If $x = 1$ and $y = 2$, then a letter of, for example, 3 ounces ($w = 3$) will cost $1 + 2(2) = 5$ cents. Substitute these values for x, y, and w into the answer choices and the correct choice will return the value 5:

A. $w(x + y) = 3(1 + 2) = 3(3) = 9$ ✗
B. $x(w - y) = 1(3 - 2) = 1(1) = 1$ ✗
C. $x(x - 1) + y(w - 1) = 1(1 - 1) + 2(3 - 1) = 1(0) + 2(2) = 4$ ✗
D. $x + wy = 1 + 3(2) = 7$ ✗
E. $x + y(w - 1) = 1 + 2(3 - 1) = 1 + 2(2) = 5$ ✓

22. **(F)** (p. 608) ***Mathematics/Arithmetic/Common Arithmetic Items/Absolute Value.*** Apply the absolute value function: $|-3| = 3$, $|2| = 2$, and $\left|-\dfrac{1}{2}\right| = \dfrac{1}{2}$. Therefore, $|-3| \cdot |2| \cdot \left|-\dfrac{1}{2}\right| + (-4) = 3 \cdot 2 \cdot \dfrac{1}{2} - 4 = 3 - 4 = -1$.

23. **(C)** (p. 608) ***Mathematics/Geometry/Complex Figures*** and ***Rectangles and Squares*** and ***Circles.*** The side of the square is also the radius of the circle. Since the square has an area of 2, $s \cdot s = 2 \Rightarrow s^2 = 2 \Rightarrow s = \sqrt{2}$, and $\sqrt{2}$ is the radius of the circle. Therefore, the area of the circle is $\pi r^2 = \pi \left(\sqrt{2}\right)^2 = 2\pi$.

24. **(G)** (p. 608) ***Mathematics/Arithmetic/Common Arithmetic Items/Properties of Numbers.*** Test each statement. As for statement (I), the product of 2 (the first prime number) and any other number must be even. Thus, (I) is not part of the correct answer. As for (II), the sum of two prime numbers might be odd, (e.g., $2 + 3 = 5$), but the sum of two prime numbers might also be even, (e.g., $3 + 5 = 8$). As for (III), however, the product of two odd numbers is necessarily odd.

25. **(A)** (p. 609) ***Mathematics/Coordinate Geometry/The Coordinate System.*** The coordinates establish that this figure is a rectangle. The width of the rectangle is a, and the length is $b - a$. Therefore, the area is $a(b-a)$.

Alternatively, "test-the-test," assuming that $a = 2$ and $b = 4$. The rectangle has a width of 2, a length of $4 - 2 = 2$, and an area of $2 \cdot 2 = 4$. Substitute 2 for a and 4 for b into the answer choices and the correct formula will yield 4.

26. **(H)** (p. 609) ***Mathematics/Arithmetic/Simple Manipulations.*** Perform the indicated operations: $\sqrt{(43-7)(29+7)} = \sqrt{(36)(36)} = 36$.

27. **(A)** (p. 609) ***Mathematics/Arithmetic/Common Arithmetic Items/Proportions and Direct-Inverse Variation.*** Set up a direct proportion and solve for the unknown value:
$$\frac{\text{Cement } X}{\text{Cement } Y} = \frac{\text{Grit } X}{\text{Grit } Y} \Rightarrow \frac{4}{50} = \frac{20}{x} \Rightarrow 4x = (20)(50) \Rightarrow x = \frac{(20)(50)}{4} = 250.$$

28. **(H)** (p. 610) ***Mathematics/Geometry/Lines and Angles.*** Label the other two angles in the triangle:

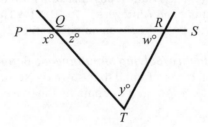

Therefore, $x + z = 180 \Rightarrow 150 + z = 180 \Rightarrow z = 30$. Furthermore, since $\overline{QT} = \overline{QR}$, $y = w$, and $x + y + z = 180 \Rightarrow 30 + y + y = 180 \Rightarrow 2y = 150 \Rightarrow y = 75$.

29. **(C)** (p. 610) ***Mathematics/Algebra/Solving Algebraic Equations with Two Variables.*** There is only one equation but two variables, so x and y cannot be solved for individually. Instead, look for a way to rewrite the first equation to give the information needed: $\dfrac{x}{y} = -1 \Rightarrow x = -y \Rightarrow x + y = 0$.

30. **(K)** (p. 610) *Mathematics/Statistics and Probability/Data Representation/Tables* and *Arithmetic/Common Arithmetic Items/Decimal-Fraction Equivalents.* Set up the cost per yard of each fabric as a decimal and compare the decimals directly:

    F. $\dfrac{\$8}{3\text{ yd.}} \approx \$2.67/\text{yd.}$

    G. $\dfrac{\$6}{2\text{ yd.}} = \$3/\text{yd.}$

    H. $\dfrac{\$9}{4\text{ yd.}} = \$2.25/\text{yd.}$

    J. $\dfrac{\$7}{5\text{ yd.}} = \$1.4/\text{yd.}$

    K. $\dfrac{\$10}{8\text{ yd.}} = \$1.25/\text{yd.}$

    Therefore, the (K) fabric costs the least per yard.

31. **(A)** (p. 611) *Mathematics/Geometry/Lines and Angles.* Since $\overline{PQ} \parallel \overline{ST}$, we know $x = y$ because the alternate interior angles of parallel lines are equal. Furthermore, since the sum of angles in $\triangle PRQ$ is $180°$, $75 + 65 + x + x = 180 \Rightarrow 2x + 140 = 180 \Rightarrow 2x = 40 \Rightarrow x = 20$. Therefore, $y = 20$.

32. **(H)** (p. 611) *Mathematics/Arithmetic/Complicated Manipulations/Simplifying.* Perform the indicated operations: $\dfrac{10^3\left(10^5 + 10^5\right)}{10^4} = \dfrac{10^5 + 10^5}{10} = 10^4 + 10^4 = 2\left(10^4\right)$.

33. **(D)** (p. 611) *Mathematics/Algebra/Solving Quadratic Equations and Relations.* Factor and solve for x: $x^2 - 5x + 4 = 0 \Rightarrow (x - 4)(x - 1) = 0$. So, either $x - 4 = 0$ and $x = 4$, or $x - 1 = 0$ and $x = 1$.

    Alternatively, substitute the values in the choices back into the equation to find the set that works.

34. **(K)** (p. 612) *Mathematics/Statistics and Probability/Averages.* Use the method for finding the missing elements of an average. The smallest possible sum for 6 different positive integers is $1 + 2 + 3 + 4 + 5 + 6 = 21$. The sum of all 7 integers is $7 \cdot 12 = 84$. Therefore, the largest that the seventh number could be (with the average of the seven numbers still 12) is $84 - 21 = 63$.

35. **(E)** (p. 612) *Mathematics/Algebra/Solving Simultaneous Equations.* To find b in terms of x and y, solve the first equation for b in terms of x and then solve the second equation for b in terms of y: $x = b + 4 \Rightarrow b = x - 4$ and $y = b - 3 \Rightarrow b = y + 3$. Combine the two equations by adding:

$$b = x - 4$$
$$\underline{+\ b = y + 3}$$
$$2b = x + y - 1 \Rightarrow b = \frac{x + y - 1}{2}$$

    Alternatively, substitute some numbers. Let $b = 1$. Therefore, $x = 1 + 4 = 5$, and $y = 1 - 3 = -2$. Substitute 5 for x and -2 for y in the answer choices. The correct choice will yield the value 1.

36. **(F)** (p. 612) *Mathematics/Arithmetic/Common Arithmetic Items/Properties of Numbers.* Since $z = 5x = 3y$, and $x, y,$ and z are integers, z is a multiple of both 3 and 5, so z is evenly divisible by 5, (G), 3,

(H), and 15, (J). And since $5x = 3y$, and x and y are integers, x is a multiple of 3 (and evenly divisible by 3), (K). However, while z is divisible by both x and y individually, z is not necessarily divisible by the product of x and y.

Alternatively, substitute some numbers. The most natural assumption is to let z equal 15, so $x = 3$ and $y = 5$. However, on that assumption, every answer choice is an integer. Try the next multiple of 15. Let z equal 30, so $x = 6$ and $y = 10$. Only (F) is no longer an integer: $30 \div (6 \cdot 10) = \dfrac{1}{2}$.

37. **(B)** (p. 612) ***Mathematics/Geometry/Rectangles and Squares.*** Use the equation for the area of a

rectangle: $\text{area}_{\text{rectangle}} = \text{width} \cdot \text{length} \Rightarrow 48x^2 = w(24x) \Rightarrow w = \dfrac{48x^2}{24x} = 2x$.

Alternatively, substitute some numbers, such as $x = 2$. The area of the rectangle is $48\left(2^2\right) = 48(4) = 192$,
and the length is 48. And 48 times the width is equal to 192, so the width is $192 \div 48 = 4$. Therefore, if $x = 2$, the correct choice yields the value 4. Only (B) works.

38. **(K)** (p. 613) ***Mathematics/Algebra/Manipulating Algebraic Expressions/Basic Algebraic***

Manipulations. Rewrite the equation: $x = \dfrac{1}{y+1} \Rightarrow x(y+1) = 1 \Rightarrow y+1 = \dfrac{1}{x} \Rightarrow y = \dfrac{1}{x} - 1 \Rightarrow y = \dfrac{1-x}{x}$.

39. **(B)** (p. 613) ***Mathematics/Coordinate Geometry/The Coordinate System.*** The length of the base of the
triangle is $4x - x = 3x$, and the length of the altitude is $3x - 0 = 3x$. Use the formula for finding the area

of a triangle to determine x: $\dfrac{1}{2}(3x)(3x) = 54 \Rightarrow (3x)(3x) = 108 \Rightarrow 9x^2 = 108 \Rightarrow x^2 = 12 \Rightarrow x = \sqrt{12} = 2\sqrt{3}$.

40. **(K)** (p. 613) ***Mathematics/Statistics and Probability/Probability.*** This question is a little tricky, but it
does not require advanced mathematics. If the room were completely dark, what is the worst thing that
might happen? You might happen to pull all the blue and white socks first (the two colors with the
largest number of socks). So you might have pulled 16 socks. Now, the only color left is the color (green)
with the smallest number of socks. Then you would need to pull 2 of the only 4 socks left. So, on the
worst assumption, $16 + 2 = 18$ picks will *guarantee* you a pair of each color.

41. **(C)** (p. 614) ***Mathematics/Geometry/Complex Figures*** and ***Circles*** and ***Lines and Angles.*** The
question supplies the area of the shaded part of the figure, which is a portion of the circle. First, find
what fraction of the circle is shaded. Then, use that value in order to determine the value of the

unshaded angle at the center of the circle. The area of the entire circle is $\pi r^2 = \pi\left(4^2\right) = 16\pi$. $\dfrac{14\pi}{16\pi} = \dfrac{7}{8}$ of

the circle is shaded, so $\dfrac{1}{8}$ of the circle is unshaded. Therefore, the unshaded angle at the center of the

circle is $\dfrac{1}{8}$ of $360° = 45°$. Now, find x: $x + 45 + 90 = 180 \Rightarrow x + 135 = 180 \Rightarrow x = 45$.

42. **(J)** (p. 614) ***Mathematics/Geometry/Circles*** and ***Triangles/45°-45°-90° Triangles.*** This is a
composite figure, so redefine one figure in terms of another. The diameter of the smaller circle is equal
to the side of the square. The diagonal of the square is the diameter of the larger circle. First, let r be the
radius of the smaller circle, so the smaller circle has an area of πr^2. The diameter of the smaller circle is
$2r$, which is also the side of the square:

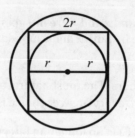

The diagonal of the square creates a 45°-45°-90° triangle with the sides of the square, so the hypotenuse of that triangle is equal to $2r \cdot \sqrt{2} = 2\sqrt{2}r$. Thus, the larger circle has a radius of $2\sqrt{2}r \div 2 = \sqrt{2}r$, and an area of $\pi\left(\sqrt{2}r\right)^2 = 2\pi r^2$. Therefore, the ratio of the area of the larger circle to the area of the smaller circle is $2\pi r^2 : \pi r^2 = 2 : 1$.

43. (D) (p. 614) *Mathematics/Arithmetic/Simple Manipulations.* Just perform the indicated operations:

$$2^0 = 1$$
$$2^3 = 8$$
$$2^{-2} = \frac{1}{2^2} = \frac{1}{4}$$
$$1 + 8 - \frac{1}{4} = 8\frac{3}{4}$$

44. (J) (p. 615) *Mathematics/Coordinate Geometry/Graphs of Quadratic Equations and Relations.* Since the axis of symmetry of the parabola is given by the equation $x = 0$, the parabola is symmetric about the y-axis. The point symmetric to the point with coordinates $(-1, -2)$ will have the same y-coordinate, and the x-coordinate of the point will be the same distance from the y-axis but in a positive direction: $(1, -2)$. It might be easier to find the solution with a sketched graph of the equation:

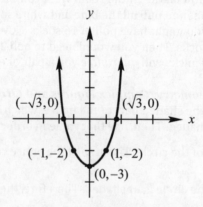

45. (C) (p. 615) *Mathematics/Coordinate Geometry/Slope-Intercept Form of a Linear Equation.* Each equation is written in slope-intercept form, so the slope of the first line is m_1, and the slope of the second line is m_2. If two lines in the coordinate plane are perpendicular to each other, then the product of their slopes is -1. Thus, $m_1 m_2 = -1$.

46. (K) (p. 615) *Mathematics/Geometry/Complex Figures* and *Triangles/Properties of Triangles* and *Rectangles and Squares.* Draw some additional lines to carve the figure into more familiar shapes, and use the Pythagorean theorem to determine the length of the shared third side of the two small triangles:

$a^2 + 8^2 = 10^2 \Rightarrow a^2 + 64 = 100 \Rightarrow a^2 = 36 \Rightarrow a = 6$. Note that this can also be immediately deduced by recognizing the triangles as Pythagorean triangles.

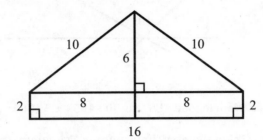

The area of the large rectangle is $16 \cdot 2 = 32$. The total area of the large triangle is $\dfrac{1}{2} \cdot 6 \cdot 16 = 48$.

Therefore, the area of the composite figure is $32 + 48 = 80$.

47. **(A)** (p. 616) ***Mathematics/Algebra/Manipulating Algebraic Expressions/Evaluating Expressions.***

Rationalize the denominator: $\dfrac{\sqrt{x}}{2\sqrt{x} - \sqrt{y}} \cdot \dfrac{2\sqrt{x} + \sqrt{y}}{2\sqrt{x} + \sqrt{y}} = \dfrac{2x + \sqrt{xy}}{4x + 2\sqrt{xy} - 2\sqrt{xy} - y} = \dfrac{2x + \sqrt{xy}}{4x - y}$.

Alternatively, assume some values for x and y. Since the problem involves square roots, pick a couple of

perfect squares, e.g., $x = 9$ and $y = 4$. The expression in the question stem becomes: $\dfrac{\sqrt{9}}{2\sqrt{9} - \sqrt{4}} =$

$\dfrac{3}{2(3) - 2} = \dfrac{3}{4}$. Now, substitute 9 for x and 4 for y into the answer choices. The correct choice will generate

the value $\dfrac{3}{4}$:

A. $\dfrac{2x + \sqrt{xy}}{4x - y} = \dfrac{2(9) + \sqrt{(9)(4)}}{4(9) - 4} = \dfrac{18 + 6}{32} = \dfrac{24}{32} = \dfrac{3}{4}$ ✓

B. $\dfrac{4x + \sqrt{xy}}{4x - y} = \dfrac{4(9) + \sqrt{(9)(4)}}{4(9) - 4} = \dfrac{36 + 6}{36 - 4} = \dfrac{42}{32}$ ✗

C. $\dfrac{2\sqrt{x} + \sqrt{y}}{4xy} = \dfrac{2\sqrt{9} + \sqrt{4}}{4(9)(4)} = \dfrac{2(3) + 2}{144} = \dfrac{8}{144}$ ✗

D. $\dfrac{2\sqrt{x} + \sqrt{xy}}{2x - y} = \dfrac{2\sqrt{9} + \sqrt{(9)(4)}}{2(9) - 4} = \dfrac{6 + 6}{14} = \dfrac{12}{14}$ ✗

E. $\dfrac{2\sqrt{x} - \sqrt{y}}{2} = \dfrac{2\sqrt{9} - \sqrt{4}}{2} = \dfrac{2(3) - 2}{2} = \dfrac{4}{2} = 2$ ✗

48. **(H)** (p. 616) ***Mathematics/Geometry/Lines and Angles.*** Since vertical angles are equal, the figure becomes:

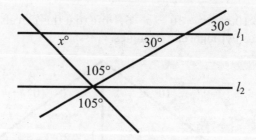

And the interior angles of a triangle total 180°, so $30 + 105 + x = 180 \Rightarrow x = 45$.

49. **(D)** (p. 616) ***Mathematics/Trigonometry/Determining Trigonometric Values.*** The graph intersects the y-axis where $x = 0$: $y = 2\cos(2 \cdot 0) + 2 = 2\cos 0 + 2$. Since $\cos 0 = 1$, $y = 2(1) + 2 = 4$.

50. **(G)** (p. 617) ***Mathematics/Geometry/Complex Figures*** and ***Rectangles and Squares*** and ***Circles.*** The shaded area is equal to the whole square minus the four circles. On the assumption that each circle has a radius of r, the side of the square must be $4r$, and the area of the square is $4r \cdot 4r = 16r^2$. Furthermore, each circle with radius r has an area of πr^2, so the shaded area is $16r^2 - 4\pi r^2$. And the ratio of the shaded area to the area of the square is $\dfrac{16r^2 - 4\pi r^2}{16r^2} = \dfrac{4r^2(4 - \pi)}{16r^2} = \dfrac{4 - \pi}{4}$.

Note that a little common sense goes a long way when applied to the answer choices. Since π is less than 4, (F) is a negative number and is therefore impossible. Both (J) and (K) are greater than 1, asserting that the shaded area is larger than the square, an equally absurd conclusion. Now, there are only two answer choices remaining: (G) asserts that the shaded area is a little less than one-quarter of the square, and (H) asserts that the shaded area is about three-quarters of the square. After careful inspection of the figure, it is safe to assume that (G) is correct.

51. **(C)** (p. 617) ***Mathematics/Trigonometry/Trigonometric Relationships.*** The Pythagorean trigonometric identity is $\sin^2\theta + \cos^2\theta = 1$. Therefore, $\dfrac{\sin^2\theta + \cos^2\theta}{\sin\theta} = \dfrac{1}{\sin\theta}$. And the reciprocal identity for the sine function is the cosecant function: $\dfrac{1}{\sin\theta} = \csc\theta$.

52. **(G)** (p. 618) ***Mathematics/Trigonometry/Definitions of the Six Trigonometric Functions.*** Since $\tan\theta = \dfrac{\text{side opposite }\theta}{\text{side adjacent to }\theta}$, $\tan 55° = \dfrac{6}{\overline{AC}} \Rightarrow 1.4 \approx \dfrac{6}{\overline{AC}} \Rightarrow \overline{AC} \approx \dfrac{6}{1.4} \approx 4.28$.

53. **(D)** (p. 618) ***Mathematics/Algebra/Manipulating Algebraic Expressions/Evaluating Expressions.*** The expression is undefined for every value of x that makes the denominator equal to zero. The denominator is zero if either $x - 1$ or $x + 2$ equals zero. Therefore, the expression is undefined for $x = 1$ or $x = -2$.

54. **(K)** (p. 618) ***Mathematics/Algebra/Solving Simultaneous Equations.*** Since $x + y \le 6$, y will have its maximum value when x has its minimum value. The minimum value of x is 0; the maximum value of y is 6. Therefore, the minimum value for $3y$ is $3(6) = 18$.

Alternatively, test the answer choices. Since the question asks for the maximum value of y, start with the largest choice: 18. If $3y = 18$, then $y = 6$. And $x + y \le 6 \Rightarrow x + 6 \le 6 \Rightarrow x \le 0$. Since x can be 0, $y = 6$ satisfies the system of inequalities.

55. **(C)** (p. 619) ***Mathematics/Coordinate Geometry/The Coordinate System.*** Find the corresponding values for y when $x = -1$, 0, and 1:

$$y(-1) = \left| (-1)^2 - 3 \right| = \left| 1 - 3 \right| = \left| -2 \right| = 2$$

$$y(0) = \left| (0)^2 - 3 \right| = \left| -3 \right| = 3$$

$$y(1) = \left| (1)^2 - 3 \right| = \left| 1 - 3 \right| = \left| -2 \right| = 2$$

Only (C) shows the correct plotting of the points $(-1,2)$, $(0,3)$, and $(1,2)$.

56. **(G)** (p. 620) ***Mathematics/Coordinate Geometry/Graphs of Linear Equations.*** Each answer choice is an equation of a line in slope-intercept form ($y = mx + b$), and each has a different slope. Calculate the slope of the line shown in the graph: $m = \dfrac{(-2)-(4)}{(2)-(-1)} = \dfrac{-6}{3} = -2$. Only (G) has the correct slope.

57. **(A)** (p. 620) ***Mathematics/Algebra/Solving Quadratic Equations and Relations.*** The best approach to solving this item is to see that the roots are expressed in a form suggestive of the quadratic formula, the solution to the quadratic equation $ax^2 + bx + c$: $x = \dfrac{-b \pm \sqrt{b^2 - 4ac}}{2a}$. Thus, $-b = -3$, so $b = 3$, which eliminates (B) and (D). Next, $2a = 2$, so $a = 1$, which eliminates (E). Finally, $b^2 - 4ac = 5$. Since $b = 3$ and $a = 1$, $b^2 - 4ac = 5 \Rightarrow (3)^2 - 4(1)(c) = 5 \Rightarrow 9 - 4c = 5 \Rightarrow 4c = 4 \Rightarrow c = 1$. Thus, the equation is $x^2 + 3x + 1 = 0$.

58. **(F)** (p. 620) ***Mathematics/Algebra/Expressing and Evaluating Algebraic Functions/Concepts of Domain and Range.*** A function is a relationship such that each element of the domain is paired with one and only one element in the range. The domain is the set of all possibilities for the first coordinate. In the relationship given in the question stem, two pairs—(0,3) and (0,5)—have the same first coordinate. So, one element of the domain, 0, is paired with two different elements in the range: 3 and 5. We need to eliminate either (0,3) or (0,5). By dropping (0,3), the element, 0, is paired only with 5, and the set becomes a function.

59. **(E)** (p. 621) ***Mathematics/Geometry/Complex Figures*** and ***30°-60°-90° Triangles*** and ***Rectangles and Squares.*** Consider the trapezoid as a composite figure. Draw a line from point B perpendicular to $\overline{CD}$: the trapezoid is a combination of a right triangle and a rectangle. Since the triangle has degree measures of 30, 60, and 90, the side opposite the 30° angle has a length half that of the hypotenuse, or a length of 4. Thus, the rectangle has sides of 4 and 9 and an area of 36. Then, the side of the triangle opposite the 60° angle has a length equal to $\dfrac{\sqrt{3}}{2}$ times the hypotenuse, or $4\sqrt{3}$. The area of the triangle is $\dfrac{ab}{2} = \dfrac{(4)(4\sqrt{3})}{2} = 8\sqrt{3}$. So, the area of the trapezoid is $36 + 8\sqrt{3}$.

60. **(F)** (p. 621) ***Mathematics/Trigonometry/Trigonometric Relationships.*** The cotangent and tangent are reciprocal functions, so if $\cot\theta = \dfrac{4}{3}$, then $\tan\theta = \dfrac{3}{4}$.

Section 3: Reading

1. **(B)** (p. 623) *Reading/Prose Fiction/Development.* The author is arguing that most of the stories in the newspaper are not really worth reading. He includes this report as an example to show how silly some news coverage is. It is an odd occurrence that does not really affect the person who reads about it—except as idle gossip. The other choices must be wrong because the event is not significant.

2. **(J)** (p. 623) *Reading/Prose Fiction/Development.* In the second paragraph, the author of Passage A is making the point that the foreign news is not really news and mentions the examples of Spain, England, and France. He writes that it is possible just to toss in some generic information about Spain, and the resulting report will be accurate. (J) best summarizes how the author uses this example. The other choices are wrong because the author is not offering real news, only a parody of the news.

3. **(A)** (p. 623) *Reading/Prose Fiction/Voice.* The point of Passage A is that the reports contained in the newspaper are really worthless, covering all kinds of events that ultimately have no significance. At key points in the passage, the author pokes fun at the news: people would come running in response to a fire alarm in the hope of seeing a good fire, even if it were the church that was burning. Since the author's attitude is negative, you can eliminate (B), (C), and (D).

4. **(H)** (p. 623) *Reading/Prose Fiction/Vocabulary.* Because this is a Vocabulary item, you can be pretty sure that the correct answer is not going to be the most common meaning of "attend." As a result, (F) is wrong. In this context, "attend" means to "pay attention to," and (H) is a good match. The other choices do not fit the meaning of the sentence; in fact, (G) and (J) are never synonymous with "attend."

5. **(A)** (p. 623) *Reading/Prose Fiction/Development.* The author says that people would respond to the fire alarm not because they want to help save property from destruction but because they want to watch a fire. The author adds that this is particularly true if the church itself is on fire. The author is adding emphasis to the point by saying that people would show up to watch their own church burn. As for (B), while it seems that these people might not care enough about property to put out the fire, this is not the point that the author wants to prove. He wants to prove that they would enjoy watching the church burn. (C) is wrong because the point is not that people are legitimately interested in local affairs but that in this case they are fascinated by something unusual. (D) has to be wrong because the point is that people are less interested in the church than in watching a fire.

6. **(J)** (p. 623) *Reading/Prose Fiction/Explicit Detail.* The author states that the people on the island had continued to act as friends even though they were enemies (meaning that the countries from which they originally came were at war). (F) and (G) are ideas mentioned in the selection but do not respond to the question asked. (H) is not discussed in that paragraph.

7. **(B)** (p. 623) *Reading/Prose Fiction/Explicit Detail.* The "plight" that both the islanders and the residents of Europe shared was the delay in the news reporting. Though the delay may have been longer (in the case of the islanders) or shorter (in the case of Europeans nearer to the events), there was still a delay during which people were in the position of acting on outdated and wrong information. As for (A), the reporting was not wrong; it was merely delayed. As for (C), even regular reports can be outdated. As for (D), the problem was not biased news but late news.

8. **(F)** (p. 624) *Reading/Prose Fiction/Implied Idea.* In the final paragraph, the author states that from our perspective we can see that results were achieved even though people were working with outdated or wrong information. The author offers overseas exploration as an example; with the backing of the Spanish government, Columbus set sail for India only to land in what is now the Americas, and was credited with a significant achievement. As for (G), while the Spanish government and Columbus worked with wrong information, this is not the author's point—the results are what matters. As for (H), the author talks about hindsight and does not fault those who made errors because their information was limited. (J) represents a misunderstanding of the final paragraph.

9. **(A)** (p. 624) *Reading/Prose Fiction/Application.* The author of Passage A thinks that the news is only gossip. The author of Passage B thinks that news is important, even if it arrives a little late. As for (B), the author of Passage A does not really care whether news is accurate or not; it's just gossip. As for (C), again, the author of Passage A insists that the news has no value at all. As for (D), the author of Passage B really does not hold out much hope for the news, though he or she might allow that faster reporting is better than slower reporting. As for (E), while it is true that Passage A mentions some local events, the author does not say that one type of event is more suitable for coverage than the other. Similarly, while the second author talks about international events, he does not say that reporting on international events is particularly suited to all newspapers.

10. **(F)** (p. 624) *Reading/Prose Fiction/Implied Idea.* We do not know what the authors would have said about the web because they obviously died before it was invented, but we can make a good guess. The author of Passage A would probably say, "See I told you so, more and faster junk." Figuring out author two is a little harder. The point of the second passage is that no matter how fast the news comes, there is always some delay between the event and the report, and during that time, we are operating on wrong information. That point is nicely summarized by the first sentence of the third paragraph: how indirectly we know the environment. Thus, the second author would probably say that while the web closes the gap somewhat, it does not eliminate it. As for (G), there is no way that author one is going to buy into this point. As for (H), surely author two would allow that the web is faster and therefore at least a little better. In any event, author one is going to say that both sources are terrible. The same reasoning applies to (J).

11. **(B)** (p. 625) *Reading/Social Science/Main Idea.* (B) is the correct answer choice. It accurately summarizes the main idea developed in the passage; in addition, it is the only statement general enough to cover the full range of information discussed in the passage. As for the other answer choices, (A) is incorrect because it is contradicted by the passage; as the author says, the current lack of regulation may have led to events that have "had harmful effects not only on stockholders but also on the economy as a whole" (lines 6–8). (C) and (D) are incorrect because they are only two points or opinions presented during the passage; in other words, neither is a statement broad enough to encompass the main idea of the passage. In addition, it is hardly clear that the author shares or would endorse either of these opinions.

12. **(G)** (p. 626) *Reading/Social Science/Application.* (G) is the correct answer choice. In lines 47–51, the author outlines the basic details of how a "golden parachute clause" works. The description in this item stem matches what is described in the passage.

13. **(C)** (p. 626) *Reading/Social Science/Implied Idea.* (C) is the correct answer choice. In lines 9–12, the author gives the defining characteristic of a hostile takeover; specifically, the current management is opposed to it.

14. **(F)** (p. 626) *Reading/Social Science/Explicit Detail.* (F) is the correct answer choice. In the third paragraph, the author explains how raiders must raise substantial capital to buy large quantities of a targeted company's stock (usually at above market price). According to the author, the raiders acquire "debt" (line 29) that they then attempt to liquidate by selling parts of the targeted company or by running the targeted company more efficiently.

15. **(D)** (p. 626) *Reading/Social Science/Explicit Detail.* (D) is the correct answer choice. In lines 51–53, the author outlines the basic details of a "poison pill" strategy. The description in (D) matches what is outlined. As for the other answer choices, (A) is incorrect because it describes the "greenmail" strategy (lines 54–58). (B) is incorrect because it describes the "golden parachute" strategy (lines 47–51). Finally, (C) is incorrect because it is not supported by any material in the passage.

16. **(G)** (p. 626) *Reading/Social Science/Explicit Detail.* (G) is the correct answer choice. In the final paragraph, the author explicitly says that supporters of corporate takeovers believe "the threat of a

takeover...makes managers more efficient" (lines 60–61). As for the other answer choices, they are all incorrect because there is no evidence in the passage to suggest that supporters of corporate takeovers would hold these beliefs.

17. **(D)** (p. 626) *Reading/Social Science/Explicit Detail.* (D) is the correct answer choice. A proxy fight is defined in lines 16–20. The description in (D) matches what is outlined in lines 16–20. As for the other answer choices, they are all incorrect because they are unrelated to proxy fights.

18. **(H)** (p. 626) *Reading/Social Science/Application.* (H) is the correct answer choice. In the final paragraph, the author says that supporters of corporate takeovers believe "the threat of a takeover...makes managers more efficient" (lines 60–61). Selling unprofitable subsidiaries to raise cash and cut expenses is an example of being more efficient. As for the other answer choices, see the second to last paragraph of this passage for correct definitions of these terms.

19. **(B)** (p. 627) *Reading/Social Science/Explicit Detail.* (B) is the correct answer choice. In the first sentence of the passage, the author explains that the Securities and Exchange Commission is a federal agency that regulates American financial markets.

20. **(H)** (p. 627) *Reading/Social Science/Explicit Detail.* (H) is the correct answer choice. In the fourth paragraph, the author explains that people have been sent to jail for "selling inside information about future takeover attempts" (lines 35–36).

21. **(A)** (p. 628) *Reading/Humanities/Main Idea.* Although the passage includes an abundance of detail, nearly all of these details can be grouped into two main categories: first, a general introduction to Josquin des Prez; and second, an explanation as to why he is relatively unknown. (A) is the correct answer choice because it mentions both of these main points.

22. **(J)** (p. 629) *Reading/Humanities/Explicit Detail.* (J) is the correct answer choice because the author never mentions any of Josquin's students. As for the other answer choices, (F) is answered in the second paragraph (*El Grillo, Allegez moy*, etc.). (G) is answered in the final paragraph (sackbuts, krummhorns, etc.). (H) is answered in the second paragraph (Ockeghem).

23. **(D)** (p. 629) *Reading/Humanities/Implied Idea.* In the fourth paragraph, the author lists several difficulties associated with reading a musical score from the Renaissance. The author specifically mentions that no tempos are given, flats and sharps are not specified, and no instructions are provided as to which instruments are to play each part. It is logical to assume that, since these are mentioned as difficulties associated with musical scores from the Renaissance, modern musical notation must contain all of these features.

24. **(G)** (p. 629) *Reading/Humanities/Implied Idea.* In the third paragraph, the author discusses a distinction between concept and performance. The author states that music does not exist in notes printed on a page; instead, the author argues, a musical score is merely a set of instructions for producing music. Therefore, the author would agree with (G).

25. **(D)** (p. 629) *Reading/Humanities/Application.* Each answer choice provided here has a certain amount of merit. On the one hand, (A) seems like a good choice because the author mentions that members of *collegia musica* are generally the only ones who attempt to perform Renaissance music; however, the author also lists several shortcomings associated with these organizations. (B) seems like a good choice because study in general is an excellent method for producing positive results; however, the author mentions several deficiencies associated with musical scores from the Renaissance that even a lifetime of dedicated study could never overcome. (C) might seem like a good choice for the same reason as (B) since additional study or attention normally leads to positive results; however, the essay gives no specific evidence that merely adding Renaissance music to a college curriculum would increase public appreciation of this remote and esoteric art form. In the end, (D) is the best answer choice because it is

actually supported by evidence from the essay. In lines 62–63, the author explicitly mentions that musicians cannot afford to study the type of music written by Josquin des Prez due to lack of financial support from an audience. If financial support were available from another source, though, musicians could afford to study and promote the music of Renaissance composers like Josquin des Prez.

26. **(G)** (p. 629) *Reading/Humanities/Explicit Detail.* (G) is the correct answer choice because, although the author says that musicians who read modern musical notation have difficulty reading Renaissance notation, the author never says that these musicians cannot play Renaissance instruments. As for the other answer choices, (F) is mentioned in the fourth paragraph. (H) and (J) are mentioned in the final paragraph.

27. **(A)** (p. 629) *Reading/Humanities/Implied Idea.* (A) is the correct answer choice because there are at least two reasons to believe that the author admires Galileo. First, in lines 28–29, the author says that both Josquin and Galileo "asserted a new importance for man." The author does not qualify or give any reason to doubt the goodness of this accomplishment. Second, the author has only praise and admiration for Josquin. If the author then says that Josquin and Galileo were comparable figures in their respective fields, we can assume that the author would have similar praise and admiration for Galileo.

28. **(H)** (p. 629) *Reading/Humanities/Implied Idea.* In line 6, the author states that the dominant theme of liturgical music "was reverence." So, (H) is the correct answer choice.

29. **(A)** (p. 629) *Reading/Humanities/Implied Idea.* (A) is the correct answer choice. In lines 32–33, the author says that "in fine art, concept and performance are one." Specifically, in arts such as painting and poetry, there is a permanent and physical artifact (i.e., a mural or a book of poems) that does not change. In contrast, the author says there is a "separation of concept from performance in music" (lines 31–32). Specifically, a composer writes a musical score that consists of notes on a page. However, the music itself does not exist until musicians perform it; the music then varies from performance to performance based on the quality and the interpretation of the musicians. Similarly, a choreographer creates a ballet and leaves instructions as to its performance. However, the ballet itself does not exist until dancers perform it; and, again, the ballet varies from performance to performance based on the same factors mentioned above.

30. **(H)** (p. 629) *Reading/Humanities/Implied Idea.* (H) is the correct answer choice. In lines 1–2, the author says that Western music was only liturgical up until the time of Josquin des Prez. The author then says that, while Josquin des Prez wrote liturgical music, he also "stepped with the other [foot] into the human world" (lines 12–14). In other words, Josquin des Prez also wrote nonreligious music. For example, the author cites the *Deploration d'Ockeghem*, a musical piece written in tribute to a fellow composer, as well as *Allegez moy*, a musical piece about a beautiful woman.

31. **(C)** (p. 630) *Reading/Natural Science/Explicit Detail.* (C) is the correct answer choice. In the first sentence of the passage, the author says that a supernova occurs about "twice every century" (line 1) or about once every fifty years.

32. **(J)** (p. 630) *Reading/Natural Science/Explicit Detail.* (J) is the correct answer choice. The passage never mentions or implies that supernovas are caused by the collision of large galaxies. As for the other answer choices, (F) is incorrect because supernovas are described as extremely bright (lines 30–31). (G) is incorrect because supernovas are described as a type of explosion (lines 2–4). Finally, (H) is incorrect because supernovas are said to emit large quantities of X-rays (lines 35–36).

33. **(A)** (p. 630) *Reading/Natural Science/Development.* (A) is the correct answer choice. Starting at line 12, the author compares a star to a leaky balloon. An analogy is a comparison.

34. **(H)** (p. 631) *Reading/Natural Science/Implied Idea.* (H) is the correct answer choice. The key word used to describe these meteorites is "anomalous," which means "uncharacteristic." These meteorites are

758 • CAMBRIDGE PRACTICE TEST REINFORCEMENT

uncharacteristic because they contain "certain isotopes" (line 42) not found in our solar system. If these isotopes are not found in our solar system, it can be inferred that they came from a supernova that gave birth to our solar system. As the author notes, elements such as these isotopes "are manufactured deep in the interior of stars and would...remain there if it were not for the cataclysmic supernova explosions that blow giant stars apart" (lines 49–52).

35. **(A)** (p. 631) ***Reading/Natural Science/Implied Idea.*** (A) is the correct answer choice. In the second paragraph, the author explains that the hot gas from a supernova "will emit most of its energy at X-ray wavelengths, so it is not surprising that X-ray observatories have provided some of the most useful insights into the nature of the supernova phenomenon" (lines 35–38). The author also notes that X-ray studies have detected "more than twenty supernova remnants" (line 39). In short, the author implies it is easiest to find evidence of a supernova using equipment that detects X-rays (rather than equipment that views visible light).

36. **(J)** (p. 631) ***Reading/Natural Science/Explicit Detail.*** (J) is the correct answer choice. In the first paragraph, the author describes how a star becomes a supernova. The sequence of events begins when, within the star, "the nuclear fuel is exhausted...[and] the matter in the center of the star collapses inward" (lines 19–21).

37. **(B)** (p. 631) ***Reading/Natural Science/Explicit Detail.*** (B) is the correct answer choice. In the first paragraph, the author begins the process of describing how a star becomes a supernova. According to the author, once a star completes its initial collapse, its "nuclei and electrons are fused into a super-dense lump of matter known as a neutron star" (lines 23–24). In the second paragraph, the author explains what follows this stage—namely, a supernova. Therefore, a neutron star is an intermediate stage between an ordinary star and a supernova.

38. **(J)** (p. 631) ***Reading/Natural Science/Main Idea.*** (J) is the correct answer choice for two reasons. First, it accurately summarizes the author's main purpose, which is to describe the sequence of events that precedes and follows a supernova. Second, it is the only statement general enough to cover the full range of information discussed in the passage. As for the other answer choices, they are all incorrect because they focus on only one element of the passage; in other words, (F), (G), and (H) are all too narrow to describe fully the author's main purpose in writing this passage.

39. **(D)** (p. 631) ***Reading/Natural Science/Explicit Detail.*** (D) is the correct answer choice. In line 44, the author says our galaxy was formed "more than four and a half billion years ago."

40. **(H)** (p. 631) ***Reading/Natural Science/Implied Idea.*** (H) is the correct answer choice. In the last paragraph, the author says "supernovas produce clouds of high-energy particles...[which] are responsible for many of the genetic mutations that are the driving force of the evolution of species" (lines 53–57).

Section 4: Science

1. **(B)** (p. 633) ***Science/Data Representation/Analysis.*** Generally, the Wright data show lower lift at a given angle than the Lilienthal data.

2. **(H)** (p. 633) ***Science/Data Representation/Comprehension.*** The highest point on the graph is at 14 degrees (approximately 5.7 pounds/sq. ft.).

3. **(A)** (p. 633) ***Science/Data Representation/Comprehension.*** By extending both lines to the 50° mark, the difference between them is clearly less than 1 pound/sq. ft.

4. **(H)** (p. 633) *Science/Data Representation/Comprehension.* According to the graph, the greatest difference in lift for the two experiments (corresponding to the greatest distance between the two curves for a given angle of incidence) occurs at approximately 30 degrees.

5. **(B)** (p. 634) *Science/Data Representation/Comprehension.* The widest region is between 18 and 43 degrees: $43 - 18 = 25$ degrees.

6. **(J)** (p. 635) *Science/Research Summary/Analysis.* Since plastic beads are not alive, they cannot possibly carry out cellular respiration. This control is designed to detect any atmospheric changes (in the laboratory) that may cause a change in pressure inside the tubes.

7. **(A)** (p. 635) *Science/Research Summary/Comprehension.* Oxygen in the air of the tube is consumed by the peas during cellular respiration (see summary equation).

8. **(F)** (p. 635) *Science/Research Summary/Analysis.* Without KOH to remove the carbon dioxide produced during cellular respiration, the same number of gas molecules ($6CO_2$) would always be added to the tube as gas molecules were being consumed in the tube ($6O_2$) and the pressure would remain constant.

9. **(C)** (p. 635) *Science/Research Summary/Analysis.* Experiment 2 was conducted at a higher temperature than Experiment 1. The greater decrease in pressure in the same time period demonstrates a faster consumption of oxygen.

10. **(G)** (p. 636) *Science/Research Summary/Analysis.* If results are identical in light and dark, then light/dark conditions are irrelevant to cellular respiration rates in the experiment; only temperature conditions are important.

11. **(A)** (p. 636) *Science/Research Summary/Comprehension.* Glucose must be consumed in order for cellular respiration to occur, eliminating (B) and (D). Cellular respiration did not occur at equal rates in Experiments 1 and 2, eliminating (C), so (A) is the only possible answer: peas are seeds containing a supply of glucose.

12. **(G)** (p. 637) *Science/Conflicting Viewpoints/Analysis.* Scientist 1 believes that processes associated with sudden events in the past shaped the earth, whereas Scientist 2 believes that the processes are continuing in the present.

13. **(D)** (p. 637) *Science/Conflicting Viewpoints/Analysis.* Mountains could not have formed only when land masses were raised at the beginnings of the earth if recent fossils of sea creatures are found at mountain tops. This evidence suggests that the rocks were underwater relatively recently.

14. **(H)** (p. 638) *Science/Conflicting Viewpoints/Analysis.* The two scientists agree that the changes that have shaped the landscape have operated over a long time span, but they disagree as to whether those changes were sudden and violent (catastrophism) or constant and gradual (principle of uniform change). Furthermore, catastrophism holds that the cataclysmic events happened in the distant past, not recently, eliminating (F).

15. **(A)** (p. 638) *Science/Conflicting Viewpoints/Comprehension.* According to Scientist 1, the worldwide ocean precipitated granite first, so it must be the lowest layer, with other precipitated materials covering it later.

16. **(F)** (p. 638) *Science/Conflicting Viewpoints/Comprehension.* According to Scientist 1, the three major rock types formed when the worldwide ocean precipitated different materials on three occasions, so no further types can be expected since this ocean no longer exists (possibly due to evaporation).

17. **(C)** (p. 638) *Science/Conflicting Viewpoints/Analysis.* By arguing that processes that formed the earth at its origin differed from those that maintain and mold the earth as an existing planet, Scientist 1 would be refuting Scientist 2's view that processes are uniform from the beginning.

18. **(G)** (p. 638) *Science/Conflicting Viewpoints/Analysis.* Scientist 1 refers to three rock types forming during three separate precipitations. Regions of lava (with no present volcanoes), rivers presently continuing to cut their channels, and "related" fossils that could not have immigrated from other geographic areas are factors that support the views of Scientist 2.

19. **(D)** (p. 639) *Science/Research Summary/Comprehension.* Ten individuals had their heart rates recorded every 10 minutes during a 30-minute experiment (three times each). Therefore, 10(3) = 30 values were used to calculate the average heart rate for each of the experiments.

20. **(G)** (p. 639) *Science/Research Summary/Analysis.* Since Species B had an increase in heart rate when environmental temperature increased, it is the likely species to be cold-blooded (Species A's heart rate stayed about the same).

21. **(C)** (p. 639) *Science/Research Summary/Analysis.* Just by chance alone, any one individual might have an extremely high or extremely low heart rate. The larger the sample of individuals tested, the lower the chances of getting extreme average values.

22. **(J)** (p. 639) *Science/Research Summary/Analysis.* Since Species B (cold-blooded) had an increase in average heart rate when environmental temperature increased, a decrease in average heart rate is likely when temperatures drop. Species A should have approximately the same average heart rate at all three temperatures.

23. **(A)** (p. 639) *Science/Research Summary/Analysis.* At 22°C, Species A had an average heart rate of 150 beats/minute, while Species B averaged 100 beats/minute.

24. **(F)** (p. 640) *Science/Research Summary/Analysis.* The cold-blooded Species B should have an increase in body temperature in Experiment 2 (35°C conditions in the incubator compared to 22°C in Experiment 1). The warm-blooded Species A should have no significant change in body temperature during the experiments.

25. **(A)** (p. 641) *Science/Data Representation/Comprehension.* Each photon can promote an electron from level 1 to level 2 since the difference in energies is 0.60 eV. (Note that the actual value of level 1 alone, which happens to be 0.60 eV also, does not determine the answer. Differences in energy are what matter.)

26. **(J)** (p. 641) *Science/Data Representation/Comprehension.* There is no way to distinguish between the emission from level 3 to level 4 or from level 5 to level 4 since each releases a photon of 0.32 eV.

27. **(D)** (p. 641) *Science/Data Representation/Comprehension.* Only the level 3 to level 1 emission has an energy difference of 0.92 eV.

28. **(J)** (p. 641) *Science/Data Representation/Comprehension.* Each electron can go from level 5 to any other level, with each of the four transitions requiring the emission of a photon of a different energy.

29. **(C)** (p. 641) *Science/Data Representation/Analysis.* Since absorption of photons occurs first, then emission, electrons must be promoted (gaining the necessary energy from the absorbed photons), then emitted. Transitions between levels 3 and 4 have the necessary energy: 0.23 eV.

30. **(J)** (p. 641) *Science/Data Representation/Comprehension.* Although 2.07 eV is the absolute energy of level 5, there is no difference of energy levels anywhere on the diagram that equals 2.07 eV; hence, the photons will not be absorbed: no electron transitions will occur between levels 1 and 5.

31. **(C)** (p. 642) *Science/Research Summary/Comprehension.* Note how θ_1 and θ_2 are defined on the original drawing, then imagine how the diagram will change as the angles become smaller approaching zero: they would align along the vertical axis. Note that (B) would be correct if the angles were defined as those between the ray and the horizontal, not vertical, axis.

32. **(J)** (p. 642) *Science/Research Summary/Analysis.* In Experiment 1 the angle in water is equal to the angle in air. In Experiment 2 the angle in water is less than the angle in air. So, only the last choice fits both experiments.

33. **(A)** (p. 642) *Science/Research Summary/Comprehension.* This question simply requires interpretation of the meaning of the diagram: in Experiment 3, the beam is shown hitting the water surface and reflecting back, but not back on the beam itself.

34. **(H)** (p. 643) *Science/Research Summary/Comprehension.* The beam of light only passes into the air for observation in Experiment 2.

35. **(C)** (p. 643) *Science/Research Summary/Analysis.* Only this response covers all elements of the three diagrams.

36. **(H)** (p. 644) *Science/Data Representation/Comprehension.* The number of butterflies captured for marking is found under the heading "Marked." Reading across the table for each size group, the "dark brown" category always has the fewest butterflies marked.

37. **(D)** (p. 644) *Science/Data Representation/Comprehension.* Compare the number of butterflies recaptured to the number marked to derive a proportion that represents how easy it is to recapture each type of butterfly. The proportion for small, white butterflies (30/35) is much higher than that for any of the other choices.

38. **(G)** (p. 644) *Science/Data Representation/Analysis.* An examination of the table shows that for all colors, as size increases, the number of butterflies marked increases.

39. **(B)** (p. 644) *Science/Data Representation/Application.* A poisonous chemical will have adverse effects on the butterfly after marking (perhaps by killing or by preventing flight). The group with the lowest number (and proportion) of individuals recaptured in flight ($10/40 = 1/4$ recaptured) is the group consisting of small, tan butterflies.

40. **(G)** (p. 644) *Science/Data Representation/Analysis.* For medium–sized butterflies, the proportion of individuals recaptured in each color is as follows: white ($15/30 = 1/2$), tan ($20/40 = 1/2$), and dark brown ($10/20 = 1/2$).

Sample Essay Responses and Analyses

Section 5: Writing (p. 646)

Above Average Response

With online systems, Americans could easily register and vote without leaving their homes. While this method is a practical solution to increase voter registration, it should not be used for voting on Election Day because of the potential for technical problems and voter fraud. Online voter registration would make the process more convenient and would not necessarily result in less informed voters. However, since errors due to technical problems could skew election results, this system should not be used for voting itself.

Online systems could make voter registration a faster, easier process and, therefore, accessible to more people. As Perspective 3 states, a high voter turnout is crucial for a healthy democracy. The ability to register online would especially encourage younger voters who are used to the convenience of online services and may not take time out of their schedule to travel to a designated place to register. States that have implemented online registration have recorded an increase in youth voter turnout. Moreover, this option would also help people who cannot leave their homes due to illness or disability, and it would make it easier to register for an absentee ballot if you are living out of state. With one obstacle to registration removed, voter turnout could increase.

Online voter registration or voting would not necessarily lead to less informed voters. While the task of going to a designated place to register or to vote demands more effort from voters, this does not prevent people who are uninformed about the candidates from traveling to a polling station. One can accomplish many important tasks online, such as financial or legal transactions, and the online convenience does not make these actions any less important. Onsite registration and voting does, however, stop citizens who do not have the ability to reach a polling place, such as people with illnesses or inflexible work or childcare schedules. Although employers in some states are legally required to give employees time off for voting, employees may not be aware of this right, and in many states, they would lose pay while leaving work to vote.

While the convenience of online voting and registration would make voting accessible to more people, technological problems might lead to unfair elections. For example, an unreliable Internet connection might prevent one's vote from being counted, or it may be possible to tamper with an online system to skew election results. Voting remotely might also allow someone to vote multiple times. It is true that more traditional voting methods are not foolproof; for example, during the Presidential Election of 2000, problems with punch cards called into question the election results in Florida. However, a new method of voting could introduce even more technological problems. Voter registration could be moved online, since one can always verify whether the registration worked. However, voting itself is a time-sensitive issue, and accidental or intentional errors in an online system may go unnoticed until the election is over.

Online registration could make voter registration more accessible and therefore increase voter turnout. However, while the convenience of online voting may also increase turnout, there are too many technological risks involved to rely on it.

Ideas and Analysis: The writer clearly states his or her thesis in the introduction: an online system should be used for voter registration, but realistically, not for voting itself. The body paragraphs consider arguments for and against online registration and/or voting. The first paragraph addresses the accessibility of online voting (Perspective 3), and the second paragraph argues against the correlation between online voters and uninformed voters (Perspective 1). The third paragraph acknowledges the technical problems that could occur (Perspective 2).

Development and Support:

- The introduction states the thesis in its second sentence and previews the arguments that will support it.

- The body paragraphs begin with topic sentences that clearly state the main point or argument to be made in the paragraph.

- The body paragraphs include a mix of arguments and examples to support the author's opinion.

- The writer develops a "compromise" position on the subject by arguing for online registration but recognizing that online voting could cause too many technological problems. The writer is able to acknowledge both sides without contradicting his or her own arguments.

Organization:

- The writer introduces each paragraph with a topic sentence.

- The writer uses transitions to connect ideas between and within paragraphs. For example, the third body paragraph begins with the clause "While the convenience of online voting and registration would make voting accessible to more people" because the paragraph introduces an opposing argument to online voting.

- The second body paragraph could be stronger without the last sentence (about leaving work to vote). The argument of the paragraph is that online voting would not lead to uninformed voters, so this sentence might be seen as off-topic.

- The essay could also be improved with a longer and slightly more developed conclusion.

Language Use and Conventions:

The essay contains at least three principal strengths in this area:

- The essay does not have any mechanics/usage errors. As a result, the reader's attention is not distracted from the substance of the essay.

- The writer does not use any informal language.

- Stylistically, the writer varies sentence structures.

- The writer uses vivid verbs and avoids vague language. The verb choice shows a sophisticated vocabulary.

Summary and Conclusions: This essay demonstrates writing skills that are very well developed and analyzes multiple viewpoints of the issue. The writer incorporates all three perspectives in his or her argument. This essay would likely receive a score of 10.

Below Average Response

Online voting and registration is a great idea because it would allow more people to vote and would make our democracy stronger. It is elitist to assume that more people voting would lead to less informed voters. I also don't think that we should be afraid of using this technology we do so much online and it works really well, so why not vote online?

Online voting is a good idea because it is more convenient than going to a polling place or a government building and waiting in line to vote or to register. Our lives are much busier now since we work so much, so why not make voting easier to do? Young people are also used to doing everything online, and as these people make up more and more of the voting population, it makes sense to adapt to their ways and vote online.

I don't think that online voting would necessarily lead to less informed voters. The purpose of a democracy is to have citizens elect their leaders, not to only allow an elite group to vote. Also, so many people keep up with current events by reading online news. The internet has made people more informed, not less.

Some might worry about the technological problems involved with online voting and what would happen if the system didn't work. However, we do so many important things online, like transfer money and enter important information onto websites. If we can do this, why can't we vote?

Online voting seems like a logical, practical solution that will make voting more accessible to more people.

Ideas and Analysis: The writer clearly expresses his or her point of view in favor of online voting. However, the arguments are superficial because the writer offers little concrete evidence in favor of his or her argument and does not give enough consideration to opposing viewpoints.

Development and Support:

- The introduction clearly states the writer's opinion, but the writer should use more specific language rather than saying that online voting "is a great idea."

- The writer attempts to support the arguments with generalizations, rather than using concrete examples or clear logic.

  - In the first body paragraph, the writer has one relevant argument (that online voting would engage younger, technology-oriented voters). However, the statement that "our lives are much busier" is too general to be used as an argument.

  - In the second body paragraph, the writer claims to argue that online voting will not lead to uninformed voters. However, the writer attempts to support the argument with a generalization: "The purpose of a democracy is to have citizens elect their leaders, not to only allow an elite group to vote." This generalization does not answer the question that the writer needs to address: *Why* wouldn't online voting lead to uninformed voters?

  - In the third body paragraph, the writer acknowledges that there might be technological problems involved with online voting. However, the writer simply dismisses this argument without thoroughly engaging with it. He or she does not reflect on how technological problems could influence elections.

- The conclusion should be more developed and should revisit the writer's three main arguments.

Organization:

- The introduction has three separate sentences that show that the writer agrees with Perspective 3 and argues against Perspectives 1 and 2. However, the introduction would be stronger if the writer combined these opinions into a coherent thesis.

- The topic sentences should have transitions to introduce new ideas in the following paragraph.

- The last two sentences of the second paragraph do not support its main topic. ("Also, so many people keep up with current events by reading online news. The internet has made people more informed, not less.") The prompt does not ask whether the Internet makes people better informed about the news in general; it asks whether online voting could lead to less informed voters.

Language Use and Conventions:

The essay contains several weaknesses in this area:

- The essay contains some usage and mechanics errors.

  o Introduction: "I also don't think that we should be afraid of using this technology we do so much online and it works really well, so why not vote online?" is a run-on sentence. The first sentence should end after "technology."

- The writer uses informal language, such as "so many important things" (Body paragraph 3).

- The writer uses vague language. In the first body paragraph, when the writer says "**Our** lives are much busier now since **we** work so much" it is unclear what "our" and "we" are referring to.

Summary and Conclusions: The writer's opinion is clear, but the essay relies too much on generalizations and does not give enough consideration to opposing arguments. The body paragraphs do not have enough evidence to support their arguments. This essay would likely receive a score of 5.

ITEM INDEX

In the following index, all of the numeric references are designed as follows: **Page #**/Item #. The parenthetical information beside each item category refers to the subject-area in which that item category appears.

30°-60°-90° Triangles (Mathematics)

Lesson: **236**/205; **239**/219; **242**/232
Quiz I: **253**/11
Quiz IV: **266**/11
Practice Test III: **621**/59

45°-45°-90° Triangles (Mathematics)

Test Mechanics: **194**/4
Lesson: **236**/203–204; **239**/219
Quiz III: **263**/20
Practice Test I: **486**/25
Practice Test II: **550**/31
Practice Test III: **614**/42

Absolute Value (Mathematics)

Lesson: **212**/63–65
Practice Test II: **549**/25; **555**/45
Practice Test III: **608**/22

Adjectives versus Adverbs (English)

Test Mechanics: **22**/2, 8
Lesson: **27**/22–25; **28**/26–28
Quiz I: **51**/25
Quiz IV: **66**/7
Directed Study Practice Test: **362**/3; **373**/28; **385**/55
Practice Test II: **533**/31; **540**/75
Practice Test III: **586**/3

Algebra (Mathematics)

Test Mechanics: **193**/2-3; **199**/8
Lesson: **201**/2-3; **202**/4-6; **216–227**/94–169
Quiz I: **252**/4, 9; **253**/12, 14; **254**/15
Quiz II: **256**/3; **257**/6, 8, 10; **258**/15–16
Quiz III: **261**/9; **262**/12, 14
Quiz IV: **264**/3, 5; **265**/6; **266**/14, 16; **267**/18, 20–21, 23, 25
Review: **271**/14; **272**/17, 19; **273**/22, 24, 26
Directed Study Practice Test: **395**/3, 5; **396**/7; **397**/9, 11; **398**/14; **399**/18; **400**/19–20; **401**/21;
404/27–28; **408**/36; **409**/39; **410**/40; **411**/42; **414**/51; **415**/52–54; **416**/56; **417**/58
Practice Test I: **478**/1–2; **480**/8; **481**/10–11; **482**/14; **484**/20; **485**/21, 23; **487**/29; **488**/31, 33; **489**/36; **490**/37; **491**/42–43; **494**/52; **495**/53–55; **496**/57
Practice Test II: **542**/2; **546**/15–16; **547**/19–21; **548**/24; **552**/35; **553**/37–38; **554**/43; **556**/50; **557**/54; **559**/59
Practice Test III: **602**/2; **603**/3; **604**/8–9; **605**/12; **607**/19–21; **610**/29; **611**/33; **612**/35; **613**/38; **616**/47; **618**/53–54; **620**/57–58

Analysis (Science)

Test Mechanics: **288**/2–3; **290**/1–3; **291**/4–6
Lesson: **295**/1; **296**/6–9; **297**/11; **298**/12–13; **299**/19–22; **302**/28–31; **303**/32–33; **304**/36–39; **305**/43–45; **306**/47–49; **307**/50–51; **308**/55–57; **311**/58, 60–63; **313**/66–68; **315**/70; **316**/72–73; **317**/77–78; **318**/79, 82–83; **319**/84–85, 87; **320**/88–91; **323**/102–103
Quiz I: **326**/3–5; **327**/6; **328**/11–13; **329**/14–16
Quiz II: **331**/5; **332**/7–9; **333**/10; **335**/14, 16
Quiz III: **337**/1, 3–5; **338**/7; **339**/11–12; **340**/13–15
Review: **341**/2–3; **342**/4–5; **343**/11; **344**/16, 18; **346**/28–30; **347**/32–33; **348**/35–36; **349–351**/46–54; **352**/56, 58, 60; **353**/63–65
Directed Study Practice Test: **436**/2; **439**/9; **441**/12–13; **443**/17; **444**/19; **445–448**/22–27; **450**/29; **451**/30; **453**/33–35; **454**/36–37; **455**/39–40
Practice Test I: **510**/2; **511**/7; **514**/11, 13; **516**/18–20; **517**/22; **518**/24; **519**/27; **520**/31; **521**/32, 34; **522**/37–38; **523**/39–40
Practice Test II: **569**/1, 5–6; **570**/9; **571**/11; **573**/13–16, 18; **574**/20, 23; **575**/24–26, 28; **576**/29; **578**/32; **579**/37–38; **580**/39
Practice Test III: **633**/1; **635**/6, 8–9; **636**/10; **637**/12–13; **638**/14, 17–18; **639**/20–23; **640**/24; **641**/29; **642**/32; **643**/35; **644**/38, 40

Apostrophes (English)

Lesson: **38**/112, 114
Review: **73**/23
Directed Study Practice Test: **365**/9; **384**/54

Application (Reading)

Lesson: **99**/12–13; **101**/20; **105**/38; **106**/43;
117/92; **126**/129, 132; **130**/145, 148
Quiz I: **132**/5, 7
Quiz II: **138**/16–17
Quiz III: **140**/3; **141**/8; **142**/10; **143**/15, 17–18
Quiz IV: **148**/17; **152**/29
Review: **154**/7; **155**/12; **158**/20; **160**/29; **162**/37
Directed Study Practice Test: **434**/40
Practice Test I: **502**/20; **503**/24
Practice Test II: **562**/14; **565**/28; **566**/35; **567**/36,
38–39
Practice Test III: **624**/9; **626**/12, 18; **629**/25

Application (Science)

Test Mechanics: **288**/4
Lesson: **295**/2; **298**/14; **303**/34; **304**/40; **306**/46;
308/54; **313**/69; **316**/74; **320**/92
Quiz III: **337**/6; **338**/8–10; **340**/16
Review: **342**/6; **343**/12; **344**/17, 19; **348**/37–41;
352/57
Directed Study Practice Test: **437**/5; **442**/16;
444/18, 20–21
Practice Test I: **510**/3–6; **514**/14; **517**/21; **519**/26
Practice Test II: **570**/10; **571**/12; **575**/27; **578**/31,
33
Practice Test III: **644**/39

Appropriate Supporting Material (English)

Test Mechanics: **19**/2
Lesson: **39**/116; **42**/125
Quiz I: **50**/17
Quiz II: **55**/16; **56**/17; **57**/28
Quiz III: **61**/15; **64**/31
Review: **72**/16; **76**/38
Directed Study Practice Test: **368**/16; **369**/18;
380/45; **392**/72
Practice Test I: **471**/46; **473**/59; **475**/72
Practice Test II: **531**/16; **535**/47; **536**/48; **539**/65
Practice Test III: **592**/33; **593**/38

Approximation (Mathematics)

Lesson: **208**/37–39

Arithmetic (Mathematics)

Test Mechanics: **193**/1, 3; **198**/2–4; **199**/5, 7, 10
Lesson: **201**/1; **205**/17–19; **206**/20–26;
207/28–30, 32; **208–216**/33–93
Quiz I: **251**/2; **252**/5–7; **253**/13; **254**/16
Quiz II: **256**/4; **257**/11; **258**/14
Quiz III: **260**/2, 4; **261**/6; **262**/11, 16; **263**/17
Quiz IV: **264**/1–2, 4; **265**/7; **266**/13, 15
Review: **269**/1, 3, 5; **270**/8–9; **271**/10, 12–13;
272/20; **273**/21, 25; **274**/27
Directed Study Practice Test: **394**/1; **396**/8;
397/12; **398**/15–16; **403**/26; **406**/31–33;
409/38; **413**/47; **414**/50; **416**/55; **418**/60
Practice Test I: **479**/3–4; **480**/6; **481**/11; **482**/13;
483/16, 17; **484**/19; **486**/27; **487**/30; **489**/35;
490/38; **491**/40–41; **492**/44; **494**/50–51
Practice Test II: **542**/1, 3; **543**/4–6; **544**/9;
545/12; **548**/23; **549**/25, 27–28; **550**/29–30;
552/34, 36; **554**/41–42; **555**/45; **558**/57–58
Practice Test III: **602**/1; **603**/5–6; **604**/10; **605**/11;
605/13; **606**/15–16; **607**/18; **608**/22, 24;
609/26–27; **610**/30; **611**/32; **612**/36; **614**/43

Audience (English)

Lesson: **40**/119
Quiz I: **50**/15; **52**/32
Quiz III: **64**/30
Review: **71**/14
Directed Study Practice Test: **372**/26; **377**/37;
388/62; **393**/74
Practice Test I: **469**/32; **475**/73

Averages (Mathematics)

Test Mechanics: **198**/1
Lesson: **203**/11; **244**/240–243; **245**/244
Quiz I: **252**/8
Quiz II: **257**/9
Quiz III: **260**/1; **261**/7
Quiz IV: **266**/14
Review: **270**/7
Directed Study Practice Test: **397**/10; **398**/13
Practice Test I: **481**/12; **485**/22; **494**/49
Practice Test II: **545**/10; **546**/14; **549**/26
Practice Test III: **612**/34

Bar, Cumulative, and Line Graphs (Mathematics)

Lesson: **204**/12; **247–249**/252–256

Basic Algebraic Manipulations (Mathematics)

Lesson: **216**/94; **217**/95
Review: **271**/14
Directed Study Practice Test: **396**/7; **404**/27; **411**/42
Practice Test I: **481**/10; **490**/37
Practice Test II: **548**/24; **553**/38
Practice Test III: **613**/38

Circles (Mathematics)

Lesson: **202**/8; **207**/27; **238**/211, 216; **239**/217, 220
Quiz I: **255**/20
Quiz II: **258**/12
Quiz III: **261**/10; **262**/15
Quiz IV: **266**/12, 17
Directed Study Practice Test: **394**/2; **399**/17; **402**/23; **403**/25
Practice Test I: **484**/18; **493**/47–48
Practice Test II: **548**/22
Practice Test III: **605**/14; **608**/23; **614**/41–42; **617**/50

Clarity of Meaning (English)

Lesson: **43**/134
Quiz I: **52**/29
Quiz IV: **66**/8; **68**/17, 19-20

Colons (English)

Lesson: **37**/106–107
Review: **72**/18
Practice Test I: **470**/40

Comma Splices (English)

Lesson: **31**/59–60
Practice Test III: **589**/19; **592**/34

Commas (English)

Test Mechanics: **19**/1; **22**/3, 6
Lesson: **34**/81–82; **35**/87–88, 90; **36**/91–92, 95–100; **44**/136
Quiz II: **53**/3; **54**/5; **56**/19
Quiz III: **60**/7–8
Review: **72**/17–18; **76**/42
Directed Study Practice Test: **365**/10; **369**/17; **374**/29; **376**/36; **379**/42
Practice Test I: **467**/22, 24; **470**/42; **474**/62
Practice Test II: **534**/37
Practice Test III: **586**/3; **590**/25

Common Arithmetic Items (Mathematics)

Test Mechanics: **193**/3; **198**/2–3; **199**/10
Lesson: **205**/17–19; **206**/20, 23, 25; **207**/28–29; **210–216**/45–87
Quiz I: **252**/5–6; **253**/13; **254**/16
Quiz II: **258**/14
Quiz III: **260**/2, 4; **262**/11, 16; **263**/17
Quiz IV: **264**/2, 4; **265**/7; **266**/13, 15
Review: **269**/1, 3, 5; **270**/8–9; **271**/10, 12–13; **272**/20; **273**/25; **274**/27
Directed Study Practice Test: **396**/8; **403**/26; **406**/31, 33; **413**/47; **414**/50; **418**/60
Practice Test I: **479**/3–4; **482**/13; **483**/17; **484**/19; **486**/27; **487**/30; **490**/38; **491**/40–41; **492**/44; **494**/50
Practice Test II: **542**/3; **543**/4, 6; **548**/23; **549**/25; **550**/29–30; **552**/34; **555**/45
Practice Test III: **603**/5–6; **604**/10; **605**/13; **606**/15–16; **607**/18; **608**/22, 24; **609**/27; **610**/30; **612**/36

Complex Figures (Mathematics)

Lesson: **202**/8; **238–240**/216–221; **242**/231
Quiz I: **253**/10; **255**/20
Quiz II: **258**/12
Quiz III: **262**/15; **263**/18
Quiz IV: **266**/11
Review: **271**/11; **272**/15, 18
Practice Test I: **488**/32; **492**/45; **493**/47–48
Practice Test II: **548**/22; **550**/31
Practice Test III: **605**/14; **608**/23; **614**/41; **615**/46; **617**/50; **621**/59

Complex Numbers (Mathematics)

Lesson: **213**/70–71
Practice Test I: **494**/50

Complicated Arithmetic Application Items (Mathematics)

Lesson: **209**/43–44
Quiz I: **251**/2; **252**/7
Quiz II: **256**/4
Quiz III: **261**/6
Quiz IV: **264**/1
Review: **273**/21
Practice Test I: **481**/11; **483**/16; **489**/35
Practice Test II: **549**/27; **552**/36
Practice Test III: **606**/16

Complicated Manipulations (Mathematics)

Test Mechanics: **193**/1; **199**/5

Lesson: **208**/34–39; **209**/40–42
Quiz II: **257**/11
Directed Study Practice Test: **406**/32; **416**/55
Practice Test II: **543**/5; **544**/9; **554**/41; **558**/57
Practice Test III: **605**/11; **611**/32

Comprehension (Science)

Test Mechanics: **288**/1
Lesson: **295**/3; **296**/4–5; **297**/10; **298**/15;
299/16–18; **300**/23–27; **304**/35; **305**/41–42;
307/52–53; **311**/59; **313**/64–65; **315**/71;
317/75–76; **318**/80–81; **319**/86; **323**/98–101
Quiz I: **326**/1–2; **327**/7–10
Quiz II: **330**/1–2; **331**/3–4; **332**/6; **334**/11–13;
335/15
Quiz III: **337**/2
Review: **341**/1; **342**/7–8; **343**/9–10; **344**/13–15;
345/20–25; **346**/26–27; **347**/31, 34; **349**/42–45;
352/55, 59; **353**/61–62, 66
Directed Study Practice Test: **436**/1, 3–4; **439**/6–8,
10; **440**/11; **442**/14–15; **450**/28; **451**/31–32;
454/38
Practice Test I: **510**/1; **513**/8–10; **514**/12;
516/15–17; **518**/23, 25; **520**/28–30; **521**/33;
522/35–36
Practice Test II: **569**/2–4; **570**/7–8; **573**/17;
574/19, 21–22; **578**/30, 34; **579**/35–36; **580**/40
Practice Test III: **633**/2–4; **634**/5; **635**/7; **636**/11;
638/15–16; **639**/19; **641**/25–28, 30; **642**/31, 33;
643/34; **644**/36–37

Concepts of Domain and Range
(Mathematics)

Lesson: **223**/142–145
Practice Test I: **496**/57
Practice Test III: **620**/58

Conciseness (English)

Lesson: **42**/128–130; **43**/131–133; **45**/143;
46/144
Quiz I: **48**/3, 7; **50**/18; **51**/27
Quiz II: **54**/7–8; **55**/15; **57**/24
Quiz III: **62**/16
Quiz IV: **66**/9
Review: **70**/9; **72**/19; **73**/24; **74**/30
Directed Study Practice Test: **362**/2; **370**/21;
375/32; **381**/46; **390**/67–68
Practice Test I: **464**/1, 3; **466**/13; **472**/53, 55;
473/57; **474**/63; **475**/70
Practice Test II: **528**/4; **532**/27; **533**/30; **534**/35,
40; **515**/53, 57; **516**/58

Practice Test III: **590**/27; **592**/37; **595**/52; **597**/61;
599/70

Conflicting Viewpoints (Science)

Test Mechanics: **290**/1–3; **291**/4–6
Lesson: **317–323**/75–103
Quiz II: **334**/11–13; **335**/14–16
Review: **344**/13–19; **347**/34; **348**/35–41;
352/55–60
Directed Study Practice Test: **453–455**/33–40
Practice Test I: **520**/28–31; **521**/32–34
Practice Test II: **579**/35–38; **580**/39–40
Practice Test III: **637**/12–13; **638**/14–18

Coordinate Geometry (Mathematics)

Lesson: **202**/7; **227–234**/170–196
Quiz I: **255**/19
Quiz II: **257**/7; **258**/13; **259**/19
Quiz III: **262**/13
Quiz IV: **266**/17; **267**/19
Review: **270**/6
Directed Study Practice Test: **396**/6; **401**/22
Practice Test I: **480**/7; **486**/26
Practice Test II: **553**/40; **555**/47; **556**/49, 51;
557/55; **558**/56; **559**/60
Practice Test III: **609**/25; **613**/39; **615**/44–45;
619/55; **620**/56

The Coordinate System (Mathematics)

Lesson: **227**/170–171; **228**/172–174
Quiz IV: **266**/17
Review: **270**/6
Practice Test I: **480**/7; **486**/26
Practice Test III: **609**/25; **613**/39; **619**/55

Creating Algebraic Expressions
(Mathematics)

Lesson: **218**/105–106; **225–227**/158–169
Quiz III: **262**/14
Quiz IV: **264**/5; **265**/6; **266**/14
Directed Study Practice Test: **398**/14; **415**/54
Practice Test II: **553**/37
Practice Test III: **602**/2; **607**/21

Dashes (English)

Lesson: **38**/109–110
Review: **76**/42
Directed Study Practice Test: **381**/47

Data Representation (Mathematics)

Test Mechanics: **193**/2
Lesson: **204**/12; **247–250**/252–260
Quiz I: **254**/16–17
Quiz III: **261**/5; **263**/17
Quiz IV: **264**/2
Review: **274**/27
Practice Test I: **479**/5; **484**/19
Practice Test III: **610**/30

Data Representation (Science)

Lesson: **295–304**/1–40
Quiz I: **326**/1–5; **327**/6–10
Quiz II: **330–333**/1–10
Quiz III: **337**/1–4; **339**/11–12; **340**/13–16
Review: **341**/1–3; **342**/4–6; **345**/20–25; **346**/26–27; **349**/42–48; **353**/61–66
Directed Study Practice Test: **436–445**/1–22
Practice Test I: **510**/1–6; **511**/7; **518**/23–25; **519**/26–27
Practice Test II: **569**/1–6; **574**/19–23; **578**/30–34
Practice Test III: **633**/1–4; **634**/5; **641**/25–30; **644**/36–40

Decimal-Fraction Equivalents (Mathematics)

Test Mechanics: **199**/5
Lesson: **209**/41–42
Quiz II: **257**/11
Practice Test II: **543**/5
Practice Test III: **605**/11; **610**/30

Definitions of the Six Trigonometric Functions (Mathematics)

Test Mechanics: **194**/5
Lesson: **203**/10; **242**/233; **243**/234
Quiz I: **253**/11; **254**/18
Quiz II: **258**/17
Quiz III: **263**/20
Review: **274**/28, 30; **275**/32
Practice Test I: **496**/59
Practice Test III: **618**/52

Determining Trigonometric Values (Mathematics)

Quiz IV: **267**/24
Review: **275**/31
Directed Study Practice Test: **417**/59
Practice Test I: **495**/56
Practice Test II: **555**/48
Practice Test III: **616**/49

Development (Reading)

Test Mechanics: **89**/2
Lesson: **98**/7; **99**/8; **100**/18; **104**/34–35; **106**/41; **108**/46, 50; **109**/57; **113**/76; **116**/90; **117**/93; **119**/99, 103; **126**/131
Quiz II: **138**/15
Quiz III: **140**/5
Quiz IV: **147**/12; **152**/28
Review: **154**/5; **160**/31
Directed Study Practice Test: **431**/29
Practice Test I: **501**/15–16; **503**/21
Practice Test III: **623**/1–2, 5; **630**/33

Diction (English)

Lesson: **30**/51–55; **31**/56
Quiz I: **49**/11; **51**/25–26
Quiz II: **54**/11; **57**/25, 27
Quiz III: **59**/2; **62**/22; **63**/26
Review: **75**/35, 37; **76**/44
Directed Study Practice Test: **362**/4; **364**/7; **370**/20; **371**/23; **374**/31; **378**/40; **379**/43; **381**/48; **384**/53; **386**/58–59; **389**/65; **390**/66; **391**/69; **391**/70
Practice Test I: **464**/2; **465**/6; **466**/11; **467**/18; **468**/28–29; **469**/34; **470**/38; **472**/48; **473**/60
Practice Test II: **528**/2; **529**/5; **532**/25; **533**/29, 34; **534**/36; **535**/45–46; **536**/50; **537**/52
Practice Test III: **586**/1; **587**/4, 7, 10; **588**/13–14; **591**/30–31; **594**/48; **596**/55; **598**/66; **599**/72

Distance Formula (Mathematics)

Lesson: **230**/184–186; **231**/187
Quiz IV: **267**/19
Practice Test II: **553**/40; **557**/55

Double Negatives (English)

Lesson: **28**/29–30

Effective Concluding Sentence (English)

Lesson: **42**/126
Quiz I: **49**/13
Review: **73**/21
Practice Test I: **465**/8
Practice Test III: **595**/50

Effective Opening Sentence (English)

Lesson: **40**/117; **41**/122
Review: **75**/36
Directed Study Practice Test: **373**/27

Effective Transitional Sentence (English)

Quiz III: **59**/3
Review: **69**/2; **73**/22
Practice Test I: **467**/19; **472**/54
Practice Test II: **529**/8; **531**/19; **537**/54
Practice Test III: **590**/23; **592**/35; **599**/69

End-Stop Punctuation (English)

Lesson: **37**/108
Directed Study Practice Test: **385**/56

Equations Involving Absolute Value (Mathematics)

Lesson: **202**/6; **221**/129–130
Quiz I: **253**/14
Directed Study Practice Test: **400**/20
Practice Test I: **480**/8
Practice Test II: **557**/54

Equations Involving Integer and Rational Exponents (Mathematics)

Lesson: **220**/123; **221**/124–126
Quiz II: **256**/3
Quiz IV: **267**/21
Directed Study Practice Test: **415**/52

Equations Involving Logarithms (Mathematics)

Lesson: **221**/127–128
Quiz IV: **267**/23
Review: **273**/24

Equations Involving Radical Expressions (Mathematics)

Lesson: **220**/119–122
Quiz II: **258**/16
Directed Study Practice Test: **399**/18

Equations Involving Rational Expressions (Mathematics)

Lesson: **201**/3; **219**/115; **220**/116–117
Quiz II: **258**/15
Directed Study Practice Test: **399**/18
Practice Test I: **478**/1

Evaluating Expressions (Mathematics)

Test Mechanics: **193**/3
Lesson: **217**/96–99
Quiz II: **257**/8

Quiz III: **261**/9
Review: **273**/26
Directed Study Practice Test: **395**/5; **397**/11; **401**/21; **415**/53
Practice Test I: **488**/31, 33; **489**/36
Practice Test II: **547**/20; **556**/50
Practice Test III: **603**/3; **616**/47; **618**/53

Evaluating Sequences (Mathematics)

Test Mechanics: **193**/2
Lesson: **201**/2; **219**/109–112
Quiz I: **253**/12

Explicit Detail (Reading)

Test Mechanics: **87**/2
Lesson: **98**/3–5; **100**/19; **104**/28; **108**/48; **109**/53; **111**/65; **113**/77; **114**/78, 81; **115**/84; **116**/89; **119**/98, 100, 102; **120**/105, 107; **121**/108–112; **122**/113; **123**/117, 119; **124**/124–125; **126**/126–128; **127**/133–135; **129**/139–141; **130**/144, 146–147
Quiz I: **132**/4; **133**/10; **134**/13, 16–18
Quiz II: **136**/3–4, 6–7
Quiz III: **140**/4; **141**/7; **142**/9, 11; **143**/12–14, 16
Quiz IV: **145**/2–4; **146**/8; **147**/11; **148**/16; **150**/20–21; **152**/25–27
Review: **155**/10–11; **156**/13–14; **157**/17; **158**/22; **159**/26; **160**/28, 30; **161**/35, 36; **162**/39; **163**/41; **164**/43–46
Directed Study Practice Test: **420**/3; **421**/6; **424**/11–13; **425**/15–16; **426**/17–18; **430**/27; **433**/31–33; **434**/36–38
Practice Test I: **499**/2, 6; **501**/11; **502**/19; **503**/23; **504**/28; **506**/31–34, 36; **507**/39
Practice Test II: **561**/5–6, 10; **562**/12; **563**/16, 20; **564**/21–23; **565**/24–25, 27, 30; **566**/31, 34; **567**/40
Practice Test III: **623**/6–7; **626**/14–17; **627**/19–20; **629**/22, 26; **630**/31–32; **631**/36–37, 39

Expressing and Evaluating Algebraic Functions (Mathematics)

Lesson: **202**/4–5; **222**/134–140; **223**/141–146
Quiz I: **254**/15
Quiz II: **257**/6
Quiz III: **262**/12
Quiz IV: **264**/3; **266**/16
Directed Study Practice Test: **397**/9; **400**/19; **409**/39
Practice Test I: **478**/2; **487**/29; **494**/52; **495**/54; **496**/57
Practice Test II: **547**/21

Practice Test III: **607**/19; **620**/58

Factoring (Mathematics)

Test Mechanics: **193**/1
Lesson: **208**/35–36
Practice Test II: **544**/9; **554**/41

Factoring Expressions (Mathematics)

Lesson: **218**/102–104
Quiz IV: **265**/9; **267**/20
Directed Study Practice Test: **414**/51
Practice Test I: **484**/20; **495**/55
Practice Test II: **542**/2
Practice Test III: **604**/9; **605**/12; **607**/20

Faulty or Illogical Comparisons (English)

Lesson: **28**/34–36; **29**/37–38
Quiz IV: **67**/14
Review: **74**/31
Directed Study Practice Test: **389**/65
Practice Test I: **473**/61
Practice Test II: **528**/1; **534**/41; **538**/62

Faulty Parallelism (English)

Lesson: **33**/71–73
Quiz III: **60**/10; **63**/28
Quiz IV: **65**/1; **66**/5
Review: **71**/10; **72**/20; **74**/32
Directed Study Practice Test: **371**/22
Practice Test I: **468**/30; **474**/64
Practice Test II: **539**/63
Practice Test III: **589**/18; **593**/40; **598**/64

The "Flying-X" Method (Mathematics)

Lesson: **209**/40

Fragments (English)

Test Mechanics: **22**/1
Lesson: **31**/61; **32**/62; **45**/142
Quiz II: **54**/4; **55**/14
Quiz III: **60**/5; **62**/18
Review: **70**/4
Directed Study Practice Test: **364**/8; **371**/24; **356**/36
Practice Test I: **467**/17, 21; **471**/47; **472**/51
Practice Test II: **535**/44; **540**/74
Practice Test III: **594**/46; **599**/73

Function Notation (Mathematics)

Lesson: **202**/5; **222**/134–140; **223**/141

Quiz I: **254**/15
Quiz II: **257**/6
Quiz III: **262**/12
Quiz IV: **264**/3
Directed Study Practice Test: **397**/9; **400**/19; **409**/39
Practice Test I: **478**/2; **487**/29; **494**/52; **495**/54
Practice Test II: **547**/21
Practice Test III: **607**/19

Functions as Models (Mathematics)

Lesson: **202**/4; **223**/146

Geometry (Mathematics)

Test Mechanics: **194**/4; **199**/6, 9
Lesson: **202**/8; **203**/9; **204**/13–14; **205**/15–16; **207**/27, 31; **235–242**/197–232
Quiz I: **251**/1, 3; **253**/10, 11; **255**/20
Quiz II: **256**/1–2, 5; **258**/12, 17; **259**/20
Quiz III: **260**/3; **261**/8, 10; **262**/15; **263**/18, 20
Quiz IV: **265**/8, 10; **266**/11–12, 17; **267**/24
Review: **269**/2, 4–5; **271**/10–11; **272**/15–16, 18; **273**/23, 25
Directed Study Practice Test: **394**/2; **395**/4; **399**/17; **402**/23–24; **403**/25; **405**/30; **407**/34; **410**/41; **411**/43; **412**/44; **413**/45; **416**/57; **417**/59
Practice Test I: **481**/9; **482**/15; **484**/18; **485**/24; **486**/25; **487**/28; **488**/32; **489**/34; **490**/39; **492**/45, 46; **493**/47, 48
Practice Test II: **544**/7–8; **545**/11, 13; **546**/17; **547**/18; **548**/22; **550**/31; **551**/32–33; **552**/34; **553**/39; **554**/44; **557**/53
Practice Test III: **603**/4; **604**/7; **605**/14; **606**/17; **608**/23; **610**/28; **611**/31; **612**/37; **614**/41–42; **615**/46; **616**/48; **617**/50; **621**/59

Grammar and Usage (English)

Test Mechanics: **19**/3; **22**/2, 4, 7–8
Lesson: **25–31**/1–56; **45**/139
Quiz I: **48**/5, 8; **49**/11; **50**/19; **51**/24–26
Quiz II: **53**/1, 3; **54**/11; **55**/13; **56**/20; **57**/22–23, 25, 27
Quiz III: **59**/1–2; **60**/11; **61**/12; **62**/17, 19, 22; **63**/24, 26
Quiz IV: **66**/6–7; **67**/10, 14
Review: **69**/1; **73**/26; **74**/29, 31; **75**/35, 37; **76**/44; **77**/47
Directed Study Practice Test: **362**/3–4; **363**/6; **364**/7; **366**/11; **367**/13; **370**/20; **371**/22–23; **373**/28; **374**/31; **375**/33; **378**/40; **379**/43;

380/44; 381/48; 383/51–52; 384/53; 385/55; 386/57–58; 386/59; 389/63, 65; 390/66; 391/70
Practice Test I: 464/2; 465/6, 10; 466/11, 14; 467/18; 467/24; 468/25, 28–29; 469/34; 470/37–38, 41; 472/48; 473/58, 60–61; 474/64–65
Practice Test II: 528/1–3; 529/5, 9, 11; 530/13–14; 531/18; 532/25–26, 28; 533/29, 31, 33–34; 534/36, 38, 41; 535/42, 45–46; 536/49–50; 537/52; 538/62; 539/66–67; 540/71, 73, 75
Practice Test III: 586/1, 3; 587/4–5, 7, 9–10; 588/13–14; 589/22; 591/30–31; 592/36; 594/44, 47–48; 595/49, 53–54; 596/55, 58; 598/65–66; 599/71–72

Graphs of First-Degree Inequalities (Mathematics)

Lesson: 232/190

Graphs of Linear Equations (Mathematics)

Lesson: 231/188–189
Directed Study Practice Test: 396/6
Practice Test II: 559/60
Practice Test III: 620/56

Graphs of Quadratic Equations and Relations (Mathematics)

Lesson: 232/191; 233/192
Quiz IV: 267/19
Practice Test II: 556/49, 51
Practice Test III: 615/44

Humanities (Reading)

Lesson: 100–102/16–24; 106/40–43; 118/95–97; 119–124/98–125
Quiz I: 133/9–10; 134/11–18
Quiz IV: 149/18–19; 150/20–23
Review: 161/33–36; 162/37–40
Directed Study Practice Test: 428–431/21–30
Practice Test I: 503/21–25; 504/26–30
Practice Test II: 564/21–23; 565/24–30
Practice Test III: 628/21; 629/22–30

Idiomatic Expression (English)

Lesson: 43/135
Quiz III: 60/9
Quiz IV: 65/4; 67/10; 68/19–20
Review: 75/34
Directed Study Practice Test: 367/14; 376/34; 378/39; 383/52
Practice Test II: 539/64

Practice Test III: 591/32

Implied Idea (Reading)

Test Mechanics: 87/3
Lesson: 99/9–11; 100/17; 102/22–23; 104/36; 105/37; 106/40; 108/49, 52; 109/55; 111/58–63, 66–67; 113/69–73, 75; 114/80, 82; 115/85–86; 117/91; 118/96; 120/104, 106; 122/114–115; 124/122–123; 128/137; 129/138
Quiz I: 132/3; 134/11–12, 15
Quiz II: 135/1; 136/2, 8–10; 137/12; 138/13
Quiz IV: 145/5–7; 147/13; 148/15; 149/19; 150/23
Review: 154/3–4, 6; 157/18; 158/19, 24; 159/27; 162/40
Directed Study Practice Test: 420/2; 421/5, 7; 422/9–10; 424/14; 427/20; 429/21, 24; 430/25–26; 431/28; 434/39
Practice Test I: 499/1, 3–5, 7–10; 501/12; 504/26–27, 29–30; 506/37, 507/38
Practice Test II: 561/1–4, 7–9; 562/13; 563/15, 17–18; 565/26, 29; 566/32–33; 567/37
Practice Test III: 624/8, 10; 626/13; 629/23–24, 27–30; 631/34–35, 40

Incomplete Split Constructions (English)

Lesson: 33/74–75
Quiz IV: 65/2

Inequalities Involving Absolute Value (Mathematics)

Lesson: 221/131 ; 222/132–133

Inequalities Involving Rational Expressions (Mathematics)

Lesson: 220/118

Lines and Angles (Mathematics)

Lesson: 204/13–14; 205/15–16; 207/31; 235/197–200; 236/201; 241/226, 228–229
Quiz I: 251/1–3; 255/20
Quiz II: 256/2
Quiz III: 261/8; 263/18
Quiz IV: 265/8
Review: 272/18; 273/25
Directed Study Practice Test: 394/2; 395/4; 403/25; 407/34; 411/43; 413/45
Practice Test I: 482/15; 490/39
Practice Test II: 544/7–8; 545/11; 548/22; 551/32; 557/53

Practice Test III: **603**/4; **610**/28; **611**/31; **614**/41; **616**/48

Logarithmic Expressions (Mathematics)

Lesson: **218**/107; **219**/108
Review: **272**/19; **273**/22

Main Idea (English)

Lesson: **40**/118; **42**/127
Quiz III: **61**/13
Practice Test I: **466**/16; **476**/74
Practice Test II: **530**/15

Main Idea (Reading)

Test Mechanics: **87**/1, **98**/1–2
Lesson: **98**/1–2; **100**/16; **102**/21; **103**/25–26; **104**/27; **115**/83; **117**/94; **118**/97; **123**/120; **124**/121; **129**/142
Quiz I: **132**/2, 8; **133**/9
Quiz II: **136**/5; **137**/11
Quiz III: **141**/6
Quiz IV: **144**/1; **147**/10; **150**/22; **152**/24
Review: **154**/2; **156**/15; **158**/21; **160**/32; **160**/34; **164**/42
Directed Study Practice Test: **420**/1; **426**/19; **431**/30; **433**/34
Practice Test I: **506**/35; **507**/40
Practice Test II: **562**/11
Practice Test III: **625**/11; **628**/21; **631**/38

Manipulating Algebraic Expressions (Mathematics)

Test Mechanics: **191**/3
Lesson: **216–219**/94–108; **225–227**/158–169
Quiz II: **257**/8
Quiz III: **261**/9; **262**/14
Quiz IV: **264**/5; **265**/6, 9; **266**/14; **267**/20
Review: 271/14; **272**/19; **273**/22, 26
Directed Study Practice Test: **395**/5; **396**/7; **397**/11; **398**/14; **401**/21; **404**/27; **411**/42; **414**/51; **415**/53–54
Practice Test I: **481**/10; **484**/20; **485**/23; **488**/31, 33; **489**/36; **490**/37; **495**/53, 55
Practice Test II: **542**/2; **546**/16; **547**/20; **548**/24; **553**/37-38; **556**/50
Practice Test III: **602**/2; **603**/3; **604**/9; **605**/12; **607**/20–21; **613**/38; **616**/47; **618**/53

Manipulating Expressions Involving Exponents (Mathematics)

Lesson: **212**/66; **213**/67–69; **217**/100–101

Practice Test I: **485**/23; **495**/53
Practice Test II: **546**/16

Matrices (Mathematics)

Lesson: **212**/66; **213**/67–69
Quiz IV: **265**/7
Review: **270**/8

Median (Mathematics)

Lesson: **245**/245
Directed Study Practice Test: **407**/35

Misplaced Modifiers (English)

Lesson: **33**/76–77; **34**/78; **46**/145
Quiz IV: **65**/3; **67**/11; **68**/18
Practice Test I: **474**/65
Practice Test III: **589**/20

Mode (Mathematics)

Lesson: **245**/246
Directed Study Practice Test: **414**/49

Natural Science (Reading)

Test Mechanics: **89**/1–2; **90**/3
Lesson: **125–126**/126–132; **127**/133–135; **128**/136–137; **129**/138–143; **130**/144–148
Quiz II: **137**/11–12; **138**/13–17
Quiz III: **142**/9–11; **143**/12–18
Quiz IV: **146–147**/10–13; **148**/14–17; **151–152**/24–29
Review: **153-154**/1–8; **155**/9–12; **156**/13–15
Directed Study Practice Test: **432–434**/31–40
Practice Test I: **505–506**/31–37; **507**/38–40
Practice Test II: **566**/31–35; **567**/36–40
Practice Test III: **630**/31–33; **631**/34–40

Nouns and Noun Clauses (English)

Lesson: **28**/31–33
Quiz I: **50**/19
Quiz II: **53**/3
Directed Study Practice Test: **371**/22

Organization (English)

Lesson: **40**/120; **41**/121, 123; **45**/138
Quiz I: **49**/10, 14; **50**/16; **52**/31
Quiz II: **58**/29
Quiz III: **61**/14; **63**/29
Review: **70**/3, 6; **71**/11; **72**/15; **76**/43; **77**/48
Directed Study Practice Test: **372**/25; **377**/38; **382**/50; **393**/75

Practice Test I: **466**/12, 15; **469**/31; **471**/45; **476**/75
Practice Test II: **531**/21; **533**/32
Practice Test III: **588**/15–16; **590**/24; **591**/29; **597**/60; **600**/74–75

Paragraph-Level Structure (English)

Lesson: **40**/120
Review: **70**/3, 6; **71**/11; **76**/43
Practice Test I: **466**/12; **469**/31; **476**/75
Practice Test II: **531**/21
Practice Test III: **590**/24; **591**/29

Passage-Level Structure (English)

Lesson: **41**/121, 123
Quiz I: **49**/14; **50**/16; **52**/31
Quiz II: **58**/29
Quiz III: **61**/14; **63**/29
Review: **72**/15; **77**/48
Directed Study Practice Test: **372**/25; **377**/38; **382**/50; **393**/75
Practice Test I: **466**/15; **471**/45
Practice Test II: **533**/32
Practice Test III: **588**/15–16; **600**/75

Percents (Mathematics)

Test Mechanics: **194**/4; **199**/10
Lesson: **206**/25; **207**/28; **214**/72–78
Quiz I: **254**/16
Quiz IV: **264**/2
Review: **269**/3, 5; **271**/13; **274**/27
Directed Study Practice Test: **396**/8; **414**/50
Practice Test I: **479**/3; **484**/19; **487**/30; **490**/38; **491**/41
Practice Test II: **543**/6; **548**/23; **550**/30
Practice Test III: **606**/15–16

Pie Charts (Mathematics)

Lesson: **249**/257–258
Quiz III: **261**/5

Probability (Mathematics)

Lesson: **245**/247–248; **246**/249–251
Quiz II: **259**/18
Quiz III: **263**/19
Directed Study Practice Test: **413**/46
Practice Test III: **613**/40

Problems of Coordination and Subordination (English)

Test Mechanics: **22**/4
Lesson: **32**/63–70
Quiz I: **51**/21; **52**/28
Quiz II: **57**/24
Quiz IV: **67**/13
Directed Study Practice Test: **390**/69
Practice Test I: **468**/27; **472**/49; **474**/67
Practice Test II: **530**/12, 14
Practice Test III: **597**/63; **598**/68

Pronoun Usage (English)

Test Mechanics: **22**/7
Lesson: **26**/13–16; **27**/17–21
Quiz I: **48**/5, 8
Quiz II: **53**/1; **56**/20; **57**/23
Quiz III: **59**/1; **61**/12; **62**/19
Review: **77**/47
Directed Study Practice Test: **366**/11; **375**/33; **380**/44; **383**/52; **389**/63
Practice Test I: **465**/10; **466**/14; **467**/24; **470**/41; **473**/58; **474**/64
Practice Test II: **528**/3; **530**/13–14; **531**/18; **532**/26; **533**/34; **535**/42; **539**/66
Practice Test III: **592**/36; **598**/65

Properties of Numbers (Mathematics)

Test Mechanics: **191**/3; **193**/2
Lesson: **205**/19; **207**/29; **210**/45–52; **211**/53
Quiz II : **258**/14
Quiz III: **262**/11, 16
Quiz IV: **264**/4; **266**/13, 15
Review: **271**/12
Directed Study Practice Test: **406**/32
Practice Test I: **479**/4; **492**/44
Practice Test II: **543**/4; **550**/29; **552**/34
Practice Test III: **603**/5; **604**/10; **605**/13; **608**/24; **612**/36

Properties of Tangent Lines (Mathematics)

Lesson: **199**/9; **238**/212–215

Properties of Triangles (Mathematics)

Lesson: **237**/206–207; **239**/217–218; **240**/221; **241**/227;
Quiz I: **253**/10
Quiz II: **256**/5; **258**/12
Review: **269**/4; **271**/10–11; **272**/15, 18
Directed Study Practice Test: **405**/30; **407**/34; **410**/41; **412**/44; **416**/57

Practice Test I: **482**/15; **484**/18; **486**/25; **487**/28; **488**/32
Practice Test II: **552**/34; **553**/39
Practice Test III: **606**/17; **615**/46

Proportions and Direct-Inverse Variation (Mathematics)

Test Mechanics: **191**/3; **199**/7, 9
Lesson: **206**/20; **215**/81-86; **216**/87
Quiz I: **252**/5
Quiz III: **260**/4; **263**/17
Review: **270**/9; **271**/10; **272**/20
Directed Study Practice Test: **406**/31; **413**/47; **418**/60
Practice Test I: **483**/17; **486**/27; **491**/40
Practice Test II: **542**/3
Practice Test III: **607**/18; **609**/27

Prose Fiction (Reading)

Lesson: **107-108**/44-52; **109**/53-57; **110-111**/58-67; **112**/68; **113**/69-77; **114**/78-82
Directed Study Practice Test: **419-422**/1-10
Practice Test I: **498-499**/1-10
Practice Test II: **560-561**/1-10
Practice Test III: **622-623**/1-7; **624**/8-10

Punctuation (English)

Test Mechanics: **19**/1; **22**/3, 6
Lesson: **34**/81-82; **35**/87-88, 90; **36**/91-92, 95-100; **37**/103-108; **38**/109-110, 112, 114; **44**/136
Quiz I: **52**/28
Quiz II: **53**/3; **54**/5; **56**/19
Quiz III: **60**/7-8
Review: **72**/17-18; **73**/23; **76**/42
Directed Study Practice Test: **361**/1; **365**/9-10; **366**/12; **369**/17; **376**/36; **379**/42; **381**/47; **384**/54; **385**/56; **388**/61; **369**/64
Practice Test I: **467**/22, 24; **470**/40, 42; **474**/62, 69
Practice Test II: **529**/9; **534**/37
Practice Test III: **586**/3; **590**/25; **593**/41

Pythagorean Theorem (Mathematics)

Test Mechanics: **191**/4
Lesson: **202**/8; **236**/202; **241**/230
Quiz II: **258**/17
Quiz IV: **265**/10; **267**/24
Directed Study Practice Test: **402**/23; **417**/59
Practice Test I: **492**/45; **493**/47

Qualitative Behavior of Graphs of Functions (Mathematics)

Lesson: **233**/193-194
Quiz I: **255**/19

Quotation Marks (English)

Directed Study Practice Test: **388**/61
Practice Test I: **474**/69
Practice Test III: **593**/41

Ratios (Mathematics)

Lesson: **205**/17-18; **206**/23; **215**/79-80
Quiz I: **252**/6
Review: **273**/25
Practice Test I: **482**/13
Practice Test III: **603**/6

Rectangles and Squares (Mathematics)

Test Mechanics: **198**/2; **199**/6, 9
Lesson: **237**/208-210; **238**/216; **239**/218-220; **242**/231
Quiz III: **260**/3; **262**/15
Review: **269**/2; **272**/15, 18
Practice Test I: **481**/9; **485**/24; **486**/25; **488**/32
Practice Test II: **545**/13; **546**/17; **550**/31; **551**/33; **554**/44
Practice Test III: **604**/7; **605**/14; **608**/23; **612**/37; **615**/46; **617**/50; **621**/59

Research Summary (Science)

Test Mechanics: **288**/1-4
Lesson: **305-316**/41-74
Quiz I: **328**/11-13; **329**/14-16
Quiz III: **337**/5-6; **338**/7-10
Review: **342**/7-8; **343**/9-12; **346**/28-30; **347**/31-33; **351**/49-54
Directed Study Practice Test: **447**/23-26; **448**/27; **450**/28-29; **451**/30-32
Practice Test I: **513**/8-10; **514**/11-14; **516**/15-20; **517**/21-22; **522**/35-38; **523**/39-40
Practice Test II: **570-573**/7-18; **575**/24-28; **576**/29
Practice Test III: **635**/6-9; **636**/10-11; **639**/19-23; **640**/24; **642**/31-33; **643**/34-35

Rhetorical Skills (English)

Test Mechanics: **19**/2
Lesson: **39**/116; **40**/117-119; **41-43**/121-135; **45**/138; **45**/143; **46**/144

Quiz I: **48**/2–3, 7; **49**/10, 13–15; **50**/16–18; **51**/27; **52**/29, 31–32
Quiz II: **53**/2; **54**/6–8, 10; **55**/15–16; **56**/17, 21; **57**/24, 28; **58**/29
Quiz III: **59**/3; **60**/4, 9; **61**/13–15; **62**/16, 20, 23; **63**/29; **64**/30–31
Quiz IV: **65**/4; **66**/8–9; **67**/10; **68**/16–17, 19–20
Review: **69**/2; **70**/3, 6–9; **71**/11, 13–14; **72**/15–16, 19; **73**/21–22, 24, 28; **74**/30, 33; **75**/34, 36; **76**/38, 41, 43; **77**/48
Directed Study Practice Test: **362**/2; **367**/14; **368**/16; **369**/18; **370**/21; **372**/25–26; **373**/27; **375**/32; **376**/34; **377–378**/37–39; **380**/45; **381**/46; **382**/50; **383**/52; **388**/62; **390**/67–68; **391**/71; **392**/72; **393**/74–75
Practice Test I: **464**/1, 3; **465**/5, 8; **466**/12–13, 15–16; **467**/19; **469**/31–33, 35; **471**/43, 45–46; **472**/50, 52–55; **473**/57, 59; **474**/63, 68; **475–476**/70–75
Practice Test II: **528**/4; **529**/7–8, 10; **530**/15; **531**/16–17, 19, 21; **532**/22–24, 27; **533**/30, 32; **534**/35, 40; **535**/43, 47; **536**/48; **537**/53–54; **537**/57; **538**/58–61; **539**/64–65; **570**/70
Practice Test III: **586**/2; **587**/6, 8; **588**/11, 15–16; **589**/17; **590**/23–24, 27–28; **591**/29, 32; **592**/33, 35, 37; **593**/38, 42; **594**/43; **595**/50, 52; **596**/59; **597**/60–62; **599**/69–70; **600**/74–75

Run-On Sentences (English)

Lesson: **31**/57–58
Quiz I: **49**/12
Quiz II: **57**/26
Quiz III: **63**/27
Directed Study Practice Test: **385**/56
Practice Test I: **465**/4, 10; **468**/26
Practice Test III: **596**/56

Scatterplots (Mathematics)

Lesson: **250**/260

Scientific Notation (Mathematics)

Lesson: **211**/54–57
Quiz III: **260**/2
Review: **269**/1

Semicolons (English)

Lesson: **37**/103–105
Quiz I: **52**/28
Directed Study Practice Test: **361**/1
Practice Test II: **529**/9

Sentence Structure (English)

Test Mechanics: **21**/1
Lesson: **31-34**/57–80; **45**/142; **46**/145
Quiz I: **47**/1; **49**/12; **51**/20–21; **52**/28, 30
Quiz II: **54**/4; **55**/14; **57**/24, 26
Quiz III: **60**/5, 10; **62**/18; **63**/27–28
Quiz IV: **65**/1–3; **66**/5, 7; **67**/11, 13; **68**/15, 18
Review: **70**/4; **71**/10; **72**/20; **74**/32
Directed Study Practice Test: **364**/8; **371**/22, 24; **385**/56; **391**/69
Practice Test I: **465**/4, 10; **467**/17, 21; **468**/26–27, 30; **470**/39; **471**/47; **472**/49, 51; **473**/56; **474**/64–65, 67
Practice Test II: **530**/12, 14; **535**/44; **539**/63; **540**/74
Practice Test III: **589**/18–20; **592**/34; **593**/40; **594**/46; **596**/56; **597**/63; **598**/64, 68; **599**/73

Sentence-Level Structure (English)

Test Mechanics: **22**/4
Lesson: **45**/138
Quiz I: **49**/10
Practice Test III: **597**/60; **600**/74

Sequence and Verb Tense (English)

Lesson: **30**/47–50
Quiz II: **57**/22
Quiz III: **60**/11; **62**/17
Review: **73**/26
Practice Test I: **470**/37; **473**/58; **474**/65
Practice Test II: **529**/11; **530**/13; **533**/33; **540**/71
Practice Test III: **587**/5; **588**/14; **594**/44, 47; **595**/53; **596**/58

Sets: Union, Intersection, and Elements (Mathematics)

Lesson: **211**/58–59; **212**/60-62
Quiz I: **253**/13
Quiz IV: **264**/4
Directed Study Practice Tests: **403**/26

Simple Equations (Mathematics)

Test Mechanics: **191**/3
Lesson: **219**/113
Quiz I: **252**/4, 9
Quiz IV: **264**/1
Directed Study Practice Test: **404**/28
Practice Test I: **482**/14; **485**/21

Simple Inequalities (Mathematics)

Lesson: **219**/114
Quiz IV: **264**/5

Simple Manipulations (Mathematics)

Test Mechanics: **190**/1; **191**/4; **198**/3; **199**/7
Lesson: **206**/22; **207**/32; **208**/33; **216**/88-93
Directed Study Practice Test: **394**/1; **397**/12; **398**/15–16; **409**/38
Practice Test I: **480**/6; **494**/51
Practice Test II: **542**/1; **545**/12; **549**/28; **554**/42; **558**/58
Practice Test III: **602**/1; **609**/26; **614**/43

Simplifying (Mathematics)

Lesson: **208**/34
Directed Study Practice Test: **406**/32; **416**/55
Practice Test II: **558**/57
Practice Test III: **611**/32

Slope of a Line (Mathematics)

Lesson: **228**/175; **229**/176-178
Quiz II: **257**/7; **258**/13
Quiz III: **262**/13
Directed Study Practice Test: **401**/22
Practice Test II: **558**/56

Slope-Intercept Form of a Linear Equation (Mathematics)

Lesson: **202**/7; **229**/179–180; **230**/181-183
Quiz II: **259**/19
Practice Test III: **615**/45

Social Science (Reading)

Test Mechanics: **86-87**/1–4
Lesson: **97-99**/1-15; **103–105**/25–39; **115–117**/83–94
Quiz I: **131**/1; **132**/2–8
Quiz II: **135**/1; **136**/2–10
Quiz III: **139-141**/1–8
Quiz IV: **144–146**/1–9
Review: **157–160**/16-32; **163**/41; **164**/42–46
Directed Study Practice Test: **423-427**/11–20
Practice Test I: **501**/11–18; **502**/19-20
Practice Test II: **562**/11–14; **563**/15-20
Practice Test III: **625–627**/11–20

Solids (Mathematics)

Lesson: **240**/222–225
Quiz II: **259**/20

Review: **273**/23

Solving Algebraic Equations or Inequalities with One Variable (Mathematics)

Test Mechanics: **193**/3
Lesson: **201**/3; **202**/6; **219–222**/113–133
Quiz I: **252**/4, 9; **253**/14
Quiz II: **256**/3; **258**/15–16
Quiz IV: **264**/1, 5; **267**/21, 23
Review: **273**/24
Directed Study Practice Test: **399**/18; **400**/20; **404**/28; **415**/52
Practice Test I: **478**/1; **480**/8; **482**/14; **485**/21
Practice Test II: **546**/15; **557**/54
Practice Test III: **604**/8

Solving Algebraic Equations with Two Variables (Mathematics)

Lesson: **223**/147
Review: **272**/17
Practice Test I: **491**/43
Practice Test II: **547**/19
Practice Test III: **610**/29

Solving Quadratic Equations and Relations (Mathematics)

Test Mechanics: **199**/10
Lesson: **224**/153-156; **225**/157
Quiz IV: **267**/18
Directed Study Practice Test: **395**/3; **408**/36; **410**/40
Practice Test II: **552**/35; **559**/59
Practice Test III: **611**/33; **620**/57

Solving Simultaneous Equations (Mathematics)

Test Mechanics: **199**/8
Lesson: **223**/148; **224**/149-152
Quiz II: **257**/10
Quiz IV: **265**/6
Directed Study Practice Test: **416**/56; **417**/58
Practice Test I: **481**/11; **491**/42
Practice Test II: **554**/43
Practice Test III: **612**/35; **618**/54

Statistics and Probability (Mathematics)

Test Mechanics: **190**/2; **193**/2; **198**/1
Lesson: **203**/11; **244–246**/240–251
Quiz I: **252**/8; **254**/16-17
Quiz II: **257**/9; **259**/18
Quiz III: **260**/1; **261**/5, 7; **263**/17, 19

Quiz IV: **264**/2; **266**/14
Review: **270**/7; **274**/27
Directed Study Practice Test: **397**/10; **398**/13;
407/35; **413**/46; **414**/49
Practice Test I: **479**/5; **480**/6; **481**/12; **484**/19;
485/22; **494**/49
Practice Test II: **545**/10; **546**/14; **549**/26
Practice Test III: **610**/30; **612**/34; **613**/40

Strategy (English)

Lesson: **39**/116; **40**/117-119; **41**/122; **42**/125-127
Quiz I: **49**/13; **50**/15, 17; **52**/32
Quiz II: **55**/16; **56**/17; **57**/28
Quiz III: **59**/3; **61**/13, 15; **64**/30, 31
Review: **69**/2; **71**/14; **72**/16; **73**/21–22; **75**/36;
76/38
Directed Study Practice Test: **368**/16; **369**/18;
372/26; **373**/27; **377**/37; **380**/45; **388**/62;
392/72; **373**/74
Practice Test I: **465**/8; **466**/16; **467**/19; **469**/32;
471/46; **472**/54; **473**/59; **475**/72, 73; **476**/74
Practice Test II: **529**/8; **530**/15; **531**/16, 19;
535/47; **536**/48; **537**/54; **539**/65
Practice Test III: **590**/23; **592**/33, 35; **593**/38;
595/50; **599**/69

Style (English)

Lesson: **42**/128–130; **43**/131-135; **45**/143; **46**/144
Quiz I: **48**/3, 7; **50**/18; **51**/27; **52**/29
Quiz II: **54**/7–8; **55**/15; **57**/24
Quiz III: **60**/9; **62**/16
Quiz IV: **65**/4; **66**/8-□ **67**/10; **68**/19□20
Review: **70**/9; **72**/19; **73**/24; **74**/30; **75**/34
Directed Study Practice Test: **362**/2; **367**/14;
370/21; **375**/32; **376**/34; **378**/39; **381**/46;
383/52; **390**/67–68
Practice Test I: **464**/1, 3; **466**/13; **472**/53, 55;
473/57; **474**/63; **475**/70
Practice Test II: **528**/4; **532**/27; **533**/30; **534**/35,
40; **537**/53, 57; **538**/58; **539**/64
Practice Test III: **590**/27; **591**/32; **592**/37; **595**/52;
597/61; **599**/70

Subject-Verb Agreement (English)

Test Mechanics: **19**/3; **22**/4
Lesson: **25**/1-6; **26**/7-12
Quiz I: **51**/24
Quiz III: **62**/17
Quiz IV: **67**/10
Review: **69**/1; **74**/29
Directed Study Practice Test: **367**/13; **383**/51
Practice Test I: **467**/24; **468**/25

Practice Test II: **532**/25, 28; **534**/38; **535**/46;
536/49; **539**/67
Practice Test III: **591**/31; **595**/54

Tables (Mathematics)

Test Mechanics: **193**/2
Lesson: **250**/259
Quiz I: **254**/16–17
Quiz III: **263**/17
Quiz IV: **264**/2
Review: **274**/27
Practice Test I: **479**/5; **484**/19
Practice Test III: **610**/30

Transformations and Their Effects on Graphs of Functions and Figures (Mathematics)

Lesson: **234**/195-196

Triangles (Mathematics)

Test Mechanics: **191**/4
Lesson: **202**/8; **236**/202–205; **237**/206-207;
239/217-219; **240**/221; **241**/227, 230; **242**/232
Quiz I: **253**/10-11
Quiz II: **256**/5; **258**/12, 17
Quiz III: **263**/20
Quiz IV: **265**/10; **266**/11; **267**/24
Review: **269**/4; **271**/10-11; **272**/15,18
Directed Study Practice Test: **402**/23; **405**/30;
407/34; **410**/41; **412**/44; **416**/57; **417**/59
Practice Test I: **482**/15; **484**/18; **486**/25; **487**/28;
488/32; **492**/45; **493**/47
Practice Test II: **550**/31; **552**/34; **553**/39
Practice Test III: **606**/17; **614**/42; **615**/46

Trigonometric Relationships (Mathematics)

Lesson: **243**/235–236
Quiz IV: **267**/22
Review: **274**/29
Directed Study Practice Test: **405**/29; **409**/37;
414/48
Practice Test I: **496**/58
Practice Test II: **555**/46; **557**/52
Practice Test III: **617**/51; **621**/60

Trigonometry (Mathematics)

Test Mechanics: **194**/5
Lesson: **203**/10; **242**/233; **243**/234–237;
244/238–239
Quiz I: **253**/11; **254**/18
Quiz II: **258**/17

Quiz III: **263**/20
Quiz IV: **267**/22, 24
Review: **274**/28–30; **275**/31–32
Directed Study Practice Test: **405**/29; **409**/37;
414/48; **417**/59
Practice Test I: **495**/56; **496**/58 -59; **497**/60
Practice Test II: **555**/46, 48; **557**/52
Practice Test III: **616**/49; **617**/51; **618**/52; **621**/60

Trigonometry as an Alternative Method of Solution (Mathematics)

Lesson: **243**/237; **244**/238–239
Practice Test I: **497**/60

Unintended Meanings (English)

Lesson: **34**/79–80
Quiz I: **47**/1; **51**/20; **52**/30
Quiz IV: **66**/7; **67**/13; **68**/15
Practice Test I: **470**/39; **473**/56

Usage and Mechanics (English)

Test Mechanics: **18**/1; **19**/3-4; **21**/ 1; **22**/2-8
Lesson: **25-38**/1–114; **44**/136–137; **45**/139–142;
46/145
Quiz I: **47**/1; **48**/4–6, 8–9; **49**/11–12; **50**/19;
51/20–26; **52**/28, 30
Quiz II: **53**/1, 3; **54**/4–5, 9, 11; **55**/12–14; **56**/18–
20; **57**/22–27
Quiz III: **59**/1–2; **60**/5–8, 10–11; **61**/12; **62**/17–19,
21–22; **63**/24–28
Quiz IV: **65**/1–3; **66**/5; **67**/10–14; **68**/15, 18
Review: **69**/1; **70**/4–5; **71**/10, 12; **72**/17–18, 20;
73/23, 25–27; **74**/29, 31–32; **75**/35, 37; **76**/39–40,
42, 44; **77**/45–47
Directed Study Practice Test: **361**/1; **362–369**/3–
17; **370**/19-20; **371**/22–24; **373**/28; **374**/29–31;
375/33; **376**/35–36; **378**/40–41; **379**/42–43;
380/44; **381**/47–48; **382**/49; **383**/51-52; **384**/53-
54; **385**/55-56; **386**/57-59; 387/60; 388/61; **389–
392**/63–66, 69, 70, 73
Practice Test I: **464**/2; **465**/4, 6–7, 9–10; **466**/11,
14; **467**/17–18, 20–24; **468**/25–30; **469**/34;
470/36–42; **471**/44, 47; **472**/48–49, 51; **473**/56,
58, 60–61; **474**/62, 64–67, 69
Practice Test II: **528**/1–3; **529**/5–6, 9, 11; **530**/12–
14; **531**/18, 20; **532**/25–26, 28; **533**/29, 31, 33–34;
534/36–39, 41; **535**/42, 44–46; **536**/49–50;
537/51–52, 55–56; **538**/62; **539**/63, 66–68;
540/69, 71–75
Practice Test III: **586**/1, 3; **587**/4–5, 7, 9–10;
588/12–14; **589**/18–22; **590**/25–26; **591**/30–31;
592/34, 36; **593**/39–41; **594**/44–48; **595**/49, 51,
53–54; **596**/55–58; **597**/63; **598**/64–68; **599**/71–
73

Verb Tense (English)

Test Mechanics: **22**/5
Lesson: **29**/39–44; **30**/45–46; **45**/139
Quiz II: **55**/13
Quiz III: **63**/24
Quiz IV: **66**/6
Review: **73**/26
Directed Study Practice Test: **363**/6; **386**/57
Practice Test I: **470**/37; **473**/58; **474**/65
Practice Test II: **529**/9; **534**/36; **540**/73
Practice Test III: **587**/9; **589**/22; **595**/49; **599**/71

Vocabulary (Reading)

Test Mechanics: **87**/4
Lesson: **98**/6; **100**/17; **104**/29–33; **106**/42;
108/44–45, 47, 51; **109**/56; **111**/64; **112**/68;
113/74; **116**/88; **118**/95; **123**/118; **126**/130;
128/136
Quiz I: **131**/1
Quiz II: **138**/14
Quiz III: **140**/1–2
Review: **154**/1; **155**/9; **157**/16; **159**/25; **161**/33
Directed Study Practice Test: **421**/4, **422**/8; **429**/22
Practice Test I: **501**/14, 18; **503**/22
Practice Test III: **623**/4

Voice (Reading)

Lesson: **99**/14–15; **102**/24; **105**/39; **109**/54;
114/79; **115**/87; **119**/101; **123**/116; **129**/143
Quiz I: **132**/6; **134**/14
Quiz IV: **146**/9; **148**/14; **149**/18
Review: **154**/8; **158**/23; **162**/38
Directed Study Practice Test: **429**/23
Practice Test I: **501**/13, 17; **503**/25
Practice Test II: **563**/19
Practice Test III: **623**/3

Cambridge *Victory for the ACT® Test, 13th Edition*
Error Correction and Suggestion Form

Name/Location: _____ Day Phone: _____ E-mail Address: _____

Part of Materials: ☐ Student Text, Specify Subject: _____ Page: _____ Item: _____

☐ Teacher's Guide, Specify Subject: _____ Page: _____ Item: _____

☐ Test Explanations, Specify Year/Code: _____ Page: _____ Item: _____

Error/Suggestion: _____

_____

_____

Part of Materials: ☐ Student Text, Specify Subject: _____ Page: _____ Item: _____

☐ Teacher's Guide, Specify Subject: _____ Page: _____ Item: _____

☐ Test Explanations, Specify Year/Code: _____ Page: _____ Item: _____

Error/Suggestion: _____

_____

_____

Part of Materials: ☐ Student Text, Specify Subject: _____ Page: _____ Item: _____

☐ Teacher's Guide, Specify Subject: _____ Page: _____ Item: _____

☐ Test Explanations, Specify Year/Code: _____ Page: _____ Item: _____

Error/Suggestion: _____

_____

_____

Part of Materials: ☐ Student Text, Specify Subject: _____ Page: _____ Item: _____

☐ Teacher's Guide, Specify Subject: _____ Page: _____ Item: _____

☐ Test Explanations, Specify Year/Code: _____ Page: _____ Item: _____

Error/Suggestion: _____

_____

_____

Part of Materials: ☐ Student Text, Specify Subject: _____ Page: _____ Item: _____

☐ Teacher's Guide, Specify Subject: _____ Page: _____ Item: _____

☐ Test Explanations, Specify Year/Code: _____ Page: _____ Item: _____

Error/Suggestion: _____

_____

_____

Mail form to Cambridge Educational Services, Inc. or fax form to 1-847-299-2933. For teacher's assistance, call 1-800-444-4373 or e-mail solutions@CambridgeEd.com. Visit our Web site at www.CambridgeEd.com.